THE CLASSICS OF WESTERN SPIRITUALITY
A Library of the Great Spiritual Masters

ALBERT&THOMAS

SELECTED WRITINGS

TRANSLATED, EDITED, AND INTRODUCED BY

SIMON TUGWELL, O.P.

PREFACE BY

LEONARD E. BOYLE, O.P.

PAULIST PRESS

NEW YORK • MAHWAH

Cover art: KEVIN NOVACK, C.S.P., is a free-lance artist, and is currently assigned to the St. Thomas Aquinas University Parish, Boulder, Colorado

Nihil Obstat
Herbert McCabe, O.P.
Timothy Radcliffe, O.P.

Imprimi Potest
Peter Edgar, O.P.
February 3, 1988

Library of Congress Cataloging-in-Publication Data

Albert and Thomas : selected writings / edited and translated by Simon
    Tugwell : preface by Leonard Boyle.
        p.   cm. — (The Classics of Western spirituality)
        Bibliography: p.
        Includes index.
        ISBN 0-8091-0417-2 : $24.95. ISBN 0-8091-3022-X (pbk.) :
$17.95.
        1. Spiritual life—Catholic authors—Early works to 1800.
I. Tugwell, Simon. II. Albertus, Magnus, Saint, 1193?–1280. Super
Dionysii Mysticam theologiam. English. 1988. III. Thomas,
Aquinas, Saint, 1226?–1274. Selections. English. 1988.
IV. Series.
BX2349.A575 1988
248.4'82—dc19

Published by Paulist Press
997 Macarthur Boulevard
Mahwah, New Jersey 07430

Printed and bound in the United States of America

Contents

CONTENTS

Editor of This Volume

SIMON TUGWELL OP, STD, MA, teaches theology in the University of Oxford and at the Dominican house of studies there, where he has been Regent of Studies since 1976. He also teaches for part of each year at the Pontifical University of St Thomas in Rome (the Angelicum) and at the Dominican sisters' study house in Rome. He is a member of the Dominican Historical Institute.

He has published numerous articles in a wide variety of journals, both scholarly and popular. His books include *Reflections on the Beatitudes*, *Ways of Imperfection* and, more importantly for readers of this present volume, *The Way of the Preacher* and, in the Classics of Western Spirituality series, *Early Dominicans*. He is editor of the series, Dominican Sources in English.

He was educated at Lancing College, Sussex, England and at Corpus Christi College, Oxford, where he read classics and English before entering the Dominican Order.

Author of the Preface

LEONARD BOYLE, OP, STM, D. PHIL, FRHS is Prefect of the Vatican Library and a member of the Irish Province of the Dominicans. He formerly taught at the Pontifical Institute of Mediaeval Studies, Toronto.

Foreword

In a previous volume, *Early Dominicans* (Classics of Western Spirituality, 1982), I expressed a hope that the two outstanding thirteenth-century Dominican doctors of the church, St. Albert the Great and St. Thomas Aquinas, would find their own place among the Classics of Western Spirituality. This present volume is the fulfilment of that hope.

Neither of the two is a "spiritual writer" in the sense to which we have become accustomed, but both are, in different ways, significant for the history and understanding of Christian piety. Both represent instances, recognized and canonized by the church, of a type that has not always enjoyed a good press in devout circles: both are unambiguously Christian intellectuals. Albert, we may say, is almost the apotheosis of curiosity, while Thomas stands for fearless lucidity. In their different ways both were men who kept their eyes open and were not afraid to look at what they saw, though in the case of Thomas the eyes of the mind were paramount.

It is obviously not possible in a single volume to do justice to the range of interests of either of the two saints. From the voluminous works of Albert I have selected only one, his commentary on the *Mystical Theology* of the elusive Greek writer of about A.D. 500 who hid behind the name of Dionysius the Areopagite. In my introduction I have tried to situate Albert in the Western Dionysian tradition. He is significant as a theologian who resisted both the obscurantism of twelfth-century negative theology and the devotionalist reading of Dionysius, which eventually led to *The Cloud of Unknowing* and St. John of the Cross. Even he was unable to recapture the full breadth of the authentic Dionysian vision, but he did manage to retrieve a fair amount of it, in spite of the obstacles posed by inadequate Latin translations and a somewhat misleading tradition of interpretation. And his appreciation of Dionysius is something that he passed on to his German Dominican disciples and followers, not the least of whom is Meister Eckhart. One of the many exciting scholarly projects currently going on is the rediscovery of the German Dominican tradition, of which Albert is undoubtedly the progenitor, and which has a characteristic stamp of its own, distinct from the Thomist tradition with which the Dominicans are normally and naturally identified.

The writings I have chosen from the corpus of Thomas' works are more immediately related to some of the standard topics of spirituality. In particular I have presented a substantial dossier on prayer, ranging from near the beginning of Thomas' career to near its end. Thomas more or less created the scholastic treatise on prayer and achieved a clarity on the subject that it is hard to find elsewhere except in his disciples. It is fascinating to watch as he gradually achieves this clarity. The subject of contemplation and the contemplative life seems not to have interested him nearly so much, and his treatise on it in the *Summa Theologiae* is, in some respects, disappointing; but it is still instructive to see what he has to say and to note what he does not say. Finally, I have selected a variety of texts illustrating Thomas' views on religious life, many of them shaped by the controversial needs of his own time and, as a result, perhaps surprisingly, all the more pertinent to the controversies (including some "undeclared controversies") of our own time.

I have made no attempt to provide a general introduction to the thought of either writer as a whole. Since Albert is the less well-known, I have tried to give some idea at least of the temper of his thought. In the case of Thomas there are excellent books available to help us understand his philosophy and his theology, so I have contented myself with a few remarks on the texts actually included in this volume.

Since the language of thirteenth-century theology is not always easy for the modern reader, I have not been shy of supplying notes. No doubt everyone will find some places where my notes are unwanted and others where a note is looked for in vain; such is the lot of commentators and those who read them. But I have done my best to anticipate puzzles and, insofar as I could, to shed light on them.

Unfortunately there is still a great deal of obscurity surrounding the lives of both saints. I have therefore thought it best to offer a fairly long biography of each of them and to indicate at every step the evidence on which I have based myself. Anyone who wants to can of course ignore the documentation, which is cited extensively in the notes, but it should be borne in mind that much of what I say is controversial and that we are still a long way from having a "standard" biography of either Albert or Thomas. The main outlines are tolerably secure, but the details have to be fought for. I have tried always to find such solid evidence as is available and then, ruthlessly at times, eliminate even those fantasies that have been hallowed by generations of historians. It would have been unworthy of our two subjects to do otherwise. How far I have succeeded in reaching the truth about their lives, time will perhaps tell; I hope that at least I have taken a small step forward.

Both Albert and Thomas make frequent references to earlier sources, and I have tried to identify these sources as precisely as possible, a task in which I have naturally been much helped by the work of earlier editors. Biblical references are cited in accordance with the Latin text of the traditional Vulgate, which was the bible used by our two writers, and biblical texts are translated afresh from the Vulgate in the light of contemporary commentaries and the specific purposes for which they were quoted by Albert or Thomas.

It remains to thank the many people who have helped me during the many years that have gone to the gestation and the making of this book. I must especially mention the late Osmund Lewry, O.P., who read through the typescript of the section devoted to St. Albert with meticulous care, even though he was already a very sick man; his comments were invaluable to me. I must also express my gratitude to Ulrich Horst, O.P., for sending me material on Albert that I was unable to find either in Rome or in Oxford. My treatment of St. Thomas has benefited from the kindness of several of my confrères. Various members of the Leonine Commission—and they are the real experts—have helped me in sundry ways, and Louis Bataillon, O.P., in particular has been most generous in sharing his learning with me. Albert Patfoort, O.P., in a series of lengthy conversations, sparked off several profitable trains of thought and put me straight on a number of points. Leonard Boyle O.P. helped and encouraged me in a variety of ways and, in the final stages of the composition of the book, he kindly read through the typescript and commented on it, as well as generously agreeing to write the Preface. No English Dominican can approach St Thomas without being conscious of Herbert McCabe O.P., who has made himself, for generations of students, the interpreter par excellence of Thomas'

FOREWORD

thought. Not least I must thank the Paulist Press and the editors of this series for their patience and indulgence, and also the friends, colleagues and students, who have allowed me to try out on them all or parts of the typescript in successive phases of its evolution, and particularly Marcus Hodges O.P., Michael Doyle O.P. and last, but far from least, Brian Davies O.P.

Preface

By any measure, this is a remarkable volume. It is not simply a translation, with commentary, of passages from Albert the Great and Thomas Aquinas on prayer, the contemplative life, the ideal of the theologian, the religious life or mystical theology. It is really two books in one. For there is also, and with much originality, an unravelling of the tangled sources of the life of Albert and a pruning, at times ruthless, of some traditional accounts of that of Thomas.

The selection of passages for translation is adroit. The translations are deft and the annotations scholarly. As an introduction to the lives and spiritual teaching of two of the greatest Dominican authors of the Middle Ages, Father Tugwell's work here is easily the most clear-headed and stimulating in English, or indeed in any language.

ALBERT THE GREAT

Introduction

I. The Life and Works of Albert[1]

When Albert died in 1280 he was already something of a legend. Even in his own lifetime, contrary to all normal academic etiquette, he was being treated as an "authority" in the schools, on a par with the ancients;[2] and a Dominican preacher in Paris could refer with evident proprietary satisfaction to "*our* philosopher, bishop Albert."[3] Albert's friend, fellow-Dominican and pupil, Ulrich of Strasbourg, describes him as "so godlike (*divinus*) in every branch of knowledge that he can aptly be called the wonder and the miracle of our time."[4] Unfortunately, though, there is still a great deal of uncertainty about the biographical details of this remarkable man.

At the time of his death he was more than eighty years old; that is solidly attested.[5] So he was born toward the end of the twelfth century. He called himself "Albert of Lauingen,"[6] but this might mean either that he was born in Lauingen, a small town on the Danube not far from Ulm, or that Lauingen was his family name. The medieval biographers mostly assume the former interpretation,[7] and they have in general been followed by modern writers; Scheeben found confirmation of Albert's childhood in Lauingen in a text in *De Animalibus* 7.1.6.65, where Albert comments on the habits of fish that he had observed "in my estate on the Danube,"[8] but this can equally well, if not better, be understood not of the family home, but of the episcopal residence where Albert lived as bishop of Regensburg.[9] There do not appear to be any explicit childhood reminiscences in Albert's works which unambiguously indicate where he grew up.[10]

Recently the possibility that Lauingen should be taken as a family name has received more attention.[11] Albert's brother Henry, also a Dominican, was known as Henry of Lauingen,[12] and there is some evidence that the Lauingen family had Austrian connections as well as those closer to the place from which the family name derived.[13] This makes it possible that we should look much further afield for Albert's birthplace.[14] But in the absence of any more conclusive evi-

3

dence, it is best to retain the traditional belief that he was born in Lauingen.

Medieval sources say that Albert came of knightly stock,[15] which in the usage of the period would mean that his family did not belong to the nobility.[16] But they were presumably quite well off, since as a young man Albert and his friends used to go out into the fields with retrievers and catch birds with the help of half-tamed falcons.[17] And if, as seems likely, another personal reminiscence refers back to Albert's youth, it also suggests a background of leisure and prosperity: Albert tells us that he and his companions sometimes stood around for hours watching eagles fighting with swans; when eventually the eagle won and brought the defeated swan back to earth, a servant would run and pick up the swan, scaring off the eagle in the process.[18]

According to several medieval biographers Albert became a Dominican at the age of about sixteen,[19] which is impossible if he was over eighty in 1280, unless he was one of the first people to join the Order, in which case we should expect this fact to have been noticed and commented on. Johannes Meyer simply says that he was a "young man" when he became a Dominican,[20] and this tallies with Bacon's comment that he entered the Order as "a boy," allowing for Bacon's intentions as a debunker.[21]

The earliest sources give us no precise information about when or where Albert became a Dominican, though they leave it to be inferred that it was in Germany.[22] Thereafter there is a double tradition, which is something of an embarrassment to Albert's biographers. The anonymous Cologne legenda, whose date is controversial but which precedes Peter of Prussia (c. 1485), says that Albert was received into the Order by Jordan of Saxony while he was a student in Italy,[23] and it is clear that the source of this report is an autobiographical account in the *Vitae Fratrum* of how an unnamed student in Padua was converted by Jordan's preaching and, after various doubts and delays, sought and received the Dominican habit from Jordan.[24] A fairly early German manuscript of the *Vitae Fratrum* (Leipzig 818) identifies this Paduan student as Albert. The Cologne legenda goes on to tell how, after a few years, Albert was sent to Cologne to be the priory lector there.[25] On the other hand there was also a Cologne tradition that it was in Cologne itself that Albert joined the Order.[26] Peter of Prussia is plainly aware of both traditions and is conscious of being controversial in arguing for Padua, on the evidence of the *Vitae Fratrum* and of Albert's own writings.[27] He goes on to suggest that Jordan, having received Albert in Padua, sent him on more or less immediately to Cologne.[28] Peter's interpretation of the evidence did not convince everybody. Johannes Molitoris, more or less Peter's contemporary, stated very precisely that Albert entered the Order in Cologne under the second prior, Leo,[29] who succeeded Jordan's friend Henry in 1229.[30] Rudolph of Nijmegen tried to reconcile all the evidence on the assumption that Albert was received by Jordan in Padua and was then sent to Cologne as lector under the priorship of Leo,[31] which is only a chronologically more precise version of what we find in the anonymous Cologne legenda. The main difficulty with Rudolph's theory is that there seems to have been a relatively early tradition that it was not in Cologne but in Hildesheim that Albert began his career as a lector.[32] Probably the theory that he was first a lector in Cologne was intended to reconcile the evident fact that Cologne was his home convent with the belief that he joined the Order in Padua.[33]

That Albert visited Italy as a young man is certain. He tells us that he was in Venice when he was young and went to see a "picture" of a king's head that had been found in a freshly carved piece of marble: "All of us who were there knew it had been painted by nature." Evidently the young Albert had a reputation among his associates as a natural philosopher, because they asked him why the "forehead" was distorted and he duly gave them a physical explanation.[34]

That he studied in Padua is also very likely. We know that he was in Padua at some stage in his life,[35] and it is surely significant that in his list of cities he singles out for comment "Padua, in which a studium of letters has long flourished" and "Paris, the city of philosophers."[36] There is no reason, then, why the identification of Albert as the hero of the story in the *Vitae Fratrum* should not be correct. And since it is improbable that there was anything like a formal university faculty of Arts in Padua when Albert was young,[37] Bacon's charge that he had never received a proper training in philosophy would be to some extent substantiated, if it was in Padua that he studied.[38] It would be true that he had not graduated in any recognized faculty, and Bacon was certainly right in pointing out that at this time the arts and philosophy were not being taught within the Order. But this does not mean that Albert had not received quite a good education from some school, presumably one run privately by some Master. As we have seen, he is already treated as a scientific "expert" by his friends in Venice, and also it must have been before his entry into the Order that he acquired his familiarity with some of the writings of Aristotle.[39]

So we may take it as true, then, that Albert was a student in Padua, in which case it was probably there that he succumbed to the preaching of Jordan, who was famous for his ability to "lure" students into the Order.[40] But far too little is known of the early development of the teaching of arts and sciences in Padua for us to be able to base any dating of Albert's moves on it.[41] We have only one reasonably secure date. Albert several times mentions that he was in Lombardy during a severe earthquake,[42] and this has convincingly been identified as the one that caused considerable damage and was felt throughout northern Italy at Christmas 1222.[43]

We can assume, then, that Albert was in Lombardy by the end of 1222, but this does not necessarily mean that he was in Padua. According to the *Vitae Fratrum* his uncle was with him when he made the acquaintance of the Dominicans and prevented him from joining the Order impetuously without time for reflection. It is possible that this uncle was living in Italy in the service of the German emperor[44] and that Albert was with him there for some time before he became a Dominican.

It has come to be commonly asserted that it was in 1223 that Albert received the habit in Padua, but this assertion seems to rest solely on one of the letters of Jordan of Saxony, which Scheeben is quite right to dismiss as irrelevant.[45] The letter in question describes how successful Jordan has been in recruiting students in Padua, including the sons of "two great German counts,"[46] and Albert has been assumed to be one of the latter. But, as we saw earlier, Albert was not, so far as we know, the son of a great German count. The dating of almost all of Jordan's letters is conjectural, and Scheeben quite properly points out that Jordan was in Padua on several different occasions.[47]

Peter of Prussia cautiously abstains from attempting to date Albert's reception of the habit, but his reconstruction of what happened is well-argued and is probably correct: Albert was received into the Order in Padua, but was sent, more or less immediately, to

Cologne, in accordance with Jordan's known practice of sending new recruits back to their own countries.[48] And if Molitoris' evidence is sound (and it may well come from some document in Cologne), Albert's actual arrival in Cologne must be dated to late 1229 or early 1230, in which case it was presumably in 1229 that he heard Jordan preaching and yielded to his charm.[49] This is the only date directly proposed by our sources, and there does not seem to be any warrant for rejecting it. Albert was then in his thirties when he became a Dominican, and that is within the conventional meaning of "young man" (*iuvenis*).[50]

Our next date is supplied by the well-attested tradition noted above, that Albert's first appointment as lector was in Hildesheim. The Dominican priory in that city was founded in 1233,[51] so Albert cannot have been an official lector before that date.[52] As a relatively mature recruit, it is quite likely that he opted to make his vows without a probationary period or without a full year anyway,[53] and we may guess, though we cannot know, that he began his theological studies as soon as he arrived in Cologne. By 1235 the Dominican constitutions contained a law that nobody could be appointed a "public doctor" without first doing four years of formal study, but we do not know when this rule was introduced.[54] Certainly at least one year of formal study was envisaged in the 1220 constitutions.[55] It is, I suggest, not unlikely that Albert spent his first year in Cologne as a student and then, in view of his maturity and talents, was given some teaching to do while he completed his own studies. It is well-attested that he lectured on the Sentences twice in Cologne,[56] and this appears to refer to the period before his graduation in Paris.[57] It could well be that he lectured on them as a kind of apprentice lector, on the analogy of a bachelor of the Sentences, before he was formally appointed lector of Hildesheim.

In 1233 at the earliest, then, Albert was officially appointed a lector and sent to Hildesheim where, if we may trust a late report, he put his knowledge of natural philosophy to good effect by ridding the priory refectory of flies.[58] Thereafter he was lector *in Vriburgo*, at Regensburg ("for two years") and at Strasbourg, from where he was sent to Paris.[59] *In Vriburgo* could mean either Freiburg-im-Breisgau, where the Dominicans accepted a site in 1233 and began to establish themselves in about 1235,[60] or Freiberg in Saxony, where the Dominican priory was founded in 1236.[61] In either case

7

Albert would almost certainly have been the priory lector required by the constitutions as part of the founding community in any new house.[62] It has generally been assumed that it was to Freiburg-im-Breisgau that Albert was sent,[63] but there is nothing to prevent the alternative interpretation, which is favored by Weisheipl,[64] and indeed there is some evidence to support it. In 1240, Albert tells us, he was in Saxony and "saw a comet near the north pole,"[65] which squares with his being the lector of Freiberg in Saxony at the time. Also we know that at some stage in his life he visited the mines in Freiberg and Goslar,[66] going far out of his way to do so, because of his interest in mineralogy,[67] and this could well refer to his journey from Hildesheim to Freiberg and to expeditions made from Freiberg.

On the basis of these considerations, it is tempting to infer that Albert remained in Hildesheim and Freiberg for some years, and then spent his two years in Regensburg in 1240–42 or 1241–43 and moved to Strasbourg in 1242 or 1243 and Paris in 1243 or 1244. The difficulty with this chronology is that it does not seem to allow enough time for Albert to have achieved all the writing that we know he did in Paris before 1246. We know that he was working on book II of his commentary on the Sentences in 1246,[68] and before that he had already commented on books I and III, and before that he had already completed a fairly substantial *Summa de Creaturis*.[69] If he only arrived in Paris in 1243, it is difficult to see how he could have accomplished so much, particularly as he had first to absorb the Aristotelian learning, which is much in evidence even in the *Summa de Creaturis*. So we cannot rule out the possibility that Albert visited Saxony for some reason that we do not know in 1240, and that he was lector in Freiberg rather earlier. If we assume that he went there as a member of the founding community, he could have been lector there in 1236–37, in Regensburg in 1237–39 and in Strasbourg in 1239–40, in which case he could have been in Paris as early as 1240.[70]

At some period during this first phase of his teaching career Albert composed his earliest known work, *De Natura Boni*,[71] which reflects a familiarity with those works of Aristotle that had been available in Latin for some time, as well as the standard classical and theological authorities (Cicero, Seneca, Augustine, the Glossa Ordinaria); there is no sign of any of the new material that was causing such excitement in Paris (new and more complete translations of Aristotle and the works of Arab and Jewish philosophers).

From the tasks he was given it appears that Albert was held in some esteem by his brethren and that he was expected to contribute to the development of his rapidly expanding province.[72] According to Scheeben, Albert enjoyed other, even more impressive signs of his brethren's confidence in him: they elected him diffinitor to a Provincial Chapter during this period, and probably also sent him as diffinitor to the General Chapter in Bologna in 1238, where he secured half the votes in the election of the new Master of the Order.[73] But the sole authority for all this is a statement by Galvano della Fiamma,[74] whose fantastic improvements upon historical facts are notorious. Most scholars properly discount the whole alleged episode.[75]

The real honor paid to Albert by the Order was the decision that he should lecture on the Sentences in Paris with a view to becoming a Master in Theology. At this time Paris was the only international study-house that the Dominicans had, and even to be sent there as an ordinary student was no mean privilege, seeing that each province was only allowed to send three students there a year.[76] But the chances of becoming a Master were even more restricted. The Order possessed two chairs of theology in Paris and, although we are in the dark about many of the details concerning the early Dominican Masters, it seems probable that the Order had so far done little to exploit these chairs systematically for the benefit of the provinces at large. No clear procedure was yet established for providing friars to hold the chairs, and Guerric of St. Quentin and Godfrey of Bléneau had apparently been left in possession of them for quite some time.[77]

In 1246 the General Chapter initiated a move to extend the possibilities of study at the highest level by creating four new international study-houses (*studia generalia*), one each in the provinces of Provence, Lombardy, England and Germany.[78] It is tempting to wonder whether sending Albert to Paris was not already part of a plan to open up the academic resources of the Order more effectively. The decision to send him there was presumably made by the Master of the Order. If it was in 1241 or 1242 that the decision was made, it can be seen as one of a series of moves characteristic of the generalate of John of Wildeshausen. In the late 1240s it is noticeable that there is a rapid turnover of Dominican Masters in Paris,[79] and sending Albert from Germany, then a few years later the lector of Montpellier, Elie Brunet,[80] and finally Thomas Aquinas of the Roman province in 1251,[81] indicates at least a rudimentary policy of not allowing the two Parisian chairs to be totally dominated by the Parisian brethren. And a concern about the supply of lectors is also evident in the ruling of the 1245 General Chapter that all priors who could be usefully employed as lectors must stop being priors.[82]

When Albert arrived in Paris, perhaps in 1241 or 1242 and certainly not later than 1243, the renowned scripture scholar, Hugh of St. Cher, was provincial of Paris, a position he held until he was made a cardinal in May 1244.[83] He was succeeded by Peter of Rheims, who himself became a bishop in 1245, and then Humbert of Romans became provincial.[84] The two Dominican Masters were still Guerric and Godfrey, though we do not know whose bachelor Albert became. Guerric probably died either toward the end of 1244 or at the beginning of 1245.[85] By 1247 Godfrey was in the pope's entourage.[86]

In Paris Albert encountered a whole new intellectual world. By now almost the whole Aristotelian corpus was available in Latin and was being avidly studied, in spite of considerable uneasiness on the part of the ecclesiastical authorities. But it was largely through the Arabs that Aristotle had been brought back to the West, and their Aristotle was part of an essentially Neoplatonist package. He brought with him the pseudo-Aristotelian *Liber de Causis*, derived from the *Elements of Theology* by Proclus, one of the last great pagan Neoplatonists, and he was accompanied by the works of the Arab commentators, especially Avicenna and, slightly later, Averroes. And in addition to this wealth of supposedly Aristotelian learning, which was often in fact more Platonist than Peripatetic, a veiled Platonism was also exercising a considerable influence through the writings of "Dionysius the Areopagite," which had begun to enjoy a new vogue in the twelfth century.

Albert eagerly absorbed all this new intellectual nourishment. In his earliest Parisian writing, the *Summa de Creaturis*, finished (insofar as it was finished) by about 1244 at the latest, he is already confidently handling most of the available works of Aristotle, and he shows himself well-acquainted with a range of Islamic philosophers. And, as we shall see, he was not afraid to tackle some of the more controversial topics being debated in the schools.

After lecturing on the Sentences, Albert became a Master in Theology in 1245, perhaps taking over the chair that had been vacant since the death of Guerric. He taught for a further three years as Regent Master and then, in 1248, he was sent back to Germany to preside over the new studium generale in Cologne.[87]

While he was still a Master in Paris an aristocratic young Neapolitan had been sent to join the Dominican community in St. Jacques by the Master of the Order, to put him beyond reach of his family, whose ambitions for him were devastated by his decision to become a Dominican and who had resorted to all possible means to divert him from his chosen path. This young man, Thomas d'Aquino by name, arrived in Paris in 1246, and he seems to have attached himself to Master Albert. He copied down in his own hand the lectures that Albert was giving on the *Celestial Hierarchy* of Dionysius, and his copy served as the original on the basis of which the university stationers proceeded to publish the work. When Albert was sent to Cologne, young Thomas went with him and continued to record the lectures on the rest of the Dionysian corpus.[88]

Thomas was a reserved, quiet young man, whom the brethren nicknamed "Dumb Ox"; but bit by bit his talents emerged, and Albert is said to have commented one day, "We call him a dumb ox, but the time will come when he will make such a bellowing in his teaching that it will sound in the whole world."[89]

Among Albert's other students at this time were his devoted admirer, Ulrich of Strasbourg,[90] and Bl. Ambrose Sansedoni.[91]

From now on Albert was an increasingly public figure and the relative abundance of documentation makes it easier to keep track of him. The "lector of Cologne" was called upon to intervene and advise in a variety of local affairs and in 1252 he was appointed, together with Hugh of St. Cher (at this time papal legate in Germany), to negotiate a settlement in the long-standing dispute between the archbishop of Cologne and the citizenry.[92] In the course of his life he was frequently to be asked to undertake similar diplomatic missions.[93]

In 1254 he was elected provincial of the German Dominicans at the Provincial Chapter of Worms.[94] He had apparently already been appointed vicar of the province, presumably either by the General Chapter or by the recently elected Master of the Order, Humbert of Romans,[95] and in this capacity he presided over the Provincial Chapter. The German provincial had responsibility for a dauntingly large territory. By now there were thirty-six priories and perhaps almost as many monasteries of nuns scattered over an area including Switzerland, Austria, Belgium and the Netherlands in addition to the whole of Germany, and the province spilled over into parts of what is now France and Yugoslavia. There was also a missionary house attached to the province in Riga, Latvia.[96] The provincial was supposed to visitate all the houses in his charge,[97] and the very chapter at which Albert was elected insisted that the brethren must observe the traditional practice of travelling everywhere on foot, barring very exceptional circumstances.[98] The General Chapter of 1255 was clearly determined not to make life any easier for provincials and forbade them to have private bedrooms (as a lector Albert would have got used to having his own room),[99] and it also warned people not to travel to chapters except on foot and called for a stricter observance of the ban on carrying money when on a journey.[100] The German Provincial Chapter of 1257 fired three priors for travelling on horseback.[101] According to Peter of Prussia, Albert fully conformed to the Order's constitutional requirements, covering the length and breadth of his enormous province on foot, begging his bread as he went.[102] We cannot be certain that Albert visited every single house in person, but the extent of his travels can be seen from the widely separated places mentioned in his writings in connection with his observations of natural phenomena, from Latvia to France, from the Alps to the English Channel.[103] It seems likely that a great many of these observations were made in the course of Albert's travels as provincial. He also had to attend Provincial Chapters at Regensburg (1255) and Erfurt (1256),[104] and the General Chapter in Paris in 1256.[105]

Our sources do not give us a very personal or intimate picture of Albert as provincial. Three new priories came into existence during his term of office, but it is not known that he was personally involved in any of them. He also received the vows of the first nuns in the recently established monastery near Soest, the famous "Paradisus."[106] The excerpts quoted from Provincial Chapters during his provincialate show him insisting on such traditional observances as poverty and silence, and on a careful screening of preachers before they are allowed to preach in public.[107] He was clearly a conscientious superior, but we may wonder how far his heart was in this kind of work. As we have seen, his long journeys on visitation gave new scope to his unbounded curiosity about the world around him, and his responsibilities as provincial did not make him abandon his writing. It was while he was provincial that he wrote his important *De Anima*.[108]

In 1256 Albert got caught up, in a small way, in the conflict between the seculars and the mendicants, which had at one stage looked like crippling the work of the mendicants entirely.[109] Early in the year the Parisian secular Master, William of St. Amour, the friars' most virulent opponent, had produced a particularly inflammatory pamphlet, *De Periculis*, and this had been delated to the pope, thus bringing to a crisis the long and bitter dispute in which the heads of the two main mendicant Orders, Humbert of Romans and John of Parma, and the leading mendicant theologians in Paris, including St. Thomas Aquinas and St. Bonaventure, had been involved. All was now set for a decisive condemnation of William. In September the pope, Alexander IV, appointed a commission of cardinals to examine *De Periculis*. All that remained was the formal judgment. And at this stage, rather mysteriously, Albert turns up at the papal court in Anagni. One early source implies that he had gone there on his own initiative, which seems an unlikely thing for a conscientious provincial to have done.[110] The other major sources claim that he had been sent for by the pope precisely in view of the condemnation of William,[111] but this seems rather implausible too. The mendicant theologians had had ample opportunity to present their case, and the matter was now in the hands of the pope's commission of cardinals, which included two distinguished Parisian theologians, Eudes of Chateauroux and the Dominican Hugh of St. Cher; it is not at all clear why they should need any further theological advice from Germany.[112] So why send for Albert?

It is most unlikely that Albert, with the responsibility for his province on his shoulders, went to Italy without being summoned. So the suggestion is tempting that maybe he was sent for in connection with some quite different affair.[113] Anyway, however he came to be there, there is no doubt that he was consulted about the condemnation of *De Periculis* and his reaction is revealing. He tracked down a copy of the book, paid to have the use of it, and managed to get it transcribed overnight, with the help of several scribes, and then studied it in the twenty-four hours before the consistory met.[114]

Apart from assisting at the condemnation of William of St. Amour, we know that Albert gave a public refutation, at the papal court, of the Averroist doctrine of the non-individual nature of the agent intellect, which he later wrote up as a book, *De Unitate Intellectus*.[115] It is tempting to suppose that this was the real purpose for which he had been summoned to Anagni. In 1255 the Arts faculty in Paris had issued new regulations, in which the study of the books of Aristotle played an important part.[116] It is quite conceivable that Alexander IV was disquieted by this. Already William of Auvergne (†1249) had felt obliged to argue against the "Aristotelian" and Islamic doctrine of the non-individual soul.[117] If the pope wanted to consult someone about how he should react to the new Arts syllabus in Paris, Albert would by this time be well-established as the leading ecclesiastical authority on Aristotelianism, and so he would be an obvious person to send for. And the fact that Alexander IV made no move to censure the Parisian syllabus might reflect Albert's conviction that the philosophers have to be met on their own ground with "arguments and syllogisms," not just with dogmatic censures.[118]

How long Albert remained at the papal court we do not know, but there is no reason to suppose that he remained in Italy until the General Chapter due to meet in Florence at Pentecost 1257,[119] because this was a diffinitors' Chapter and did not involve provincials.[120] We may reasonably suppose that, as a dutiful provincial, Albert returned home to his province, though it seems he took time to see the sights of Rome on the way.[121]

The General Chapter of 1257 absolved Albert from the chore of his office, but he appears nevertheless to have been at the subsequent Provincial Chapter in Augsburg, and our sources give the impression that he presided at it.[122] Conceivably the news of his absolution from office had not yet reached Germany.[123] We do not know when the Provincial Chapter was held, but Albert was certainly in Augsburg at the end of August. He preached a series of sermons during the octave of the feast of St. Augustine in various churches, including that of the Dominican nuns, of whom he was evidently fond since he later remembered them in his will.[124] In his sermon on 30 August, which was preached in the Dominican church, he refers to his recent trip to Italy, mentioning his sight-seeing in Rome and the reflections it prompted (how much better the ancient Romans were than we are today, saving only that we have the faith and they did not). In another public sermon on Sunday he reported how he had confessed to the pope that he was overawed by him, to which the pope replied, "I am earth, I am dust, I am nothing."[125]

By March 1258 at the latest Albert was back in Cologne in his old job of lector (Regent of the studium generale).[126] And as usual we find him being called upon to advise and arbitrate and act as witness to various transactions. At least once the pope used him as his agent.[127] Clearly people trusted his judgment and his impartiality.

In June 1259 he was appointed by the Master of the Order, Humbert of Romans, to a special commission at the General Chapter of Valenciennes, whose brief was to draw up a plan for the organization of studies throughout the Order. It is clear from the membership of the commission that Humbert wanted Dominican studies to be modelled on the pattern of the University of Paris: apart from Albert, the other members of the commission were Bonhomme, Florent de Hesdin, Thomas Aquinas and Peter of Tarentaise, who were all Parisian Masters. As a result of their work, the Order for the first time officially adopted a policy of providing a full program of studies, at least for the brighter students, including the arts (and therefore philosophy) as well as theology. This was a momentous innovation and represented a triumph for Albert, who had been insisting for years on the importance of philosophy. Other points of interest are that all the brethren are expected to attend the classes given by the lectors, including priors and other lectors who are free; study of a fairly formal kind is evidently envisaged as a full part of Dominican observance, not just as something that the friars pass through as part of their formation. Also lectors in the more important studia are to have a bachelor, just like the Masters in the universities.[128]

Albert had secured for his Order an educational program after his own heart, but his personal work as an educator was rudely interrupted early in 1260. On 5 January Alexander IV appointed him bishop of Regensburg, and at the same time wrote to the canons of

Regensburg telling them to accept Albert as their pastor;[129] their own candidate had refused the bishopric.[130] A rumor of what was going on reached the ears of Humbert, who promptly sent an impassioned letter to Albert, pleading with him to refuse the papal injunction. This famous document, which incidentally reveals what an important man Albert was in Dominican eyes, is worth quoting in full:

Brother Humbert, useless servant of the friars of the Order of Preachers, to his dearest brother in Christ, Albert, lector of Cologne, eternal salvation in heaven and may he shine in the world with the splendour of his merits and example.

A rumour has just reached me, in a letter from the Roman curia, and it has pierced my heart to the quick and would have shattered me completely if it had not been counteracted by the holy and firm confidence that I have in you in all good. We have been given to understand that they are saying in the curia that a decision has been made that you are to be raised to some episcopal rank.

It is not difficult to believe that the curia might have made such a decision, but no one who knows you would ever think it possible that you might be inclined to consent to such a decision. How could anyone believe that at the end of your life you would be willing to blot your own glory like this and that of the Order which you have made so glorious? Dearest, dearest brother! If you yield like this, no one in our Order or in any other kind of poor religion will ever resist again the temptation to pass over to a position of rank; they will all cite your example as an excuse. If people in the world hear of this, they will all misunderstand you and everyone else who has made profession in a religion like ours, thinking that we do not love poverty but only put up with it for as long as we cannot escape from it.

Please do not let yourself be moved by any advice or entreaties from our lords in the curia; such things quickly and easily become a matter of ridicule and mockery there. And do not be defeated by any annoyances you have received in the Order—the Order loves and respects everyone, but it specially boasts of you in the Lord. Even if you had suffered far worse annoyances than you ever have or ever will, annoyances which would have defeated anyone else, you are quite sensible enough to know that your own gigantic shoulders can support them cheerfully, as is proper. Do not let yourself be turned aside by any papal precepts; in cases like this such precepts are reckoned to be mere words, not meant sincerely, and they have never been known finally to constrain anyone who seriously wanted to resist them, and this kind of holy disobedience for a time usually enhances rather than damages people's reputations.

Consider what has happened to people who have allowed themselves to be drawn into this kind of thing. What do people say of them? What do they achieve? What is their position? How do they end up? Turn over in your heart the enormous difficulties and perplexities involved in ruling the churches in Germany and how difficult it is there to avoid offending either God or man. And how will your soul endure being tangled up all day long in worldly business and living with the continual risk of sin, when it has such a love for the scriptures and for purity of conscience? If it is a harvest of souls that they want from you, bear in mind what a countless harvest of souls will be utterly lost if you change your status like this—all those souls which you undoubtedly gain not only in Germany but almost everywhere in the world by your reputation and example and writing. And it is far from certain what sort of harvest you might gain as a bishop. Dearest brother, you see our whole Order rescued from the greatest tribulations and enjoying anew the greatest consolation; what will it be like if you plunge it into even deeper distress by any act of yours?

I would rather hear of my favourite son being laid out on a bier than of his being exalted on a bishop's throne, if this would mean that I did not lose my hope of firmness in such matters and that everyone would not have to depart from this world in sorrow. I kneel before you in my heart, I adjure you by the humility of the undefiled Virgin and her Son, do not abandon your position of humility. What the enemy's pride and cunning has perhaps obtained for the harm and upset of many people, I hope it will rebound on his own head, to your and our double glory and honour. Write me something to comfort me and all my and your brethren, to deliver us from our fear. Pray for us. The grace of Jesus Christ be with you. Amen.[131]

The question of whether Dominicans should become bishops or not had been bothersome from the beginning. St. Dominic was known to have refused several bishoprics,[132] and this was interpreted as a gesture of humility and refusal of grandeur, though in fact it is probably better seen as the expression of a concern to prevent the preaching ministry becoming confused with or being limited by other kinds of responsibility or authority.[133] The story that Dominic specifically rejected the idea of his friars becoming bishops is almost certainly apocryphal.[134] From quite early on there were Dominican bishops whose reputation remained high in the Order, like Guala, bishop of Brescia; Constantine, bishop of Orvieto; and Humbert's own predecessors as provincial of Paris, Peter of Rheims and Cardinal Hugh of St. Cher. What complicated the issue was that ecclesiastical preferment provided the obvious way out for people who had entered the Order, maybe with enthusiasm, but who then found its discipline and austerity irksome; according to Jordan of Saxony it is not surprising if they turn out not to be very edifying bishops.[135] From Jordan onward successive Masters of the Order and successive General Chapters tried to shut off this possibility of escaping from the Order by seeking promotion in the church. In 1260 the constitutional position was that no Dominican could accept a bishopric without permission from his provincial or from the Master of the Order, unless he was "constrained by such a command that it would be mortal sin to disobey it"; the penalty for becoming a bishop contrary to this ruling was expulsion from the Order.[136] But Humbert was almost certainly exaggerating when he suggested that everyone, inside and outside the Order, would be scandalized if Albert became a bishop. The almost exactly contemporary *Vitae Fratrum* certainly reports Jordan's explanation of why friars make bad bishops, but Hugh of St. Cher is mentioned several times without embarrassment as having become a cardinal,[137] and in his slightly earlier Chronicle Gerald de Frachet gives the impression of being rather proud of the Dominican bishops and cardinals.[138] Thomas of Cantimpré only heard about Albert becoming a bishop when he had already written about three quarters of his *De Apibus*— up to II 49.5 he refers to *magister Albertus*, but in II 51.11 he adds *postea Ratisponensis episcopus*—but Albert's elevation seems in no way to shock him, and he continues to cite him as an edifying example (for example, in II 57.50). In the 1270s Stephen Salagnac regards the Dominican bishops as one of the glories of the Order, though he also notes with approval the friars who refused such honors.[139]

Albert must have pondered deeply the ambiguities of his situation. On 1 March he is still functioning as "lector of Cologne,"[140] and by then he must have had both the papal letter and that from Humbert for several weeks. In the end, as Bernard Gui tells us, "he accepted the bishopric of Regensburg under constraint."[141] "Under constraint" echoes the very language of the constitutions, and it is more than likely that Gui is correctly indicating Albert's verdict, that the pope's command was such that it could not be disobeyed without mortal sin. Humbert could dismiss such papal precepts lightly, but then he was far more familiar with the curia than Albert was, and he had witnessed the devastating volte-face of Innocent IV who turned against the friars at the end of his life, becoming a figure of malevolent myth in some Dominican circles. Thomas of Cantimpré tells us with evident glee that he was struck down as soon as he signed the Bull that effectively hamstrung the work of the mendicants and never left his bed again, and when he died soon afterward his soul was seen by a convenient visionary being handed over to Francis and Dominic for judgment.[142] Humbert could be cynical about popes and their curias, but Albert, as we have seen, was overawed by the papal majesty and edified by the papal humility. After two months or so of reflection he evidently came to the conclusion that the pope's behest must be obeyed. On 29 March he quietly entered Regensburg and spent the night in the Dominican priory, and the following day, which was Maundy Thursday, he formally took possession of his see.[143] When and where he received episcopal consecration is not known.

It was no easy task that had been assigned to Albert. His predecessor had been induced to resign the previous October, after a spate of very serious accusations, and was saved from being censured only by meekly retiring into obscurity. He had incurred enormous debts and, according to Alexander IV, his diocese was in a thoroughly bad way, materially and spiritually. Albert was appointed in the hope that his sound judgment and eloquent doctrine would set the diocese back on its feet.[144]

According to the Dominican constitutions even friars who were exempt from the Order's jurisdiction, such as those who were bishops, were expected to abide by the Order's discipline in fasting and in their style of dress.[145] Whatever Humbert's fears may have been, Albert did not find much opportunity for self-indulgence, even if he was looking for it. When he took possession of his episcopal residence there was "not a drop to drink in the cellar nor a single grain of wheat and not even an egg to eat."[146] As for his style of dress, all we know is that his footwear amused the populace, who gave him a nickname that Weisheipl pleasantly translates "Boots the bishop."[147]

The medieval biographers mainly give us an edifying picture of Albert's humble and spiritual way of life as a bishop,[148] but Tolomeo of Lucca is probably nearer the truth when he suggests that Albert found himself in a "pit" of secular affairs most unlike the tranquillity he had enjoyed in Cologne.[149] On the very day of his enthronement he was approached by the emissaries of an abbey wanting the renewal of an exemption from tithes,[150] and he cannot have paid off the debts of his diocese, which apparently he did,[151] without devoting at least some of his attention to financial matters. It may be true that he entrusted the secular business of his diocese to "reliable people in whom there was no greed,"[152] but it is not the work of a day establishing a good staff to handle all the business of a diocese.

Apart from restoring the finances of his see, Albert was expected by the pope to improve its spiritual condition. He must have travelled around a certain amount to acquire his nickname, so he presumably visited the parishes of his diocese,[153] and he at least made arrangements for the visitation of the monasteries in his territory, though it is not clear whether he visited them himself.[154] In September 1260 he attended a meeting of the bishops of the province of Salzburg, which took certain steps to bolster up church discipline and prevent financial abuses.[155]

As always, Albert found time to pursue his studies as a naturalist and to do some writing. During his short episcopacy he apparently wrote a commentary on Euclid[156] and more or less completed his massive *De Animalibus*.[157] In the Middle Ages an autograph copy (or so it was supposed) of his commentary on Luke was preserved in the Dominican priory of Regensburg, which was believed to have been written while Albert was bishop of the city,[158] but this is probably not quite accurate.[159]

In the spring of 1261 Albert set off once again for the papal curia, evidently with the intention of resigning his see.[160] He reached Viterbo after the pope's death on 25 May, but he seems not to have returned to Germany. A document of 23 December shows that his vicars were still running the diocese in his absence.[161] But although Urban IV was elected on 29 August, it was not until the following spring that Albert's resignation was accepted.[162]

It was no doubt while he was at a loose end in Italy that Albert went travelling. In some place, which he describes as *Campania iuxta Graeciam*, he was delighted to discover a translation of Aristotle's *De Motu Animalium*.[163] Presumably the place in question was in southern Campania, near the Greek-speaking community in Calabria.

What happened after Albert's resignation is not entirely clear from the sources, which, in any case, have a rather garbled account of the whole episode of Albert's episcopacy. He appears to have retained a pension from his diocese,[164] and he probably stayed on in the papal court.[165] In October 1262 the papal court moved to Orvieto, and by this time Thomas Aquinas was probably already in residence there in the Dominican convent,[166] so presumably Albert enjoyed renewing his acquaintance with his talented pupil.

In his regained leisure Albert continued to work on various writings. He probably completed the *De Animalibus*, if he had not already done so,[167] and a book based on his new-found translation of *De Motu Animalium*.[168] He was also perhaps working on some New Testament commentaries. If there is any substance to the story that the commentary on Luke was written during Albert's time as bishop of Regensburg, it could be that he did some work on it during his stay at the papal court at the time of his resignation. His comment on Luke 22:26 reflects the tone of a man still sore from the trials of office:

> In the early church not much attention was paid to power, but people took note of humility and examples of charity. . . . Nothing is less burdensome than to govern your subjects in humility and meekness, so long as the times permit it. But when the number of wicked people obliges a prelate of the church to proceed with severity and grim discipline, then it becomes intolerable for him, as it did for Moses, unless you enjoy pomp so much that you are willing to put up with or even encourage the wicked, as the prelates of our time do, who are representatives of Sardanapolus rather than of Jesus Christ.[169]

The commentary on Luke was apparently not completed until later, and it was preceded by that on Matthew,[170] so Albert was presumably writing that too while he was in the papal entourage.

From February 1263 until the death of Urban IV on 2 October 1264 Albert, now nearly seventy if not already in his seventies, was the pope's special envoy in Germany. His initial mandate was to organize support for the pope's plans for a new crusade to liberate the holy places, and he was given full power to recruit assistant preachers, to raise money, to grant dispensations to people willing to become crusaders.[171] Urban was clearly deeply committed to his rather unrealistic hope that a crusade could be mounted, and he relied on Dominicans for help in propagating the idea.[172] Albert seems also to have become the pope's troubleshooter in a more general way in Germany. We find him engaged in a variety of tasks, including being vicar general of the archdiocese of Cologne, presumably because relations between the archbishop and the city were making it impossible for the diocese to function normally.[173] The extent to which Albert's probity and impartiality were trusted is indicated by the readiness of the bishop of Augsburg and Count Ludwig von Öttingen to give him the decisive voice in settling a long-standing dispute between them.[174]

Albert was certainly in Germany by early May 1263, and he celebrated the feast of the Ascension (10 May) with his beloved Dominican nuns in Augsburg, to whom he granted an indulgence. But, considering his age, he seems to have travelled around with impressive speed and energy (though presumably no longer always on foot).[175] He was in Polling on 5 May, Augsburg on 10 May, Donauwörth on 13 May, Würzburg on 27 May, Frankfurt on 5 June. . . .[176]

With the death of Urban IV Albert's papal commission automatically lapsed. On 4 December 1264 Albert, no longer styling himself "Preacher of the Crusade," is named as one of the arbitrators in a dispute in Würzburg, and since one of the witnesses is a Dominican called Henry it has been suggested that Albert had settled in Würzburg because his brother, Henry, was living there.[177] But another document from Würzburg from December 1265 is witnessed by no less than two Dominicans called Henry, neither of whom is Henry of Lauingen, so it would be rash to assume that the Henry of 1264 was Albert's brother.[178] It is not until 1274 that we have any sure evidence that Henry of Lauingen was at Würzburg.[179] But whether or not his brother was there, it does seem likely that Albert did settle at Würzburg with the Dominicans. We hear of him there several times between 4 December 1264 and 23 December 1265, and we do not hear of him anywhere else.[180] For 1266 we have no documentation, but in the spring of 1267 we find him at Würzburg again,[181] so the presumption is that he had been living there continuously since 1264, working as always at his writing and responding to the calls of those who needed the help of his prudence and authority. It was almost certainly in Würzburg that he completed his commentary on Luke.[182]

In 1267 the energetic old man set off on another round of travels. On 6 May he granted an indulgence to those who visited the Dominican church of Regensburg on certain days, but we cannot be sure that he went to Regensburg in person. On 14 July he was at the Cistercian nuns' monastery of Burtscheid, near Aachen. In August and September he was in Cologne, and on 29 April 1268 he consecrated the Dominican church in Esslingen. After that he seems to have settled for a while in Strasbourg,[183] where his friend and disciple Ulrich of Strasbourg was the Dominican lector.[184]

As a retired bishop, Albert was not subject to the jurisdiction of the Dominicans, and we have seen that the medieval biographers' claim that when he resigned his bishopric he returned immediately to the discipline of the Order and to his teaching in Cologne[185] is untrue. But there are two, unfortunately rather enigmatic, letters from the Master of the Order that seem to indicate Albert was and was known to be willing to undertake work for the Order. One of them thanks Albert for what he has done for the Order in Strasbourg in terms which imply that he has been teaching there. The other shows that he had been asked to go to Paris to teach and had expressed a willingness to do so in principle "if only he had a lector" (this condition is mysterious to us); instead he is now asked to go and lecture in Cologne, where the clergy are apparently clamoring for his presence. The language of these letters makes it clear that Albert is being addressed not as a subject, but as a bishop willing to do the Order any favor that is within his power.[186] Since we know that Albert was in or around Strasbourg in 1268–69 and that he was certainly back in Cologne in 1270, these letters can safely be dated to this period, and it was presumably in 1269 that he was asked to go to Paris, no doubt to replace Peter of Tarentaise, who had vacated his chair of theology in that year to become provincial of Paris.[187]

So Albert, in spite of his pension and his independence of the Order's jurisdiction, is still very much a Dominican, and in some of his letters he refers to himself as "of the Order of Preachers," not just as "ex-bishop of Regensburg";[188] and his will leaves us in no doubt about the genuine bonds of mutual affection that linked him with his brethren.[189] He had the good of the Order at heart and was still willing to do what he could to foster it, and in accordance with his own special gifts that meant in particular a readiness to go on being a teacher.

So in 1269 or 1270 Albert returns at last to his beloved convent of Cologne, to spend his remaining years as the grand old man of the studium. But he was by no means left in peace. Right through to August 1279 he is still being called upon to do all sorts of episcopal odd jobs and to lend his wisdom and authority to sundry transactions and negotiations, and at least sometimes these motley tasks involved travelling quite a distance from Cologne.[190] When Ulrich of Strasbourg was provincial (1272–77)[191] he leaned heavily on Albert's support.[192]

On 7 May 1274 the second Council of Lyons opened and it seems reasonably certain that Albert was there.[193] According to Peter of Prussia he spoke on behalf of Rudolf of Hapsburg's candidacy for the kingship of the Romans,[194] and this is not implausible. Rudolf was certainly a considerable benefactor of the Dominicans later on,[195] and it looks as if the Dominicans, including Ulrich of Strasbourg, had supported his candidacy before he became king.[196]

The facts about Albert's declining years are difficult to disentangle from the legends. In January 1279 he declared in his will that he was in good health,[197] and as late as 18 August he was still capable (or was regarded as being capable) of doing routine ecclesiastical business.[198] On the other hand, fears that he was going senile are ascribed to the brethren as early as 1274.[199]

In the canonization process of St. Thomas we are told, on the authority of Albert of Brescia, that Albert learned miraculously of the death of Thomas in 1274 and suddenly burst into tears.[200] We learn from Bartholomew of Capua, on the other hand, that when Albert "heard of" Thomas' death (with no suggestion of a miracle) he wept so much and so often that the brethren were afraid that he was "light-headed" because of his old age.[201] Bartholomew's source is Ugo of Lucca, whom he calls "provincial of Tuscany," but Ugo stopped being provincial in 1304[202] and Bartholomew was giving his evidence on 8 August 1319,[203] so it is not unreasonable to doubt the accuracy of some of the details of his story. Ugo was apparently a student of Albert's in Cologne at some time, but not necessarily in 1274; it is not until 1277, as we shall see, that his presence in Cologne is most securely attested. But if Albert was still teaching in 1277, he can hardly have been senile in 1274.

The source of Albert of Brescia's story can only be conjectured, but it looks as if the Italian Albert had been a student of the German Albert, and it is probably a Cologne story that he is reporting. In that case it is not absurd to believe that there was a tradition in Cologne that Albert was deeply upset to hear of the death of Thomas (which is not difficult to accept), and that Albert of Brescia, in accordance with his own taste for miraculous revelations, added a supernatural spice to what was originally a fairly ordinary human occurrence. If some of the brethren found Albert's reaction excessive, which is not impossible, that does not suffice to prove that Albert was in fact light-headed because of old age. After all, he was probably far more aware than most of his students were of the importance of the philosophical and theological enterprise in which he and Thomas had been engaged, and in the ordinary course of events it should have been the younger man, not the older, to carry on the struggle for it.

Bartholomew of Capua also informs us, still on the authority of Ugo of Lucca, that a rumor reached Albert in Cologne that Thomas' writings were being impugned in Paris, and Albert determined to go to Paris to defend them. The brethren were afraid that he was too old for such a journey, and in particular they were worried that he might tarnish his reputation if he should turn out to be failing in his memory and intellect. But Albert would not be dissuaded; he went to Paris, summoned the university (*studium generale*) and delivered a rousing defense of Thomas. Ugo apparently accompanied him. Then the old man went back to Cologne and had all the works of Thomas read to him and declared that "Thomas had completed everyone's work until the end of the world and that it was useless for anyone to work thereafter."[204]

This much loved story of Thomas' venerable master going to Paris to defend his works has been severely criticized,[205] but it is unlikely that Bartholomew, who is normally a reliable witness, simply made it up or that Ugo had fabricated it out of nothing. On the other hand, it is odd that the fairly numerous Parisian accounts that survive of the events of 1277 contain no mention of any visit by Albert, nor does the Cologne tradition (apart from the evidence of Ugo as mediated by Bartholomew) preserve any memory of Albert undertaking such a momentous journey.

What makes the story historically attractive is that an intervention by Albert could help to explain what actually happened in 1277. The stage was all set for a formal censure of Thomas in Paris, and it was only prevented by a direct veto from some of the cardinals meeting in conclave to elect a new pope. The bishop of Paris, Stephen Tempier, had to content himself with a condemnation of a list of mostly Thomistic propositions taken from the writings of Giles of Rome. As early as 1277 Godfrey of Fontaines was able to use Albert's barely finished *Summa Theologiae* precisely in support of Giles' condemned theses.[206] Either a copy of Albert's *Summa* had found its way remarkably quickly to Paris, or specially tailored excerpts had been made available for use in the controversy over Thomas' doctrines.

It seems likely that the Master of the Order, John of Vercelli, who was in Paris at this time, had taken steps to thwart Tempier's moves against Thomas. And it is surely not improbable that he had solicited the support of Albert. It may be difficult to believe that Albert actually went to Paris in person—Bartholomew of Capua may have misunderstood Ugo's story or remembered it in an exaggerated form. But he may well have sent some extracts from his *Summa* that he thought would be useful. And it is quite conceivable that he summoned his own studium generale in Cologne to listen to an address based on the text, "What praise is it to the living to be praised by the dead?" applying "living" to Thomas and "dead," surely, to himself and not, as Bartholomew says, to "the others." If this is the story brought back by Ugo, it could have grown in Bartholomew's mind during the intervening fifteen years into the much more dramatic tale of the old man actually going to Paris and summoning a meeting of the Parisian studium generale (the university).

It is also obviously possible that Albert then set himself to a study of the writings of Thomas (which he may well not have read exhaustively before). But it is highly unlikely that he declared that Thomas had put all future theologians out of business for the rest of time.[207]

If Ugo's testimony is to be trusted thus far, then Albert was still teaching in 1277. But according to Tolomeo of Lucca, Albert's memory, at least in matters of learning, failed badly about three years before his death, "as an example to others."[208] More vaguely Henry of Herford reports that "at last, broken by all his work and by old age, his mind began to wander"; as an illustration of this he tells us how one day the archbishop of Cologne went to visit Albert and when he knocked on the door Albert replied from within, "Albert is not here."[209] Tolomeo's source is probably Ugo or some other Italian student of Albert's, while Herford is drawing on a German tradition. Their agreement makes it reasonable to conclude that there is a basis of truth in the allegation that Albert became a bit absent-minded in his last years. The "three years" specified by Tolomeo suggest that the story brought home by Ugo (or whoever it was) was that Albert's memory actually failed while Ugo (or whoever) was there as his student; and the comment "as an example to others" implies that this failure of memory was fairly sudden and public. And this must be what underlies the tradition, first found in Luis of Valladolid, that Albert actually had to abandon a lecture in mid-course and then never lectured again.[210] Maybe it was not literally in mid-lecture that Albert failed, but it is not difficult to believe that he had to abandon a projected lecture course and, since the old man seems to have been a living legend, word would no doubt have got round and been exaggerated.

There seems to be no reason, then, why we should not accept that Albert taught until 1277, then had to give up because of his failing memory, and that in the period immediately before his death his mind began to wander a bit.

The more elaborate stories that some of the sources relate can without hesitation be regarded as legendary accretions.[211]

On 15 November 1280 Albert died in the Dominican convent in Cologne. He was beatified in 1622 and canonized as a doctor of the church in 1931. In 1941 he was officially made the patron saint of natural scientists.

*

Albert's career shows that he was a competent administrator and a conscientious religious and ecclesiastical superior. The number of occasions on which people had recourse to his arbitration indicates his reputation for integrity and fairness, and his fearlessness in dealing with people is illustrated by a story he himself told in one of his sermons:

> A thief was caught once and I interceded for him with an important judge. The judge refused to listen to me, so I said to him, "What are you talking about? You are a greater thief than he is. He stole three pence, but you have stolen a thousand marks." When he heard this he had the man freed, and he blushed.[212]

If this is how Albert talked, it is a wonder that he did not make more enemies. But it looks as if all sorts of people felt confident in his honesty and in his practical wisdom, and so he kept on being asked to resolve tedious disputes and seems not to have refused his services when they were wanted.

But his life's work and his great joy was in study and teaching, whether in the classroom or by writing.

That enjoyment is best which is happiest. And the happiest is one which cannot be touched by guilt or pain. And that is the enjoyment which people have in their hearts with wisdom, because no sin ever approaches wisdom. I have often spent the whole night like this, never suspecting that even two hours of the night had passed.[213]

Of Albert's devotion to study there can be no doubt. The breadth of his reading and the volume of his writings, composed in the course of a life busy with other duties, make it easy to believe that he did indeed often sit up all night. Since he travelled on foot he could not, like John Wesley, read while he rode, but he could make use of his travels in other ways. Great reader that he was, he was also an inveterate looker at things and he clearly liked talking to the people he met about everything under the sun in the hope of gleaning bits of information. His works reveal observations made all over the place and give us charming glimpses of him chatting to elderly fishermen about the noise made by fish when they mate[214] or to veteran hunters and falconers.[215] He liked his friends to tell him about curiosities they had encountered. One of his colleagues in Cologne, whom he describes as *curiosus experimentator*, delighted him with his report of a peculiar magnet possessed by the emperor Frederick.[216] And he must have had a reputation for appreciating such things, because while he was teaching in Paris he was given a pearl full of images of snakes.[217] He apparently once possessed (perhaps before he joined the Order) a horse that suffered from a cold in the nose, and after he returned to Cologne in 1257 he seems to have kept a snake that got drunk one day and went flopping round the cloister; he also had a puppy with one white eye and one black eye.[218]

Nothing seems to have eluded Albert's interest. He studied the laying habits of different kinds of flies,[219] checked out (and found to be untrue) a common belief about the nesting of vultures,[220] noticed that people's urine goes a different color when they fast ("as we sometimes do");[221] he doggedly offered pieces of metal to any ostriches he met, to see if it was true that they would eat them (he found that they refused).[222] Albert could unhesitatingly endorse Aristotle's sentiment: "There are wonders to look at in all the things of nature."[223] "The whole world is theology for us, because the heavens proclaim the glory of God."[224]

Albert was not only an omnivorous student, he was also a dedicated teacher, and he particularly enjoyed it when he could share his intellectual enthusiasms and discoveries with his brethren. Although he was patently a very zealous pedagogue, what delighted him most was the intellectual companionship that he found in a Dominican studium. In his writings he generally refers not to his "students" but to his "companions" (*socii*). It was his great joy "to seek the truth in the pleasure of companionship" (*in dulcedine societatis quaerere veritatem*).[225] It was in this context that Albert could venture at times to be somewhat outrageous. When he was appointed Regent of the new studium generale in Cologne the Dominican constitutions still forbade the study of "the books of the pagans," except with special permission from the Master of the Order or from a General Chapter; the brethren were to confine their studies to "theological books."[226] But within two or three years Albert was lecturing on Aristotle's *Ethics*, of which a new translation (the first to contain the whole work) had recently been completed by Grosseteste. His lectures were faithfully recorded by his student, Thomas Aquinas.[227] When he returned to Cologne in 1258 he apparently lectured on Aristotle's works on animals.[228]

As a Regent Master, though, Albert's official responsibility was the teaching of theology and, in particular, the exposition of scripture,[229] and there is no reason whatsoever to believe that he neglected this task or that he would have been allowed to retain his position as Regent for long if he had neglected it. Nor is there the slightest reason to imagine that Albert was reluctant to devote his attention to the word of God. "Anyone who lacks the consolation of the Spirit falters spiritually through thirst and hunger; the body needs food if it is to stand firm in the battle, and it is the same with the spirit: unless it is fed with the word of God and with God's charm (*dulcedo*), it will inevitably abandon its work, power will fall from its hands. So we need often to be nourished by the charm of the word of God."[230] At the end of his life Albert was working on theological writing and especially on his scriptural commentaries.[231] And this final phase of his writing is the fulfilment of his many years of teaching; the vast bulk of his philosophical writings did not originate in lecture courses.[232]

Albert's reputation as being chiefly a philosopher[233] is not entirely fair to him, but it is not difficult to see how it arose. He was firmly persuaded of the importance of philosophical studies and in response to the persistent demands of his students (his "companions") he undertook the colossal task of "making intelligible to the Latins all the parts of philosophy."[234] He could see that this was needed, and his aim was to produce what would be "useful to students."[235] His project was a far more elaborate and developed version of the more traditional one undertaken at approximately the same time, in about 1250, by his English confrère, Robert Kilwardby, whose *De Ortu Scientiarum* may well have been composed at the request of his superiors to provide an introduction to the whole range of philosophy and the arts for Dominican students.[236] But although much of his life was devoted to expounding Peripatetic thought, Albert was not prepared to be cowed by the authority of "the philosopher": "If you believe that Aristotle was a man, then no doubt he could make mistakes like the rest of us."[237] Albert was no uncritical partisan: "You cannot be a complete philosopher without knowing both philosophies, Aristotle's and Plato's."[238] And he seems to have been rather annoyed when people regarded him as necessarily adhering to the Aristotelianism he was concerned, for pedagogical reasons, to expound.[239]

The gigantic exposition of Peripatetic philosophy was the largest, but it was not the only work written for the sake of others. At some time in the mid-1270s Albert replied seriously, if perhaps somewhat speedily, to a letter from Giles of Lessines in Paris, who asked him—addressing him as "true enlightener of minds"—to comment on fifteen propositions ascribed to some university Masters supposed to be among the best philosophers and clearly related to the thirteen propositions condemned by the bishop of Paris in December 1270.[240]

The *Summa Theologiae* was also written in response to the request "of the brethren and many others."[241] More specifically it was written for the sake of lectors who have only limited access to books,[242] evidently lectors working outside the main study-houses.[243]

Albert's output was enormous, even though the authenticity of some of the writings ascribed to him is still in dispute. The current critical edition is envisaged as running to thirty-nine volumes of certainly genuine works. Unfortunately there is still much uncertainty about the exact chronology of all these works. The *Summa de Crea-*

turis must have been completed by about 1244. The commentary on the Sentences was well under way by 1246, but was not completed until after Albert's return to Cologne, in about 1249. The Dionysian commentaries were also begun in Paris, but the lectures on most of the Dionysian works were delivered in Cologne, the whole corpus being finished in 1250. The exposition of Aristotle, complete with extra treatises to fill the gaps left by the philosopher's own works and not excluding the pseudo-Aristotelian *Liber de Causis*, occupied Albert from about 1250 until about 1270. The scriptural commentaries, which may have been revised more than once, probably date between about 1262 and 1274 or even later. The *Summa Theologiae* was certainly not completed until after the Council of Lyons in 1274, to which Albert refers.[244] Albert also wrote some devotional verse, but it is not known how much or when he wrote it.[245]

The popular *De Adhaerendo Deo* is certainly not by Albert, in spite of its traditional ascription to him,[246] and the two treatises on the Mass have recently been subjected to a close scrutiny resulting in the conclusion that they are probably not genuine.[247] The treatise on prayer, which was attributed by its editor to Albert, is also not at all likely to be by him.[248]

Albert was evidently prepared to give unstintingly of his time and energy for the sake of his brethren and others, as St. Dominic had done before him. All the same, a certain tetchiness does from time to time appear in his writings. In 1271 he, like St. Thomas and Kilwardby, received from the Master of the Order, John of Vercelli, a list of forty-three questions with a request that he comment on them.[249] Apparently the trouble had started in Venice. Someone, presumably one of the lectors there, was propounding ideas that were found disturbing. Baxiano of Lodi, also a lector there, had written to Thomas asking for an urgent response and shortly afterward the students too had written to Thomas, adding a few extra perplexities. Thomas replied courteously and clearly,[250] but plainly the situation was not eased and the Master of the Order became involved and decided to seek the opinion of three of the Order's leading theologians. Thomas dropped all he was doing—and does not disguise from the Master the inconveniences caused to him, and he hints fairly clearly that he considers that he has gone beyond the call of duty in taking all this trouble. He also complains that he has received the list of questions with no indication of the contexts in which they were raised. But, once again, he responds patiently and generously. He insists that most of the questions are not properly doctrinal at all, and he warns that dogmatic interventions in philosophical disputes can easily lead to a fiasco. Wherever possible he tries to find a benign interpretation of the matters raised, even though it is clear that some of the questions arouse little interest in him.[251]

Kilwardby, in his response, also seems concerned to provide a serious answer, and on one mathematical question he expatiates at considerable length. He seems to have found it quite an interesting task responding to the Master's letter.[252]

Albert, by contrast, intimates that he is replying only because of his affection for John of Vercelli; he is nearly blind from old age and would rather be attending to his prayers, he says, than replying to "the questions of an undisciplined mind."[253] He actually deals with the questions at greater length than Thomas does, but clearly he is getting more and more annoyed as he goes on. He makes no attempt to sympathize with what the propounder of the disputed theses might have been trying to get at, and he generally gives the impression that only someone who was philosophically illiterate would ever have raised such questions. From question 15 onward his comments become positively rude. "This question is not much good" (15), "this comes from some silly fancy" (17), "utterly silly" (19), "this is ridiculous" (25), "only a madman would say this" (26). To the question whether the names of the saints will be written up in the sky for all to see, Thomas says calmly that he doubts it, but it is a harmless idea, and Kilwardby even seems quite sympathetic to it;[254] all Albert has to say is that anyone suggesting such a thing must be out of his mind.[255] Thomas sees nothing wrong, in an appropriately academic context, in debating whether the soul of Christ came *ex traduce*; Albert says the question is "fatuous."[256]

Albert may have suffered from failing eyesight in 1271 as he claims, but he was far from having abandoned writing. He was still as concerned as ever to provide books that would be useful to his brethren. But he had his own ideas about what would be useful and did not like wasting his time on fools.

And he had worse than fools to contend with. Every now and then he gave vent to his anger at those among his own brethren who made light of philosophy, mocking what they could not be bothered to understand,[257] who could see no point in his laborious efforts to make Peripatetic philosophy intelligible to the Latins. And the opponents of philosophy in the Order were not just the people who looked back nostalgically to the early days when (or so it was maintained) the brethren were usually to be found in church saying their prayers (like the friar who was believed, according to Humbert, to have gone "silly from too much devotion" and expressed profound disapprobation of the brethren in Paris who were not generally to be found in church).[258] There was clearly a "market" for stories about friars who lost their faith through too much philosophical speculation,[259] and Jordan complains about people who sacrificed study to "unintelligent devotions;"[260] but the most troublesome problem was posed by the attitude of some of the Order's academics. In 1231 a Dominican theologian, preaching a university sermon in Paris, criticized people "who have learned the language of the Spirit perfectly well, I mean theology, but then they speak it like barbarians, corrupting it with philosophy; once people have learned metaphysics they never stop talking about points and lines in their theology. People like that clothe the king in soiled, torn raiment."[261] Not long before Albert went to Paris, Richard Fishacre, a Dominican Master in Oxford, expressed surprise at people who "so enjoy the embrace of the vulgar servant (philosophy) that they pay no attention to the mistress (theology)" and who can scarcely be torn from secular studies "when they are too old to beget children."[262] Even the founder of one of the Dominican chairs in Paris, John of St. Giles, had preached that the saints study only those things they will have to answer for on the day of judgment, while "we want to know how the world and the sun were made and other irrelevant things, instead of caring about the things for which we shall be held to account." The business of scholars, he declared, is to study the scriptures and in particular to study in the book of conscience.[263] Even after Humbert's commission on studies had secured a recognized place for philosophy in the Dominican curriculum, the traditional ban on secular learning retained its place in the constitutions[264] and there is evidence of a continuing embarrassment about Dominicans studying philosophy,[265] in spite of Humbert's own explanation of why it should be studied.[266] Even in the development of the biography of Albert we can detect a certain uneasiness about his philosophical interests.[267]

Although Albert's wholehearted acceptance of scientific and philosophical studies was in the mainstream of the Dominican tradition, as it unfolded in subsequent centuries, he must sometimes have felt that he was a lone voice crying in an unsympathetic wilderness. But, even apart from the apostolic need for Dominicans to be able to deal competently with the speculative questions with which they were faced by their contemporaries—and intellectual innocence often raises questions with profound implications for faith, which it takes considerable intellectual sophistication to deal with—Albert could not have begun to understand the attitude of people who go through their lives in devout unawareness of all the fascinating traces of God that can be found in all his works. "The whole world is theology for us." In *De Animalibus* 11.2.3.84–85 Albert paraphrases Aristotle's famous apologia for the study of even the most dingy creatures, and his slight adaptation of Aristotle's words strongly suggests that he was recreating the philosopher's sentiments from his own heart. It is difficult, he says, to study the heavens, but it is worth it, even if the results are meager, because "the lover of anything, when he really loves it a lot, is in anguish and strives to comprehend anything he can of what he loves, however little. This is what it means to be a lover. His comprehension of that little bit is dearer to a lover than the comprehension of anything else which he does not love so much, even if he can understand much more of it." On the other hand, he goes on, it is worth studying the creatures of earth too, even the least attractive of them: "That nature which creates the animals, as the cause of all causes, as that which gives them shape, when it is known it will be a cause of great delight to those naturalists who can understand the true proximate causes of their natures, even if he looks at them in some dingy, ignoble animal. That is why we ought to look at the forms of animals and rejoice in him who is their artificer who made them, because the artistry of the maker is revealed in the way he works."[268]

It was as a teacher and writer that Albert made his most notable contribution to the church of his time, but he was far from being exclusively an academic. He was always a preacher and a priest as well. The study of his sermons has only relatively recently been seriously undertaken, but it seems likely that a considerable number of them have survived.[269] Albert appears to have been in demand as a preacher in the vernacular as well as in Latin, and it is interesting to see how integrated his philosophy is into his Christian vision. Even in sermons addressed to ordinary congregations he establishes his points by an entirely harmonious use of philosophical and theological authorities.

Albert gives us a clue to his ideals as a pastor in his comment on John 10:1. "The sheepfold is the Christian religion. . . . It is made up of seven things, if it is going to be useful to the sheep. It must be soft with bedding to lie down on, clean to rest in and warm, it must offer solid protection, it must be provided with food for nourishment, it must have spacious accommodation and it must have unity so that the flock can congregate there. The softness comes through the gentleness of prelates, the cleanliness through chastity, the warmth through charity, the solidity through fortitude, nourishment through instruction in the word of God, spaciousness through a generous distribution of material goods and unity through unanimity." The gentleness of prelates is contrasted with ecclesiastics who are quick to resort to punishments and condemnations.[270]

The ideal of "unanimity" is spelled out in one of Albert's published sermons: "The apostle says, 'Rejoice with those who rejoice, weep with those who weep, sharing each other's feelings.' He means that if you want to be in unity with everyone, you should make your heart like your neighbor's heart, so that when he is happy, you are happy, and you grieve with him when he is grieving. But some people are like stones that have so many rough edges that they cannot possibly be put together with other stones to make a wall; wherever you put them their awkward shape immediately pushes out other stones. There is no way they can be joined together. Similarly if my heart is in distress and you are happy, your happiness sticks into me like an ill-shaped stone, so that our feelings cannot possibly come together." Albert goes on to point out that some people are far more truly "excommunicated" than the objects of the most formal ecclesiastical censures, because they are separated from their neighbors in their hearts, refusing to enter into their joys and griefs.[271] Albert was surely speaking from his own experience here. What must it have been like for a man who so enjoyed "seeking the truth in the pleasure of companionship" to be faced only with a pompous inquiry, "What has that to do with salvation?" when he was eager to impart some fascinating titbit of zoological lore he had just discovered?

Albert evidently brought to his pastoral work the same bluntness that made him so successful as an arbitrator. "I have sometimes enjoined a long fast of bread and water on people who never sinned mortally, not actually as a penance, but to mortify a root of evil in them, because I could see that they were inclined to self-indulgence."[272] He had a high ideal of freedom and was convinced that there could be no human freedom for people who were at the mercy of their own comforts.[273] But he was not taken in by false austerity. Visiting the convents of his Order he noticed that some friars were exaggeratedly enthusiastic in their participation in the liturgy or in undertaking fasts beyond the norms of the community, and his comment on them is brutally frank: "They are aspirants to the infirmary and in no time they are clamoring to be cosseted, with their headaches and their backaches and so on."[274] He liked people to enjoy their religion and had no objection to them showing it in rather rowdy ways of celebrating in church.[275]

Of Albert's own piety we know little. He had a great devotion to our Lady, that seems certain.[276] Thomas of Cantimpré, who sat at Albert's feet for some time, assures us that Albert was so devoted to prayer by day and by night that he recited the whole psalter almost every day,[277] which it is difficult to believe; maybe he recited the penitential psalms every day.[278] It is not difficult to accept the story that Albert used to declare that he often obtained by prayer the understanding of something that he could not master by study.[279] What sane Christian intellectual would say otherwise?

Henry of Herford gives us a charming picture of Albert's last years in Cologne, which there is no reason to disbelieve and which surely depicts the accumulated habits of a lifetime, adapted to the realization of impending death:

He prayed fervently and freely proclaimed the word of God to the people at suitable times and he pleasantly and affectionately gave good advice and useful counsel to people who asked for it. With the charm of his eloquence he led the minds of his hearers wherever he wanted. In sum, living in Cologne he studied, dictated, wrote, prayed, sang psalms and often wept pleasantly from devotion. Every day he visited the place where he would be buried, reciting the vigils for himself as if he were already dead. In a garden or some other secluded place he used frequently every day to retire alone to sing some song to the blessed Virgin with sighs and tears. He was honored and venerated by everybody, regulars and seculars, old and young, small and great.[280]

*

Albert's fame has for long been overshadowed by that of his pupil Thomas Aquinas, but, even apart from his role in shaping Thomas' intellectual development, he had a distinct and lasting influence on subsequent philosophy and theology. The independence and vitality of the German Dominican tradition is only now becoming fully apparent, and Albert is at the source of it.[281] Hugh Ripelin of Strasbourg, within Albert's lifetime and under his influence, wrote one of the most successful theological handbooks of the period, the *Compendium Theologicae Veritatis*.[282] Other followers of Albert include Ulrich of Strasbourg, Dietrich of Freiberg, Meister Eckhart, Berthold of Moosburg. The translations of Proclus made by William of Moerbeke made the Platonist affinities of Albert's "Peripateticism" more obvious,[283] and the German Dominicans are characterized by an avowedly Platonist bias,[284] culminating in the great commentary on Proclus by Berthold.[285] Dietrich of Freiberg also continued Albert's scientific interests and made some quite important contributions of his own.[286]

In the fifteenth century "Albertism" came to be recognized in some circles as a distinct school, which could at times enter into conflict with Thomism.[287] In his own alma mater of Padua Albert came to be very influential in the fifteenth and sixteenth centuries and indeed he was held in high esteem in Italy as a whole in this period.[288] Dominican intellectuals were currently more engaged in a revival of Thomism, and it was chiefly lay philosophers who were attracted to Albert, but the Dominicans certainly did not forget him. Albert retained a prominent position in Dominican bibliographies[289] and there was a succession of more or less ample biographies of him, culminating in those of Peter of Prussia and Rudolph of Nijmegen in the late fifteenth century.[290] Early in the sixteenth century Alberto di Castello commented that Albert was "a very famous teacher" and that "the number of his writings is almost infinite and they are very well-known."[291]

II. ALBERT AND THE DIONYSIAN TRADITION

By the middle of the thirteenth century, when Albert began to lecture on the Dionysian writings, "Dionysius the Areopagite" was well-established as an important source for Western theologians. His books were available to scholars in Paris in large volumes containing more than one translation and a rich abundance of glosses and commentaries.[1] His assumption of the persona of St. Paul's Athenian convert went unchallenged,[2] with the result that he enjoyed almost apostolic authority. It is not surprising that, after lecturing on the standard textbook of Latin theology, as he was obliged to do as Bachelor of the Sentences, Albert should turn his attention to this outstanding monument of Greek theology.

The first significant appearance of Dionysius in the West occurred in 827 when the Byzantine emperor Michael the Stammerer presented a copy of the Dionysian corpus to Louis the Pious.[3] "Dionysius" the author was promptly identified with St. Denis of France and, on the eve of the latter's feast day, the manuscript was solemnly deposited in the abbey of St. Denis, a few miles from Paris, where we are told it immediately yielded a good crop of miracles. In about 832–35 the abbot of St. Denis, Hilduin, produced the first Latin translation. Abbot Hilduin's knowledge of Greek was rather inadequate to the task and his translation was decidedly opaque.[4]

Later in the century Charles the Bald commissioned a new translation from an eccentric Irish scholar who had been at his court since about 850, John the Scot, generally known by the rather Homeric name he gave himself, Eriugena. He completed his version in about 862. He also composed a commentary on the *Celestial Hierarchy*. The discovery of Greek theology made a deep impression on him, and he proceeded to translate other works, including the very Dionysian *Ambigua* of St. Maximus. He also wrote a book of his own, *Periphyseon*, in which he tried to synthesize the Augustinian tradition with that of the Greeks.[5]

In 875 another excellent Greek scholar, Anastasius the Librarian, made a translation of the scholia found in many Greek manuscripts of the Dionysian works and added a few extra comments of his own. The Greek scholia derive from St. Maximus and John of Scythopolis and Anastasius was careful to distinguish between the two scholiasts, but later copyists were less careful and the whole commentary was known to Albert simply as the work of Maximus.[6]

In the twelfth century there was a revival of interest in both Eriugena and Dionysius. Honorius Augustodunensis produced a book, *Clavis Physicae*, which is little more than a précis of Eriugena's *Periphyseon*,[7] and substantial parts of the *Periphyseon* were interpolated into the Anastasian scholia (which is how they were known to Albert).[8] Hugh of St. Victor wrote a large commentary on the *Celestial Hierarchy*, which enjoyed a considerable success.[9] And John of Salisbury persuaded his tame translator, John Sarracenus, who had probably already composed his own commentary on the *Celestial Hierarchy*, to make a new translation of the entire Dionysian corpus, a project whose usefulness was greatly enhanced by the abbot of St. Denis' success in acquiring new Greek manuscripts for Sarracenus to work on.[10]

The degree to which Eriugenist and Dionysian ideas had penetrated, often anonymously, into Western theology by the end of the twelfth century can be seen, for instance, in a passage in John of Salisbury to which E. Jeauneau has recently drawn our attention:

> As Augustine says in his *De Ordine*, "God is best known
> by not knowing." . . . And elsewhere, "Ignorance of God
> is the truest wisdom."[11]

The first quotation does genuinely come from Augustine, but the second is derived from Dionysius by way of Eriugena, and the combination of the two texts is also found in Eriugena.[12] As Jeauneau comments, "We are here in the presence of a theology more radically negative than that of Augustine. The Augustine cited in this passage is an Augustine revised and corrected by Dionysius." And the result has an unmistakably "Eriugenist flavor."

The Latin tradition had always, in a mild way, acknowledged the transcendence of God and the consequent impossibility of any created mind attaining to full knowledge of him, but both philosophically and theologically its tendency was far less insistent on this point than that of the Greeks. Marius Victorinus was prepared to follow the Neoplatonists in saying that God is above being and, as such, above mind and knowable only by not-knowing;[13] but the exigencies of Trinitarian theology obliged him all the same to abandon the Plotinian strict separation between the utterly transcendent One and Being. And so, as R. A. Markus observes, "we find the 'negative theology' characteristic of the Neoplatonic framework receding into the background with Victorinus."[14] Augustine, in common with a widespread Christian tradition, simply identifies God with Being.[15] And Plotinus' confidence that the human mind has it in itself to rise to the highest heights had not yet been superseded by the later Platonists' belief that the mind is completely fallen and can only be united with God by the gracious act of his own condescension to us.[16] Nor did the succession of crises that sharpened Augustine's doctrine of grace[17] do anything to make Augustine rethink his position on this point; it underlined the helplessness of the human will rather than the incompetence of the mind. There was no serious challenge to the view espoused in the *Confessions*, that the mind can rise to the vision of God, but we are morally incapable of sustaining this vision.[18]

In the Christian East the controversy with Arianism forced a much more emphatic development of the belief that God dwells in "inaccessible light" (1 Tim. 6:16), beyond the reach of any created intellect. Arius' contention that it is impossible for God really to have a Son provoked the response that we do not know and cannot know enough about God to set such limits to what is possible for him. Some of the Arians apparently retorted that we can know God as well as he knows himself. The orthodox in return insisted even more strongly on the unknowability of God.[19] Some of the Greek fathers developed a corresponding spirituality of unknowing, such as we find in Gregory of Nyssa and Evagrius Ponticus.[20] Where Augustine looks forward to a final, beatifying vision of God as he is in his own substance,[21] Gregory of Nyssa and Evagrius are inspired rather by the lure of the unfathomable and inexhaustible mystery of God.

Fifth-century Platonism, as we find it in Proclus, goes even further than Plotinus in emphasizing the mysteriousness and elusiveness of God. To safeguard the utter transcendence of the One a new intermediary is postulated between It and the realm of multiple beings, namely the Henads, representing the origin of participated unity.[22] Of the One itself we cannot strictly say anything, not even that It is one.[23] But our minds can be directed toward the One by a meticulous analysis of all that they can understand and at the end they are carried beyond themselves by entrusting themselves to the inspiration and act of God, so becoming united with him. Where Plotinus attributes this final self-transcending move to love,[24] Proclus attributes it to faith and connects it with religious ritual (theurgy), in which God acts upon us to take us beyond the limits attainable by philosophy.[25] The theme of God's love for us, which had in general only been adumbrated in earlier Platonism, receives a remarkable exposition in Proclus.[26]

Whether or not it is Proclus himself who provided Dionysius with the philosophical tool that lent itself so admirably to the exposition of his deeply Christian worldview, it is clearly Proclus' kind of Neoplatonism that he adopted.[27] With its help he evolved a statement of Christian truth in which the utter transcendence of God is affirmed as strongly as ever, so that no names or concepts strictly reach the reality of what he is; but at the same time God can and should be named by all names.[28] The structured complexity of created beings is nothing less than the structured and riddling revelation of God. All that we find in creatures comes ultimately from God and so must, in some higher way, pre-exist in him. The God who makes darkness his hiding-place beckons us to himself through the alluring but unfulfilling creatures with which he has surrounded us. Everything is at once a revealing and a hiding of God; it is both like him and unlike him.[29] We are therefore raised to the knowledge of God by conjugating affirmative and negative theologies:[30] God *is* everything that can be said about anything because nothing exists that does not in some way derive from him, but at the same time he *is not* anything that we can see or grasp with our minds. The negations may, in a sense, be more accurate than the affirmations,[31] if only because they make a more cautious claim, but they must not be misunderstood. To say that God is not whatever it may be is not to say that he lacks some characteristic or property, but rather to indicate that he transcends the limits connoted by our normal use of words.[32] For instance, we might say that someone who is totally insensitive to music is "not musical"; in so doing we are indicating simply a lack on the part of that individual. But we might also hesitate to say that Mozart was "musical"; the little boy next door may be musical, but Mozart—? The word hardly begins to do justice to his talent. In the same way, but with more metaphysical rigor, we can say that God is "good," but we must also insist that he is not "good" in the trivial way that a meal or an opera or even a saint is good. The goodness of a saint is only a pale reflection of what God is. There is thus a close relationship between Dionysius' negative theology and his liking for the prefix *hyper:* both are ways of intimating that God is always *more than* whatever we can say about him.[33]

If God is revealed in his creatures, he is also revealed in his words. We have no access to him apart from his self-disclosure and should not venture beyond what he has said about himself;[34] and his whole revelation of himself is centered upon Christ,[35] who is his Word and the foundation of all his creatures. But this revelation of God in Christ involves the whole range of teaching offered to us in the bible, whose words share in the riddling quality of the things that make up creation. What is said of God in scripture must therefore be interpreted once again by the conjunction of affirmative and negative theology.[36]

But God is beyond both our affirmations and our negations.[37] We are united with him in the darkness of unknowing[38] by submitting ourselves in faith to the deeds of God, wrought in the Incarnation and made available to us in the sacred rites of the liturgy. Christ is the principle of "theurgy"[39] as well as of "theophany"; in him we are acted on by God as well as enlightened. Where earlier negative theology had, perhaps, tended to foster a rather narrow kind of spirituality, bidding us concentrate on God by leaving behind all that is not God, Dionysius' negative theology is more subtle, inviting us into a kind of dialectical relationship with the lush richness of biblical language, metaphysical speculation and, above all, liturgical celebration. Even while passing beyond everything, we have to accept everything as being the indispensable vehicle for us of God's act and his self-disclosure.[40] This is particularly evident if it is correct, as has been suggested, that Dionysius' *Mystical Theology* is a kind of hinge linking the *Divine Names* (together with the lost or perhaps unwritten *Theological Outlines* and *Symbolic Theology*) with the *Celestial* and *Ecclesiastical Hierarchies.*[41] If this interpretation of the Dionysian corpus is correct, as I believe it to be, then the more or less speculative endeavor to understand the significance of the various ways in which God is talked about comes to its head and its apparent bafflement in the *Mystical Theology*, and then we move on by entering into the hierarchical ministration of the acts of God in the angelic choirs and then in the rites of the church. The words of God ("theology") are fulfilled and completed in the deeds of God ("theurgy").[42]

Unfortunately when Dionysius' writings came to the West the full, rich content of his doctrine seems not to have been much appreciated, except perhaps by Eriugena himself. The main consequence of his arrival and of Eriugena's own works was a greatly enhanced sense of the transcendence of God. This can be seen, for instance, in some glosses on Boethius emanating from Auxerre, where Eriugena's influence was strong.[43] Eriugena's insistence on the inadequacy of human language to talk about God[44] was taken to heart and its influence was boosted during the eleventh and twelfth centuries by a growing interest in grammar and semiotics and, in due course, logic.[45] But the need to combine negative theology with affirmative theology was much less appreciated, and the link between negative theology and the sacraments was lost sight of entirely.

What remained, then, was a rather isolated conviction that none of our words properly apply to God. But without the genuine Dionysian complement, that our negations do not properly apply to God either, we are left simply with a vacuum, in which it is far from clear that we can talk meaningfully about God at all. And the vacuum can hardly help but be filled with some kind of affirmative theology, which will in turn operate without the moderating influence of negative theology.

Thus Abelard, in his discussion of the problem of reconciling the unity of the Godhead with the Trinity of Divine Persons, says,

> I do not find it surprising if the nature of the Godhead, unique as it is, calls for a unique way of talking. It is only fair that something widely removed from all creatures should be talked about in a widely different way of speaking and that that unique majesty should not be constrained

by a common, public form or speech, that what is utterly
incomprehensible and ineffable should not be subject to
the same rules as everything else.

Abelard then quotes Plato (on the authority of Macrobius) as not
having dared to say what God is, "knowing of him only that he cannot be known by any human being."[46] But this does not commit
Abelard to any really negative stance on talking about God. When
we use words about God they are "shifted from their usual meanings,"[47] but the crucial point is that God has reserved it to himself
to give us knowledge of himself, "and so he has himself manifestly
disclosed to us what he is."[48] A similar position is adopted in the
Abelardian *Sententiae Parisienses*, which again quote Macrobius and
insist that the philosophers "could not fit any words to God by
which they could define or demonstrate what God is"; but Christ
himself has taught us about "the essence of God."[49] The subtle
Dionysian attitude both of confidence in and of reserve toward *all*
that we say about God, including the words of revelation, has
turned into a much simpler dissociation between philosophy and
faith, and between words in their ordinary senses (which cannot do
justice to God) and words of faith (which apparently can do justice
to God).

Gilbert of Poitiers makes a similar and even more rigid distinction between the theological use of words and their use in other "faculties" or disciplines.[50] And he goes much further than Abelard in
limiting the extent to which the human mind can know God. God
is not any kind of "something," and so the mind is deprived of the
help of its usual concepts in trying to understand him. The only way
we can understand God—and Gilbert maintains that we can understand him—is by stripping away from him all the usual ways in
which we qualify things, leaving only the bare notion of "Being."
And this stops far short of any "complete understanding" or "comprehension" of God, because there is no positive characterization of
him for us to latch on to.[51] Nevertheless Gilbert evidently felt free
to develop a highly technical and sophisticated theology.

As is well known, people like St. Bernard were not at all happy
with the more speculative theology that was developing in the
schools. Abelard was denounced by William of St. Thierry to Bernard and Bernard forced a public confrontation, resulting in the con-

demnation of Abelard. One of the points raised against Abelard was his contention that the names "Father," "Son" and "Holy Spirit" do not strictly apply to God, and William of St. Thierry is clearly impatient of any subtle distinction between senses of words in such matters.[52] Later on similar moves were made against Gilbert of Poitiers.[53] It is fairly clear that Abelard's opponents did not understand what he was trying to do, and Gilbert seems to have escaped condemnation chiefly because nobody could keep up with his subtle explanations or compete with his patristic erudition. The opposition accused both Abelard and Gilbert of being too "philosophical," and at least in germ there is probably a valid point there: the separation of negative theology from affirmative theology makes possible a very technical theological language uncontrolled by either the norms of ordinary discourse or the modesty attendant upon negative theology.

In Thierry of Chartres there seems to be a more genuinely Dionysian or Eriugenist influence, and he does not claim such a radical autonomy for theological language as Gilbert does, but he leaves it unclear how any real knowledge of God can be possible. "It is the practice of authors, when they speak about God, since God has no name, to use many names to speak about him so that they can thereby intimate what they think about him."[54] This has an authentically Dionysian ring about it. The impossibility of forming ordinary sentences about God is stated in a way which anticipates Albert: strictly speaking God can be neither a subject nor a predicate, so sentences about God can never work in quite the same way as ordinary sentences. When we form propositions about him, we are using words only in a metaphorical sense (*translative*), to "hint" at what God is through some image or negation. We hint at what he is like, at his "quality which is above all quality and is a quality-less quality" and so on.[55] We apply words to God without their normal substance (*res*), as when we say that the fields are "smiling" without meaning that there is a real smile there.[56] Since God eludes all our categories, he cannot be signified by any word or comprehended by any intellect. He is not even to be called a "being," since he is rather the "beingness" of all beings, and our words apply properly only to beings. That is why we can understand what he is not better than what he is[57]—a sentiment ascribed to Augustine, but it is in fact surely more Dionysian and Eriugenist than Augustinian.[58] The

46

only real problem in all this is that if *all* our talk about God is metaphorical, how can we actually understand any of it? As Albert points out, metaphorical language is parasitic on non-metaphorical language.[59]

In the mid-twelfth century we find a very extreme statement of the autonomy of theological language from Hugh of Rouen:

> Whatever can be said of God as God must be understood in his way, not ours. . . . Whatever words and utterances are adopted to signify God no longer belong to any of the grammarians' parts of speech, but they mean something in a divine way, not in the manner of grammarians, rhetoricians or logicians. God is always what he is and cannot be delimited or described or defined, because he is incomprehensible.[60]

As Evans says, "These are words of proper caution . . . but they are also, in a sense, a counsel of despair."[61]

In the course of the twelfth century this negative streak in Latin theology was reinforced from several directions. Translations were being made of some of the Muslim and Jewish philosophers who had themselves been influenced by the same kind of Neoplatonism as Dionysius. Avicebron, for instance, whose *Fons Vitae* was translated by Gundissalinus, while maintaining that knowledge of the "First Essence" is the very goal for which the human race was made, declares that we can have no direct knowledge of it, since it is "above everything" and "infinite"; the only knowledge we can have of it is indirect, through creatures.[62] And we can only know "that" it is, not what it is or what sort of thing it is or why it is.[63]

In addition, extra Greek sources were becoming available in Latin, including John Damascene's *De Fide Orthodoxa*, which begins with an emphatic denial of the possibility of any created intellect grasping God,[64] and Chrysostom's homilies on St. John, which contain an equally strong denial that God in himself can be seen by any angelic or human mind.[65]

A curious indication of how these various currents could flow together is provided by the anonymous *De Causis Primis et Secundis*,[66] in which Avicenna, Eriugena, Dionysius (known apparently only through Eriugena) and Augustine are all exploited, and which concludes with an unmitigatedly negative declaration that "the principle of principles defeats all thought and understanding and all the powers which rank after it, and it is God most glorious."[67]

Our Avicennist, writing probably around the turn of the twelfth and thirteenth centuries, represents somewhat of an aberration. More typical is Alan of Lille, in whom an avowedly Dionysian-Eriugenist tradition merges with an easily recognizable though unacknowledged dependence on Gilbert of Poitiers. His *Summa "Quoniam Homines,"* written c.1160, begins with a typically Gilbertist denunciation of people who do not understand the special nature of theological language, the meaning of whose words is not "natural but miraculous." "Terms taken from the natural order are transferred to theology and wonder at their new meanings and seem to clamor for their old meanings." Because of a failure to appreciate the distinctness of theological discourse, people "who are scarcely capable of understanding a pantomime" force their way into "divine conversations" and, because they have not first consulted the liberal arts (the "queen's doorkeepers") and so lack a proper introduction to the "royal way of theology," "sink into various errors, ineffably ruined" when they try to ascend to what is ineffable.[68]

In the more or less contemporary *Regulae Theologicae* Alan spells out in considerable detail how words work in theology. His guiding principle is taken from Dionysius: affirmations about God are *incompactae*, whereas negations are true.[69] By *incompactae* Alan understands *incompositae*: all genuine propositions involve "composition," they propose a connection between two properly distinct notions ("This piano is out of tune": it is not intrinsic to pianos to be out of tune, nor is out-of-tuneness confined to pianos). But in the case of God no such distinct notions are strictly appropriate because of the well-known principle that "whatever is in God is God."[70] So when we say that "God is just," we are not making a connection between a God who is in principle conceivable without justice and a justice which is distinct from the very being of God, so it is only in appearance that we are predicating something of God; our affirmation is *incompacta*.[71] The second presiding principle is that no name is properly applicable to God, not even "Being," though that seems to be less improper than most.[72] There seems to be an unbridgeable gap between the reality of God (to whom in fact "being" belongs most properly) and our words (we can only improperly *say* that

"God is"),[73] which leaves us perplexed as to how we can even know that "being" does most properly belong to God or indeed what it might mean to make such a claim. Alan's explanations are far from satisfying. Taking up the doctrine we have already met in Thierry he contends that when we apply words to God it is only the "name," not the "reality" (res) that is being transferred to him.[74] Even in the case of an attribute like "justice," the word applies only "causatively" to God; what we mean in calling God "just" is that he causes justice.[75] So even if this is intended to say something about what God actually is (and Alan is explicit that such causative predication is intended to refer to God's "substance"),[76] it is not clear that it can ever succeed.

In the *Summa "Quoniam Homines"* Alan produces a massive battery of authorities, both theological and philosophical, to support a radically negative theological position.[77] We cannot really know God nor, obviously, can we name him, except negatively, in the sense that we can know what God is not. Even "being" is only ascribed "equivocally" to God.[78] Our minds (and here Alan is again following Gilbert) can only understand things by latching on to their properties, and God has no properties.[79] This obviously raises the question whether even in heaven we can have any positive knowledge of God, and if we cannot, what of the promise that we shall see God "face to face"? To this Alan can only say that we shall see and understand God differently in the hereafter, but for the moment we cannot understand how this is possible. Somehow in heaven our "intellect will be changed so that it will not require the help of forms."[80]

At two points, then, Alan has to resort to unexplained, miraculous changes: theological language acquires its meaning "miraculously" and the beatific vision is possible only because of an alteration in our intellect that we cannot hope to understand here and now. Because of this, he can on the one hand enunciate a negative theology that is far more confident of itself than Dionysius would allow, while at the same time developing an almost aggressively positive system of theological propositions, which seems to be largely unchecked by the precautions of negative theology. At the beginning of his *Regulae* he gives the impression of revelling in the technical and abstruse nature of theological language: it is a Fachsprache like any other, calculated to confuse the uninitiated.[81] It is not hard to feel about him as some people felt about Gilbert, that he is engaged in verbal sophistry which has little to do with the realities of Christian faith and life.[82] Such a response would certainly be unfair, but it would not be incomprehensible.

The penetration of Greek theology and, to a lesser extent, Islamic philosophy into Western thought resulted, then, chiefly in a rather exaggerated negative theology that, precisely because of its exaggeration, did not seriously interact (as it does in Dionysius and Eriugena) with affirmative theology. The perfectly sound claim that it is something to do with what God is, not just a temporary accident, that no created intellect can grasp him as he really is,[83] leaves a real epistemological problem about how we can aspire to the vision of God in heaven. And if all our talk about God rests simply on an *equivocal* use of words, it is not clear that we can ever succeed in really talking about God at all, in which case all theology, however sophisticated it may seem to be, is no more than an empty playing with words.

In the twelfth century this "orientalizing," negative theology was by no means unchallenged. As we have seen, an attempt was made to secure the condemnation of Gilbert of Poitiers, who was famous for his knowledge of the Greek fathers.[84] And Hugh of St. Victor, for all his interest in Dionysius, protested warmly against what he understood to be Eriugena's doctrine that even in heaven we see God only indirectly, by way of "theophanies": "Away with their fancies with which they try to cloud the light of our minds! They must stop coming between us and our God with these images of theirs! Nothing can satisfy us except God himself."[85]

The most influential of all the products of twelfth-century theology, the Sentences of Peter Lombard,[86] seems largely unaffected by Greek theology, and it was this text that became the basis for the teaching of systematic theology in the universities in the thirteenth century.

It was in the thirteenth century, though, that matters really came to a head. According to the very plausible interpretation proposed by Contenson, it was not oriental theology as such that precipitated the crisis, but the attempt to apply Aristotelian epistemology to the problem left unresolved, as we have seen, by twelfth-century theologians; namely, how it is possible for our minds to know God.[87]

Early in the thirteenth century David of Dinant ventured on a very optimistic appropriation of the Aristotelian doctrine that the intellect and its object become identical in the act of understanding; the results were rather pantheistic and were condemned in 1210.[88]

In reaction to this condemnation, some theologians moved toward the other extreme. Even William of Auvergne, whom we shall be meeting again shortly, toyed with the idea that we see God only through a "likeness" of him received by our minds (clearly the Aristotelian *species intelligibilis*).[89] Alexander of Hales at first opted for a frankly Eriugenist position, that God's essence becomes apparent to us only in its conjunction with his intellectual creatures, just as light becomes visible only because it illuminates the air.[90] Others, including the Dominican Master Guerric of St. Quentin maintained that God's essence is seen, but not *as* essence.[91] Hugh of St. Cher's postil on John 1:16 declares bluntly that even in heaven we shall not see the essence of God; we shall see him "as glory, as goodness, as truth."[92]

All of this must have seemed very small beer to people looking forward to the "full" enjoyment and vision of God promised by Peter Lombard.[93] William of Auvergne for one was not content, in spite of his own earlier doctrine, with anything less than "the most complete and clear vision of the Creator" (*perfectissima lucidissimaque visio creatoris*).[94] And William of Auxerre, in his highly popular *Summa Aurea*, espouses a purely Augustinian theory, basing our knowledge of God on his essential presence in the soul: at the moment, even though by grace the veil of sin and the veil of "the letter" is removed, our intellect is too weak to apprehend God directly, without the "veil of creatures," in spite of his immediate presence in us; but in the hereafter this obstacle will be removed.[95]

In 1241[96] William of Auvergne, by now bishop of Paris, together with the Masters of the University, issued a formal condemnation of several propositions, of which the first is that "the divine essence will not be seen in itself either by any human being or by any angel."[97] The ninth proposition is that "whoever has better natural endowments will of necessity have more grace and glory,"[98] which almost certainly reflects a Neoplatonist doctrine of hierarchy, apportioning divine illumination strictly according to ontological

51

status.[99] The other condemned propositions do not directly concern us here but, as M. D. Chenu has shown, they all seem to derive from an essentially oriental theology.[100]

Exactly who was the author of the condemned propositions is not known for certain, but they are presented in some sources as emanating from mendicant circles, and it is clear that the Dominicans were immediately affected. Successive Dominican chapters insisted on the books of the brethren being corrected to eliminate the condemned doctrines,[101] and the manuscripts of Hugh of St. Cher show various attempts to implement this ruling.[102] Guerric of St. Quentin, who had previously maintained that God's essence, as such, is not known to the blessed, made a sort of public retraction by presiding over a new disputation on the subject and pronouncing the opposite conclusion.[103]

The condemnation of 1241 represented a victory for those who were disillusioned with the attempt to accommodate the Christian hope of the beatific vision to a general, philosophical epistemology. The conviction that we can have a real knowledge of God was taken to be a primary datum; if philosophical epistemology could not cope with it, so much the worse for epistemology. Before the condemnation William of Auvergne denounced the "Aristotelian" doctrine that there can be no true knowledge of individuals on the grounds that "this error prevents and altogether denies the glory of human souls, which is the most complete and clear vision of the Creator," since, in William's view, the Creator is "very individual" (*singularissimus*).[104] Some years later, probably in the mid-1250s, St. Bonaventure alludes to the epistemological problem posed by the lack of proportion between God and the soul and, instead of trying to deal with it, he simply dismisses it, on the grounds that "if proportionality were necessary for knowledge, the soul would never reach the knowledge of God . . . by nature, by grace or by glory."[105] This is tantamount to saying that it *must* be possible for us to know God, even if there is no way that we *can* know God.

Before we turn to Albert himself, there is another Dionysian tradition that must be noted, which seems to have been entirely unaffected by the epistemological controversies or the condemnation of 1241. Where Eriugena and his conscious or unconscious followers tended to reinterpret Augustine in the light of Dionysius, this other tradition absorbed Dionysius into an essentially Augustinian tradition, according to which we know God precisely by loving him.[106] In the twelfth century one of the most persistent exponents of this doctrine was William of St. Thierry, according to whom:

> As our outward senses are related to bodies and bodily things, so our inward sense is related to the things that are like it, that is, the things of reason and the things of God or spiritual things. The interior sense of the soul is the understanding. But it has a greater and worthier sense and a purer understanding than these, namely love. It is by this sense that the Creator himself is perceived by his creatures, it is by this understanding that he is understood, inasmuch as God can be perceived or understood by any creature.[107]

The absorption of Dionysian negative theology into this perspective can be seen in the treatise *De Natura et Dignitate Amoris:*

> The natural light of the soul, the power of sight created by the author of nature for us to see God with, is charity. There are two eyes involved in this power of sight, always trembling with a natural eagerness to see that light which is God: love and reason. When one of them strives without the other, it does not achieve so much, but when they help each other, when they become a single eye, they can do much. . . . Each of them has its own kind of burden: one of them, reason, can only see God in what he is not, but love refuses to rest except in what he is. What can reason grasp or discover, for all its endeavours, of which it would dare to say, "This is my God"? All it can discover of what he is is what he is not. . . . But love prospers the more because of its failure and grasps the more by means of its ignorance. Reason seems to progress through what he is not to what he is, but love disdains what he is not and rejoices to fail in what he is.[108]

William's doctrine of knowledge by love is summed up in his famous phrase, "love itself becomes (our) understanding" (*amor ipse intellectus est*),[109] a phrase which must be taken at its face value, as J. M. Déchanet has shown.[110]

In the early thirteenth century Thomas Gallus, a canon of St. Victor in Paris who later became abbot of Vercelli, developed the theme of knowledge by love in his extensive Dionysian writings, which included a paraphrase of the *Mystical Theology*, brief notes on it and finally a substantial commentary on it.[111] In his view Dionysius' references to union with God have to be taken as indicating a special faculty in us that goes beyond the limits of our understanding, and this faculty is the "peak of our affectivity," which gives us a supra-intellectual "knowledge" of God:

> Our mind has a faculty of understanding (which we may call the "theoric intellect"), by which the mind looks at what is intelligible. The mind also has a faculty of union, which we understand to be the peak of our affections, which is properly brought to perfection by the love of God, and this extends the nature of the mind through its exercise, and by it the mind is joined in contemplations (*theoriis*) which surpass both its nature and its exercises. It is by this faculty of union that we have to know the things of God, not in the sobriety of our understanding, but placing ourselves above ourselves, united to God with all our power.[112]

Gallus wrote his Dionysian paraphrases and commentaries in Vercelli, between his arrival there in 1224 and his death in 1246. According to the dating established by G. Théry, the paraphrase of the *Mystical Theology* and the large commentary both belong precisely to the period of the Parisian condemnation.[113]

After Gallus' death another distinguished scholar, Peter of Spain (later Pope John XXI), wrote a series of commentaries on the Dionysian corpus, in which he closely follows Gallus' interpretation. The unknowability of God is strongly affirmed, in spite of the condemnation of 1241, and knowledge is even taken to be a hindrance to the "contemplation of the divine incomprehensibility." God is "beyond the notion of being and beyond the understanding of any mind, so he is neither knowable by us nor comprehensible." But nevertheless there is another kind of knowledge: in this life "the most worthy knowledge of all that could fall under the heading of 'understanding' is perfect union with God by means of an ecstasy of love."[114] This kind of union "suspends all intellectual activity."[115]

After Peter of Spain the doctrine of the "peak of affectivity" is maintained by Hugh of Balma, who again insists that at this level there is no room for any activity of the intellect.[116] From Gallus and Balma this affective and at least unintellectual reading of Dionysius passes to its most famous exponent, the author of the *Cloud of Unknowing*.[117]

When Albert came to Paris in the 1240s, the issue of "Eastern" theology was a live and delicate one in Dominican circles. The attempt to provide a viable epistemological account of how we know God had apparently reached an impasse and had, in the process, brought negative theology into a certain disrepute; the only form of negative theology that was quite unaffected was one which posited a non-intellectual way of knowing God by love, which by-passed rather than settled the epistemological problem.

Albert, it is quite clear, was not prepared simply to abandon the attempt to interpret Christian claims to present or future knowledge of God in terms of some coherent epistemology, and it is precisely on the subject of epistemology that he found himself most seriously at odds with the Latin tradition. On just the issue that had provoked the "anti-oriental" backlash, he aggressively opted for a frankly "oriental" view.[118] For a full statement of his doctrine of how the intellect functions and how it comes to the knowledge of God—and it is evident that his position is Aristotelian with a strong dose of Neoplatonism, both Dionysian and Islamic—we have to wait for books written after the completion of the Dionysian commentaries. But at least in germ the same doctrine is already contained in the commentary on the first book of the Sentences[119] and in the Dionysian commentaries themselves, so there does not seem to have been any essential change in his attitude.

At the beginning of the section of his *De anima* devoted to the intellect Albert announces emphatically that "in settling these questions we utterly abhor what the Latin doctors say." His objection to the Latins is that they follow Plato too much and suppose that the mind somehow contains within itself all that is needed for knowledge, with its own private supply of universals. Albert makes fun of these private universals, which could never be the basis for any objective knowledge of reality as it exists outside the soul and which would mean that no two individuals could ever be said to have the same knowledge. And against the idea of knowledge being somehow innate he affirms the Peripatetic doctrine that the mind acquires knowledge from things, not from itself.[120]

One of the main points of controversy arising out of this concerns the soul's self-knowledge. The Augustinian tradition maintained that the soul has, in principle, a direct, immediate knowledge of itself and all that is in itself, including God. This theory is mentioned in the commentary on the *Mystical Theology*, and Albert opposes it firmly.[121] He insists, with Aristotle, that we acquire knowledge of our own minds in the same way that we acquire knowledge of anything else.[122] What we are is not intrinsically luminous to us, it has to *become* an object of understanding to us.

On certain crucial points, then, Albert is a loyal Peripatetic. But this is far from being the whole of his epistemology, as we see in his fascinating treatment of Augustine's recantation of the claim that "any truth that is known is inspired by the Holy Spirit":

Four things are needed in the soul if it is to receive any knowledge of truth: the possible intellect, which is ready to receive it; secondly the agent intellect, by whose light the abstraction occurs of the forms in which the truth or the particular truth resides; thirdly the reality (*res*) which is present as an object either through an image of itself or in its own right—this is what the truth is about; and fourthly the principles and axioms which are as it were the instruments which arrange in due proportion the possible, impossible and necessary connections and separations, on the basis of which the particular truth is received. Of these four the first is purely receptive, the second is simply a source of light, the third is what receives light from the agent intellect and gives to the possible intellect the light of a specific truth, and the fourth is moved as an instrument and in turn moves the conceptual connections and separations with regard to the matter in which truth is known or sought. Some philosophers have concluded that these four things suffice for the knowledge of any truth which is subject to our reason. But we must rather say that the light of the agent intellect is not sufficient by itself without being directed by the light of the uncreated intellect. . . . This can happen in two ways, depending on whether there is simply a twofold light or whether there is a threefold light. The light is twofold if the mind is joined to the light of the uncreated intellect, and that light is the "interior teacher." But sometimes the mind is joined to an angelic intellect as well as to the divine. . . . This is what Dionysius calls the leading back of our hierarchy through the hierarchy of the angels. Augustine says this happens in many ways. And this is what some philosophers call the "link-up of intellects," because they too said that nothing is seen except by way of the first light.

So, to return to the question whether a new grace is needed, we must say that if any gift freely given by God is called "grace," then no knowledge comes about without grace. Indeed one philosopher has said that even if we have a habitual knowledge of something, that knowledge will not become actual unless the mind turns to the light of the uncreated intellect.[123]

Even without identifying all the sources of this remarkable passage, we can see at once that its doctrine is essentially Neoplatonist, though Albert himself may have been unaware of this;[124] and Albert seems to have remained faithful to it throughout his life.[125]

The combination of this Neoplatonist illuminationism and the Aristotelian denial of any immediate and primitive intellectual self-knowledge gives Albert a philosophical basis for a very rich and profound Christian intellectualism, such as we find in several passages in the *De Intellectu et Intelligibili*, in which we are surely entitled to recognize his own convictions, not just his interpretations of what he took to be Peripatetic doctrine:[126]

Our intellect is more closely joined to imagination and the senses than it is to the first agent intellect, and so it is dark and, with regard to things which are in principle thoroughly separate from matter, it is like the eye of a bat with regard to sunlight. For this reason it has to be imbued with physics first, and then with mathematics, so that once it has been strengthened in this way by many lights coming from many intelligibles it can rise to the understanding of the things of God. And in all these intelligibles, when it becomes an effective understanding of any of them, it discovers both itself and the agent intellect. . . . But though it is closer to physics and mathematics because of its connection to the body, it is really more akin by nature to the things of God, and so it discovers more of itself in the intelligibles which pertain to God than it does in those which belong to mathematics and physics.

Furthermore it seems true to say that, since anything which is only potentially a knower actually knows nothing at all, the intellect knows nothing at all unless it becomes effective. And from this it follows that anyone who does not study philosophy knows nothing at all, neither himself nor anything other than himself. . . . As long as the intellect remains potential and in no way effective, it is impossible to know anything other than oneself or oneself or even to know that one does not know. . . . So Hermes reproached the uneducated in antiquity, saying that such people paid no attention to anything human in their lives, but spent their days like pigs. . . .

The possible intellect is potentially everything that can be understood. So it is not actually received except in as much as what is potentially understood becomes effectively understood, and it is completely obtained and received when it attains to the effective realisation of all the intelligibles which it potentially is. This is how human beings take possession of their own intellect.

Plato accordingly said that the truest definition of philosophy is "knowledge of oneself," and Alfarabi said that the soul is placed in the body in order to discover and know itself, and he claims that Aristotle said this, but I have not found where he said it. . . . The reason for all this is that the first image of the light of the first cause to be joined to space and time is the human intellect, and so it must be a kind of likeness of everything that comes into being through the light of the first cause, it must enfold all these things, being a receptacle of some in as much as it is an image of the first cause and of others in as much as it is joined to space and time; in both it has to take possession of itself. . . .

This makes it evident that the contemplation of wonderful truths is the highest delight and the most natural occupation, in which people's whole human nature, precisely as such, blossoms, particularly in the contemplation of the things of God, because it is particularly in these that the intellect discovers itself in its proper nature, because human beings, precisely as human, are essentially intellect. . . . This reveals how it is by study that the intellect takes possession of itself.

Now let us talk about the understanding which some of the oldest philosophers call "assimilative" or "assimilating," and in doing so let us also clarify the soul's perfection, which arises from all the kinds of understanding alluded to. "Assimilative understanding" is that in which human beings rise to the divine intellect, which is the light and cause of everything, insofar as it is possible and lawful and in a way which is proportionate to them. This comes about when the intellect has become fully actual and has taken possession of itself and of the light of the agent intellect and, on the basis of the lights received from everything and of its self-knowledge, it reaches out in the lights belonging to the intelligences and so gradually ascends to the simplicity of the divine intellect. From the light of its own agent intellect it passes to the light of intelligence and from there it reaches out to the intellect of God. . . .

Strengthened in that light (of intelligence) the intellect rises to the divine light, which has no name and is unutterable, because it is known by no name of its own, becoming known only as it is received. And it is received first in intelligence, which is the first effect to be caused, and when it is uttered it is uttered with the name of intelligence, which is the effect it causes, not with any name of its own. So Hermes said that the God of Gods is improperly grasped by a name which is not properly his own. . . . So the human intellect is joined to its final goal and its light and united with that light it shares in somewhat of his Godhead. . . .

Notice that in all these kinds of understanding the possible intellect is as it were primary and the foundation. The light of the agent intellect is a disposition in it and a kind of basis for the understanding of principles, and the understanding of principles is the basis for effective understanding, and effective understanding is the basis for taking possession of the intellect, because here particularly the soul acquires knowledge of itself; and possession of one's own intellect is the basis for the assimilative intellect, which rises step by step from lower light to higher light up to the light of the divine intellect, and there it stops as having reached its destination. Since everyone naturally desires knowledge, the goal of everyone's desire is to come to rest in the divine intellect.[127]

There is a similar message in the commentary on the *Metaphysics:*

Since all human beings naturally desire knowledge and desire is not unlimited, it must be possible to bring this desire to an end in some form of knowing. And this can be nothing other than the knowledge of that which is the cause and light of all beings and all objects of knowledge, and this is no other than the divine intellect. . . . This is why Averroes says in his comment on book XI of the *Metaphysics* of Aristotle that the question of the divine intellect is the one which all human beings desire to know.[128]

The human intellect becomes aware of itself by understanding other things, and by an "analysis" (*resolutio*) of its own light (once it has discovered this through coming to understand things) it comes to the "first, pure intellect." "This is what is most pleasant and most desirable in contemplation (*theoria*), this is what every being that has an intellect naturally desires to have actual knowledge of and to contemplate."[129] The "first, pure intellect" is, of course, God.[130]

In these writings Albert is not expressly developing his own views, and he objected to people supposing that he endorsed all that he said in his expositions of what he took to be Peripatetic philosophy. But so much of the same doctrine of the intellect recurs in his other works, and his comments are sometimes so enthusiastic, that it is difficult to believe that he would really insist on disowning it.

> The highest thing that the soul can have while it is in the body is at least sometimes to reach the pure intellect in its mind. And if, once it is freed from the body, what it sometimes fleetingly attains in the body becomes continuous, that will be supreme joy and the kingdom of heaven.[131]

The intellectual nature of beatitude is affirmed already in the early work *De Resurrectione* with the same quotation from Averroes that we find in the *Metaphysics* commentary,[132] and it is reaffirmed in the commentary on Dionysius' *Divine Names*, again with the same text from Averroes.[133]

The hypostatized "intelligence" that is the *primum causatum*, mentioned in the text cited from *De Intellectu et Intelligibili*, is easily identified with suprahuman intellectual beings, that is, the angels,[134] and as we have seen, Albert is quite willing to ascribe an important role to the angels in the illumination of the human mind, so the passage through the light of "intelligence" to the divine light needs little comment, if any, to make it acceptable to him.

Above all, Albert's illuminationist doctrine of the intellect allows him to develop a theory of how we come to know God. In the early *De Resurrectione* he was content to say, like William of Auxerre, that God "is in the intellect in his own right, that is, substantially, because he is in every essence. So for him to be seen all that is needed is the removal of any obstacle that is in the way. And there are two such obstacles: the imperfection that goes with this present wretchedness and our being turned in another direction. Since both of these are removed by beatitude, in beatitude we shall see him as he is."[135]

In the commentary on the *Divine Names* Albert gives us a much more precise account of how God is in the soul, and it presupposes already the doctrine later expounded in *De Intellectu et Intelligibili*: "God is essentially present in the soul, not as any kind of nature of the soul, but as a certain light of the intellect, and this is sufficient for him to be known by the intellect; indeed because of his being in the soul like this he is known under the appearance of anything that is understood, as the philosophers say about the agent intellect. In the same way we know of God 'that' he is by way of our knowledge of any creature."[136]

We know God through his works, then, essentially because he is implicitly present in our actual *knowing* of creatures. The divine being of God is the principle of all knowledge, because it is the "first light";[137] our intellect receives him as a "principle," and if we could know him perfectly (which we cannot) we should be able to derive a knowledge of everything from our knowledge of him.[138] All knowledge derives from God's own knowing, the light which is the causal principle of all knowing; but actual knowledge is received by different creatures in different ways, and our human way is laborious and circuitous.[139]

The divine intellect is the "cause and light of all beings,"[140] the "intellect which is the mover in all of nature,"[141] and for Albert this does not just mean some remote Aristotelian deity moving all things simply by attracting them, without in any way being concerned for them, nor does it mean a remote Platonist principle acting in all things, but not deigning to be cognizant of individuals or particulars: it means the creator God whose knowledge is the source of the whole reality of all things in all their particularity.[142]

God is the source of the existence of all things, and at the same time, as the primordial Intellect, he is the source of the intelligibility of all things, and it is this latter which most interests Albert.[143] Our minds approach God by way of the intelligibility of his creatures, discovering themselves and the light that is in them in the process. Bit by bit, as they exercise their own intellectual powers, they move toward an ever simpler, more comprehensive view of things, in which the light, which comes from God and enlightens angelic and (in a more diffuse and obscure way) human intellects, is apprehended more clearly.

The Aristotelian principle that it is only in understanding other things that the mind takes possession of itself is, of course, an admirable justification for Albert's own wide-ranging interests. He evidently took seriously and found congenial the belief that the intellect takes full possession of itself only when it realizes to the full its capacity to understand all that can be understood. But this is not simply a justification of curiosity; it is an application of the Dionysian principle that God, who is not adequately named by any name, must be given *all* names. Any narrowing of our intellectual interests would in fact shut out ways in which we are meant to be led to God. Precisely because the light of God is discovered only indirectly through the intelligibility of his works theology cannot profitably be undertaken as a narrow specialization. The link between negative and affirmative theology is fully restored in all its amplitude.

Albert's view of how we ascend to the knowledge of God leaves no room for any kind of shortcut. Nor does it leave room for any kind of specialized faculty for union with God, such as Gallus posited. And the idea that there might be some kind of non-intellectual knowledge of God receives very short shrift from Albert: if we cannot know God by the intellect, "it is clear that we cannot know him in any other way."[144] And if we are to know God by the intellect, it must be by the whole, ordinary process of intellection, beginning with the "possible intellect." (Albert cannot really accommodate the popular distinction between a "higher" intellectual power directed toward God and a "lower" power directed toward creatures.)[145]

If all intellectual activity depends on an illumination that comes from God, it is obvious that there can be no radical division between natural knowledge and faith. The proper object of faith is the First Truth, which is the source of all knowledge, not just knowledge of the truths of faith,[146] so the distinction between faith and natural knowledge is a distinction within an essentially coherent illumination from God: "Without a light to enlighten the intellect our possible intellect cannot receive any knowledge; it is by this light that the possible intellect becomes an eye to see with. This light is natural with regard to our receiving knowledge of natural things, it is freely given (*gratuitum*) with regard to our receiving the objects of belief, and it is glory with regard to our receiving what beatifies us."[147] And the illumination of faith functions in the same way as any other illumination: light enables us to see but does not determine what we see, and the light of the agent intellect enables us to know but does not determine any particular object of knowledge; in the same way the light of faith enables us to believe, but does not of itself specify any object of belief.[148] The actual content of faith comes to us, like any other kind of knowledge, through the senses[149]—through hearing sermons, reading the bible and so on. This is why, as Albert says in the *Mystical Theology*, there is need both for the inward teaching of God and for an "external teacher."[150]

The salient characteristic of faith, as distinct from ordinary knowledge, is that by it we believe certain things to be true that are not susceptible of rational proof,[151] though it is important to note that they are not susceptible of rational refutation either: if they could be refuted, we should have to believe the refutation as well as the refuted article of faith, so two contradictories would have to be true at the same time, which is impossible.[152] Natural knowledge is limited in its scope, but it is not, in Albert's view, unnatural for the mind to be carried beyond the limit of its own resources. The abandonment of intellectual activity recommended in the *Mystical Theology* is interpreted by Albert to mean only the abandonment of the intellectual activity which is "connatural" to the intellect,[153] that is to say, the activity which is sustained by the powers with which the human mind is born. But it is precisely the *intellect* that is carried beyond its innate capacity by the higher illumination it receives from God, and this does not involve any essential change in its nature.[154] It is, as Albert makes clear in his commentary on the *Mystical Theology*, an *intellectual* union with God that is our final goal.[155]

The light of faith is not an alternative to, let alone a negation of, the mind's natural way of functioning, it is precisely a strengthening of the mind, enabling it to do better and more surely the very thing that it is naturally designed to do. "The bodily vision of some creatures, like the bat, is totally shattered by the light of the sun, but the vision of other creatures, like human beings, is capable to some extent of looking at the sun, but because it is weak it cannot do so without the eyes trembling; other creatures, like the golden eagle, have their vision so strengthened that they can see the sun in the round. In the same way the mental vision of people who are held down by earthly affections and bodily images is material and is totally rebuffed by the divine radiance, but if their vision draws away from these things into intellectual speculation then it becomes immaterial, but it is still trembling, because it looks upon the things of God from afar, as it were, with the principles of reason. But if it is strengthened by the light of faith it ceases to tremble."[156]

There is a fine passage in the commentary on the *Divine Names* that develops a similar point:

> "This reason" (divine reason) "is the simple truth of what exists, which itself exists . . . and divine faith is about it" (it is the proper object of the faith we have about God). "It is pure," by contrast with the truth there is in other sciences, inasmuch as some impurity overflows into them from the things on which they are based; "it is not erroneous," as against the truth which is derived from reasoning, which is often liable to error because of the way things shift around. "It is knowledge of all things," in that it pours out knowability on all things, which is the situation of the first truth.
>
> Next he defines faith, of which this truth is the object. First he gives the definition and comments on it, then he explains why he said, "If knowledge unites those who know. . . ."
>
> So first he says that "faith is an abiding" and firm "establishment of believers," and this is interpreted in two ways: it "establishes" believers "in the truth" through their assent to it and it establishes the truth in them, placing it in their minds, in the minds, that is, of "believers who have a simple knowledge of the truth" in the first truth, "in unalterable steadfastness," inasmuch, that is, as someone remains unalterably in the one faith which also unites all the faithful. And the cause of this unchangeable steadfastness is indicated next: it is of the nature of knowledge to be "unitive," and this is understood in two ways: of the object of knowledge, because perfect knowledge makes us stand firm in the one, simple "whatness" of something, and also of the act of knowing, because at first the act of knowing is unsteady and wanders round various ideas, but once it gets a probable idea of something it sticks to one idea, but is nervous there because it is afraid of its opposite; but when it has perfect knowledge and enters into the proper and essential cause of something, then it stands firmly in one place, and this is the reason why all those

who know something are at one in a single knowledge of the truth.[157]

Neither Dionysius nor Albert would actually want to claim that faith gives us "perfect knowledge" in this life, but it is clearly implied that faith does give us the same kind of solidity as perfect knowledge. Whereas opinion is always unsettled because of its "fear of the opposite," both faith and knowledge give us a kind of certainty, and faith has at least some advantages over any other kind of knowledge, because of its direct reliance on the "first truth." And Albert seems to have no hesitation in treating faith as a kind of knowledge: although faith and reason differ in us, "they belong to the same genus, namely *natura cognoscitiva*."[158]

Faith, however, cannot be regarded simply as a "given," allowing us to rest on our laurels. It shares with the investigation of truth the responsibility for bringing our reason to perfection,[159] presumably by sharing in its own way the task of reason, which is to explore reality so that the general principles known by our intellect are applied and we come to a real understanding of things. By faith we have access to more material, which we can explore; and theology is the exploration of it.[160] In his commentary on St. John, Albert says he likes the "ancient" view of faith, found in St. Gregory, which differentiates between two facets of faith: "believing is thinking together with assent" (*cogitare cum assensu*). As assent, it is simply a given, a "changeless foundation"; but as "thinking" it is clearly open to all kinds of development.[161] "In faith . . . we first assent to the first truth for its own sake, then we look for reasons, so that we can to some extent understand what we believe."[162]

The wonderful humane and intellectual perspective opened out to us by faith is indicated by St. Albert in his comment on John 8:31–2, "Jesus said to the Jews who believed in him, 'If you abide in my word, you will truly be my disciples and you will know the truth and the truth will set you free.' ":

"Jesus said to those who believed in him." They were already beginning to be free, in that they had been called to faith. "You have been called into freedom, brethren, only do not make freedom an occasion for the flesh" (Gal. 5:13). Faith is the beginning of freedom, because it makes people know what freedom there is in grace. Therefore he speaks to these believers as to people who already understand freedom. "Let people with understanding speak to me, let a wise man hear me" (Job 34:34). "If you abide" with perseverance, intelligence and obedience "in my word." With perseverance, so that you meditate on it by study; with intelligence, so that you understand the mystery of the Holy Spirit in it; with obedience, so that you fulfill it by practicing it in what you do. On the first of these it says, "Persevere in discipline; God offers himself to you as to his children" (Heb. 12:7), and God's children are free. On the intelligibility of the words it says, "Understand what I say, for the Lord will give you understanding in everything" (2 Tim. 2:7), and "I will give you understanding" (Ps. 31:8). On obedience, "Cursed is anyone who does not abide in the words of this law and who does not accomplish them in practice" (Deut. 27:26), and "If you hear the voice of the Lord your God in order to do and to keep all his precepts, which are my command to you today, the Lord your God will make you higher than all the peoples who live on the earth" (Deut. 28:1), than those who live in earthly desires, that is, because you will be free and will be master of them. See how it is the beginning of true freedom thus to abide in the Lord's word.

"You will truly be my disciples." A true disciple is one who is truly imbued, without any error, with the teachings of his master. And this is how freedom grows. As the philosopher says, we call people free if they are their own cause.[163] And as it says in book ten of the *Ethics*, a human being is just intellect[164]—all the rest that is in us is not human but animal. And the intellect is perfected in the study of the things of God, not in anything else. "If you are outside the instruction of which all have been made partakers, then you are bastards and not children" (Heb. 12:8), as if to say, "You were not born of free stock, but of a bastard, servile stock." "The Lord God opened my ear and I do not contradict, I have not gone away" (Is. 50:5). "In this everyone will know that you are my disciples, if you have love for one another" (John 13:35), because it is love which makes you hold to my instruction. "If anyone loves me, he will keep my word" (John 14:23). A true disciple is one who holds to the instruction he received, just as it was imparted by his master. "Learn from me, for I am meek and humble of heart" (Matt. 11:29).

"And you will know the truth." This brings true liberty to perfection. Knowledge of the truth is the knowledge of that by which things truly are what they are, and this is no other than the divine art and wisdom which is proposed to us in the words of God. It is by God's art and wisdom that things truly are what they are. Because of certain other principles things fall from the truth of their being, inasmuch as they are material and mutable and inclined to sag away from what is true. "Sanctify them in truth; your word is truth" (John 17:17). And it says of the Word in John 1:14, "Full of grace and truth." "I am the way and the truth and the life" (John 14:6). "Truth abides and is strong for ever" (3 Esdras 4:38). "Truth prevails over everything" (ibid. 3:12). And so it frees us from the futility of changeability and is the principle which makes freedom itself perfect.

There follows, "And the truth will set you free." And this is the completion of true liberty. "Creation itself will be set free from enslavement to corruption into the freedom of the glory of the children of God" (Rom. 8:21). "The Jerusalem which is above is free, and that is our mother" (Gal. 4:26). So the word of the Lord, as being the truth, frees us from the coercion and constraint of futility. As the word of grace, it frees us from enslavement to guilt and sin. As the word of almighty God, it frees us from enslavement to wretchedness. First it gives us the freedom of nature, then it gives us the freedom of grace and thirdly it gives us the freedom of glory.[165]

If the study of the liberal arts already gives us a certain freedom, faith leads us into a far greater freedom, because it gives us access to the word of God, the study of which, if undertaken perseveringly and obediently, will eventually bring us to the complete fulfilment of our intellectual nature and to complete moral freedom.

The theological study, which alone is fully satisfying to our minds, cannot be isolated from the study of the arts though. At the end of his life Albert is still insisting on this. "Theology in itself is the first of all sciences, but it comes last in the order of our study and investigation. This is why Alfarabi says that it is in the study of theology that the philosophers have ended their lives."[166]

It is rather surprising, at first sight, that Albert was not prepared to regard theology as essentially and simply a speculative science, for all his intellectualism. Both in the early commentary on the Sentences and in the late *Summa Theologiae* he cites Titus 1:1–2 to identify theological truth as being *secundum pietatem*, inseparable therefore from the practice of the Christian life and the hope of salvation and everlasting bliss. In the *Summa* he concludes that theology is a practical science, in the commentary on the Sentences that it is neither speculative nor practical, it is an "affective science," bringing both mind and heart to their proper perfection.[167] This does not mean that theology is not a genuine science; it is a science, an organized body of knowledge with its own proper consistency. And even in the commentary on the Sentences it is indubitably correct to say that Albert's view of beatitude is an intellectual one: the "truth which beatifies" beatifies precisely by being the truth which fully satisfies the intellect.[168] What Albert is concerned to deny is surely the tendency we have noticed in the twelfth century for theology to become just another specialization which could, in principle, be mastered by anyone who was competent, without its engaging and shaping a whole human and Christian life. In calling theology an "affective science" Albert is by no means proposing to subject theology to the control of that affective piety that was already beginning to define itself against learning and intellectualism. On the contrary, he is refusing to concede that there is any tension between piety and theology; he is locating piety in the heart of the intellectual discipline of theology.

In the commentary on the Sentences Albert is still struggling to find the best way to express himself and he uses phrases like *intellectus affectivus* that suggest an affinity which is certainly not really there between his doctrine and that of Gallus. In his later works he abandons this kind of terminology almost entirely.

One of the crucial problems involved in the attempt to determine the nature of theology was the very vexed question of the precise nature of faith. The traditional data made it difficult for early thirteenth-century scholastics to see faith precisely as a form of knowledge. St. Augustine had insisted on the voluntary nature of belief, which suggested that faith had to be located in the will. Faith had also to be interpreted as a virtue, and it was generally accepted that the object of all virtues was some practical *good*, whereas the object of knowledge was always some *truth*.[169] In accordance with this problematic Albert locates faith, in the commentary on the Sentences, as not being a kind of *scientia*, because the knowledge (*cognitio*) it involves comes more from affection than from reason,[170] from love in the will rather than from rational proof. Faith is situated in "affective" rather than speculative understanding.[171] Knowledge may be the "matter" of faith, but it is affection that actually makes it faith and has the dominant role in faith.[172] Faith is a kind of virtue, rather than a kind of *scientia*.[173] If it is objected that faith's object is truth and that therefore it belongs to the domain of the speculative intellect (and could therefore not be a virtue unless we are prepared to say that *all* speculative achievements count as a virtue), Albert proposes in reply a distinction between the kind of truth that is the goal of speculation and the kind of truth that "beatifies the intellect." Speculative truth consists in "the complete account of something" and involves a "kind of movement from the thing to the intellect." Beatifying truth, by contrast, is outside the mind and is not an "account of something" but a "something" (*res*), "a light of eternal happiness" that is the "goal of an understanding which is moved by love for this truth."[174]

Albert is well aware of the awkwardness of this position. It seems to entail that the object of faith is not truth as such, but truth viewed as good (*secundum rationem boni*), and this was indeed the doctrine, for example, of Philip the Chancellor and of the first Dominican Master in Paris, Roland of Cremona.[175] But in Albert's judgment this is "no solution," because the truth has to be valued in its own right, precisely as truth.[176] Otherwise it is difficult to see how we can escape saying that we believe something to be true just because we find it attractive (or "helpful," as people say these days), which would be a disastrous concession to wishful thinking. But then it is hard to see how Albert has not already made such a concession in declaring that the light of faith "convinces the reason by a kind of love in the will."[177]

In the Dionysian commentaries we find Albert telling a very different story. The essentially cognitive nature of faith is affirmed there, as we have seen. He can still allude, without comment, to the voluntary quality of faith as a virtue that informs our conscience rather than persuading us with arguments, so that we are not constrained to believe by any rational proofs.[178] But there is no longer any question of our being "convinced by love" to go beyond what can be demonstrated by the principles of reason. The divine light is not a proposition, it is true, but "it is a reality (*res*) which convinces the intellect."[179] It convinces the intellect directly, it seems, by its sheer actuality.

On one point, at least, the development of Albert's theory of the intellect enabled him to come to a clearer understanding of faith. In the commentary on the Sentences one of his concerns was to insist that faith directs us toward a reality outside our own minds, in which our hope of beatitude is vested, and he contrasts this with the "account of a thing" that is the goal of intellectual speculation. But when he turned his attention to the subject of the intellect, he acquired, as we have seen, a hearty distaste for the "Latin" theory, which made the whole intellectual process a purely private, internal affair going on within the individual mind. His own view gave the intellect itself more of an outward orientation. What makes our understanding an understanding of some specific reality is the reality itself which is being understood (*ipsa res*).[180] On this view it is precisely as an intellectual virtue that faith directs us to something outside our own minds, and this is no doubt why Albert is now able to say that faith unites all believers, which he was earlier not prepared to say.[181]

The orientation of the intellect toward that which is outside itself means that there is no essential contradiction between the "ecstatic" structure of its natural workings[182] and the "ecstatic" nature of faith, on which the text of Dionysius obliges Albert to comment. Exploiting the ambiguity of the word ἔκστασις[183] Dionysius remarks that many people will suppose the believer to be "beside himself" (to have suffered an "ecstasy"), not realizing that he has indeed undergone an "ecstasy" (in a good sense) in "stepping out" quite properly from error.[184] Albert, willfully or otherwise, misconstrues the sentence and takes *extasis* in a stronger sense than was intended here by Dionysius: "The believer has undergone an ecstasy for truth, that is, he has been placed outside himself in divine truth."[185]

This is the *excessus* referred to in *MT* 1, on which Albert comments that it means "not holding oneself back within reason's own principles"[186]—it does not, as Albert explains at some length, necessarily involve *excessus* in the sense of rapture or ecstatic trance.[187]

The insertion of faith into a more general account of the working of the intellect does not mean that Albert has lost interest in the affective component in our knowledge of God. Even apart from his lifelong conviction that knowledge of God is our highest and most satisfying joy, he still wishes to ascribe a certain role to our affections in the very process whereby we come to know God; but his more developed intellectual theory allows him to state more precisely what this role is. "There is a kind of science which is about things beyond the reach of reason, so the knowledge of these things has to be received from some higher nature by participating in its light. . . . Although science is the perfection of our understanding, yet it is by the perfection of our affectivity (*affectus*) that we draw near to God and participate in his light; this is how our understanding is brought to perfection with regard to things which cannot be had simply by human reason."[188] There is no question of affectivity taking over the role of the intellect, but if we are to get beyond the limits of our own rationality we need a greater share in the divine light than is given to us in purely natural knowledge, and there are moral presuppositions for such a sharing. Purity of heart is what immediately disposes us to receive the vision of God.[189]

There is also an affective coloring to any genuinely Christian knowledge of God. In a famous passage in the *Divine Names* Dionysius refers to Hierotheos as "not just learning about the things of God, but undergoing them (οὐ μόνον μαθὼν ἀλλὰ καὶ παθὼν τὰ θεῖα)."[190] Albert comments on this: " 'Also he was perhaps taught the things of God by a diviner inspiration,' diviner than teaching or study, that is, 'not only learning' from others 'but also undergoing divine things,' being moved in his affection about them, 'and by his very sympathy for them,' by his affection for the things of God . . . 'he was made perfect for union with them,' union with the things of God in heart and mind, 'and for faith,' that is, for the certain knowledge of spiritual things. . . . This is called a diviner way because thus the things of God are perceived, in a way, experientially, just as someone who is suffering from a wound has a more certain knowledge of what a wound is than someone who only hears about it or sees it, and someone who tastes wine has a better knowledge of its pleasant flavor."[191] A text like this does not contradict Albert's conviction that our union with God is fundamentally intellectual,[192] it draws out one aspect of what intellectual union with God means: the certainty of faith is not like the certainty that a cogent rational argument produces, it is much more like the certainty which comes from a direct perception of something. What convinces the mind to assent to the first truth is not a proposition but a *reality*, and the reality of God cannot properly be apprehended dispassionately. In the commentary on the *Mystical Theology* Albert distinguishes between the ability to form propositions and *real* knowledge (*realis scientia*), that is, knowledge which actually touches in some way the *res*, the reality, of God, and this knowledge is "part of beatitude" and so cannot be divorced from its affective component.[193] The idea that we could have a real knowledge of God that was not, to some extent, beatifying is simply incoherent.

So faith has a necessary affective component precisely because it is concerned with the reality of God, not just with words about him;[194] but this very insistence on the reality of God means that the status of our talk about God has to be examined carefully. If, as several twelfth-century theologians maintained, the relationship between theological and non-theological use of words is one of equivocation, then theology will tell us nothing about the reality of God unless we can unscramble the equivocation and determine what the words actually mean when they are used theologically. And if we can do no more than say that they have "miraculous new meanings," then all we shall be able to achieve is the arrangement of more or less coherent verbal patterns, without having the remotest idea what we are actually talking *about*. If the only kind of bank that I am familiar with is the kind that deals in money, and have no acquaintance with the other kind "whereon the wild thyme blows" (and perhaps try to arrive at some idea of what "wild thyme" is by imagining a nightmarish world in which savage clocks chime irregular hours according to some scheme of chronometry untamed by arithmetic), then I shall quite strictly not have a notion what the bard is talking about, and shall not be any the wiser for being told that he is using words in miraculous new senses. Similarly if all theological language is metaphorical, theology will at most be a vaguely suggestive expression of people's religious aspirations; it will not have any capacity to tell me anything about what God really is. If none of our language properly applies to God and all we can do is transfer words to him without the "things" (*res*) they signify, then we can never be sure we are really saying anything about God at all. And it is no good appealing to some kind of direct experiential knowledge of God, which would render words superfluous, if it is true, as Albert believed in common with most of his contemporaries, that in this life we never have a direct encounter with God unmediated by creatures.[195] In Albert's view the *res* that convinces the mind to cleave to the first truth is the divine light itself, but this does not in itself present us with any specific *object*. It would be more correct to say that it is like the sheer fact of daylight than that it is like direct perception of any particular thing. You cannot argue with daylight (though you can draw the curtains and shut your eyes, if you want to); it "convinces the mind." But if we actually want to see something, there has to be something there for us to see. The light of faith enables us to believe, but it does not of itself give any content to belief, and the content comes largely from words (the words of the creeds, the words of the bible, and so on). So if faith does in some way confront us with the reality of God it must be, in this life, largely through the medium of words. And these must, then, be words that really do succeed, however inadequately, in putting us in touch with God himself.

Thirteenth-century theologians had learned from Aristotle at least one linguistic gambit they could use to escape from the twelfth-century dilemma. Instead of having to decide simply whether theological usage was univocal, metaphorical or equivocal, they could also consider the possibility that it might be analogical. Barclays and Chase Manhattan are both banks in the same sense (univocally). The bank where I keep my overdraft and the bank where I keep my wild thyme are banks in two quite unrelated senses, apparently connected only because of a linguistic accident, so here "bank" is equivocal. As for yon Cassius' lean and hungry look, he may indeed have been dieting and he may be pining for his lunch, but his look is "hungry" with reference to a different appetite and can properly be regarded as metaphorically hungry, a use of language justified by the evident similarities between different kinds of appetite. But what about that shockingly fine specimen, the Earl of Blandings' brother? He has a healthy look, a healthy body and a healthy appetite. Here, according to medieval Aristotelianism, we have a case of analogy. The look and the appetite are certainly not healthy in the same way as the body, but they are called healthy with reference to the same health that makes us call the body healthy.[196]

This notion of analogy suggests a promising way of upgrading theological language. If we say (in the manner of Alan of Lille) that words like "good" are applied to God causally (we call God "good" because he causes goodness), then it is not clear that they really tell us anything about God, though Alan evidently wanted them to do so. But in the Platonist perspective of an Augustine or a Dionysius any goodness in creatures is not just caused by God, it is a participation of some kind in God's goodness. We certainly cannot say that God is good in just the same way that a sausage is good. Sausages, unfortunately, can be bad, so being a sausage is not the same as being a good sausage, whereas for God to be God and for God to be good are exactly the same, in accordance with that most basic of medieval theological rules that God is whatever he has. But could it not be the case that there is some real common referent involved in both God's goodness and that of the sausage, like the common referent involved in the healthy appetite and the healthy body? Albert is not prepared to go so far as that. Full-fledged analogy requires that there be something in common, and there is nothing that is strictly common to God and creatures; it would never be proper to cite God and a creature as two instances of the same thing, even with all the refinements introduced by the notion of analogy. But there is a kind of halting analogy, after all: even if there is, strictly, nothing in common between God and creatures, creatures do, in their various ways, "imitate" God. We call a sausage good with reference to its being a sausage, not with reference to the divine nature; but a good sausage is still, in its own dim way, a reflection of the goodness of God. There is something in God that is responsible for there being a world in which things like sausages can attain to excellence. Creatures are obviously unlike God, but they are also, however palely, like the God who made them. Albert therefore concedes that there is an "analogy of imitation" between God and creatures, even if there is no full analogy.[197]

On this basis we can now take a further step. Of course all our language is human language and, as such, is inadequate for talking about God. But does that mean that we are confined to transferring words to God without the reality which they signify? If in at least some cases the link between our talking about creatures and our talking about God is an "analogy of imitation," that suggests that in some cases God has a prior claim on certain words. Albert therefore makes a distinction between what words mean (the reality they signify) and the way in which we learn how to use them. It is from God the Father that all fatherhood is named, according to St. Paul (Eph. 3:15), but it is obviously from the fatherhood we encounter among creatures that we learn to talk about fathers. So the meaning of the word can be said to apply properly to God; what is inadequate is its *modus significandi*, the way it functions in our human language.[198] This means, then, that we must distinguish between words that properly refer to creatures, which can only be used metaphorically of God, and words that really do indicate genuine attributes of God. And when negative theology bids us negate all that we say of God, we must distinguish between different kinds of inadequacy in our language: in some cases we are not denying that the reality indicated by the word belongs to God; we are just reminding ourselves that we cannot properly state what it means for it to belong to God.

Instead of a simple declaration, then, that all human language is inadequate, Albert gives us a rather more nuanced doctrine:

> Divine names are formed in two ways: (1) from things which in reality belong to God first and only secondarily to creatures, and these are the names which blessed Dionysius calls "mystical," such as "being," "life," "intellect," "wisdom," "goodness." "Mystical" in Greek is the same as "secret" in Latin, and a "mystical name" is so called because (owing to the character imparted to words by the way they are instituted) it signifies imperfectly and partially something that exists in God perfectly and totally, and sometimes it suggests that something is an accidental property which exists substantially in God and is the divine substance. Because of this the divine reality which it names remains hidden from us, because we know that the reality is higher than the name and that our tongues fall short of declaring it. . . . Affirmations are inadequate because the way that names function in our language (their

modus significandi) is at odds with the divine reality, particularly in three ways: they present as complex a reality which is of infinite simplicity; they present imperfectly what is absolutely perfect; and they sometimes present as an accident something which is really substance. So Anselm says that "Father" and "Life" and so on actually come down to our level from God, but we are more at home with "father" meaning a human, fleshly father than we are with "Father" meaning God. (2) In the case of symbolic names God is designated by transferring some property that belongs to bodies to a spiritual sense. He is called "stone," for instance, because stone is solid and provides a solid basis for building on, so in a spiritual sense God's truth is solid and is the foundation for our whole spiritual edifice.[199]

So only some names of God are metaphorical, and in their case negative theology has the simple task of reminding us that God is not really a stone or a lion, that he is not really angry or drunk. But some names of God are not metaphorical, they are "mystical" and apply primarily to God; in their case negative theology comes in to insist that they do really apply to God, and that therefore we cannot fully know what they mean. It is particularly with reference to these mystical names that the importance of holding together negative and affirmative theology is apparent: affirmative theology must not exaggerate its competence in talking about the reality of God, but negative theology must not degenerate into pure negation,[200] its aim is to clarify how we *are* talking about God, not simply to stop us talking about God. The mystical names of God are, according to Albert, the subject of two books of the Dionysian corpus, the *Divine Names* and the *Mystical Theology*, corresponding to the two ways in which these names can be considered: "They can be viewed in terms of the flowing out from the cause of the effects it causes, which participate in a secondary way in the content of some name, and this is how they are dealt with in the *Divine Names*; or they can be viewed in terms of the way in which an analysis of the caused effects traces them back to their cause and the meaning of the name, as it exists in the cause, is left unknown because of the transcendence of the cause, and this is how the names are dealt with in the *Mystical The-*

ology."[201] These are obviously complementary approaches: one emphasizes that we are *talking* about God and explores the manifestation of God in the intelligible structure of creation, while the other emphasizes that we are talking about *God* and so leads us back from creation to the transcendent mystery that lies hidden within the whole process of revelation.

It is, incidentally, interesting to contrast Albert's interpretation of the distinction between mystical and symbolic names with that of William of Auxerre. According to William, "Mystical theology, which is called 'mystical,' that is, 'hidden,' names God by means of what it hiddenly perceives about God through some intellectual vision or contemplation, as when it calls God 'sweet,' 'beloved,' and so on. In both symbolic and mystical theology God is named by means of creatures, but in symbolic theology he is named from external creatures, whereas in mystical theology he is named by way of inner, hidden and more worthy effects which the soul receives above itself from the contemplation of God, and the soul imposes such names through the gift of wisdom, to which it belongs especially and properly to know experientially what God is like (*qualis sit deus*)."[202]

Albert's much more objective understanding of what the mystical names signify is patently facilitated by metaphysical considerations, but it would be wrong to see it as a purely philosophical doctrine. At the beginning of the *Divine Names*, as in the *Celestial Hierarchy*, Albert points out that the *habitus regens* in this science is faith, and specifically "the faith, as it is passed on to us in sacred scripture."[203] And, following Dionysius, he interprets this strictly. "Our intellect might think that, though it has to be guided by the practice of sacred scripture in its exposition of the divine names, it could legitimately discover something about God by reason beyond what is in scripture. Dionysius excludes this and says that we must say and think nothing about God except what is passed on to us by sacred scripture, so that we reserve to God himself the knowledge of himself in anything which is not given to us in scripture."[204] Every science has its own basic principles, and in the case of theology its "principles" consist of scripture.[205] And it should not be forgotten that in this period any intellectual discipline was intimately associated, if not identified, with its "set books," so that the very word *scientia* could be used to refer to such authoritative writings.[206] *Theologia* as a science is inseparable from *theologia* as the word of God in scripture. In the case of other disciplines it would be a sign of intellectual weakness to follow "authority" too uncritically. But in theology the "authority" in question is not just human authority; it rests on the infallible "reason" of God, and so it is rational for us to submit to it unhesitatingly, even if we do not always understand the reason for what is said.[207] It is this submission to scripture that gives theology its special solidity and certainty.

Intellectual speculation has no right to try to supplement or to criticize the data of revelation. But scripture is meant "to enlighten our intellect,"[208] and this calls for sustained and intelligent study, and this is where we may benefit from the tools supplied by philosophy and other disciplines. A naive devotion to the mere text of scripture will lead only to "childish fancies." It may be true, as St. Gregory said, that "sacred scripture is a river in which sheep paddle and elephants swim," but this does not justify even the simple faithful in resting content with the mere symbols in which the scriptural message is often clothed, because even the literal meaning of the text should be located, not in the symbols themselves, but in what they signify.[209]

Mystical theology, then, is located firmly within the enterprise of Christian reflection on the word of God, and it is an intellectual discipline, even if it requires a mind strengthened by a supernatural light so that it can go beyond its natural limits in the "ecstasy" of faith.

Albert's analysis of theological language leads him to a relatively optimistic view of our ability to say things that do really apply to God, to ascribe the substance, the *res*, of at least some of our words to him, and not just the words without their *res*. But at the same time he is keenly aware of how little we actually know God, and he is clearly far from unsympathetic to the "oriental" theology that provoked the condemnation of 1241.

The epistemological problem of how any created intellect can know God, which Bonaventure could dismiss so breezily in his *quaestio disputata*, was for Albert a very serious question.

In the *De Resurrectione*[210] Albert makes a valiant, if not very successful, attempt to deal with the issues involved in the claim that we shall see God directly in heaven, a claim which the 1241 condemnation made it necessary to endorse, and in any case Albert seems to be persuaded that if we cannot ever attain to a genuine knowledge of God then our whole intellectual life (and therefore our whole life) will be eternally doomed to frustration. But there are problems. Only an infinite act of understanding could cope with an "infinite intelligible," and that is what God is; and our intellectual capacity is finite and so there seems to be an irremediable disproportion between it and God. We also need to show that there is some procedure whereby our minds could know God without either actually being God (which would bring us back to the pantheism condemned in 1210) or needing some intelligible form of God, which would leave us with a knowledge of God by way of something which is not God, and that would be merely a "vision in theophanies," such as Hugh of St. Victor had reprobated and which some people believed to have been condemned as heretical in 1241.[211] To evade the second kind of difficulty Albert falls back on an Augustinian notion of immediate knowledge of God by virtue of his real presence in the intellect, which we cannot see now because of the conditions of life in this world (particularly the flesh and sin) and because our attention is turned elsewhere, hindrances which will both be removed in the hereafter. Our immediate knowledge of God is thus to be understood on the model of our immediate knowledge of ourselves, and Albert even goes so far as to say "God will present himself to us without any medium, just as he sees himself without any medium."

To deal with the problem of disproportion and with the patristic authorities marshalled against the possibility of any direct vision of God, Albert resorts to distinctions in true scholastic vein. Taking up a phrase from 1 John 3:2 he distinguishes between seeing something "as it is" and seeing what something is, the latter meaning an exhaustive vision of all that something is. Clearly in this sense we cannot see what God is, and in this sense, as Damascene says, God is "incomprehensible and boundless, known by none, the sole contemplator of himself." But we can see God "as he is," Albert maintains, and seeing something "as it is" means "seeing its existence (*esse*) or being (*essentia*)." This rather underdeveloped distinction seems to rely heavily on the analogy of bodily vision: when the long-awaited visitors from Alpha Centauri eventually decide to land, we shall no doubt see many exotic pieces of equipment "as they are," without having the remotest idea what they are.

This still leaves the problem of disproportion. The only possibility of coping with something infinite, Albert suggests, is by finding some way in which it is finite. There is no chance of our intellect being able to delimit *what* God is, but it can handle God's attributes, and in reality any of God's attributes *is* God, so if our minds can reach any of them they will in fact be reaching God's essence. This also provides the answer to the problem raised by Chrysostom:[212] if God's essence is simple, then all those who see it must be seeing the same thing, yet "one praises it as glory, another as majesty, another as holiness and another as wisdom." The answer is that "though any attribute, as it exists in God, is the divine essence, yet as perceived by the intellect the attributes are distinguished by what they connote. And that is why one praises God as glory, another as wisdom and another as majesty." What is "connoted" by the divine attributes is their derivatives in creation[213] (their reality in God being what they denote), and if this is the source of their distinction it might be felt that Albert has not sufficiently established that knowledge of God by way of his attributes is any different from knowledge of him through creatures, and his implied suggestion that the attributes of God are somehow "finite," which must mean that we can "define" them in a way that is impossible with the question "what" God is, surely prompts us to wonder whether it is not at the level of their created counterparts that they are thus definable, rather than at the level of their existence in God. And if these anxieties are legitimate, we may further suspect that Albert has not sufficiently distinguished between the vision of God that we shall have in heaven and the knowledge of God we can have by faith here on earth.

In his account of the "mechanics" of the vision of God, at this stage, Albert is essentially at one with the Augustinian critics of "oriental" theology, but in his account of what we shall be able to see he stops a long way short of the utterly complete and clear vision of God to which William of Auvergne aspired, and he concedes a great deal to the Dionysian contention that "complete ignorance is the way to know him who is above all that is known": " 'Complete ignorance' means 'ignorance of the complete,' that is, ignorance of what God is; the most perfect knowledge of God is the vision of him together with the recognition that we are powerless to reach 'what' he is. He is thus known to be above all knowledge and all mind. And this is what Job says, that all who see him look on him from afar" (cf. Job 36:25).[214]

In the commentaries on the Sentences and on Dionysius' *Celestial Hierarchy* we can see that Albert's position has already matured considerably. He now repudiates the suggestion that the divine attributes might provide a way round the problem of God's infinity: God is "infinite in any one of his attributes." Precisely as infinite he cannot be known, except in the sense that we can know that he is infinite. But because he is simple and because we are not talking of any kind of infinite bulk, knowing God incompletely does not mean knowing just a "part" of God (as we might see just the tail of a mouse, which would not of itself tell us much about the rest of the animal). So there is no radical impossibility about our knowing God (who is infinite), even though we cannot know him precisely in his infinity—only God can have that kind of thorough knowledge of himself.[215] God, according to a phrase inspired by Damascene, is "an infinite ocean of substance," entirely eluding any attempt to say what he is. So our minds are rather in the position of people gazing out to sea: they are definitely looking at the sea, but at the same time they are not looking at anything precisely defined.[216]

The question of proportionality was largely sidestepped in *De Resurrectione* by means of the Augustinian doctrine of knowledge by presence in the intellect. If God is really there the whole time and it is only the nuisance of this present life that prevents us from seeing him, then clearly the soul just *is*, as Augustine claimed, capable of God (*capax Dei*).[217] Our inability to see him is no more than a temporary, if tiresome, fact about us. In the commentary on the Sentences Albert becomes less and less happy with this scenario. In book I he is still essentially relying on the model of the intellect's awareness of itself: "The divine substance is seen by all the blessed; as to how it is seen, without wishing to preempt further discussion we say that it is seen unmediatedly by conjunction, in such a way that God offers himself to our intellect in his own substance, just as the intellect does to itself." But there is no longer any hint that this immediate vision of God was all along a possibility lurking within the soul. The lack of proportion between God and us has to be taken seriously, and Albert now maintains that naturally there really is no such proportion; it is only "by the help of God" that our minds can rise up to become capable of seeing God.[218]

Once a more active role is ascribed to God in making it possible for us to see him, the question of "theophanies" begins to demand more attention. The use of this term was integral to the Eriugenist interpretation of the Dionysian hierarchical worldview, and had been interpreted to involve (a) that God is seen, even by the angels and the blessed, only indirectly by way of "images," and (b) that the vision of God is accorded to the angels and saints strictly in accordance with their position in the hierarchy of being, so that lower beings receive only the illumination that passes down to them through higher beings and therefore do not actually see God.[219] Both conclusions were condemned in 1241 and "theophany" became a word to be avoided. But Albert is now no longer prepared to leave the word in the hands of its enemies, whom he accuses of "insulting holy books" and "presumption."[220] His own maturing theory of the intellect makes possible an interpretation of theophanies that allows for a direct vision of God: in intellectual as in bodily vision there has to be some kind of light to make things visible (or intelligible), but there has also to be a specific visible (or intelligible) object, and it is this that determines what in particular is seen (or known). A created intellect needs to be reinforced by a light from on high if it is to see God, and this light may come either directly from God or through the mediation of higher created beings, but the role of intelligible object, which determines the content of the act of understanding, is God himself, God's own substance.[221] So Albert distinguishes between purely symbolic theophanies, which have no place in the beatific vision, and theophanies that are perfectly compatible with the beatific vision: We may see an object which is truly God in a divine light that is not God (that is, a light which flows to us from God through created intermediaries, which fortifies the mind to see God himself). We may also see an object which is truly God in a divine light which is God: "God himself is in all the blessed as a kind of light, making them into a likeness of himself through their participation in him."[222] In this way Albert is able to revive the Eriugenist doctrine that we see God by participating in God and to allow room even in heaven for a process of illumination that respects the structural interdependence of created intellects, without any denial of the immediacy of the vision of God. The spiritual solipsism which can, even if rather unfairly, be deduced from Plotinian or Augustinian doctrine, is thus shown to be unnecessary: the richly coherent cosmos of later Neoplatonism in which all beings are connected with each other in multiple ways does not exclude the possibility of direct intellectual union between any created mind and God.

In the commentary on the fourth book of the Sentences Albert formally and finally rejects the Augustinian knowledge by presence: substantial presence of something in the soul is not a sufficient basis for understanding. The mind understands itself in the same way that it understands anything else. Albert concedes this, but with an unexpected reservation: there is no other way of interpreting understanding, "provided we know what we are saying or understanding. But in heaven it will not be like this. There the unbounded light of the Godhead, which is God himself, is united with the agent intellect and poured out substantially over the whole soul and fills the soul, and in this way the soul will be full of God who is its bliss."[223] It is by being united directly with God like this that the blessed soul will "understand" him, but it seems to be a rather odd kind of understanding, if it excludes knowing what we are talking about or understanding. In fact Albert seems to be proposing to us a state of complete, but rather vague, luminosity, in which nothing in particular is understood.

In the later Dionysian commentaries Albert moves with much greater confidence toward a coherent and surprisingly Eriugenist doctrine, in which the notion of theophanies plays an important part. It is in terms of theophanies that Albert manages to do justice to both sides of the dispute that resulted in the 1241 condemnation, showing that it is possible for a created intellect to have a direct vision of God's essence, that such a vision is not ineluctably confined to the natural capacity of any given being, and that in spite of the simplicity of the divine essence it can truly be seen directly by different intellects in different ways.

Let us look at some texts from the commentary on the *Divine Names*:

> "Seeing" means actually making contact with the thing seen. . . . It also means running your eye over something. As Euclid shows, anything that is seen is seen from the vantage point of the corner of a triangle, whose apex is in the eye and whose base is in the thing seen. . . . The thing is seen along a line dividing the triangle, and so it is not

seen all at once, but by passing from one point to another. When we have run our eye over the whole thing, we can be said to have seen the whole thing. In this sense God cannot be seen by running our mind's eye over all that he is.

. . . Although God is simple in his substance, he is multiple in his attributes, whose principle (*ratio*) exists truly in him without any real plurality. If we saw God by surveying his substance with the knowledge of "what" he is, then all who see him would see and praise him in the same way. But as it is he is seen only in the sense of an immediate contact with his substance, in whatever way he makes himself present (*se obiicit*). And since he makes himself present to one in one light (*secundum unam rationem*) and to another in another light, one sees what another does not see, although they are all seeing his substance, because knowledge and goodness and everything that can have a *ratio* [i.e., more or less, everything that can properly be predicated of God] is God's substance.

. . . A created intellect has no proportionate capacity to know God by its own natural endowments, but it is made proportionate inasmuch as it is helped by enlightenments or theophanies coming down to it from God; even so it is not made capable of seeing "what" God is, but only of seeing him by a real contact with his substance, in accordance with whatever way he makes himself present in one or another light (*sub tali vel tali ratione*).[224]

The life of glory is a perfection above nature, in which nature without grace is incompetent; so since it is not granted in accordance with the power of nature, since it increases the capacity of nature, though without destroying nature, it can come about that a being whose nature is lower can be brought to the level of some being of a higher nature or even beyond it.[225]

The intellect, making contact with God's substance, knows him either in some image, as in this life in which we know God in a mirror and enigmatically, or immediately, as in heaven. The intellect is not proportionate just by its nature to this contact, but it is made proportionate by the light of glory coming down to it and strengthening it and raising it above its nature; and this is what is meant by saying that God is seen by way of theophany and participation, inasmuch as different intellects are strengthened in different ways to see God.[226]

Albert's whole scheme presupposes that no created intellect can see "what" God is, so that we are all entirely dependent on the various ways in which God strengthens our minds and the various lights in which he proposes himself to our thus strengthened minds. And Albert's doctrine is quite unambiguous on this point. Even the highest angels do not know "what" God is.[227] All that is proportionate to our understanding is "that" God is (*quia est*).[228] And even this is perhaps going too far: "A created intellect cannot perfectly reach God in such a way that no knowledge of him remains outside it; it is joined to him as to something transcending its capacity, indistinctly (*sub quadam confusione*) because there can be no knowledge 'what' he is, since he is unlimited, or of 'why' he is, since he has no cause, or even a distinct knowledge 'that' he is, since he has no remote cause or effect proportionate to him,[229] so neither on earth nor in heaven can anything be seen of him except an indistinct 'that he is' (*quia confusum*), although God himself is seen more or less luminously according to different kinds of vision and different kinds of seer."[230]

The knowledge "that" God is is apparently "proportionate" to our minds, and this calls for a more precise statement of what is meant by saying that our minds do not naturally have any "proportion" or capacity for the knowledge of God. There was a tradition, going back to St. Paul, that some kind of knowledge of God is possible to us by way of his creatures, independent of the gift of faith. St. John Damascene specified that the knowledge "that" God is is implanted in us by nature, and Albert accepts this.[231] Such a claim is entirely coherent with Albert's belief that God is present in us as a light in our minds, so that he is known, implicitly, in our knowledge of anything, as the ground of all intelligibility. But if knowledge "that" God is is natural to us, and knowledge "that" God is is all we shall have even in heaven, what becomes of the alleged "strengthening" of our intellect by some supernatural influx of light?

In response to a suggestion that our knowledge of God is perfected in heaven and must therefore move on from knowledge "that" to knowledge "what" or "why," Albert replies very firmly, "Our knowledge will not be perfected with a different kind of knowledge, either knowledge 'what' or knowledge 'why,' but with another way of knowing 'that': we shall have an unmediated vision 'that,' where now we have only a veiled and enigmatic vision in a mirror."[232] The supernatural reinforcement of our minds does not enable them to do something quite different from what they could do naturally; it enables them to do more fully what they could already, to some extent, do. Albert is fully serious in his concern that the supernatural should not be envisaged in any way that jeopardizes the natural. However much a created intellect may be enhanced by grace or glory, its understanding will always be conditioned by its own nature.[233] Albert does not believe that some miraculous change will overtake our intellectual or perceptual powers in heaven. The text in the pseudo-Augustinian *De Spiritu et Anima*, which suggests that in heaven our senses will be turned into reason and our reason into intellect and our intellect into understanding (*intelligentia*),[234] is interpreted by Albert to mean only that the lower powers turn *to* the higher powers and receive a kind of overflow from them so that they too can share in their enjoyment; he explicitly denies that they are "drawn out of their own natures."[235]

All that our minds are capable of, then, is an indistinct knowledge "that" God is, a knowledge which is, to start off with, simply implicit in the sheer fact that we can understand anything at all. This purely natural and indirect knowledge of God can be enhanced in various degrees, for instance, by the light of faith, that *res convincens intellectum*, the sheer fact of illumination contained in the fact that we find the articles of belief credible. Inasmuch as we are united with the light of God, we can come to know the unknown God more and more,[236] but even in heaven, even with the light of glory, we cannot get beyond an indistinct knowledge "that" God is; he remains for us an "infinite ocean" of which we know more truly what it is not than what it is.[237] What is new in heaven is that we shall meet this brute fact of light directly, instead of meeting it indirectly in its reflection in the intelligibility of God's works, whether of grace or of nature. But does this mean, then, that there is nothing for us to see except a vague, unbounded luminosity?

Vistas of infinite and indeterminate light no doubt appeal to some people, and if that is all that there is to be known about God, the comparative mysticists will have no difficulty in proving that all religions are really one and that the systems of doctrine that divide them are no more than hopeless attempts to formulate the ineffable. There have presumably always been people who prefer their religion to provide uplift and inspiration, without requiring them actually to believe anything in particular. In the Middle Ages Eriugena could perhaps be read (inaccurately, to be sure) as recommending a rather nebulous deity, when he announced that even God does not know what he himself is, because he does not have any particular "what" to know. This doctrine was duly passed on in Honorius Augustodunensis.[238] Avicenna also denied that God has an essence or quiddity.[239]

William of Auvergne had little sympathy for any such imprecise divinity. In his view it is impossible to speak either about God or to God unless God is "intelligible and nameable as an individual (*singulariter*)," unless he can be clearly picked out and distinguished from everyone and everything else. Any philosophy that could not accommodate this clearly locatable individuality of God was automatically disqualified. If we cannot identify God as an individual, to whom shall we pray, whom shall we worship, how shall we know we are not worshipping the wrong God?[240]

St. Albert is definitely not happy about calling God "individual." Apart from the problem that God is not "an individual" (he is three Persons), the term *individual* suggests only improperly the real uniqueness of God. In principle, wherever there is one individual there could conceivably be more than one; even if in fact we have only one sun in our sky, there is no absolute reason why we should not have half a dozen. To call God "an individual" (*singularis*) suggests that he might always turn out to be merely one God among several, and "God," according to St. Albert, properly has no plural.[241] On this view William of Auvergne's anxiety is somewhat misconceived. The problem is not how we identify the right God, so that we do not worship the wrong one, but how we make sure we do not worship anything which is not God. And if this is the right way to formulate the problem, it is not really necessary to "pick out"

God, so long as we remember not to worship anything that we can pick out. But this still leaves the other side of William's anxiety, which was mentioned earlier on, that if we cannot know God as an individual, our whole hope of beatitude collapses. Are we really looking forward only to an eternity of gazing out into (supernatural) space?

Albert certainly does not accept that God actually *is* indeterminate. The contention that God has no *quid est* is explicitly repudiated: God is "a kind of quiddity and essence"; there is something "intrinsically intelligible in God, by which he is distinguished from others."[242] Although God "is infinite in every way, in his essence, in his power and in every other way that is conceivable in him,"[243] Albert does not want this to be understood as implying that God is fuzzy at the edges: "Though God is not measured or limited by anything created, he is measured by himself and so in a way he is finite to himself, though not to us."[244]

The trouble is that God is "infinite" as far as we are concerned and "what" he is is therefore indeterminate in our minds. He is not properly to be thought of as an "object" to any created intellect.[245] All the same, Albert is not prepared to leave us simply with a vast, unfocused luminosity to gaze at. In his commentary on Dionysius' fifth epistle he formally raises the question: If it is God who enlightens us, then how can it also be God who perfects our intellect, since the perfection of the intellect requires that it should have some definite object to know? And it is not light that provides the mind with any definite object; the mind comes to intellectual fulfilment in the form of actual understanding because its intellectual light is particularized by the thing understood.

Albert answers that God brings the intellect to its fulfilment by acting in two ways. He enlightens the mind (this picks up the doctrine formulated in the commentary on the fourth book of the Sentences that God unites himself with our agent intellect), but he also "brings it to a particular knowledge, inasmuch as he is something particular (*quiddam determinatum*), particularized not by matter, but by his nature and the attributes of his nature and inasmuch as there are Persons with their own particular properties."[246]

So God is not in any ordinary sense an "object" for the intellect, yet he takes the place of the thing known. How are we to understand this? In the commentary on the fifth epistle Albert refers us back for the rest of his discussion of the vision of God to the commentary on the first epistle, where Dionysius makes the devastating comment, "If anyone who sees God understands what he has seen, then he has not seen God himself, but only something that is his. . . . Perfect ignorance in the best sense is how we know him who is above all that is known." Since understanding and mental vision are essentially the same thing, Albert takes Dionysius to be propounding the startling paradox that "anyone who sees God does not see God, but only something that is his," that is, something that derives from him, and he comments accordingly:

> When he says that anyone seeing God does not see him, this must be understood in terms of a vision of "what" God is or a distinct vision "that" he is, and God is not seen in either of these ways; all there is is an indistinct and inadequate vision "that" he is, and this is true both on earth and in heaven, as we have already said.
>
> When he says, "but only something that is his," this must be understood with reference to the starting-point of vision, because vision always begins with some effect of God's, either one in which the intellect sees, as in a mirror, or one by which it sees, as with light. But the intellect is fixed on God himself as the goal (*terminus*) of its vision, because the intellect receives God's effects and plunges itself in him and sees God himself. . . .

The "perfect ignorance" Dionysius recommends is taken to mean that "we know ourselves to be failing completely to comprehend God because of his excellence. . . . And so it is clear that Dionysius does not mean that God is not seen in any way, but that he is seen precisely in our ignorance of him."[247]

If we put these comments on the epistles together with the passages cited earlier from the *Divine Names*, it is reasonably clear what Albert's doctrine is. God unites himself with our minds as light; he also confronts us with himself, indirectly on earth and directly in heaven, but our minds cannot really take him in as an "object" because we can only attain to an indistinct knowledge "that" he is. But God presents himself to us, *obiicit se*, almost "objectifies himself" for us, "under this or that *ratio*," as goodness or wisdom or whatever.

These are surely the "somethings that are his" that we see and that are a way of reaching a real vision of God, which begins with some effect of his. It is through God's effects that we have a distinct grasp of his attributes (which in him are simply himself). And in as much as it is by participating in God that we know him, it is surely not least by discovering the effects of his attributes in ourselves that we see him in the light of them. Thus we do have a real and immediate vision of God in heaven, but simply as such it provides no specific content for our intellect. Inasmuch as God provides the content as well as the light for our intellect, it is in terms of his attributes, on which we can get some intellectual purchase because of their visibility in God's effects. Starting from these effects, we see through them to God who is presenting his substance to us (which is not really distinct from his attributes) precisely by knowing that we are not capable of comprehending what God is. It is quite literally in our ignorance, our not-knowing, that we actually see God in himself, because it is the not-knowing that takes us beyond the intelligible effect of God to the reality of the attribute of God that it manifests, and so to the essence of God, that sheer presence whose very transcendence delights the intellect supremely.[248]

If this interpretation of Albert's doctrine is correct, then the position he has reached by the end of his Dionysian commentaries is, as I have suggested, surprisingly Eriugenist. Unlike Eriugena he does formally allow for an unmediated vision of God's essence, but as such this unmediated vision is unintelligible to us. What makes it intelligible is that God presents himself to us in the light of his attributes, which are distinct and intelligible to us because of their manifestation in creatures. So what actually gives intelligible shape to our vision of God is the vision of God's effects become entirely transparent to himself, and this is precisely what Eriugena believed. It is God who is seen, but he, as it were, nuances the vision of himself in different ways for different people, so that it is in terms of theophanies that the vision of God becomes, as it were, manageable to them. And this is just how Eriugena's twelfth-century follower, Honorius Augustodunensis, interprets the "many mansions" of John 14:2.[249]

It is clear that any theory like this of how we see God requires the sort of theory we were looking at earlier of how we talk about God. If theophanies are to provide a real, direct vision of God, then it must be possible to ascribe real attributes to God which, in him, actually *are* his substance but which are at the same time real in their own right, so that the affirmation of them does genuinely succeed in saying something about God, even if, because of the inadequate *modus significandi* of all our language, the affirmation needs to be capped by a negation.

We can also see how important the *Mystical Theology* is in Albert's view of the Christian life. There is real continuity between the vision of God in heaven and our attempts to develop our faith into a theological science on earth. Even in heaven we have only an indistinct vision of God's essence, as such, and whatever distinctness there is comes from an increasingly perspicuous knowledge of how the attributes of God are manifested in his works. Thus there has to be a rich affirmative theology, culling signs and riddling disclosures of God from all his creatures and all his words. But if this elaborate and no doubt lengthy process is to debouch into a vision of God himself, every light has to be transcended. If it is "transcended" without first being affirmed, there will be no revelation, no theophany; but equally if it is affirmed without being transcended, then we shall stop short of the knowledge of God that is possible to us.

*

"God is seen precisely in our ignorance of him." This is the abrupt conclusion to Albert's commentary on Dionysius' first epistle. And it might appear to make God painfully remote. But if this is how it strikes us, we need to look carefully at our reaction. There is a very proper way to make God remote from us, namely, the removing of our comfortable false gods, our idols. Negative theology reminds us of just how many things are not God. The patron saint of a later and rather different kind of "mystical theology," St. John of the Cross, tears away our domesticated deities with almost insolent ruthlessness. If we feel that St. Albert is "taking away our God,"[250] maybe our "God" was never really worth having anyway.

But if we are concerned, not with some comfortable godling, but with the God who is the maker of all things, visible and invisible, the God who is the Father of immeasurable majesty, the God who is the Son in whom all things were made, the God who is the

Holy Spirit, the Lord, who spoke through those very uncomfortable gentlemen, the prophets, then it is surely not really true that it is negative theology, as presented by Dionysius, as interpreted by Albert, that makes God "remote." Precisely because God is inaccessible and incomprehensible, there can be no shortcuts to him, and in that sense he is "remote"; nor can there be any specialist faculty in us that can by sheer concentration of energy get through to him. But what this leaves us with is the incredible abundance of ways in which God gives himself to us. If Dionysius and Albert are right, we are bumping into God the whole time. It is negative theology, properly understood, which validates the apparent paradox that God has no name and yet every name is God's name. If there is, strictly speaking, no entirely adequate way of talking about God, there is also no way of talking about God that is entirely inadequate either. And this means that theology can never be allowed to degenerate into an esoteric Fachsprache. And it is not only academic theology that is prone to the temptation to false expertise; piety too has its experts and its jargon. Negative theology dethrones the idols with their professional guardians and gives us back the breadth and richness of the church, with its innumerable ways of talking and behaving, in which, of course, some of us have competences others lack, but the most important thing about all of us is that we are incompetent with reference to God.

If we take Dionysian negative theology seriously, it frees us from the various tyrannies that narrow our religious language and practice. Unduly self-confident affirmative theologies take some ways of talking and some ways of behaving too seriously, and deprive all the rest of any significance. But it is surely trivial gods who make most of life trivial. The God of St. Albert, who is the source of all being and of all intelligibility, of course cannot be seen simply as "a being" or as "an intelligible object,"[251] but this means that we do not turn to him by naively turning away from other beings and other possible objects of our mental attention; he sheds a light of intelligibility and significance upon *everything* and it is in everything that we encounter him. This gives us back the whole giddy vocabulary of the bible,[252] it gives us back a whole world of fascinating creatures to study, it gives us back the whole range of sacraments and sacramentals,[253] of liturgies and devotions. Of course it warns us not to be duped into supposing that any of these things "is" God, but it also warns us not to be taken in by any simplistic assertion that they are *not* God. In knowing them we are, at least implicitly, beginning to know God.

Precisely because God is incomprehensible, a variety of ways of approaching God can be real ways of approaching him. If we forget this, we cannot help but subvert the lawful freedom of God's children. Conversely, no way is entirely adequate. If we forget this, then our ways of piety will become impenetrable barriers between us and God; as Albert's follower Meister Eckhart warns us, if we seek God "with some particular way," we shall find a way and lose God.[254] If certain particular ways of talking about God come to be taken as fully clear and satisfactory accounts of what God is like, our very clarity will do much to obscure our apprehension of him. The modern dogma, for instance, that "God is a person" can be given a perfectly serviceable sense, as long as we do not imagine that it tells us *what* God is in a way that we can understand. If we omit the negative corrective, as most of the devotees of this slogan appear to do, then not only do we produce some rather bizarre theologies, not only do we cut ourselves off from many centuries of Christian tradition, but we also trap ourselves in assumptions about the Christian life that may actually make life rather miserable for us. When we pray, according to the ancient definition, we are talking to God. If "God is a person," then talking to God must be talking to a person. But then very often saying our prayers is not a bit like talking to a person in any ordinary sense.[255] If God's love for us and our love for him have to be interpreted rigorously and relentlessly as "personal" love on both sides, this is likely to conjure up all kinds of associations, which will in many cases be frequently disappointed. Why not allow ourselves other and more varied ways of talking? Why not, just for a treat, see what it is like to call God "Truth" and see what light the love of truth can shed on what it means to love God? Neither "person" nor "truth" will alone be enough for us to live off indefinitely, but the more numerous our avenues of approach are, the more likely it is that we shall find God infinitely intimate to us and supremely enjoyable.

St. Albert gives us a vastly spacious view of life, but he too was drawn to God in his own way. His most famous disciple, St. Thomas Aquinas, did not agree with his master on how we shall see God in heaven. Even as a child, we are told, young Thomas wanted an answer to the question, What is God?[256] As an adult theologian he ventured to assert that in heaven we shall get the answer to this question and see what God is (*de ipso Deo videtur non solum quid non est, sed etiam quid est*).[257] H. F. Dondaine suggests that the difference in doctrine between the two saints reflects a difference in spirituality: "St. Albert likes to imagine the vision of God as an encounter with the Infinite, a being plunged into it or a blind gazing over the limitless ocean of substance. But St. Thomas defines the essential desire of the spirit as an aspiration to see *what something is*; he has understood the agony of the great philosophers, dissatisfied with only knowing of God 'that' he is."[258]

Dondaine may well be right in supposing that there was a difference of spiritual temperament between Thomas and Albert, and it is perhaps true that Albert had more of a taste for infinity than Thomas did. St. Catherine of Siena certainly liked the idea of God as a "boundless ocean."[259] But I do not believe that the crucial factor lies there. For Thomas the question, What is it? may well have been paramount, but Albert—in this perhaps more truly Aristotelian than Thomas—harps at least as much on the further question, Why? May we not perhaps detect a personal note in Albert's comment near the beginning of his exposition of the *Metaphysics?*

> God does not put to rest our desire for knowledge precisely inasmuch as he is God or as a particular nature existing in its own right, but rather inasmuch as he is the highest cause of things, whose knowledge causes being, because this is how he is the principle and light of all that is known, just as an art is the principle and light of all artifacts.[260]

Would it be too far from the truth to suggest that the *ratio* under which God especially showed himself to Albert was that of being the cause of all intelligibility, the ultimate explanation of everything? My suspicion is that for Albert beatitude would have to include, even if only as the minutest part of it, the opportunity to say, "So that's why flies lay their eggs on white walls!"[261]

95

Notes

Part I

1. The major sources for the life of Albert are cited according to these editions: Henry of Herford, *Liber de Rebus Memorabilibus* (c.1355), ed. A. Potthast (Göttingen, 1859). Luis of Valladolid, *Tabula Alberti Magni* (1414), ASOP 20 (1932) pp. 752–61 (there is another ed. of this text in *Catalogus Codicum Hagiographicorum Bibl. Regiae Bruxellensis* I ii [Brussels, 1889], pp. 95–105). *Legenda Coloniensis* (mid-fifteenth century), ed. P. von Loë, *Analecta Bollandiana* 19 (1900) pp. 272–84. Peter of Prussia, *Legenda Alberti Magni* (c.1485), ed. with *De Adhaerendo Deo* (Antwerp, 1621). Rudolph of Nijmegen, *Legenda Alberti Magni* (c.1488), ed. H. C. Scheeben (Cologne, 1928). Alberto di Castello, *Cronica de Magistris Generalibus*, in *Tabula Privilegiorum* (Venice, 1504) (on which see R. Creytens, AFP 30 [1960] pp. 233, 239–41) (the 1506 ed. of this chronicle is reprinted in E. Martène and U. Durand, *Veterum Scriptorum . . . Amplissima Collectio* VI [Paris, 1729], the passage concerning Albert being in cols. 358–62). The main modern studies of Albert's life are: P. von Loë, "De vita et scriptis B. Alberti Magni," *Analecta Bollandiana* 20 (1901) pp. 273–316 (cited as Loë). H. C. Scheeben, *Albert der Grosse: zur Chronologie seines Lebens*, QF 27 (Vechta, 1931) (cited as Scheeben). F. Callaey, "La vita del B. Alberto Magno," ASOP 20 (1932) pp. 475–530 (cited as Callaey). There are useful articles in various encyclopedias: A. Fries–K. Illing, "Albertus Magnus," *Die deutsche Literatur des Mittelalters: Verfasserlexikon* I (Berlin, 1978), cols. 124–39. P. Simon, "Albert der Grosse," *Theologische Realenzyklopädie* II (Berlin, 1978), pp. 177–84. W. Kübel et al., "Albertus Magnus," *Lexikon des Mittelalters* I (Munich/Zurich, 1980), cols. 294–99. Finally there is a study of Albert's life by Weisheipl on pp. 13–51 of J. A. Weisheipl, ed., *Albertus Magnus and the Sciences* (Toronto, 1980) (this whole book is cited as Weisheipl, *Albert*), and by W. P. Eckert in A. Fries, ed., *Albertus Magnus: Ausgewählte Texte* (Darmstadt, 1981), pp. VII–XXX (cited as Eckert).

2. Roger Bacon, *Opus Tertium* 9, ed. J. S. Brewer, *Opera Quaedam Hactenus Inedita* (London, 1859), p. 30. On Bacon's attitude to Albert, cf. Weisheipl, *Albert* pp. 53–72.

3. MS Troyes 1956 f.24ᵛ, cited by J. G. Bougerol in *Le Scuole degli Ordini Mendicanti*, Convegni del Centro di Studi sulla Spiritualità Medievale XVII (Todi, 1978), p. 266.

4. *Summa de Bono* IV tr. 3 ch. 9; see J. Daguillon, *Ulrich de Strasbourg: La "Summa de Bono" Livre I* (Paris 1930), p. 30*. Quoted in Peter p. 260.

5. Tolomeo of Lucca, *Hist. Eccl.* XXII 19 (L. A. Muratori, *Rerum It-*

alicarum Sciptores XI [Milan 1727], col. 1151). Bernard Gui, MOPH XXII p. 125. J. Meyer, QF 12 p. 50, QF 29 p. 40. Luis (p. 755) says that he was "about 87" and Peter says that he was exactly 87 (p. 303); the value of this more precise figure is uncertain, but it could be correct.

6. Loë p. 276; Weisheipl, *Albert* p. 15. J. B. Freed, "St. Albert's Brother Henry of Lauingen OP," AFP 48 (1978) p. 63.

7. Luis p. 752; Meyer, QF 12 p. 49; Peter p. 78; Alberto f. 139^r. Also some manuscripts of Albert's *Metaphysica* (cf. Col. XXI i p. XV). Rudolph (p. 8) adds that the family name was Bollstadt, but this is almost certainly his own conjecture (cf. Scheeben pp. 5–7).

8. Scheeben, *Albertus Magnus* (Bonn, 1932), p. 22; cf. Scheeben p. 7 n. 28; Freed pp. 63–64.

9. This view has most recently been espoused by Weisheipl, *Albert* p. 38. Since then it has been attacked by B. Schmidt (Col. XXI i p. XV) on two grounds: Albert would not have referred to his episcopal palace of Donaustauf as *villa mea*, since it was not a *villa* but a *castrum;* and there are reasons for believing that *De Animalibus* was completed before Albert became a bishop. But if, as Schmidt contends, *villa* has to be translated "town," it seems odd that Albert should refer to Lauingen as "*my* town"; and it is far from proved that *villa* cannot refer to an episcopal estate (cf. J. F. Niermeyer, *Mediae Latinitatis Lexicon Minus* [Leiden, 1976], p. 1102). And, as Schmidt concedes, his arguments for the dating of *De Animalibus* are not conclusive. It seems certain that the *Quaestiones de Animalibus* can be dated to 1258 (Schmidt, p. XVI), and this work does refer, once, to "our book *De Animalibus*" (Col. XII p. 169:58), but the reference is totally vague (cf. Col. XII p. XLIV) and could be taken as a sign that the *De Animalibus* was still more of a project than a reality. Little can be inferred with any certainty from the fact that a Parisian manuscript contains an earlier draft of a single page from the beginning of *De Animalibus;* the dating of this manuscript no later than 1260 is not controversial (cf. Schmidt, p. XVI), but there seems to be no reason why someone should not have culled a page discarded by Albert from a work that was still in progress. Unless better arguments are proposed against it, it seems to me that Albert's "estate on the Danube" can most naturally be taken as referring to his episcopal residence, not his birthplace.

10. *Anim.* 8.2.6.110 is an explicit but not localized reference to the childhood experience of Albert and his friends, so it is not unreasonable to take *nobis* in 8.2.6.111 as referring to the same period—no other group has been mentioned to which the plural could refer (Albert does not use the plural when he only means himself); and 8.2.6.111 is explicitly located in "upper Swabia."

11. Freed pp. 63–70.

12. Freed p. 66. That Henry was Albert's blood brother is proved by Albert's will (QF 16 p. 33).

13. Freed pp. 68–9: a Henry of Lauingen is known in Austria c.1176; ibid. p. 64 for a late thirteenth-century Lord Hartmann of Lauingen in Augsburg, known as "the Bavarian" (which could in this period refer to Austria). Freed argues fairly plausibly that Albert's brother Henry could be identical with the Henry of Lauingen who is known as a canon of Friesach in Carinthia between 1232 and 1241 (ibid. pp. 66–7).

14. Freed pp. 63–4, is lured by Scheeben into looking for a place on the Danube (cf. note 8), and so wonders why Henry became a canon so far from home (ibid. p. 68). But it is not impossible that the family home was in Carinthia. Albert gives us presumably first-hand information that the peasants in that part of the world lure dormice to hibernate in specially prepared places in the woods and then use them for food (*Anim.* 22.2.1.103). The medieval biographers did not necessarily have any evidence for Lauingen being Albert's birthplace except their knowledge of his name. The fact that a chapel was built in Lauingen in Albert's honor in view of his hoped-for canonization in about 1320 (Luis, p. 757) proves only that people believed or at least wanted to claim that Albert was born there.

15. Herford p. 201; Meyer, QF 29 p. 103; Peter p. 78; Alberto f. 139^r.

16. Freed pp. 64–5. But if Lord Hartmann of Lauingen, attested in Augsburg in 1280, is to be connected with Albert's family, then they had clearly gone up in the world (as did some other knightly families according to Freed, ibid. p. 65).

17. *Anim.* 8.2.6.110.

18. *Anim.* 8.2.4.72.

19. Herford p. 201; Luis p. 752; Peter p. 78. Peter's story is self-contradictory: Albert cannot both have been 87 in 1280 and been received into the Order by Jordan at the age of 16. Rudolph (pp. 9–11) clearly saw the contradiction and abandoned the claim that Albert joined the Order when he was 16.

20. Meyer, QF 12 p. 49.

21. Bacon, *Compendium Studii Philosophiae* 5, ed. cit. p. 426. It is not clear that Bacon is even intending to make a specific point about Albert; he remarks generally that a great many Dominicans enter the Order as "boys" under 20 years of age. Although he specifically mentions Albert and Thomas, he does not, in so many words, claim to have any knowledge of the ages at which they became Dominicans.

22. Herford p. 201; Luis pp. 752–3.

23. *Leg. Col.* pp. 272–3.

24. MOPH I pp. 187–8.

25. *Leg. Col.* p. 273.

26. Meyer QF 29 p. 110; Alberto f. 139ʳ. Both probably depend on the lost chronicle of Jakob of Soest.

27. Peter pp. 79–82.

28. Peter pp. 83–5.

29. Vincentius Justiniani, *Compendiosa Vitae Descriptio . . . B. Alberti,* with *Bibliae Mariae Opus a B. Alberto Magno . . . Conscriptum* (Cologne, 1625), pp. 40–1. Apart from Justiniani's quotations, the chronicle of Iohannes Molitoris is lost.

30. Scheeben, QF 35 pp. 165–6.

31. Rudolph pp. 10–13.

32. Herford p. 201. Peter, p. 90, follows Herford very closely, but changes "first" to "next," to allow for a previous period as lector in Cologne. Meyer has clearly received a confused tradition that has Albert lecture on the Sentences in Cologne and then become a lector "for the first time" in Hildesheim (QF 26 p. 156). It is clear that the traditional datum, which has to be accommodated, is that Albert was first a lector at Hildesheim.

33. Justiniani p. 11 implies that Molitoris maintained that Albert was sent to Cologne as a lector under the priorship of Leo, but the text actually quoted (pp. 40–41) does not substantiate this. As Scheeben suggests (pp. 11–12), Molitoris' reference to Albert's assignation to Cologne may well concern a later occasion.

34. *Mineralia* II 3.1 (B 5 pp. 48–9; AT 82).

35. *Meteora* III 2.12 (B 4 p. 629a; AT 123); *Summa de Creaturis* II 10.5 (B 35 p. 119b).

36. *De Natura Loci* 3.2 (Col. V ii pp. 33–34).

37. Cf. N. G. Siraisi, *Arts and Sciences at Padua* (Toronto, 1973), esp. p. 24.

38. Bacon, *Compendium Studii* 5, ed. cit. pp. 425–26.

39. *De Natura Boni,* written before he went to Paris (cf. P. Simon, Col. XXV i pp. V–VI), reveals a knowledge of those texts of Aristotle that had been available for some time, including the *Metaphysics* and some of the *Naturalia.* The public study of these works was banned in the University of Paris in 1210 and 1215 (*Chart.* I pp. 70–1, 78–9) and the ban was renewed in 1231 until such time as a suitably bowdlerised version could be produced (ibid. p. 138), but in some other places a more liberal attitude prevailed (e.g. Toulouse, see *Chart.* I p. 131).

40. MOPH I pp. 108–9, 174.

41. As Scheeben tries to do (pp. 12–13).

42. *Meteora* III 2.9, 2.20 (B 4 pp. 626, 638; AT 121, 122).

43. Cf. Caesarius of Heisterbach, *Dialogus Miraculorum* X 49; Tolo-

meo of Lucca, *Annales* 1222 (MGH SS NS VIII [Berlin, 1955], pp. 111, 303); Chronicle of the Villolas, Muratori, RIS XVIII i vol. 2 (Bologna 1938–46), p. 85.

44. This is suggested by Scheeben p. 13.

45. Scheeben p. 11. The historians who give 1223 as the date of Albert's entry into the Order all rely on B. M. Reichert, "Das Itinerar des zweiten Dominikanergenerals Jordanis von Sachsen," in S. Ehses, *Festschrift zum 1100 jährigen Jubiläum des deutschen Campo Santo in Rom*, Freiburg i. Br. 1897, pp. 154–5, or more recently on B. Altaner, QF 20 p. 70, both of whom base themselves on the presumed dating of Jordan's letter 20.

46. MOPH XXIII p. 24.

47. QF 35 p. 17 n. 20.

48. Cf. MOPH I p. 108.

49. Scheeben p. 12; accepted without comment by Freed p. 67.

50. *Iuventus* was as imprecise a term as "youth" is today, in spite of various attempts to define it, but it was readily extended well beyond the age of 30. Isidore regards it as continuing to the age of 50 (*Etymologiae* 11.2.5). Thomas of Cantimpré actually regards *adolescentia* (which comes before *iuventus* in the usual scheme) as lasting up to the age of 35 (*De Natura Rerum* I 80, ed. H. Boese [Berlin 1973], p. 81).

51. J. B. Freed, *The Friars and German Society in the Thirteenth Century* (Cambridge, Mass., 1977), p. 140.

52. The claim that he was already a lector in 1228 (Loë p. 277) rests on the evidence of *Leg. Col.* and Justiniani (not Molitoris, if Scheeben pp. 11–12 is correct) and it is to be explained as an attempt to reconcile the statement that Albert entered the Order in Cologne under Leo with the belief that he entered the Order in Padua. It is of no guaranteed historical value.

53. For the Dominicans' tendency to do without a probationary period before profession, see S. Tugwell, AFP 53 (1983) pp. 5–52. M. H. Vicaire, AFP 54 (1984) pp. 24–5 note 76, denies my contention that before 1220 the Order made no provision at all for a probationary period, but he does not answer my arguments and his case rests (a) on *Prim. Const.* I 13 (on the novice master), which he dates to 1216, and (b) on a papal Bull of 7 February 1217 (MOPH XXV no. 81). But the Bull only refers to profession and cannot prove anything about the presence or absence of provision for a probationary period before profession. And Vicaire himself acknowledges elsewhere that it is not certain that *Prim. Const.* I 13 antedates 1220 (*Histoire de St Dominique*, 2d ed. [Paris, 1982], II p. 48 n. 118), and in any case *novitius* only means "newcomer" and can apply without the slightest difficulty to someone who has already made profession (cf. Tugwell, p. 21).

54. *Prim. Const.* II 30, ed. A. H. Thomas, *De oudste Constituties van de Dominicanen* (Louvain, 1965); for the dating cf. ibid. pp. 289–90. During Albert's life there were several different editions of the constitutions, which are cited here according to their chronological appropriateness: the edition made by Raymund of Peñafort can be found in AFP 18 (1948) pp. 29–68, that promulgated by Humbert of Romans in ASOP 3 (1897–8) pp. 31–60, 98–122, 162–81. "*Prim. Const.*" refers to the text edited by Thomas.

55. *Prim. Const.* II 31. II 20 (also from 1220) allows for the possibility of some people being sent for further study.

56. Herford p. 201; Peter p. 90.

57. In the sources the lectures on the Sentences are mentioned before the appointment as lector of Hildesheim, and this leads to a rather awkward text in Meyer (QF 26 p. 156), whose very awkwardness confirms that we are dealing with traditional material. And once Cologne was erected as a studium generale it is likely that Albert, as Regent, would not be expected to lecture on the Sentences, anymore than a Regent Master would in Paris (cf. Weisheipl, *Albert*, p. 21).

58. Alberto f. 140ʳ (presumably from Jakob of Soest).

59. Herford p. 201.

60. Freed, *The Friars and German Society*, p. 214. J. Steinhart, "Ein unbekannter Brief des Konstanzer Bischofs Heinrich von Tanne an die Freiburger Dominikaner aus dem Jahre 1237," *Zeitschrift des Breisgau-Geschichtsverein* 101 (1982) pp. 47–64.

61. QF 4 p. 11.

62. *Prim. Const.* II 23; for the date, see Tugwell, "Dominic the Founder," *Dominican Ashram* 4 (1985) p. 140.

63. Cf. the index to Potthast's ed. of Herford; Scheeben, p. 20; H. Wilms, *Albert der Grosse* (Munich, 1930), p. 27; W. A. Hinnebusch, *History of the Dominican Order* II (New York, 1973), p. 123; and the articles in the *Verfasserlexikon*, the *Realenzyklöpadie* and the *Lexikon des Mittelalters* (cf. above, note 1).

64. Weisheipl, *Albert*, p. 20.

65. *Meteora* I 3.5 (B 4 p. 504). The comet appeared at the end of January and was visible for several months (Scheeben pp. 20–1).

66. *Mineralia* III 1.10 (B 5 p. 72).

67. Ibid. 1.1 (B 5 p. 59).

68. *II Sent.* d.6 a.9 (B 27 p. 139a).

69. See R. A. Gauthier, Leonine XLV i pp. 256*–7*.

70. See Scheeben pp. 20–21 for a reminder that we do not necessarily know all of Albert's moves in these years.

71. See above, note 39.

72. There were five houses at the time of the first Provincial Chapter

in 1225 and thirty houses by 1241. Cf. Freed, *The Friars and German Society* pp. 210–5.

73. Scheeben pp. 21–22.

74. AFP 10 (1940) p. 354.

75. Cf. Loë p. 278; Callaey and Weisheipl simply do not mention it.

76. *Const.* II 14 (AFP 18 [1948] p. 66).

77. A pioneering study of the Dominican Parisian Masters by H. Denifle in *Archiv für Literatur- und Kirchengeschichte des Mittelalters* 2 (1886) pp. 167–182 indicated the importance of the list of Masters in the Chronicle of Gerald de Frachet (MOPH I pp. 334–5). In *Revue Thomiste* 8 (1925) pp. 501–521 P. Mandonnet attempted to attach precise dates to Gerald's list, and in the process advanced the theory that the two Dominican chairs, at least from the time of Albert, were allocated in accordance with the principle of retaining one chair for the Paris province and one for members of the other provinces; this alleged principle of one 'intern' chair and one 'extern' chair has apparently acquired canonical status; according to Weisheipl, *Thomas* p. 65, it was laid down by a General Chapter. The dating of the Masters was taken further by P. Glorieux in his standard *Répertoire des Maîtres en Théologie de Paris au XIIIᵉ siècle*, Paris 1933–4. Unfortunately both Mandonnet and Glorieux resorted to extremely fanciful procedures in order to arrive at their dating, and it is highly doubtful whether the alleged principle governing the allocation of the two chairs has any validity, at least in the time of Albert and Thomas. It is only in the fourteenth century that there is clear evidence for a principle of alternating between intern and extern candidates for the two chairs, and even then it is misleading to speak of intern and extern chairs. Gui provides dates for the accession of new Dominican Masters for a few years at the beginning of the fourteenth century (MOPH XXII pp. 131–4), which seem to be mostly accurate. We learn that in 1301 both Masters were members of the Paris province. In 1302 a German (Eckhart) became a Master, together with another Frenchman. In 1303 or 1304 (cf. *Memorie Domenicane* NS 10 (1979) pp. 219–220) Remigio dei Girolami received the title of Master, but he had already been away from Paris for two or more years and never taught there as a Master. In 1304 two more members of the Paris province became Masters. Thereafter there seems to be an alternation between the Paris province and other provinces up to 1314. From 1311 onwards the General Chapter assigned people to be bachelors of the Sentences in Paris, and it is clear that there is a rigorous principle of alternating between the Paris province and other provinces at work (MOPH IV pp. 55, 60, 62, 69, 75, 86, 104, 110, 118, 125 etc.). Alternating intern and extern bachelors did not necessarily lead to an alternation between intern and extern Masters, and the 1316 General Chapter ruled that the practice of alternating Masters should be dropped,

in favour of a system whereby the first to lecture on the Sentences would automatically be next in line for a chair (MOPH IV pp. 91–2). The 1317 Chapter, however, ruled that the principle of alternation was to be resumed and retained (MOPH IV p. 102). This did not necessarily mean that the chairs as such, though, were to be designated as 'intern' and 'extern'; the 1317 Chapter itself decreed that *whoever* was the next to incept in Paris should take over the chair which Pierre de la Palu had been holding since 1314 (MOPH IV p. 104; MOPH XXII p. 133). The 1317 Chapter refers to alternation as an 'approved custom' in the Order, but insufficient dates have been established to enable us to know when it became customary. At any rate any such principle is clearly excluded by the earliest known capitular legislation: the 1264 Chapter said that the two chairs must be filled 'without regard for nationality' (MOPH III p. 125). In principle, the 1220 Constitutions made the General Chapter responsible for the deployment of Dominican manpower, but in practice it is likely that this responsibility devolved upon the Master of the Order and the provincials. The 1264 Chapter (loc. cit.) refers to 'superiors' promoting people to Parisian chairs, and tries to tidy up the situation by deputing the Master of the Order to take control of such promotions himself, and this thereafter seems to have been the normal practice (cf. MOPH III pp. 125, 126, 130, 142, 150, 155, 161). Already in 1251 it was clearly the Master of the Order who felt responsible for sending someone to prepare for Mastership in Paris, the someone, in the outcome, being Thomas Aquinas (Tocco, FVST pp. 80–1, Ferrua p. 48), and it is hard to see who sent Albert to Paris, if it was not the Master of the Order. If we take Gerald's list of Masters as being arranged in chronological sequence, then Albert was the first to graduate after Guerric and Godfrey, who succeeded Hugh of St Cher and John of St Giles. John of St Giles left Paris in 1233 (QE I p. 100), and Hugh was certainly provincial of France by March 1237 (M. C. Guigue, *Grand Cartulaire de l'Abbaye d'Ainay*, Lyons 1885 II pp. 134–5) and may well have been provincial some years earlier, and he was possibly prior of Paris before that (QE I p. 195).

78. MOPH III pp. 34–5. Since this was a proposal to change the constitutions, it only became law after it had passed through two more chapters, so it became effective in 1248 (MOPH III p. 41).

79. In Gerald's list we find, following Albert, Laurence de Fougières, Stephen de Venizy, William of Étampes and John Pointlasne. Stephen and John are already Masters in 1248 (*Chart.* I p. 210), so if Gerald's list is chronological and accurate, this must mean that Laurence became a Master in 1245 or 1246, Stephen in 1246 or 1247, and William in 1247 or 1248. If Stephen was, as one manuscript suggests, the author of the propositions condemned in Paris in 1241 (*Chart.* I p. 171), he must have been

at least bachelor of the Sentences by then, but he need not have been a Master, and if he was censured it would have been likely to delay his graduation as a Master.

80. Élie was lector of Montpellier in May 1247 (J. Guiraud, *Cartulaire de Prouille* [Paris, 1907], II p. 240). By 1253 he and Bonhomme were the two Dominican Regent Masters (*Chart.* I p. 280, referring back to document no. 219). In Gerald's list Bonhomme is mentioned before Élie, but this still leaves several possibilities open. Perhaps the succession was William—Bonhomme and Albert—Pointlasne—Élie. Granted the anti-Dominican statute of February 1252 (*Chart.* I pp. 226–7), we should presumably have heard complaints about it if the Dominicans had had a new Master incept between then and 1253, so Élie and Bonhomme were surely both already in possession in the academic year 1251–52. Laurence de Fougières, although probably a member of the Paris province, went from Paris to teach in Toulouse in 1235 (QE I p. 100), so sending him back to Paris to graduate as a Master can also be seen as part of a policy of increasing the supply of Masters to the provinces.

81. Cf. below, p. 211.

82. MOPH III p. 32.

83. MOPH XVIII pp. 79–80; Eubel I p. 77.

84. There has been some confusion about the succession of provincials in Paris. Salagnac and Gui both state that Peter of Rheims was provincial when he was made bishop of Agen in 1245 (MOPH XVIII p. 80, MOPH XXII p. 31), so the common assertion that Humbert was provincial immediately after Hugh cannot be correct. But he must have been provincial in time for the General Chapter of 1246 (MOPH III p. 36:3–5 cannot refer to Peter, who was a bishop by this time).

85. According to a story reported by Gerald de Frachet (MOPH I pp. 274–5), Guerric's death occurred in Paris, while Jean de la Rochelle was still there. Jean died in February 1245 (cf. P. Michaud-Quantin, ed., *Jean de la Rochelle, Tractatus de Divisione Multiplici Potentiarum Animae* [Paris, 1964], p. 8), but he was apparently already in Lyons, in connection with the preparations for the forthcoming council, by Advent 1244, since he is known to have preached there for the curia (Schneyer, *Repertorium* III p. 710, no. 97). So Guerric must have died in about November 1244, or at the very latest before February 1245. Gerald's story implies that Guerric was still Regent Master at the time of his death. Godfrey's presence in Paris is attested up to January 1247, judging from a sermon in MS Arras 759, which appears to be a collection of Parisian sermons (Schneyer, *Repertorium* VI p. 104 no. 168), but he was not necessarily still Regent Master.

86. Kaeppeli, *Scriptores* II p. 16.

87. Albert's presence in Paris is attested in May 1248 (*Chart.* I p. 210);

his presence in Cologne is attested in January 1249 (Scheeben pp. 24–5). That he was Regent Master for three years in Paris is formally stated by Herford p. 201. 1245 as the date of Albert's accession to his chair in Paris and 1248 as the date of his return to Cologne seem secure and are not disputed.

88. P. Simon, Col. XXXVII pp. VI–VIII. Thomas' manuscript of Albert's Dionysian lectures is now Naples, Bibl. Naz. I B 54.

89. Tocco FVST p. 79, Ferrua p. 46.

90. M. Grabmann, *Mittelalterliches Geistesleben* I (Munich, 1926), p. 154; H. C. Scheeben, "De Alberti Magni discipulis," *Alberto Magno, Atti della Settimana Albertina Celebrata in Roma 9–14 Nov. 1931* (Rome), pp. 207–8.

91. M. H. Laurent, ed., *Fontes S. Catharinae Senensis* XX, Florence 1937, pp. 2–3.

92. Loë, p. 282. It appears that it was in fact Albert who arranged the settlement, which Hugh did little more than confirm (Scheeben pp. 33–4).

93. For a convenient summary, see Callaey pp. 486–91.

94. Loë p. 282.

95. Scheeben p. 36. Cf. G. Gieraths, *Die Dominikaner in Worms* (Worms, 1964), pp. 24–6. On vicars of provinces, see G. R. Galbraith, *The Constitution of the Dominican Order* (Manchester, 1925), pp. 149–50. In principle the prior of the house where the provincial chapter was to be held automatically became vicar in the absence of a provincial (*Const.* II 3, AFP 18 [1948] p. 50), but judging from an inchoation made in 1246 this system was not found to be ideal [MOPH III p. 35:12–21]; however the 1247 Chapter did not approve the inchoation, so no change was made in the constitutions.

96. For the priories, see Freed, *The Friars and German Society* pp. 210–15. In the case of the nuns it is often difficult to know exactly what their relationship was to the Dominicans in this period, but in one way or another the German Dominicans probably had responsibility for a great many monasteries; see H. Wilms, *Das älteste Verzeichnis der deutschen Dominikanerinnenklöster*, QF 24 (Leipzig, 1928).

97. *Const.* II 3 (AFP 18 [1948] p. 51).

98. Peter p. 204.

99. MOPH III pp. 37:1–2, 76:12–3.

100. MOPH III pp. 76–7.

101. Peter p. 205.

102. Peter pp. 203–4 (from *Leg. Col.* p. 274).

103. Albert's personal observations are conveniently listed in P. Hossfeld, *Albertus Magnus als Naturphilosoph und Naturwissenschaftler* (Bonn,

1983), pp. 76–93; also "Die eigenen Beobachtungen des Albertus Magnus," AFP 53 (1983) pp. 147–74.

104. Meyer (Scheeben pp. 157–8) gives Regensburg as the place of Albert's second provincial chapter and Erfurt as that of the third, and this corresponds to the sequence in QF 1 p. 31. Rudolph (p. 25) gives Augsburg second place and puts Regensburg in fourth place, but he is probably dependent on Peter (p. 205) and misunderstands the significance of what Peter says (cf. Scheeben, p. 39). The sermons ascribed to Albert at the Regensburg chapter indicate that the chapter coincided with the feast of the Nativity of Our Lady, 8 September (AFP 34 [1964] pp. 73–4).

105. Milan (1255) was a diffinitors' chapter, which would not involve Albert as provincial, but Paris (1256) was a provincials' chapter (Galbraith, p. 255).

106. For the new priories see Freed, *The Friars and German Society* pp. 210, 215. For the Paradisus see QF 24 p. 92.

107. Scheeben pp. 157–61.

108. This is indicated by one of the manuscripts; see Col. VII i p. v.

109. On this controversy see D. L. Douie, *The Conflict between the Seculars and the Mendicants at the University of Paris in the Thirteenth Century* (London, 1954); Weisheipl, *Thomas* pp. 80–92; M. M. Dufeil, *Guillaume de Saint-Amour et la Polémique Universitaire Parisienne 1250–1259* (Paris, 1972) and "Signification historique de la querelle des Mendicants: ils sont le progrès au 13e siècle" and "Gulielmus de Sancto Amore, Opera Omnia (1252–70)" in A. Zimmermann, ed., *Die Auseinandersetzungen an der Pariser Universität im XIII Jahrhundert* (Berlin, 1976), pp. 95–105, 213–19.

110. Cf. vol. V of the Quaracchi ed. of Bonaventure, p. VIIa.

111. Thomas of Cantimpré, *De Apibus* II 10.23; Herford, p. 197.

112. Dufeil pp. 197–282; Dufeil makes it clear that neither Bonaventure nor Thomas was at the papal court at the time of the condemnation of William (p. 261).

113. This is suggested by Dufeil, p. 261.

114. Herford p. 197. Loë p. 284 confidently asserts that Albert arrived in Anagni on 4 October and that the consistory was held on 6 October, but none of the sources he lists actually mentions either date. The Bull condemning William is dated 5 October (Potthast 16565; *Chart.* I pp. 331–33; BOP I pp. 317–18), so if Herford's report is accurate Albert must have arrived on 3 October.

115. Albert recounts the circumstances in *Summa Theol.* II tr. 13 q. 77.3 (B 33 p. 100b).

116. *Chart.* I pp. 277–9.

117. William of Auvergne, *De Universo* Ia IIae ch. 11 (Paris, 1674), I p. 819.

118. *De Unitate Intellectus* Prol. (Col. XVII i p. 1); *Summa Theol.* II tr. 13 q. 77.3 (B 33 p. 75a). Cf. Peter pp. 238–9. Albert adopted the same position later on in *XV Problemata* (Col. XVII i p. 34:53–7). If a philosophical opinion were to be condemned simply on dogmatic grounds, it would appear that the issue was reducible to a contradiction between philosophy and theology, which could lead either to a theory of "two truths" (this is alluded to in the passage referred to from *Summa Theol.*, and it is clearly what Bishop Tempier was afraid of: cf. *Chart.* I p. 543; cf. P. Wilpert, ed., *Beiträge zum Berufsbewusstsein des mittelalterlichen Menschen* [Berlin, 1964], pp. 149–52) or to a general rejection of philosophy by theologians. This is why Albert insists on a philosophical refutation of the Averroists; their tenets must be shown to be bad philosophy, not just dogmatically erroneous.

119. Contrary to what is affirmed by Weisheipl, *Albert* p. 36.

120. Galbraith p. 255; we know it was a diffinitors' chapter, for instance, from the appointment of a diffinitor at the previous Roman provincial chapter (MOPH XX p. 20).

121. AFP 34 (1964) p. 59; RTAM 36 (1969) p. 114. The claim that Albert became Master of the Sacred Palace at this time (*Leg. Col.* p. 275) derives from Thomas of Cantimpré's statement that while Albert was at the papal court he expounded St. John's gospel and epistles at the request of the pope and cardinals (*De Apibus* II 10.24). This part of the *De Apibus* antedates Albert's episcopacy, so there can be no question of any confusion between Albert's earlier visit to the papal court and his later stay there in 1261–63. But Thomas explicitly presents the exposition of St. John as part of the refutation of William of St. Amour, not as a course of lectures in the papal studium (on which see R. Creytens, "Le 'Studium Romanae Curiae' et le Maître du Sacré Palais," AFP 12 [1942] pp. 5–83), so there are no good grounds for inferring that Albert stayed on at Anagni for any length of time after 5 October.

122. MOPH III p. 89:1; Meyer (Scheeben p. 158); Peter p. 205.

123. There was no fixed time for the holding of provincial chapters; each chapter appointed the time and place for the next one, the only proviso being that it had to be later than the General Chapter (*Const.* II 7, AFP 18 [1948] p. 55). Thus provincial chapters could be held any time from June onward (cf. Scheeben, p. 37). But there is something mysterious about German provincials. Albert was absolved in 1257, but his successor was not elected until 1258; his successor was absolved in 1259 (MOPH III p. 101:1), but the next provincial was not elected until 1260. He was absolved in 1263 (MOPH III p. 121:5), but seems to have taken no notice; he was absolved again in 1265 (MOPH III p. 131:1), and this time a successor was elected immediately (QF 1 p. 13; cf. *Archiv der deutschen Dominikaner* 4 [1951] p. 83). There was perhaps an ambiguity about the consequences of

absolution from office; in 1263 the General Chapter directs that when priors are absolved from office a specific time has to be indicated beyond which they are not to go on being prior (MOPH III p. 120:25–27), which implies that an absolved superior could be regarded as remaining in office until his successor took over. In the case of provincials this would mean interpreting *amoto* in *Const.* II 3 (ASOP 3 [1897–88] p. 106) as meaning literally "moved away," not just "removed from office" (as the provincial of England was absolved and assigned to Germany in 1261, MOPH III p. 110:32–5).

124. QF 16 pp. 32–3 (the date must be interpreted as January 1279, the year being regarded as beginning at the Annunciation, not on 1 January).

125. RTAM 36 (1969) pp. 114, 132. Schneyer shows that the only possible dates for these sermons are 1257 and 1263 (AFP 34 [1964] p. 67); since the report refers to *fratri Alberto* it is clear that Albert was not yet a bishop, so 1257 must be the date.

126. Loë pp. 285–6.

127. Loë pp. 285–7.

128. *Chart.* I pp. 385–6; MOPH III pp. 99–100. The General Chapter of 1261, in furtherance of the new policy, called explicitly for the erection of studia for the teaching of logic (MOPH III p. 109:25–9). Cf. L. Robles, 'Les *Artes Liberales* en la primitiva legislación dominicana', in *Arts Libéraux et philosophie au Moyen Age* (Actes du quatrième Congrès International de Philosophie Médiévale), Montreal/Paris 1969, pp. 599–616.

129. Loë pp. 287–8; Potthast 17737–8.

130. Scheeben p. 54.

131. Scheeben pp. 154–6.

132. MOPH XVI pp. 146, 177.

133. Vicaire, *Histoire* I pp. 308–9.

134. Thomas of Celano, *Vita Secunda S. Francisci* II 148 (*Analecta Franciscana* X pp. 215–6). For a brief critique of this story see Simon Tugwell, *Early Dominicans* (New Jersey, 1982), p. 43 note 85.

135. MOPH I pp. 141–2.

136. MOPH III p. 72; *Const.* II 13 (ASOP 3 [1897–8] p. 170).

137. MOPH I pp. 32, 173.

138. MOPH I p. 335.

139. MOPH XXII pp. 37, 118.

140. Loë p. 288.

141. MOPH XXII p. 34.

142. Thomas of Cantimpré, *De Apibus* II 10.21.

143. *Leg. Col.* pp. 275–6; Loë p. 289; Scheeben p. 57.

144. BOP I p. 387; C. Bourel de la Roncière et al., *Les Régistres d'Al-*

exandre IV, Paris 1902–1953, nos. 2327, 2545, 2557, 3012–4, 3058–9 (in 3058 *tulerat* should be corrected to *tulerit*, as in BOP). Cf. A. Hauck, *Kirchengeschichte Deutschlands* V 1 (Berlin/Leipzig, 1953), pp. 20–1.

145. *Const.* II 13 (ASOP 3 [1897–98] p. 170).

146. The sixteenth-century historian, Lorenz Hochwart (†1570), quotes this report from "an ancient codex" in book 3 of his *Catalogus Episcoporum Ratisponensium*, ed. A. F. Oefele, *Rerum Boicarum Scriptores* I (Augsburg, 1763), p. 207.

147. Loë p. 291; Scheeben p. 63; Weisheipl, *Albert* p. 38.

148. *Leg. Col.* pp. 276–7; Peter pp. 263–6; Rudolph pp. 45–8.

149. Tolomeo of Lucca, *Hist. Eccl.* XXII 19, ed. cit. col. 1151; cf. Herford p. 201, Alberto f. 140ʳ.

150. Loë p. 289; Scheeben p. 58.

151. Scheeben p. 59.

152. *Leg. Col.* p. 276.

153. Cf. *Leg. Col.* p. 276; Peter p. 264.

154. Loë pp. 290–1; Scheeben p. 60.

155. Loë p. 290; Scheeben p. 61.

156. This dating is suggested by P. Hossfeld at the conclusion of his article in AFP 52 (1982) pp. 115–33. P.M.J.E. Tummers still proposes the much vaguer dating "between c.1235 and c.1260" in his edition of part of the text, *Albertus (Magnus) Commentaar op Euclides Elementen der Geometrie* (Nijmegen, 1984), I, pp. 72–3.

157. Weisheipl, *Albert* p. 38.

158. *Leg. Col.* p. 276; Peter pp. 264–5; Rudolph pp. 47–8.

159. Cf. B. Schmidt, Col. XXI i pp. XIV–XVI (and see above, note 9).

160. The date is secured by a document dated 1261 indicating that the abbot of Oberaltaich gave Albert a sum of money to take to Alexander IV which he was unable to deliver owing to the pope's death (*Monumenta Boica* XII [Munich, 1775], p. 101). Albert must have set off before Alexander's death was known, and he must have reached Viterbo after 25 May 1261.

161. Loë p. 292.

162. On 25 February 1262 Albert is still referred to as bishop of Regensburg (Loë p. 292). On 11 May Urban IV confirmed the election of Albert's successor (Loë p. 292; Potthast 18309).

163. *De Princ. Motus Proc.* 1.2 (Col. XII p. 48:69–71). For the date see Weisheipl, *Albert* p. 574 (correcting ibid. p. 36); there is no reason to suppose that Albert made any significant detour in 1256.

164. Herford p. 201; Alberto f.140ʳ. This is confirmed by Albert's will (QF 16 p. 32). Gui's statement that Albert immediately "returned to

the Order's poverty" (MOPH XXII p. 34), taken up in the later tradition (Meyer in Scheeben p. 156; *Leg. Col.* p. 277; Peter p. 267; Rudolph p. 50) seems not to be based on any precise knowledge of what happened straight after Albert's resignation.

165. Heinrich of Würzburg ("the Poet"), in his *De statu curiae Romanae* 879–82, refers to an outstanding philosopher at the papal court, probably with reference to these years:

Est illic aliquis qui, si combusta iaceret,
Inventor fieret, philosophia, nove;
Erigeret meliore modo novus editor illam
Vinceret et veteres artis honore viros.

Grabmann suggested that this is an allusion to Albert ("Ist das 'philosophische Universalgenie' bei Mag. Heinrich dem Poeten Thomas von Aquin?" *Historisches Jahrbuch* 38 [1917] pp. 315–20). On Heinrich, see F. J. Worstbrock, *Verfasserlexikon* III (Berlin, 1981), cols. 924–6. Grabmann's identification of Heinrich's philosopher as Albert has been accepted by several scholars: Scheeben p. 70; Weisheipl, *Thomas* p. 148; H. Stehkämper, "Über die geschichtliche Grösse Alberts des Grossen," *Historisches Jahrbuch* 102 (1982), pp. 73–4.

166. See below, pp. 218–19.

167. Cf. AMDU pp. 136–7.

168. Cf. B. Geyer, Col. XII p. XXIV (except that Geyer dates Albert's discovery of the text to 1256, on which see above, note 163).

169. B 23 p. 682; quoted in this connection by Peter, p. 268 and by Scheeben, p. 64.

170. AMDU pp. 134, 136.

171. Loë pp. 293–4.

172. BOP I pp. 421–6.

173. Loë p. 313; Scheeben p. 74.

174. Loë p. 296; Scheeben pp. 72–3.

175. Cf. Scheeben p. 76.

176. Scheeben pp. 72–7.

177. Scheeben p. 78; Weisheipl, *Albert* p. 40.

178. Scheeben p. 142.

179. Freed, AFP 48 (1978) p. 66.

180. Loë pp. 298–9.

181. Scheeben, pp. 142–3.

182. AMDU p. 138.

183. Loë pp. 299–301.

184. Cf. M. Grabmann, *Mittelalterliches Geistesleben* I pp. 159–61. On Ulrich see F. J. Lescoe, *God as First Principle in Ulrich of Strasbourg* (New York, 1979).

185. Tolomeo of Lucca, *Hist. Eccl.* XXII 19; Herford, pp. 201–2; *Leg. Col.* p. 277; Peter pp. 270–1; Alberto f. 140ʳ.

186. H. Finke, *Ungedruckte Dominikanerbriefe des 13 Jahrhunderts* (Paderborn, 1891), pp. 51–2.

187. See below, p. 225.

188. Loë, p. 315; Scheeben, pp. 149, 153. He is also referred to as "OP" by others: Scheeben pp. 152–3. It may be significant that all these documents date from after Albert's return to Cologne.

189. QF 16 pp. 32–3.

190. Loë pp. 302–9.

191. QF 1 p. 13.

192. Finke pp. 80, 82, 84–5.

193. Weisheipl, *Albert* p. 42, claims that "there is no evidence whatsoever" that Albert was at the council. It is true that Albert's name is not found among the bishops who signed some of the conciliar documents (cf. P. Frowein, "Der Episkopat auf dem 2 Konzil von Lyon (1274)," *Annuarium Historiae Conciliorum* 6 [1974] pp. 307–31), but as a retired bishop Albert would not have been at the council in a diocesan capacity, so this is not surprising. But we do possess a letter of his written in Lyons on 12 May 1274 (Scheeben pp. 151–2), and if he was in Lyons at this time it was surely in order to assist at the council, as Peter claims he did (pp. 279–80). Also in *Summa Theol.* II tr. 18 q. 122 a. 2 (B 33 p. 396) Albert claims that the council obliged the Greeks to recognize simple fornication as a mortal sin; there is nothing in the conciliar decrees to justify this remark, but the letter of Girolamo d'Ascoli to the pope in preparation for the council contains the comment that the Greeks "do not believe simple fornication to be a mortal sin" (B. Roberg, *Die Union zwischen der griechischen und der lateinischen Kirche auf dem II Konzil von Lyon* [Bonn, 1964], p. 230; cf. A. Franchi, *Il Concilio II di Lione* [Rome, 1965], pp. 171–2). It looks as if Albert had inside information about the council, and this reinforces the likelihood that he was there himself.

194. Peter p. 280.

195. Finke pp. 120–1.

196. Finke pp. 87–8, plausibly identified by Finke as belonging to this period.

197. QF 16 p. 32.

198. Loë p. 308.

199. Cf. FVST p. 382, Ferrua p. 324.

200. FVST p. 358, Ferrua p. 299. This was adopted into Gui's legenda (FVST p. 208, Ferrua p. 179), from where it passed to Luis (p. 754) and Peter (pp. 277–78).

201. FVST p. 382, Ferrua p. 324.

202. AFP 4 (1934) p. 137.

203. FVST p. 370, Ferrua p. 313.

204. FVST pp. 382–3, Ferrua pp. 324–5; the story of Albert's intervention in Paris is also mentioned by Galvano, AFP 10 (1940) p. 359.

205. Scheeben, "De Alberti Magni discipulis," pp. 201–7; Weisheipl, *Albert* pp. 43–5; Eckert p. XXVII.

206. On this episode, see below pp. 236–38.

207. In fact Albert appears to be challenging Thomas in *Summa Theol.* I tr.1 q.3.2 (Col. XXXIV i p. 12:35–8; cf. ibid. p. XVII).

208. Tolomeo of Lucca, *Hist. Eccl.* XXII 19.

209. Herford p. 202.

210. Luis p. 754.

211. Luis pp. 754–5; Peter pp. 300–2; Rudolph pp. 68–9; Alberto ff. 139, 141^r. They all connect Albert's sudden loss of memory with a promise alleged to have been made to him by our Lady at the beginning of his Dominican life, but the details are different in each source. According to Luis and Rudolph, Albert was afraid that his faith would be corrupted by philosophy and our Lady promised that before he died all philosophical "cunning" would be taken from him and he would end his days in "childlike innocence"; according to Peter and Alberto, he was not very bright as a student and asked our Lady for a gift of understanding of philosophy, which she gave him, but with the warning that it would be taken away before he died. Alberto adds that this was to be a punishment for choosing philosophy instead of theology. There is absolutely no reason to believe that Albert was lacking in intellectual ability as a young man; his alleged fear that he would be unable to stay in the Order because of his intellectual incompetence is no more than a distorted version of the dream reported in MOPH I p. 188 (which does not mention any intellectual inadequacy). The anxiety that philosophy might corrupt faith does not square with anything we know about Albert. And all these stories seem to rest on the assumption that Albert spent his life teaching philosophy, which is untrue. The divergences between the different accounts make it clear that this is legendary and apologetic material being developed according to the whim of each writer. The whole lot of it can safely be disregarded.

212. RTAM 36 (1969) p. 118.

213. From one of Albert's sermons, AFP 34 (1964) p. 56.

214. *Anim.* 5.1.2.18.

215. *Anim.* 5.2.2.65; 23.1.9.

216. *Mineralia* II 2.11 (B 5 p. 40b).

217. *Mineralia* II 3.1 (B 5 p. 49; AT 83).

218. *Quaest. de Anim.* I 29–31, VII 17–19 (Col. XII pp. 99:47–8, 178:33–6, 99:52–4).

219. *Anim.* 5.1.4.31.

220. *Anim.* 8.2.4.69.

221. *Quaest. de Anim.* VII 17–19 (Col. XII p. 178:12–16).

222. *Anim.* 23.24.139.

223. Aristotle, *Part. Anim.* 1.5 (645a16–17); Albert, *Anim.* 11.2.3.86.

224. *Comm. Matt.* 13.35 (Col. XXI i p. 412:35–37).

225. *Politica* Epil. (B 8 p. 804, AT 8). Cf. Y. Congar, "*In Dulcedine Societatis Quaerere Veritatem,*" AMDU pp. 47–57.

226. *Const.* II 14 (AFP 18 [1948] pp. 65–6). This was insisted on at the General Chapter of 1249 (MOPH III p. 47:22–4) and reaffirmed in 1277 (MOPH III p. 190:32–4) in terms suggesting that some lectors were not giving as much time to lecturing on the bible as they were expected to.

227. Col. XIV i pp. V–VI.

228. Col. XII p. XLV.

229. Cf. Weisheipl, *Albert* p. 40.

230. From one of Albert's sermons, RTAM 36 (1969) p. 109.

231. The Job commentary is dated to 1272 or 1274 in the manuscripts (cf. AMDU p. 139). The *Summa Theol.* refers to the Council of Lyons in 1274 (cf. above, note 193); the authenticity of the work, which had been called into question (cf. Col. XXXIV i pp. V–XVI for a discussion of this), seems to be placed more or less beyond doubt by the fact that Godfrey of Fontaines was already citing it as Albert's as early as 1277 (R. Wielockx, ed., *Aegidii Romani . . . Apologia* [Florence, 1985], pp. 40–1).

232. Weisheipl, *Albert* p. 40.

233. Cf. Herford pp. 195–6.

234. *Physica* I 1.1 (Col. IV i p. 1).

235. *Politica* Epil. (B 8 p. 803).

236. A. G. Judy, ed., *Robert Kilwardby OP, De Ortu Scientiarum* (London, 1976), pp. xiv–xvii.

237. *Physica* VIII 1.14 (B 3 p. 553b; AT 33b).

238. *Metaphysica* I 5.15 (Col. XVI i p. 89:85–7).

239. *Politica* Epil. (B 8 pp. 803–4); *Metaphysica* XI 2.1, XIII 2.4 (Col. XVI pp. 482:23–9, 599:61–6); *De Causis* II 5.24 (B 10 p. 619; AT 5).

240. Albert's reply is in Col. XVII i pp. 31–44. For the date and circumstances, see below, pp. 237 with note 359.

241. *Summa Theol.* I 1 Prol (Col. XXXIV i p. 5).

242. *Summa Theol.* II tr.18 q.122.4.2 (B 33 p. 402b).

243. For a fascinating glimpse of how such lectors worked, see L. E. Boyle, "Notes on the education of the *fratres communes* in the Dominican Order in the 13th century," in R. Creytens and P. Künzle, eds., *Xenia Medii Aevi* (Rome, 1978), I, pp. 249–67.

244. For the dating of the *Summa de Creaturis* see R.A. Gauthier in

Leonine XLVI i pp. 256*–57*; for the Sentences commentary and the Dionysian works, see P. Simon, Col. XXXVII pp. VI–VII, XXV. For the Aristotelian works, see Weisheipl, *Albert* pp. 565–77. For the scriptural commentaries, see A. Fries, "Zur Entstehungszeit der Bibelkommentare Alberts der Grossen," AMDU pp. 119–39.

245. See A. Fries, *Die Gedanken des hl. Albertus Magnus über die Gottesmutter* (Fribourg, 1958), pp. 342–4; Fries, "Albertus Magnus prosator," AMDU pp. 141–65.

246. Cf. M. Grabmann, *Mittelalterliches Geistesleben* I pp. 489–524; C. Stroick, *Unpublished Theological Writings of Johannes Castellensis* (Ottawa, 1964), pp. 3–4.

247. A. Fries, *Der Doppeltraktat über die Eucharistie unter dem Namen des Albertus Magnus*, Beiträge NF 25 (Münster, 1984).

248. A. Wimmer, ed., *De Forma Orandi* (Regensburg, 1902). Wimmer edited the work from a manuscript without any ascription and argued for Albert's authorship, but the work is elsewhere attributed to Vincent of Beauvais (QE I p. 238b). The fact that it follows the writings of Peraldus very closely makes me wonder whether it should not be ascribed to him. In any case, there is absolutely no warrant for the ascription to Albert.

249. D. Callus, "Une oeuvre récemment découverte de S. Albert le Grand," RSPT 44 (1960) pp. 243–61. The work is edited in Col. XVII i pp. 45–64.

250. On this episode, see J. Destrez, "La lettre de St Thomas d'A-quin dite lettre au lecteur de Venise," *Mélanges Mandonnet* I (Paris, 1930), pp. 103–89; H. F. Dondaine, Leonine XLII pp. 299–301.

251. Leonine XLII pp. 327, 335:614–9.

252. On Kilwardby's response, see M. D. Chenu, "Les réponses de St Thomas et de Kilwardby à la consultation de Jean de Verceil (1271)," *Mélanges Mandonnet* I pp. 191–222. The full text is edited by H. F. Dondaine in AFP 47 (1977) pp. 5–50. For the mathematical question see ibid. pp. 45–50.

253. Col. XVII i p. 64:42–49.

254. Leonine XLII p. 332:429–30; AFP 47 (1977) pp. 34–5.

255. Col. XVII i p. 59:9.

256. Leonine XLII p. 333:447–66; Col. XVII i p. 60:9.

257. *Politica* Epil. (B 8 pp. 803–4); *Comm. Dion. Ep.* 7 (Col. XXXVII p. 504:27–32).

258. Ed. Berthier I p. 172; cf. MOPH I p. 148.

259. MOPH I p. 112.

260. Jordan's encyclical of 1233 (Tugwell, *Early Dominicans* p. 123).

261. M. M. Davy, *Les Sermons Universitaires Parisiens de 1230–1231* (Paris, 1931), pp. 340–41. "Points and lines" were much used in discussions

of how we know God and of the relationship between God and creatures (e.g., Albert, *DN* 1.21, 2.48, Col. XXXVII p. 11:41–59, pp. 75–6).

262. Davy p. 84.

263. Davy p. 279.

264. *Const.* II 14 (ASOP 3 [1897–88] pp. 172–3); Galbraith p. 250.

265. General Chapters often give the impression of a fear that philosophy is liable to oust theology: e.g., MOPH III pp. 159:33–4, 174:23–4, 197:3–4, 209:3–5. In 1278 the Roman provincial chapter decreed that outsiders were not to be admitted to philosophy lectures (MOPH XX p. 49).

266. Ed. Berthier I pp. 435–9, II pp. 42–4. The suggestion made by Stehkämper, p. 89, that Humbert was attacking Albert in his commentary on the Rule, ed. cit. I p. 465, is absurd; Humbert is ridiculing people who drop names just to show off. It is clear that Humbert held Albert in high esteem. It may well be Albert who is the 'quidam philosophus' referred to in his sermon material II 70 (*Humberti quinti generalis sacrosancti Ordinis Predicatorum magistri sermones ad diuersos status*, Hagenau 1508, f. K 1ʳ) for a saying about magistrates being worse thieves than the crooks they sentence (cf. above, p. 28).

267. Cf. above, note 211.

268. Cf. Aristotle, *Part. Anim.* 1.5.

269. Cf. J. B. Schneyer, "Predigten Alberts des Grossen in der Hs. Leipzig Univ. Bibl. 683," AFP 34 (1964) pp. 45–106; Schneyer, "Alberts des Grossen Augsburger Predigtzyklus über den hl. Augustinus," RTAM 36 (1969) pp. 100–147. B. Geyer, *Die Universitätspredigten des Albertus Magnus* (Munich, 1966). P. Hossfeld and E. Nellessen, *Die Predigt des hl. Albertus Magnus zu Honnef* (Bad Honnef, 1980) (I have not seen this last work). Cf. W. Fauser, *Die Werke des Albertus Magnus in ihrer handschriftlichen Überlieferung* I, *Die echten Werke* (Münster, 1982), pp. 337–8.

270. *Comm. Io.* 10.1 (B 24 pp. 396–7), cited to illustrate Albert's own practice in Peter pp. 208–9.

271. RTAM 36 (1969) p. 121.

272. From one of Albert's sermons, AFP 34 (1964) p. 57.

273. Cf. Albert's sermon in RTAM 36 (1969) pp. 126–30.

274. From one of his sermons, AFP 34 (1964) pp. 55–6.

275. Ibid. p. 55.

276. Cf. A. Fries, *Die Gedanken des hl. Albertus Magnus über die Gottesmutter*. Fries notes that Albert is one of the medieval theologians who wrote most copiously about our Lady: *Die unter dem Namen des Albertus Magnus überlieferten Mariologischen Schriften*, Beiträge XXXVII/4 (Münster, 1954), p. 138.

277. *De Apibus* II 57.50.

278. Suggested by Scheeben, p. 29.

279. Peter, p. 86.

280. Herford, p. 202.

281. Cf. M. Grabmann, *Mittelalterliches Geistesleben* II (Munich, 1936), pp. 324–412; A. de Libera, *Introduction à la Mystique Rhénane* (Paris, 1984). A series of texts and studies is being published in the *Corpus Philosophorum Teutonicorum Medii Aevi* (Hamburg). Cf. also AMDU pp. 89–110.

282. Cf. Kaeppeli, *Scriptores* II pp. 260–9.

283. Cf. Kaeppeli, pp. 122–9. For the Neoplatonist character of Albert's Peripateticism, cf. Lescoe p. 91.

284. Cf. R. Imbach, "Le (néo-)Platonisme médiéval, Proclus latin, et l'école dominicaine allemande," *Revue de Théologie et Philosophie* 110 (1978) pp. 427–48.

285. Part of the text is published in L. Sturlese, ed., *Bertoldo di Mossburg, Expositio super Elementationem Theologicam Procli* (Rome, 1974). A complete edition is promised in the *Corpus Philosophorum Teutonicorum;* so far two volumes have been published (1984, 1986).

286. Cf. W. A. Wallace, *The Scientific Methodology of Theodoric of Freiberg* (Fribourg, 1959).

287. On Albertism, see G. G. Meersseman, *Geschichte des Albertismus,* 2 vols. (Paris, 1933; Rome, 1935); Z. Kuksewicz, "Le prolongement des polémiques entre les Albertistes et les Thomistes vu à travers le *Commentaire* du *De Anima* de Jean de Glasgow," *Archiv für Geschichte des Philosophie* 44 (1962) pp. 151–71; I. Craemer-Ruegenberg, *Albertus Magnus* (Munich, 1980), pp. 147–54; AMDU pp. 7–46.

288. See Weisheipl, *Albert,* pp. 537–63.

289. E.g., MOPH XVIII pp. 2–3, 57–8, 70; P. Auer, *Ein neuaufgefundener Katalog der dominikaner Schriftsteller* (Paris, 1933), pp. 88–9.

290. On the biographical tradition, see Scheeben pp. 1–3.

291. Alberto f. 140^v (cf. AFP 30 [1960] p. 263).

Part II

1. On the form in which the Dionysian corpus was available to Albert, see H. F. Dondaine, *Le Corpus Dionysien de l'Université de Paris au XIIIe siècle* (Rome, 1953).

2. H. Urs von Balthasar, *Herrlichkeit* II (Einsiedeln, 1962), p. 154, suggests that St. Thomas realized that Dionysius was later than Proclus, since in *Super Lib. de Causis Expos.* 3, ed. H. D. Saffrey (Fribourg/Louvain, 1954), p. 20 he says that Dionysius corrects Proclus; but in fact Thomas only claims that Dionysius corrects a Platonist doctrine illustrated by Pro-

clus, and there is no clear evidence that he ever called into question the traditional ascription of the Dionysian writings to the apostolic period.

3. G. Théry, *Études Dionysiennes* I (Paris, 1932), pp. 1–9. The manuscript presented to Louis is now Paris, Bibl. Nat. gr. 437.

4. On Hilduin see Théry; volume II (Paris, 1937) contains an edition of his text.

5. Eriugena's translation, together with the Greek text and all the other Latin versions, is found in P. Chevallier, *Dionysiaca* (Bruges, 1937). His commentary on the *Celestial Hierarchy* is edited by J. Barbet in CC Cont. Med. XXXI (Turnhout, 1975). The first three books of the *Periphyseon* have been edited by I. P. Sheldon-Williams (Dublin, 1968, 1972, 1981); otherwise we are still dependent on the unsatisfactory edition in PL 122. On Eriugena, see R. Roques, ed., *Jean Scot Érigène et l'histoire de la philosophie* (Paris, 1977); G. Schrimpf, *Das Werk des Johannes Scottus Eriugena*, Beiträge NF 23 (Münster, 1982); J.J. O'Meara, *Eriugena* (Oxford, 1988).

6. Cf. Dondaine, *Le Corpus Dionysien*, p. 35.

7. The most significant part of the text is edited by P. Lucentini, *Honorius Augustodunensis: Clavis Physicae* (Rome, 1974).

8. Dondaine *Le Corpus Dionysien*, pp. 84–88, 137–8.

9. The text can be found in PL 175:923–1154. On the large number of surviving manuscripts see R. Goy, *Die Überlieferung der Werke Hugos von St. Viktor* (Stuttgart, 1976), pp. 181–96.

10. On Sarracenus see G. Théry, "Jean Sarrazin, 'traducteur' de Scot Érigène," *Studia Mediaevalia in hon. A.R.P. R. J. Martin* (Bruges, 1948), pp. 359–81; Théry, "Documents concernant Jean Sarrazin," *Archives d'Histoire Doctrinale et Littéraire* 18 (1951) pp. 45–87.

11. John of Salisbury, *Metalogicon* 4.40. See E. Jeauneau, "Jean de Salisbury et la lecture des philosophes," in M. Wilks, ed., *The World of John of Salisbury* (Oxford, 1984), pp. 99–100.

12. The first text is Augustine, *De Ordine* 2.16.44. For the second, cf. Dionysius, *Ep.* 1 (PG 3:1065A), but none of the translations has "wisdom" (*sapientia*) here; the Dionysian text (with "wisdom") together with the text from Augustine occurs in Eriugena, *Periphyseon*, ed. Sheldon-Williams, I p. 190:32–3, II p. 162:26–8.

13. *Ad Candidum* 13–4 (ed. P. Henry and P. Hadot, SC 68 [Paris, 1960], p. 148).

14. A. H. Armstrong, ed., *The Cambridge History of Later Greek and Early Medieval Philosophy* (Cambridge, 1970), pp. 334–5.

15. Cf. *Dieu et l'Être*, Études Augustiniennes (Paris, 1978), pp. 87–164. For a pagan identification of the One and Being and its philosophical background see ibid. pp. 57–63.

16. Cf. C. G. Steel, *The Changing Self, A Study of the Soul in Later Neoplatonism* (Brussels, 1978).

17. On which see J. Patout Burns, *The Development of Augustine's Doctrine of Operative Grace* (Paris, 1980).

18. *Conf.* VII 9.13–10.16, 18.24–20.26. On Augustine's "toning down" of negative theology, cf. R. Mortley, *From Word to Silence* (Bonn, 1986), II pp. 218, 220.

19. Cf. Simon Tugwell, "The Incomprehensibility of God," *New Blackfriars* 60 (1979) pp. 479–91.

20. Gregory of Nyssa, especially his *Life of Moses;* Evagrius Ponticus, especially his *De Oratione*, of which a translation by Simon Tugwell is available from the Faculty of Theology, Oxford University (published in 1987).

21. Cf. Augustine, *Ep.* 147, especially 8.20. See H. F. Dondaine, "L'objet et le 'medium' de la vision béatifique chez les théologiens du XIII siècle," RTAM 19 (1952) pp. 62–3; Mortley pp. 211–4.

22. Cf. R. T. Wallis, *Neoplatonism* (London, 1972), pp. 147–53.

23. Proclus, *Commentarium in Parmenidem* VII, ed. C. Steel, II (Louvain, 1985), p. 498:1–2.

24. Cf. Armstrong, pp. 261–3.

25. Proclus, *Platonist Theology*, ed. H. D. Saffrey and L. G. Westerinck (Paris, 1968ff.), I 25 and IV 9. In the later Platonists, it should be emphasized, "theurgy" does not mean a magical acting *on* God, but an acting *of* God on us: cf. Iamblichus, *De Mysteriis* II 11, ed. E. des Places (Paris, 1966) pp. 95–96; cf. E. des Places in *De Jamblique à Proclus*, Entretiens Hardt XXI (Geneva, 1975), pp. 82–3.

26. Especially in the *Commentary on the First Alcibiades of Plato*, ed. A. P. Segonds (Paris, 1985, 1986); there is an English translation and commentary by W. O'Neill (The Hague, 1965). Cf. J. M. Rist, *Eros and Psyche* (Toronto, 1964); G. Quispel, "God Is Eros," in W. R. Schroedel and R. L. Wilken, eds., *Early Christian Literature and the Classical Intellectual Tradition* (Paris, 1979), pp. 189–205.

27. On Dionysius, see: H. Urs von Balthasar, *The Glory of the Lord* II (Edinburgh, 1984), pp. 144–210; I. P. Sheldon-Williams, "The Pseudo-Dionysius," in Armstrong, pp. 457–72; A. Louth, *The Origins of the Christian Mystical Tradition* (Oxford, 1981), pp. 159–78; P. Rorem, *Biblical and Liturgical Symbols within the Pseudo-Dionysian Synthesis* (Toronto, 1984).

28. *DN* 1.6 (PG 3:596A).

29. *DN* 9.7 (PG 3:916A).

30. On the need to practice affirmative and negative theology simultaneously, see the perceptive comments of Rorem, pp. 88–90.

31. *CH* 2.3, ed. R. Roques, G. Heil and M. de Gandillac, SC 58bis (Paris, 1970), p. 79.

32. *MT* 1.2 (PG 3:1000B), *Ep.* 1 (PG 3:1065A); cf. *CH* 2.4 (p. 82), *DN* 8.6 (PG 3:893C).

33. Cf. Rorem, p. 90; Eriugena makes an excellent comment on this in *Periphyseon* I, ed. cit., pp. 76–78.

34. *DN* 1.2 (PG 3:588C).

35. *CH* 2.5 (p. 86).

36. Rorem remarks quite correctly that Dionysius' whole theological method is essentially a technique of exegesis (pp. 88–9).

37. *MT* 1.2 (PG 3:1000B).

38. *MT* 1.3 (PG 3:1001A).

39. *EH* 1.1 (PG 3:372A).

40. Cf. Rorem, pp. 104–5.

41. Rorem pp. 126–31; Rorem, "The Place of *The Mystical Theology* in the Pseudo-Dionysian Corpus," *Dionysius* 4 (1980) pp. 87–97.

42. *EH* 3.5 (PG 3:432B).

43. The glosses were edited by E. K. Rand in *Johannes Scottus* (Munich, 1906); Eriugena's influence is visible, for instance, at pp. 40–1 and 59. On their provenance, see D. M. Cappuyns, "Le plus ancien commentaire des 'Opuscula Sacra' et son origine," RTAM 3 (1931) pp. 237–72. On the Eriugenism of the school of Auxerre see ibid. pp. 263–4. Cf. also J. Marenbon, *Early Medieval Philosophy* (London, 1983), pp. 73–7.

44. E.g. *Periphyseon* I, ed. cit. pp. 76, 86, 220.

45. Cf. G. R. Evans, *Old Arts and New Theology* (Oxford, 1980).

46. *Theologia Christiana*, ed. E. M. Buytaert, CC Cont. Med. XII (Turnhout, 1969), III 116. Cf. Macrobius, *Comm. in Somnum Scipionis* 1.2.15.

47. Ibid. I 7.

48. Ibid. III 116.

49. A. Landgraf, *Écrits théologiques de l'école d'Abélard* (Louvain, 1934), pp. 5–7.

50. N. M. Häring, ed., *The Commentaries on Boethius by Gilbert of Poitiers* (Toronto, 1966), p. 193. The importance of this principle in Gilbert's teaching is highlighted by John of Salisbury, *Historia Pontificalis* 12–13, ed. M. Chibnall (Oxford 1986), pp. 27, 38.

51. Gilbert, ed. cit. pp. 247, 249.

52. William's letter to Bernard is edited by J. Leclercq in *Revue Bénédictine* 79 (1969) pp. 376–8; for his fuller treatment see PL 180:253–4.

53. Cf. M. L. Colker, "The trial of Gilbert of Poitiers, 1148: a previously unknown record," *Mediaeval Studies* 27 (1965) pp. 152–83.

54. N. M. Häring, ed., *Commentaries on Boethius by Thierry of Chartres and His School* (Toronto, 1971), p. 170.

55. Ibid., pp. 99, 190–1.

56. Ibid., p. 191.

57. Ibid., p. 195.

58. Cf. Dionysius, *CH* 2.3 (p. 78); Eriugena, *Periphyseon* I p. 84.

59. Albert, *Dion. MT* 1 (Col. XXXVII p. 455:58–61). The claim that is sometimes made that "metaphor is primary" (e.g., J. Coulson, *Religion and Imagination* [Oxford, 1981], p. 11, interpreting Coleridge) may well be true, in the sense that often we use metaphorical language first, and only by a process of subsequent reflection move on to less metaphorical language, and in the sense that the less metaphorical language may often do less justice to what we want to say; but non-metaphorical language still presupposes the possibility of saying *something* that is not metaphorical. It may be very right and proper for Romeo to say,

> But, soft! what light through yonder window breaks?
> It is the east, and Juliet is the sun.
> Arise, fair sun, and kill the envious moon,
> Who is already sick and pale with grief
> (*Romeo and Juliet*, Act 2 Scene 2).

It would be much less right and proper for him simply to recite the stage direction, "Juliet appears above at a window." Nevertheless it would not be right for Romeo to talk like this were it not for the truth of the literal statement contained in the stage direction.

60. PL 192:1252AB.

61. G. R. Evans, p. 118.

62. *Fons Vitae* I 4–5, ed. C. Baeumker, Beiträge I/2-4 (Münster, 1895), p. 6.

63. Ibid. V 24, p. 301.

64. Burgundio's Latin version of John Damascene, *De Fide Orthodoxa*, ed. E. M. Buytaert (New York, 1955), chap. 1, especially pp. 11–12. This translation was probably made c.1153–4; cf. ed. cit. p. XIV.

65. Translated by Burgundio in 1171–3. Text in RTAM 19 (1952) pp. 100–2.

66. R. de Vaux, *Notes et Textes sur l'Avicennisme latin* (Paris, 1934), pp. 83–140.

67. Ibid. pp. 139–40.

68. Alan of Lille, *Summa "Quoniam Homines"* (hereafter *SQH*), ed. P. Glorieux, *Archives d'Histoire Doctrinale et Littéraire* 20 (1954) pp. 113–364; the reference here is to *SQH* 1, p. 119. Alan also insists on the special nature of theological language in his *Expositio super Orationem Dominicam* 4, ed. N. M. Häring, *Analecta Cisterciensia* 31 (1975) p. 159.

69. Dionysius, *CH* 2.3 p. 79.

70. This principle is all-pervasive, but cf. Boethius, *De Trinitate* 2–3; Lombard, I *Sent.* d.8 8.1; William of Auxerre, *Summa Aurea* I 2.1.3, ed. J. Ribaillier (Grottaferrata, 1980), p. 25. For a modern interpretation of this doctrine, see B. Davies, "Classical theism and the doctrine of divine simplicity" in B. Davies, ed., *Language, Meaning and God* (London, 1987), pp. 51–74. Cf. also D. B. Burrell, "Distinguishing God from the world," in Davies pp. 75–91.

71. Alan of Lille, *Regulae Theologicae* XVIII; this work is edited by N. M. Häring, "Magister Alanus de Insulis, Regulae Caelestis Iuris," *Archives d'Histoire Doctrinale et Littéraire* 48 (1982) pp. 97–226.

72. Ibid. XX–XXI, XXXIX; cf. *SQH* 9b, p. 143.

73. *Regulae* XX.

74. Ibid. XXVI.

75. Ibid. XXI.

76. Ibid. XXI 4.

77. *SQH* 8, pp. 134–5.

78. Ibid. 10, p. 145.

79. Ibid. 8b, p. 137.

80. Ibid. 8e, pp. 138–9.

81. *Regulae* Prol., pp. 121–3.

82. Cf. Colker p. 154 note 15.

83. Cf. Alan of Lille, *SQH* 8d, p. 138.

84. On Gilbert and the Greek fathers, see N. M. Häring, "The Porretans and the Greek fathers," *Mediaeval Studies* 24 (1962) pp. 181–209.

85. PL 175:955A.

86. Edited by the fathers of the Collegio S. Bonaventura (Grottaferrata, 1971, 1981).

87. P. M. de Contenson, "Avicennisme latin et vision de Dieu au début du XIIIᵉ siècle," *Archives d'Histoire Doc. et Litt.* 26 (1960) pp. 29–97.

88. *Chart.* I pp. 70–1; *New Catholic Encyclopaedia*, "David of Dinant," vol. 4 (1967), p. 659.

89. P. M. de Contenson, "La théologie de la vision de Dieu au début du XIIIᵉ siècle," RSPT 46 (1962) pp. 410–20.

90. Alexander of Hales, II *Sent.* d.8, Quaracchi (1952), pp. 79–80; cf. Eriugena, *Periphyseon* I, ed. cit. pp. 54–6.

91. RSPT 44 (1960) pp. 230–33.

92. Text in RTAM 19 (1952) pp. 119–20.

93. I *Sent.* d.1 ch. 3.2 (ed. cit. I p. 57).

94. William of Auvergne, *De Universo* II.II ch.92, ed. cit. I p. 946bG.

95. William of Auxerre, *Summa Aurea* III 37.3, ed. Ribaillier (Grottaferrata, 1986), pp. 704–8.

96. There has been some controversy over the date of the condem-

nation; it now seems reasonably certain that it occurred in 1241 and was repeated in 1244. See J.G. Bougerol, AFH 80 (1987) pp. 462–66.

97. Cf. H. F. Dondaine, "L'objet et le 'medium' de la vision béatifique chez les théologiens du XIIIe siècle," RTAM 19 (1952) pp. 60–130; W. J. Hoye, "Gotteserkenntnis per essentiam im 13 Jahrhundert," in A. Zimmermann, ed., *Die Auseinandersetzungen an der Pariser Universität im XIII Jahrhundert* (Berlin, 1976), pp. 269–84.

98. For the full text see *Chart.* I pp. 170–2.

99. Cf. Albert, *CH* 3.3 (B vol. 14 p. 88); Guerric of St. Quentin, RSPT 44 (1960) p. 239 lines 28–37.

100. M. D. Chenu, "Le dernier avatar de la théologie orientale en Occident au XIIIe siècle," *Mélanges Auguste Pelzer*, (Louvain, 1947) pp. 159–81.

101. MOPH III p. 27:10–1, p. 80:32–81:2; C. Douais, *Acta Capitulorum Provincialium* (Toulouse, 1894), pp. 66–8.

102. H. F. Dondaine, "Hugues de St Cher et la condamnation de 1241," RSPT 33 (1949) pp. 170–4.

103. B. G. Guyot and H. F. Dondaine, "Guerric de Saint-Quentin et la condamnation de 1241," RSPT 44 (1960) pp. 225–42.

104. William of Auvergne, *De Universo* II.II ch.92, loc. cit.

105. Bonaventure, *Quaestio Disputata de Trinitate* 1 a.1 n.10, Quaracchi vol. V (1891), p. 46.

106. Cf. S. Tugwell, *Ways of Imperfection* (London, 1984), p. 98; Eriugena, *Periphyseon* I, ed. cit. p. 52.

107. *Speculum Fidei* 97 (SC 301 [Paris, 1982], pp. 166–9).

108. *De Natura et Dignitate Amoris* 8 (PL 184:393).

109. E.g., *Golden Epistle* 173 (SC 223 [Paris, 1975], p. 282).

110. J. M. Déchanet, "Amor Ipse Intellectus Est," *Revue du Moyen Age Latin* 1 (1945) pp. 349–74.

111. On Gallus see G. Théry, "Thomas Gallus: aperçu biographique," *Archives d'Hist. Doct. et Litt.* 12 (1939) pp. 141–208; Théry, "Chronologie des oeuvres de Thomas Gallus, abbé de Verceil," *Divus Thomas* (Piacenza) 37 (1934) pp. 265–77, 365–85, 469–96. Alexander of Hales also states that in heaven we shall see God "by love alone," I *Sent.* d.3.12 II, Quaracchi, 1951, p. 43.

112. Paraphrase of *DN* 7; text in *Dionysiaca* p. 696.

113. Théry, *Divus Thomas* 11 (1934) pp. 371–72.

114. Ed. Manuel Alonso, *Exposição sobre os livros do beato Dionisio Areopagita*, (Lisbon, 1957), pp. 497–8.

115. Ibid. p. 267.

116. Until the long-awaited SC edition of Balma is published, the

most convenient text is in A. C. Peltier, ed., *Omnia Opera S. Bonaventurae* VIII (Paris, 1866), pp. 2–53.

117. On Gallus and Balma as sources for the *Cloud*, cf. James Walsh's introduction to his translation of *The Cloud of Unknowing*, Classics of Western Spirituality (New York, 1981); Balma's influence has been disputed by A. Minnis, "The Sources of *The Cloud of Unknowing:* a Reconsideration," in M. Glasscoe, ed., *The Medieval Mystical Tradition in England* (Dartington, 1982), pp. 63–75; Minnis, "Affection and Imagination in 'The Cloud of Unknowing' and Hilton's 'Scale of Perfection,'" *Traditio* 39 (1983) pp. 325–50.

118. Albert, *De Anima* III 2.1 (Col. VII i p. 177:58–63).

119. Cf. I *Sent.* d.1 a.15 (B 25 p. 37).

120. *De Anima* III 2.1, 2.11 (Col. VII i p. 177:59–60, pp. 191–2). For a popular statement of the "Latin" view, cf. Ps.Augustine, *De Spiritu et Anima* 2 (PL 40:781), 32 (PL 40:801–2).

121. *MT* 2 (Col. XXXVII pp. 466–7). On Augustine's theory of self-knowledge cf. J. Geyser, "Die Theorie Augustins von der Selbsterkenntnis der menschlichen Seele," in A. Lang, J. Lechner and M. Schmaus, *Aus der Geisteswelt des Mittelalters*, Beiträge Suppl. III (Münster, 1935), pp. 169–87.

122. *MT* 2 (Col. XXXVII p. 467:10–1).

123. I *Sent.* d.2 a.5 (B 25 pp. 59–60).

124. Albert's intention was to expound Peripatetic doctrine, including only such Platonism as was compatible with it (*De Intellectu et Intelligibili* 1.1, B 9 p. 478a). But then Albert took the thoroughly Neoplatonist *Liber de Causis* to be the crown of Peripatetic philosophy (*De Causis* 2.1.1, 2.5.24, B 10 p. 434a, 619a), though he was aware that it was not a genuine work of Aristotle's (B 10 pp. 433–35). Thanks to William of Moerbeke's translation of Proclus' *Elements of Theology* St. Thomas was able to identify the *Liber de Causis* for what it was (*Super Lib. de Causis*, Proemium, ed. cit. p. 3).

125. Cf. A. Schneider, *Die Psychologie Alberts des Grossen*, Beiträge IV/5–6 (Münster, 1903–6), pp. 347–8.

126. Cf. Schneider's caution, pp. 302–8; on Albert's real commitment to the philosophy of the commentaries cf. Craemer-Ruegenberg pp. 137–40.

127. *De Intellectu et Intelligibili* II 6–9 (B 9 pp. 513–7).

128. *Metaph.* 1.1.5 (Col. XVI pp. 7–8).

129. Ibid. 11.2.11 (p. 498).

130. Ibid. (p. 498:42).

131. Ibid. (p. 497:65–9).

132. *De Resurrectione* IV 1.9.1 (Col. XXVI p. 328:27–36).

133. *DN* 3.16 (Col. XXXVII pp. 111–2); cf. *DN* 6.3 (p. 329:17): the essential constituent of eternal life is knowledge.

134. Cf. *DN* 4.67 (Col. XXXVII p. 175:65–70), *Dion. Ep.* 5 (ibid. p. 497:31–3). Albert rejects, however, the Neoplatonist emanationism that requires there to be a single *intelligentia* as the first step toward the production of multiplicity from the first cause: *DN* 7.3 (Col. XXXVII p. 339).

135. *De Resurrectione* IV 1.9 (Col. XXVI p. 328:40–46).

136. *DN* 7.25 (Col. XXXVII p. 356:67–74).

137. Ibid. 1.50 (p. 31:48–51).

138. Ibid. 7.25 (p. 357:3–4, 53–5).

139. Ibid. 4.69 (p. 179).

140. *Metaph.* 1.1.5 (Col. XVI p. 7:86–8).

141. Ibid. 11.2.11 (p. 497:51).

142. Cf. *DN* 7.3 (Col. XXXVII p. 339:45–51); *XV Problemata* X (Col. XVII i pp. 41–2).

143. Cf. E. Wéber in E. Zum Brunn et al., *Maître Eckhart à Paris* (Paris, 1984), pp. 29–40.

144. *DN* 7.24 (Col. XXXVII p. 356:1–2).

145. Cf. Schneider pp. 446–55. The Islamic doctrine of the soul's two faces is united with the Augustinian distinction between "wisdom" and "knowledge" to suggest a fairly sharp dichotomy in, for instance, Gundissalinus, *De Anima* 10, ed. J. T. Muckle, *Mediaeval Studies* 2 (1940) pp. 98–101.

146. *DN* 7.35 (Col. XXXVII p. 363:49–57).

147. *Summa Theol.* I 3.15.3.3 (Col. XXXIV i p. 81:9–15).

148. I *Sent.* d.1 a.15 (B 25 p. 37a).

149. *Comm. Io.* 9.38 (B 24 p. 391b).

150. *MT* 1 (Col. XXXVII p. 456:25–38).

151. *CH* 1.1 (B 14 p. 8b, AT 36); *DN* 2.19 (Col. XXXVII p. 56:56–7).

152. *DN* 2.19 (Col. XXXVII p. 56:57–62).

153. *MT* 1 (Col. XXXVII p. 458:16–8). Cf. E. Wéber, "L'interprétation par Albert le Grand de la Théologie Mystique de Denys le Ps.-Aréopagite," AMDU pp. 409–39.

154. Cf. below, note 38 to *MT* 1.

155. *MT* 1 (Col. XXXVII p. 460:74).

156. *CH* 1.1 (B 14 p. 12b).

157. *DN* 7.36 (Col. XXXVII pp. 363–4).

158. *DN* 7.31 (Col. XXXVII p. 360:6–8). On *natura cognoscitiva* see *DN* 4.69 (p. 179): it refers quite generally to any created knowing faculty, and is then differentiated into different specific kinds of intellectual capacity in angels, human beings, etc.

159. *DN* 7.1 (Col. XXXVII p. 337:37–8).

160. *CH* 1.1 (B 14 p. 8, AT 36).

161. *Comm. Io.* 20.29 (B 24 p. 694). *Cum assensione cogitare* comes from Augustine, *De Praedestinatione Sanctorum* 2.5, and is frequently quoted: e.g., Lombard's Gloss on 2 Cor. 3:4 (PL 192:23C); Lombard, II *Sent.* d.26 4.4, ed. cit. I p. 475; Philip the Chancellor, *Summa de Bono*, ed. N. Wicki (Berne, 1985), p. 587; William of Auxerre, *Summa Aurea* III 12.3, ed. cit. III p. 205. I am not aware of any other attribution of the phrase to Gregory.

162. III *Sent.* d.23 a.2 (B 28 p. 407b, AT 240).

163. Aristotle, *Metaph.* A 2 (982b25–6).

164. Aristotle, *Eth. Nic.* X 7 (1178a7).

165. B 24 pp. 351–3.

166. *Summa Theol.* I Prol. (Col. XXXIV i p. 3:50–4).

167. I *Sent.* d.1 a.4 (B 25 pp. 18–19); *Summa Theol.* I 1.2, 1.3.3 (Col. XXXIV i pp. 8–9, 13).

168. Beatifying truth is *afficiens per intellectum* (*De Resurrectione* IV 1.9.2, Col. XXVI p. 330:36–7). Cf. W. Senner, "Zur Wissenschaftstheorie der Theologie im Sentenzenkommentar Alberts des Grossen," AMDU pp. 323–43.

169. On this whole problem, see G. Englhardt, *Die Entwicklung der dogmatischen Glaubenspsychologie in der mittelalterlichen Scholastik*, Beiträge XXX/4–6 (Münster, 1933).

170. III *Sent.* d.23 a.1 (B 28 p. 405a). Cf. M. D. Chenu, "La Psychologie de la Foi dans la Théologie du XIIIe siècle," *Études d'Histoire Littéraire et Doctrinale du XIIIe siècle* II (Ottawa, 1932), pp. 174–91.

171. I *Sent.* d.3 a.3 (B 25 p. 95a).

172. III *Sent.* d.23 a.1 (B 28 p. 405b).

173. III *Sent.* d.23 a.2 (B 28 pp. 406–8).

174. Ibid. p. 408a.

175. Philip the Chancellor, ed. cit. p. 589; Roland of Cremona, *Summa* III 98.13, ed. A. Cortesi (Bergamo, 1962), p. 300.

176. III *Sent.* d.23 a.2 (B 28 p. 408a).

177. I *Sent.* d.3 a.3 (B 25 p. 95a).

178. *DN* 4.62 (Col. XXXVII p. 170:20–6); this is cited in an objection, but Albert does not criticize it in his response.

179. *MT* 1 (Col. XXXVII p. 455:15–8). For the translation, cf. below p. 139 note 14.

180. *DN* 4.12 (Col. XXXVII p. 121:37–42).

181. Earlier Albert denied that faith unites believers: *De Incarnatione* V 2.2 (Col. XXVI pp. 214–5). We noticed above Albert's complaint that the "Latin" view of the intellect makes it impossible for there to be any shared knowledge.

182. In *Maître Eckhart à Paris*, p. 35, Wéber speaks of the "structure extatique" of the activity of created intellects, with reference to the doctrine of Meister Eckhart.

183. Iamblichus, *De Mysteriis* III 25, ed. E. des Places (Paris, 1966), p. 133, distinguishes between good and bad senses of ἔκστασις, and this ambiguity is taken for granted by Dionysius (cf. his *Ep.* 9.5, PG 3:1112C).

184. Dionysius, *DN* 7.4 (PG 3:872D).

185. *DN* 7.36 (Col. XXXVII p. 364).

186. *MT* 1 (Col. XXXVII p. 457:60–1).

187. *MT* 1 (Col. XXXVII pp. 462–3).

188. *DN* 3.6 (Col. XXXVII pp. 104–5). Albert makes a rather partisan comment on this point in one of his sermons: "That we also surpass others in study is clear. We see that many young men in the order within four or five years overtake prominent masters who have studied for many years in Paris. Why is this? Because they learn to understand the scriptures by being inspired by the same Spirit who composed them" (AFP 34 [1964] p. 55).

189. *Dion. Ep.* 8 (Col. XXXVII p. 515).

190. Dionysius, *DN* 2.9 (PG 3:648B). On the ritual connotations of this passage see the excellent comments of Rorem, *Biblical and Liturgical Symbols*, pp. 133–8.

191. *DN* 2.76 (Col. XXXVII p. 92). The standard Latin gloss on this passage interpreted *passum* to mean *affectum*, in line with Eriugena's translation (Vat. lat. 176 f.197ᵛ).

192. *MT* 1 (Col. XXXVII pp. 460:74, 463:53–7).

193. Ibid. p. 458:54–62.

194. Cf. *DN* 2.18 (Col. XXXVII p. 56:1–5).

195. There might be a few exceptions such as St. Paul, but they do not talk about it; cf., for example, Rupert of Deutz, *De Victoria Verbi Dei* 1.4 (Monumenta Germaniae Historica, Quellen 5 [Weimar, 1970], p. 8).

196. Aristotle himself does not actually call this kind of situation "analogy," though he recognizes that this is one of the ways in which words work; cf. J. Owens, *The Doctrine of Being in the Aristotelian Metaphysics* (Toronto, 1951), p. 59. Aristotle discusses it in *Metaphysics* Γ 2.

197. *MT* 1 (Col. XXXVII p. 459:24–31). For an identical doctrine in the earlier Dominican theologian, Richard Fishacre, see Englhardt p. 480. I take this occasion to mention that it would be beyond my competence and the scope of this introduction to attempt to define exactly the limits of Albert's originality.

198. *MT* 5 (Col. XXXVII pp. 473:49–474:6).

199. I *Sent.* d.2 a.17 (B 25 p. 73).

200. Cf. *MT* 2 (Col. XXXVII p. 466:79).

201. *DN* 1.3 (Col. XXXVII p. 2).
202. William of Auxerre, *Summa Aurea* I 4.1.4, ed. cit. pp. 40–1.
203. *CH* 1.1 (B 14 p. 8b, AT 36); *DN* 1.4 (Col. XXXVII p. 2:68–9).
204. *DN* 1.11 (Col. XXXVII pp. 5–6).
205. *DN* 2.54 (Col. XXXVII p. 80:35–6).
206. Cf. L. J. Bataillon, RSPT 67 (1983) p. 421.
207. *DN* 1.12 (Col. XXXVII p. 6:54–60).
208. *DN* 1.14 (Col. XXXVII p. 7:44–5).
209. *Dion. Ep.* 9 (Col. XXXVII p. 534); cf. Gregory, *Moralia*, Ep. ad Leandrum, PL 75:515A, CC 143 (Turnhout, 1979) p. 6.
210. IV 1.9.1 (Col. XXVI pp. 326–9).
211. Cf. Bonaventure, II *Sent.* d.23 a.2 q.3, Quaracchi, vol. 2 p. 543b.
212. See RTAM 19 (1952) p. 101. This problem is frequently alluded to: e.g., Alexander of Hales, II *Sent.* d.8.11 (Quaracchi, vol.2 pp. 78–9); Hugh of St. Cher on John 1:16 (in RTAM 19 p. 120); Guerric (in RSPT 44 [1960] pp. 238–9).
213. Cf. I *Sent.* d.3 a.4 (B 25 p. 95b).
214. *De Resurrectione* IV 1.9.1 (Col. XXVI p. 329:21–8).
215. I *Sent.* d.1 a.15 (B 25 pp. 34–37); Albert tries to explain how we can know something infinite in I *Sent.* d.2 a.4 (B 25 pp. 58–9).
216. *CH* 2.7 (B 14 p. 44a); Damascene, *De Fide Orthodoxa* 9, ed. cit. p. 49.
217. Augustine, *De Trinitate* XIV 8.11; cf. St. Thomas, *Summa Theol.* I.II q.113 a.10.
218. I *Sent.* d.1 a.15 (B 25 pp. 34–6).
219. Cf. *CH* 3.3 (B 14 p. 88).
220. II *Sent.* d.4 a.1 (B 27 p. 105); *CH* 3.3 (B 14 p. 88).
221. I *Sent.* d.1 a.15 (B 25 p. 37); II *Sent.* d.4 a.1 (B 27 p. 105); *CH* 8.5 (B 14 p. 237).
222. *CH* 4.6 (B 14 p. 118).
223. IV *Sent.* d.49 a.5 (B 30 p. 670). This is in part inspired by Avicenna's idea that after death the soul can be united with the agent intellect and so find eternal bliss (*De Anima* V 6, ed. cit. II pp. 148–50); cf. Contenson, *Archives d'Hist. Doct. et Litt.* 26 (1960); pp. 59–62.
224. *DN* 1.21 (Col. XXXVII pp. 10–11).
225. *DN* 6.9 (Col. XXXVII p. 332:75–81).
226. *DN* 13.27 (Col. XXXVII p. 448:38–47).
227. *DN* 7.25 (Col. XXXVII p. 356:84–357:2).
228. *DN* 7.25 (Col. XXXVII p. 356:61–6).
229. Cf. below notes 70–1 on *MT* 1.
230. *Dion. Ep.* 5 (Col. XXXVII p. 495:33–43).

231. *DN* 7.25 (Col. XXXVII p. 357:43–4); cf. Damascene, *De Fide Orthodoxa* 1, ed. cit. p. 12, and 3, p. 16.

232. *DN* 1.24, 27 (Col. XXXVII pp. 12:28–33, 13:53–7). At p. 13:56 *quid* must be emended to *quia*, even though the manuscript reading is definitely *quid*; cf. F. J. Catania, " 'Knowable' and 'Namable' in Albert the Great's Commentary on the *Divine Names*," in F. J. Kovach and R. W. Shahan, eds., *Albert the Great, Commemorative Essays* (Norman, 1980), p. 99 note 10 and p. 107 note 37.

233. *Dion. Ep.* 1 (Col. XXXVII p. 481:37–48).

234. *De Spiritu et Anima* 12 (PL 40:788). This seems to originate in Eriugena, *Periphyseon* I p. 56. It is also found in the *Sententiae Anselmi*, ed. F. P. Bliemetzrieder, Beiträge XVIII/2–3 (Münster, 1919), pp. 152–3.

235. *DN* 1.38, *Dion. Ep.* 5 (Col. XXXVII pp. 21:43–6, 497:23–7). Already in *Res.* 2.4.160 (Col. XXVI p. 344:16–23), when Albert still accepted the ascription of *De spiritu et anima* to Augustine, and in I *Sent.* d.1 a.23 (B 25 p. 51b), where he denies Augustine's authorship, a similar interpretation is proposed. On Albert's relationship to *De spir. et an.*, see A. Hiedl, "Die pseudo-Augustinische Schrift 'De Spiritu et Anima' in den Frühwerken Alberts des Grossen," in T. W. Köhler, ed., *Sapientiae Procerum Amore* (Rome, 1974), pp. 97–121.

236. *MT* 1 (Col. XXXVII p. 463:71–5).

237. *DN* 7.15 (Col. XXXVII p. 348:71–3).

238. Eriugena, *Periphyseon* II pp. 138–48; Honorius, *Clavis Physicae* 107, ed. cit. pp. 78–9.

239. Avicenna, *De philosophia prima* tr.8 ch.4, ed. S. van Riet (Louvain/Leiden, 1980), pp. 398–9.

240. William of Auvergne, *De Universo* II.II ch.10, ed. cit. I pp. 853–4.

241. *MT* 3 (Col. XXXVII p. 469:30–46); I *Sent.* d.2 a.22 (B 25 p. 84).

242. *DN* 7.25 (Col. XXXVII p. 356:45–57); *DN* 1.51 (Col. XXXVII p. 32:38–40).

243. *DN* 7.24 (Col. XXXVII p. 356:12–5).

244. *DN* 7.25 (Col. XXXVII p. 357:8–32). Cf. F. J. Catania, "Divine Infinity in Albert the Great's Commentary on the "Sentences" of Peter Lombard," *Mediaeval Studies* 22 (1960) pp. 27–42.

245. *Dion. Ep.* 1 (Col. XXXVII p. 481:65–70). *Obiectum* was a "modern" word when Albert was writing, and its precise connotations in different authors need to be studied; in Albert's usage it seems to be closely linked to the idea of the natural "object" of our natural powers. See L. Dewan, " 'Obiectum': notes on the invention of a word," *Archives d'Hist. Doct. et Litt.* 48 (1982) pp. 37–96, especially p. 38.

246. *Dion. Ep.* 5 (Col. XXXVII pp. 495–6).

247. *Dion. Ep.* 1 (Col. XXXVII pp. 481–2).

248. Cf. *Dion. Ep.* 5 (Col. XXXVII p. 495:63–4).

249. PL 172:1246B–D.

250. This was the cry of the Egyptian monk trying to pray after being confounded by the anti-anthropomorphites: Cassian, *Conf.* 10.3.

251. For William of Auvergne, God is the "first and most noble intelligible": *De Universo* I.II ch.8, ed. cit. I p. 816aG.

252. Cf. Albert's defense of the poetical language used in scripture: *Summa Theol.* I tr.5 n.2 ad 1 (Col. XXXIV i p. 18:11–23).

253. Cf. *De Sacramentis* 1.1 (Col. XXVI p. 2:7–13, 21–2).

254. Meister Eckhart, *Die deutschen Werke*, ed. J. Quint, I p. 91.

255. Cf. B. Davies, "What Happens When You Pray?," *New Blackfriars* 61 (1980) pp. 537–42.

256. Petrus Calo, *Vita S. Thomae* 3 (FVST p. 19).

257. Thomas Aquinas, *De Veritate* q.8 a.1 ad.8. Cf. H. F. Dondaine, "Cognoscere de Deo 'quid est,' " RTAM 22 (1955) pp. 72–8.

258. Dondaine, "Cognoscere de Deo 'quid est,' " pp. 77–8.

259. Catherine of Siena *Il Dialogo* ch. 165, ed. G. Cavallini (Rome, 1968), p. 493.

260. *Metaph.* 1.1.5 (Col. XVI p. 7:89–94).

261. Cf. *Anim.* 5.1.4.31.

ALBERT THE GREAT

COMMENTARY ON
DIONYSIUS'
MYSTICAL THEOLOGY

This translation is based on the critical edition by Paul Simon in volume XXXVII of the Cologne edition of the works of St. Albert. I have occasionally ventured to express some doubts about the received text, but only in one case have I actually adopted an emendation into the translation. All such places are pointed out in the notes.

In attempting to render Albert intelligible for English-speaking readers I have probably rather fallen between two stools. An unduly literal translation would yield the kind of version that is serviceable as a "crib," but which can scarcely be understood without constant reference to the Latin original. On the other hand I did not want to drift too far from the words that Albert actually wrote: a paraphrase is not a translation. So I have tried, where it can be done without paying too high a price, to avoid barely anglicized Latin jargon, and this has meant a certain degree of paraphrase, or at least elaboration of the text. But there are still some passages where the uninitiated reader is likely to be puzzled, and I hope I have provided sufficient commentary to deal with such eventualities. Above all I have tried— though the results are perhaps a bit cumbersome—to avoid using latinate jargon that immediately suggests some totally irrelevant meaning in modern English. Thus, although it would be highly convenient to render sensibilis "sensible," I have respected the fact that the English word has taken on an entirely different career of its own, even though the alternative has been to use unwieldy phrases like "the things of the senses."

In addition to the text of Albert's commentary I have included a translation of Dionysius' Mystical Theology. For this I have used a Greek text edited by myself on the basis of the manuscripts available in Oxford, but the translation was actually made on the basis of Sarracenus' Latin version (which is what Albert used) in the light of Albert's comments. That is to say, I have tried to present the text of Dionysius as it was read and interpreted by Albert. Where the Latin version (or Albert's reading of it) is unusually bizarre, I have added a note explaining what seems to be going on.

To help the reader I have provided a fairly substantial commentary of my own, in which I have tried to shed light (a) on the arguments used by Albert, and (b) on the sources he cites. In this latter task I have obviously been much helped by Mgr. Simon's notes, but I have nevertheless pursued all Albert's explicit citations for myself, and I have sometimes come to conclusions that differ from those of Mgr. Simon. One of the difficulties is that Albert often cites imprecisely and the texts he has in mind have in fact matured in his own use of them, sometimes to the point where they bear little resemblance to their originals.

CHAPTER ONE

John Sarracenus' prologue. To Odo, abbot of St. Denis.

The *Symbolic Theology* ought to have come before the *Mystical Theology*, because St. Dionysius' own words make it clear that this was the work composed after the *Divine Names*. But, although I looked for it carefully, I was not able to find it in the parts of Greece where I was. If by any chance you manage to obtain it and the other books I mentioned to brother William, thanks to your monk who is said to have gone to Greece, please let me know.[1] In the meantime here is my translation of the *Mystical Theology*. It is clearly called "mystical" because it is hidden and closed; in this kind of theology we rise to the knowledge of God by way of abstraction and at the end it remains a closed and hidden secret what God is. It can also be called "mystical theology" because it too is a way in which much teaching about God can be obtained. The word *myo*, from which "mystical" comes, means "close" and also "learn" and "teach."

*

"Truly God of Israel, the Savior, you are a hidden God" (Is. 45:15). From these words we can deduce four things about this teaching which is entitled *Mystical Theology:* its nature, its content, its audience and its objective.

Its nature is alluded to in the word "truly." This is a feature common to the whole of sacred scripture; because we do not receive

---

1. Sarracenus says literally, "to me your cleric," which is probably only a formula of politeness; it certainly refutes the suggestion that he was actually a monk of St. Denis.

it on the authority of human arguments, which involve a large admixture of uncertainty and error, but on the authority of divine inspiration, which cannot contain any falsehood, it rests on undoubted truth. So Christ says to the Father, "Your word is truth" (Jn. 17:17). "God is truthful" (Rom. 3:4). "Which God promised, who does not lie" (Tit. 1:2). "God is not like us, that he should change or lie" (Num. 23:19). "It is impossible that God should lie" (Heb. 6:18).

The content of this teaching is alluded to in the words "hidden God." It is called "mystical," that is, hidden, as the translator says in his prologue, because "in this kind of theology we rise to the knowledge of God by way of abstraction and at the end it remains a closed and hidden secret what God is." And so because the Godhead is hidden like this it says, "He dwells in inaccessible light and no human being has seen him or can see him" (1 Tim. 6:16). "No one has ever seen God" (Jn. 1:18). On this last text Chrysostom says that not even the heavenly beings have ever been able to see him as he is.[2] "No human being shall see me and live" (Exod. 33:20). "Each one beholds him from afar; see how God in his greatness defeats our knowledge" (Job 36:25–26).

The sort of people to whom this kind of teaching is meant to be addressed is alluded to in the word "Israel," which means "very straight" and "a man who sees God."[3] This reveals the twofold perfection which is required of the student of this science: clarity of understanding in order to see God and right behavior in practice, which is how we come to such clarity or sharpness of understanding. The student should not be a child either in years or in manners,

---

2. Cf. Chrysostom, *Hom. on the Gospel of John* 15.1 (PG 59:98); Latin text in RTAM 19 (1952) p.101. In I *Sent.* d.1 a.15 (B 25 p.34) Albert claims to have found this text "in the original" (i.e., in the actual translation of Chrysostom, as distinct from a florilegium or someone else's citation of the text); in *CH* 4.5 (B 14 p.115) a similar text is ascribed to Damascene. The actual words cited by Albert are not found in Chrysostom or in Damascene, and "heavenly beings" (*coelestes essentiae*) perhaps suggests an influence from Eriugena (cf. *Periphyseon* I, ed. cit. p.66:34–6). Presumably Albert originally received this text as an unattached "authority," which he subsequently located in Chrysostom, but whose wording he did not bother to correct in the light of what Chrysostom actually said.

3. The interpretation of Israel as meaning *vir videns deum* was classic (cf. Lombard's comment on Ps. 75:2, PL 191:706A), in spite of Jerome's refutation of it (*Hebr. Quaest. in Gen.* 32:28, CC vol. 72 p.41), cited both in the Glossa Ordinaria and in Hugh of St. Cher's postil on Gen. 32:28. Jerome favors the interpretation "straight," which he gives in Greek: εὐθύτατος θεόυ.

as the philosopher says in the *Ethics*[4] about the student of political science. So Bernard also says, "It is presumptuous when impure people unworthily undertake holy reading before their flesh has been tamed and subjected to the spirit by the practice of discipline and before they have cast off and spurned the pomp and the burden of the world."[5] "To whom will he teach knowledge and whom will he make to understand his message? People who are weaned from milk and torn away from the breast" (Is. 28:9). "We speak wisdom among the perfect . . . no one with the resources merely of the human soul can grasp the things of God's Spirit" (1 Cor. 2:6,14). "Do not give what is holy to dogs" (Mt. 7:6).

The objective of this teaching is alluded to in the word "Savior." Its goal is not just that we should acquire knowledge or, as in ethics, that we should "become good"[6] by doing good works, but that we should go further and attain to everlasting salvation, where we shall encounter openly and without veil what is at present left hidden from us about God by way of negations. "To know you is the consummation of righteousness, and the knowledge of your righteousness and truth is the root of immortality" (Wis. 15:3). "I have seen the Lord face to face and my soul is saved" (Gen. 32:30).

After this preamble we must proceed to inquire about the name of this science, and ask why it is called "mystical." At the same time its aim will become clear to us.

(1) On the face of it, no science ought to be called "mystical." Anything that is known systematically is laid out in the open on the basis of its first principles, and once it is out in the open it is not hidden. So it would seem that no science, including this one, should be called "mystical" or hidden.

(2) Something which is completely hidden has more right to be called "mystical" than something which is at least clear in its starting point. But this science, as we shall see in the third chapter, proceeds by denying things of God, and it starts with things that are clearly perceived by the senses, which it separates from God. But the divine Persons, which our author deals with elsewhere, are completely hid-

---

4. Aristotle, *Eth. Nic.* 1.3 (1095a2–9).
5. Bernard, *On the Canticle* 1.3.
6. Aristotle, *Eth. Nic.* 2.2 (1103b26–8) says that the purpose of ethical study is not just speculative, it is that "we may become good."

den, so it seems that that is the science which should be called "mystical," not this one.

(3) "Mystical" or "hidden" ought to apply particularly to whatever is furthest removed from our knowledge. But the distinction of the Persons in the Trinity is particularly remote from our knowledge. As Ambrose says, "It is impossible for me to know the secret of the Son's birth; our mind fails, our voice falls silent, and not only ours but that of the angels too."[7] So the teaching which discusses the distinction of the Persons appears to be the one which should be particularly called "mystical."

(4) Augustine says that in some fashion he read in the books of Plato everything else contained in the prologue of St. John, but what he did not find there was "the Word was made flesh." So it is said of him that he could not even have an inkling of the mystery of "the Word was made flesh."[8] But the less something is amenable to the philosophers, the more hidden it must be from human reason. And Dionysius deals elsewhere with the mystery of the Incarnation, together with the distinctive properties of the Persons, as he implies in the chapter on Peace in the *Divine Names*,[9] so it is that science rather than this which should particularly be called "mystical."

(5) Although we say that the philosophers had some kind of knowledge of the divine Persons by way of attributes appropriated to them, they had absolutely no knowledge of their proper attributes.[10] So surely the science which has the best claim to be called "hidden" and "mystical" is the one which deals with these proper attributes.

---

7. Ambrose, *De Fide* 1.10.64 (PL 16 [1845]:543B).

8. Cf. Augustine, *Confessions* 7.9.13–4, 7.19.25. Albert does not perhaps make it as clear as he should that it is Augustine who did not have an inkling of the mystery of the Incarnation, not Plato, and that the words are Augustine's own.

9. Dionysius, *DN* 11.5, though this actually does not make it clear that the divine Persons and the Incarnation are discussed in the lost (or perhaps unwritten) work, *Theological Outlines*. But *MT* 3 makes it clear that the book did (or was intended to) include such a discussion.

10. The proper attributes of the divine Persons (Fatherhood, Sonship, procession) are known only by revelation; but certain terms that apply strictly to the essence of God are traditionally "appropriated" to particular Persons, even though they belong to all three: for example, "power" can be ascribed to the Father, "wisdom" to the Son and "goodness" to the Holy Spirit. It is within the competence of philosophy to apply such terms to God, but since they properly belong to all three Persons, they do not lead to any real knowledge of the Trinity. Cf. I *Sent.* d.3 a.18 (B 25 pp.113–4); St. Thomas Aquinas, *Summa Theol.* I q.32 a.1, q.39 a.7–8.

(6) The certainty which any science possesses derives entirely from its first principles. So a science which is hidden even in its starting point is more to be called "mystical" than one which at least starts from something which is out in the open. But this science starts from things which are out in the open, because its procedure is to start with the objects of the senses and separate them from God. But the science of God's names is hidden in its starting point, because it shows how all the things which are manifest to us proceed from the hiddenness of the Godhead. So it is that teaching, not this, which should be called "mystical."

(7) That which transcends all beings is obscure to our knowledge, in that our knowledge is caused by beings. But in the *Divine Names* Dionysius taught us how to interpret all the divine names by way of transcendence.[11] Therefore that is the science which ought to be called "mystical."

(8) As it says in the second and also in the first chapter of the *Celestial Hierarchy*, sacred scripture depicts the things of God with symbols, so that we will be led to the things of God in a way which is adapted to us via things which are known to us.[12] So if this science is to be called "mystical" because it leads us from the things which are manifest to us and leaves us finally in the dark, then symbolic theology too should surely be called "mystical" because it too ends in darkness.

In response to these points we may say that negative ways of

---

11. Albert begins his exposition of the *Divine Names* with a comment on the *eminentia* (transcendence) of the names that are given to God (Col. XXXVII p.1), and this interpretation of Dionysius' exegetical principle is justified especially by *DN* 7.2 (cf. St. Thomas, I *Sent.* d.8 q.4 a.3). In Albert's view both *DN* and *MT* deal with God's "mystical" names; on the relationship between the treatments of them in the two works, see above, pp.77–78.

12. The first two chapters of *CH* contain an apologia for the use of symbolic language in scripture, stressing that such language can both communicate the mystery of God to us in a way adapted to our capacity and at the same time protect the mystery from the profane. It also makes clear the link there is between symbolic theology and negative theology. *Ep.* 9.1, in fact, appears to identify symbolic theology with mystical theology, but in his commentary (Col. XXXVII pp.535–6) Albert points out that mystical theology, in the sense appropriate to the treatise of that name, is "materially" opaque, in that it takes away from us any "matter" which our minds can grasp, whereas symbolic theology is not, in that sense, opaque, in that it deals precisely with the "veils" that hide God from our direct vision, but which are not themselves obscure. So Albert does not want to deny that symbolic theology is "mystical," only to insist that the mystical theology of *MT* has a distinct quality of its own, namely, that it leads us further and further into the dark, whereas symbolic theology is, in its own way, concerned with a kind of divine condescension to the clarity we naturally prefer.

doing theology begin, as it says in the third chapter, by taking what is clear to us and perceptible to our senses and denying it of God. They proceed in this way, separating everything from God, so that our understanding is left with something unclear, from which all that it knows has been taken away and about which it cannot say what it is. Affirmative ways of doing theology, on the other hand, bring the hiddenness of the Godhead out into the open, inasmuch as they indicate how the things that are manifest to us proceed from a transcendent cause. For example, when God is called "good" this signifies that he is the one from whom all goodness in creatures is derived, and when he is called "Father" this means that he is the one "from whom all fatherhood in heaven and on earth is named."[13]

So because this teaching with which we are concerned here deals with the kind of separation performed by negations, whereas others deal with what we affirm about God, this teaching has more right to be called "mystical" than any others, because it leaves us in the dark, whereas other sorts of teaching bring us out of the darkness into what is manifest to us.

So we may reply to the points raised above as follows:

(1) A science which proceeds from our own reason's first principles lays open the conclusions to which it leads us. But this present kind of teaching does not start from principles like this, it begins rather with a kind of divine light, which is not a statement by which something is affirmed, it is a kind of reality which convinces the understanding[14] to adhere to it above all else. And so it raises the understanding to something which transcends it, and this is why the mind is left with something of which it has no clearly defined knowledge. This light is analogous to the light by which our bodily vision is empowered to see things; the light as such does not give us specific knowledge of any particular visible thing, since it is not the visible form of anything in particular. By contrast the light of rational principles in the mind is more like the specific forms of visible objects,

---

13. Eph. 3:15.

14. *Res convincens intellectum.* R. A. Gauthier, in his introduction to the Leonine edition of St. Thomas' *De Anima* (vol. XLV i pp.290*–293*), insists that in medieval Latin *convincere* means "convict" or "refute," not "convince," and the *Dictionary of Medieval Latin from British Sources* fasc. II (London, 1981), certainly does not list "convince" as one of the meanings of the verb. But A. Patfoort, *Thomas d'Aquin, Les Clés d'une Théologie* (Paris, 1983), pp.114–18, argues cogently that in St. Thomas "convince" is sometimes the most natural interpretation of *convincere*, and it is hard to see what else Albert means in this present passage.

by which our vision grasps particulars, and so these principles lead to the specific knowledge of some definite object.

(2) Although the reality of the divine Persons is hidden, yet there is nothing hidden about the way in which we treat of them, because the affirmations made about them in Trinitarian theology, such as that the Father begets or that there are three Persons, bring our understanding out of the darkness of the Godhead into things which are clear, in which some pointer is found which is left in them by the first cause.[15] The science under discussion here is called "mystical" with reference to the nature of its method, as has been said above.

This shows us the answer to points 3, 4 and 5 as well.

(6) A science, like anything else, ought to be designated chiefly with reference to its end-product.[16] So this science, which leaves us in the dark at the end, has a better right to be called "mystical" than the science of the divine names which shows us how to move from hiddenness to clarity, particularly as this latter science does not even consider its starting point precisely as something hidden, but as something which is made manifest by the procession of things from it, which resemble it analogously inasmuch as they imitate it.

(7) The transcendence which is considered in the *Divine Names* is the transcendence of the cause, and so the theology of the divine names does not stay in it as something hidden, it moves from it by way of its causality toward effects which are manifest.

(8) *We* begin any symbolic theology with things that are clear to us, but the natural direction in this kind of teaching is from what is hidden to what is manifest, because what is said metaphorically is secondary with respect to what is said properly. A metaphor cannot work except because of some relationship to what is said properly; for instance we cannot know why God is said to be "sleeping" without first knowing in what sense he refrains from acting.[17] But

---

15. Albert is not denying that the Trinity is an incomprehensible mystery to us; his point is that the language used in Trinitarian theology is not in itself unfamiliar to us. We know what it means for someone to be a father, and there are various triadic structures in creation that point to the Trinity of divine Persons; these pointers are genuine traces (*vestigia*) of the Trinity stamped on creation by its maker (cf. I *Sent*. d.3 a.13–18, B 25 pp.102–14).

16. Aristotle, *De Anima* 2.4 (416b23–4).

17. Dionysius comments on God's "sleep" in *Ep*. 9.6, and Albert suggests that the scriptural reference is to Psalm 43:23, "Wake, Lord, why do you sleep?"; Albert's interpretation, that God's "sleeping" means that he appears to be turning a blind eye to what is going

what belongs properly to God is hidden, whereas metaphors are taken from what is manifest, so the movement of symbolic theology too is from what is hidden to what is manifest.

We must now proceed to the analysis of the book's structure.

As the philosopher says in the second book of the *Metaphysics*, we should not try to investigate at the same time both the way in which some object is clarified and the object itself.[18] We must investigate first how it is to be clarified. So this book falls into two parts: the first determines how this kind of teaching proceeds, and the second, beginning in chapter four, contains the actual teaching.

The method involved in this teaching comprises two factors: the situation of the person conducting the discussion, and the method of the discussion itself. So the first part of the book falls into two parts, the first dealing with the situation of the person conducting the discussion, the second (in chapter three) dealing with the method of the actual discussion.

There are two facets of the situation of the person conducting the discussion: first knowledge and then union with God, because, as it says in the *Celestial Hierarchy*, "hierarchy is knowledge and action and, as far as possible, likeness to God and union with him."[19] So this first section is in two parts, the first dealing with how we know God, the second (in chapter two) with how we become one with him.

The first subsection is also in two parts, the first dealing with the situation of the teacher, the second with the situation of the student.

The procedure for someone teaching the things of God is to seek by prayer the gift of that truth about the things of God which is to be passed on to others, because any theological business has to begin with prayer, as it says in the third chapter of the *Divine*

---

on and not doing anything about it (*dissimulans*) is in line with that of the standard commentary by Peter Lombard (PL 191:434C). But Dionysius takes the "sleep" to mean also the hiddenness of what God keeps to himself and does not share with his creatures, and in his commentary (Col. XXXVII p.545) Albert interprets this as the transcendence of God's majesty.

18. Aristotle, *Metaph.* α 3 (995a13–4); in the Middle Ages book α was called "book two."

19. *CH* 3.1 (p.87).

Names.[20] So this first section falls into two parts, a prayer and a re-capitulation.

(1) But surely prayer is not the proper procedure for teaching. It is the teacher's role to implant truth in the soul of the student, and the only way this can happen is by means of a quite different sort of utterance, indicating that something is true or false.[21] But the utterance of a prayer does not indicate anything to be true or false, so it seems that prayer is not the proper procedure for a teacher to adopt.

(2) Teaching is meant to pass from the teacher to the student. But in the case of truth that is won by praying for it the student can be in exactly the same position as the teacher, because what is in question there is not the relationship between teacher and pupil but their respective holiness. So again prayer appears not to be a proper procedure for a teacher.

(3) Against this, though, truth which is higher than our own knowledge cannot be received by us unless its own generosity is moved and it bestows itself upon us. And the truth which is being sought in the present instance is of this kind. Now it is only by prayer that God's generosity is moved, so prayer apparently has to be the procedure adopted by a teacher in this domain.

In response to this problem we may say, as Gregory does at the beginning of his *Moralia,* that we arrive at a grasp of the things of God more by prayer than by discussion.[22] The reason for this is that, since divine truth exceeds our rational powers, we cannot of ourselves lay it bare unless it deigns to give itself to us. It is itself the inner teacher, without whom the external teacher toils in vain, as Augustine says.[23] But this does not mean that external teaching is superfluous, because it is a kind of tool as it says in the psalm ("My tongue is the pen of a scribe," Ps. 44:2), and it makes an impression on the hearer's soul by means of utterances signifying truth or false-

---

20. *DN* 3.1 (PG 3:680D).

21. *Oratio* in Latin can mean either "statement" or "prayer"; the definition of it in the former sense as "signifying something true or false" comes from Boethius (PL 64:454D).

22. There is a text very similar to this at the end of St. Bernard, *De Consideratione* 5.14.32, but no such text has been found at the beginning of Gregory's *Moralia.*

23. Albert is here summing up the essential thesis of Augustine's *De Magistro* in much the same way as he had done a few years earlier in I *Sent.* d.2 a.5 (B 25 p.59b).

hood. So, because of the two teachers involved, both kinds of utterance are necessary: statements (and this concerns the relationship between teacher and student) and entreaty.

This shows us how to answer the points raised above.

On Mystical Theology. Dionysius, presbyter, to his fellow-presbyter Timothy. Chapter One.

> Supersubstantial Trinity, more than divine, more than good, inspector of the divine wisdom of the Christians, direct us to the more than unknown, more than resplendent and highest peak of the mystic Oracles, where the simple, separate and changeless mysteries of theology are veiled in the darkness of instructed silence which is hiddenly more than resplendent, which makes that which is most excellently luminous to shine down in utter obscurity and fills minds which have no eyes with more than beautiful brilliances in what is utterly impalpable and invisible. Let this then be my demand in prayer.

*

Several questions arise about details of the text which need clarifying.

(1) Splendor is by its nature a kind of manifestation; but "manifest" and "unknown" are opposites. So the author appears to be contradicting himself when he says "unknown" and "more than resplendent."

(2) A thing is simple precisely because it is separate from matter, so the author seems to be wasting words in saying both "simple" and "separate." It is also superfluous to add "changeless," since immobility goes with both simplicity and immateriality.

(3) All instruction is given by means of some kind of word, whether inner or outer. And when a word is uttered, silence is broken. So the author seems to be harnessing two incompatible terms when he says "instructed silence."

The answer to these points is as follows:

(1) God is called "more than resplendent" in himself, but hid-

den with regard to us, because things which are naturally the most manifest are related to our understanding as a bat's eye is related to sunlight.[24] Or we can say that God is hidden in himself in the exaltedness of his nature, but more than resplendent inasmuch as he gives himself to us.

(2) Among lower realities some things are simple from the point of view of our way of understanding them, though in their actual existence they are composite and dependent on matter; such are the essences of things that exist in nature. Realities of this kind are immobile and indestructible in themselves, but they are accidentally prone to corruption in the subjects in which they inhere.[25] But God is both notionally simple and in reality separate from matter, not dependent on anything, because he is complete in himself, and he does not move or change in any sense, not even accidentally.[26]

(3) There is "silence," simply speaking, because we cannot say of God "what" he is; but it is, relatively speaking, an "instructed silence" inasmuch as we can say "that" he is.

The introductory greeting needs no comment, because it has been expounded elsewhere[27] and its meaning is obvious, and the sig-

---

24. Aristotle, *Metaph.* α 1 (993b9–11).

25. Although a poodle, say, is a complex organism, and there cannot be any poodle in existence that is not compounded of a considerable number of parts, the *idea* of a poodle is simple—I do not have to piece together the idea of a tail, the idea of fur, and so on, to arrive at it, nor do I review a succession of thoughts when I think "poodle." The *idea* of a poodle is "separate from matter"—I could still think "poodle" even if there were no poodles left alive anywhere in the world. And when I take my poodle for a walk, I am not really taking "poodleness" for a walk, nor does "poodleness" suffer when my beloved pet expires. Nevertheless, inasmuch as "poodleness" only exists either in poodles or in people's minds, as the various poodles in the world go about their business, "poodleness" too, in a sense, shifts its location, and when a poodle dies "poodleness" ceases to exist in that particular part of the world. This is what it means to say that things like "poodleness" are "accidentally" (though not in themselves) liable to movement and corruption. Albert's point is that it is not superfluous for Dionysius to list "simple," "separate" and "immutable" as distinct items.

26. Unlike "poodleness," God actually exists independently of all materiality, nor is there any kind of complexity that can truly be ascribed to him. Even such abstruse distinctions as that between his essence and his existence are no more than a concession to our own intellectual convenience and do not correspond to any real distinction in God. And there is no sense at all in which God is liable to change or corruption.

27. The greeting, "Dionysius, presbyter, to his fellow-presbyter Timothy," is identical with that at the beginning of *DN*, on which Albert's only comment is that "presbyter" means "bishop" and that they were both bishops (Col. XXXVII p.3).

nificance of the title is clear from what has already been said above, so without further ado let us pass on to the preliminary prayer.

So the author prays, "O supersubstantial Trinity," Trinity, that is, who make all things exist,[28] "more than divine," providing, that is, for things that do now exist,[29] "more than good," inasmuch as it directs all things to their goal,[30] "inspector of the divine wisdom" (wisdom about God) "of the Christians" (possessed by Christians), because he alone is perfectly able to contemplate himself; this is why Dionysius says "inspector," which suggests a very intimate kind of looking.[31] And he says "of the Christians" to distinguish this wisdom from the knowledge of God which even philosophers possessed, which was mixed up with a great many errors because of the weakness of human reason. "Direct us," because you alone perfectly see yourself, "to the highest peak of the mystic oracles," along the way by which we come as it were to something hidden by denying everything of him, as has been said above; "to the peak which is more than unknown . . . , where" (on that peak) "the mysteries of theology are veiled," that is, hidden from us, "in the darkness of instructed silence which is hiddenly more than resplendent." Just as the light of the sun is too bright for us and produces a kind of darkness in our feeble eyes even though there is no darkness in the sun, so "in God there is no darkness at all,"[32] but our eyes are darkened by the excess of his radiance, because they are powerless to cope with such splendor, and it is by this darkness that the things of God are hidden from us, the "simple mysteries, etc." This peak "makes that which is most excellently luminous" (the divine light) "shine

---

28. "Supersubstantial," taken in accordance with Albert's principle that all the divine names are to be expounded along the lines of *eminentia causae*, means that God is "more than substantial" because he is not just "a substance," he is the cause of all created substance, that is, the cause of the existence of all creatures. Cf. his comment on *DN* 1.54 (Col. XXXVII pp.33–4).

29. "Godhead" is interpreted by Dionysius as meaning the providence which "sees" everything and "runs around" everything to bring creation to its fulfilment (θεότης being derived from θεᾶσθαι or θεωρεῖν in the first sense and from θέειν in the second): *DN* 12.2 (PG 3:969C), and cf. Eriugena, *Periphyseon* I p.60 (a text incorporated into the Latin interpolated Gloss). See Albert, I *Sent.* d.2 a.11 (B 25 p.65a); *DN* 12.7 (Col. XXXVII p.430).

30. According to Dionysius, *DN* 4.1–2, it is the outpouring of good from the primary Good that inspires all beings with the desire to be assimilated to the Good and so to come to their own perfection; cf. Albert's commentary on this (Col. XXXVII p.129).

31. A typical medieval etymology, linking *inspectrix* with *intime spectans*. Dionysius' Greek actually means "inspector" in the sense of "overseer."

32. 1 John 1:5.

down" (into our minds) "in utter obscurity," the obscurity of divine transcendence, because although the excess of this radiance leaves a darkness in us so that we fall short of comprehending God's transcendence, nevertheless because in some way we do attain to it by abandoning everything, our minds are deified and enlightened. And so he goes on: "and fills minds" (our minds and those of the angels) "which have no eyes" (no bodily eyes) "with more than beautiful brilliances" of divine illuminations in that highest point which is "utterly impalpable," because it is known by none of our outward senses, and "invisible" to our inner sight.

Then he recapitulates, "Let this then . . . "; the meaning is obvious.

*

As for you, my friend Timothy, with regard to mystic visions, with a strong contrition abandon the senses and the workings of the intellect and all that is known to the senses or the intellect and all that is non-existent or existent and, as far as possible, rise up in unknowing to imitate him who is above all being and knowledge. It is by an unrestrainable and unbound[33] ecstasy from yourself and from everything that you will be carried upward in purity to the supersubstantial ray of divine darkness, removing everything and cut loose from everything.

See that no one who is uninstructed hears these things; none of those, I mean, who are shaped within beings and imagine that nothing exists supersubstantially above beings, who think they can know him who makes darkness his hiding place[34] with their own kind of knowledge. If the divine teaching of the mysteries is above them, what are we to say of those who are more uninstructed, who construct an image of the cause which is above everything out of the lowest among beings and claim that it has nothing higher than these impious and manifold shapes

---

33. I have not been able to retain the density and consistency of Albert's Latin vocabulary. "Unbound" here and "cut loose" a few lines on, like "separate" (from materiality) elsewhere, all translate forms of the Latin *absolutum*.

34. Psalm 17:12.

which they themselves have constructed? Of this cause we have both to posit and affirm all that is affirmed of beings, and, more properly, to deny it all, because the cause transcends everything. And we must not think that the negations contradict the affirmations; seeing that the cause is above all negation and all affirmation, we must believe it to be all the more above all lack.[35]

*

Next Dionysius deals with the stance of the student, and this section falls into two parts, the first indicating what the student's stance should be, the second proving it by authority.

The first part is divided into two: first the author deals with the student's stance in receiving teaching, then he deals with the communication of it to others.

The procedure which he teaches Timothy, to whom he is writing and who epitomizes the student, is to "abandon the senses and the workings of the intellect" with regard to mystic understanding, and to do so with "strong contrition," crushing them, as it were, under the divine light, and to abandon "all that is known to the senses or the intellect," because none of these things is God. "Known to the intellect" here means "comprehended by the intellect."[36] Similarly he must abandon "all that is existent" in fact and "all that is non-existent," being merely potential, because God is not categorized with other things that exist, as if he formed a class with them. And thus he should "rise to imitate God who is above all being and knowledge," inasmuch as the mind in which the image of God is reformed by habitual grace or glory actually imitates God. Another reading has "rise to be united with God," and this corresponds

---

35. If the negations were taken simply to be contradicting the affirmations, we should end up ascribing to God a *lack* of something, whereas God is actually beyond both affirmations and negations. The affirmation says that God does not lack whatever it may be; the negation insists that he does not have it in the limiting way in which we have our properties. But neither comes anywhere near actually describing God.

36. In the more common, weaker sense, God is obviously among the *intelligibilia* (things known by the intellect rather than perceived by the senses); so Albert takes Dionysius to be meaning something stronger here: God is not among those things of which the mind can have a comprehensive understanding.

to the other translation, which has "rise to unity,"[37] that is, simplicity. And in this way he is to be "carried upward to the ray of divine darkness, removing everything" (abandoning everything) and "going out of himself unrestrainably," that is, not holding himself back within reason's own principles.

Several questions arise out of this.

(1) Why does the author instruct his student more carefully here than in his other books?

(2) Without the workings of the intellect nothing can be known. So since his aim is to bring his student into some kind of knowledge, he ought not to tell him to abandon the workings of the intellect, he ought rather to encourage him to take them up energetically.

(3) In the theological negations which are the concern of this science it is necessary to begin with the things of the senses, so he ought not to tell his student to abandon the senses.

(4) Nothing goes outside itself, so in bidding his student to do so he is apparently bidding him do something impossible.

The answers to these points are as follows:

(1) In his other books about God the things of God are brought to us by way of what is manifest to us, but in this book we have to go to God and become united with him. So this is the complete perfection of the knowledge of God, and therefore it calls for a greater perfection in the student.

(2) Dionysius bids us abandon the workings of the intellect which are connatural to us, not those which are in us by virtue of the divine light.[38]

(3) He bids us abandon the senses only inasmuch as we have to

---

37. Albert seems to have had a defective text of Sarracenus, reading *ad eius imitationem* instead of *ad eius unitionem*. The "other translation" is that of Eriugena, which has *ad unitatem*.

38. The intellect, simply with its own resources, is not adapted to the knowledge of God, but it is made capable of knowing God by the illuminations which come down to it from God (*DN* 1.21, Col. XXXVII p.11:28–35); and this is not unnatural to the intellect, because the intellect possesses an inherent potentiality for such enlightenment by God (*potentia obedientiae*, ibid. 1.27, p.13:61–3) and, as we saw in the Introduction, all intellectual activity in fact requires some such enlightenment from on high (I *Sent.* d.2 a.5, B 25 pp.59–60; *Dion. Ep.* 5, Col. XXXVII p.496). And however much any created mind is boosted by supernatural illumination from God, it still works in the way which is natural to it (*Dion. Ep.* 1, Col. XXXVII p.481). "Far from being radically abolished, our natural or philosophical ways of grasping things are henceforth integrated, by means of their being subjected to the supernatural light, into the new epistemological edifice constituted by the mystical darkness of faith" (E. H. Wéber, AMDU p. 439).

abandon the delight we can have in them; he does not mean that it is wrong for us to go to God by way of the negation of things perceived by the senses.

(4) Nothing goes out of itself in the sense that it could exist outside itself, but its power can be extended above itself inasmuch as it is carried toward an object which is higher than itself, and this is what is being recommended here.

Next (a) he lays down the proper procedure in communicating this doctrine to others; after that (b) he replies to a question.

(a) First he debars philosophers from sharing in this science, then idolaters. So first of all he says that Timothy must be careful here not to let anyone who is "uninstructed" in the doctrine of God "hear" these mystical teachings. He calls "unlearned" those whose hearts and minds are "shaped" by "beings," from which we receive knowledge, and so they do not believe that anything "exists supersubstantially above beings," incommensurably, that is, with beings. So even philosophers say that the first mover is proportionate to the first thing moved.[39] What they do believe is that they can know "him who makes darkness his hiding place" (God, that is) "with their own kind of knowledge," that is, by way of rational principles. In this way Augustine is said to have wanted in the conceit of his vain philosophy to comprehend with his human reason what the devout mind strives to apprehend with the liveliness of faith.[40]

But there are two difficulties:

(1) On the face of it, those who are not shaped like this by beings are already instructed, and as such they do not need to be instructed, and so it looks as if it is rather the people whose minds are shaped by beings who should be offered instruction.

(2) As the philosopher says, there are many people who have knowledge, but act in a way which contradicts their knowledge.[41] So there is no reason why some people should not be able to know the things of God, even though in their emotions they are shaped by beings.

---

39. Albert is probably thinking of the kind of discussion we find in Aristotle, *Physics* 8.6 and *De Caelo* 2.6, in which the first mover and the first moved are discussed strictly with reference to each other, so that little room is left for any real transcendence in the first mover.

40. The source of this citation is unknown, but cf. Bernard, *Ep.* 338.1 (where a similar comment is made about Abelard, not Augustine).

41. Cf. perhaps Aristotle, *Eth. Nic.* 7.1 (1145b12–3).

The answer is that we must say that we do not receive the things of God by means of rational principles, but experientially, in a way, by a kind of "sympathy toward them," as Dionysius says of Hierotheus, who learned the things of God "by undergoing the things of God."[42] But if our emotions are infected by an unlawful love of things, we shall not feel the sweetness of God's inspiration, and so, because of the lack of experiential knowledge, we may be able to form syllogisms and utter propositions, but we shall not have that real knowledge which is a part of beatitude.

So we may respond to the points raised as follows:

(1) It is not those who are already instructed who are to receive instruction, but people who are ready for the divine teaching because their hearts and minds have been purged from errors and lusts.

/ (2) What the philosopher is saying has to be taken as referring to the kind of knowledge which is based on rational principles, not on experiential knowledge.

Next Dionysius excludes idolaters from sharing in this teaching. He says that if the "divine teaching" about mystic realities is beyond all those who follow reason, it is much more beyond the "even more uninstructed" who only follow the senses and do not think that there is anything beyond the realm of the senses, but "construct an image" of God on the basis of "the lowest among beings." Such people are referred to in Romans as having "changed the glory of God into images of birds and serpents" (Rom. 1:23). They do not think that God is anything greater than these "impious" images which they themselves make.

(b) Since in defense of this error it might be possible to argue that God is the cause of everything and therefore everything must be predicated of him, so God is man and ought to be worshipped in human images, and similarly he ought to be worshipped in images of serpents and other things, Dionysius responds with an *anthypophora*[43] and says that God is the cause of everything yet in his

---

42. *DN* 2.9 (PG 3:648B).

43. A rhetorical technical term; *hypophora* is when a speaker raises an objection that might be made against the position he is expounding, *anthypophora* is the response to it (cf. Fortunatianus, *Rhet.* 2.27, in C. Halm, *Rhetores Latini Minores* [Leipzig, 1863], pp. 117–8; Fortunatianus' definition is quoted by Martianus Capella, *De Nuptiis* 5.563). Albert interprets the

essence he is above everything. And so it is true that everything is predicated of him as cause, yet much more essentially everything is separated from him and he is not any one of them. And these "negations do not contradict the affirmations," because they do not concern the same point; the cause of all has to be situated above both negations and affirmations, because the "whatness" of God cannot be comprehended by way of either of them.

But this raises four questions:

(1) It does not seem possible to predicate everything of God. A cause which has nothing in common with what it causes does not share in the predicates which apply to what it causes. We do not say that the sun is a human being, but we do say that sun shining on the earth is the day, because the form of the sun, namely light, is what makes it day.[44] But God has nothing in common with any creature, generically, specifically or analogously.[45] Therefore things which are affirmed of creatures cannot be predicated of God.[46]

---

sequence of Dionysius' thought on the assumption that the conclusion of this paragraph is a response to a tacit objection raised by the people accused of idolatry.

44. According to Aristotelian physics human beings are generated "by human beings and the sun" (*Physics* 2.2 (194b13); cf. Albert, *De Resurrectione* tr.1 q.2.10, Col. XXVI p.243:12–15; *De Anima* 3.1.5, Col. VII i p.171:10–2). The sun, as the primary physical cause of all that happens in the world, is the cause of human beings coming to birth, but it does not share in the predicates which apply to human beings, so it would be patently silly to call the sun a human being.

45. These are the three ways of having something in common that Aristotle lists, *De Partibus Animalium* 1.5 (645b27–8).

46. This point is stated more fully in the commentary on *DN* 13.22 (Col. XXXVII p.445:50–68). Two things have something in common in the sense that they belong to the same genus: a caterpillar and an orangutan have it in common that they are both animals. Or in the sense that they belong to the same species: two violins have it in common that they are both violins, though they are made of different wood, etc. In the case of analogy there has to be some common term and, if the analogy is to be a strict one, it has to be a term understood univocally: thus substance and accidents have "existence" in common; even though a red nose and a Red Indian exist in different *ways*, they exist in the same *sense* (red noses have only the kind of parasitic existence which is proper to accidents, but they could still be included in a list of red objects in the room on exactly the same footing as Red Indians, whereas red deans and redness could not be so included without the risk of objections being raised). But God is not of the same *kind* as any creature (no genus includes both God and creatures), nor is he of the same species as any creature, and we have to beware even of saying that there is an analogy between God and creatures in that both God and creatures "exist." When we say that "God is there" we are not making the same kind of statement as when we say "my pet gorilla is there." They are not items in the world in anything like the same sense. All that Albert will concede, as we shall see from his answer to this point, is that there is a reduced sort of analogy, an "analogy of imitation," between God and creatures: whatever it is that entitles us to say

(2) We do not say that a knife-smith is a knife, even though he works by means of the concept of a knife, which he has in himself. So it does not look as if we should predicate creatures' names of God, even though the idea of all things is in him.

(3) The proximate causes of things are not always predicated of their effects or vice versa. Much less, then, the first and most distant cause.[47]

(4) Affirmation and negation contradict each other formally when the same thing is both affirmed and denied with regard to a single object. And this is the case here. So it seems that the affirmations and negations involved do contradict each other.

In answer to this problem we must say that if an effect is to be predicated of its cause, there has to be something in common between the cause and the effect. This is why we say that, although God has nothing in common, generically, specifically or analogously with his creatures (in the sense that there is no single item found identically in him and in other things), nevertheless he does have something in common with creatures in the form of an imitative kind of analogy, in as much as other things imitate him to the extent that they are able. Some things imitate him only in being formed by his idea, such as things which do not pre-exist in him— for example, asses and stones in their own forms. These are not predicated essentially of God, but only causally. Other things imitate him as an image or likeness of him, and these pre-exist primarily in him, such as wisdom, goodness and so on. These things are predicated essentially and causally of him.[48] The situation of the crafts-

---

that some creature "is" or "is good" must be true in a prior (and, to us, incomprehensible) way in God.

47. A sculptor is a proximate cause of a statue, but we do not say that a sculptor is a statue; and remote causes are further from their effects than proximate causes and are therefore even less plausibly called by the name of their effects (cf. Albert on *DN* 5.31, Col. XXXVII p.321). But proximate causes do receive names from their effects when they operate at least causally by the transmission of some form from themselves (ibid. 5.32, p.322); the example of the sun and daylight cited above would be a case in point (and in Latin it is slightly more natural than in English to suggest that we talk of the sun in terms of day: for instance, in Latin you can say indifferently that the sun is rising or that the day is rising). So the point being made here is that proximate causes do not *always* share a common name with their effects; this means that the real question is whether there is anything in common between God and his effects. Once this has been clarified, Albert is quite right to say that no specific answer is needed to the point raised here.

48. By "essential predication" is meant claiming that some attribute genuinely belongs

man is different, because he is not the idea of the knife, although he has the idea of the knife in himself, whereas God is the idea of everything, as well as containing it, because he is whatever he has.[49] Therefore God in a certain way is susceptible of having all the names of things applied to him, just as we can apply the word "house" to the design and plan from which the house made of stone and wood is derived, as the philosopher says.[50]

This makes it clear what the answer is to the first three points.

(4) In answer to the fourth point we must say that we affirm things of God only relatively, that is, causally, whereas we deny things of God absolutely, that is, with reference to what he is in himself. And there is no contradiction between a relative affirmation and an absolute negation. It is not contradictory to say that someone is white-toothed and not white.

*

So the divine Bartholomew says that theology is both plentiful and minimal, and the gospel is broad and large and then again it is concise; it seems to me that he is noticing supernaturally that the good cause of all things is a matter of many words and at the same time of short utterance, and it is non-rational, having neither reason nor understanding, because it is placed supersubstantially above all things, and it appears unveiledly and truly only to those who pass over all that is impure and all that is pure and who climb above every ascent of all the holy limits and leave behind all divine lights and sounds and heavenly words and enter into the darkness where he truly is, as the Oracles say,[51] who is above all.

---

to what something is in itself; by "causal predication" is meant calling A "x" because A causes x.

49. Cf. above, Introduction, Part II note 70.

50. Aristotle, *Metaph*. Z 7 (1032b12–4); cf. Albert, *DN* 4.62 (Col. XXXVII p.170:84–6), where there is the same phrase "stone and wood," apparently conflated from two other passages in Aristotle (1032b30 and 1033a15).

51. Exod. 20:21.

*

Dionysius has shown us the perfection required even of a student of this science because of the exaltedness and difficulty of its subject matter. So now he adduces two authorities to prove its difficulty, one from the apostle Bartholomew, the other from Moses.

The first falls into two parts: the citation of the authority and then the comment on it.

So he first says that we have explained that with reference to God's essence everything is denied of him because of the height of his divine majesty, while at the same time everything is affirmed of him causally. "So therefore," because of this, "the divine Bartholomew" (the apostle) "says" in the gospel he wrote, which we do not use,[52] "that theology" (talking about God in general) is "plentiful" because of all God's effects and images and "minimal" with regard to what we can truly grasp of God in the conditions of this life. And the gospel in particular, containing the teaching about the Word incarnate, is "broad" because of the number of its parables and "large" because of the depth of its meaning and its mysteries, "and then again it is concise," that is, short, with reference to its purpose, which is to reveal God to us, of whom we can grasp little at present. This is why the apostle cites Isaiah in connection with the gospel, "The Lord will make his word shortened upon the earth" (Rom. 9:28).[53]

Next Dionysius comments on the authority he has cited. "It seems to me" (this expresses humility) "that the divine Bartholomew is noticing supernaturally," moved, that is, by the divine light, "that the good cause of all things" (God) "is a matter of many words" inasmuch as he is talked about with the names of the things he causes, "and at the same time of short utterance" (of few words) because there is little we can say of him as he is in himself. And he says that he is "non-rational," because we cannot reason about him, "having neither reason" (definition)[54] "nor understanding"—this is to be

---

52. The existence of an apocryphal Gospel of Bartholomew is attested by several church fathers (cf. E. Hennecke, *New Testament Apocrypha* I [London, 1963], pp.484–507), but it is extremely unlikely that Dionysius is really quoting from it. His alleged quotation is designed to give added substance to his pseudonymous persona.

53. Isaiah 10:23, as found in the Septuagint.

54. This passage is held together by the word *ratio*, which Albert takes here to mean "definition." The underlying Greek probably means that God is "wordless" (ἄλογος), rather

taken passively, in the sense that he cannot be comprehended by any understanding—"because it" (the cause) "is placed above all things" (in the exaltedness of its nature) "supersubstantially" (this refers to its manner of existing) "and it appears unveiledly" (as to our way of receiving it) "and truly" (as to its objective truth), and this is seen only by those who, in their movement toward God, "pass over" (transcend) "all that is impure" (material creatures) "and all that is pure" (immaterial creatures) "and climb above every ascent of all the holy limits." This refers to the angelic "limits" and "limits" means the point at which a lower nature touches a higher, the highest point of the lower nature touching the lowest point of the higher. Since God is above all natures, all these limits have to be transcended if we are to come to him. "And leave behind" even "all divine lights and sounds and heavenly words," that is, the illuminations which God sends us but which are not God, "and enter into the darkness," that is, the hiddenness of the Godhead, the darkness being caused by our insufficiency, "where God truly is, who is above all, as the Oracles say," in the verse of the Psalm, "Darkness is under his feet" (Ps. 17:10).

There are several questions which arise out of this:

(1) The author seems to be contradicting himself. In the first chapter of the *Celestial Hierarchy* he said that "it is impossible for the divine ray to shine on us except veiled in a variety of sacred coverings,"[55] but here he says that it appears unveiledly to those who transcend everything. So on the face of it he is contradicting himself.

(2) To receive divine illuminations unveiledly is to be the first recipient of them, but this is not natural to human beings, because this is precisely where the human soul differs from the angels, as Alexander says.[56] So at least in this life we apparently cannot see the things of God unveiledly.

---

than "non-rational"; this is how it is taken by A. Louth, p.173, and P. Scazzoso in his translation, *Dionigi Areopagita: Tutte le Opere* (Milan, 1983), pp.407–8, and also by C. Luibheid in his translation of the Paulist Press Classics of Western Spirituality 1987 volume on Dionysius, p. 136.

55. *CH* 1.2 (p.72).

56. This is a reference to the often quoted definition of the soul in Alfred of Sareshel, *De Motu Cordis* Prol. 1 (ed. C. Baeumker, Beiträge XXIII/1–2 [Münster, 1923], p.2): the soul "is the last to receive the illuminations which come from the first." This work was dedicated to Alexander Neckham and, as a consequence, was very often ascribed to him.

(3) In the *Celestial Hierarchy* it says that a lower nature at its highest point touches the lowest extremity of a higher nature.[57] So it is impossible for it to go beyond its limit. But the angels have a higher nature than ours, so it seems to be impossible for us to transcend the limits of angels, which is what the text literally says here.

(4) In the chapter on peace in the *Divine Names* he said that souls must first be united in themselves and then, through that intellect which is immaterial and simple, come to union with God.[58] So it seems that we ought not to leave the angels behind (they are the immaterial intellects), we ought rather to unite ourselves with them as far as possible in order to come to God.

(5) Divine lights are given to us to strengthen our understanding so that it can know God. But if you are moving toward some goal, you ought not to abandon what facilitates your ascent toward that goal. So apparently we ought not to abandon divine lights in order to know God, we ought rather to cleave to them strongly.

(6) What is the difference between divine lights and heavenly sounds and words?

The answer to these questions is as follows:

(1) The contemplation of God can be viewed in two ways. It can be viewed (a) with reference to the medium in which we contemplate God or the starting point of contemplation, and it is in this sense that Dionysius says in the *Celestial Hierarchy* that we cannot see the divine ray in this life without its covering of signs and effects, because "we now see in a glass and enigmatically."[59] Or (b) contemplation can be viewed in terms of the goal of contemplation or the object which we seek by contemplation, and this is God himself, unveiled. And this is where we arrive ultimately, when we reach the level of purely intellectual natures. Rational investigation would be futile if it never arrived at intellectual union. And it is in this sense that Dionysius speaks here.

(2) All contemplators of God desire to see the same thing. So from that point of view there is no diversity at all. Diversity arises

---

57. Albert uses this formula several times in his commentary on *DN* (e.g., Col. XXXVII p.129:66, p.137:56–7, p.359:64–7), but it does not appear as such in Dionysius. St. Thomas quotes the same principle and gives Dionysius, *DN* 7 as his reference (cf. 7.3, PG 3:872B): I *Sent.* d.3 q.4 a.1 ad 4; *Summa Theol.* I q.78 a.2.

58. *DN* 11.2 (PG 3:949D).

59. 1 Cor. 13:12.

in the way in which God is seen, because it is natural for some of them to receive God without any veil, whereas for others it is natural to receive him under a veil.

(3) "Transcending" something in contemplation can mean two different things. If it refers to our power of contemplation, in that sense we cannot transcend or even equal the angels in this life, even though we are raised by the divine light above the capacity of our own nature; if it refers to the object of contemplation, in that sense we do transcend even the angels in contemplating, because what we are looking for is above everything. This is what it says in the Canticle, "Shortly after I had passed on from them, I found him whom my soul loves" (Cant. 3:4).

(4) We ought not to be united with the angels as if they were our object, but we should be united with them through the lights which come down to us through them, by which we are raised up to the contemplation of God.

(5) We ought to cleave to the divine lights, that is, the illuminations sent us by God, but not as if they were our object; we should regard them as the medium in which our object is seen and as strengthening our intellect, but our desire does not stop at them, as if they were our highest good.

(6) There are two ways in which our intellect is raised toward God. One is the way of discovery, in which the intellect, as it were, rises up of its own accord toward God, and in this sense the divine lights guide it on its way, because light brings our faculty of sight to perfection and sight is the chief instrument of discovery. The other way is when our intellect is raised toward God by means of various signs which he sends us, in which we have a kind of experience of him, like the way in which words give us an impression of the things which they signify. Signs like this may be directed toward our emotions, filling us with a joy which cannot be explained or even conceptualized, and this is what Dionysius refers to as "sounds." Since our emotions cannot be enunciated, they are expressed by interjections, like the *jubilus* mentioned in the commentary on Psalm 46:6 ("God goes up with a *jubilus*"), "This is an unspeakable joy which it is impossible either to contain in silence or to express in words."[60] Or signs may be addressed to the intellect,

---

60. Lombard's gloss on Ps. 46 (PL 191:456A).

inasmuch as it receives some conception of God, and this is what "words" refers to, because words express the concepts of the mind. And all this kind of thing has to be transcended, because none of them is the object we are looking for in contemplation.

*

It is not simply that the divine Moses is first of all commanded to be purified himself and then to separate himself from those who are not such, and after all this purification he hears the many-voiced trumpets and sees many lights brilliantly emitting pure and widely-radiating beams. Then he separates himself from the crowd and, with select priests, reaches the height of the divine ascents. And even so he is not with God, he contemplates not God himself—who is invisible—but the place where God is. I think this signifies that the most divine objects of sight or intellect are certain subordinate principles of things which are subordinate to him who transcends everything, by means of which his presence, which is above all thinking, is shown riding above the intellectual heights of his holiest places. And then he breaks loose from all that is seen and all that sees and enters the darkness of unknowing, the darkness which is truly mystical, in which he shuts off all his cognitive impressions, and comes to be in that which is entirely impalpable and invisible, belonging totally to him who is above all, and to no one, neither himself nor anyone else, united to him who is utterly unknown by the cessation of all knowledge, for the best,[61] knowing beyond mind by knowing nothing.

---

61. *Secundum melius* (κατὰ τὸ κρεῖττον) properly qualifies the "cessation of all knowledge" and means "in a good sense," to prevent misunderstanding—there are obviously bad ways of abandoning knowledge. The construction and the meaning have generally been missed by commentators and translators here, in spite of the parallel passage in *Ep.* 9.5 (which the translators generally get right) and the similar discussion in Iamblichus, *De Mysteriis* 3.25 and the comparable use of the contrasting phrases κατὰ τὸ χεῖρον, κατὰ τὸ κρεῖττον elsewhere (e.g., several times in Damascius, *De Principiis*). The word order, both in the Greek and in the Latin, has tempted modern scholars, as it tempted Albert, falsely to link *secundum melius* with *unitus*, resulting in the translation "united for the best," which has to be adopted if Albert's commentary is to make sense.

DIONYSIUS' MYSTICAL THEOLOGY

*

Next Dionysius demonstrates both the difficulty of the subject matter and the need for serious preparation on the part of the student by using the example of Moses (Exod. 19:10ff).

This part falls into two sections: first, the story itself, then its meaning.

So he says first that we have stated that anyone wanting to ascend to the mystery of the divine darkness must be cleansed of everything. For "it is not simply" (not without a mystery of great significance) "that the divine Moses is first of all commanded to be purified himself," both in his emotions, which must be purged of all earthly affections, and in his understanding, which must be purged of all that is not God. "And then" secondly he is commanded "to separate himself from those who are not such" (not pure, that is), to ensure that he is not defiled by consorting with them and that he does not share with them the holy things he sees. Thirdly, "after all this purification he hears the many-voiced trumpets," the multiple divine precepts, that is, resounding in his soul. And fourthly "he sees many lights" (divine revelations) "emitting beams" (different kinds of knowledge), "pure beams" (uncontaminated by material appearances), "widely-radiating" (covering many objects of knowledge which become known through these beams). Fifthly, "he separates himself from the crowd" (the people), as it says in Exodus 20:21, "The people stood afar off and Moses went toward the darkness, where God was." Anyone who contemplates the things of God is separated not only from the impure but also from the imperfect. Sixthly, "with select priests" (priests chosen by God) "he reaches the height of the divine ascents," that is, the highest levels of divine contemplation, as it says in Exodus 24:1, "God spoke to Moses, 'Go up to the Lord, you and Aaron, Nadab and Abiu and the seventy elders of Israel.' " "And even so he is not with God," that is, he does not see God himself, "but" seventhly "he contemplates, not God himself—who is invisible—but the place where God is," that is, he sees him in his most outstanding creatures, in which he is, as it were, enthroned. And this comes from Exodus 33:20–21, where the Lord says to Moses, "No human being shall see me and live. . . . Lo, here is a place by me, and you shall stand on the rock."

Next comes Dionysius' commentary on all this. "I think that

this" (what has just been described) "signifies that the most divine objects of sight or intellect," whatever we see concerning God, that is, by the most noble revelations or whatever we come to understand by the highest contemplation in this life, are not God, but "certain principles" (appearances)[62] "of things which are subordinate" to God "who transcends everything," and these "principles" are "subordinate," that is, they are lower than God, though they are relevant inasmuch as God is in his noblest creatures and effects; through them his (God's) most divine "presence, which is above all thinking, is shown," for he is present in all his effects and in a special way he is present in the effects of grace or glory. "His presence is shown riding above the intellectual heights of his holiest places," God's holiest places, that is, and these "places" mean the angels who receive in their highest powers the presence of God coming upon them through its effects of glory, and it is in their light that our soul sees the things of God, in that it is enlightened by them about the things of God. "And then," when Moses sees these most divine things, "he breaks loose from all that is seen" (the visible beams), because they are not the object of his contemplation, and from the others who see (the priests mentioned above); this is why the others are told, "You shall worship from afar, and Moses alone will go up to the Lord" (Exod. 24:1–2). And being thus separated from all "he enters the darkness of unknowing," in which God is said to have been, because he is unknown to us; and this "darkness is truly mystical" (hidden, that is) "in which he shuts off all his cognitive impressions," that is, all the natural powers of the soul which know things by receiving impressions and which, if they are separated from everything else, are filled solely with the divine darkness. And thus, by the adherence of his intellect, "he comes to be in that which is entirely impalpable and invisible," because what he finds in this way cannot be perceived by the senses or comprehended by the intellect, "belonging totally to him who is above all" (God), by being completely turned toward him, "belonging to no one" (no one other than God), "neither himself nor anyone else," because he is turned to nothing except God, but being "united for the best" (in the best possible way

---

62. "Principles" translates *rationes* (λόγους); "appearances" translates *species*. The link between them is the notion of "form"—the *ratio* of something (the principle of its intelligibility) is its "form" (*species*). But here *species* seems also to carry its more basic meaning, "appearance."

of being united) "with him who is utterly unknown" (God) "by the cessation of all" natural "knowledge," because he does not turn to other things which are naturally known, but only to God, who is known by no natural knowledge, "by knowing nothing" with any natural knowledge, "knowing beyond mind," beyond the nature of his own mind; this is made possible by the divine light infused from above, by which the mind is raised above itself.

To clarify all this, we need to discuss three questions:
(I) Is all such contemplation of God rapture?
(II) Is it "for the best" that our mind should be united to the utterly unknown?
(III) Did Moses see God himself?

(I) (1) It appears that this kind of contemplation always involves rapture. Whenever we are abstracted from our lower powers and only the higher power[63] remains active, that is rapture. But this is what happens in this kind of contemplation, because the contemplator is united with the unknown God for the best by the cessation of all knowing. Therefore the contemplation of God appears always to involve rapture.

(2) When our lower nature follows the impetus of our higher nature, it is caught up, rapt, into it. And this happens when we are contemplating God, because the contemplator, as our text says here, becomes totally his who is above everything. So rapture appears to be always involved in the contemplation of God.

(3) The darkness of unbounded light appears not to shut off all our cognitive impressions. The senses are a capacity for knowledge which functions by receiving impressions of forms, as the philosopher says,[64] but they are not capable of receiving the divine light nor can they reach out toward it, because it is immaterial. So they are not shut off by its darkness. If they are shut off by going idle themselves, that is surely always a case of rapture.

(4) If the contemplator is in no way his own, as Dionysius says, then he is abstracted from all that is his. And this includes his nat-

---

63. According to Albert's commentary on *Ep.* 9 (Col. XXXVII p.537:25–26) the "higher part" of the soul is the intellect.

64. Aristotle, *De Anima* 2.12 (424a17–9).

ural processes. Therefore he is abstracted from his own natural processes. And this is plainly false, because the workings of nature, such as digestion and the absorption of nourishment, do not cease.

(5) The soul of anyone contemplating in this life is in some way in the body. But the primary powers of the soul are those which work in our natural functions, and so if we are abstracted from these, the soul will not remain in the body at all, and this is not the case.

(6) What is the difference between the knowledge obtained by this kind of contemplation in this life and the comprehension of truth in heaven? Since in both cases there is an absorption in the divine light, there appears to be no difference at all.

In response we must say that rapture is not involved in all contemplation of God, and what is said here of contemplation applies to all contemplation, not just to rapture, which is the best part of contemplation.

The answers to the points raised are as follows:

(1) In rapture there is an abstraction from the use of our lower powers, because no use at all is being made of them. But in the contemplation of God in general there is no such abstraction from their use, because some use of them remains; but there is an abstraction in the sense of a relaxation of their intensity, because the soul pays no attention to their workings and their action is weakened, because when one of our powers is working with particular intensity, another power is weakened in its operation, as the philosopher says.[65]

(2) In the contemplation of God our lower nature follows the impetus of our higher nature in the sense that our higher nature becomes its object, and it directs itself exclusively toward it as such, but not in the sense that it is totally fixed in attendance upon our higher nature and separated from its own functioning, which is what happens in rapture.

(3) The unbounded light shuts off some of our cognitive powers

---

65. The source of this dictum appears to be Aristotle, *De Sensu* 7 (447a14–5); cf. Albert, *De Homine* q.48 a.1 (B 35 pp.429–30); *Super Ethica* 3.3.171 (Col. XIV p.153); *De Sensu et Sensato* 3.3 (B 9 p.83); *De Anima* 3.1.1 (Col. VII i p.167). Its development in Albert's mind owes something to Averroes, *Compendium Libri Arist. de Somno et Vigilia* (ed. E. L. Shields [Cambridge, Mass: 1949], p.113). The point can be illustrated from Albert's sermons: people can be so engrossed in their studies that they do not know whether or not they have eaten and that they look for things that they are actually holding in their hands; hours can go by without their noticing (AFP 34 [1964] pp.55–6).

directly, namely, the powers of our understanding, which are capable of reaching out to it. Our other cognitive powers, those of the senses, it shuts off by an indirect influence, inasmuch as the higher powers move the lower powers and a kind of token of higher things results in the lower powers.

(4) The contemplator is separated even from his natural powers, not in the sense that they stop functioning, but in the sense that he is not doing anything with them, both because the soul pays no attention to what they are doing and because they do not act with any intensity and so little energy is taken up by them, so that they are capable of enduring a long fast just as, at the other end of the scale, as the philosopher says, our digestion does its work better when we are asleep, when our animal powers are idle, than when we are awake, with our senses free.[66]

(5) This shows what the answer is to the fifth point: the soul is in the body with reference to the functioning of the natural powers.

(6) The two kinds of knowledge are different, because in heaven God is seen directly, whereas in this life he is contemplated in the effects of grace and light which flow from him into the soul. Also in heaven the vision of God will free us perfectly from all wretchedness, and this does not happen here. Finally in heaven we shall know God by being in a state of glory, whereas here we know him by being in a state of grace.

(II) (1) On the face of it, it is not "for the best" that the intellect is united with the utterly unknown. Any power is destroyed by being joined to something which exceeds its capacity, and it is not "for the best" to be united with anything if the result is going to be destruction. So since the "unknown" in question is unknown because of the excess of its light, our mind is surely not united with it for the best.

(2) Our understanding is better united with something known than with something unknown, because knowledge is the way in which it comes to be united with things. So it is apparently not for the best that it is united with the unknown.

(3) If we know of something "that" it is, it is not utterly unknown, and we do know of God "that" he is, so he is not utterly unknown.

---

66. Aristotle, *De Somno* 1 (454b32–455a2).

(4) Nothing enjoys being absorbed. And the best kind of union is one which results in enjoyment. So if the contemplative intellect is absorbed in the divine light, its union with it appears not to be for the best.

In response we must say that the best kind of union for anything is when it is united with its own ultimate perfection and when it is united with what is best. But God is what is best and he is the ultimate perfection of our intellects, so for our intellect being united with him is for the very best.

The answers to the points raised are as follows:

(1) This claim is true with regard to the powers of the senses; because they are material and attached to material organs, they are destroyed by any object which is too much for them because it ruins the sense organ. But, as the philosopher himself says, the case is different with regard to the intellect; when the intellect takes to itself the most intelligible objects, its ability to grasp lesser objects is enhanced, not reduced.[67] So the intellect is strengthened, not ruined, by being united to the divine light. Or we can say that even if it would be ruined by being united in its natural condition to too brilliant a light, nevertheless since it is by means of a supernatural condition that it is united with this light, it is not ruined, it is made perfect.

(2) The intellect is not profitably united with something which is intrinsically unknown, but it is excellent for it to be united with what is unknown to us, but in itself supremely knowable, because by being united with it it acquires more and more knowledge of it; and God is this kind of unknown, as the philosopher says.[68]

(3) Inasmuch as knowing "that" is a particular mode of natural knowledge identified by the philosophers,[69] we do not know God in this way. The philosopher identifies knowledge "that" as deriving either from a remote cause, or from an effect which is convertible

---

67. Aristotle, *De Anima* 3.4 (429a29–b4).

68. The reference is presumably to Aristotle, *Metaph.* α 1 (993b7–11), which Albert uses in a similar context in the commentary on *DN* 7.25 (Col. XXXVII p.356:32–40).

69. In Aristotelian philosophy, full-fledged knowledge means knowing "why," that is to say, being able to give an explanation of why something is the case, such that the thing being explained can be shown to follow *necessarily* from the alleged cause. If we can do no more than demonstrate "that" something is the case, the result is a second-class kind of knowledge, knowledge "that."

with and proportionate to its cause.[70] And we cannot know anything of God in either of these ways, and so there is no kind of natural knowledge by which he is known, neither knowledge "that" or knowledge "why," nor is he known by the senses or by the reason or by the understanding.[71] Instead we have a supernatural knowledge of him in an indistinct kind of way.

(4) Anything which is absorbed in such a way as to lose its own nature is rendered insensible and does not rejoice in it, but whatever is absorbed by its own perfection becomes perfect by being absorbed and its enjoyment is brought to the full.

(III)   (1) Moses appears to have seen God himself. It is God himself

---

70. Aristotle, *Post Anal.* 1.13 (78a22–38). The first way of arriving at knowledge "that" is illustrated by Albert with the question why a wall does not breathe. To answer, "Because it is not an animal," is insufficient, since it does not isolate the crucial factor. It is true that only animals breathe, so if a wall is not an animal, it follows that it does not breathe; but not all animals breathe, so even if a wall were an animal it would not follow that it does breathe. For a real explanation of why a wall does not breathe we need to identify the physiological conditions which produce breathing, whose presence genuinely explains the presence of breathing and whose absence therefore genuinely explains the absence of breathing (I *Post Anal.* 3.6, B 2 p.84). It should be noticed that "knowledge" in this context means more than sheer knowledge of a brute fact, it means being able to give an account of something (cf. Aristotle, *Post. Anal.* 2.19, 100b10), so J. Barnes is justified in translating ἐπίστασθαι "understanding" (*Complete Works of Aristotle* [Princeton, 1984], I p.127). The second way of arriving at knowledge "that" is illustrated by Aristotle himself: a "convertible" effect is one which is so linked to its cause that the presence of the one will always mean the presence of the other, but the cause will *explain* the presence of the effect, thus giving us knowledge "why," whereas the presence of the effect does not explain the presence of the cause, it merely allows us to infer it. So, according to Aristotle, the reason why planets do not twinkle is that they are too close to the earth; thus we can demonstrate *why* they do not twinkle from their closeness to the earth, but from the fact of their not twinkling we can only demonstrate *that*, not *why*, they are close to the earth.

71. Albert is here talking about knowledge "that" as a precise, if inadequate, brand of philosophical knowledge, and in the case of God all that we have is a confused and indeterminate knowledge "that" he is, which is innate in us, but falls short even of Aristotle's definition of knowledge "that" (cf. *DN* 7.25, Col. XXXVII pp.356–7). Albert's "proofs" of the existence of God are far less rigorous and ambitious than those of Thomas (cf. Craemer-Ruegenberg pp.52–5) and rely essentially on *reductio ad absurdum* of the claim that God does not exist (cf. *Summa Theol.* 3.17, Col. XXXIV i pp.84–5). The fact of God is essentially a mystery of intelligibility that we have to take for granted and can explore but not comprehend (cf. ibid. 3.13.1, pp.40–1). As F. J. Catania remarks, "Albert could have espoused a fideism. And, in fact, there are aspects of his position that could support such a judgment in the end. But if Albert's position is fideistic after all, it is a fideism which is held off as long as possible as he returns again and again to those aspects of our ordinary processes of knowing that seem to be open to the sorts of extension that are necessary with the unique object, God" (" 'Knowable' and 'Namable' " in Kovach and Shahan, p.102).

who is seen in face-to-face vision, because this is what is promised us in heaven by the apostle (1 Cor. 13:12). But this is how Moses saw God, because it says of him in Exodus 33:11, "The Lord spoke to Moses face to face." Otherwise his prayer would have been in vain, "Show me your face" (Exod. 33:13). So he appears to have seen God himself.

(2) How is it possible that one could be contemplating God in the noblest kind of contemplation and yet not see God himself, as Moses did? And since many things come together in our natural intellectual processes—the abstraction of forms from images, their union with the possible intellect and the illumination by the agent intellect—to which of these is the knowledge involved in such exalted contemplation to be assimilated?

In response we must say that Moses did not see God himself in himself, he saw him in his most noble effects, effects of grace and of theophanies, the latter being manifested images of the divine goodness.

So we may answer the points raised as follows:

(1) "Seeing the face" can mean two different things. If it is taken to mean seeing God's face in itself, without any veil, then this is how it will be seen in heaven, but it is not how Moses saw it; Moses saw God's face in certain signs of God's effects, which Dionysius here calls "subordinate principles," and in the passage of scripture referred to they are called God's "back" (Exod. 33:23). So the Lord said to him, "You will see my back, but my face you will not be able to see."

(2) There is a link-up of lights in sense-perception, and there is a similar link-up of intellectual lights.[72] Now the things of God cannot be learned from any kind of probable or necessary inferences from first principles, and the light of the agent intellect has no other tools which it can wield as its own except first principles; so if it is

---

72. On the link-up of "lights" involved in bridging the gap between the visible object and the sense-organ, cf. Albert's *Quaestio Disputata de Prophetia* 83.1 (ed. J. P. Torrell, RSPT 65 [1981] p.27); on Albert's theory of sense-perception, see L. Dewan, "St. Albert, the Sensibles and Spiritual Being," in Weisheipl, *Albert*, pp.291–320. On the intellectual "link-up" cf. I *Sent.* d.2 a.5 (B 25 pp.59–60), translated above in Part II of the Introduction, pp.56–57. Albert's theory of how our minds receive light from on high enables him to answer the objection raised above: such illumination does not have to be identified with any of the "lights" listed in the objection, and it is possible for the mind to be raised to considerable heights without actually attaining to the direct vision of God.

to know the things of God it needs the light of the angels' intellect to come to it, which effects a variety of appearances in our souls in which the things of God are seen, reflecting the more unified way in which these appearances exist in the angels themselves, as was explained in the *Celestial Hierarchy*.[73] The philosopher too says in his *Divination in Dreams* that because they cannot be arrived at by way of any systematic speculation on the basis of first principles; the intellect receives them by being united to some higher moving powers.[74] It is much more the case that the soul is fortified to see the things of God by having the divine light coming down into it. Maybe both procedures are combined.[75] And this light is called the "mirror of eternity," in which the prophets saw their visions. But it is not God,[76] it merely comes from God, and it is the equivalent of the light of the agent intellect in the case of natural knowledge. These are the "declarations" of which Dionysius speaks here, which he also calls "divine objects of sight." This makes it clear how it is not God himself who is seen even in the most noble forms of contemplation, and this answers our question.

CHAPTER TWO

How we must be united and offer hymns to the cause of all, who is above all.

To this more than radiant darkness we pray to be brought, by not seeing and not knowing, to see and know him who is above seeing and knowing, in this very not-seeing and not-knowing. For this is truly to see and know him who is above substance and to praise him supersubstantially by separating from him all beings, as if we were making an

---

73. Cf. Dionysius, *CH* 15.3 (p.175), and Albert's comment, 15.6 (B 14 p.424).

74. This has only a tenuous connection with Aristotle, but *De Homine* q.50 a.1 and a.3, q.51 (B 35 pp.436–7, 440, 441) show how Albert developed his own theory on the basis of Aristotle, *De Div. Somn.* 1–2 (462b25–6, 463a31–b3, 463b14).

75. I.e., both angelic illumination and direct divine illumination (as suggested in I *Sent.* d.2 a.5, B 25 p.60a).

76. On the *speculum aeternitatis* cf. *QD de Prophetia* II.1, ed. cit. pp.24–8 with Torrell's comments, pp.212–4.

image of his very nature, removing the obstacles which get in the way of a pure vision of what is hidden and revealing the hidden beauty for what it is simply by this removal. But, as I think, we must celebrate the removals in a way opposite to the affirmations. When we were making affirmations, we began with the first and moved down through the intermediate ones to the most remote, but here we ascend from the most remote toward those that are more primary and then again through the intermediate ones to the topmost ones, removing them all so that we may have an unveiled knowledge of that unknowing which is veiled all round by all that is knowable in all beings, and see that supersubstantial darkness which is hidden by all the light in beings.

*

In the previous chapter Dionysius laid down the proper attitude of someone practicing this science, whether as a teacher or as a student, with regard to the reception of this teaching. Now, because the reception of this teaching leads to that union in which we are made one with the things of God, in this chapter he specifies the position with regard to union itself, telling us how we have to be united with God in our understanding and praise him with our voices. This is apparent from the title of the chapter, "How we must be united and offer hymns to the cause of all, who is above all."

The chapter falls into two parts: in the first Dionysius lays down the manner in which we are united with God, namely, by way of negations; in the second part he indicates the difference between theological negations and theological affirmations.

In the previous chapter, in which he specified the proper way of receiving this teaching, he began with a prayer because of the exalted nature of the teaching, and here he does the same: "We pray to be brought" (by God) "to this darkness," in which God is, a darkness which is obscure to us but is "more than radiant" in itself; and we pray that "in this very not-seeing and not-knowing," that is, precisely in the cessation of all our natural forms of knowledge, "by not seeing and not knowing" (these being a kind of route by which we pursue our course) we may "see and know him who is above all seeing and knowing," namely, God. "Seeing" should be taken as referring to the way in which our understanding simply "sees" first principles; "knowing" refers to the way in which we know conclusions which follow from first principles. Thus God will be known as a principle, when we receive him as the light of our intellect, and by means of this divine light we are led to the attributes of God as to a kind of conclusion, knowing him to be wise, good and so on. And we pray "to praise him" (God) "who is above substance supersubstantially," that is, in a way which transcends all beings, "by separating from him all beings, as if we were making an image," shaping a representation, "of his very nature, removing" (by removing, that is) from our mind's eye "the obstacles which get in the way of" (interfere with, damage) "the pure vision of" the God who is "hidden," the sort of vision by which we want to see God without any reference to any of his effects, thereby "revealing the hidden beauty" (of God) for what it is; as if to say that precisely by having everything denied of it, the transcendence of the beauty of God is represented as by a formed image. Alternatively, as the commentator suggests[1], it is like stone-cutting: when you cut a piece of stone and take it away, the surface that was previously hidden by the piece you have removed can now be seen to bear certain images of things, something that looks like an ear or a lamb or a dog, though of course these are only images, not the real things. Similarly when we separate things from God we discover something like the divine nature, though it is not the divine nature in itself, only something which reveals the divine nature. For instance, by separating from him all the non-living, what we are left with is that he is alive, even though life, as we use the word, means the coming forth of life and this is not the divine nature, though it is a likeness of it which reveals it.

Next Dionysius indicates the difference between theological negations and theological affirmations and says that in affirmative theology "we begin with the first" and nobler affirmations "and

---

1. This interpretation comes from the Latin scholia of Anastasius, derived from the Greek (cf. PG 4:421–4), and it is clear that it is what Dionysius had in mind: an αὐτοφυὲς ἄγαλμα is an image found naturally in a piece of stone or wood (such as Albert himself witnessed in Venice as a young man: *Mineralia* II 3.1, B 5 pp. 48–9, AT 82); Sarracenus' rendering, *ipsius naturae insigne* is thoroughly misleading.

move down through the intermediate ones" as far as "the most remote." Accordingly he first, in the *Outlines*[2], spoke about the properties of God in himself, then in the *Divine Names* he dealt with the
spiritual qualities that flow from God and belong properly to him,
beginning there too with the most noble, such as "good" and
"being"; finally he discussed the symbols taken from the realm of
the senses, in the *Symbolic Theology*. But in negative theology it is the
other way round: in denying things of God, we have to begin with
"the most remote," the lowest things, that is, and, proceeding via
"those that are more primary," which are "intermediate," "ascend
to the topmost." For instance, we could begin by saying that God
is not a stone and that he is not a lion and so on, with reference to
other things belonging to the realm of the senses, then we could go
on to say that he is neither living nor life and so on, so that, proceeding in this way, we might "have knowledge of that unknowing,"
of that divine transcendence which is unknown to us, "unveiled
knowledge," without any veil of creatures, knowledge of that "unknowing which is veiled all round by all that is knowable in all
beings." In all the things that are known by their forms[3] the forms
themselves are images of God's own beauty, and by denying them
we arrive at that hidden reality which was expressed in them in a
veiled way. Dionysius returns to the same point in what follows:
"And see that supersubstantial darkness" of the divine transcendence, "which is hidden by all the light" that is "in beings," just as
the reality of something is hidden in an image which represents it in
an alien nature.

To clarify what is said in this chapter we need to raise three
questions:

(I) Can we know and see God by not-seeing and not-knowing?

(II) What about the manner in which he says we are united with
God?

(III) What about his statement that the order of negations is the
opposite of the order of negations?

---

2. Cf. chapter 1 note 9. It seems that Albert actually took the title, *Theologicae Hypo-
typoses* to mean "theological hypostases" (cf. *DN* 1.6, Col. XXXVII p. 3:63–4).

3. To know an object is to know what it means for it to be what it is (cf. Aristotle,
Metaph. Z 6, 1031b6–7), i.e., to know its "form."

(I) (1) On the face of it, God cannot be known by not-seeing. Everything which serves as a means by which something else is known must have something about it permitting what is to be known to be inferred from it, as in the case of a syllogism, or at least it must provide some sort of access to what is to be known, as the infused light of faith gives us access to the articles of the faith. But there is nothing of the kind in not-seeing and not-knowing, so they cannot be a way of coming to know God.

(2) Privation is not a way of coming to have something; it is rather the other way about.[4] And not-seeing and not-knowing means being deprived of seeing and knowing. So they are not a possible way of attaining to the knowledge and vision of God.

(3) Either the not-seeing by which God is seen posits something or it does not posit anything. If it does not posit anything, then no kind of knowledge will result from it, because nothing can be inferred from pure negatives, since there is no syllogism made up entirely of negatives. If it does posit something and denies something else, it must be a starting point for or a way to the knowledge of God either by virtue of what it denies or by virtue of what it posits. The first is impossible for the reasons given. But in the second case, it should be identified as leading to the knowledge of God by the affirmation of vision, not its denial.[5]

(4) The noblest way of seeing things is at the furthest remove from all denial of vision, just as the most completely white object is at the furthest remove from black. But, according to Augustine, the noblest kind of vision is when we see what is essentially present in

---

4. Albert seems to be rather unnecessarily complicating a commonsense observation with a logical point. The commonsense observation is clear: lacking something is not a means whereby we acquire something. The logical point is that the idea of "privation" presupposes the idea of possession, not vice versa, a point made by Albert in *DN* 4.169 (Col. XXXVII p. 255:17–9) in connection with Aristotle's definition of privation in *Metaph.* Γ 2 (1004a 15–6); you do not have to be stupid in order to be intelligent, but you do have to be intelligent in order to be stupid—something entirely devoid of intelligence, such as a stewed prune, is not properly called "stupid."

5. It is a commonplace of scholastic logic that no syllogism can be formed on the basis of two negative propositions (cf. Albert, I *Prior. Anal.* 2.7, B 1 p. 498; Petrus Hispanus, *Tractatus (Summulae Logicales)* 4.4, ed. L. M. de Rijk [Assen, 1972]; T. Gilby, *Barbara Celarent* [London, 1949], pp. 211–2). There is no reason why a useful syllogism should not be formed out of one positive and one negative proposition, but Albert is within his rights in claiming that the capacity of such a combination to yield information depends on the positive proposition.

our own soul, and this includes God.[6] So the way in which we see God is at the furthest remove from any non-seeing.

In response we must say that in the case of God all our natural ways of knowing, which are the basis of systematic understanding, lapse. He is not known per se, as first principles are, nor do we know "why" he is, because he has no cause, nor do we know "that" he is, because he produces no effect which is proportionate to himself. Instead our minds receive a certain divine light, which is above their own nature and raises them above all their natural ways of seeing things, and this is how our minds come to see God, though only in a blurred and undefined knowledge "that" he is. This is why it is said that God is seen by not-seeing: he is seen by the absence of natural seeing.

The answers to the points raised, then, are as follows:

(1) A kind of light is received in the soul which causes an absence of seeing in all our natural ways of seeing, and this light does provide a way to a blurred knowledge of God, and in this sense not-seeing does provide a way.

(2) This is not simply a case of privation, there is a reception of a kind of habitual light, which leads to the actuality of some vision of God.

(3) This indicates the answer to the third point too, because we are not dealing with pure negation; what is being denied is our natural way of seeing, and what is left is a receiving of a supernatural light which is, all the same, best indicated by negations, because we find nothing which is known to us which we can properly predicate of God because of his transcendent simplicity; genuine predication is always based on some kind of complexity[7]. As Gregory says, we "echo the high mysteries of God" by "stammering."[8]

(4) There are two senses in which we can talk about the "noblest way" of seeing things. We may be thinking of the noblest medium in which to see something, like knowledge "why," and this kind of

---

6. Augustine, *De Gen. ad Lit.* XII especially 10.21 and 31.59. That this is the passage Albert had in mind is suggested by Kilwardby's identical interpretation of it, *De Ortu Scientiarum*, ed. cit. para.222; cf. also St. Thomas, *Summa Theol.* I–II q.112 a.5.

7. Predication always involves making a connection between two distinct notions; such complexity is foreign to the nature of God.

8. Gregory, *Moralia* 5.36.66 (PL 75:715C), as reworded by Lombard, I *Sent.* d.9 c.4.2.

seeing is at the furthest remove from not-seeing.[9] And in the case of God, this "noblest way" of seeing does not exist. Or we may be thinking of the object of vision, so that the noblest kind of vision will be the vision of the noblest object. In this sense there is such a thing as the noblest kind of vision in connection with God.[10] But because of the transcendence of its object it carries with it the highest degree of non-vision, as the philosopher says.[11]

It should also be appreciated that what Augustine is saying is open to objection, because more is required for the knowledge of something than that it should be in our possible intellect: the possible intellect has to be shaped by its form and so become actual, just as matter actually becomes something through the form, not the essence, of the thing that acts upon it, even if it is something present in it.[12] This is why the philosopher says that the intellect understands itself in the same way as it understands other things.[13]

(II) (1) Creatures do not obviously interfere with our seeing of God. Nothing is at the same time both a support and an obstacle, and creatures, carrying in themselves as they do the trace and image of God, help us toward the knowledge of God. Therefore they are not an obstacle.

(2) Building up a complex understanding of something and analyzing something into its elements both proceed in the same way, because the process from first to last passes by the same intermediate

---

9. The manuscript text appears to be corrupt here. I read *non-visione* for *visione*; the Borgnet edition reads *visione Dei*.

10. Since this passage is remarkably obscure and I am not entirely confident that I have understood it correctly, I give the Latin text: *nobilissimus modus videndi est dupliciter: vel ex parte medii, sicut in scientia propter quid, et iste modus maxime remotus est a <non> visione, et sic non est modus nobilissimus divinae visionis; vel ex parte obiecti, ut dicatur nobilissimus modus visionis, per quam nobilissimum obiectum videmus, et sic est nobilissimus modus divinae visionis.* Knowledge "why" is the "noblest" form of vision, in the first sense indicated here; in Aristotle's view it is the only full-fledged form of knowledge (*Post. Anal.* 1.2, 71b9–16).

11. The reference is presumably to Aristotle, *Metaph.* α 1 (993b9–11).

12. Cf. *DN* 7.24 (Col. XXXVII p. 355:59–75). Matter is not acted upon simply by the presence of something—the presence of my rubber duck in the bath water has no effect on the water, whereas the elaborate hot water system does have an effect on the water, even though it may not actually be in the water; in Aristotelian terms the heating system communicates a form of heat to the water, and this is because it itself possesses such a form.

13. Aristotle, *De Anima* 3.4 (429b5–9), naturally without Bywater's emendation in b9 of δὲ αὐτὸν to δι'αὐτοῦ; cf. Albert, *De Anima* 3.2.15 (Col. VII i p. 199).

terms as the process from last to first. But the way from the first cause to its effects, into which it pours itself out, is a way of building up a complex understanding and it proceeds by way of affirmations, because we affirm everything of it causally. Similarly then it will be by way of affirmations that we return to it to be united with it, not by way of negations.

(3) Nothing can be concluded from negations, except in the context of some general affirmation. For instance we can say, "It is an animal, and it is not rational, therefore it is irrational," and so on. But God does not share a common category with anything else. Therefore nothing can be deduced about him by way of negations.

In response we must say:

(1) There are two different ways of considering a creature. If we take it precisely under the rubric of "trace of God," leading us to God, then it helps us to know God qua cause; but if we take creatures precisely as what comes forth from God with all the variety that means in terms of essence, species, genus and principle—like being, which is common to substance and to accidents—then in this way they do interfere with our knowledge of God in his own nature, and it is that kind of knowledge which Dionysius calls "pure vision," because it is without reference to the effects caused by God.

(2) When we are building up a complex understanding out of the essential elements of something, then both the synthesis and the analysis proceed affirmatively; for instance, this is how we build up our picture by predicating "substance" and then moving on to "body" and "animal" and so on until we reach individuals, and we move back through the same predicates when we are working our way up to more and more general ways of describing things. This is because there is no difference of essential being involved. But when we build up our complex picture by moving from some cause which is separate in its essential being to the effects produced by that cause, this is indeed also done affirmatively, because this is how the cause is revealed qua cause, and as such it can be designated by its effects, but in the reverse movement from the effects to the cause what we are seeking is the very essence of the cause and, since this is separate from all the caused effects, we have to proceed by way of negations.

(3) There is nothing in common between God and creatures, they share no common species or genus, no common factor to justify

strict analogy; all there is is the kind of sharing involved in imitation: the effects imitate their cause as far as they can. And this does not really mean that there is anything genuinely in common between them. And so we have no real way of saying anything about God, but we talk about him as best we can.

(III)   (1) It is not clear that we must necessarily start with the lowest things in our negations. The intermediates and the highest things are separated from what God is in himself just as much as the lowest things, so it makes no difference where we start.

(2) Whatever has everything separated from it is not anything at all. So if everything is denied of God, which is what Dionysius is saying here, then he is nothing at all, and in that case he will not exist. And that is what "the fool has said in his heart."[14]

(3) When we deny something of anything, it is because of some contrariety or dissimilarity, and these presuppose that there is some common ground.[15] But there is no common ground between God and creatures; if there were, he would be analyzable into a genus and his distinguishing specific characteristics, and so would not be simple. It seems to follow from this that nothing can be denied of him, whether it be elevated or lowly.

The answer to these points is as follows:

(1) When we deny something of anything, it is because there is a certain gap between them, and so it is natural to begin by denying of God the lowest kinds of thing, which are the furthest removed from him; theological affirmations on the other hand are based on the outflow from the cause into what it causes, and since it is the primary effects which influence lower things and not the other way round, it is natural to move in this case from higher things to lower.

(2) What follows from the separation of all things from God is that he is not one thing among others, as if he were on the same level as other things; but this is not to deny that he is above everything and that everything imitates him.

---

14. Psalm 13:1.

15. We can deny that "white" is "black" because both white and black are colors, but they are opposite colors ("contrariety"). We can deny that Jones is energetic, because he resembles other human beings enough in other ways to make it reasonable to suppose that he might have been energetic ("dissimilarity"). Where there is no common ground at all, denial is meaningless; we are not often tempted to deny that the color pink is smelly.

(3) The answer to the third point is already clear from what has been said; although there is no common ground between God and other things, such as there is between other things, nevertheless there is some common ground in the sense that things imitate him.

CHAPTER THREE

Cataphatic and apophatic theologies.

In the *Theological Outlines*, then, we celebrate particularly the items belonging to affirmative theology, how the divine and good nature is called "single" and how it is called "threefold," what the Fatherhood is taken in itself and what the Sonship, and what the theology of the Spirit intends to show; how from the immaterial and simple good there sprouted lights of goodness which remain in the heart, and how they have remained inseparable from their stability in it and in themselves and in each other in their coeternal burgeoning; how the supersubstantial Jesus was made substance with the true properties of human nature, and all the other things revealed in the Oracles which are celebrated in the *Theological Outlines*. In the *Divine Names* we celebrate how he is called "good," "being," "life" and "wisdom" and "power" and all the other things which form part of intellectual God-naming. In the *Symbolic Theology* we celebrate the designations of God taken over from the things of the senses and applied to the things of God, what God's "forms" are, and his "shapes" and "parts" and "instruments," his "places" and "ornaments," his "anger," "sadness" and "madness," his "drunkenness" and "carousing," his "oaths" and "curses," his "sleep" and his "waking up," and all the other holy compounded images which are part of symbolic God-shaping.

*

In this chapter Dionysius proposes to establish the proper way of treating our subject, as we have already seen from our analysis of the book as a whole. And since the subject is treated by way of negations, his principal objective is to establish the procedure involved in negative theology. And since the procedure of negative theology is learned from that of affirmative theology, he begins with an account of affirmative theology. This is clear from the title, "Cataphatic and apophatic theologies."

This chapter accordingly falls into two parts, the first dealing with the procedure of affirmative theology, the second with that of negative theology.

The first part falls into two sections. In the first, Dionysius lays down the procedure of affirmative theology; in the second he encourages Timothy to ponder this procedure.

The first section has three subdivisions, in line with the author's three books on theological affirmations; he first mentions those dealt with in the *Theological Outlines*, then those dealt with in the *Divine Names*, and finally those dealt with in the *Symbolic Theology*.

Before we actually look at the text, there is a question about whether these three books cover the ground sufficiently.

(1) The task of theology with regard to affirmations about God does not appear to be sufficiently communicated in these three books. In addition to the proper attributes of the Persons, there are certain attributes which are appropriated to them, and no teaching about this is contained in the three books, so it looks as if they are insufficient.

(2) In none of these books does the author deal with God's will, foreknowledge or predestination, yet all of these belong to the theologian's task and demand particular treatment, as the Master says in the Sentences.[1] So these three books, it seems, are inadequate on their own.

(3) In addition to the eternal processions of the Persons, there are certain temporal processions, and there is nothing about these in any of the three books; so they are, on the face of it, incomplete.

(4) Dionysius wrote other books too, such as the *Ecclesiastical Hierarchy*, in which he teaches us how to approach the things of God by way of symbols, and similarly his book on *Things Visible and In-*

---

1. Peter Lombard, I *Sent*. d.35 c.1.

visible, and these are not listed here. So his account seems to be incomplete.

In response we must say that the task of theology being described here is not that of manifesting God in any of his effects or gifts, but that of manifesting him in himself, and the affirmative aspect of this task is sufficiently contained in the three books listed, because there are only three ways of talking about God: metaphorically, and this is what the *Symbolic Theology* is about; or literally (a) with reference to the properties which belong to the Persons, and this is what the *Theological Outlines* is about; or (b) with reference to the properties of the divine nature, and this is what the *Divine Names* is about. This analysis of the different ways of designating God comes from Ambrose.[2]

So we can answer the points raised as follows:

(1) Terms which are appropriated to the Persons are in themselves common and belong to the divine nature; they are terms like "goodness," "wisdom" and "power," and they are discussed in the *Divine Names*.

(2) Predestination and foreknowledge differ from knowledge and wisdom only in being antecedent, which is what the prefix signifies. For this reason they are included in the discussion of God's wisdom in the *Divine Names*. The specific nuance which they add calls for some special conclusions, but these belong more to the discussion of creatures than to the treatment of God in himself. Similarly what needs to be said about God's will is indicated by the discussion of his goodness, which is the disposition of his will.[3] As it says at the end of the *Divine Names*, other words which are used to the same effect must be taken in accordance with the same rules of interpretation.[4]

(3) The temporal processions are a manifestation of the eternal processions, and so both are explained together; the temporal processions are contained in the interpretation of the divine names,

---

2. Ambrose, *De Fide* II Prol. 2 (PL 16 [1845]: 559D–560C), taken up by Lombard, I *Sent.* d.22 c.1, on which see Albert's comment, B 25 pp. 566–7.

3. Albert's contention is that predestination is part of divine foreknowledge (cf. I *Sent.* d.40 a.1, B 26 pp.304–5), and that foreknowledge is not, in this context, significantly different from knowledge, which Dionysius discusses in *DN* 7.2. The specific nuance added by "fore–" is relevant to a quite different area of theology. Similarly God's will is taken to be sufficiently discussed in Dionysius' treatment of goodness in *DN* 4.

4. Dionysius, *DN* 13.6 (PG 3:981C).

in the guise of effects, where Dionysius talks about the divine processions into creatures.[5]

(4) In these other books God is not revealed in himself, but in some of his effects, such as sacramental grace (in the *Ecclesiastical Hierarchy*) or visible creatures (in the other book).

So Dionysius begins by saying, "In the *Theological Outlines*, then," (the book he wrote about the divine Persons) "we celebrate particularly," or according to the other translation, "we celebrated particularly," "the items belonging to affirmative theology," that is, the affirmations about God which belong properly to the Persons, namely, "how the divine and good nature is called 'single.' "

There are several objections to this:

(1) Hilary says that in God there is neither singleness nor aloneness.[6]

(2) Single individuals are distinguished from others by their accidents,[7] but in God there are no accidents, therefore he is not single.

(3) Single individuals are individuated by matter,[8] but God is utterly immaterial, therefore he is not single.

(4) Single individuals presuppose some common nature which is individuated in them,[9] but God is not an individual member of

---

5. Cf. Dionysius, *DN* 2.11, with Albert's commentary (Col. XXXVII pp. 96–100).

6. Hilary, *De Trinitate* 7.38 (PL 10:231B), as cited and exploited by Lombard, I *Sent.* d.23 c.5.

7. The doctrine that individuals are distinguished only by their accidents goes back to Boethius, *De Trinitate* 1 (ed. H. F. Stewart and E. K. Rand, Loeb classics [1918], p.6:24–6), who probably got it from Porphyry, *Isagoge*, ed. Busse 7.22–5 (text in *Aristoteles Latinus* I 6–7 [Bruges and Paris, 1966], pp. 13–14). In the later Middle Ages it was defended by William of Champeaux (cf. Abelard, *Hist. Cal.* 2, PL 178:119AB), but it was attacked by Abelard, *Glossae super Porphyrium*, ed. B. Geyer, Beiträge XXI/1 [Münster, 1919], p. 13; later on it was attacked by William of Auvergne, *De Universo* I.II ch.11, ed. cit. I p.819aD, and by Thomas, *in Metaph. Comm.* 1626 (Marietti ed.). Elsewhere Albert seems to concede only that accidents are one way in which individuals differ from one another (*Metaph.* 10.2.9, Col. XVI p.455:78–9). I am indebted to Osmund Lewry, O.P., for the reference to Porphyry.

8. This is the standard medieval Aristotelian doctrine, that matter is the principle of individuation (cf. Averroes, *De Somno et Vigilia*, ed. cit. p.103; Thomas, *in Metaph. Comm.* 1496); whether or not the principle is genuinely Aristotelian is disputed: cf. J. Owens p.244.

9. To say that something is "an individual" normally implies that it is "an individual X" (an individual cat, teacup or whatever), which means that there is more to X than is contained in the individual. My favorite beer mug, however splendid, does not exhaust the whole notion of beer mugs. If God were an individual in this sense, he would be only a partial instantiation of what it means to be God.

any class, because otherwise there would be something more primary and more simple than God. Therefore God is not single.

In response we must say that what Hilary was denying in God
is that there is only one divine Person, but Dionysius is talking about
the singleness of the divine essence; and even that is not strictly "single" in the same way that single individuals are found in lower
beings. It is called "single" in the sense that it is not in fact nor could
it in principle be multiplied, as individuals generally can be.[10]

This makes it clear what the answer is to all the points raised.

So, to return to the text, Dionysius is talking about "how the
divine nature is called 'single' " (unique, not multiplied, in the three
Persons), "and how it is called 'threefold' " (in the Trinity of Persons), "what the Fatherhood is, taken in itself, and what the Sonship" and how it is revealed in the temporal procession, and "what
the theology of the Spirit intends to show", that is, what is meant
by talking about "Holy Spirit" in God, and "how lights of goodness"
(the Son and the Holy Spirit) "sprouted from the simple and immaterial good" while nevertheless "remaining in the heart," which
is clearly contrary to the way lower beings work, because when
something sprouts, it does not remain in the source from which it
has sprouted.

There are several difficulties about this:

(1) "Good" is a name belonging to the divine essence, and the
essence neither generates nor is generated, so it does not look as if
there is anything "sprouting" from the good.

(2) What does "heart" mean?

(3) The image of light is inappropriate, because light is not a
substance, whereas the Persons are substances existing in their own
right, so they are not well signified by "lights."

In response:

---

10. Normally even unique individuals are not necessarily unique, but God is necessarily unique, the word "God" properly has no plural (I *Sent.* d.2 a.22, B 25 pp.83–4). For a
modern discussion of problems about calling God an "individual," see B. Davies, *Thinking
about God* (London, 1985), pp.118–28. Albert's argument here becomes much clearer if we
emend the text by deleting *sed* at p.469:45; this would yield: "Even that is not strictly 'single'
in the same way that single individuals are found in lower beings, because it is not in fact nor
could it in principle be multiplied, as individuals can be." The last clause would thus become
the explanation of why God is not an individual, rather than of why he is so called in spite
of the difficulties. One great advantage of this emendation is that it gives us a text which really
does answer points (2)–(4).

(1) "Good" is being used here for the divine nature as it is in the Father, in whom it is the principle of generation, because the Father begets in virtue of the divine nature, even though taken in itself the divine nature is not relative and is not confined to any one of the Persons; but taken with reference to the act of begetting, it is peculiar to the Father and has to be called "relative," just as the power of begetting does.[11] So to the objection that "good" is a name belonging to the divine essence, we may say that this is true, but because it signifies the essence concretely in the divine Person, it can be taken over because of this connection to stand for the Person, as the word "God" is in "God from God."[12]

(2) The coming forth of feelings and thoughts from the heart is an immaterial procession, and so, to symbolize the immateriality of the divine begetting, the divine nature is compared to a heart, inasmuch as it is in the Father as the principle from which the Son and the Holy Spirit proceed. And because they proceed from the Father as Persons, yet remain in his essence, they are said to "remain in the heart."

(3) The word "lights" is not being used to display the perfection of the divine Persons, but to show that their procession is a procession of form:[13] just as light comes from light, so God comes from God.

Dionysius goes on, "and how they have remained inseparable from their stability in it" (the heart), in that they remain in one essence, "and in themselves," in that each Person remains in himself, "and in each other," in that the Son is in the Father and the Father is in the Son, even though one Person proceeds from another "in a

---

11. The essential point is that, though all three divine Persons are God (and so the divine nature is common to them all), nevertheless it is qua God that the Father begets the Son, so in a sense we have to say that the divine nature is the principle of divine generation (cf. I *Sent*. d.5, B 25 pp.173–91).

12. The phrase from the Nicene Creed justifies the claim that we can say that "God begets God," not just that "the Father begets the Son." The divine essence does not subsist on its own, somehow, independently of the divine Persons, and the Father is not some kind of compound of divine essence and Fatherhood. In him the divine nature is the Father and he is the nature.

13. The procession of the Son and the Holy Spirit from the Father is a "formal procession," because it involves the transmission of "form": what comes from God in this way is God. There are obviously other ways in which one thing can come from another, which do not involve any such passing on of form: if I write a book, the book is not human, even if I am.

coeternal burgeoning," because the generation of the Son does not precede the Son, nor does the breathing-out precede the Spirit, because there is no question here of any movement from potency to act,[14] and also "how the supersubstantial Jesus" (supersubstantial with reference to his Godhead) "was made substance," dwelling in "the true properties of human nature," that is, a genuine body and a genuine soul, "and all the other things revealed in the Oracles" (the canonical scriptures) "which are celebrated" by us "in the *Theological Outlines.*"

But surely it is not part of the business of that book to explain about the Incarnation of the Word. Conclusions and explanations which rest on different principles belong to different areas of instruction. Even if one and the same conclusion is demonstrated on the basis of different principles, that conclusion belongs to different sciences; thus for instance the sphericity of the earth is demonstrated on different grounds by physicists and by astronomers. But the Incarnation of the Word involves different principles from the distinctions between the Persons; the latter is explained in terms of their eternal relationships, but the Incarnation involves certain temporal deeds performed by God. So they do not belong to the same area of doctrine.

In response we may say that since the Incarnation of the Word belongs exclusively to the Son, it is appropriate to deal with it at the same time as the other features which are proper to the different Persons. The theological explanation of it relies on the same general principles, namely, the eternal relationships which distinguish between the Persons, because it is by one and the same Sonship that the Son is eternally the Son of the Father and that, from a certain point in time, he is the Son of his mother, and it is as the same Person that he is identified both in his Godhead and in his humanity.[15]

---

14. This is Albert's comment on "coeternal": the generation of the Son and the spiration of the Spirit are not processes, which could be measured in time; it makes no sense to think of a time when the Son was *being generated* but was not yet actually generated (and so was only potentially the Son, the Son "in the making").

15. The Son of Mary and the Son of God are one and the same person and one and the same Son. When we read in our papers that Mabel and Ebenezer Twiggins have had a son, we do not infer that there must be two sons, one son of Mabel and one son of Ebenezer; no more are there two sons in Jesus, one son of God and one son of Mary. If there were two distinct filiations involved, there would be two distinct persons in Jesus (which is the Nestorian heresy). Cf. III *Sent.* d.4 a.5 (B 28 p.86).

Even if certain further special principles are brought in to explain the Incarnation, this does not matter, since the same science can perfectly well contain conclusions which have different specific principles.

Dionysius goes on to say that "in the *Divine Names*" he has explained how God is called "good" and "all the other things which form part of intellectual God-naming," that is, names whose meaning does not express anything to do with the senses.

Then he says that "in the *Symbolic Theology*" he has explained the designations of God which are "taken over from the things of the senses and applied" to God, such as "God's 'forms' and 'shapes';" "form" and "shape" refer to the same thing, but from a different point of view, referring respectively inward and outward—form is not here being used in the sense of "substantial form."[16] And so on in the same vein with regard to everything else which is said symbolically about God.

*

And I think you have recognized how this last is more verbose than the previous two. The *Theological Outlines* and the exposition of the *Divine Names* ought to be less wordy than the *Symbolic Theology*, because the higher we turn our regard, the more our talking about intelligibles contracts in our sight, just as now, as we enter the darkness which

---

16. Albert's rather cryptic comment on the distinction between "form" and "shape" is elaborated in the commentary on *DN* 1.43 (Col. XXXVII p.25:24–9) and much more fully in *De Praedicamentis* 5.8 (B 1 p.259). "Substantial form" determines what something *is*. "Form" as a kind of quality, which is what Albert supposes Dionysius to be referring to here, is closely connected with substantial form (hence its "inward" orientation): it is shape considered precisely as the shape of a particular kind of thing. Substantial form means that something *is* a tiger. This other sort of form means that it *has the shape of* a tiger, it defines the outer limits of this particular lump of flesh as having the contours proper to a tiger. "Shape" (*figura*) refers to the same phenomenon, but with an "outward" reference: the tiger is shaped in such a way that it is well-adapted to make certain kinds of movements, its claws are not merely the right shape for a tiger's claws, they are also excellent for clawing with. Another way of looking at it is to say that you might be interested in a nose precisely as a human nose, part of a human body (this would be an interest in "form"), or you might be interested in it as a curious geometrical shape (this would be an interest in "shape").

is above mind, we shall find not brevity of speech but complete irrationality and foolishness.[17]

*

Dionysius next bids Timothy consider how the more lowly names are "more verbose" than the previously mentioned names, because in the *Theological Outlines* and the *Divine Names* he was "less wordy" than in the *Symbolic Theology*. The reason for this is that the higher we extend our reach, "the more our talking about intelligibles contracts" and shortens "in our sight." And so in this teaching, in which we reach out, as far as we can, to the very transcendence of the divine nature, we do not even find few words to affirm about it, but we find there nothing but "complete irrationality and foolishness" because our intellect, seeing nothing identifiable in God's nature, cannot express it in any affirmations, but only in negations, and therefore this science comes to its fulfilment solely with negations.

*

There our speech, descending from the heights to the lowest limits, expanded into multiplicity in proportion to its descent, but now that it is going upward from lower things to the heights, it contracts in proportion to its ascent and, after the end of the whole ascent, it will be totally voiceless and totally united with the ineffable. But why, you ask, when we begin positing our divine affirmations altogether with the most primary, do we start our separation of things from God with the last and lowest? Because when we were

---

17. Albert has been misled by Sarracenus' translation: he takes *sermones conspectibus intelligibilium contrahuntur* to mean "our talking about intelligibles contracts in our sight," but the Greek shows that it must be intended to mean "our talking contracts because of the synoptic view (we have) of intelligibles" (at a higher level of abstraction more significance is packed into fewer words). Also "irrationality and foolishness" (*irrationabilitatem et imprudentiam*) is infelicitous for ἀλογίαν καὶ ἀνοησίαν ("absence of words, absence of understanding").

affirming what is above all affirmation we had to posit one presiding affirmation[18] on the basis of what is most kin to it, but now that we are negating what is beyond all negation we must begin with things that are most distant from it. Is God not more truly life and goodness than he is air or stone? Is it not more the case that he is not carousing or madness than that he is neither spoken nor understood?

*

Next Dionysius lays down the procedure for negative theology as opposed to affirmative theology. And first he says what the procedure is, then he raises and answers a question.

So first he says that in his treatment of affirmations he began with "the heights" and the more he descended, the more he "expanded his speech," following "the proportions" of reality: the further things are from what is primary, the more numerous they are[19] and their properties are better known to us than those of the first things. But in negative theology, which is our present concern, we go "upward from lower things to the heights," separating everything from God. And so, as we ascend, our "speech contracts" (becomes shorter) because there is little there that we comprehend. And at the end, when we have separated everything from God, our whole speech will be "voiceless" because it will be "united" with him who is "ineffable," namely God. And that is why this science more than any other is called "mystical," because it ends in a darkness, about which, since everything has been taken away, we cannot properly affirm anything.

Then he asks why we have to begin affirmative theology with higher things and do negative theology the other way round. And

---

18. I presume that this is what Sarracenus meant by *superpositivam affirmationem;* if so, it is not a bad rendering of τὴν ὑποθετικὴν κατάφασιν. But cf. below, note 20.

19. This echoes Neoplatonist ontology: from the inconceivable simplicity of the One we descend into ever greater multiplicity the further we go. The compact richness of higher levels of reality can be imaged at lower levels only by the provision of a far greater number of beings carrying various more or less fragmentary and pale representations of the glory that is on high.

he gives the answer as follows. Affirmation rests on appropriateness, so when we want to state something about God, who is "above all affirmation," when we want to "posit one presiding affirmation," since we cannot affirm anything of him as he is in himself, but can only name him with some name taken from what he causes, as the philosopher says,[20] and this will be something subordinate to him, we have to begin with those things which are closest to him. But negation rests on separation or unlikeness, and therefore it is "things that are most distant from" him that should first be separated from him. God is "more truly life and goodness than he is air or stone," so it is the former names that should be given to him first. But "it is more the case that he is not carousing and madness than that he is neither spoken nor understood," that is, drunkenness and madness are further removed from him than utterability or intelligibility, which are closer to him; so it is things like drunkenness and madness which are the first to be denied of him.

CHAPTER FOUR

He who is the pre-eminent cause of all that the senses perceive is not anything perceptible by the senses.

So we say that the cause of all which is above all is not without substance or life or reason or mind. Neither is it a body nor is it a shape or form, nor does it possess any quality or size or weight. Neither is it in any place, nor is it seen, nor can it be touched by the senses. It is not per-

---

20. The reference is probably to the pseudo-Aristotelian *Liber de Causis*, proposition 5(6) (ed. A. Pattin, *Tijdschrift voor Philosophie* 28 [1966] p.147), which Albert cites in I *Sent.* d.2 a.16 (B 25 p.72). It is possible that Albert intends his comment that names are taken from some effect which is "subordinate" (*supponitur*) to God to explain why Dionysius (Sarracenus) talks of an *affirmatio superpositiva*; if so, this latter phrase could be translated "super-affirmative": God is beyond affirmations, any affirmations we make are based on effects which are "placed (posited) beneath" him, so making them of God we have to make them in a special way, affirming (positing) them "above" that to which they ordinarily refer. But I think it is more likely that the juxtaposition of *superpositiva* and *supponitur* is accidental. *Supponitur* must in any case be taken to mean "placed beneath"; when this verb is used to mean "stand in for," it requires more than a simple dative to accompany it, so we should expect *pro se supponitur*, not *sibi supponitur*, if that were what Albert meant.

186

ceived or perceivable by the senses, nor does it admit of any disarray or disturbance from being troubled by any of the things which affect matter. Neither is it powerless, nor is it subject to the chances which go with the things of the senses, nor is it in need of light. Neither does it admit of change or corruption or division or deprivation, it has no passibility or flux, it neither possesses nor is anything else that belongs to the realm of the senses.

*

Here Dionysius actually begins his treatment of the subject, in which he intends to separate everything from God. It falls into two parts: first he separates the things of the senses from him, then (in chapter five) the things of the mind. This is the analysis suggested by the titles of the chapters.

Another, more technical, analysis is also possible: Dionysius first lays down what God is not without, and then shows what God is not (beginning with "Neither is it a body").

So first of all he says that, since it is in this way that we have to go into the divine darkness, "we say"—or, according to the other translation, "let us say"[1]—because he is here beginning his treatment of the subject—that God, who is "the cause of all" and "above all, is not without substance or life or reason or mind," although none of these things can be affirmed of him. He is not without them, since they proceed formally from him.[2]

Alternatively, if we prefer the first analysis of the text, he is here separating from God various conditions which characterize things of the senses: it is characteristic of accidents to be without substance, and of inanimate beings to be without life, and similar comments can obviously be made about the other items listed.

Next, if we follow the second analysis of the text, Dionysius separates from God all that God is not, beginning with the things of the senses, because they are the furthest from God, and then the

---

1. The "other translation" is, as usual, that of Eriugena.
2. In the case of "formal procession" (cf. chapter 3, note 13) the source of the form in the recipient has to be (in some sense) the same form in the source. Therefore anything that proceeds "formally" from God must (in some sense) be in God.

things of the mind and spiritual things; this is in accordance with the techniques Dionysius has been teaching us.

So he says first that God is "not a body" nor is he "shape or form." "Form" can be taken here in two senses. It could mean the kind of form that matter has,[3] in which case it refers to something different from "shape," and it is found only in the things of the senses. Or it could mean the kind of "form" which belongs to the fourth kind of quality,[4] in which case "form" and "shape" refer to the same thing, though from different points of view, because "shape" refers outward, since it indicates the outline limiting something's size, whereas "form" refers inward, since it makes the thing it inheres in into a particular kind of being.[5] Artificial forms are "shapes."

"Neither is he in any place" as if he were contained in a place in the same way that material objects are contained in a place; he is everywhere as the one who contains all place. "Nor is he seen" by any bodily sight "nor can he be touched by the senses," because he has no tactile quality. Dionysius means us to understand by these two senses all the other sensual means of perception; one of the two he mentions is the most spiritual of all the senses, the other is the most material. "He is not perceived" (in fact) "or perceivable" (potentially) "by the senses, nor does he admit of any disarray," as imperfect beings do, such as deformed creatures, nor does he, the cause of all, admit of any "disturbance from being troubled by any of the things which affect matter," as if he could be weakened in his activities by having anything happen to him. "Neither is he powerless, subject to the chances which go with the things of the senses," in the way that matter is rendered powerless when it is separated from its form by the action of bodily things.[6]

Or we could say that Dionysius began by separating from

---

3. The "form of matter" means the kind of form which yields some specific kind of matter (e.g., putty or wood), and this is quite independent of any shape that may be imposed on such matter.

4. Cf. Aristotle, *Categ.* 8 (10a11–2).

5. Cf. chapter 3 note 16.

6. Albert's comment shows that he takes *casibus sensibilibus* to mean "chances brought about by *sensibilia*," but the phrase should probably be taken to mean "the chances that affect *sensibilia*."

God all bodily things and their various conditions, then he separated from him all the things of the senses. Now he is going to separate from him the defects to which beings of sense are prone, beginning with defects in their emotions, whether caused by innate passions (so "disarray" must go[7]) or by things inflicted from outside (so "disturbance" is taken away); and since it is impossible that anything should be inflicted on him, Dionysius goes on that he is "not subject to chances" nor is he "powerless." "Chance" applies to beings devoid of intelligence, whereas "fortune" applies only to rational beings.[8] "Nor is he in need of light," bodily light, that is; this eliminates any defectiveness in his capacity to know. Sight is the noblest of the senses, and it is light which brings it to its fulfilment.

After this Dionysius separates from God all bodily defects in general: "neither does he admit of change" (such as occurs in the accidents of things) "or corruption" (in his substance) "or division" (which would break him up into pieces) "or deprivation" (either in the sense of matter losing its form or in the sense of losing his natural state); "he has no passibility" in face of anything external, which would leave him open to being affected by any outside force, "or flux," either in the sense of any contrary components of his interacting on each other or in the sense of any kind of movement or change from one situation to another.

Finally Dionysius sums it all up: "He neither possesses nor is anything that belongs to the realm of the senses." He has none of the conditions or defects which go with the senses, nor is he any of the things which the senses perceive.

---

7. I have been unable to think of a single English word to cover *inordinatio* in both of Albert's comments. In his first interpretation it means bodily disorder (misplaced or misshapen limbs and so on); here it means disorder in one's appetites and emotions.

8. This distinction comes from Aristotle, *Physics* 2.6 (197a36–b22); cf. Albert's comment, II *Phys.* 2.17 (Col. IV pp. 123–5). "Fortune" is taken to indicate something that contributes to the kind of weal or woe which only intelligent beings can appreciate; it is therefore a much narrower term than "chance." The birth of a freak is "chance," and no doubt has some physical explanation, even though it is contrary to the normal workings of nature. But if I courteously help an old lady across the street and she "happens" to be a millionairess looking for someone to leave her oil wells to, that is my good "fortune" and strictly speaking has no natural cause whatsoever. Granted this distinction, then clearly it is "chance," not "fortune," which belongs in this present elimination of *sensibilia* from God, since "fortune" is a kind of country cousin of *intelligibilia*.

Chapter Five

He who is the pre-eminent cause of all that the mind understands is not any of the objects of our understanding.

Ascending further, we say that he is neither soul nor mind, nor does he possess fantasy or opinion or reason or intellect, neither is he reason or intellect. Neither is he spoken of or understood. He is neither number nor order, greatness or smallness or equality, likeness or unlikeness. He neither stands still nor moves, nor is he silent. Neither does he have power, nor is he power or light. Neither does he live, nor is he life or substance or eternity or time. He cannot be touched by our understanding, nor is there knowledge of him or truth. He is neither kingdom nor wisdom, nor is he one or unity, Godhead or goodness. Nor is he Spirit in such a way that we could see him,[1] nor is he Sonship or Fatherhood. Nor is he any of the things which are known to us or to any other being, nor is he anything non-existent or existent. Neither do beings know the Cause as it really is, nor does it know beings qua beings. It has no explanation or name or knowledge or darkness or light or error or truth. Neither is there any affirmation or negation of it whatsoever, but when we make affirmations or negations of things which come after it we neither affirm nor deny it in itself, since the perfect and unitive cause of all is above all affirmation, and the transcendence of what is simply free of all things and above them all is beyond all negation.[2]

---

1. Why Sarracenus translates εἰδέναι as *videamus* is far from clear. Since Albert does not comment on this phrase, we do not know what he made of it. The Greek means "he is not spirit in any sense that we could understand."

2. There is some ambiguity about how Dionysius' string of nouns should be interpreted syntactically, and since Albert's commentary is far from exhaustive it is not always clear how he construed some parts of this chapter.

DIONYSIUS' MYSTICAL THEOLOGY

*

In this chapter Dionysius means to separate from God all that the understanding apprehends, such as life, substance and so on. But surely these things should not be separated from him:

(1) As Anselm says, God is designated with the names of everything of which it is true, simply speaking, to say that it is better that it should exist than that it should not.[3] But life, wisdom and so on are of that kind. So they should be used to name God, in which case they ought not to be denied of him.

(2) An attribute which properly belongs to something names that thing and is predicated of that thing more truly than it is of anything else to which it does not properly belong. And, as Jerome says, being belongs properly only to God.[4] Therefore talk of "essence" or saying that "he is" applies more truly to God than to creatures; so since we do not deny these things of creatures, they should be even less denied of the creator.

(3) A property that belongs to something in its own right belongs to that thing more truly than to other things with only a derivative claim to it. But all these things belong to creatures only derivatively, because it is from God that they have life, substance, and so on. But they belong to God in his own right. So they are more truly ascribed to God than to creatures, so the same conclusion follows.

(4) Anything that has being has it either necessarily or possibly, and whatever has it necessarily has a better claim to it than anything which has it possibly.[5] Now Avicenna demonstrates that God alone is necessary being, while everything else possesses only possible being.[6] Therefore being is more truly ascribed to God than to any-

---

3. Albert discusses Anselm's "rule for naming God" in I *Sent.* d.2 a.17 (B 25 pp. 72–4) and *CH* 2.7 (B 14 p. 43), and it is clear that the passage he has in mind is Anselm, *Proslogion* 5, 11–12 (PL 158:229C, 234A).

4. Cf. Lombard, I *Sent.* d.8 c.1, citing Jerome, *Ep.* 15.4.

5. The distinction between "necessary" and "possible" beings is an Aristotelian commonplace, which is often misunderstood. "Necessary beings" are those that have no principle of decay within themselves, so they cannot cease to exist or undergo any major alteration because of any natural cause; "possible beings" are produced by and so can be ruined or destroyed by natural causes. Cf. Patterson Brown, "St. Thomas' doctrine of necessary being," in A. Kenny, ed., *Aquinas* (London, 1970), pp. 157–74.

6. Avicenna, *De Philosophia Prima* 1.6–7. On Avicenna's rather un-Aristotelian notion

thing else, and the same principle applies to all these names. So once again the same conclusion follows.

(5) It might be argued that the reality to which these names refer exists more truly in God, but our use of the names depends on the way in which such things come to our knowledge, so that in this sense the names apply more truly to creatures, of which we do have some understanding, and are more truly separated from God, the knowledge of whom defeats our comprehension. But the fact that from our point of view something does or does not apply does not justify the conclusion that it absolutely does or does not apply because, as the philosopher says, the things that are naturally the most manifest of all are, from our point of view, unknown.[7] So it does not follow from the fact that these names, as we use them, belong more truly to creatures that they ought absolutely to be denied of God.[8]

(6) It is fallacious to argue, "The heavens do not have the same consistency as the elements, therefore they have no consistency,"[9] or "Human beings are not animals in the same way as asses, therefore they are not animals." So there appears to be a similar fallacy in saying that God is not wisdom in the same sense in which there is wisdom among us, therefore he is not wisdom in any sense.

In response we must say with Anselm[10] that the realities sig-

---

of possible and necessary beings, see G. Verbeke's introduction to S. van Riet's edition of this work (Louvain/Leiden, 1977) I pp. 42*–62*.

7. Aristotle, *Metaph. α* 1 (993b9-11).

8. The argument is this: we cannot infer anything at all about what things are in themselves from the way they appear to us; therefore we have no right to say that terms derived from our own lowly experience do not apply perfectly well to some higher reality.

9. The fallaciousness of the argument is obvious, but some comment is perhaps needed on what the argument is about. In *DN* 13.15 (Col. XXXVII p. 441) Albert gives an argument against the *continuitas* (which I have somewhat uneasily translated "consistency") of the heavens: if the heavens "held together" there could not be the uncoordinated movement which we perceive in the heavenly bodies. By contrast the elements do "hold together" (not, obviously, in the sense that the whole stock of fire, air, earth and water is all in one place, but in the sense that any given dollop of any of the elements is continuous). Albert rejects the suggestion that even fire is "discontinuous," though it certainly looks as if it might be no more than an aggregate of separate bits (*De Causis Propr. Elem.* 1.2.11, Col. V ii pp. 80–81). Nevertheless the sky does form a continuous body, according to Albert (ibid. p. 81:7–8); at least each heavenly sphere is an undivided whole (*De Caelo* 2.3.8, Col. V i p. 158:15-7). It would be odd to say that the sky is "bitty."

10. I cannot find any place where Anselm actually says this; Albert appears to have in mind his own discussion of Anselm's "rule" in I *Sent.* d.2 a.17 (B 25 p. 73), and cf. *CH* 2.7 (B 14 p. 43). His interpretation of Anselm finds some justification in texts like *Proslogion* 17 and 24 (PL 158:236B, 239CD).

nified by names like this are not foreign to God, they are more truly present in him than they are in the creatures into which they descend from him. In creatures they are a kind of image of the primary life and wisdom and so on. But the way in which we use these words to mean something is more truly applicable to creatures, and it is in this sense that they are foreign to God, because we attach names to things in accordance with the conception we have of things in our mind. As Damascene says, words announce our understanding.[11] But our knowledge derives from things and so the meaning of our words follows the nature of the things from which our knowledge is taken, with all the complexity and temporality and other limiting factors which that involves. And so in this way they do not apply to God at all. This is why he says[12] that although all fatherhood derives from the Father in heaven,[13] nevertheless the word "father" is more familiar to us as meaning our kind of fatherhood.

Or we can say that even the reality these names refer to does not justify their application to God. In any predication you have to have a subject and something of which it is the subject, something, that is, that is in it and can be taken with it in some sense, and also there has to be the sort of relationship between them that makes one of them a proper subject and the other a proper predicate; you cannot predicate absolutely anything of absolutely anything. But God is utterly simple, and so in him it is not true that one thing is in another or that one thing is the subject of another, therefore the actual reality of God transcends any possibility of there being subjects and predicates. This means that no proposition can truly and properly be formed about God, as the commentator shows on *Metaphysics* XI;[14] when we talk about God we use borrowed words and both subject and predicate refer to the same reality and the distinction between them is not a real one, but only one which we make in our understanding on the basis of God's relationship to things outside himself.

This makes it clear, then, that both from the point of view of the way in which we name things and from the point of view of the

---

11. *De Fide Orthodoxa* (Burgundio's version), ed. cit. p. 131.

12. "He" is apparently Anselm, but Albert is thinking of his own reflections on Anselm; cf. I *Sent.* d.2 a.17 (B 25 p. 73).

13. Eph. 3:15.

14. Cf. Averroes, *Metaph.* 11 (12) comm. 39 (last half).

reality of God nothing can properly be predicated of him, and for this reason it is more true to separate everything from him. This is why it says in the *Celestial Hierarchy* that in theology negations are true, while affirmations are ill-adapted.[15]

The answer to the first four points raised above should now be clear.

(5) Sometimes things as we know them are contrasted with things as they are in their own nature, when what does not really come first comes first for us and from our point of view. In such a case what we know of something is only what it is relative to something else, and we cannot deduce what it is in itself. But if we take "knowledge" in its general sense, as including all that we know, both a priori and a posteriori, then unconditional inferences can be made from the way things are as known by us. If something is not known to us and cannot be known by us in any way at all, then there is no way in which we can give it a significant name.[16]

(6) The heavens do possess some kind of consistency and human beings do have some kind of animal nature, but it cannot properly be said of God that he has anything or that he is anything or that anything is in him, because all such phrases signify some sort of differentiation and complexity[17] and this is quite foreign to God. So the case is not the same.

---

15. Dionysius, *CH* 2.3 (p. 79). Alan of Lille (*SQH* 9, ed. cit. p. 140) takes *incompactae* to mean that there is no real *compositio*, which fits Albert's own doctrine, but Albert actually interprets Dionysius' phrase as meaning only that affirmations "are not straightforwardly true" (B 14 p. 46, and cf. *DN* 7.30, Col. XXXVII p. 359:46–9).

16. In response to the skeptical attack on negative theology (cf. note 8 above) Albert makes a distinction: if all we have is knowledge a posteriori (based on arguing from effects to causes), then indeed we cannot claim to know anything about the causes in question as they are in themselves. If I see a beam of light, I can infer that there is some sort of light-producer around, but without a different kind of evidence I cannot know whether there is a lighthouse there or a castle or a police search-party or what. But in theology we are not confined to a posteriori inferences; there is an interplay between inferences from creatures to the creator and inferences from what the creator must be, if he is to count as the creator (cf. the moves made by Albert in I *Sent.* d.3 a.3, B 25 pp. 94–5). It is, in fact, only in the context of this kind of interplay between different kinds of theological argument that negative theology can function. An excessively skeptical or radical negative theology defeats itself as well as knocking out affirmative theology.

17. We can only say things like "My cat has whiskers" or "My tortoise is green" or "There are signs of native wit in that fellow" because in each case we can both distinguish between the two (or more) elements involved and make some connection between them, and this is not possible with God, in whom there is no such complexity. God simply *is* whatever

So Dionysius begins by saying, "Ascending further" from the things of the senses to the things of the mind "we say that he" (God) "is neither soul nor mind," referring respectively to the lower part of the soul, viewed as that which makes a body alive, and to the higher part which is the eye of the soul, taking *mens* (mind) as coming from *metiri* (measure).[18] Or "soul" can be referred to human beings and "mind" to the angels.[19] "Nor does he possess phantasy." The commentator here distinguishes between two kinds of phantasy, "of which neither can be ascribed to God. One is the sort which comes first, arising in our sensory apparatus from something naturally perceptible by the senses, and this is properly called an image expressed in the senses. The other is the sort which follows from this image and is shaped by it, and this is the phantasy proper which is commonly given the precise name of interior sense. The first is always attached to the body, the second to the soul. And although the first is in the senses it does not perceive itself, but the second both perceives itself and is the receiver of the first."[20] This appears to mean that the first sort of phantasy is the common sense and the second is what we usually call imagination,[21] which the philosopher defines

---

may properly be said about him, so that there is no room for any real distinction between subject and predicate. Therefore any argument (such as that proposed in point 6) based on the way we may or may not attach predicates to other subjects is ineluctably irrelevant.

18. Various etymologies of *mens* were current (cf. *DN* 1.31, Col. XXXVII p. 16: 62–5; St. Thomas, I *Sent.* d.3 q.5). The alleged connection with *metiri* is derived from Burgundio's version of Damascene, *De Fide Orthodoxa* 36.6, which Albert cites in *De Homine* q.73 a.2 (B 35 p. 609a).

19. The angels are called "minds" in Dionysius, *DN* 4.1 (PG 3:693C), on which see Albert's commentary (Col. XXXVII p. 125:69–70).

20. This is quoted more or less verbatim from the interpolated Gloss (on which see Dondaine, *Le Corpus Dionysien* pp. 84–9); it comes in fact from Eriugena, *Periphyseon* II, ed. cit. p. 108.

21. In the absence of convenient modern equivalents I have simply anglicized the medieval jargon here. In the older terminology *phantasia* (originally "appearance") was used to mean "sense" (capacity for sense-perception); cf. Bernardus Silvestris, *Cosmographia*, Micr. 13.13, ed. P. Dronke (Leiden, 1978), p. 149. Eriugena distinguishes between the physical reception of an image and the conscious registering of it, the latter being the "phantasy" proper, which Eriugena says is rightly and properly called the "external sense" (but in the Gloss, at least as found in Vat. lat. 176 f.251ʳᵃ and in Albert, this has turned into "interior sense"!). Albert's account of sense-perception (on which see N. H. Steneck, "Albert on the psychology of sense perception" in Weisheipl, *Albert* pp. 263–90) depends on Aristotle, for whom "phantasy" was a power of the soul; the conventional translation was "imagination." First the sense-organ receives the "perceptible species" from the perceived object; the various sense-impressions received by the different organs are put together into a composite sense-

as "a movement taking place because of actual sense-perception."[22] The commentator himself implies this definition. And it is true that neither can be ascribed to God, but it is not true that the common sense is unaware of itself, because its proper function is to see itself see and to put together and distinguish between sense-objects.[23] If we wish to save what the commentator says, we must say that phantasy is named after seeing, as the philosopher says,[24] and so the first kind of phantasy must refer to external vision and the second to the inner powers of sense, such as the common sense and imagination; then there will be no problem in what he says.

"Nor does he have opinion," opinion being a matter of accepting something merely on the basis of symptoms, with the fear therefore that the opposite might be true.[25] "Nor does he have reason," which tracks external symptoms down to essential inner principles, "or intellect," which gets no further than the limits of rational thought, namely, understanding what something is and grasping first principles.[26] He neither has nor is any of these things. Neither can he be "spoken of or understood": we have no well-defined understanding "what" he is or "that" he is, only a blurred knowledge

---

impression by the "common sense," which then passes it on to "imagination," where it becomes a mental image that can be stored away.

22. Aristotle, *De Anima* 3.3 (429a1–2).

23. In Eriugena's terminology the first kind of "phantasy" is simply the physical reception of an image by the sense-organ, so of course it is not self-conscious. Albert's difficulty arises from his interpretation of it to mean the "common sense." When I see a bedbug, I know that I am seeing a bedbug, but this knowledge is not the result of any kind of inference; it is actually part of my seeing the bedbug that I should be conscious of seeing a bedbug. But clearly it is not with my eyes that I see myself seeing a bedbug, so it must be thanks to the "common sense" that sense-perception is aware of itself (cf. Albert, *De Homine* q.36 a.1, B 35 pp. 319–20). It is also the job of the "common sense" to make distinctions and connections between sense-impressions, judging that my perception of whiteness and my perception of sweetness are both due to one and the same object (a sugar cube, maybe), but that nevertheless whiteness and sweetness are not the same thing (ibid. q.35 a.1, pp. 306–10).

24. Cf. Aristotle, *De Anima* 3.3 (429a1–4) (φαντασία comes from φάος, light, which is the sine qua non for seeing); cf. Albert, *De Anima* 3.1.9 (Col. VII i p. 176:31–6).

25. Arguing from symptoms or clues rather than from causes leads only to probable, not certain, conclusions (cf. Albert, *Topica* 1.1.2, B 2 pp. 241–2). The definition of opinion seems to come from Avicenna, *De Anima* 5.1, ed. van Riet (Louvain/Leiden 1968) II p. 79; cf. also Gundissalinus, *De Anima* 10, ed. cit. p. 85.

26. The proper objects of understanding (intellect) are (a) fundamental principles (which cannot be argued for, they have to be presupposed in all arguments) and (b) the actual "whatness" of things. These are the "limits" of rational thought (or its "terms"), because reasoning has to begin from (a) and, with any luck, it leads to the knowledge of (b).

"that" he is. "He is neither number nor order": order follows from number, because until there is number there cannot be any before and after. Nor is he "greatness," spiritual greatness, that is, and all the other terms which follow have to be understood in the same way in line with the explanation given in the *Divine Names*.[27] "Nor is he silence" (this refers to his name of "peace") "or light" (intellectual light), nor can he be "touched by our understanding," by an understanding, that is, that would enfold the outer limits of something. As Augustine says, to touch God with one's mind is great bliss,[28] but there "touching" means merely reaching the edge of him. "Nor is there knowledge of him" (enabling us to form conclusions about him) "or truth," in the sense in which "truth" is contrasted with falsehood with reference to the facts, truth being an "equivalence between reality and our understanding."[29] And so on. The meaning is clear.

"Or to any other being": the angels, that is.

"Nor is he anything non-existent": anything merely potential.

"As it really is": that is to say, with a clearly defined knowledge "that" or with knowledge "what" it is.

"Nor does it know beings qua beings": in such a way that God's knowledge, like ours, would be caused by beings.[30]

"It has no explanation": which would make it possible for us to reason about it.

"Or darkness": darkness on God's side, that is.

"Or error": that is, going astray in knowledge because of a wrong application of basic principles.

"Or truth": as opposed to appearance, so it does not mean the same as "truth" a few lines back.

---

27. Dionysius, *DN* 9 deals with greatness, smallness, equality, likeness, unlikeness, standing and moving.

28. Augustine, *Serm.* 117.3.5 (PL 38:663).

29. This famous definition of truth was ascribed to all kinds of people in the Middle Ages (cf. note to St. Thomas, *De Veritate* q.1 a.1, Leonine XXII i p. 6:186); it seems to derive from the Arab philosophers: cf. Averroes, *Destructio destructionum*, trans. S. van den Bergh (London, 1954), p. 60, where it is cited as a commonplace. This work of Averroes' cannot be Albert's actual source, since it was not translated into Latin until the following century. Cf. L. Baur. *Die Philosophie des Robert Grosseteste, Bischofs von Lincoln (†1253)*, Beiträge XVIII/4–6 (Münster, 1917), p. 203 note 3.

30. God's knowledge, unlike ours, is creative knowledge: things are what they are because he knows them, whereas we know things because they are what they are. Cf. I *Sent.* d.36 a.7 (B 26 pp. 217–8), d.38 a.3 (pp.286–7).

"Or negation": no strictly accurate negation, because any negation rests on some affirmation, so where there is no true affirmation there will not be any true negation either, although when we are dealing with God negation is truer than affirmation. But in negative and affirmative theology "we neither affirm nor deny" God himself, but only "things which come after" him, for instance, when we say that God is wisdom or that he is not wisdom; the word "wisdom" designates our kind of wisdom, and that is not God's wisdom. So it is clear that the perfection and unity of the first cause is "above all affirmation," because all excellences are in him, but in him they are really identical, while any affirmation implies that there is some linking up of separate things. And the "transcendence" of him who is above all transcends all negation. The names which are denied of him are denied because of his transcendence, not because he lacks anything, which is why we deny things of creatures. And so his transcendence defeats all negation. And so neither negations nor affirmations arrive at any sufficient praise of him, to whom belong power and infinite splendor and eternity, forever and ever. Amen.

THOMAS AQUINAS

Introduction

I. THE LIFE AND WORKS OF THOMAS AQUINAS[1]

Thomas was born into a large, aristocratic family[2] in 1226,[3] ten years after the establishment of the Order of Preachers,[4] five years after the death of St. Dominic. It was the year in which the first signs appeared of the conflict between pope and emperor that was to dominate the next quarter of the century.[5] Some of Thomas' ancestors had borne the title "Count d'Aquino",[6] but this title had been lost several generations back and his father was known simply as "Lord Landulph d'Aquino"[7] and is described in the necrology of Monte Cassino as a "knight."[8] The family's main residence, where Thomas almost certainly first saw the light of day, was the castle of Roccasecca[9] in the kingdom of Naples, ruled at this time by the flamboyant and ambitious King Frederick II, who had been crowned emperor by Honorius III in 1220. Thomas' father, Landulph, was one of Frederick's barons[10] and in 1220 he had been appointed judge for the district round Naples, the Terra di Lavoro.[11] At least two and probably more of Thomas' brothers served at different times in the imperial army.[12] Politically the most important member of the family was a cousin of Landulph's, also called Thomas d'Aquino, whose staunch and adventurous support for Frederick was rewarded early in 1221, when he was named Count of Acerra.[12a]

Thomas' mother, Theodora, came of noble Neapolitan stock,[13] and there was a family tradition that before Thomas was born, and indeed before she realized she was pregnant, a local hermit visited her at Roccasecca and prophesied that she would give birth to a son called Thomas, who would be unrivalled in holiness and knowledge and that, in spite of his family's intention that he should be a monk at Monte Cassino, he would join the Dominicans. This story was told by Theodora herself to her granddaughter, Catherine, who told it to Thomas' biographer, William of Tocco.[14] It is not inconceivable that something of the kind took place, but there are reasons for suspecting that Theodora may have "edited" the story to some extent;[15] in particular it is difficult to believe that it was actually prophesied that Thomas would be a Dominican.[16]

A family friend was responsible for the memory of an incident in Thomas' infancy which, in the light of his later tastes, could be seen as significant: Theodora had gone to Naples to the baths, but when baby Thomas was about to be given his bath, he seized a piece of paper and would not keep quiet if it was taken away from him. His mother found that the Hail Mary was written on it, and she had to let it go into the bath with the determined child.[17] Ever after, according to Tocco, the only way to stop young Thomas crying was to give him a piece of paper with something written on it.[18] His taste for books apparently antedated his ability to read!

On 18 March 1227 Honorius III died and the next day St. Dominic's friend Cardinal Ugolino became pope as Gregory IX.[19] He immediately intimated his intention of taking a firm line with Frederick II[20] and on 10 October he formally excommunicated him.[21] Open hostilities soon broke out, and papal and imperial armies faced each other in the kingdom of Naples.[22] Landulph d'Aquino showed himself a loyal supporter of the emperor.[23]

In 1230 negotiations between Frederick and Gregory IX, in which the Dominican, Guala, shortly to become bishop of Brescia, was the chief papal negotiator,[24] resulted in a peace treaty agreed on 23 July.[25] Whether Landulph was directly involved or not, we do not know.[26]

During the period of hostilities the monastery of Monte Cassino suffered its fair share of trouble,[27] but in 1231 all was calm again and Thomas, at the age of five, was entrusted to the monks there for his education.[28] It was normal practice for upper-class families to present their younger boys as oblates to monasteries with which they were connected, and the connection between the d'Aquinos and Monte Cassino was an ancient, if not always a happy, one.[29] Thomas' parents, we are told, hoped that he would one day become abbot of Monte Cassino.[30]

At Monte Cassino Thomas started his education in earnest, acquiring the fundamental literary culture needed for any further studies.[31] According to the family tradition culled by Tocco, the young Thomas already displayed the taste for solitude and silence, which marked his later years, and he is said to have been notably pious at his prayers. Most significantly, Tocco was told that even at this tender age Thomas was chiefly interested in God.[32] Petrus Calo specifies that he often used to ask his teacher, "What is God?"[33]

In the course of 1239 Monte Cassino fell victim to renewed hostilities between the emperor and the pope. Frederick was excommunicated again on 24 March and proceeded to turn the monastery into a fortress. More and more monks were expelled until in July only eight were left there.[34] It was probably during these months that Thomas was sent home to his family, with a recommendation from the monks that he should go to study at the University of Naples.[35] At thirteen, Thomas would probably have been only slightly younger than most of his fellow freshmen.[36]

At Naples Thomas began to study philosophy, especially logic and natural science, under a certain Master Martin, about whom nothing seems to be known, and Master Peter of Ireland,[37] some of whose works have come to light in the course of this century. It seems that Peter was particularly interested in Aristotelian philosophy and that he formed part of a sort of Aristotelian movement associated with the court of Frederick II, one of whose most significant achievements was the introduction of the works of Averroes to the Latins. The university of Naples, therefore, provided a markedly Peripatetic (Aristotelian-Averroist) milieu.[38] It was no doubt partly because of his early studies in Naples that Thomas had a much sharper awareness than Albert did of the differences between Aristotelianism and Platonism.

While he was a student at Naples, Thomas got to know the Dominicans, whose priory had been founded there in 1231.[39] In particular he was befriended by John of S. Giuliano, who encouraged him to join the Order.[40] We have no direct evidence as to what attracted Thomas to the Dominicans, but it seems reasonable to suppose that it was their commitment to study and preaching. Later on, in his writings, Thomas shows himself keen to resist the common assumption that religious life means essentially "contemplative life,"[41] and he gives the highest rating to forms of religious life in which a contemplative life debouches into teaching and preaching.[42] He would surely have been responsive to the plea made by Jordan of Saxony in an Ash Wednesday sermon: we are called to bring forth fruits worthy of repentance; people say they want to bring forth fruit, but "I won't enter religion, because I should be shut in and would not bring forth any fruit." Now, says Jordan, this excuse is out of order "because here they can study and preach."[43]

Exactly when Thomas received the Dominican habit is not known. It was generally believed later on that he had entered the Order very young.[44] Tolomeo of Lucca says that he was sixteen,[45] and this may well be right. Although theoretically the Dominicans, like most other religious, did not accept novices below the age of eighteen,[46] it is clear that this rule was not being observed in the Roman province, to which Naples belonged, any more than it was elsewhere.[47] Thomas himself, in due course, defended the practice of receiving children into religious life, the only caveat being that they cannot validly make profession before puberty (i.e., fourteen).[48] So we may conclude that Thomas probably became a Dominican in 1242 or 1243. He received the habit from Thomas Agni of Lentini.[49]

In spite of papal pressure, the Dominicans at this time did not require a full year before profession. The constitutions established a probationary period of six months, with the proviso that this could be waived in the case of enthusiastic recruits who wished to make profession immediately,[50] and in fact there is evidence from precisely this period that the Dominicans preferred their novices to make profession at once.[51] But at whatever stage they made their profession, the novices were regarded as forming a separate group for a full year, having their own chapter and receiving instruction from their novice master.[52]

We know nothing of whether Thomas waited for six months before making profession, but, at least if he joined the Order in 1242, he may well have spent a full year in Naples. Then began one of those dramas which sometimes occurred when well-born young men became Dominicans against the wishes of their families.[53] The brethren in Naples were aware that Thomas' family was opposed to his entry into the Order,[54] and they were suspicious of his mother's persistent attempts to visit him.[55] The d'Aquinos were quite powerful enough to get him turned into a monk in spite of any Dominican profession he might have made.[56] It was therefore decided to send the young man away, in the hope that he would be safer from the molestation of his parents. He was accordingly despatched to the convent of Santa Sabina in Rome.[57]

The d'Aquinos did not give up. Theodora, it seems, followed

her son to Rome and renewed her efforts to gain access to him.[58] And the new pope, Innocent IV, was apparently persuaded to lend his support. The papal court was in Rome between 16 October 1243 and 7 June 1244[59] and it was presumably there that Thomas was summoned to be lured out of the Dominicans with the offer of high ecclesiastical preferment.[60] But Thomas was unimpressed. He wanted to be a Dominican.

At this stage the Master of the Order, John of Wildeshausen, probably took matters into his own hands and decided that Thomas had better go to Paris, to the studium generale there.[61] So Thomas set off with four other friars.[62] But he was not destined to reach Paris. His mother arranged to have him intercepted. She sent a message to her sons who were encamped with Frederick II and his army at Acquapendente, bidding them capture Thomas and bring him to her.[63] Frederick was based at Acquapendente during March and April 1244,[64] which gives us a secure date at last. Thomas' brothers probably obtained the emperor's support, or at least his connivance,[65] and set a watch along the various roads that might be taken by the travelling friars. In due course they found Thomas, resting with his companions by a spring (it should be remembered that the friars had to walk everywhere, so their journey would be tiring). The rest of the party was allowed to go on its way,[66] but Thomas was taken to the family castle at Montesangiovanni, near Frosinone, and then, probably, on to Roccasecca.[67] It looks as if Thomas' mother, Theodora, was waiting for him at Montesangiovanni and tried to persuade him to put off the Dominican habit; having failed in her attempt, she seems not to have known what to do next, so "she had him kept securely guarded at Montesangiovanni and Roccasecca until the return of her sons."[68] This must mean that she was waiting until her sons returned from their military service before attempting anything more with Thomas; presumably the stubborn friar was left to cool his heels at Montesangiovanni for a time and then brought home to Roccasecca.

Although Thomas' freedom of movement was restricted, he was not kept in idleness; in fact, apart from his enforced separation from his Order, he seems to have been allowed to live precisely the kind of life that suited him. Before being parted from his companions he managed to ask them to make sure that he received a breviary and a bible, and these were speedily brought to him.[69] According to Tocco he read through the bible in its entirety and also studied the Sentences of Peter Lombard.[70] And he made himself useful: he acted as tutor to his sisters and persuaded one of them, Marotta, to become a Benedictine nun at St Mary's, Capua, where in 1254 she became abbess.[71] And he is said to have written a treatise on logic, De Fallaciis, though the authenticity of this writing is not certain.[72]

Meanwhile the brethren had taken steps to secure Thomas' release. They lodged a complaint with Innocent IV against the emperor[73] and the emperor, evidently not wishing to add yet another item to the pope's list of grievances against him, arrested the guilty parties. But the Order decided not to press charges, for fear of causing scandal.[74] So poor Thomas remained in captivity, though the brethren were able to visit him, especially John of S. Giuliano, and they ensured that he had a wearable Dominican habit.[75]

When Thomas' brothers came home, the pressure on him was increased. They resorted to a tactic of which it is unlikely his mother approved: they sent to his room an attractive girl, seductively got up, no doubt in the hope that a good dose of fornication would bring young Thomas to his senses and make him less idealistic.[76] Instead young Thomas, feeling his sensuality aroused, seized a burning log from the fire and drove the lady from his room with it and then used its hot tip to draw the sign of the cross on the wall. Falling to the ground, he implored from God the gift of chastity. In response, we are told, his loins were tightly bound by two angels, so tightly that he came to with a cry.[77] The dramatic conclusion to this episode is not particularly well-attested and may have become more dramatic and more supernatural in the narrator's imagination. But Thomas' virginity was famous,[78] and one of his confessors remarked that he never mentioned suffering even from carnal thoughts.[79] And one of his students circulated the report that Thomas always shunned the company of women.[80] So, with or without the intervention of the angels, it is probably true that the would-be seduction of the young friar did have a profound effect on his personality, even if not the one that had been intended.

How long Thomas was held in captivity by his family is not entirely certain. Estimates in the sources range between about one year and three years. Tocco, who seems to be our most reliable informant, says that he was held for "about two years" and this is probably correct.[81] If he was kidnapped in March or April 1244, kept first at Montesangiovanni and then brought to Roccasecca and able to study the whole of the bible and the Sentences, while his mother waited for her other sons to come home, more than a few months must be allowed. The would-be seduction must have occurred in the winter, if Thomas had a fire in his room, so it is reasonable to date it to the winter of 1245–46.

After the failure of the attempted seduction, things were evidently at an impasse. And now Theodora seems to have taken the lead. She arranged for Thomas to escape through the window, like St. Paul, by climbing down a rope to where his Dominican brethren (who had been alerted to what was going to happen) were waiting to receive him.[82]

So, probably in the early months of 1246, Thomas was free again and restored to his brethren, who found him "as well-educated as if he had been spending a long time in the schools."[83]

What happened next does not appear clearly from the sources. He was probably taken first to Naples,[84] but plans were soon made to send him elsewhere to pursue his studies. What was remembered in the fourteenth century was that he was sent to Cologne, and that there he studied under Albert the Great.[85] It looks as if the whole tradition of Thomas' student days in the Order derives from the story of Albert as told in Cologne.[86] But in 1246 Albert was in Paris, not in Cologne, and there was as yet no studium generale in Cologne. So why should Thomas have been sent to Cologne before 1248?[87]

It must have been the Master of the Order who decided what to do with Thomas,[88] and Tocco mentions casually that he took Thomas first to Paris and then on to Cologne.[89] Earlier sources allow us to flesh out this part of the story. Gerald de Frachet, entirely ignoring Thomas' studies in Cologne, says that Thomas was sent to Paris, where he became a Master in Theology,[90] and it is probably significant that, after Thomas' death, the University of Paris, and the Arts faculty in particular, claims that it first educated and fostered him.[91] But it is Thomas of Cantimpré who seems to be the best-informed. According to him, Thomas was first sent to Paris. While he was there, his family made one last attempt to dislodge him from the Order by getting the pope to send for him and offer him the abbacy of Monte Cassino. When Thomas refused to leave the Dominicans, the pope offered to let him be abbot of Monte Cassino while remaining a Dominican, but Thomas was still unmoved. Slipping unobtrusively away from the papal court, he went to Cologne and studied there under Albert.[92]

Thomas of Cantimpré dates this whole sequence to a time before Albert went to Paris, which is patently incorrect, but otherwise he appears to have the story right.

Tocco knows that Thomas attended Albert's lectures on Dionysius' *Divine Names* in Cologne,[93] and we have the best possible proof that he did so in the form of a transcript of these lectures written in Thomas' own hand.[94] What Tocco did not know was that Albert began his lecture course on Dionysius in Paris, probably in 1247–48, and these lectures too were transcribed by Thomas.[95] The Cologne tradition, not surprisingly, carried no memories of Thomas as a student of Albert's in Paris, but there is no doubt that he was Albert's student there for at least a year. And there is nothing to prevent us believing that he was sent straight to Paris in 1246. Tocco is probably right that it was after, not before, his captivity that he set off for Paris in the company of the Master of the Order;[96] and in 1246 the Master of the Order had to go to Paris for the General Chapter.[97]

There is also some reason to believe that, during this period in Paris, Thomas attended lectures in the Arts faculty on Aristotle's *Ethics* and *De Anima*.[98]

In 1245, at the first Council of Lyons, Frederick II was solemnly excommunicated and deposed, and his subjects were freed from all bonds of allegiance to him; anyone who obeyed or supported him thereafter would be automatically excommunicated too.[99] At what stage the d'Aquinos transferred their loyalty from the emperor to the pope we do not know, but Tolomeo says that they were banished from the kingdom of Naples,[100] and Thomas' brother Reginald was put to death by Frederick[101] and seems to have been considered by his family to have been a martyr because of his fidelity to the church.[102] It is not unlikely that they solicited some favor from Innocent IV in return.

In 1248 the papal court was still at Lyons,[103] and there is nothing inherently implausible in Cantimpré's story that Thomas visited the pope in between Paris and Cologne. And the abbacy of Monte Cassino was in fact vacant in 1248.[104] And since the monastery was still depopulated,[105] the abbot was not really required to be a monk,

208

so a Dominican abbot would not be totally incongruous. At the very least, then, we can say that Cantimpré's account might well be true.

It was no doubt to remain with Albert that Thomas went to Cologne. And he was certainly there from 1248, as he continued to copy Albert's lectures on Dionysius, which were completed in 1250 and represent a good two years' worth of lecturing.[106] Thomas also attended and wrote out Albert's lectures on the *Ethics*, which can hardly have been finished before 1251.[107]

From Cologne we have two much-loved stories about the discovery of Thomas' talents. Thomas was habitually so taciturn, we are told, that he was known to everyone as "the dumb ox," and it was assumed that he was not very bright. One of his fellow students, trying to be helpful, offered to go over Albert's lectures with him; Thomas meekly accepted the proffered help. But the would-be helper soon ran into difficulties and Thomas ended up explaining the lecture to him. The student was so impressed that he went to the student master and said, "This Neapolitan Thomas is frightfully clever! Today he went over the lecture with me so thoroughly that I understood it better from him than I did from the Master." Next day, when the exercise was repeated, the student master secretly listened in and was likewise impressed and went and told Albert what a gifted student he had.[108]

Round about the same time, one of the students discovered some notes Thomas had taken on a difficult question that Albert had been disputing, and he took the notes to show Albert. Albert, as a result, decided to give Thomas what was evidently his first experience of taking an active part in a disputation. The student master was told to put a tricky question to Thomas in preparation for the disputation. Thomas tried to get out of it, in all humility, but was not allowed to escape; so he betook himself to prayer. When the time came, he responded to Albert's questions so authoritatively that Albert commented that he appeared to have taken the place of the Master rather than of a student, "determining" the question rather than "responding." After trying in vain to out-argue Thomas, Albert declared, "We call him the dumb ox, but one day he will emit such a bellowing in his teaching that it will be heard throughout the world."[109]

It is incredible that Albert should not have discovered Thomas' talents long before they went to Cologne. It was Thomas who had written up his lectures on Dionysius' *Celestial Hierarchy* for publication,[110] and Albert must have appreciated that Thomas had at least a rare talent for note-taking and editing. But it is quite possible that Albert's students in Cologne did not know of Thomas' abilities, even if they knew he was, as it were, the class "secretary." And it is easy to imagine their surprise when they began to realize that he could explain things better than Albert could.

It is also probable that Albert, even if he was aware of Thomas' unusual ability to pass on the teaching he had received, had not yet had the occasion to try him out in a disputation. Under the Dominican constitutions, the students held their own sessions with their student master to discuss "difficulties and questions,"[111] and in university disputations only bachelors and senior students played an active role,[112] so it was probably in Cologne that Albert first discovered that Thomas instinctively took on the role of the Master rather than that of the student in such a situation, and that he had every right to do so and was too humble to pretend to a stupidity he did not possess.[113]

So even if Albert himself already had some notion of Thomas' calibre before they left Paris, there is no need to jettison either of these two anecdotes from Cologne.

We also possibly have a little work written by Thomas during his time in Cologne, *De Principiis Naturae*. Tolomeo dates it to the period before Thomas' inception as a Master,[114] and its modern editors favor an early date for it.[115] Since it is closely connected with the beginning of Aristotle's *Physics* and seems to be indebted to Albert's commentary on that work,[116] can we not attribute it to Thomas' time as a student in Cologne, which is probably when Albert was writing his commentary?[117] It could be an instance of how Thomas helped his fellow students to understand their professor.

Thomas' stay in Cologne came to an end when he was sent back to Paris to begin the process of becoming a Master in Theology. The Master of the Order, John of Wildeshausen, had asked Albert to recommend someone suitable and Albert proposed Thomas. Hugh of St. Cher endorsed Albert's proposal and the Master accordingly sent Thomas to Paris.[118] But when did this occur?

We know that Thomas received his license to teach in 1256 before 3 March,[119] and shortly afterward he incepted formally as a

Master.[120] He was barely thirty years old, or perhaps still slightly under thirty[121] at the time, five years below the official minimum age for becoming a Master in Theology.[122]

According to Tolomeo, Thomas was twenty-five when he arrived in Paris,[123] which brings us to 1251. And on other grounds this seems the most plausible date. An earlier date would make it impossible for Thomas to have attended all the lectures we know he did attend in Cologne. John of Wildeshausen died early in November 1252,[124] so that gives us a firm limit in the other direction. But in February 1252 the faculty of Theology in Paris issued a deliberately anti-Dominican rule that no religious Order could possess more than one chair of theology[125]—the Dominicans being the only Order in fact to possess two chairs. In the circumstances, it would have been sheer madness to send Thomas to Paris in 1252 to become a Master, since he was far too young to satisfy the regulations.[126] In 1251, on the other hand, in spite of some anti-mendicant rumbles,[127] the situation did not look all that threatening, so the only consideration in John of Wildeshausen's mind had to be to find a candidate of sufficient intellectual ability.

University rules required that before becoming a Master all candidates had to do at least some lecturing on the bible and on the Sentences,[128] and at least five years of theological study were required before anyone could start lecturing on the Sentences.[129] Thomas had satisfied the second requirement already, if indeed he had been studying with Albert in Paris and Cologne from 1246 to 1251. So his first task when he arrived in Paris in 1251 was to give introductory lectures on the bible, as *cursor biblicus*. He chose to lecture on Isaiah, and his lectures survive, written up and edited by Thomas as a literal commentary on the text.[130] It is in connection with this commentary that we first encounter Thomas' lifelong companion, Reginald of Piperno,[131] who later became his permanent official socius.[132]

In 1252 or 1253, after lecturing on the literal sense of Isaiah and, perhaps, Jeremiah,[133] Thomas became bachelor of the Sentences and started his full-scale course of lectures on Peter Lombard's standard textbook of theology, writing them up for publication as he went. Tocco remarks on the freshness of his approach to his task: confident in his own judgment, he did not hesitate to propound new opinions and support them with new arguments, raising new topics and, above all, looking for a new clarity in his exposition.[134] It is unlikely that Tocco actually had any direct information about the impression Thomas made on his first students in Paris, and it took Thomas longer than Tocco implies to find his own intellectual way, but from the outset it is clear that Thomas is going to go his own way, politely but firmly, bringing his great gift of lucidity to bear on theological problems and, even in his earliest years as a teacher, exploring ways of making things clearer by reformulating questions, asking new questions, involving a wider range of arguments, and in particular trying to make full use of the resources of philosophy in dealing with theological problems.

Apart from his lectures on the Sentences, Thomas also wrote the short philosophical work *De Ente et Essentia* during these years before he graduated as a Master.[135] Its precise date is not known, but linguistic arguments have been proposed, suggesting that it is contemporary with the last half of the commentary on book I of the Sentences,[136] and it is quite likely that it was a spin-off from the unavoidable discussion of "essence" and "existence" in Thomas' comments on the doctrine of the Trinity and, particularly, on the nature of the angels, both of which fall within the scope of book I of the Sentences. *De Ente et Essentia*, according to an early tradition, was written by Thomas for his "brethren and companions,"[137] and it is certainly not a formal, scholastic product. Not surprisingly, it differs on some points from Thomas' later doctrine, and it is very dependent on Avicenna and William of Auvergne.[138] All the same, it announces some of Thomas' distinctive views, and especially it already reveals his desire to upgrade "existence": the real mystery of things is not *what* they are, but *that* they are, and it is their sheer existence which leads us to talk about God. Here we can recognize both one of the major differences between Thomas and Albert and one of Thomas' most basic and pervasive convictions. Albert was fascinated by all the details of *what* things are and rejoiced to find traces of God in all the intricacies of his handiwork; Thomas was profoundly uninterested in the world around him, except inasmuch as it contained books and people. Although it is probably true to say that Thomas never meant the argument in *De Ente et Essentia* 4 to be a "proof of the existence of God," and he certainly never uses it when he is formally presenting such proofs, it is still one of the ways and perhaps it is the most direct way in which the human mind is led to talk about God.[139] For Thomas, it is not really the marvelous complexity and ingenuity of things that alerts the mind to the reality of God, it is rather the metaphysical implications of very simple observations about things, beginning with the primary fact of their being there at all. And the immediate connection in Thomas' mind between existence and God is implicit in much of his theology, because it underlies his deep conviction that there can never be any separation between God and his creatures. The idea that God somehow "withdraws" in order to give his creatures space to be could never begin to make sense to Thomas; if God withdrew then being is the last thing any creature could achieve. The freedom and inner consistency of creatures is not something that has to be defended against divine interference; it is precisely the gift that is made by the divine presence. The fact that things exist and act in their own right is the most telling indication that God is existing and acting in them. Without this fundamental conviction, Thomas would never have developed his doctrines of creation and providence and grace.

While Thomas was studying and lecturing in Paris, the Dominican Order was passing through the worst crisis in its history. There had, from the beginning, been some opposition to the new mendicant Orders; their way of life was on many points quite unlike what was expected of religious and they had, not surprisingly, been viewed with suspicion.[140] Their increasingly effective public ministry cut across the traditional structures of pastoral responsibility, which antagonized some (though by no means all) of the clergy.[141] And their powerful presence in the universities threatened the prestige and corporate identity of the secular Masters.[142] Also the friars represented a new internationalism in the church, with their direct dependence on the pope and their considerable independence of the bishops, and the popes had not failed to take advantage of them as troubleshooters, who could be seen as meddling in things that were not their business by people accustomed to a less centralized view of the church.[143] They had accordingly had to defend their right to be what they were, in particular the legitimacy of their living in towns among people rather than in secluded monastic strongholds, and their right to live off alms and to preach and teach rather than engaging in manual labor and aiming at financial self-sufficiency.

The legitimacy of the mendicants' way of life had been debated in the University of Paris before Thomas' time. For instance, Jean Pointlasne, who was one of the Dominican Masters at the end of the 1240s,[144] conducted a disputation on manual labor.[145] But previously the opposition to the friars had lacked a leader and was spontaneous rather than orchestrated. From 1251–52 the situation changed. A virulent enemy of the friars, William of Saint-Amour, emerged to become the focus for a far more deliberate attack on them, in which their very right to exist was challenged and a coordinated attempt was made to destroy the whole basis of their work. William himself published a succession of tracts in which the friars were depicted in lurid terms as harbingers of the Antichrist, culminating in his book "On the Dangers of These Last Times."[146]

In 1252, as we have seen, the faculty of Theology adopted a measure designed at least to curb the power of the friars in the university. But this was only the beginning. Led by William of Saint-Amour, the secular Masters put pressure on the pope to withdraw his support from the friars and drastically to curtail their rights, and on 21 November 1254 Innocent IV issued a Bull, *Etsi animarum*, in which the freedom of the friars to preach and hear confessions was severely restricted.[147] But within a few weeks Innocent was dead—struck down by divine judgment, as the friars were inclined to say[148]—and his successor, elected with extraordinary promptness, a known supporter of the friars, Alexander IV, immediately cassated *Etsi animarum* and restored the friars to their former position.[149] This goaded some of the seculars, in particular William of Saint-Amour, to increase their denunciations.

At the Dominican General Chapter of 1254, held at Buda in Hungary, Humbert of Romans was elected Master of the Order.[150] He brought his considerable diplomatic skills to bear on the desperate situation, urging the brethren not to provoke confrontations, trying to arrive at a compromise with the University of Paris, attempting to forge an alliance with the Franciscans.[151]

By early 1256 it is clear that the mendicants are not going to be defeated. One of the immediate results of the changing situation is that the chancellor of the university, Aymery de Ver, apparently on his own initiative, gave Thomas Aquinas the license to teach, which was the first step toward becoming a Master. In doing so he was probably anticipating a demand from the pope that Thomas should be licensed.[152] Although Thomas was well below the regular age, he was instructed to prepare for his inception as a Master.

One of the most popular stories about Thomas concerned this turning point in his life. Conscious of his youthfulness and, no doubt, of the opposition he faced among the secular Masters, he was unable to decide what to talk about in the inaugural lecture that was an essential part of the process of becoming a Master. As usual, he turned to prayer and a venerable friar appeared to him and told him to take as his text Psalm 103:13, "Watering the mountains from above, the earth will be filled with the fruit of your works."[153] And that is exactly what he did. Basing himself on this text, he devoted his inaugural lecture to elaborating a splendid account of the vocation of a theologian. A text of this lecture is included in this volume. By the end of the century the Dominican tradition in Paris had identified the "venerable friar" who appeared to him as St. Dominic himself.[154]

In spite of the pope's support and that of the chancellor, Thomas was not received without complaint into the ranks of the Masters. Some of them were trying to stop people from attending the lectures of the friars and in particular they tried to prevent anyone from attending Thomas' inauguration.[155] Even after Thomas' inception the enemies of the mendicants refused to acknowledge either him or Bonaventure as members of the magisterial body, and it was not until August 1257 that this refusal was, however grudgingly, withdrawn.[156]

Soon after he became a Master, and maybe even as part of the ceremonies of his inception, some time in the spring of 1256, Thomas entered into the fray with a disputation on manual labor.[157] Then, probably during the summer, he embarked on a substantial defense of the mendicants against all the objections raised against them, *Contra Impugnantes*.[158]

It used to be maintained, on the authority of Tocco, that the *Contra Impugnantes* was written on the instructions of the pope.[159] But Tocco's account is quite extraordinarily confused and can safely be disregarded.[160] There is in fact no reason to believe that the work was specially commissioned or that Thomas was directly involved at all in the process leading up to the formal condemnation of William of Saint-Amour by the pope on 5 October 1256.[161] Since he does not mention the condemnation, it is likely that his book was more or less completed before the pope's Bull was known in Paris, but long before that it was quite clear that some such condemnation was in the wind. Thomas' concern is pedagogical. The *Contra Impugnantes* is not designed to secure a political victory for the friars; it is designed to explain and justify a particular view of religious life. It is not merely legitimate, Thomas argues, it is highly appropriate that there should be religious devoted to study, teaching and preaching (with the hearing of confessions an important pastoral adjunct of preaching). Poverty, in the rigorous sense of mendicancy, is not merely permissible, it is a crowning glory of religious life. Manual labor, by contrast, is not an essential feature of religious life. Thomas bases his exposition of the life of the friars on a general view of what religion is, and what religious life must therefore be, and he develops his case at length before turning to the more immediately practical questions about whether it is right for religious to defend themselves against slander and to the business of clearing the friars' good name. *Contra Impugnantes* is not Thomas' last word on religious life, but it is a highly competent piece of work and represents the seriousness with which Thomas undertook an important facet of his responsibilities as a teacher.

After 1256 the fourteenth-century biographers seem to have known next to nothing about Thomas' moves. Tocco, Gui and Calo abandon the attempt to present his life in any kind of chronological sequence,[162] and Gui also gives up his rather hopeless outline of Thomas' dates.[163] Tolomeo does little better.[164] Judging from the state of the tradition available to Tocco's conscientious researches, nobody had been terribly interested in the "life" of Thomas; what was treasured was the memory of his way of life, illustrated by a sprinkling of anecdotes, and the awareness of his importance as a teacher and writer.

More modern historiography has, with waning confidence, compensated for the lack of direct evidence by assuming that after the end of his Parisian regency Thomas became lector in the Dominican studium associated with the papal curia and therefore followed the vagaries of successive papal residences.[165] The resulting chronology was dogmatically summed up by Mandonnet in 1920,[166] and even the most modern biographies of Thomas have not entirely escaped being bewitched by his assurance.

Since there is not the slightest evidence to support the premise that Thomas followed the papal curia around, we need to begin again at the beginning and ask what we can actually assert on the basis of such data as we possess.

According to Tolomeo, Thomas taught for three years in Paris after his inception as a Master and then returned to Italy "for certain reasons."[167] That Thomas did indeed remain in Paris until 1259 is confirmed by other evidence. We know that he preached there on Palm Sunday in 1259.[168] Less surely, but still fairly confidently, we can also say that the first series of Quodlibetal disputations must at least take us into the academic year 1258–59.[169]

It is also reasonably certain that Thomas vacated his professorial chair in 1259. By 1260 his successor is already in possession.[170]

One small detail from this period is worth noting. A manuscript belonging to Thomas has survived, containing some anonymous disputations, which are now generally ascribed to Albert, together with Thomas' first two Quodlibets. A note on one of the pages indicates that at some stage the section containing Thomas' quodlibets must have been borrowed by Albert.[171] It is pleasing to see how Thomas and his old Master have kept in touch.

At the beginning of June 1259 Thomas was present, with Albert, at the General Chapter at Valenciennes; both were members of a commission appointed to suggest ways of promoting study in the Order.[172] It is clear that the members of this commission were chosen by the Master of the Order, Humbert of Romans, before the beginning of the Chapter[173] and, since all five were Parisian Masters, it is safe to infer that Humbert's intention was that Dominican studies should be developed along university lines, a policy already adumbrated by his predecessor.[174] Since the successful pursuit of this policy required a steady supply of university graduates in theology and made it necessary that such graduates should be available to the various provinces of the Order, there is no reason to believe that the decision to move Thomas from Paris was due to anything more mysterious than a desire to make room for another Dominican to graduate as a Master and to free Thomas for service elsewhere.[175] The fanciful speculation prompted by Tolomeo's cryptic allusion to "certain reasons"[176] is quite gratuitous.

After the end of the academic year in 1259, then, Thomas was probably no longer a professor in the University of Paris. And by the end of September 1260 he was presumably back in his province, since the Provincial Chapter meeting at that time created him a preacher general.[177]

The next secure date that we have is that in 1265 the Provincial Chapter instructed Thomas to set up a studium in Rome.[178] And in 1268, as we shall see shortly, Thomas was reassigned to Paris and by 1269 at the latest he had resumed his Parisian chair.

Apart from these dates we have a certain amount of undated information. Fontana discovered in Orvieto an assignation of Thomas to that convent as lector,[179] and we know from the testimony of Conrad of Sessa that Thomas lived in Orvieto during the pontificate of Urban IV,[180] that is, 1261–64, though this does not have to mean that Thomas was in Orvieto *only* while Urban was pope or that he was there for the whole of Urban's pontificate.

We also possess two Advent sermons, whose authenticity is generally accepted, one delivered in Bologna, the other in Milan.[181] That Thomas visited Bologna at some time is confirmed by Tocco.[182]

As a preacher general, Thomas was automatically a member of the Provincial Chapter[183] and, as such, also a member of the General Chapter whenever it was held in his own province,[184] so we may presume that he attended the Provincial Chapters in Orvieto (1261), Perugia (1262), Rome (1263), Viterbo (1264), Anagni (1265), Todi (1266) and Lucca (1267), and the General and Provincial Chapters at Viterbo in 1268.[185]

According to a late report, Thomas was also present at the General Chapter in London in 1263,[186] and a fourteenth-century writer also claims that he was present at the Bologna Chapter in 1267,[187] but both these assertions are highly questionable.[188]

What we have secured so far, then, is only a rather meager outline and a few details. Thomas was back in Italy by the end of September 1260, was assigned to Orvieto as lector some time before 1264, was assigned to Rome to set up a studium in 1265 and was reassigned to Paris in 1268.

In view of Thomas' close association with Urban IV, it seems reasonably safe to conjecture that Thomas was living in Orvieto at least since 1262, in October of which year the pope took up residence there.[189] Before the end of 1263 Thomas had completed, at Urban's request, the first part of the so-called *Catena Aurea*,[190] a running commentary on Matthew compiled from an impressively wide range of patristic sources. Also, early in 1263 he was entrusted by the pope with the task of "reviewing" Nicholas of Cotrone's attempt to use Greek patristic sources to refute modern Greek doctrines where these were at odds with Western doctrine, chiefly on the subject of the procession of the Holy Spirit.[191] We can probably infer that Thomas was assigned to Orvieto no later than 1262.[192]

As lector of Orvieto Thomas seems to have had ample time to pursue his researches and to get on with his writing. We are told that he made use of a variety of monastic libraries to assemble material for the *Catena Aurea*[193] and somewhere, perhaps at Monte Cassino, he appears to have discovered a collection of texts from the early dogmatic councils of the church, which provided him with an important source for his subsequent theological work.[194]

Some time in about 1264 Thomas seems to have been at Montesangiovanni,[195] presumably to pay a visit to whatever members of his family may have been there. And it must also have been during his years in Orvieto or Rome that he went to spend one Christmas at Molara at the invitation of Cardinal Richard degli Annibaldi, a holiday made memorable by his success in converting two Jews to the faith.[196]

If we want to pin down Thomas' moves more precisely, we have little solid evidence to go on. The acts of the Provincial Chapters survive only in a truncated form, generally missing out such details as assignations. We obtain a few more nuggets of information from a sixteenth–seventeenth century document, published by Masetti.[197] Its anonymous compiler was chiefly interested, on his own account, in facts relating to the foundation of convents in the Roman province, but he seems to have had a tolerably complete text of the Provincial Chapters to work on, and it looks as if his procedure was to select only those Chapters at which a convent was founded or something of the kind,[198] but to note down from those Chapters other little titbits which he considered interesting, including anything they said about St. Thomas.[199] Thus in 1260 he duly records that Thomas was made a preacher general, and we may cautiously infer that if the same Chapter had said anything else about Thomas (e.g., an assignation) he would have told us about it. On the same basis we can, still cautiously, infer that, since he was interested in the 1259 Chapter, he would have noted anything it said about Thomas, and since he does not mention Thomas in connection with it, presumably there was nothing about Thomas in the acts of that Chapter. If this reasoning is accepted (and its fragility must be borne in mind), we may conclude that Thomas was not assigned to Orvieto or anywhere else in 1259 or 1260. After that our compiler passes straight on to 1268,[200] so that Thomas may have been assigned anywhere, for all we know to the contrary, in any of the intervening Chapters except 1265.

In 1260, according to our compiler, the Chapter created several preachers general, including "Thomas d'Aquino who had returned from Paris a Master in Theology." The mention of Thomas' return from Paris is presumably to be ascribed to the acts of the Chapter, not to the compiler, but strictly speaking it would not be illogical to say that Thomas "had returned from Paris" even if he had actually come back well over a year before. All the same, we cannot help but wonder why the 1259 Chapter did not make Thomas a preacher general if he had already rejoined his province by then. Even if Thomas went back to Paris after the Valenciennes General Chapter to complete the academic year,[201] he could easily have reached his province before Michaelmas, which was when the Provincial Chapter met that year.[202]

So what did Thomas do after the Valenciennes Chapter? In principle it was still term-time in Paris, and in any case he presumably needed to return to Paris to collect his papers. Nor would Paris be out of his way, even if he was intending to go straight on to Italy. But did he in fact propose to go straight on to Italy? It has been suggested that maybe he stayed on in Paris, not as a professor, but to work on the *Summa contra Gentiles*.[203] The difficulty with this suggestion is that Thomas had been assigned to Paris for a specific function and, once this function ceased, his assignation there would automatically lapse and he would be expected to return to his home convent. It is hardly conceivable that he was reassigned to Paris simply to write books. And anyway we know that he left Paris just after he started writing chapter 53 of book I of the *Contra Gentiles*[204] and before he had finished editing the *De Veritate*.[205] It does not look as if he was left to write at his leisure for very long. So where did he go?

In the absence of other evidence we must follow Weisheipl and say that Thomas' destination when he left Paris was Naples.[206] But if we are right to surmise that he had not yet reached his province by the end of September, it follows that, for some reason or another, he took his time over the journey.

The two Advent sermons to which allusion has already been made can perhaps shed a little light on the matter. The text for the Bologna sermon comes from the epistle for the first Sunday in Advent, that for the Milan sermon from the gospel for the third Sunday, so it has generally been assumed that Thomas was heading north at the time. Mandonnet dates both sermons to 1268, when he believed Thomas was on his way to Paris.[207] But serious difficulties have been raised against this suggested winter journey across the Alps.[208] In 1267 Thomas was allegedly in Bologna at Pentecost for the General Chapter, but even if this story is true, which it probably is not, there would be no reason for Thomas to be still in the north in Advent. Thomas presumably passed through northern Italy again in 1272, when he was returning from Paris for the second time, but he was probably in Florence for the General and Provincial Chapters at Pentecost and by September he was in Naples.[209] So when was Thomas in the north in December? It is at least not implausible to suggest that the two sermons were preached in 1259 during Thomas' journey back to his province after his first Parisian regency. And the apparent order of the sermons may be misleading. In the Ambrosian rite, used in Milan, there are six Sundays of Advent instead of four,[210] so if we assume that a sermon preached "to the clergy and people" in Milan may have been based on the local liturgy, then both sermons may have been preached in the same week: one on Sunday in Milan (where it was the third Sunday of Advent) and one during the week in Bologna (where it was the first week of Advent).[211]

On this view, Thomas had only got as far as Milan by late November 1259. Why was he so slow to return to Naples? The obvious and correct answer is that we do not know, and indeed we do not know for certain that the question even arises, though the evidence we have been considering, taken cumulatively, seems to warrant the provisional conclusion that he did not go straight back to Naples. One possible explanation is that he was held up in Paris waiting for the graduation of the friar who was to succeed him in his professorial chair, and there is actually some evidence to support this theory. Gerald de Frachet gives us a list of Dominican Masters in Paris up to 1259,[212] and he includes Peter of Tarentaise who only incepted in 1259.[213] In 1260 the two regent Masters were Peter and William of Alton.[214] It is tempting to infer that there was some delay over the inception of William, to explain why Peter is on Gerald's list and William is not.

There are, however, considerations that weigh against this suggestion. First of all, it seems highly improbable that the Dominicans would deliberately change professors in the middle of the academic year. If Thomas' successor was not ready to take over the chair at the beginning of term, Thomas would surely have been left in Paris for another year—it is clear enough that there was no other particular job waiting for him elsewhere. And Peter does not really belong on the 1259 list anyway: it is meant to be a list of Masters who have actually taught in Paris,[215] and this was not true of Peter until the new academic year started; so his presence in Gerald's list is probably due to his known role at the Valenciennes chapter.

Even if we accept that William only incepted later, we cannot infer that Thomas retained his chair. In February 1260 an otherwise unknown "fr. Gerard Reveri" was buried in the Dominican choir in Paris; he died as a Regent Master. Destrez suggested that he may have been a secular Master who took the habit on his deathbed, in which case he would never have functioned as a Dominican Master.[216] He is certainly not mentioned in any Dominican list of Masters. But we cannot rule out the possibility that he was actually Thomas' successor and fell ill too soon for Gerald de Frachet to learn about him, leaving a vacancy that William was then called upon to fill. But in that case there was no foreseeable reason why Thomas should have to stay on in Paris, even though in the outcome there was a delay in getting his effective successor graduated.

Much better evidence needs to be adduced, then, before we can conclude that Thomas stayed on in Paris into the autumn of 1259 as a professor.

We have to fall back, after all, on Tolomeo's "certain reasons," no longer to explain why Thomas returned to Italy, but to explain why he apparently took so much time getting there. It would have been out of character for him to linger over the journey just for fun. We can only conclude that he had received some kind of instructions either from Humbert of Romans or from his provincial. At the time of the Valenciennes Chapter the Roman province lacked a provincial and was apparently unable to elect one, so Humbert appointed a provincial during the chapter, a Frenchman, currently prior of Rouen, known to the Italians as Robert the Norman.[217] He evidently issued some kind of edict on the subject of study,[218] so he must have been concerned about the intellectual life of his new province. It is possible that he commissioned Thomas, the first Parisian Master in the province, to see what other provinces were doing on his way home to Naples. If, in the outcome, nothing came of Thomas' investigations, it could be explained by the fact that in 1260 Robert was replaced by a new, elected provincial.[219] If this conjecture is right, Bologna would certainly have been an obvious place for Thomas to visit, and Tocco gives us the impression that Thomas stayed there long enough to become known in the city.[220] Before that, he could profitably have visited at least Toulouse and Montpellier. It is pleasant to think that he may have travelled south with Gerald de Frachet and his socius, Peter of Listrac![221] But we have now strayed uncomfortably far from our evidence.

To sum up, we have reason to believe that Thomas gave up his Parisian chair at the end of the academic year in 1259. We know that he was at Valenciennes in early June, but then we lose track of him. There are grounds for supposing that he was in Milan at the end of November and in Bologna in early December. Then we must presume he eventually reached his home convent of Naples. There, so far as we know, he stayed until his assignation to Orvieto, where he was appointed lector in 1261 or 1262. There he probably remained until 1265, when he was ordered to erect a new studium in Rome.

The acts of the Roman Provincial Chapters survive in an incomplete form and perhaps give us a misleading impression, but it looks as if so far the province had done little to develop its scholastic institutions. Every house was required to have a lector[222] and it was part of his job to educate the Dominican students belonging to his convent.[223] This is what Thomas had been doing in Orvieto. But before 1265 we hear nothing of any specialized or more advanced study houses. Indeed, the 1264 Chapter complains that "we see that study is being neglected in this province."[224] The appointment of Thomas in 1265 to create a new studium in Rome seems to be the province's first attempt to provide a more worthwhile course for students who were capable of something more intensive than the average house lector could supply, but were not of sufficient ability to be sent to one of the Order's international study houses. It seems that Thomas was given a free hand to run his own show; at least he explicitly had the right to dismiss students who were not up to scratch[225] and it looks as if he had effectively been given a "personal studium,"[226] in which he could develop his own ideas about how young Dominicans should be educated. As we shall see, he did not waste the opportunity offered him by his province. For a few years the convent of Santa Sabina[227] must have housed one of the most remarkable study houses the Order had ever possessed.

At some stage during this period, according to Tolomeo, Clement IV asked Thomas to be archbishop of Naples. This must have been in 1265 or 1266.[228] Thomas declined the invitation.

Meanwhile in Paris things had been ticking over peacefully enough after the fierce troubles of the mid-fifties. The friars were secure in the support of successive popes, Alexander IV (1254–61), Urban IV (1261–64) and Clement IV (1265–68). In the Dominican chairs we do not know exactly how long Peter of Tarentaise and William of Alton remained, but by 1262, when he became a cardinal,[229] Thomas' friend and student, Annibaldo degli Annibaldi, had graduated as a Master, and either his colleague or his successor was the Frenchman, Baudouin.[230] Baudouin was probably soon joined by a member of the German province, Gilbert van Eyen.[231]

In the Order, the 1263 General Chapter in London allowed Humbert of Romans to resign as Master of the Order[232] and in the following year John of Vercelli was elected in his place.[233]

Probably in 1265, or soon after, somebody "delated" Peter of Tarentaise to the Master of the Order and a hundred and eight "suspect" points in his doctrine were listed. John of Vercelli evidently referred the list to Thomas, whose own teaching was implicated to some extent since Peter, on one of the controverted points, was following Thomas. Thomas prepared a painstaking comment on the document submitted to him, sometimes criticizing Peter, but on the whole vindicating him and showing that his attacker was unfair and rather inept. John seems to have been satisfied, because no more is heard of the matter.[234]

The new Master of the Order appears to have been less concerned than his predecessors with maintaining the flow of Masters in Theology in the Order. Baudouin retained his chair at least until 1267,[235] and it was probably as his replacement that Peter returned to the university in that year to teach for another two years until he became provincial again in 1269.[236] The other chair also seems to have fallen into French hands in the person of William of Luxi.[237] In 1269 it looks as if Albert was asked to return to Paris, but then John changed his mind and asked him to go to Cologne instead.[238] The 1264 Chapter, at which John was elected, evidently wanted to ensure that the provision of Masters was not left entirely at the mercy of provincials and string-pullers, so the Master of the Order was made responsible for seeing that the Parisian studium was run for the good of the whole Order,[239] but this does not necessarily mean that it was John in person who always appointed the holders of the two Dominican chairs. In 1268, as usual, the General Chapter routinely charged him to make sure that Paris and the other studia generalia were properly provided with Masters, bachelors and so on.[240] The Order was apparently happily unaware that another storm was brewing and that the death of the pope on 29 November[241] was going to give the enemies of the friars the chance they had been waiting for to launch another bitter attack in Paris.[242]

By 1269 the Roman province had lost the services of Thomas. The Provincial Chapter, which assembled on 7 September,[243] had to devise a replacement for Thomas' personal studium, and it designated three convents of the province as special study houses, Perugia for philosophy and Naples and Orvieto for theology.[244] By then Thomas had been in Paris for some time. At the General Chapter held in Paris at Pentecost we know that he served on a commission of Masters that seems to have been set up on the spur of the moment,[245] so he must already have been in residence there.[246]

Exactly when or why Thomas returned to Paris we do not know for certain. His travelling companion when he made the journey was Nicholas Brunaccio, who later went on to study with Albert in Cologne and was highly commended by Albert, who called him "a second Thomas Aquinas."[247] Nicholas can only have been going to Paris as a student,[248] so we must infer that he and Thomas aimed to be there in time for the beginning of the academic year in 1268; unless evidence to the contrary is discovered,[249] we can presume that Thomas was in Paris at least from September 1268.

The obvious reason for sending Thomas back to Paris was that he should occupy one of the Dominican chairs of theology in the university, and we know that he was in possession of a chair at least for the academic years 1269–72.[250] But why did the Master of the Order want Thomas back in Paris?

The simplest explanation would be that the chair was vacant[251] and John of Vercelli found it convenient to reuse people who were already Masters; in 1267, after all, Peter of Tarentaise had been sent back to his teaching, and in 1269 it seems that Albert was asked to return too.

It has been suggested that Thomas may have been reassigned to Paris because of the revival of the anti-mendicant campaign there,[252] but it is far from proven that the Order was anticipating any renewal of hostilities until they actually broke out in December 1268, by which time, I have argued, Thomas was already there.

A more convincing proposal is that sending Thomas back to his professorship was the Order's response to the threat to faith posed by the so-called "radical Aristotelianism" developing in the Arts faculty,[253] to which Bonaventure had drawn attention in 1267 and again in 1268.[254] On this theory we can even consider retrieving a nugget of truth from Tocco's garbled account of the genesis of the *Contra Impugnantes*.[255] It was presumably after the two chapters in Viterbo that John of Vercelli gave Thomas his assignation, and it is quite conceivable that the pope had asked John to make some response to the situation in Paris. And if Thomas' mission was primarily to the Arts faculty we could even, if we have to, make sense of the possibility that it was not until 1269 that Thomas resumed his chair in theology.

However there is another factor, to which sufficient attention has not been paid in this connection.[256] Bonaventure's intervention in Paris was preceded by a series of disputations held by the Franciscan Master for 1266–67, William of Baglione, and it may well have been William who first raised the alarm and persuaded Bonaventure to speak out.[257] And William unambiguously implicates Thomas in the propositions he is attacking; he does not accuse Thomas of heresy, as such, but he makes clear his conviction that some of Thomas' tenets encourage precisely the two heretical beliefs denounced by Bonaventure, the eternity of the world and the non-individual nature of the intellect.[258] The "blind leaders of the blind" decried by William evidently include Thomas as their chief.[259]

Quaestiones Disputatae were public occasions in the university, attended not just by a Master's own students, but by other students as well and possibly by other Masters.[260] William's attack on Thomas would not have gone unnoticed by the Dominicans. There was little love lost between the two Orders of friars[261] and if Thomas' doctrine were to be implicated in a Franciscan campaign against heterodox philosophy, it could have serious repercussions on the Dominicans. It is at least not unlikely that it was this situation whose seriousness induced John of Vercelli to send Peter of Tarentaise back to his chair in 1267 and Thomas himself a year later, and to consider asking Albert to join him in 1269. On this view, there can be no question of Thomas delaying until 1269 before resuming his professorship.[262]

Thomas' position in Paris during his second regency was in some ways less happy than it was in 1256–59. By now he was developing a distinctive and original theology, which sometimes left him rather isolated among his fellows. One important factor in this theology was the conviction he shared with Albert that philosophy has to be taken seriously. The faith is not served by invoking dogmatic considerations to impose solutions to philosophical problems, nor is sound theology fostered by disowning philosophical conclusions that are genuinely cogent. Against the background of the continuing problem of heterodox philosophy, it is not surprising that Thomas was sometimes seen as conceding too much ground to the philosophers, but what was at stake in Thomas' position was the very possibility of a coherent Christian understanding: if Christianity is true, then it must make sense and it must make sense in terms which are related to the ordinary, untheological ways in which human beings try to make sense of things; in the long run, a faith which tries to create a new sort of "sense" of its own sooner or later ends up abandoning the attempt to make sense of things.[263] And Thomas was not prepared to give up so easily. Thus he accepted as philosophically necessary the belief that matter cannot exist without form, even though this poses problems for the doctrine of the Eucharist.[264] And he stoutly defended the view that there is nothing incoherent in the notion of an eternal creation—indeed, he argued that it was contrary to belief in divine omnipotence to deny a priori the possibility of an eternal creation; theology must therefore content itself with affirming that revelation teaches us that the world that actually exists did have a beginning in time and with showing that the philosophical argument about the eternity of the world is inconclusive.[265] His most contentious view was that Aristotle was correct to identify the soul as the form of the body and as the only substantial form involved in making this or that collection of matter into a human body. What Aristotle's doctrine secures is a strong statement of the coherence of the whole human person, as both bodily and spiritual at once, but it appears to have disastrous consequences for faith: if the soul is the only form of the body and death is the separation of soul and body, then there is no real continuity of identity between a living body and a corpse. How then can we identity as Christ's body the body that hung dead on the cross and was buried?[266]

Thomas' refusal to sidestep philosophical issues makes it easy to see why he manifestly enjoyed cordial relationships with the Arts faculty.[267] Even Siger of Brabant, who was one of the more adventurous of the ultra-Aristotelians, took Thomas' criticisms very seriously[268] and referred to him and Albert as being "outstanding in philosophy."[269] Thomas could argue with the best against the "Averroistic" doctrine that the intellect is essentially one, not personal to each individual,[270] but he argued philosophically and it seems that his arguments made more impact, at least on Siger, than the bald dogmatic condemnation issued in December 1270 by the bishop of Paris, Stephen Tempier.[271]

Among the theologians, by contrast, Thomas was faced with one controversy after another. First of all, there was the revived campaign against the mendicants. In the 1250s it had been a straight fight between seculars and mendicants and, at least after the election of Alexander IV, there was little doubt that the mendicants were winning. But during the interminable conclave that followed the death of Clement IV there was for nearly three years no pope to support the friars,[272] and so the hopes of those who wanted to clip their wings began to revive and flourish.[273] And this time the fight was a confused one, with the mendicants arguing against each other as well as against the seculars.

The leader of the seculars was now Gerard of Abbeville. The most provocative outstanding statement of the mendicant case was the Franciscan work, *Manus quae contra Omnipotentem*, probably by Thomas of York; its thesis is that perfection consists in the complete abandonment of all property, whether held individually or in common.[274] In December 1268 Gerard opened the new campaign with a Quodlibet and a public sermon attacking this thesis and suggesting instead that the highest perfection belongs to the state of pastoral responsibility and that this perfection is in no way diminished by the possession or administration of temporal goods.[275] Round about the same time he also published a more extended refutation of the Franciscan claims.[276] His Easter Quodlibet in 1269 pursued the same topic,[277] and at Christmas he set about showing that all beneficed clergy with cure of souls are in a state of perfection superior to that of religious.[278]

The Franciscans, naturally, were not slow to retort, Bonaventure and John Pecham among them.[279] Pecham was particularly insistent on the claim that renunciation even of common ownership is essential for the highest perfection.[280] This is a claim that Thomas was no more able to accept than Gerard of Abbeville was. In his Easter Quodlibet in 1270, and then more fully in his book De Perfectione, written in the same year,[281] he presented his own doctrine of perfection: Perfection consists in the perfection of charity, to which all Christians are called; poverty, like chastity and obedience, is no more than a means toward perfection, it is not a perfection in itself. But a state of perfection requires a solemn, public commitment to the pursuit of perfection. Religious are in a state of perfection, inasmuch as they bind themselves by vow to poverty, chastity and obedience, which are the outstanding means toward the perfection of love of God. Bishops are in an even higher state of perfection, because they are solemnly consecrated and pledged to a situation in which they must be prepared to lay down their lives for their flock, in which they have to use their worldly resources selflessly and be the servants of all their people and, like religious, they are obliged to celibacy. Religious, as such, are only committed to pursuing perfection for themselves, but bishops are meant to lead others to perfection, and making others perfect presupposes a higher state of perfection than is involved in simply becoming perfect on one's own. Apart from bishops, though, Thomas does not accept that any other pastoral clergy are in a state of perfection, not even archdeacons (Gerard was archdeacon of Pontieu and Cambrai).[282] The last few chapters of De Perfectione are obviously aimed at Gerard of Abbeville, but it is clear that most of the book is essentially an attack on the Franciscan doctrine. And the significance of Thomas' position for the Dominicans is not hard to see: they too needed to defend their position against the Franciscan claims and to show that it did not detract from the perfection of their state to own things in common, and it was Thomas' boast that the highest way of life was that of teachers and preachers, who, like the bishops, enlighten others as well as seeking enlightenment for themselves.[283] And it was not just vanity that was at stake. The Franciscans were not above trying to lure away Dominican vocations on the grounds that their state was the higher one, because of their higher poverty,[284] and Pecham even turned secular arguments against the Dominicans, alleging that Dominican possessions proved them to be monks, therefore they have no right to claim to be preachers.[285]

Pecham apparently wrote his response to Gerard without being aware of the line Thomas was taking, and argued against Gerard that poverty carried to the extreme of renouncing even common ownership is the highest perfection, higher than that of the pastoral clergy (including, by implication, even the bishops). He was then horrified to discover Thomas' "betrayal" of the cause, and appended some furious pages devoted to an attack on his doctrine of poverty as only a means.[286]

On other fronts too Thomas found himself at odds with Pecham. It seems likely that an episode reported by Tocco refers to Pecham: A new Master chose to attack a known doctrine of Thomas' on the occasion of his inception (when all the Masters of the faculty would be present). Thomas did not say a word, and evidently his brethren rebuked him for letting the side down, but he explained that he did not want to spoil the new Master's day.[287] Tocco specifies that this somewhat aggressive new Master was a religious, and it so happens that Pecham incepted in 1270, and it is highly probable that his *quaestio* on the eternity of the world, in which he argues against Thomas that there is a radical incoherence in the idea of an eternal creation, was part of the ceremonies of his inception.[288]

But it was not only Pecham who was suspicious of Thomas' attitude. Thomas' own bachelor, Romano of Rome, mentions Thomas' position, but says that it is not very cogent and so it is better to follow the commoner view, that an eternal creation is impossible.[289] And Thomas' vigorous defense of his own stance, *De*

Aeternitate Mundi, which surely dates from this period, seems not to have been allowed to circulate at all widely.[290]

According to a letter of Pecham's from some years later, Thomas was on one occasion called upon to defend his doctrine that there is only one substantial form in human beings at a gathering of Masters with the bishop, and no one, not even the Dominicans, agreed with him. Pecham claims that he alone stood up for him "as far as truth would permit."[291] Thomas must have found it very galling being patronized by Pecham, and it is quite likely that this was the occasion remembered in the Dominican tradition as one on which Pecham publicly insulted Thomas, without succeeding in ruffling his patience.[292] All the same, Pecham was probably telling the truth when he said that no one was prepared to agree with Thomas.

Even at the General Chapter of 1269 Thomas had found himself in disagreement with his fellow Dominican Masters: on two points in the report submitted by the commission of Masters Thomas expressed a lone dissenting opinion, advocating a subtly nuanced position on how far a superior could go in obliging his subjects to reveal secrets concerning matters of conscience. Thomas maintained that, if the matter was already in some sense public, then a superior could use his authority to probe further, whereas something that was genuinely secret should not be divulged and therefore no superior should demand to have it divulged.[293]

Among the seculars, an up-and-coming bachelor, Henry of Ghent, was lecturing on the Sentences and, although no direct record of his lectures survives, there is reason to believe that he expressed his opposition to a variety of Thomistic theses and argued that they were not merely wrong, but contrary to faith.[294]

Thomas was not entirely alone, of course. Judging from the Quodlibets of this period, his controversial beliefs aroused considerable interest among his students, though we cannot tell whether they were sympathetic or not to his views.[295] And people appreciated his lectures on the bible. Reginald took down his lectures on John at the request of the provost of Saint-Omer and others,[296] and two people independently took down his lectures on Matthew, one of them a Dominican, Peter d'Andria, who was evidently an admirer of Thomas,[297] the other a secular cleric, Léger of Besançon.[298]

Among the other Dominican students in Paris at this time, we know that the young Remigio dei Girolami was deeply impressed by Thomas[299] and John of Caiazzo seems to have been a friend of his,[300] though we have no direct evidence of what he made of Thomas' teaching.

Not least, on Thomas' side, there was the Augustinian bachelor, Giles of Rome.[301] He was no uncritical follower of Thomas, but on many points he espoused his doctrine. He was well-aware of the evolution of Thomas' thought and sometimes used his later writings in order to criticize what he had said earlier.[302] Evidence of his enthusiasm for Thomas was produced later on in the course of Thomas' canonization process.[303] His was probably just the kind of support Thomas most appreciated: he took Thomas seriously and respectfully as a theologian, but never sacrificed the autonomy of his own mind to the authority of "the Master." He was never a "Thomist," perhaps, but he arguably had a better understanding of what Thomas was about than some of the later partisans who could not tolerate even the slightest hint of criticism of anything Thomas had ever written.

Thomas himself, no doubt, went about his business, calm and cheerful as usual,[304] in spite of all the controversies that surrounded him. But the scene was already being set and the dramatis personae were assembling for the attempted condemnation of some of his tenets in 1277 and for the ensuing dramas that culminated, paradoxically, in the excommunication of an English Dominican for Thomist teaching and the formal adoption of that same teaching by the Dominican Order as a whole.

In 1272, because of a dispute with the bishop, the whole university went on strike and all lectures were cancelled from the beginning of Lent.[305] Thomas apparently held his usual Lenten Quodlibet,[306] but by June it was known that he was being withdrawn from Paris.[307] His colleague in the other chair, William of Quinsac, a member of the Provence province, was withdrawn at the same time.[308] His enemy, John Pecham, also probably left Paris and went to teach in Oxford.[309] Thomas was succeeded by the short-lived Romano the Roman;[310] William, it seems likely, was succeeded by the Catalan Dominican, Ferrer.[311]

There was no point in staying on idly in Paris, so Thomas presumably returned to Italy in time for the General and Provincial Chapters in Florence. The General Chapter initiated legislation which, had it become law (which it did not, as the 1274 Chapter threw it out), would have created a new international studium in the Roman province.[312] The Provincial Chapter, rather jumping the gun, gave Thomas full authority to set up such a studium anywhere he liked in the province.[313] He plumped for Naples, where there was already a provincial studium for theology.[314] No doubt he started his courses there in the autumn.[315]

Thomas had been away from his home convent for ten years or more, but there were at least some familiar faces among his brethren there. There was Reginald, of course, who arrived with him, and two of his students from Paris, John of Caiazzo and Peter d'Andria. There was the ex-provincial, Troiano. And, most marvelously of all, old John of S. Giuliano, the mentor of his youth, was still alive there.[316] And Thomas' decision to settle in Naples was appreciated by the civil authorities too; King Charles I undertook to pay the convent a stipend for as long as Thomas was teaching there,[317] which probably means that he was co-opted as professor of theology for the University of Naples.[318]

At Michaelmas 1273 he was a diffinitor at the Provincial Chapter in Rome.[319] Returning to Naples he was accompanied, as ever, by his faithful companion Reginald, and also by his student, Tolomeo of Lucca. On the way, as we learn from Tolomeo, both Thomas and Reginald fell ill while the party was staying with Cardinal Richard degli Annibaldi. Reginald's condition appeared to be serious, so Thomas gave him a relic of St. Agnes he was bringing from Rome. To the surprise of the doctors, Reginald recovered. In commemoration of this miracle, Thomas arranged for a solemn celebration among the brethren in Naples, "together with a good meal," which he wanted to become an annual event.[320]

On about 6 December 1273 something happened to Thomas, which left him physically very weak and psychologically unable to go on working. The nature of this occurrence is not entirely clear; we shall return to it later and see what we can make of it. At any rate it marks the end of Thomas' teaching and writing. Thereafter he was obviously a sick and rather helpless man. Presumably in the hope of perking him up, he was sent to visit his sister, the Countess Theodora of San Severino, but the visit was not a success; Thomas appeared to be in a dazed condition and hardly spoke a word, greatly to the distress of his sister. So he was taken back to Naples, although he was evidently finding it difficult to travel.[321]

Not very long after this Thomas had to set off again. He had been asked by the pope to assist at the forthcoming Council of Lyons, due to begin in May 1274.[322] He left Naples with Reginald and a lay servant to look after him; on the way they were joined by some other ecclesiastics.[323] Between Teano and Borgonuovo Thomas bumped his head against a tree that had fallen across the road. The accident left him a bit stunned, but he made light of it. To distract him, Reginald began to talk about the Council and his hopes for it. "You and brother Bonaventure," he said to Thomas, "will become cardinals and bring glory to your Orders"; but Thomas rather sternly put an end to this banter.

At Maenza they broke their journey at the home of Thomas' niece, Countess Francesca di Ceccano, and there Thomas became seriously ill. Some of the monks of the nearby Cistercian monastery of Fossanova, of which the Ceccanos were patrons,[324] visited and ministered to the sick friar. Some time in February, feeling his end approaching, Thomas remarked that he would rather the Lord found him in a religious house, so he was taken to Fossanova. As he entered the monastery he was heard to say, "Here is my rest forever" (Psalm 131:14).[325] About a month later he received the last rites with great devotion and, two days afterward, he died, attended by Reginald and a few other Dominicans, the monks of Fossanova and the Franciscan bishop of Terracina with his Franciscan companions.[326]

The monks of Fossanova were in no doubt about the greatness or the sanctity of their Dominican guest. One of the laybrothers later testified that he had heard it said that Thomas had been invited to the Council "because he was considered to be one of the wisest and holiest men in the world."[327] As a gesture of respect, we are told, the monks personally carried the wood for Thomas' fire, and he received their service with a corresponding humility.[328] They were impressed by the uncomplaining way he endured his infirmity[329] and remembered that he had been no trouble to the people who were looking after him.[330]

Once he was dead the monks unashamedly began to treat him

as a saint. They hid the body, for fear it would be taken from them,[331] but Thomas appeared to the prior in a vision and demanded to be put back in the sanctuary, so his body (which they found still incorrupt) was solemnly translated and the Mass of a Confessor was sung.[332] In 1276, when Thomas' old colleague, Peter of Tarentaise, became pope, the monks were afraid that the Dominicans would obtain possession of the precious corpse, so they removed and hid Thomas' head.[333] A few years later the body, still incorrupt, was translated to a more honorable place by the new abbot, Thomas' admirer, Peter of Montesangiovanni.[334] By 1288 other people were beginning to take an interest. Thomas' sister, the Countess Theodora of San Severino, asked to see the relics and, at her request, a hand was detached and given to her,[335] and some years later a thumb from this hand was presented by Reginald to the Dominican cardinal, Hugh de Billom.[336] In 1309 the chaplain at San Severino regarded Thomas' hand as the choicest relic in his keeping, as a visiting canon discovered to his cost when he fell ill after refusing to take it seriously on the grounds that Thomas was "not a saint, he was only a Dominican."[337] Later the hand was given to the Dominicans in Salerno.[338]

Miracles began to occur in connection with Thomas' tomb.[339] One which made a particular impression on the monks happened a few years after Thomas' death: no less a person than the community physician, Dr. Reginald, was cured of his gout.[340] By the end of the century the monks regarded Thomas as their habitual "medicine."[341] Little by little Thomas acquired a reputation in the neighborhood, and pilgrims started arriving at the monastery seeking supernatural remedies for their ailments through his intercession.[342]

In Naples Thomas' holiness seems to have been widely believed and talked about.[343] Thomas' students, both lay and Dominican, related their various stories about him to their friends,[344] and Reginald of Piperno, who had apparently taken over Thomas' job as lector in Naples, publicly commented in his lectures on how Thomas had always resorted to prayer when he was unable to understand something.[345] A young man who had only known Thomas by sight,[346] Bartholomew of Capua, became fascinated by what he heard about him and, through his Dominican friend John of Caiazzo, who had been Thomas' student in Paris and in Naples, gained access to other friars who could talk to him about Thomas' earlier life, including old John of S. Giuliano, whose protégé Thomas himself had been as a youth.[347] Bartholomew interested himself in Thomas' works too, and procured a catalogue of them; he says he spent several years reading them.[348] It is to him that we owe the comment that would probably have pleased Thomas most of all, that "people of all sorts can easily benefit from his writings according to whatever little intellectual capacity they have, and that is why even the laity and people who are not very bright look for his writings and desire to have them."[349] When James of Viterbo became archbishop of Naples in 1302, one of the first things he did was to visit the Dominican priory in order to see Thomas' room and the place where his desk had been, and Bartholomew heard him speaking in the most glowing terms of Thomas' doctrine,[350] in which he had probably become interested as a result of the enthusiasm of his fellow Augustinian, Giles of Rome.[351]

Elsewhere in Italy those who had stories to tell about Thomas were obviously pleased to relate them.[352] In Brescia a former student of Albert's in Cologne, the Italian Albert of Brescia, made no secret of his conviction that Thomas was a saint and evidently used his position as house lector to propagate the teachings of Thomas. In the mind of one of his students, Anthony of Brescia, the highest accolade that could be bestowed on someone was to call him "a follower of the teaching of Thomas."[353] Behind Albert of Brescia we can probably recognize the influence of Albert the Great, who was very upset when he heard of Thomas' death and whose appreciation of Thomas' greatness is not in doubt.[354]

In Paris Thomas' reputation was more ambiguous. The Arts faculty expressed its grief at his death in a surprisingly emotional letter to the General Chapter of 1274 and asked to have his body sent back to Paris,[355] and there is evidence that Thomas' writings exercised a serious influence on the philosophers there.[356]

The theologians, on the other hand, were mostly hostile. The "neo-Augustinianism" pioneered by Pecham[357] was for the moment carrying the day, sustained by the Franciscans and by some of the seculars, notably Henry of Ghent.[358] The bishop, Stephen Tempier, and most of the theologians were deeply suspicious of some of Thomas' philosophical options and so the "cause" of Thomas continued to be embroiled in the affair of heterodox Aristotelianism, which was far from having been resolved by the 1270 condemnation. It is tempting to suppose that this is why the Dominican Giles of Lessines, sometime in the middle of the decade, wrote to Albert about some of the worrying propositions current in the Arts faculty;[359] with Thomas gone, there was no one else to carry on (and defend?) the policy of dealing with philosophical problems philosophically, on their own ground.

In 1274–75 the English Franciscan who was soon to emerge as the official spokesman for Franciscan anti-Thomism, William de la Mare, was Regent Master,[360] and he attacked Thomistic positions in his disputations.[361] Giles of Rome continued to support some of Thomas' contentious doctrines, including unicity of form,[362] but he was fighting a losing battle, as he was to discover to his cost.

Rumors of doctrinal disarray, first in the Arts faculty and then even among the theologians, reached the Master of Arts who had become pope under the name of John XXI, and in 1277 he sent two letters to Bishop Tempier demanding an inquiry and a full report,[363] but Tempier had his own plans and apparently took no notice of the pope's intention that the Holy See should deal with the affair.[364] He set up a commission of sixteen Masters,[365] including Henry of Ghent,[366] whose brief was clearly an extensive one, to examine "errors" current in the Arts faculty and to consider the doctrines of Giles of Rome and Thomas Aquinas.[367] The commission seems to have been hustled fairly overtly by the bishop and his henchmen, including the papal legate, Simon de Brion. Giles of Rome reports that the hesitation of the Masters over some of the points raised was overridden by a headstrong minority.[368] On 7 March a long list of propositions allegedly emanating from the Arts faculty was condemned by the bishop.[369] The commission then turned its attention to the theologians, beginning with Giles of Rome. A list of fifty-one propositions, many of them Thomistic, was drawn up, which Giles was required to recant; when he defended them instead, he was forbidden to receive the license to teach, so could not become a Master.[370] One of the condemned theses was that of unicity of form, and the bishop was obviously determined to prevent its being taught. Henry of Ghent, in his 1276 Quodlibet, had left the matter open and he was summoned by the papal legate, with the bishop and the chancellor in attendance, and was told that in the future he must explicitly declare the doctrine of unicity of form to be unacceptable; and he got the impression that he was being threatened with unpleasant consequences should he fail to obey.[371]

After Giles of Rome the bishop turned to Thomas Aquinas, and apparently all the available Masters were called in to discuss a list of Thomistic propositions. Again one of the suspect theses was unicity of form, and we are told that all the Masters condemned it except two (presumably the two Dominican Masters).[372] We do not know all the details, but there was clearly a whole list of theses and the overwhelming majority of Masters agreed to their condemnation.[373]

All was now set for a formal censure of Thomas. For some reason it did not happen.[374] It is probable that John of Vercelli, the Master of the Dominican Order, who was in Paris at this time on a papal diplomatic mission,[375] intervened and insisted on the whole affair being referred to the Holy See.[376] It also appears that Albert lent his authority to the defense of Thomas.[377] In any case, we know that some of the cardinals, gathered in Viterbo to elect a new pope after the death of John XXI on 20 May,[378] forbade Tempier to proceed any further.[379]

Thomas thus escaped being publicly censured in Paris. But his Franciscan opponents did not leave the matter there. Very soon after the Masters' condemnation of Thomas, William de la Mare wrote a detailed critique of his doctrine and also a more compact catalogue of some of his teachings, in which he tried to show that the positions maintained by Thomas were a danger to faith and, in many cases, implicitly condemned by the bishop on 7 March.[380] At the Franciscan General Chapter of 1282 the Minister General committed the Order to following William's critique: copies of Thomas' *Summa* were to be restricted to lectors who would be able to make "intelligent" use of them, and in every case they were to be accompanied by William's comments; rather conspiratorially, the Minister General adds that in no circumstances were these comments to be given to seculars to copy.[381]

In Paris Thomas was only condemned privately. In Oxford the Dominican archbishop of Canterbury, Robert Kilwardby, secured the agreement of the Masters and issued his own list of condemned propositions on 18 March 1277, and this list did affect Thomas unambiguously, though he was not mentioned by name. In particular the thesis of unicity of form was condemned outright.[382]

Kilwardby's action seems to have precipitated a fairly dramatic crisis among his brethren. We do not know exactly what happened in England, but it attracted the attention of the Order; in 1278 the General Chapter despatched two special visitators in haste to look into the scandal caused by Dominicans who were criticizing the writings "of the venerable father, friar Thomas d'Aquino," and they were given full authority to punish the offenders and even to banish them from the province, whatever their status.[383]

In Paris Giles of Lessines quickly published a defense of Thomas' doctrine of unicity of form,[384] and Kilwardby received a stern letter from the Dominican archbishop of Corinth, Peter of Conflans,[385] who had been in Paris at the time of William of Baglione's attack on Thomas.[386]

In 1279 the Dominican General Chapter, while recognizing that some of the brethren might not always agree with Thomas, declared it to be "intolerable" that any of them should speak disrespectfully about him or his writings, which are a great "honor" to the Order; priors, provincials and visitators are commanded to punish severely any offenders they discover.[387] But in England by this time the situation had become even more acute, with the appointment of our old friend John Pecham as archbishop of Canterbury on 28 January of that year.[388] Pecham's hostility to the Dominicans was no secret,[389] and he readily saw doctrinal disagreements in terms of a more or less systematic opposition between Franciscans and Dominicans.[390] Nevertheless, at first he held his fire, and Kilwardby's condemnation of Thomistic theses was effectively left in abeyance. Ignoring Kilwardby and keeping silent about the Parisian condemnation by the Masters (which was not public anyway), the Dominicans hastened to defend Thomas against William de la Mare. Four separate books appeared in rapid succession, responding to William's *Correctorium* (which the Dominicans all nicknamed *Corruptorium*); three were by Englishmen, Richard Knapwell, Robert Orford and William Macclesfield, and the fourth was by a Frenchman, John Quidort of Paris.[391] Robert also wrote a treatise on unicity of form.[392] All of these works were composed by 1284 at the latest.[393]

All this while Pecham apparently did nothing, but the Dominicans must have been anxiously waiting for him to make a move. In 1284 the English provincial, William Hothum, told the archbishop to his face that the brethren had repeatedly voiced their fears to him and that they were convinced that Pecham was going to take partisan and unfair action against them.[394] Nothing daunted, on 29 October 1284 Pecham convened the Masters of Oxford and formally renewed Kilwardby's 1277 condemnation, including in particular the thesis of unicity of form,[395] a doctrine of which Kilwardby's successor obviously had a keen abhorrence.[396] The Franciscan archbishop denied that his action was prompted by any anti-Dominican sentiments, but in the very process of justifying himself he slips instinctively into partisan language.[397] It was no doubt this suspicion of his motives that rallied the Dominicans to fight back, as they had not done in 1277, and that inspired the university authorities effectively to withhold their support from the archbishop's campaign. The Dominican Richard Knapwell was rash enough to publish another tract on unicity of form. Pecham was not amused.[398]

In Paris, meanwhile, the situation was improving. On 28 March 1285 Martin IV died,[399] none other than Tempier's old crony, Simon de Brion. On 2 April Giacomo Savelli became pope as Honorius IV.[400] Giles of Rome seized the opportunity and appealed to the new pope, who ordered the bishop of Paris, now Ranulph de la Houblonnière (another associate of Tempier's),[401] to review the articles Giles had been ordered to recant in 1277, with the chancellor and all the Masters of the university. The bishop was to follow the opinion of the Masters: whatever they decided Giles must recant must be recanted, and if Giles complied, no further obstacle should be placed in the way of his receiving his license to teach.[402] The result was a definite rehabilitation of Giles and, indirectly, of Thomas; none of the Thomistic doctrines on whose recantation Tempier had insisted seems to have featured in the 1285 recantation.[403] Honorius also appears to have referred the dossier on Thomas Aquinas back to the Parisian Masters,[404] and in the outcome even the vexatious thesis of unicity of form was merely declared to be wrong, without being contrary to faith.[405] A group of twelve Masters issued a public statement to the effect that, to their knowledge, it never had been condemned as heretical.[406] Even Henry of Ghent, who thought that the Thomistic thesis did have heretical implications, was forced to acknowledge that Pecham's condemnation of it in England was misguided.[407]

Pecham, however, was in no mood to compromise. On 30 April 1286 he condemned Knapwell as a heretic. Perhaps under pressure from Hothum, he seems to have relented almost immediately to the extent of not mentioning Knapwell by name in the official record of his act, but the doctrine was still condemned as heretical. Knapwell himself appealed to the pope. Unfortunately for him, his appeal arrived too late to be heard by Honorius IV, who died on 3 April 1287.[408] His successor, Nicholas IV, was the former Franciscan Minister General, Jerome d'Ascoli.[409] When Knapwell's case was eventually dealt with in 1288, Knapwell was condemned to perpetual silence. He retired to Bologna and, apparently, did not observe the ban that had been imposed on him and shortly afterward he died in miserable circumstances.[410]

In Dominican circles Pecham rapidly acquired an almost legendary reputation as a persecutor of the Order. In the mid-1290s a story reached Dietrich of Apolda in Erfurt concerning this era, which he duly incorporated into his life of Dominic: Allegedly a pitched battle was fought between the champions of the two Orders of friars. In spite of having a much larger army, the Franciscan champion was roundly defeated and mortally wounded. After the battle he rudely dismissed the Franciscans who wanted to tend him and demanded to be taken to the Dominicans to die.[411] Not a very likely tale, perhaps, and it is even less likely that Thomas would have wished his doctrine to be defended in such a violent way.

The squabble with Pecham was nasty enough for those immediately involved in it, but the rehabilitation of Thomism in Paris in 1285 was a much more significant event. It amounted to an official recognition of the legitimacy of Thomist theology, and the Dominicans were not slow to take advantage of it. In 1286 the General Chapter, while still acknowledging that not everyone in the Order necessarily agreed with Thomas, issued a strict ruling that all the brethren must do everything in their power to foster and defend Thomas' doctrine as a legitimate theological option.[412]

The most lasting effect of Pecham's "persecution" was probably that it united the Dominicans in their defense of Thomas. His partisanship created a corresponding partisanship among the Dominicans. It is surely no accident that the most emphatic counterattack in support of Thomas came from England during Pecham's time as archbishop.[413] And this is all the more remarkable if we remember that in 1278 it was the English who had alarmed the Order by their criticism of Thomas. It is tempting to say that the growth of self-conscious Thomism owes a great deal to Pecham.

It is the background of Pecham's "persecution" that perhaps explains a certain extremism in English Thomism. Robert Orford, probably in the mid-1280s, turned his pen to defending Thomas against Henry of Ghent and then, perhaps at the turn of the decade, proceeded to defend Thomas even against Giles of Rome, apparently not recognizing that Giles was sometimes attacking early Thomas precisely in support of Thomas' own later positions. Robert was seemingly reluctant to acknowledge any serious development in Thomas' thought.[414] Another writer, probably Knapwell, also defended Thomas against Giles and seems not even to notice that Thomas sometimes changed his mind.[415] Elsewhere a much more sensible line was taken, embodied in an anonymous work drawing attention to the points on which "Brother Thomas wrote better in the *Summa* than he did in the commentary on the Sentences."[416] This latter work was no doubt intended to assist Dominican lectors who wanted to use Thomas in connection with lecture courses still tied to the Sentences as the basic theological textbook.[417]

The Franciscans liked Thomism no more than they had done before, and over the years found new things to dislike in it.[418] William de la Mare's *Correctorium*, of which he had produced a second, enlarged edition in about 1284,[419] was still their official response to Thomas. And Henry of Ghent went on hoping for a condemnation, at least of the doctrine of unicity of form.[420] But Thomism had weathered the storms, and no further serious threat was posed to its survival.

What Thomas would have made of Thomism is another question. He did not succeed in revolutionizing the Order's educational procedures, as he had tried to do in his studium in Rome. It was not until the latter part of the fifteenth century that his *Summa Theologiae* began to be adopted as a theological textbook instead of the Sentences,[421] and his attempt to secure a broad theological formation for the friars who were not up to university level came to nothing. Instead, his doctrine filtered down to the ordinary Dominican students in the form of isolated extracts inserted into practical handbooks of moral and pastoral theology[422] and selected questions treated in the classroom.[423] The great intellectual adventure, which had been his life's work, soon turned into an orthodoxy to be defended and propagated, instead of being carried on as a task that can never be completed, but which is supremely worthwhile even in its failure.[424]

In 1309 the Dominican General Chapter made "Thomism" the official doctrine of the Order, bidding all lectors throughout the Order to follow the teaching of Thomas,[425] and similar and even stronger statements followed in 1313, 1314 and 1315, together with the first indications that parts of his works were henceforth to be used throughout the Order in Dominican study houses. No Dominican student could go to Paris unless he had first spent at least three years studying Thomas.[426] In 1315 the Master of the Order, Berenger of Landorra, himself a graduate of Paris,[427] expressed a desire that all studia generalia and all convents where there were Masters in Theology should have the complete works of Thomas in their libraries.[428]

In 1303 we have evidence that Bartholomew of Capua and, apparently, William of Tocco were collecting stories about Thomas and, since Bartholomew also passed on at least one such story to the newly elected Dominican pope, Benedict XI, who heard it "carefully and with great enthusiasm,"[429] it can be inferred that some people were hoping to interest the pope in getting Thomas canonized; but nothing came of it.

In 1317 the Provincial Chapter of Naples commanded Tocco to assemble the evidence of Thomas' miracles and to present it to the pope, now John XXII.[430] Tocco, possibly prior of Benevento at the time, was already an old man.[431] But he had lived with Thomas in Naples[432] and may also have had family connections with the d'Aquinos,[433] and he set about his task immediately. He probably did not need to do very much new research to produce his dossier, but in November he interviewed Thomas' nephew, Count Thomas of San Severino[434] and in the following February he visited Thomas' niece, Lady Catherine of Morra, at Marsico.[435] By August 1318 he was able to submit his report to the pope in Avignon, backed by an appeal from the Queen of Sicily, the University of Naples and various noblemen,[436] and while he was there he renewed his acquaintance with Thomas' former student, Tolomeo of Lucca, who confirmed one miracle story for him and told him another.[437]

John XXII was already interested in Thomas. In 1317 he had spent quite a lot of money procuring copies of his works for the papal library,[438] and shortly afterward he commissioned a "de luxe" edition of Thomas' major writings, which took seven years to complete and which the pope evidently read, since many of the volumes are annotated in his own hand.[439] On 13 September 1318 he formally launched the canonization process. In 1319, between 21 July and 18 September, the depositions of a range of witnesses were received in Naples.[440] In 1320 the Dominican General Chapter notes that there is a "good hope" of Thomas being canonized, and orders funds to be collected for the purpose.[440a] On 1 June 1321, presumably feeling that not enough evidence of a real cult of Thomas had so far been produced, the pope commissioned a further enquiry, to investigate specifically the miracles alleged to have been occurring at Fossanova.[441] He himself was probably chiefly interested in canonizing Thomas precisely as a theologian,[442] but the formal procedures were strict by this time and a careful examination of the evidence for miracles was necessary.[443] Eventually, on 14 July 1323, the ceremonies for the canonization began, with the pope himself preaching a sermon in which he highly commended the Order of Preachers and affirmed that, after the apostles and the doctors of the early church, Thomas was the teacher who had most enlightened the church.[444] On 18 July Thomas was officially pronounced a saint.[445] Soon afterward the pope commissioned the Dominican John Dominic of Montpellier to produce a "potted" *Summa*, presumably for his own use.[446]

On 14 February 1325 the bishop of Paris, after consulting all the Masters and bachelors in the faculty of Theology, withdrew the condemnation of the articles proscribed in 1277 insofar as they implicated or appeared to implicate the doctrine of St. Thomas.[447]

St. Thomas' Writings

In the course of his relatively short lifetime, Thomas produced an impressive number of writings, covering a considerable range of topics.[448] Unfortunately it is often difficult to be sure of the dating of these various writings. Recent scholarship, based particularly on the evidence of Thomas' citation of Greek sources, the date of whose translation into Latin is more or less known, has tended to push an embarrassing number of his writings into the last few years of his life; since it is unlikely that in fact he wrote quite as much as has been suggested in such a short period, the possibility has to be kept in mind that several of his works, and particularly the commentaries that originated as lecture-courses, were revised, maybe several times, so that Thomas could incorporate material he had not previously known.[449] If this is correct, then of course we need to ask exactly what we are dating when we attempt to fix the chronology of Thomas' works. One and the same work, as we have it now, may contain passages from widely separated periods.

In what follows I shall not attempt to give an account of all Thomas' works; instead I shall take the major categories into which most of these works fall and give some indication of the sequence in which the individual works were written, insofar as it is possible.

As a Master in Theology, whether in the university or in the studia of the Dominican Order, Thomas' first responsibility was the theological exposition of scripture.[450]

During his first regency in Paris (1256–59) we can be sure that Thomas lectured on some books of the bible, but it is not clear that we have any record of these lectures, since the written commentaries, as they stand, must all be dated to a later period, though it is possible, particularly in the case of some of the Pauline commentaries, that they incorporate material dating from the first regency.

While he was at Orvieto Thomas undertook a remarkable work at the request of Urban IV: a commentary on all four gospels, culled from patristic sources. The first part, on Matthew, was presented to Urban in 1263.[451] The rest was completed after Urban's death and dedicated to Thomas' friend, Cardinal Annibaldo degli Annibaldi. This commentary, generally known as the *Catena Aurea*, is an impressive testimony to the seriousness with which Thomas tried to document his theological work. Matthew was already well-provided with available commentaries, and the Greek tradition was represented by a Latin translation of the authentic homilies of Chrysostom and by another set of homilies falsely ascribed to Chrysostom.[452] This Eastern (and supposedly Eastern) material had already been absorbed into the postils of Hugh of St. Cher. But when he turned to the remaining three gospels, Thomas was evidently struck by the lack of Greek material, and so he procured the services of a translator and had a Greek catena translated for his use.[453] Like Albert, Thomas was plainly not content to rest snugly within a purely Latin tradition, and though he knew little Greek for himself, he did what he could to enrich his reading with Greek material.

The *Catena Aurea* is not the product of Thomas' teaching. But it provided him with an admirable tool that he could use in his teaching, and his later works show that he did use it.[454]

There seems little doubt that it was also at Orvieto, probably early in his stay there, that Thomas wrote his commentary on Job.[455] It is a highly polished work, and it is impossible to tell whether or not it originated in the classroom. Tocco points out, with some justification, that Thomas was doing something that no one else had dared to do: a systematic exposition of the literal sense of Job,[456] a book that had generally been used in a very free and allegorical way, in the wake of Gregory the Great's famous *Moralia*. Why Thomas elected to comment on Job we can only conjecture. It is obviously a crucial biblical text for anyone concerned with the theology of providence, and providence was a topic in which Thomas was very interested, not least at this time, during which he undertook an extended study of the subject in book III of the *Contra Gentiles*. We can probably see in his commentary an example of his habitual way of working: while pursuing speculative theology, he wanted to be sure that he understood his main sources properly, and the best way to ensure that was to comment on the sources in detail, either in the classroom or in writing.

During his second regency in Paris many of Thomas' biblical lectures were taken down and, more or less, prepared for publication. We know that he lectured on the gospel of John, and these lectures were written up by Reginald of Piperno at the request of the provost of Saint-Omer and others.[457] Thomas is said to have revised the text of the comments on the first five chapters himself.[458]

The lectures on Matthew have traditionally been ascribed to Thomas' first Parisian regency,[459] but it has now been shown that they are certainly later than that.[460] They survive in the form of two *reportationes* by people who attended them; there is a fairly full report of the comments up to Matthew 12:50, almost certainly due to Peter d'Andria,[461] later to become the first Dominican provincial of Naples.[462] There is a less full report of the comments from Matthew 6:9 to the end (except for a few verses near the beginning, which are curiously missing), due to the Parisian cleric, Léger of Besançon.[463] The presence of Léger, together with some references to Paris in the text, make it probable that the lectures were given in Paris, in which case they must be dated to the second regency. And there are signs that they were given after Thomas had written *De Perfectione*, in which case they cannot antedate the academic year 1270–71.[464] Since Thomas patently completed his course, we can probably rule out the academic year 1271–72 because of the strike, so the Matthew lectures must belong to 1270–71. Since the course on John was also completed, it must have been given in 1268–69 or 1269–70.

Thomas also lectured on the epistles of Paul. The ancient catalogues ascribe to him a formally written commentary on Romans and part of 1 Corinthians, and mention a *reportatio* by Reginald of the remaining epistles.[465] This distinction is borne out by the manuscripts: there is a clear break at 1 Corinthians 7:19; after that there is an interpolated extract from a quite different author, running up to the end of 1 Corinthians 10.[466] Bernard Gui also mentions a commentary on the first eleven chapters of Hebrews actually written by Thomas,[467] and this too is borne out by the manuscripts.[468]

Tocco records a tradition, whose source is unknown, that while Thomas was expounding St. Paul in Paris he had a vision of the apostle.[469] If this is not a garbled version of the story of Peter and Paul appearing to him to help him over a difficulty in his exposition of Isaiah,[470] it is evidence that Thomas lectured on Paul in Paris. On the other hand, Tolomeo reports a vision that one of the brethren had in Naples shortly before Thomas' death, while Tolomeo himself was living in Naples as Thomas' student: the Master was lecturing on St. Paul in Naples and the apostle came in and assured him that he had grasped the meaning of his epistles to the limit of what is possible in this life.[471] Such a vision surely presupposes that Thomas did actually lecture on Paul in Naples.

The evidence is unsatisfactory, but provisionally we may take it that Thomas lectured on Paul both in Paris and in Naples. The commentary on Colossians appears to contain an allusion to Proclus' *Elements of Theology*,[472] which was not translated into Latin until the middle of 1268;[473] so as it stands the *reportatio* cannot be earlier than the second regency. Thomas may well have lectured on the epistles in 1268–69 or 1269–70. However, since it is clear that Thomas did rework at least some of his Pauline material, it is not impossible that the bulk of the *reportatio* goes back to the first regency, and that Thomas did some editorial work on it later on.

There can be little doubt that the commentary on Romans and the beginning of 1 Corinthians represents a much more mature text, which can therefore be ascribed to Thomas' last years in Naples.[474]

Also extant is a set of lectures on the first fifty-four psalms, and this too is usually ascribed to Thomas' teaching in Naples at the end of his life, but there is little reason for such a late date.[475]

Some of the early catalogues also list a work on the Canticle,[476] but no such commentary survives. Tocco claims that Thomas expounded the Canticle immediately before his death, at the request of the monks of Fossanova,[477] which makes a pious conclusion to Thomas' teaching career, but it is unlikely to be true. All the evidence is that Thomas would not and could not do any more teaching after December 1273, and none of the many monks who gave evidence at the canonization process makes any mention of Thomas expounding the Canticle in his dying days, which they surely would have done if there had been any truth in Tocco's story.

Apart from lecturing on the bible, the main academic task of a Master in Theology was to tackle speculative issues directly in disputations.[478] The disputation was a way of involving at least advanced students immediately in a discussion, though it was reserved to the Master to pronounce the conclusion. Although the written *Quaestiones Disputatae* may often be at a considerable remove from what actually went on in the classroom, they still give us a lively impression of the way in which issues were clarified by the presentation of arguments and apparently conflicting considerations. Not all the issues raised were genuinely controversial but, as Thomas explains, if the student is to move beyond categorical doctrinal assertions resting simply on authority, it is necessary to raise questions argumentatively and test the real grounds that there are for making such assertions.[479]

Disputations were of two kinds. There were those devised by a Master, in which he could, over a number of sessions, systematically explore some area of interest; and there were the Quodlibetal disputations, in which the Master would respond to questions pro-

248

posed by anyone about anything.[480] Thomas seems to have enjoyed the Quodlibetals more than some Masters did, who perhaps did not relish the risk of being found wanting in a situation that they could not entirely control. Quodlibets were only held twice a year, and no Master was obliged to hold them at all. Thomas appears to have conducted Quodlibets on almost every possible occasion. We possess two series of his Quodlibets; one certainly belongs to his second regency[481] and the other is now generally regarded as belonging to his first regency,[482] so that the whole collection belongs to Thomas' teaching in Paris.

The major *Quaestiones Disputatae*, in which Thomas could choose his own topic and develop it at leisure, span most of Thomas' career. The lectures on the Sentences, which preceded graduation as a Master, gave scope for the exploration of isolated topics, since the lecturer was quite free to take up any point he wanted and tease it out with little reference to the actual text of the Lombard. But at least the sequence of topics had to follow the cues provided in the Sentences, so there was little opportunity to develop a more coherent overall view of theology. From the outset of his time as a Master, Thomas was aware, it seems, of the need for a more sustained theological enterprise, and between 1256 and 1259 he made his first attempt at systematic theology in a long series of disputations *De Veritate*.[483]

While he was still working on *De Veritate*, perhaps in 1258–59, Thomas embarked on a new venture in systematic theology, which was apparently meant to take the form of a commentary on all of Boethius' *Opuscula Sacra*,[484] though all that he actually completed was a plain exposition of the so-called *De Hebdomadibus* and an exposition, with appended discussions of specific questions, running as far as the second chapter of the *De Trinitate*.

Boethius' opuscula had been much studied in the twelfth century, but Thomas seems to be alone in commenting on them in the thirteenth century. Exactly why he chose to expound Boethius is not known, nor do we know whether he originally presented his exposition in the form of lectures or simply wrote it as a book.[485] Whatever it was that attracted his attention to them, the *Opuscula Sacra* suggested to him a theological pattern or schema to which he remained essentially faithful for the rest of his life: Whereas philosophy, working by the light of natural reason, can only approach God from beneath, by way of creatures, theology works by the light of faith and starts from above, moving from God outward to the consideration of his works. Theology thus has a threefold pattern: first it treats of God in himself, as Trinity and Unity; then it treats of the coming forth of creatures from him; and finally it treats of the restoration of creatures in Christ.[486]

The commentary on the De Trinitate, as far as it goes, is essentially an investigation of theological method and epistemology. Although we can obtain some knowledge of God by the use of our natural reason, without any further illumination by God (even natural reason being in its own way an illumination from God), the goal of human life is a beatitude consisting in a much fuller knowledge of God than reason could attain by itself; if we are to direct our lives toward this goal, we need even now to have some intimation of the full knowledge that will be our bliss in heaven, and this intimation is given by faith.[487] The ultimate basis of faith is God's own knowledge of himself and all that is his,[488] but in this life we share in this knowledge in the way that is appropriate to our nature and our condition; that is to say, faith provides us with principles, on the basis of which we can explore divine truth and move toward some sort of understanding of it, even though much of it cannot be fully grasped in this life.[489] It is therefore intrinsic to faith that it should seek to grow into a "science," an organized body of doctrine.[490] And in order to do this, it cannot help but draw on philosophy and philosophical arguments. There are, as it were, two phases in Christian doctrine: the doctrine is first asserted on the basis of authority, then it is investigated by the use of reason, presupposing what has already been established by authority.[491] In theology reason always has to follow faith.[492] But within this intellectual enterprise, based on faith, it transpires that faith itself has certain intellectual presuppositions; although many people may in fact just take on faith various doctrines that can in principle be proved rationally, as faith develops into "science" it has to clarify the different epistemological status of different parts of its content, so it is, paradoxically, one task of Christian teaching to demonstrate that some elements of Christian belief do not depend on revelation for their cogency. It is therefore part of the theologian's task to show that philosophical objections to the presuppositions of faith are actually bad philosophy. Those contents of the faith that are known only by revelation (such as the doctrine of the Trinity) cannot be proved by rational argument, but reason can profitably explore them, because the light of faith enhances the light of reason; it does not supersede or destroy it. And philosophical objections to revealed doctrine can never be decisive; at the very least they can be shown to be inconclusive, so that the intellectual legitimacy of belief is secured. It is a matter of faith to believe that there can be no contradiction between philosophical truth and revealed truth, since both derive ultimately, even if in different ways, from the same divine light. But, of course, the use of reason to explore revelation has its dangers; we can abuse philosophy and arrive at erroneous conclusions. So there is a third use for philosophical argument in theology: to rebut conclusions reached by a bad use of philosophy.[493]

As Thomas sees it, Boethius is doing "philosophical theology," not in the sense that he is examining what we can say about God if we ignore the data of revelation, but in the sense that he is taking for granted the data of revelation and seeing what help philosophy can give in bringing the believer to a fuller understanding of the faith. And he is doing this primarily for his own sake, so that he may "perceive the truth of God."[494] He thus provides Thomas, as commentator, with the opportunity to systematize his own thoughts on the role, within the life of faith, of the different kinds of understanding that are natural to us as human beings.

At precisely the point where Boethius begins to apply his method to the study of the Trinity, Thomas abandoned his commentary, apparently quite suddenly.[495] Why he did so, we can only guess. Probably the most plausible conjecture is that he lost interest in his exposition of Boethius because he had begun work on a new book, the *Summa contra Gentiles*.[496]

Some time in 1259 Thomas must have been informed that he was going to leave Paris, and it may have been the prospect of being freed from his university responsibilities that gave him the idea of starting on an ambitious new project, which would not be primarily concerned with the immediate demands of teaching. We know that before leaving Paris he had embarked on the great work which rapidly acquired the title, *Summa contra Gentiles*.[497] He completed it at his leisure, it seems, between leaving Paris in 1259 and starting the *Summa Theologiae* in about 1266.[498] Much of the work survives in Thomas' own handwriting, and we can see how insistently he went back over what he had written, sometimes years later, revising and correcting it.[499] Of all his writings, this is probably the one whose composition was the least hurried, the one to which the author could devote as much time and care as he wanted.

The proper title of the work is "The Truth of the Catholic Faith Against the Errors of Unbelievers," but its purpose has recently been the subject of some controversy. It used to be maintained, on the basis of a fourteenth-century life of Raymund of Peñafort,[500] that the work was commissioned by Raymund to be a textbook for missionaries, but this legend has now been decisively refuted as incoherent and unhistorical. Instead it has been argued by R. A. Gauthier that the *Contra Gentiles* is a purely reflective work, written primarily for Thomas' own sake, the "unbelievers" whose errors Thomas proposes to tackle being almost exclusively the ancients, not contemporary unbelievers who might be the object of a Dominican mission.[501] This proposal has in its turn been attacked and A. Patfoort has argued strongly that the text itself contains many indications that Thomas was intending to provide a presentation of the Catholic faith that would be useful to missionaries engaged in trying to convince modern unbelievers, particularly Muslims.[502] Thomas' pedagogical instincts may well have been aroused by the urgent call made by the Master of the Order, Humbert of Romans, in 1255 for more volunteers to go on the foreign missions,[503] a call which was evidently extremely successful, as Humbert himself reports,[504] and which resulted in emotional scenes as people scrambled to volunteer, some of them probably at the General Chapter in Paris in 1256.[505] In his later work on the officials of the Order, Humbert says that one of the tasks of the Master of the Order is to ensure that there is always available in the Order a supply of treatises against the errors of unbelievers, heretics and schismatics, and to see that there are always some suitably talented friars learning the languages necessary for the foreign missions.[506] If we assume that Humbert, as Master of the Order, had already been practicing what he was later to preach, it is not unreasonable to suppose that, just as he was certainly insisting on the need for Dominicans to learn languages,[507] so he had also expressed a desire for suitable books "against the errors of unbelievers" for the use of Dominican missionaries. There is nothing in the *Contra Gentiles* to suggest that the work was actually commissioned, but there is no reason why Thomas should not have been responding to a known desire of the Master of the Order in writing it.[508]

Even if we accept, as we surely should, that the *Contra Gentiles* was written specifically in view of the intellectual formation of missionaries, this does not imply that it is not at the same time a work of profound theological reflection. The refutation of error arises, as we have seen, within the whole context of the systematic exploration of Christian truth.[509] As Thomas says in his inaugural lecture, teachers of Christian doctrine need to be "well-armed" (*muniti*) if they are to defend the faith against people who contradict it.[510] In the *Contra Gentiles* Thomas ventures, he says, trusting in God's mercy, to take on the role of a "wise man," that is, to ponder the truth, especially about the First Principle (i.e., God) and to explain it to others, refuting error as an integral part of this pondering and exposition of truth.[511]

The tripartite schema announced in the Boethian commentary reappears in the *Contra Gentiles* in a slightly modified form, owing to the exigencies of the missionary perspective within which Thomas is now working, but it is still the "theological" rather than the "philosophical" direction that he follows: first comes the treatment of God in himself, then the treatment of his works as creator, and finally the treatment of God as the goal of all creation.[512] But these three topics are to be gone through twice, first on the basis of what can be said independently of revelation, and only secondly with reference to the specifically Christian doctrines known to us by revelation.[513] Thomas is writing as a Christian theologian for Christian readers, and it is within the faith that the distinction is made between doctrines that can be known by reason and those that can be known only by revelation, but the much more radical separation of the two kinds of doctrine in the *Contra Gentiles* allows Thomas to explore at length the extent to which Christian belief harmonizes with and indeed satisfies the intellectual yearnings of human beings as such. The universal quest for knowledge and understanding, examined with philosophical seriousness, constitutes the background against which the genuine attractiveness of the Catholic faith can become apparent.

As an educator Thomas seems to have been skeptical of the value of "crash courses" aimed at supplying only a few ideas and a few bits of knowledge that would be immediately applicable to the practical needs of the working brethren.[514] A true Christian apologetic must be the fruit of a profound Christian understanding and a sincere awareness of the intellectual community enfolding all seekers after truth, whether believers or unbelievers. The apologetic need to identify common philosophical ground that believers share with unbelievers is not so very far removed from the believer's own need to use philosophy in order to probe the mysteries of faith. Neither the philosopher nor the believer will ever in this life actually succeed in comprehending God. The immense delight that comes to us from even the most modest and hesitant reflection on God, as described in chapter 8 of book I of the *Contra Gentiles*, seems to be, in Thomas' view, something that philosophers and theologians, believers and unbelievers, can to a large extent share.

Though Thomas came to deny that teaching is part of the contemplative life,[515] he still maintained that those who propose to teach others, in whatever capacity, should ideally be "contemplatives" first.[516] That is to say, they must love the truth for its own sake and find their chief delight in investigating it for their own satisfaction,[517] if they are to be effective in communicating it to others. The most useful way to set about combatting the "errors of unbelievers" is to brood intensely on "the truth of the Catholic faith." It is a work of wisdom that is called for, with all that that implies. And for the teacher of missionaries, too, the same thing applies. If Thomas did indeed interrupt (and, in the outcome, abandon) his work on Boethius in order to write a book for missionaries, we can still see a real continuity between the theological enterprise he left behind and the one he took up. There does not seem to be any serious contradiction, after all, between the belief that the *Contra Gentiles* was written as a leisurely exercise in wisdom and the belief that it was written "in order to be useful to others."[518]

It is not known that Thomas had any teaching responsibilities when he returned to Italy in 1259–60 until his appointment to Orvieto, and his position there as house lector cannot have been very onerous. He was responsible for providing some intellectual stimulus for the community[519] and for seeing that any student friars there received sufficient education to exercise their ministry as priests and Dominicans. The education of the students probably consisted chiefly of moral "cases," the available textbooks being Raymund of Peñafort's *Summa de Casibus* and Peraldus' summas on vices and virtues.[520] Thomas had plenty of time to work on other projects, such as the *Contra Gentiles* and the commentary on Job and the books he wrote at the request of Urban IV.

In 1265 Thomas was put in a very different situation. Now he had his own studium, with selected students to deal with. He evidently decided that what they needed was a proper course in systematic theology, in which moral theology would find its place in a whole context of dogmatic theology. At first he followed the by now hallowed practice of basing himself on the Sentences,[521] and part of his lectures on book I have recently been discovered.[522] But, probably in 1266, Thomas decided to abandon the Sentences and create his own course. This is the genesis of the great *Summa Theologiae*, designed to introduce beginners to theology in an orderly, intelligible, interesting way, avoiding the boring and labyrinthine procedures that were inevitable if theology had to be taught on the basis of set texts, with all the repetitions and inconsequentiality this involved.[523]

From about 1266 onward Thomas can be regarded as essentially engaged in planning and writing the *Summa*. In spite of the distractions involved in having to produce works dealing with urgent topical issues, in spite of having to continue lecturing on the bible (a task Thomas surely did not resent), in spite of a considerable amount of other writing, there is a remarkable steadfastness of purpose discernible in Thomas' intellectual labors between 1266 and 1273.

There are several indications enabling us to date Thomas' various *Quaestiones Disputatae*. Apart from the *De Veritate* they are all after 1259, and we are informed that the questions *De Potentia* belong to his Roman period and that those *De Virtutibus* belong to the second Parisian regency.[524] It is also clear that *De Malo* comes after the *Contra Gentiles*[525] and it is fairly certain that the questions *De Spiritualibus Creaturis* and *De Anima* come toward the end of the Roman period.[526] This means that the succession of disputations follows precisely the movement of the first part of the *Summa Theologiae*, which Thomas wrote in Rome, and that the disputations on the virtues belong in the period when Thomas was writing the second part of the *Summa*, which deals with ethics. The question *De Unione Verbi Incarnati* can similarly be dated to the time when Thomas was dealing with Christology in the third part of the *Summa*.[527]

Also toward the end of his time in Rome Thomas composed what may have been his first fully-developed Aristotelian commentary, on the *De Anima*, and it is not unreasonable to postulate a connection between this commentary and the fact that Thomas was writing about the soul in the first part of the *Summa*.[528] In the same way the commentary on Aristotle's *Ethics*, at least in its final form, seems to be related to the composition of the second part of the *Summa*.[529]

It is tempting to date the commentary on Dionysius' *Divine Names* also to Thomas' Roman period, so that it would coincide with the writing of the early questions of the Prima Pars; such a date is conjectured by Weisheipl.[530] On the other hand, the commentary, as it stands, cannot be earlier than 1268–69, since Thomas clearly alludes to Proclus.[531]

The first part and the first section of the second part of the *Summa* were completed by the end of 1270. The whole of the Secunda Secundae was written, at amazing speed, between then and Thomas' departure from Paris in the spring of 1272.[532] The bulk of the third part was written in Naples, until Thomas abandoned all his writing in December 1273.

It is clear that much of Thomas' intellectual energy was focussed on the great theological and pedagogical enterprise enshrined in the *Summa*. No doubt his thought was continuing to evolve as he worked, but there is a definite and unified theological vision dominating the whole project. The "experiment" in the *Contra Gentiles* of separating the areas of doctrine that depend entirely on revelation from those that in principle are available to human reason as such has served its purpose and is now abandoned. In the *Summa Theologiae* Thomas can take it for granted that the intellectual appetite for knowledge and understanding, which is innate in all of us, finds its ultimate fulfilment only in the beatific vision and, in the meantime, it reaches the limits open to us in this life only in the context of faith seeking understanding;[533] for the believer, then, the use of reason to explore Christian doctrine is a single, harmonious enterprise, in which the achievements of philosophy and the contents of revelation no longer need to be kept apart for most purposes.

The schema announced in the commentary on Boethius' *De Trinitate* and adapted in the *Contra Gentiles* shows through again in the *Summa Theologiae*, though once more it is subtly different. The movement is still from God to creatures to Christ, but this time Thomas isolates that creature which is of most concern to us, namely ourselves.[534] The Prima Pars deals with God in himself and as the source and goal of creation in general. The Secunda Pars deals specifically with human beings as free agents, called to achieve their fulfilment in God by the exercise of their freedom, under the guidance and grace of God.[535] The Tertia Pars provides the climax of the whole work. The first two parts of the *Summa* can be seen as an elaborate statement of the dramatis personae, God and ourselves, with a supporting cast of other creatures. The drama consists in the bringing together of God and us in the bliss of eternal life, and this drama centers on Christ, who is the model and objective foundation for our movement toward God and who is himself the Way by which we come to union with God; and it is by means of the sacraments that we enter upon and proceed along this Way. If Thomas had completed the book, he would have gone through all the sacraments and then concluded with a section on the resurrection and eternal life.[536]

Apart from his expositions of scripture and his successive and increasingly absorbing attempts to articulate a comprehensive theological system, Thomas also devoted a fair amount of time and energy in his last years to interpreting philosophical texts. There is some controversy among scholars both about the dating of Thomas' philosophical commentaries and about his purpose in writing them.[537] Most of them appear to belong to the second Parisian regency and the final years in Naples,[538] but Tolomeo's statement that Thomas expounded most of Aristotle, and particularly the *Ethics* and the *Metaphysics*, while he was in Rome[539] should perhaps be given some credence. It becomes easier to believe that Thomas wrote all the works which are ascribed to the years 1268–1273 if we suppose that some of them, including the Aristotelian commentaries, were based on earlier drafts composed in Rome.

Gauthier argues that Thomas' concern was always theological, even in his "philosophical" writings, but his critics have pointed plausibly enough to signs that Thomas did have a serious philosophical purpose and that he was interested in clarifying Aristotelian philosophy in its own right.[540] Probably there is no real contradiction between the two positions. As we have seen, Thomas' own theology drove him to recognize the importance of philosophy as a distinct discipline, if only because philosophical errors that might threaten faith need to be tackled philosophically. But his philosophical interests were not just apologetic. He was surely sincere in believing that the theological attempt to understand faith is essentially at one with the universal human attempt to understand reality. In his last years, as we have noted, the philosophers seem to have been more enthusiastic about Thomas than many of his fellow theologians were; it is quite likely that he in return found the philosophers more congenial than some of the theologians. He believed that the best way to discover the truth is to have a good argument,[541] and in this he was being true to the tradition of Albert and indeed of St. Dominic.[542] He reacted sharply to stupidity and intellectual incompetence,[543] but he did not adopt the strident tones of self-conscious orthodoxy rebuking the errors of everyone else, as it were, ex cathedra. He preferred to engage his opponents in a common search for the truth, and this may well have brought him closer to the philosophers, just as it set him at odds with his critics among the theologians, some of whom at least were deeply suspicious of the amount of philosophy involved in his theology.[544]

Thomas wrote a number of commentaries on Aristotle, the occasion for which is not known. The exposition of the *Peri Hermeneias* was undertaken at the request of the young provost of Louvain, to encourage him in his pursuit of "wisdom."[545] It is likely that most of the others were composed partly because of Thomas' association with the philosophers in the faculty of Arts during his second regency, but he himself obviously believed in the pedagogical value of the study of Aristotle, and we know that he was working on several philosophical texts in Naples, where Tocco saw him writing his commentary on Aristotle's *De Generatione et Corruptione*.[546] Also at Naples he commented on the *Liber de Causis*, which he was able to recognize as deriving essentially from Proclus, thanks to William of Moerbeke's translation of Proclus' *Elements of Theology*.[547] He also apparently had it in mind to tackle other Platonist works, including Plato's own *Timaeus*,[548] though nothing seems to have come of it.

As a Parisian Master, Thomas was also required to be a preacher.[549] His preaching, both in his own time and in ours, has attracted much less attention than his teaching and writing,[550] but the oldest catalogues of his works include a collection of his sermons made by Reginald of Piperno.[551] According to Tocco, he was too engrossed in his intellectual life to be capable of learning languages,[552] so most of his preaching was confined to educated audiences whom he could address in Latin, but we do occasionally hear of him preaching in Italian. On one occasion he preached at least twice in Holy Week in Rome,[553] and during Lent in 1273 his sermons on the Lord's Prayer attracted huge crowds.[554] To what extent preaching was a regular part of his life it is hard to say.[555] One young man recalled years later how he preached with his eyes closed and his face raised toward heaven,[556] which perhaps suggests that he was an edifying spectacle rather than an animated orator. It was probably his personal fame rather than his reputation as a preacher that drew the populace to listen to him in Naples.[557]

In his preaching, insofar as it is available to us, he appears to have cultivated a simple style without rhetorical flourishes, whether he was addressing a university audience or an ordinary congregation; his aim was to provide lucid, straightforward instruction,[558] though he apparently could sometimes move his hearers quite deeply.[559] He had absolutely no use for the sort of pious fables employed by some popular preachers.[560]

Thomas the Saint

Thomas did not conform to the conventional idea of a saint. For one thing, he did not work miracles. At the time of his canonization so few miracles could be found in his life that it was raised as an objection against canonizing him, apparently, and John XXII is said to have retorted that every question he answered was a miracle.[561] Whether or not this tale is literally true, it certainly attests a conviction that Thomas' sanctity was vested essentially in his intellectual service of God rather than in the sort of display of supernatural power which attracted most people's attention.[562]

Nor did Thomas look like an ascetic. He was by all accounts very fat,[563] though he was also tall and physically robust. And he had delicate skin.[564] His hair was apparently very light brown, and he went bald in front.[565] He would, of course, like all clerics and religious, have sported the statutory tonsure.

If he did not look ascetic, it is probable that in fact he was not very ascetic, except for the kind of unconscious "asceticism" natural to the thoroughgoing intellectual.

Two anecdotes are told to illustrate the claim that he was devoted to poverty, but they prove nothing of the kind. One is about his famous remark that he would rather have a copy of Chrysostom on Matthew than the whole of Paris,[566] which only shows that he was more interested in owning books than he was in having any other kind of property.

The other story is a report that when he was writing the *Contra Gentiles* in Paris, he made do with little scraps of paper to write it on (*in cedulis minutis*).[567] We possess Thomas' own working copy of the *Contra Gentiles*, and it is true that it is written on poor quality parchment and that some of the pages are too small,[568] but there is no reason to take this as evidence of Thomas' own taste in the matter. He had to make do with the parchment he was given. And Gils has drawn attention to an interesting detail in another of Thomas' Parisian manuscripts: one page contains the note, "Here's the first, from Br. John," which presumably means that Thomas had run out of paper and was clamoring for more and the unfortunate friar responsible for such things was only able to find one folder for him to be getting on with.[569] There is not the slightest reason to suppose that Thomas chose to hamper his own work out of consideration for poverty.[570]

We are also told that he was not interested in clothes or special food,[571] but this suggests only that he was not prepared to be bothered about such things, not that he was particularly austere. There is a testimony about his last years, that he always ate in the refectory with the other friars, and only once a day at that,[572] but he does not seem to have been regarded by his brethren or by anyone else as unusually keen on fasting. It is likely that, at least at this time of his life, he preferred to stay with his books at supper time and did not consider it worth the trouble to make special arrangements to be fed separately.

In fact, when Thomas did take notice of his food, he seems to have appreciated it. Of the very few miracles that could be claimed for him during his lifetime, two involve food. One is the story we have already noted of the miraculous cure of Reginald, which Thomas wanted to be celebrated each year with a good meal. The other is reported, on excellent authority, to have occurred during Thomas' last illness at the home of his niece in Maenza. Reginald was trying to persuade Thomas to have something to eat, and Thomas expressed a desire for some fresh herring, but fresh herrings would not be available in that part of the world. Miraculously a fishmonger, who thought he only had sardines for sale, was found to have a whole box of herrings.[573]

Thomas was evidently not a great conversationalist. He was habitually silent, and if he was occasionally lured into the parlor he said little and escaped as soon as he could.[574] He seems to have had no small talk and perhaps he was rather devoid of humor.[575] He was also quite unlike Albert in his lack of interest in the world around him. He lived in his own head and in his books. From choice he hardly ever went out,[576] and he certainly did not make a habit of going out for walks, as we learn from Tocco in connection with his stay in Bologna: one day a friar who did not know him took Thomas out into the town as his socius and got rather peeved that Thomas was unable to keep up with him, however hard he tried.[577] On one occasion in Naples the brethren wanted him to join them in the garden for a bit of recreation, but Thomas wandered off alone in the opposite direction and went back to his room.[578] His favorite recreation was to walk round the cloister on his own.[579]

Today Thomas would probably be considered a workaholic. He was famous for not taking time off.[580] Occasionally, perhaps, he took a holiday. We know that he spent one Christmas at the home of Cardinal Richard degli Annibaldi,[581] and he seems to have visited members of his family every now and then.[582] He apparently went out to dinner sometimes, if there is any truth at all in the famous story of his bad behavior at the king's dinner table.[583]

There is no doubt that Thomas had his growing circle of devoted admirers, and by the end of his life his name was one to conjure with. For the sake of "the venerable brother Thomas" the abbot of Monte Cassino granted the Dominicans leave to build a priory at San Germano, and the abbot of Salerno gave the Order a church "because of the special affection we have for the venerable brother Thomas d'Aquino." The same magical name procured a passport for Thomas' niece, Francesca of Ceccano.[584] Whether Thomas had friends as well as admirers it is difficult to judge. In view of his long association with Reginald, going back to a time when there can be no question of Reginald being his official socius, we must presume that there was a real friendship between them.[585] Thomas is also said to have been fond of Annibaldo degli Annibaldi.[586] He reproduces Aristotle's doctrine of friendship with evident sympathy,[587] and treats friendship as the most appropriate model for understanding charity.[588] In one of his sermons he alludes to the kind of sensitivity we feel toward those we are fond of.[589] Evidently friendship was a significant reality for him. But it is doubtful that he ever went in for anything like the warmly emotional relationships of which Jordan of Saxony, for instance, was capable.[590] Thomas seems to have been essentially self-sufficient. His pronounced taste for solitude was commented on by people who knew him,[591] and he is indubitably an illustration of his own doctrine that the most intense joy available to us is the joy of the intellectual life.[592]

One of the most obvious qualities people observed in Thomas was his abstractedness.[593] He did not even notice what food was being placed before him or that his plate had been taken away.[594] In conversation he would be "miles away," and he had to be brought back to earth by tugging at his clothes.[595] His capacity to withdraw into himself was such that on one occasion he apparently had his leg cauterized by the doctors without even feeling it when the fire was applied.[596] In the canonization process this abstractedness is often described in terms of Thomas being "contemplative,"[597] but when applied to Thomas the word is as richly ambiguous as it is in his own doctrine. It has definite religious connotations, but means essentially that Thomas was wrapped up in higher things because he was *thinking* about them. He was "contemplative" in a religious sense because he was "contemplative" in the older sense; he was an intellectual entirely given over to the inner life of the mind.[598]

Thomas had a reputation for being imperturbable. He did not bat an eyelid when a boat he was on was overtaken by a severe storm that terrified the crew.[599] And he was kind as well as patient in dealing with other people. As we have seen, he allowed Pecham to enjoy his "triumph" at his inception, because he did not want to spoil the new Master's day.[600] He never humiliated people by speaking slightingly to them or by scoring points off them, even in the context of a disputation.[601]

He seems to have liked having a regular rhythm to the day. Early each morning he went to confession and said Mass, and immediately after that he attended another Mass, or if he did not say Mass himself he attended two Masses.[602] Then he spent the rest of the day reading, praying, writing and teaching.[603] At the end of the day he went to compline,[604] but this appears to be the only choral Office that he attended.[605] When, toward the end of his life, he says that he is "unable" to join in the rest of the conventual liturgy,[606] this probably means no more than that his way of life was so dominated by his intellectual and academic labors that it had to be allowed to dictate its own routine.[607] And such a conclusion was in accordance with the dispensations automatically granted to functioning Dominican academics.[608] There is some evidence that when Thomas was away from his own priory he attended rather more of the conventual Office.[609]

That Thomas read widely all his life is beyond doubt, and it is also clear that he kept himself abreast of the latest developments. This is very evident in the use he made of the new translations from the Greek that were being produced by his confrère, William of Moerbeke.[610]

That he habitually resorted to prayer in response to everything that confronted him is also scarcely in doubt. It was well-known that he referred his intellectual difficulties to God in this way.[611] If prayer is the most important activity of the contemplative life, as Thomas says,[612] it is because understanding is always God's gift. There is also a rather quaint little story about him finding one morning that he had sprouted an extra tooth during the night, which he feared would impede his speech and so interfere with his lecturing; so he went into church to pray and the tooth fell out into his hand while he was praying. He kept it as a souvenir.[613] At least at the end of his life he was a very early riser and liked to go into the church to pray before anyone else came in; when others started arriving, he retired to his room.[614]

Writing was obviously a major ingredient in his life. Throughout his active career, it seems, he wrote both in the sense of actually writing things down himself (even though his normal handwriting was famously so illegible that only a few people, then as now, were able to read it) and in the sense that he dictated things to a secretary.[615] He evidently sometimes had more than one secretary at his disposal and we are told, rather incredibly, that he could dictate different things to different secretaries simultaneously,[616] and that he could dictate in his sleep.[617]

The seriousness with which he applied himself to his responsibilities as a teacher we have already noticed. Judging especially from the stories told of his time as Albert's student, he had always been instinctively something of a teacher, more able to pronounce and defend conclusions than to ask questions or take part in general discussion. Where Albert loved communicating his interests to his friends and enjoyed "seeking the truth in the delightfulness of companionship," Thomas was temperamentally more able to do without intellectual companionship and more prone to being "the Master." And, we are told, the sureness of his judgment was famous.[618] But he was not vain; on the contrary, his humility is attested by nearly everyone.[619] But Thomas took human reason seriously; though we are far from being infallible, we must treat the light of reason as a reflection in us of divine truth, so disobeying our own reason is a kind of disobedience to God.[620] If you know the answer to a question, it is false humility to pretend that you do not,[621] just as it is intellectually dishonest to retain an opinion once you recognize that it has been refuted.

Thomas' deep devotion to the Mass emerges clearly from all our sources. Sometimes he evidently became deeply absorbed in it and was profoundly moved by it. Toward the end of his life he sometimes became so absorbed that he just stopped and had to be roused by the brethren to continue with the celebration.[622] Whatever the reasons that prompted Urban IV to entrust to him the composition of the Office for Corpus Christi,[623] it is fitting that a theologian whose piety was so dominated by the Eucharist should have been the author of the liturgy for such a feast.

Devotion to the Mass is but one facet of Thomas' great devotion to the person of Christ.[624] Although in many ways Thomas' thought is theocentric rather than Christocentric, his awareness of the impossibility of attaining to any direct vision of God except by way of the revelation he has made of himself in Christ and the grace he has given to us in and through Christ made Thomas focus his personal piety very much on Christ. On his deathbed there is good evidence that he made some special profession of faith in the real presence of Christ in the Eucharist and commented on how much he had himself written on the Eucharist (all of which he submitted to the judgment of the Holy See).[625] And it seems that Thomas implied that the presence of Christ in the Eucharist was somehow the focal point and motivation of all his theology. According to Tocco, he addressed the Blessed Sacrament, when it was brought to him shortly before he died, in these terms: "I receive you, price of my soul's redemption, I receive you, viaticum for my pilgrimage, for whose love I have studied, kept watch and labored and preached and taught."[626]

Other stories of a more miraculous nature also bring out—whatever we make of their preternatural content—Thomas' devotion to Christ and to the Blessed Sacrament. The sacristan at Naples, while Thomas was working on the Tertia Pars, is said to have seen Thomas raised above the ground in prayer; then he heard a voice coming from the crucifix saying, "Thomas, you have written well of me; what reward will you take from me for your labors?" Thomas replied, "Lord, nothing except you."[627] Tocco also heard a story purporting to emanate from Paris about Thomas being asked by the Masters of the university there to settle various questions about the Real Presence and checking his answer with Christ before presenting it; allegedly many of the brethren, including the prior, were called to witness Thomas floating in the air after some of them had heard Christ assuring Thomas that his answer was as correct as was humanly possible.[628] Unfortunately there are reasons for doubting at least this second story. It can only refer to the questions about the Eucharist in Thomas' seventh Quodlibet, which is undoubtedly the first he ever conducted.[629] It is hardly credible that so young a Master, not yet formally received into the company of the Masters because of the current opposition to the mendicants, should have been allowed to decide theological matters for the whole university! But at least it shows that Thomas was known in the Order's folklore as someone intimately associated with the Blessed Sacrament.

It is Thomas' love of the Mass which suggests at least a partial interpretation of his famous experience in or around 6 December 1273, which brought his writing and teaching to an end. Something happened to him while he was saying Mass, we are told, and thereafter he neither wrote nor dictated another word. Reginald was afraid that too much study had driven him out of his mind and urged him to resume his work on the Tertia Pars, but Thomas simply said, "Reginald, I can't." When pressed, he added, "Reginald, I can't, because all that I have written seems like straw." After this Thomas hardly spoke and appeared to be in a stunned condition. When urged to explain what was going on, Thomas said, "Everything I have written seems like straw by comparison with what I have seen and what has been revealed to me."[630]

It looks as if Thomas' physical strength collapsed at this time; it was "with great difficulty" that he managed the journey to visit his sister, and a story that implies that he was bedridden belongs to this period.[631] On the whole, Thomas seems to have enjoyed very good health, but now his long overworked body appears to have slumped suddenly into old age.[632] Maybe he had had a mild stroke.[633] But it is quite clear that something had also happened to his mind. Reginald at first thought that Thomas might have had a breakdown, but he speedily realized that this was not so. It looks as if Thomas had at last simply been overwhelmed by the Mass, to which he had so long been devoted and in which he had been so easily and deeply absorbed. What kind of "revelation" he may have had we do not know. There is a cryptic remark ascribed to him on his deathbed by Tocco, apparently on the authority of the tradition of Fossanova, which suggests that he hinted at the possibility of some knowledge of the Eucharist transcending mere faith.[634] Anyway, whatever happened, it completely drove out of him any desire or ability to go on writing.

But then, Thomas had already reached what was for him the high point of the *Summa*. He had reached Christ; he had reached the Mass. Now, in the early part of the discussion of penance, he suddenly lost interest.

The comment that all that he had written seemed like straw should certainly not be taken as a belated realization that his life's work had been a waste of time. He had always maintained that the object of theology is God, not talking about God; but in this life we cannot approach God except by using words.[635] "Straw" is a conventional image for the literal sense of scripture,[636] which is worth having, even if it is only a beginning. Words can lead us to reality. But if Thomas had, in some way, peered beyond faith and glimpsed something of the reality to which the words of faith point, of course the words would lose their appeal. They had served their purpose. In such circumstances Thomas was more entitled than most of us to feel what surely all writers feel, that all this verbiage of ours is utter nonsense and we cannot bear to go on with it.

This does not mean that Thomas spent the rest of his life in a happy state of supernatural elevation. On the contrary, he told Reginald that he wanted to die, now that he could no longer write.[637] He was evidently frustrated and confused.

It looks as if the collapse of his physique and some unusually overwhelming experience of the Mass, combined with the fact that he had already completed the section of the Tertia Pars which most engaged his interest, led to his sudden helpless inability to go on with his work. He did not disown his work, he would have completed it if he could, and he deliberately alluded to it on his deathbed in quite positive terms. It was simply that he could not go on with it. As far as he was concerned, he was finished. He had always been a withdrawn, rather taciturn person, from his early childhood onward, but teaching and writing had given him a way out of himself into the world of other people. Now that he could no longer write and teach, he was almost unable to come out of himself. He had, as a theologian, argued that rapture is the highest level of contemplation, and one of the ways in which it can come about is that "one's desire is so violently drawn to something that one becomes estranged from everything else."[638] Did not something like this happen to Thomas? This curiously calm, seemingly dispassionate man suddenly found that his lifelong love of Christ became too much for him. All his life he had been studying, writing, preaching and teaching for love of Christ; now that same love became momentarily so intense that it crippled him, leaving him a stranger in the world. There was indeed nothing left for him to do except to die and to enjoy forever the friendship of God.

II. INTRODUCTION TO THE TEXTS

1. Thomas' Inaugural Lecture (1256)

The earliest detailed account we possess of the ceremonies involved in the graduation of a new Master in Theology in Paris comes from the fourteenth century,[1] but it is likely that something very similar took place when Thomas graduated in 1256.[2] In the evening before the actual inception there was a double disputation; then, the next morning, the new Master was formally invested with the magisterial biretta and delivered a brief inaugural lecture (his *principium*),[3] and then he presided over a third disputation; the session concluded with yet another disputation, after which the new Master briefly determined the third disputation, the one over which he himself had presided.

The story of Thomas' *principium* was well-known. He was in a quandary about what he should take as the subject of his lecture, and a visitor from heaven came and told him to base his talk on the text *Rigans montes de superioribus suis*.[4] This edifying tale was popularized throughout the Order within a very short time, thanks to its inclusion in Gerald de Frachet's *Vitae Fratrum*,[5] completed by 1260. It is therefore not surprising that Remigio dei Girolami, who entered the Order in Paris in about 1267,[6] should have wanted a copy of the famous lecture. When we find, in a manuscript of Remigio's (Florence, Biblioteca Nazionale, Conv. soppr. G 4.936),[7] a *prologus* ascribed to Thomas, whose text is *Rigans montes*, it seems safe to conclude that what we are being offered is indeed Thomas' *principium*, and this conclusion is generally accepted by scholars.[8]

In his lecture Thomas touches on a topic he will develop more fully soon afterward in *De Veritate* q.11: In what sense can one human being be said to be the teacher of another? Christ said that his disciples were not to be called "master," because he alone is the Master of them all (Matt. 23:10), and the challenge posed by this saying to all human teaching was taken up frankly and discussed by St. Augustine in his *De Magistro*, whose conclusion could at least be read as meaning that no human being can strictly be called a "teacher."[9] In his exposition of Dionysius' *Mystical Theology* Albert had toned this down a little, to suggest that the human teacher could have a genuine role to play, even if it can only be effective if the "inner teacher," God, is also at work in the minds of the students.[10] Thomas follows suit and is indeed quite emphatic about the importance of allowing human teachers to play a real part in the transmission of knowledge. In his view, the problem of human teaching is only one aspect of the more general and extremely important question of whether secondary causes of any kind exercise any authentic causality.[11] And, in line with the Dionysian principle with which he begins his lecture, Thomas always insists that God's providence does dispose things in such a way that creatures do have a real effect on one another. To suppose otherwise, far from giving more glory to God, actually diminishes his glory by denying one of the perfections he has given to his creatures.[12]

All the same, the teacher has only a fairly modest role. The teacher is like the physician: both are in the position of helping nature to do something that can also be done without such help, and which cannot be done at all unless the patient (or student) is fully active as well. Truth cannot be implanted in the mind from outside. The basic principles of all knowledge are a kind of reflection, in the mind, of God's own truth, and the most the teacher can do is encourage the mind, using the fundamental principles of thought, to discover for itself the truth of various propositions.[13] Thomas is, perhaps, less optimistic than Origen, who declared that Paul teaches Timothy so that Timothy can become another Paul;[14] in his lecture, Thomas implies that there will remain a gap between the teacher's knowledge and that of his students. But he is still essentially in the same pedagogical tradition (and it is the genuine Christian tradition of pedagogy) that no teacher can replace the working of the student's own mind. That is why he insists that the student must be not only humble, but also critical. Meekly following the teacher is not, in Thomas' view, any excuse for error.[15] And even in the case of the saints we should not assume that their every word is inspired by the Holy Spirit.[16] Thomas fully expects that the student will be able to make all kinds of new discoveries on the basis of what the teacher says.

The teacher is, in the strictest sense, only a cooperator with God, and has no business trying to make disciples for himself.

This is why, as Albert pointed out, prayer is as much a part of the teacher's job as talking is.[17] And Thomas, conscious of the high role of the teacher as an instrument of divine providence, says the same: it is only by God's gift that anyone could be adequate for the task, so he needs to ask God to make him adequate.

But, in the perspective of Dionysius' hierarchies, the teacher, even if he is only an instrument of God, is still in a "higher" position than the student. And this means that it is necessary that the teacher can in fact be looked up to by his students; he must live in such a way that he is and is perceived to be "high." Thomas quotes from Gregory the same text that Humbert of Romans quotes to make an identical point about preachers.[18]

Thomas is not, of course, maintaining that moral qualities are a sufficient or even perhaps a necessary condition for being a teacher. He himself attacks the view that holiness of lifestyle, of itself, entitles anyone to be a preacher or teacher.[19] All he claims is that the teacher ought to live an elevated life. But in 1256 such a claim was somewhat controversial, at least in its implications.

In the spring of 1256 the feud between the secular Masters in Paris and the mendicants was at its height, and the Dominicans very readily claimed that one of the motives for the anti-mendicant polemic was jealousy. The seculars were supposed to be jealous because of the success of the mendicants in attracting students to their lectures.[20] And, only a few years later, Thomas of Cantimpré expressed the cynical view that of course the friars could give better lectures, since they stayed up at night working, while the seculars spent their time in routs and revels and so could not prepare their lectures properly.[21] Thomas Aquinas, without making any such rude comments on his secular colleagues, still argues that there is a particular appropriateness that religious should become teachers, since they are particularly committed to a way of life that gives them the opportunity for study.[22]

But it is not enough for one's life to be edifying; it must be seen to be edifying. "If your life is despised, your preaching will be too." This principle of Gregory's must have been bitter in the mouths of the mendicants in 1256, when their enemies had been doing all they could to make people despise the friars, with all too much success.[23] To retain the regard of their potential students, then, the friars had to take active steps to defend their reputation, and Thomas, soon after his inaugural lecture, undertook to justify the friars for taking such steps.[24]

In spite of the polemical context, though, Thomas' lecture in itself is not polemical. Thomas contents himself with expounding his idea of the role of the theologian, and in this exposition we can see luminously the ideal he is setting himself for his life's work.

The Leonine edition of this text, promised for volume XLIV, has not yet been published. I have made use of the text in P. Mandonnet's edition of Thomas' *Opuscula Omnia* IV (Paris, 1927), pp.

491–6, and that contained in the Marietti edition of the *Opuscula Theologica* by R. A. Verardo (Turin, 1954), I pp. 441–3.

2. Thomas' Theology of Prayer[1]

Thomas returned to the subject of prayer over and over again in the course of his writings; it seems to have been a subject that interested him, and it is certainly a subject on which he achieved a degree of clarity it would be hard to parallel in any other theologian. And the treatise on prayer, such as we find it in the *Summa Theologiae*, is largely Thomas' own creation; although there were scholastic treatises on prayer before Thomas, they had done little to sort out either the structure or the content such a treatise needed. It is therefore a matter of considerable interest to see how Thomas progressively clarified his own ideas on the subject. The whole dossier would be beyond the scope of this volume, but I have included what seem to me to be the most important texts. For convenience, I list them here, with brief notes on their dating and on the state of the text.

(1) *Scriptum super Libros Sententiarum* IV, distinction 15, question 4. This is Thomas' earliest treatise on prayer, dating from about 1255–56. I have used the edition by M. F. Moos (Paris, 1947).

(2) *De Veritate* question 6, article 6. This question dates from 1256–57. I have used the Leonine edition, volume XXII.

(3) *Contra Gentiles*, book III, chapters 95–6. This dates from Thomas' time in Orvieto, in all probability, that is, about 1263. I have used the Leonine manual edition (Rome, 1934).

(4) Commentary on 1 Corinthians 14:13–15 and 1 Timothy 2:1. These lectures, in their final form, apparently date from Thomas' second Parisian regency, but it is not impossible that in essence they go back to the first regency. If they are dated to the second regency, they surely antedate the commentary on Matthew, which must belong to the academic year 1270–71, as we have seen. Thomas' doctrine on the benefits resulting from prayer seems to have matured between the lectures on 1 Corinthians and the *Summa Theologiae*, so it looks as if 1271–72 can be excluded (though admittedly this kind of criterion is far from certain). I have used R. Cai's Marietti edition (Turin, 1953).

(5) Commentary on John 16:23. The lectures on John certainly

belong to the second Parisian regency, though whether they come before or after the lectures on St. Paul is not clear. I have used R. Cai's Marietti edition (Turin, 1972).

(6) Commentary on Matthew 6:5–15. These lectures belong to the academic year 1270–71. For verses 5 to 8 we only have the *reportatio* of Peter d'Andria, which has not yet been published in its entirety. I have used the only known manuscript, Basel, Bibl. Univ. B.V.12. For verses 9 to 15 we also have the *reportatio* of Léger of Besançon, for which I have used R. Cai's Marietti edition (Turin, 1951), which I have checked against one manuscript from the Vatican Library, Urb. lat. 25. I am grateful to Fr. L. J. Bataillon for sending me a copy of the Basel manuscript, and to Fr. L. E. Boyle, Prefect of the Vatican Library, for a copy of the Vatican manuscript.

A *reportatio* can never give us more than some hearer's impression of what a lecturer or preacher said, but in the case of Peter d'Andria's *reportatio* of Thomas' lectures on Matthew there is a further problem: there are some signs that Peter took it upon himself to edit his notes on the lectures with the help of Thomas' later, vernacular, conferences on the Lord's Prayer and the Ten Commandments, which he and Reginald took down and turned into Latin.[2] The relationship between (a) Thomas' original lectures on Matthew, (b) Thomas' conferences, delivered in Italian in Naples, and (c) the editorial work of Peter and Reginald, affecting both the lectures and the conferences, is fraught with considerable unclarity. However, there is no reason to suppose that Peter included anything in his edition of the Matthew lectures that did not derive, one way or another, from Thomas, so the main consequence of the unclarity is that we cannot be too sure of exactly when and in what circumstances Thomas formulated all the points reported.

For the purposes of translation, I have permitted myself what, in another situation, would be the unpardonable solecism of fusing the two *reportationes* into a single text. Since Peter's is the fuller text, I have taken his *reportatio* as the basis for my English version, but I have used Léger too, where his text is available; in the notes I have indicated where I have switched from one to the other.

(7) *Summa Theologiae* II.II q.83. If we reckon that the Secunda Secundae was written between the end of 1270 and the spring of 1272, Thomas averaged about twelve questions a month, so that

question 83 would fall about May–June 1271, after the lectures on Matthew, therefore. I have used the text in volume XXXIX of the Blackfriars *Summa* and Leonine volume IX.

(8) Commentary on Romans 8:26–7. I have argued above that the Romans commentary belongs to Thomas' last years in Naples (1272–3). I have used the edition, already cited, by R. Cai.

*

The English word "prayer" derives, via the French, from the classical Latin *precatio;* Christian Latin, for some reason, rapidly came to prefer *oratio,* but both words were used with the same meaning: petition, asking God for things. And this basic meaning survived intact well into the Middle Ages. Hugh of St. Victor's treatise *De Virtute Orandi,* for instance, arises from a puzzle over why, when we pray, we use psalms that contain all kinds of expressions which are in no obvious sense petition.[3] Also from the early or mid-twelfth century, there is a letter on "how to pray" from the Carthusian John of Portes, which is entirely about saying prayers of petition.[4] These works are not evidence of any narrowness of interest; they simply attest that traditional, primitive usage was still current.

However, various factors combined to extend and finally dislodge the original meaning of "prayer." First of all, the Pauline precept to "pray without ceasing" (1 Thess. 5:17), if taken literally, could only be fulfilled by extending the meaning of the word "pray." Since asking for something presupposes desiring something, Augustine suggested that praying without ceasing means desiring without ceasing; in particular, it means the desire for beatitude that should motivate all our petitions and indeed all our lives. From there, it is not far to saying that as long as charity persists, we are praying the whole time.[5] And this leads easily enough to the very general claim, enshrined in the Gloss, which was the standard commentary on the bible by the thirteenth century, that "the righteous never stop praying unless they stop being righteous."[6] Thus we arrive at what Bonaventure calls the "broadest sense" of "prayer," according to which it means "every good deed."[7]

A problem of a quite different kind was posed by the widespread assumption among educated people in the ancient world that prayer was a rather demeaning activity, and this assumption led some Christians fairly early on to seek some other meaning for the word. Thus Origen complains about certain heretics who take it for granted that when the bible talks about "prayer" it must actually mean something other than what is ordinarily understood by the word.[8] And even Clement of Alexandria is clearly embarrassed by petition, and prefers to push prayer in the direction of a vague "communing with God."[9]

In Latin a further complication is introduced by the use of the word *oratio*, which in classical Latin means "speech."[10] Because of this, discussions of prayer in Latin were for a long time dogged by the apparent need to interpret prayer as a kind of rhetoric. In the thirteenth century, for instance, we find William of Auvergne writing about prayer under the title "Divine Rhetoric."[11]

Another factor in the strange development of the word "prayer" was the list in 1 Timothy 2:1, "entreaties, prayers, pleas and thanksgiving." Where Origen merely treats this list as indicating topics which "border on prayer,"[12] within a few centuries we find it serving as the basis both for a theory of the "parts" of prayer[13] and for a theory of different "kinds" of prayer.[14] In the one case, the result is a quest for the proper rhetorical structure of a prayer; in the other case an apparent justification is found for a doctrine of progress from one kind of prayer to another.[15] This latter can then join forces with the suspicion that petition is a rather demeaning activity, to produce a theory of prayer in which petition is downgraded almost to the point of extinction.[16]

A fairly similar process led to a narrowing of the scope of prayer, so that the only object it was considered proper to pray for was God himself or union with him.[17] Since "contemplation" was also tending to be identified as consisting essentially in love of God or desire for God, "prayer" and "contemplation" began to converge,[18] and both came to be regarded as primarily affective activities or conditions. It is symptomatic of this that one of the commonest "definitions" of prayer by the early thirteenth century identified prayer as "a pious affection directed toward God."[19] Even St. Albert could say that "prayer is the fulfilment of our affections."[20]

Granted that love of God was generally regarded as something delightful ("sweet," in medieval parlance), the affective notion of prayer immediately posed a further problem. Prayer was traditionally regarded as one of the works of "satisfaction," a penance that could be enjoined on a penitent. But if it was an enjoyable work, how could it count as a penance? It was partly to deal with this problem that William of Auxerre, for instance, distinguished between two different kinds of prayer: that of the contemplative, which is pleasant and does not count as a penance, and that of other people, which is painful in some way or another and so does count as a penance.[21]

By the time of St. Thomas, then, it is far from clear quite what the word "prayer" means. Several theologians state without further ado that the word has several different meanings,[22] and the first Dominican Parisian Master, Roland of Cremona, seems to be in doubt whether these different meanings are even related to one another.[23] Roland himself, although he devoted quite a substantial treatise to prayer in his commentary on the Sentences, leaves us with the impression that there was enormous confusion on the subject in the schools, a confusion he is quite unable to resolve.[24] William of Auxerre and William of Auvergne did something to clarify the situation, and the latter, in particular, opts for a traditional definition of prayer as a form of petition, specified as "prayer" by the fact that it is addressed to God and therefore has to be characterized by a certain reverence toward the author of all things.[25] But the lack of clarity still remains.

It fell to the lot of Thomas to construct what is surely far and away the clearest and most coherent treatise on prayer since Origen. And he achieves much of his clarity by insisting on a very precise understanding of prayer as petition. In his commentary on the Sentences he still alludes to the fact that "some people" use "prayer" in more than one sense,[26] but thereafter he makes no concessions at all in that direction.

If we plump for the original meaning of "prayer" as petition, the question immediately arises about whether or not it makes sense for us to ask God for things. Surely he knows better than we do what is for the best? And in any case, has he not already decided from all eternity what is going to happen in the world? It is astounding that this crucial speculative question seems to have dropped out of the discussion of prayer throughout the whole period from Origen to St. Thomas, surviving only in the backwater of the question whether predestination can be helped by the prayers of the saints.

275

In the commentary on the Sentences, Thomas has not yet brought it back into the picture, but in the *Contra Gentiles* it is right in the forefront in the chapters on prayer, and thereafter it remains an integral element in Thomas' doctrine of prayer. As he sees it, it is only one aspect of the more general question about the relationship between providence and human activity: if human initiatives really do bring about real effects, this cannot be because we can interfere with the working out of God's plan; it must be because God himself gives to us the "dignity of causality."[27] Secondary causes, including our free acts, are a way in which God himself brings about his own purpose; they are deployed by his supreme causality. Our prayer, then, is not a way of trying to change God's mind, nor is it a charade; it is a real form of secondary causality, which is itself caused by God, but which does genuinely cause certain things to happen, inasmuch as God has chosen to bring about certain results by means of our prayer.

Apart from the speculative problem of whether prayer makes sense at all, there is a religious problem: How can asking God for what we want count as a genuinely religious act? Is it not rather an attempt to exploit God in the service of our own desires and interests? Precisely by focusing our attention on what it means to make a petition, Thomas can deal with this problem far more successfully than most of his contemporaries. As he points out, there is a crucial difference between ordering someone to do something and asking someone to do something. In the latter case, you are necessarily casting yourself on the mercy of someone else. So asking God for something is intrinsically an act of worship, in that it is a recognition of God's position as the source and Lord of everything. It is a sacrifice of our own planning minds to God.

In principle, once this basic point has been seen, a lot of other problems become much more tractable, though it took Thomas some time to work his way through them. One traditional problem was whether or not we should ask God for worldly things. Thomas gradually came to see that the real problem was whether we should ask God for anything specific. He escaped quickly enough from the idea (still present in the commentary on the Sentences) that asking for worldly things is a "low" kind of prayer; indeed, he seems to have abandoned thereafter any suggestion that there are different "levels" of prayer, because whether you are asking for the beatific vision or for a toy gun, the actual asking is the same. But it was not until the late commentary on Romans that Thomas was finally able to deal satisfactorily with the problem of specific petition. The difficulty is that, as St. Paul points out, "we do not know what we ought to pray for" (Rom. 8:26). After various false starts, Thomas eventually came to accept that this applies to everything, and that therefore St. Paul's further comment that "the Spirit helps us in our weakness" applies to everything. Even in the case of our practice of the theological virtues, we need the gifts of the Holy Spirit to free us from stupidity and ignorance;[28] similarly in the case of all our prayer, it is the Holy Spirit who forms in our wills precise desires that are aligned with the will of God. There is therefore no need to distinguish sharply between doubtful and undoubtful objects of petition; they are all doubtful in themselves, and they are all subject to the working of the Holy Spirit in our wills.

The problem of "kinds" and "parts" of prayer, generated by 1 Timothy 2:1, could not simply be ignored by any thirteenth-century theologian, but Thomas progressively broke loose from it. By the time he was writing the *Summa*, he was content simply to note that various ingredients go to the making of a fully-formed petition, without insisting on any particular rhetorical structure. Indeed, by this time Thomas had largely escaped from the irrelevant problems suggested by the ambiguities of *oratio*, and which had loomed large at the beginning of his treatise in the commentary on the Sentences. As for the "kinds" of prayer, they are reduced to a fairly down-to-earth account of the various ways in which a petition can be presented. And though Thomas still treats "the ascent of the mind to God" as being the most specific characteristic of prayer (that, within the whole act of prayer, which makes it prayer), by now he is able to confine it quite rigorously to petition: it is the equivalent of going up to someone in order to present your request to him, and there is no longer any hint that this means a kind of "meditation" (as there was even in the commentary on 1 Timothy).

As we read through the dossier on prayer, we can see Thomas progressively escaping from the clutches of the affective understanding of prayer, from the need to show that it is painful enough to count as a penance, from the need to make it religiously significant by insisting on fervor or concentration. We can see how he emerges from the fog of the traditional discussion of the "conditions for impetration," by distinguishing between merit and impetration, and showing what is involved in praying in such a way that it is a fully virtuous act, while reminding us that impetration (obtaining what we are praying for) depends simply on God's favor. He also moves ever more clearly toward identifying the specific objective of prayer as, precisely, impetration (we ask for something because we want to get it—it seems obvious), and this, in turn, makes for a great increase in clarity about the respective roles of attention and intention in prayer: If you pray deliberately, with the intention of doing reverence to God by asking for something, then that intention, as it were, validates your whole prayer, unless you actually rescind it. This is sufficient both to make your prayer meritorious, assuming you are in a state of charity, and to make it count as a real prayer that stands some chance of obtaining from God the boon that is being asked for. Attention is needed only to secure the incidental benefit of some immediate consolation. Thomas can thus eliminate the idea that the real point of praying is to obtain consolation,[29] an interpretation of prayer that could never explain half of the things we actually do or say when we pray.

The great achievement of Thomas in his treatise on prayer was to explain theologically both how prayer, in its traditional sense of petition, makes sense and how it is an authentic religious activity. He thereby shores up prayer, precisely in the sense in which all Christians are commanded to practice it. But at the same time he shows how unnecessary are a lot of the practical difficulties that people have claimed to find in prayer.

Readers nurtured in the very different linguistic world of modern piety are likely at first to find what Thomas says about prayer somewhat narrow; but historically his treatment of the subject provided a solid doctrinal basis for a critique of precisely the developments that yielded our modern usage, and in so doing it secured for ordinary Christians the right to go on saying their prayers in a perfectly ordinary way, without being deflected by the demands of apparently more elevated notions of prayer.[30] It is at least partly thanks to Thomas that in the twentieth century two great English Dominicans could put up a fight for a straightforward and traditional account of prayer: Bede Jarrett protested against the complexity that had come to surround the practice of prayer, with the result that it had become almost impossible for many people,[31] and Vincent

McNabb asserted, against the modern tendency to dismiss petition as scarcely worthy of the name of prayer, that prayer without petition is almost blasphemous.[32]

3. The Contemplative Life

Words connected with 'contemplation' have had, if anything, an even more bizarre history than the word 'prayer', and in St. Thomas' time they had already become seriously ambiguous. As Thomas noted in his commentary on the Sentences, ' "Contemplation" is sometimes taken in a strict sense, to mean the act of the intellect thinking about the things of God . . . but in another sense it is taken more generally to mean any act in which people separate themselves from worldly affairs to attend to God alone."[1] But whereas Thomas worked hard to unscramble the notion of prayer, he seems to have been much less interested in disentangling 'contemplation', so that his treatise in the *Summa* is not entirely coherent and we do not find a succession of discussions of 'contemplation' to parallel the dossier on prayer.

On the contemplative life I have selected three texts:

(1) The prologue to the commentary on Boethius' *De Ebdomadibus*, dating from about 1257–8 in all probability. I have used the text edited by M. Calcaterra in volume II of the Marietti *Opuscula Theologica*, Turin 1954, p. 391.

(2) The prologue to the lectures on St. John, dating from 1268 or 1269. Thanks to the kindness of Fr L. Reid OP, I have been able to use the text prepared for the forthcoming Leonine edition.

(3) The whole treatise on the active and contemplative lives in *Summa Theologiae* II.II questions 179–182, for which I have used volume XLVI of the Blackfriars *Summa* and volume X of the Leonine edition.

The words 'contemplation' and 'contemplative', as has been mentioned, were already, by St. Thomas' time, somewhat vague. They could have a straightforwardly intellectual sense: human beings have a 'contemplative' faculty in as much as they are endowed with reason and understanding;[2] *contemplatio*, in such a context, simply means 'study'.[3] This is at least one reason why the Dominican provincial of Paris, Peter of Rheims, can identify the students as being the 'contemplatives' within the Dominican community,[4] and why Gerald de Frachet sees fit to report a cautionary tale about a Dominican would-be philosopher who lost his faith because of too much 'contemplation'.[5]

At the other extreme, 'contemplative' words can be given an essentially affective meaning, even to the extent of becoming rather anti-intellectual. Thus Thomas' admirer, Giles of Rome, in his commentary on the Canticle, says that its way of proceeding is 'affective, yearning and contemplative'.[6] And James of Milan contrasts the simple, affective piety of the 'contemplative' with the dangerous temptations to which intellectuals are exposed.[7]

Further complications are introduced by the phrase 'contemplative life'. In the philosophical milieu in which the phrase originated, it meant a life devoted as exclusively as possible to intellectual pursuits,[8] but in some later Platonist circles it came to be used to refer to a life primarily devoted to religious interests.[9] In Christian circles St. Gregory gave it a classic definition: whereas the active life consists in works of practical charity, the contemplative life 'is to hold on to the love of God and of neighbour with all one's mind, but to rest from external activity, to cling solely to the desire for our Creator.'[10] In each case, it seems clear that the 'contemplative life' is a way of life peculiar to certain individuals.

The same phrase can also be used, though, to identify one aspect of the life of everyone. Thus, for instance, the Dominican preacher, Aldobrandino of Toscanella, whose heyday was in the last quarter of the thirteenth century, ascribes a threefold life to everyone ('contemplative, civic and sensual'), and this whole complex life has to be offered to God. As a minimum, one day a week is set aside (the 'sabbath') for 'contemplation of God', as otherwise our love for God would grow tepid.[11] It is not clear whether this means anything more than going to church on Sunday.

Religious life, as a life of concentration on God, could easily be identified with 'contemplative life', but this need not mean anything very portentous. Humbert of Romans, for example, says that all religious are 'contemplative', but interprets the word in a purely moralistic sense, as meaning that religious should be morally circumspect the whole time,[12] which would not exclude 'active' religious.

On the other hand, 'contemplative' could be attached to specific activities rather than to a whole life. By Thomas' time it was conventional to list things like reading, meditation and prayer as contemplative occupations.[13] And a corresponding list of 'active' works was provided by Gregory.[14] The attempt to allocate such tasks as teaching to one or other of the lives was thus a routine item on the theologian's agenda. There was also a similar concern to allocate different virtues to one life or the other.

In as much as 'contemplative life' was identified with love of God and 'active life' with love of neighbour,[15] a purely 'contemplative' life would be hard to justify.[16] On the other hand, there was a well-established tradition of regarding 'contemplation' as vastly superior to the active life.[17] But then again, pastors and preachers were expected to excel in both lives,[18] so it could be argued that a 'mixed life' was really the best.[19]

There was muddle enough in the thirteenth century about 'contemplation' and the 'contemplative life'. The modern reader is likely to compound the difficulty by bringing in other, more recent, notions as well, so it should be borne in mind that in St. Thomas' time there had not yet developed the technical usage which later prevailed, with its systematic distinction between 'contemplation' and 'meditation' and its talk of 'infused contemplation', nor did 'contemplation' immediately suggest 'contemplative prayer' (a phrase which came into vogue much later on). Nor had the adjective 'contemplative' yet been appropriated to monastic religious. 'Contemplative' vocabulary was still very fluid and so it could be adapted to a variety of different purposes more easily than it can now.

Thomas tried to do justice to the complex and not very coherent inheritance he had received from the Christian tradition, but his heart does not seem to have been in it. Under the influence of Aristotle he espoused, on the whole, a rigorously intellectual understanding of contemplation, and the one essential insight he had about the distinction between the active and contemplative lives is that it can very properly be interpreted as a distinction between two different kinds of personal bias. What distinguishes a human life from that of other animals is the human intellect, and intellect can be either speculative or practical, in that we can be primarily concerned to find out about things just because we want to understand them, or we can be primarily concerned to get things done. And whichever engages our interest the most can be said to constitute our life,[20] just as we might say of someone that 'he lives for baseball' or that 'knitting is her life'.

Obviously no one in this world can be purely active or purely contemplative, but there must be few people whose interests are so evenly balanced that they cannot be regarded as biased either in favour of speculative concerns or in favour of practicality. Thomas' interpretation of the distinction between active and contemplative makes good human sense. But the distinction between the two lives, formulated in this way, makes very little sense of most of the inherited language about either life.

One of the conventional questions concerned the relative meritoriousness of the two lives. In the commentary on the Sentences Thomas appears to be reluctant to ascribe greater merit without qualification to either life.[21] In the *Summa* he gives the conventional answer that the contemplative life, as such, is more meritorious,[22] but it is far from clear that he has seriously committed himself to this answer. Greater merit derives from greater love of God, and the most perfect love of God in this life must mean the most perfect readiness to do his will, not just the most intense desire to contemplate him.[23] It is not at all surprising that in his most formal treatment of perfection in the *De Perfectione* Thomas seems totally uninterested in distinguishing between actives and contemplatives. And although, in his treatise on the contemplative life, Thomas appears to accept that the contemplative life, as such, involves a greater love of God,[24] elsewhere he seems to be quite prepared to assert that contemplatives, as such, love God less than actives,[25] which would undermine the whole basis for the alleged greater meritoriousness of the contemplative life. It is easy enough for Thomas to spell out the sense in which the contemplative life is more attractive, other things being equal,[26] and he can also indicate in what sense it is more loved by God, as being more like the life of heaven;[27] but it is far from clear that Thomas could succeed in integrating into his overall doctrine a serious claim that the contemplative life, as he understands it, is more meritorious, more Christian, than the active life. The logic of his position would surely be to say that either life has to be converted into a Christian life in very much the same sort of way, and that either life is equally capable of being so converted. He might even go on to say that the more perfectly either life is converted, the less significant the distinction will be between active and contemplative. Unfortunately Thomas does not appear to have been interested enough in the topic to work through the implications of his basic premiss with sufficient ruthlessness to challenge the clutter of conventional assumptions which largely governed the discussion.

Thus, when he is not dealing ex professo with the contemplative life, Thomas is prepared to point out that the behaviour of 'contemplatives' has as much need to be regulated by prudence as that of anyone else;[28] but when he takes up the subject in its own right, he feels obliged to relegate prudence to the active life.[29] In the treatise on the contemplative life, all prayer is allowed to be part of contemplation,[30] even though in the treatise on prayer it has been made quite clear that prayer is an exercise of the practical reason.[31] The role of prayer in the contemplative life is defined very precisely by Thomas: prayer is essential because we need to obtain understanding from God by asking for it.[32] The role of 'contemplation' in prayer is also quite explicit: if we want to ask God for something, we must be, as it were, looking at him.[33] But this does not mean that all prayer is directly related to the contemplative's desire for understanding. Prayer is as much at home in the life of any kind of Christian, whether active or contemplative, in Thomas' sense of the words. But in the treatise on the contemplative life Thomas seems to lack the energy to escape from the conventions.

Particularly disappointing is Thomas' treatment of where teaching fits into the contemplative/active schema. In the commentary on the Sentences, Thomas seems to be at least on the verge of saying that teaching (though not preaching) belongs to the contemplative life.[34] In the Summa he is no longer prepared to allow that teaching, as such, is a 'contemplative' occupation.[35] And there is an obvious sense in which this is true: giving lectures and so on interrupts the teacher's own pursuit of the truth for its own sake. But Thomas drops hints of a far richer doctrine than he ever actually develops. In his account of what is meant by 'life' in phrases like 'contemplative life', he cites Aristotle as saying that the thing that most engages our interest is the thing that we most want to share with our friends.[36] He also says, without comment, that love of God and of neighbour is the proper Christian motivation for a contemplative life.[37] It would seem natural to move on from such considerations to a view of teaching as an exercise in fraternal charity which is natural to people whose temperamental bias is 'contemplative', but this Thomas never does, though he must have been aware of the many ways in which one's own intellectual life is stimulated and helped by the demands of one's students. Far from exploring the fraternal dimensions of the contemplative life, Thomas meekly follows the conventional belief that the solitary life is best, especially for contemplation,[38] and this in spite of his own contention that a life in which contemplation spills over into teaching or preaching is the best.[39]

In practice every Christian life must be in some sense 'contemplative' and in some sense 'active'. If 'active life' is taken in its older sense, as meaning the cultivation of the moral virtues, then it is obviously a necessary ingredient in any Christian life. If it is taken in its more modern sense, established by Gregory, as meaning the practice of fraternal charity, it is still fairly obvious that it is incumbent on all Christians; Thomas, at any rate, takes it for granted that there can be no Christian life at all without some acts of fraternal charity.[40] On the other hand, since human behaviour has to be governed by some kind of view of life, and for Christians this must mean a Christian view of life, it makes sense to say that the active life of Christians has to be governed by some kind of contemplative life.[41] So it makes little essential difference whether one's life as a whole is primarily directed towards practical results or whether it is chiefly devoted to the pursuit of knowledge and wisdom. If it is to count as a genuine Christian life, it must be based on what we know about God from revelation and on our orientation towards knowledge of God and union with him as our final objective; in this sense, it must be 'contemplative'. It must also include a genuine and effective fraternal charity, exercised in whatever way is appropriate to our talents, responsibilities and opportunities.

In so far as the two lives are ascribed to different sets of people—and this is Thomas' starting point in the *Summa*[42]—this can be developed quite cogently on the basis of Thomas' recognition of differences of intellectual bias in different people. But surely what follows from that is not so much two radically divergent sets of occupations, but rather two different ways of slanting much the same range of occupations. This is recognised by Thomas to some extent. At least he allows that supposedly 'active' occupations can be undertaken in view of a contemplative orientation. And elsewhere he is quite happy to subordinate 'contemplative' occupations to a practical goal, as when he recommends the 'contemplative' exercise of singing psalms and hymns and spiritual songs as a way of fostering celibacy.[43] But the conventions of the discussion of the contemplative life apparently do not allow him to allude to this when he is dealing expressly with the relationship between the two lives.

Where Thomas does emphatically break loose from the conventions is on points which engage his interest because of some other doctrinal concern. Thus in the commentary on book III of the Sentences (which he perhaps revised soon after leaving Paris in 1259)[44] Thomas follows the customary practice of dealing with the contemplative life in the context of the treatment of the Gifts of the Holy Spirit.[45] The 'contemplative life' is identified with reference to the two gifts which are regarded as belonging essentially to it, the gifts of wisdom and understanding; following Augustine, Thomas describes them as gifts which are important 'only in the contemplative life'.[46] This connection between the contemplative life and two particular gifts of the Holy Spirit secures theologically the specific supernatural identity of the contemplative life, and Thomas accordingly distinguishes between the contemplative life of philosophers, which is motivated only by self-love and aims only at the self-perfection of its practitioner, and the contemplative life of the saints, which is motivated by charity and desire for God.[47]

By the time we get to the *Summa*, Thomas' position is radically different. He is no longer interested in making a distinction between the intellectual life of the philosopher and that of the saints; on the contrary, he is eager to show the continuity between the saint and the philosopher, as the prologue to the commentary on St. John makes especially clear. The contemplative life is much more simply and straightforwardly the intellectual life, whoever is leading it. A Christian intellectual life must, of course, be motivated by charity, like any other Christian activity; but that does not mean that it becomes something quite different from anyone else's intellectual life. And in the *Summa* Thomas appears to be quite happy to treat the contemplative life as the life of reason,[48] whereas in the commentary on the Sentences he rather suggests that the contemplative life proper refers to intellectual vision and not to discursive reason.[49]

Even more strikingly, Thomas has significantly changed his

understanding of the Gifts of the Holy Spirit.[50] Already in the Prima Secundae he has dropped the suggestion that there are some gifts which belong especially to the contemplative life, and he treats all the gifts as constituting an essential element in every Christian life.[51] And in the Secunda Secundae he goes even further, and ascribes a practical as well as a speculative role to the gifts of wisdom and understanding.[52] The contemplative life as such, therefore, has no specific claim to any supernatural status or to any part of the supernatural 'apparatus' with which Christians can be endowed.

In the commentary on the Sentences Thomas toyed with the idea that the inner reality of both love of God and love of neighbour is part of the contemplative life, whereas the outward acts proper to both belong to the active life.[53] This would naturally not provide any basis for distinguishing between actives and contemplatives, but it is, perhaps, unfortunate that Thomas did not develop a clearer awareness of the different kinds of problematic involved in the traditional discourse on the contemplative life, which might have allowed him to discuss as separate topics the division of the human race into actives and contemplatives on the one hand, and the contemplative and active elements involved in every Christian life on the other. But between the commentary on the Sentences and the *Summa* he appears never to have turned his mind systematically to the subject of the 'contemplative life', and in the *Summa* he seems content to repeat conventional answers, with little attempt to relate them to what he says elsewhere or even to his own basic principle that the distinction between the two lives is a distinction of temperament. It seems fairly clear that his own interest was not engaged by the treatise on the two lives and that he was therefore ill-equipped to deal with it in a hurry when he reached the final questions of the Secunda Secundae. And perhaps that is the most interesting point to be gleaned from his treatise. Maybe he was right. Maybe there is not very much substantial value in the conventional dichotomy between active and contemplative, perhaps it could profitably be put to work in a much more humdrum fashion. And arguably that was Augustine's conclusion too: his answer to the vexed question which is the best life, the active, the contemplative or the mixed, is that none of them is; in the eyes of Christians, the best life can only be eternal life.[54]

4. Religious Life

In the course of his writings, Thomas discusses several topics that are important for the understanding of religious life and of Dominican life in particular. His two major treatises on religious life, *Contra Impugnantes* and *De Perfectione*, were composed in the context of fierce controversies, but even so, Thomas does far more than engage in topical polemic. He develops a view of religious life in the light of a fundamental understanding of what the virtue of religion means and what can properly be meant by the idea of perfection. Religion means essentially offering service and worship to God, and perfection means the perfection of charity, both love of God and love of neighbor. All the various structures and practices of religious life must therefore be related to the service of God and to the human pursuit of perfect charity.

The texts I have selected for inclusion here illustrate Thomas' views on obedience, study and poverty, and finally I have included a fine piece of Dominican one-upmanship, showing that the best form of religious life is one devoted to teaching and preaching. Most of these texts speak for themselves and do not need much introduction.

(a) Obedience

In his encyclical of 1261, more or less contemporary with the three texts I have included from St. Thomas, Humbert of Romans complains about a loss of generosity in the practice of obedience in the Order. "Will you not do what is commanded with a willing spirit," he asks, "without formal precepts and heavy penalties having to be invoked—which are contrary to the tradition of the Order?" The friars should not insist strictly on the limits of what they are obliged to by their profession, they should follow "the obedience of charity" and throw themselves into every good work "in accordance with that charity which knows no limits. Whatever concerns God's glory and honor, whatever concerns the salvation of souls, you should do it with all diligence, not only what is commanded, not only what is recommended, but whatever even a single hand can do. . . ."[1]

It is this essentially Dominican call for generosity that underlies Thomas' discussion of obedience. A vow of obedience is the most total kind of self-oblation, because by it one offers one's own will.[2] But this does not mean that thereafter one has no will.[3] On the contrary, a vow of obedience means that thereafter one's will is *given*, not extinguished, and all the acts performed under obedience are a renewal of that gift and must therefore be intrinsically free acts.[4] Thomas will not allow that there is any contradiction between freedom and obedience or vows.

On the other hand, Thomas does not believe that obedience can govern more than people's external acts. We can be told what to *do*, but not what to will.[5] A superior has the right to expect us to do what we are told, and Thomas would not dissent from Humbert's plea that we should throw ourselves into the twofold task of giving glory to God and furthering the salvation of our neighbors far beyond the limits of what we have strictly been told to do. But that is quite compatible with our sometimes being told to do something we do not want to do, and with our doing it generously even while going on not wanting to do it. Our freedom is engaged precisely in our wanting to obey, even if it means something that we do not, in any other sense, want to do. And, inasmuch as choosing to do something is, for Thomas, a rational affair,[6] we may find ourselves doing things that we do not even consider it sensible to do; we can quite properly and generously decide that it is sensible to obey, even if we reckon we have been given a stupid command.

In a Dominican context, obedience meant primarily obedience to the particular task given one within the whole functioning of the Order of Preachers.[7] Against this background it is easy to see why Thomas is unsympathetic to fussy notions of obedience, according to which the religious would be hemmed in by precepts. It is a whole life that is governed by obedience, rather than the minute details of day-to-day living. And even here it is important that religious life should not be turned into a death-trap. Thomas' complacency about the Dominican tradition is evident: he clearly thinks that it is a good thing that, in most cases, infringements of religious rules and regulations should not be regarded as constituting sin, not even venial sin.[8] As Humbert indicates, it is quite contrary to the Dominican tradition to use obedience as a way of bullying people into doing things.

(b) Study

One of the most original features of Dominican life was the role given to persistent study. Everyone was expected to make study a lifelong occupation, and some people were deputed to it as their major task, either as students or as teachers.[9] And, unlike the traditional monastic practice of reading (*lectio*), Dominican study was increasingly modelled on the pattern of the universities, and it was regarded as a serious professional obligation, important enough for routine conventual observances to have to make way for it.[10]

The practice of study was vulnerable to attack on several fronts. From outside the Order, it was vulnerable to the argument that it is a monk's business to weep, not to teach, as the much-quoted adage from St. Jerome had it.[11] The enemies of the friars maintained that, as religious, they should be engaging in manual labor, not study.

Within the Order study had to be defended against the immediate demands of the apostolic work of preaching. The Constitutions declared emphatically that the energy of the friars ought to be directed primarily to the good of souls.[12] To spend one's whole time as an academic might well seem to be contrary to this fundamental orientation of Dominican life. Thomas' defense of Dominican academics, which is given in full below, can stand as a permanent bulwark against the ever-present tendency to sacrifice the less obvious values of the intellectual life to the pressures of work that has to be done.

(c) Poverty

In the thirteenth century poverty was the most contentious issue connected with religious life. On the one side, there was those who denied the value of religious poverty entirely and those who, more moderately, denied the legitimacy of religious mendicancy; on the other side there were those, especially the Franciscans, who maintained that any kind of ownership whatsoever was incompatible with religious perfection. The Dominicans found themselves in a protracted row with the Franciscans on this last point, which often descended to such absurd questions as to whether Christ wore shoes or not.[13] The debate over whether Christ and his apostles owned anything lasted into the next century and was so bitter that it led one good lady, who was keen on the Franciscan Spirituals, to describe the canonization of Thomas as being a kind of canonization of "Cain" by the wicked pope.[14]

Thomas opts for a purely functional doctrine of poverty. Poverty is not a value in its own right, it is valuable only as a means to an end and, as such, must be practiced in a way that is appropriate to the end which one is pursuing. For an Order of Preachers, Thomas argues, mendicancy combined with a certain reserve stock of essentials is the ideal financial arrangement. He seems quite out of sympathy with those, even among his own brethren, who were attracted by poverty as such,[15] but it is likely that by this time the functional view of poverty was quite common in the Order.[16]

(d) Preaching and Teaching

As we have seen, Thomas does not seem to be deeply engaged by discussions of the "contemplative life." What he values, under the rubric of "contemplative," is a serious intellectual life and, as a conscientious teacher, he cannot have been in much doubt that the natural flowering of a serious intellectual life is a desire, or at least a willingness, to teach others in one way or another. He shows no hesitation in giving first prize, then, to a religious Order whose objective is to be "contemplative" (intellectual) and then to move on to communicating the results of its intellectual life to others, by preaching and teaching. And it does not take much imagination to attach a label to this Order. Thomas does not often talk about himself, but he was clearly pleased that he was a Dominican.

*

The sources for the texts used in this section are:
(1) *Contra Impugnantes* and *De Perfectione*, for which I have used volume XLI of the Leonine edition.
(2) *Summa Theologiae*, for which I have used volumes XLI and XLVII of the Blackfriars *Summa* and volumes IX and X of the Leonine edition.
(3) The Quodlibetal Questions, for which I have used R. Spiazzi's Marietti edition (Turin, 1949).

Notes

Part I

1. The sources for the life of Thomas are mostly contained in *Fontes Vitae Sancti Thomae Aquinatis*, edited by D. Prümmer and M. H. Laurent, published in fascicles attached to *Revue Thomiste* 1911–1937 (cited hereafter as FVST). The major sources are conveniently available also in A. Ferrua, *Thomae Aquinatis Vitae Fontes Praecipuae* (Alba, 1968) (cited as Ferrua). Some of the sources were published in English in K. Foster, *The Life of St. Thomas Aquinas, Biographical Documents* (London, 1959). The most important sources are the 1319 Naples canonization process and the biography of Thomas by William of Tocco, who had known Thomas at the end of his life and was the chief "researcher" involved in the pre-canonization inquiries. Bernard Gui, who wrote the second life of Thomas, depended heavily on Tocco, but he was a careful and well-informed historian, who had done a lot of work on Dominican history, and some of the details he supplies may well be based on good documentary evidence. Petrus Calo, who included a life of Thomas in his collection of saints' lives written around 1330 (cf. A. Poncelet, *Analecta Bollandiana* 29 (1910) p. 31), draws on the earlier lives, but the possibility cannot be excluded that he also had access to other material; no serious study of his legendary has ever been made, but I notice that for the translation of St. Dominic he makes use of fairly recherché material (his legenda is so far unpublished). There have been innumerable modern excursions into the biography of Thomas; the main recent lives are A. Walz, *Saint Thomas d'Aquin*, French adaptation by P. Novarina (Louvain/Paris, 1962), and J. A. Weisheipl, *Friar Thomas d'Aquino*, rev. ed. (Washington, DC: 1983).

2. The most important study of Thomas' family remains F. Scandone, "La vita, la famiglia e la patria di S. Tommaso de Aquino," in I. Taurisano, ed., *S. Tommaso d'Aquino OP, Miscellanea Storico-Artistica* (Rome, 1924), pp. 1–110. There is a brief account in Foster, pp. 159–61. Cf also E. Cuozzo, *Catalogus Baronum: Commentario*, Rome 1984, pp. 285–6.

3. There are many converging indications of the date of Thomas' birth, which seem to me to add up to near certainty. He died on 7 March 1274, and a competent witness at the canonization process, Bartholomew of Capua, says that he "is commonly said to have died in his 48th year" (FVST p. 384, Ferrua p. 326). Tolomeo of Lucca, who knew Thomas at the end of his life, gives various figures that are tolerably coherent: he lectured on the Sentences before he was thirty (i.e., he was thirty in 1256 at the earliest) (Ferrua p. 356), he joined the Order when he was sixteen and

lived in it for thirty-two years (Ferrua p. 355), he was "50 or 48" when he died (Ferrua p. 364). Tocco says he was in his forty-ninth year when he died (i.e., he was born 1225–26) (FVST p. 138, Ferrua p. 115). Gui says he was verging on 49 (FVST p. 205, Ferrua p. 175), but this is probably an over-literal interpretation of Tocco's fanciful thoughts about Thomas' sabbath and jubilee.

Thomas was made an oblate at Monte Cassino when he was five (FVST p. 69, Ferrua p. 34), and there are reasons for dating this to 1231 (cf. below, note 28).

James of Caiazzo gave evidence that he met Thomas in Naples, presumably in 1272, and that Thomas was "about 46" at the time (FVST p. 319, Ferrua p. 260).

All of this points to 1226 as the year of Thomas' birth. Other indications in the canonization process are too vague to be useful. Remigio dei Girolami says that he fell short of his fiftieth year, which, if taken strictly, means that he was 48 (AFP 54 [1984] p. 265).

4. 1216 is conventionally regarded as the year of the Order's official foundation, because of the first papal Bull received by Dominic after the brethren had clarified their canonical position, on 22 December 1216 (MOPH XXV pp. 71–6).

5. Although Honorius III always remained friendly with Frederick, in May and July 1226 he sent him two fairly stiff letters of complaint (MGH *Epistolae Saeculi XIII*, ed. C. Rodenberg, vol. I (Berlin, 1883), pp. 216–22, 233–4).

6. Tocco (FVST p. 66, Ferrua p. 31); cf. Scandone, pp. 41–5. The Counts of Aquino are first heard of toward the end of the tenth century; cf. Scandone, "Roccasecca," *Archivio Storico di Terra di Lavoro* 1 (1956) p. 39.

7. FVST p. 535. The last Count of Aquino was Landone IV in the previous century (Scandone, "Famiglia" p. 45). That Thomas was Landulph's son is known from Tocco (FVST p. 70, Ferrua p. 35); Bartholomew of Capua describes Thomas' father (whom he does not name) as a powerful nobleman (FVST p. 371, Ferrua p. 313). There is absolutely no reason to doubt the reliability of this information. Both Tocco and Bartholomew knew an old Dominican, John of S. Giuliano, who had befriended Thomas before Thomas even joined the Order (FVST p. 371, Ferrua p. 313), and Tocco also interviewed Thomas' niece, Lady Catherine of Morra, and learned the family tradition about Thomas from her (FVST p. 350, Ferrua p. 291).

8. FVST p. 541. There is a photograph of the entry in the necrology in T. Leccisotti, *S. Tommaso d'Aquino e Montecassino*, Montecassino, 1965, plate VIII.

9. The d'Aquino family tradition identifies Roccasecca as the place

of Thomas' birth (FVST pp. 66–7, 250; Ferrua pp. 31–2, 292). Scandone, "Famiglia" pp. 103–110, argues that it was the normal place of residence of the family.

10. FVST p. 539.

11. FVST p. 532.

12. Thomas' older brother, Aimone, was a crusader in Frederick's army and in January 1233 Gregory IX intervened to try to secure his release from captivity in Cyprus (FVST pp. 536–7); cf. Scandone, "Famiglia" p. 76. At least Reginald was in the imperial army at the time of Thomas' kidnapping in 1244 (Tolomeo, Ferrua pp. 355–6), and other sources refer to Thomas "brothers" in connection with this episode (FVST p. 351, Ferrua p. 292, passing on the family tradition as received by Tocco; Thomas of Cantimpré, Ferrua p. 387).

12a. On this Thomas d'Aquino, see M. Maccarrone, *Studi su Innocenzo III*, Padua 1972, pp. 167–219.

13. Tocco (FVST pp. 66, 68; Ferrua pp. 31, 33). There is a tradition, going back at least to the sixteenth century, that she was the daughter of the Count of Theate (cf. the life which introduces vol. I of the Piana edition of Thomas' works, published in 1570, f.2ᵛ), but it is not clear whether there is any justification for such a claim.

14. FVST p. 350, Ferrua p. 292.

15. Tocco's account of the whole saga of Thomas' harassment by his family (FVST pp. 71–77, Ferrua pp. 37–43) ascribes a far more prominent role to Theodora than do any of the other sources, and it may be presumed that he was basing himself essentially on the family tradition derived from Theodora herself. Her line was evidently that she was throughout trying to encourage and test her son's vocation, but this looks suspiciously like an attempt to put a benign interpretation on facts that could not simply be covered up. The prophecy of Thomas' vocation plays an important part in Theodora's story, which makes one suspect that it too may have been touched up to suit her "defense."

16. The Dominicans did not arrive in Naples until 1227 and did not have a house there until 1231 (see below, note 39), which makes it odd that there should have been talk as early as 1225–6 of Theodora's child joining them, though no doubt prophets have their own ways of knowing things. But the apparently unanimous opposition of the family when Thomas did become a Dominican is hard to understand if the prophecy had been as explicit as Theodora made out; and the earliest sources leave us in no doubt about the unanimity of the opposition, including Theodora's own testimony (FVST p. 351, Ferrua pp. 292, 379, 387). Assuming that Theodora did not make up the whole story of the prophecy, it seems safe to reckon that it grew and become more explicit with hindsight.

17. FVST p. 395, Ferrua pp. 337–8.

18. FVST p. 68, Ferrua p. 33.

19. A. Potthast, *Regesta Romanorum Pontificum* (Berlin 1874–75), I pp. 677, 680.

20. Only four days after he became pope, Gregory sent a firm letter to Frederick, ending on a decidedly threatening note (*Epist. Saec. XIII* I pp. 261–2).

21. Ibid. pp. 281–5.

22. Cf. the account in the contemporary chronicle of Richard of S. Germano, MGH SS XIX pp. 350–6.

23. FVST p. 532 (from Richard of S. Germano, ed. cit. p. 351).

24. Richard of S. Germano, ed. cit. pp. 359–61. Guala had already been used by Gregory as an emissary to Frederick in 1227 (*Epist. Saec. XIII* I pp. 278–80), and his role as the pope's "expert" on Frederick is brought out vividly in the list of recipients for Gregory's letter of 18 July 1229 on the emperor's goings-on in the Holy Land: all the others are prelates and princes, but Guala too gets his own personal copy (ibid. pp. 315–7). On 28 August 1230 Guala has already been elected bishop of Brescia (ibid. p. 335). In Dominican circles he was chiefly famous for the vision he had at the time of Dominic's death (MOPH XVI p. 70).

25. Richard of S. Germano, ed. cit. pp. 359–61; *Epist. Saec. XIII* I pp. 333–5.

26. All the *iustitiarii* were present (Richard of S. Germano, ed. cit. p. 359), but by this time Landulph had been replaced as *iustitarius* of the Terra di Lavoro (ibid.). Thomas d'Aquino, Count of Acerra, was there as senior *iustitiarius* (cf. Maccarrone, op. cit. p. 169).

27. The monastery suffered both from the papal forces and from those of the emperor (Richard of S. Germano, ed. cit. pp. 350–1); it was fortified, on the pope's orders, against the imperial troops (ibid. p. 351; *Epist. Saec. XIII* I p. 320), but the imperial commander, the Duke of Spoleto, expelled some of the monks (Richard of S. Germano, ed. cit. p. 353).

28. Tocco, on the authority of the family tradition (FVST p. 69, Ferrua p. 34), informs us that Thomas was five when he was sent to Monte Cassino; Bartholomew of Capua confirms that Thomas was sent there as a child, but does not specify his age (FVST p. 371, Ferrua p. 313). It is almost certainly in connection with the oblation of Thomas that Landulph made a generous gift to the monastery on 3 May 1231 (FVST pp. 535–6). Leccisotti, op. cit., plate II. In any case, Thomas could not have gone to Monte Cassino until the monks had had time to recover from the ravages of the preceding years.

29. Scandone, "Roccasecca" pp. 35–83.

30. This was the belief of the brethren in Naples, including explicitly

John of S. Giuliano (FVST p. 371, Ferrua p. 313). As an oblate, Thomas was certainly regarded as a Benedictine, but he remained free to leave the monastery unless he made profession there, at least tacitly, when he reached the appropriate age. He was therefore canonically free to join the Dominicans later on (cf. Leccisotti, op. cit. pp. 34–47).

31. Cf. Leccisotti pp. 26–33. Tolomeo says that Thomas studied logic and natural philosophy there (Ferrua p. 355), but as he often does he is conflating two separate episodes: it was later, at the University of Naples, that Thomas studied logic and natural philosophy (cf. Bartholomew of Capua, FVST p. 371, Ferrua p. 313).

32. FVST pp. 69–70, Ferrua pp. 34–5.

33. FVST p. 19. As Foster says (p. 59), this looks like a genuinely new piece of information, but it would be nice to be more sure of it.

34. Richard of S. Germano, ed. cit. pp. 377–8. For the excommunication, see also *Epist. Saec. XIII* I pp. 637–9.

35. Tocco (FVST p. 70, Ferrua p. 35); Bartholomew of Capua (FVST p. 371, Ferrua p. 313).

36. Cf. H. Rashdall, *The Universities of Europe in the Middle Ages* III (Oxford, 1936), pp. 352–3.

37. Tocco (FVST p. 70, Ferrua pp. 35–6). Cf. M. B. Crowe, 'Peter of Ireland: Aquinas' teacher of the *Artes Liberales*', in *Arts libéraux et Philosophie au Moyen Age*, pp. 617–626.

38. Cf. Weisheipl, *Thomas* pp. 17–19.

39. The Dominicans were given a site for a priory in 1231, at the pope's request (BOP I pp. 36–7; F. Ughelli, *Italia Sacra* VI, Venice 1720, col. 107–9), but the local tradition was that a party of friars, led by Thomas Agni of Lentini, was first sent to Naples in 1227 (T. Malvenda, *Annalium Sacri Ordinis Praedicatorum Centuria Prima*, Naples 1627, p. 451; AGOP lib. N p. 1191, Lll f.312ʳ), a tradition rendered plausible by the presence in the archives of S. Domenico Maggiore, Naples, of a copy of the Bull *Quoniam abundavit* issued by Gregory IX in support of the friars in September 1227 (A. Potthast, *Regesta Pontificum Romanorum* I, Berlin 1874, no. 8043; AGOP XI 1582).

40. Tocco (FVST p. 71, Ferrua pp. 36–7).

41. *Contra Retrahentes* 7 (Leonine XLI pp. C 51–2); *Summa Theol.* II.II q.188 a.2.

42. *Summa Theol.* II.II q.188 a.6.

43. Canterbury Cathedral, MS D 7 f.114 (the text quoted is on f.114ᵛᵇ); cf. AFP 26 (1956) p. 180. On the success of this formula in recruiting, cf. P. Amargier, *Études sur l'Ordre Dominicain XIII–XIV siècles* (Marseilles, 1986), p. 23.

44. Bartholomew, no doubt reporting the Dominican tradition in

Naples, claims that Thomas entered the Order before the age of puberty (FVST pp. 371–2, Ferrua p. 314), and this claim is repeated in the Bull of Canonization (FVST p. 520), from where it passes to Gui (FVST pp. 170–1, Ferrua p. 132). Tocco must have known this tradition, so he may have had some reason for not accepting it: he simply says that Thomas was a youth (*iuvenis*) when he became a Dominican (FVST pp. 71–2, Ferrua pp. 36–7). The likeliest explanation of the Dominican tradition is that the brethren, especially John of S. Giuliano, remembered Thomas from before the time of his entry into the Order. If the chronology I have suggested is correct, Thomas did become a student in Naples before the age of puberty.

45. Ferrua p. 355. Gui's attempt to attach dates to Thomas' life (FVST pp. 256–8) need not be taken seriously, as it is obviously conjectural. Working back from his death in 1274, supposedly at the age of forty-nine, Gui dates his birth to 1225, which means that his education at Monte Cassino must have begun in 1230. Then Gui is obviously perplexed. He allows Thomas seven years at Naples, presumably as the normal duration of an Arts course, but he cannot very well send him to university at the age of six, so he says that he went to Naples c.1232 at the age of seven or eight. That brings him to c.1240 for Thomas' entry into the Order, but he also has to accommodate the supposed fact that Thomas was under the age of puberty, so he tries to harmonize the data by having Thomas enter the Order c.1240 ("more or less") at "about" the age of fourteen (which does not square with his being born in 1225 and under the age of puberty when he became a Dominican). It is inconceivable that Thomas actually went to university at the age of seven, and it is obvious that Gui has no solid evidence behind him here.

46. Constitutions I 13 (AFP 18 [1948] p. 39).

47. The 1246 Provincial Chapter complains that all sorts of people are being allowed to join the Order and calls for this to stop; it particularly refers to "youths who are under age" (MOPH XX p. 5).

48. *Contra Retrahentes; Summa Theol.* II.II q.189 a.5. The minimum age for valid religious profession had been fixed at 14 by Alexander III, whose ruling was later adopted in the Decretals of Gregory IX, 3.31.8 (ed. E. Friedberg, *Corpus Iuris Canonici* II, Leipzig 1881, col. 571). For fourteen as the age of puberty, see Aristotle, *Hist. Anim.* 7.1 (581a12).

49. It is Gui who supplies the name (FVST p. 171, Ferrua p. 132) and this is the kind of detail about which he is reliable. Thomas Agni of Lentini was the first prior of Naples (cf. AFP 32 [1962] p. 312) and "founding priors" sometimes lasted a long time, like Arnold of Trier, who was prior of Freiburg from its foundation in 1235–6 until 1268, as we learn from the necrology edited in *Freiburger Diöcesan-Archiv* 16 (1883) pp. 41–2. The Dominican tradition in Naples that it was John of S. Giuliano who received

Thomas into the Order (FVST p. 371, Ferrua p. 313) is easily explained as a confused recollection of the fact that Thomas was John's protégé (and Bartholomew only says that it was "common knowledge" that John received Thomas into the Order; he does not say that John himself made any such claim). Tocco does not directly name the prior who received Thomas (FVST p. 71, Ferrua pp. 36–7), but he implies that it was John of S. Giuliano (FVST p. 76, Ferrua p. 43). Calo names John (FVST p. 20), but his evidence was presumably only the Dominican tradition in Naples.

50. Constitutions I 13 (AFP 18 [1948] pp. 38–9).

51. S. Tugwell, "Dominican Profession in the 13th Century," AFP 53 (1983) pp. 12–14.

52. The Roman Provincial Chapter of 1244 insists on this specifically in the case of "professed novices" (MOPH XX p. 3); see also Constitutions I 14 (AFP 18 [1948] p. 41).

53. For other cases of friends and relations trying by force or influence to get young recruits out of the Order, cf. MOPH I pp. 75–6, 81, 110–1, 178; Cecilia 11 (AFP 37 [1967] pp. 38–9).

54. According to the Dominican story received by Bartholomew in Naples, the brethren were particularly afraid of Thomas' father (FVST p. 372, Ferrua p. 314). The family version of the story, based on Theodora's account, ascribes the leading role to Theodora (FVST pp. 72–3, 350–1; Ferrua pp. 37–9, 292), from which Mandonnet inferred that Landulph was already dead (*Revue Thomiste* NS 7 [1924] pp. 387–90), a conjecture that other scholars have repeated (Walz-Novarina p. 50, Weisheipl, *Thomas* p. 29). But even in the family tradition we are told that eventually Thomas' "parents and brothers" returned Thomas to the Order (FVST p. 351, Ferrua p. 292), so there is little justification for disregarding the evidence that Landulph was still alive in Thomas' early years as a Dominican. Scandone, "Famiglia" p. 50, believes that Landulph was still alive, but in "Roccasecca" p. 83 he follows Mandonnet's conjecture.

55. That it was Theodora who tried to visit Thomas we learn from her own account (FVST p. 350, Ferrua p. 292), and it is presumably her story that Tocco is passing on when he says that she wanted to encourage Thomas but was misunderstood by the brethren (FVST p. 72, Ferrua pp. 37–8), a story we may take with a pinch of salt. Combining the evidence from the different sources, we can take it that the whole family objected to Thomas' entry into the Order, but it was Theodora who was most persistent in endeavoring to talk him out of it. If the brethren were afraid of the "power" of Landulph (FVST p. 372, Ferrua p. 314), it was not necessarily because they anticipated that he would try to remove Thomas by force; their anxiety was probably that Theodora would succeed in luring the young friar away and then the father's influence would be sufficient to

prevent them from getting him back again. If this is the correct interpretation, it is compatible with Thomas being left in Naples for some time, maybe even a full year, before being sent off to Rome.

56. This is shown by the later attempt to get Thomas made abbot of Monte Cassino, against which the pope raised no canonical objections (see below, pp. 207–09).

57. FVST p. 350, Ferrua p. 292; this is part of the family story. The Dominican story in Naples leaves out this episode and says that Thomas was immediately sent to the Order's studium generale (i.e., Paris) (FVST p. 372, Ferrua p. 314), but this is probably an oversimplification.

58. Tocco (FVST p. 72, Ferrua p. 37).

59. Potthast II pp. 951–69.

60. Thomas of Cantimpré (Ferrua p. 387). Cantimpré situates the whole drama of Thomas' tussle with his family before Albert's assignation to Paris, which is patently wrong, but otherwise his account of the successive moves made by the d'Aquinos seems convincing. There is nothing inherently implausible in his story that Innocent IV offered ecclesiastical preferment to Thomas. In 1244, in the first batch of cardinals he created, it is likely that Ottaviano Ubaldini was promoted in the hope that it would win over an important imperial family to the pope's side (cf. A. Paravicini Bagliani, *Cardinali di Curia e "Familiae" Cardinalizie dal 1227 al 1254* [Padua, 1972], I pp. 283–4), and it is not unlikely that the pope entertained similar hopes about the d'Aquinos. And it looks as if Guglielmo Fieschi, who was made a cardinal at the same time, was a very young man indeed (ibid. p. 329; ten years later he is still described as a *iuvenis*, RIS VIII 512), so Thomas' youth was not necessarily an obstacle. Innocent IV himself was probably only about 20 when he became a cardinal (cf. J. E. Sayers, *Papal Government and England during the Pontificate of Honorius III (1216–1227)*, Cambridge 1984, p. 41).

61. That Thomas' destination was Paris, and that he was being sent to the studium generale there, was well-known in the Order; it is mentioned by Gerald de Frachet (Ferrua p. 379) and by Bartholomew (FVST p. 372, Ferrua p. 314—bearing in mind that at this time Paris was the Order's only studium generale). Gerald also says that Thomas was travelling with the Master of the Order (Ferrua p. 379), which is probably untrue (cf. below, note 62). Tolomeo is probably combining Gerald's story with the Naples tradition (which, as we have seen, had forgotten that Thomas was first sent to Rome), when he alleges that Thomas travelled from Naples with the Master of the Order (Ferrua p. 355). Tocco seems to have the fullest account of what happened, presumably because of his knowledge of the family tradition, and he too tells us that Thomas was being sent to Paris

(FVST p. 72, Ferrua p. 38). But who sent him? The province was entitled to send three students each year to Paris (Constitutions II 14, AFP 18 [1948] p. 66), but Thomas set off in the middle of the academic year, when surely the province had already used up its quota. It must, then, have been the Master of the Order who sent Thomas to Paris, and this may be one factor in the development of the story that Thomas was actually travelling with the Master.

62. Tocco (FVST pp. 72–3, Ferrua p. 38). Tocco is probably better informed than our other sources in saying that it was after Thomas' release from captivity that he travelled to Paris with the Master of the Order (FVST p. 77, Ferrua p. 44).

63. Tolomeo ascribes the kidnap to Thomas' brother, Reginald (Ferrua pp. 355–6), but other sources refer to his "brothers" (Cantimpré, Ferrua p. 387; Theodora's account, FVST p. 351, Ferrua p. 292; Robert of Sezze, FVST p. 349, Ferrua p. 291); Bartholomew makes Landulph responsible (FVST p. 372, Ferrua p. 314), but Tocco, presumably following the family tradition, reports that it was Theodora who issued the instructions to Thomas' brothers (FVST p. 72, Ferrua p. 38). It must be from Theodora herself that the story of her involvement in the drama comes, and there is no reason to doubt it, though we may feel somewhat incredulous when we are told that her motive throughout was simply to test Thomas' vocation (Tocco, FVST p. 73, Ferrua p. 39).

64. J. L. A. Huillard-Bréholles, *Historia Diplomatica Friderici Secundi* VI (Paris, 1860), pp. 166–89, 910–1.

65. According to Tolomeo (Ferrua p. 356) the emperor at least connived, and according to Tocco (FVST p. 73, Ferrua p. 38) he formally authorized the kidnap. Gerald de Frachet says that Thomas' brothers took his support for granted (Ferrua p. 379). Only Thomas of Cantimpré exempts him from any involvement (Ferrua pp. 387–8). Just as Innocent IV may well have wanted to win over the d'Aquinos by granting them favors, it is not at all unlikely that Frederick wanted to retain their allegiance in the same way. And he had little love for the friars. In 1239 one of the first things he did after his excommunication was to banish all non-native Dominicans and Franciscans from his territories and to warn the native friars not to offend him (Richard of S. Germano, ed. cit. p. 377). On Frederick and the friars, see G. Barone, 'Federico II di Svevia e gli Ordini Mendicanti', *Mélanges de l'Ecole Française de Rome, Moyen Age* 90 (1978) pp. 607–626.

66. Tocco (FVST p. 73, Ferrua p. 38). According to Bartholomew it was widely believed that John of S. Giuliano was also taken captive, but he does not claim that John himself said this (FVST p. 372, Ferrua p. 314). If, as Bartholomew tells us, John was full of information about Thomas'

behavior during his captivity (ibid.), this was surely because, as Tocco tells us, he was able to visit him from time to time (FVST p. 76, Ferrua p. 43).

67. Only Tocco mentions both places (FVST p. 73, Ferrua p. 39); Tolomeo (Ferrua p. 356), Robert of Sezze and Bernard Gui (FVST pp. 349, 172; Ferrua pp. 291, 134) only mention Montesangiovanni, and Calo (FVST p. 22) only mentions Roccasecca. But there is no reason to doubt Tocco's account, which is presumably based on the family tradition.

68. Tocco (FVST p. 73, Ferrua p. 39).

69. Bartholomew (FVST p. 372, Ferrua p. 314).

70. Tocco (FVST p. 74, Ferrua p. 40). Thomas' study of the bible is confirmed by Bartholomew (FVST p. 372, Ferrua p. 314).

71. Tocco (FVST p. 74, Ferrua p. 40); we learn the name of the nun from the letters of Innocent IV confirming her election as abbess (FVST pp. 541–4).

72. Tocco (FVST p. 74, Ferrua p. 40) mentions the composition of *De Fallaciis* as a rumor only, and the work is not mentioned in the oldest catalogues of Thomas' works (cf. M. Grabmann, *Die Werke des hl. Thomas von Aquin*, Beiträge XXII/1–2 [Münster, 1949], pp. 92–3, 97–8) or in Bartholomew's list (FVST pp. 386–9, Ferrua pp. 328–331), though it is mentioned by Tolomeo (Ferrua p. 368). If it is by Thomas (and the same is true of the companion work, *De Propositionibus Modalibus*), it is quite possible that it does date from the time of his captivity (cf. Leonine XLIII pp. 385–8).

73. Tocco (FVST p. 73, Ferrua p. 39). Thomas of Cantimpré (Ferrua p. 387) says that the Master of the Order went to Rome to lodge a complaint with the emperor, but this is less plausible; for one thing, the emperor was not in Rome.

74. Tocco, (FVST p. 73, Ferrua p. 39); cf. Cantimpré (Ferrua pp. 387–8).

75. Tocco (FVST p. 76, Ferrua p. 43).

76. The story of the would-be seduction of Thomas was known in the late 1250s, anyway, as it is reported by Cantimpré (Ferrua p. 387). Tocco derives his much more elaborate account (FVST pp. 74–6, Ferrua pp. 41–3) from Robert of Sezze (FVST p. 349, Ferrua pp. 290–1), the text of whose deposition appears to be defective, but it looks as if he claimed to have heard the story from Reginald of Piperno, who heard it from Thomas. It is not part of the family tradition deriving from Theodora. According to Robert, the attempted seduction took place at Montesangiovanni, but it is clear from Tocco and Cantimpré that it happened near the end, not the beginning, of Thomas' captivity. Robert may have been mistaken about where it occurred (cf. above, note 67). Or we may conjecture that Thomas was at some stage returned to Montesangiovanni. The story in Tocco and

Cantimpré gives the impression that Thomas' brothers were particularly fierce against his Dominican vocation, so maybe Theodora kept Thomas quite comfortably at Roccasecca until the brothers returned, but they then took control and had him much less pleasantly incarcerated at Montesangiovanni. This would justify Cantimpré's assertion that he was actively maltreated before the attempt was made to break him down with female charms (Ferrua p. 387).

77. This part of the story comes entirely from Robert of Sezze (FVST p. 349, Ferrua pp. 290–1), whom Tocco follows almost to the letter (FVST pp. 74–6, Ferrua pp. 41–3).

78. Conrad of Sessa, who had known Thomas since about 1262, testified that he was "so chaste that he was considered to be a virgin" (FVST p. 326, Ferrua p. 268). Bartholomew reported it was commonly believed Thomas was a virgin (FVST p. 373, Ferrua p. 315). An old monk of Fossanova had reputedly heard from Reginald that Thomas had told him that he was a virgin (FVST pp. 400–1, Ferrua p. 343). And the preacher at Thomas' funeral declared publicly, on the evidence of Thomas' confession, that Thomas had been a virgin all his life (FVST pp. 332, 345; Ferrua pp. 273, 287).

79. Peter Capucci heard this from Raymund Severi, who had heard Thomas' confession every day in Paris (FVST p. 398, Ferrua p. 340). It was probably in 1270–72 that Severi was Thomas' student in Paris. He entered the Order in 1249 (C. Douais, *Acta Capitulorum Provincialium* [Toulouse, 1894], pp. 434–5), presumably young, since he was still going strong in 1302 (ibid. p. 479), so it is unlikely that he was already a priest during Thomas' first regency—the official minimum age for ordination was twenty-five (Raymund of Peñafort, *Summa de Iure Canonico* II 30:3, ed. X. Ochoa and A. Diez [Rome, 1975], col.160; MOPH III p. 23), though it is not clear how far this was observed in practice (cf. MOPH III p. 40, Douais p. 84). Also the province of Provence favored sending as students to Paris men who had already had some experience as lectors: of the students assigned to Paris in 1270 (Douais p. 150) for the years 1271–73 (students were assigned a year in advance: Douais pp. 81, 186, and normally for two years: ibid. p. 81), Hugh was lector in Arles in 1266 (ibid. p. 115), R. Mancii was second lector in Toulouse, Montpellier and Toulouse again in 1268–71 (ibid. pp. 131, 138, 150), and Arnald Rauca was lector at Orthez in 1268 and second lector in Bordeaux in 1269 (ibid. pp. 131, 138). One of the students assigned to Paris in 1272 (ibid. p. 163), Arnald, was a lector as early as 1265 (ibid. p. 107). We first hear of Severi as second lector at Béziers in 1267, then he was second lector at Narbonne and then lector at Aubenas up to 1270 (Douais pp. 124, 131, 138). The 1269 assignations do not survive; we next hear of him being assigned to Montpellier in 1272 (ibid. p.

170), so he could well have been in Paris during 1270–72. Severi was subprior of Montpellier when Capucci met him; we do not know when he became subprior, but he was absolved from that office in 1295 (ibid. p. 397).

80. This is reported by Anthony of Brescia, on the authority of Nicholas of Marcillac (FVST p. 355, Ferrua p. 297). Nicholas is said to have been Thomas' student in Paris. He was apparently reminiscing in Nicosia in 1306 (FVST p. 359, Ferrua p. 300), and according to J. Richard, *Documents Chypriotes des Archives du Vatican* (Paris, 1962), p. 51 note 1, he was still functioning there in 1310. Judging from his name, he was a member of the Provence province, like P. Pictavini de Marsiliaco, of whom we hear in 1296 (Douais p. 404), so we should not assume that he was sent too young to Paris. This makes it likely that he too was Thomas' student during his second regency. Nor does this entail the consequences feared by Weisheipl, *Thomas* p. 131, as we are not obliged to believe that Nicholas was actually present while Thomas was writing the *Contra Gentiles*.

81. The earliest accounts say "about a year" (Gerald de Frachet, Ferrua p. 379) and "two or three years" (Cantimpré, Ferrua p. 387). Bartholomew says "more than a year" (FVST p. 372, Ferrua p. 314). Tocco says "about two years" (FVST p. 76, Ferrua p. 43).

82. Tocco (FVST p. 77, Ferrua p. 43). The rope is also mentioned by Tolomeo (Ferrua (p. 356), but he makes out that Thomas arranged his own escape. Theodora's role is confirmed by Bartholomew, who says that she persuaded Landulph to let Thomas go (FVST p. 372, Ferrua p. 314). If, as I have suggested, Thomas' brothers were taking a much harder line than his parents, it is quite possible that she had to contrive his escape in some such picaresque way as Tocco describes, and Landulph may well have washed his hands of the matter, so that both Tocco and Bartholomew could be telling the true story from slightly different points of view. That the brethren were waiting for Thomas is mentioned by both Tolomeo and Tocco.

83. Tocco (FVST p. 77, Ferrua p. 43).

84. Most of the sources do not specify where Thomas was taken. Tolomeo says that he went to Rome (Ferrua p. 356). Tocco is probably right, though, to say that he went to Naples (FVST p. 77, Ferrua p. 43); Bartholomew also comments on the educational benefit Thomas derived from his captivity (FVST p. 372, Ferrua p. 314) and this appears to be part of the Dominican tradition in Naples, which suggests that the brethren there were directly involved at the time of his escape, in which case Naples would have been the obvious place to take him, until it had been decided what to do with him.

85. Tolomeo and Tocco himself in the canonization process all in-

dicate that Thomas was sent immediately to Cologne, and Tolomeo and Tocco both mention Albert (FVST p. 351; Ferrua pp. 292, 356).

86. There is no sign in Tocco or in the canonization process of any family tradition about Thomas' student days in the Order, nor does Bartholomew allude to this period, so it looks as if there was no Dominican tradition in Naples either. But there clearly is a tradition deriving from Cologne about Albert's attitude to Thomas, brought back to Italy by people like Ugo of Lucca and Albert of Brescia (FVST pp. 382–3, 358; Ferrua pp. 324–5, 299). Since all Tocco's information about this period concerns Cologne, it is likely that it derives from a similar tradition. For these few years Thomas is essentially part of the history of Albert the Great.

87. Scheeben, *Albert der Grosse* pp. 30–1, claims to find an original local tradition in Hermann von Fritzlar, according to which Thomas was indeed in Cologne before Albert's return there in 1248. But Hermann's account of Thomas, taken as a whole (ed. in F. Pfeiffer, *Deutsche Mystiker des vierzehnten Jahrhunderts* I, [Leipzig, 1845], pp. 99–101), seems plainly dependent on Gui, whose life of Thomas was well-known in Germany, as the number of German manuscripts shows (Kaeppeli, *Scriptores* I p. 209). Similarly the "common report" referred to by Peter of Prussia, chap. 7, that Thomas studied for nine years in Cologne could easily be an inference from Gui (who dates Thomas' release from captivity to 1242 and his becoming a bachelor in Paris to 1252: FVST p. 257). I do not believe that there is any genuine new information to be had from Hermann or Peter on the duration or dating of Thomas' stay in Cologne.

88. This is stated by Cantimpré (Ferrua p. 388) and Tocco (FVST p. 77, Ferrua p. 44).

89. FVST p. 77, Ferrua p. 44.

90. Ferrua p. 379.

91. FVST p. 585.

92. Ferrua p. 388.

93. FVST p. 78, Ferrua p. 45.

94. Naples, Bibl. Naz. I B 54. It is now generally accepted that this is an autograph of Thomas'; cf. H. F. Dondaine and H. V. Shooner, *Codices Manuscripti Operum Thomae de Aquino* I (Rome, 1967), p. 8.

95. Col. ed. XXXVII pp. VI–VII.

96. FVST p. 77, Ferrua p. 44; cf. above, notes 61 and 62.

97. MOPH III p. 33.

98. R. A. Gauthier, Leonine XLV i p. 267*.

99. *Epist. Saec. XIII* II (Berlin, 1887), pp. 93–4.

100. Ferrua p. 356.

101. Bartholomew, on the authority of Thomas' student, John of Caiazzo (FVST pp. 374–5, Ferrua pp. 316–7), reporting a vision Thomas

is supposed to have had, assuring him that Reginald was in heaven; presumably it is the same vision already being alluded to in Gerald de Frachet (Ferrua p. 380). Reginald's execution is also mentioned by Tolomeo (Ferrua p. 356).

102. Tocco (FVST p. 118, Ferrua p. 92).

103. Potthast I pp. 1078–1105.

104. According to P. Lugano, *L'Italia Benedittina* (Rome, 1929), p. 65, abbot Stephen reigned from 1238–51, but in fact he is stated to be already dead in a letter dated 30 April 1248 (Huillard-Bréholles, *Historia Diplomatica Friderici Secundi* VI ii [Paris, 1861], p. 620). J. F. B. de Rubeis, *De Gestis et Scriptis . . . S. Thomae Aquinatis*, originally published in 1750, reprinted in Leonine I, similarly suggests 1248 as the most likely date for this episode (Leonine I p. 1xix). Tolomeo says that Alexander IV (who became pope in 1254) offered Thomas the abbacy of Monte Cassino while Thomas was in Cologne (Ferrua p. 356), which is entirely incoherent.

105. Cf. L. Tosti, *Storia della Badia di Monte-Cassino* II (Naples, 1842), p. 280 and III (Naples, 1843), p. 7.

106. Col. XXXVII ii p. XXV.

107. Col. XIV i pp. V–VI.

108. Gui (FVST pp. 176–7, Ferrua pp. 139–40) seems to have a livelier version of the story than Tocco (FVST p. 78, Ferrua p. 45), though the essential outline is identical. Whether Gui had some other source than Tocco it is hard to say, though I think it would be out of character for him to jolly the story up simply for stylistic reasons.

109. Tocco (FVST pp. 78–9, Ferrua pp. 45–6).

110. Col. XXXVII pp. VI–VII.

111. Constitutions II 14 (AFP 18 [1948] p. 67).

112. *Les Genres Littéraires dans les Sources théologiques et philosophiques médiévales* (Louvain, 1982), p. 39.

113. On false humility, cf. *Summa Theol.* II.II q.161 a.1 ad 1 and a.3.

114. Ferrua p. 357.

115. J. J. Pauson in his edition (Fribourg/Louvain, 1950), p. 70, argues that it antedates the commentary on the Sentences, and the Leonine editor suggests it may go back to Thomas' student days (Leonine XLIII p. 6).

116. Pauson, pp. 73–4.

117. Cf. Weisheipl, *Albert* p. 565.

118. Tocco (FVST pp. 80–1, Ferrua p. 48).

119. *Chart.* I p. 307.

120. *Chart.* I p. 321.

121. Tolomeo (Ferrua p. 356); this tallies with Thomas being born in 1226.

122. *Chart.* I p. 79.
123. Ferrua p. 356.
124. MOPH I pp. 335–7.
125. *Chart.* I pp. 226–7.
126. M. M. Dufeil, *Guillaume de Saint-Amour* p. 89, interprets Tocco as saying that John of Wildeshausen wanted to provide "an unimpeachable bachelor for the disputed chair," but Tocco says nothing of the kind. What he does say is that John wanted someone intellectually and morally adequate. In 1252 Thomas was eminently impeachable, as being underage.
127. Cf. Dufeil, *Guillame de Saint-Amour* pp. 83–4.
128. *Chart.* I p. 226.
129. *Chart.* I p. 79.
130. It has now been established that the Isaiah commentary antedates at least the commentary on book III of the Sentences, and the inference must be that it represents the lectures Thomas gave as *cursor biblicus* (Leonine XXVIII p. 20*). Weisheipl, *Thomas* pp. 45, 50, argues that Thomas lectured on Isaiah in Cologne, chiefly because Tocco says that Thomas was sent to Paris to lecture on the Sentences (FVST p. 81, Ferrua p. 48), but this is hardly decisive, and if I am right that it is essentially a Cologne tradition we possess of Thomas' student days, it is easier to believe that Thomas' lectures on Isaiah were overlooked if they were given in Paris than if they were given in Cologne. Weisheipl is also wrong, I have argued, to date Thomas' assignation to Paris to 1252. Between 1251 and 1256 Thomas could easily have lectured on the bible and on the Sentences; Bonaventure did both in four years, giving two years to the Sentences (G. Abate, "Per la storia e la cronologia di S.Bonaventura," *Miscellanea Franciscana* 50 [1950] pp. 101–3; B. Distelbrink, *Bonaventurae Scripta critice recensita,* [Rome 1975] p. 5). Thomas finished writing up his massive *Scriptum super Sententias* after he graduated as a Master (Tocco: FVST p. 81, Ferrua p. 49).
131. According to a story allegedly deriving from Reginald himself, via two apparently independent witnesses, Thomas was perplexed about some passage in Isaiah while he was working on the commentary; in the night Reginald heard him talking, and eventually extracted the information that Saints Peter and Paul had visited him and explained the passage. Reginald then took down the interpretation at Thomas' dictation (FVST pp. 346–7, 399–400; Ferrua pp. 288–9, 342). By this time it was normal for Masters and lectors to have a regular socius (cf. Humbert of Romans, ed. Berthier II p. 255), but a mere cursor or even a bachelor would not be so privileged. Nor should we assume that Thomas had a personal secretary; the evidence adduced in A. Dondaine, *Secrétaires de St. Thomas* (Rome, 1956), pp. 26–53, proves only that the convent of St. Jacques had the reg-

ular services of several secretaries—Vat. lat. 718, containing Albert's *Parva Naturalia* was surely written for someone else, maybe the library, not for Thomas, who was not interested in such things. And even if Thomas did have a secretary, he would not have sent for him in the middle of the night, during the great silence; after all, he wrote part of the Isaiah commentary at least in his own hand, since we possess part of it written by him (Vat. lat. 9850 ff.105–114). But maybe Reginald was roused by the sound of Thomas' voice and came in of his own accord to see what was going on. It is quite possible that Reginald was in Paris at the same time as Thomas and became friendly with him, even if he cannot be regarded as his official socius. Since we are completely uninformed otherwise about when Reginald first became attached to Thomas, we cannot disregard the evidence of this anecdote.

132. When Reginald first became Thomas' official socius we do not know, nor do we know whether he was in Paris for the whole period 1251–9. But he is described in the sources as having been Thomas' constant companion (FVST pp. 369, 375, 394; Ferrua pp. 312, 317, 336), his companion "for a long time" (FVST p. 323, Ferrua p. 264), and Tocco calls him "the witness and companion of his whole life" (FVST p. 136, Ferrua pp. 112–3).

133. It is not certain that the Jeremiah commentaries belong to this period. Dufeil, *Guillame de Saint Amour* p. 90, suggests that Thomas would have needed two years to cover both prophets, but if Thomas' lectures on the Sentences had anything like the scope of the written *Scriptum* they would surely have needed four years, and for what it is worth, the biographers certainly do not give the impression that there was any great delay before Thomas became bachelor of the Sentences.

134. FVST p. 81, Ferrua pp. 48–9.

135. Tolomeo (Ferrua p. 357).

136. Leonine XLIII p. 320.

137. Ibid. p. 319.

138. Cf. the introduction to the English translation by A. Maurer (Toronto, 1968), pp. 8–9, 23–4.

139. Ibid. pp. 21–7. In the prologue to his commentary on John (translated below), Thomas refers to ways of coming to know God, which do not quite coincide with proofs of the existence of God.

140. Cf. Simon Tugwell, "Dominican Risks," *Dominican Ashram* 2 (1983) pp. 173–4.

141. Cf. Y. Congar, "Aspects ecclésiologiques de la querelle entre mendiants et séculiers," AHDLMA 28 (1961) pp. 35–151.

142. Cf. J. Verger, " 'Studia' et Universités," in *Le Scuole degli Ordini Mendicanti* (Todi, 1978), especially pp. 197–201.

143. Cf. W. R. Thomson, "The Image of the Mendicants in the Chronicles of Matthew Paris," AFH 70 (1977) pp. 3–33.

144. On the difficulties involved in dating the Dominican Parisian Masters, see above, pp. 102–04, notes 77, 79 and 80. Pointlasne presumably incepted in 1248 as Albert's successor. By 1251–52 Bonhomme and Élie are in possession of the Dominican chairs. Florent, the next Master in the list, is presumably the Dominican who incepted in peculiar circumstances in 1255 (*Chart.* I p. 294). Conceivably Innocent IV's letter of 30 May 1250 (ibid. p. 219), which was certainly in Dominican hands, refers to obstacles being put in the way of the inception of some Dominican, in which case the successor of either William of Étampes or Pointlasne must have incepted in that year—it is certainly unlikely, judging from the pope's letter, that two new Masters incepted in the same year. If William incepted in 1247, as seems quite likely, then perhaps Bonhomme succeeded him in 1249 and Élie succeeded Pointlasne in 1250. But this is highly conjectural. Erkenfrid's *Compendium* (on which see Kaeppeli, AFP 39 [1969] pp. 69–90) appears to preserve some of his student notes from the mid-1250s. In Vatican Library MS Barb. lat. 692 f.42^v he quotes Thomas, apparently referring to the lecture which underlies IV *Sent.* d.17 q.2 a.1, and he also apparently quotes the lectures, rather than written works, of Bonhomme, Élie and Florent; Pointlasne, on the other hand, is quoted as a literary source and precise references to his commentary on the Sentences are given, which enabled Kaeppeli to rediscover this commentary. It looks as if Erkenfrid was studying in Paris up to about 1255–56. Such evidence as there is, then, suggests that Pointlasne was probably Regent Master in 1248–50.

145. The text is printed in Dufeil, *Guillame de Saint-Amour* p. 378. Dufeil suggests dating it to 1252–53 (p. 102), but only a Regent Master would be conducting a disputation and by then Pointlasne was surely no longer Regent.

146. The fullest account of the whole affair is Dufeil, op. cit.

147. *Chart.* I pp. 267–70.

148. Cantimpré, *De Apibus* II 10:21 (Douai, 1605) p. 173. Innocent died on 7 December (Potthast II p. 1283).

149. *Chart.* I pp. 276–7. Alexander IV was elected on 12 December (Potthast II p. 1286) and his Bull is dated 22 December.

150. MOPH I pp. 336–7.

151. See Humbert's letters from this period, MOPH V pp. 21–38, 41, 43–49, one of them written jointly with the Franciscan Minister General. The 1256 General Chapter instituted a weekly litany in all Dominican houses "for the good state of the Order" (MOPH III pp. 82–3) and, if a report in Gerald de Frachet is to be trusted, the practice must in fact go

back to 1254 (MOPH I pp. 44–5), as is claimed by Galvano (MOPH II p. 97) and is in any case probable. Later it was claimed that the effect of the Dominicans' litanies was such that "the cardinals and bishops used to say, 'Beware of the litanies of the Friars Preachers, because they work miracles' " (first found, to my knowledge, in the chronicle of Alberto di Castello, ed. in E. Martène-U. Durand, *Veterum Scriptorum . . . Amplissima Collectio* VI [Paris, 1729], col.357; it presumably comes, like most of this chronicle, from the late fourteenth-century writer, Jakob of Soest). The litanies were credited with bringing about Alexander IV's prompt cassation of the anti-mendicant Bull of Innocent IV, with which Gerald of Frachet also associates a vision said to have been had by a "Master in Paris" (MOPH I p. 215) whom the context identifies as Thomas, and this identification is noted in at least one manuscript and is taken for granted by Johannes Meyer (QF 29 p. 35). In 1254 Thomas was not yet a Master, so the story cannot be correct as it stands.

152. *Chart.* I p. 307.

153. The story quickly gained currency and is already present in Gerald of Frachet (MOPH I p. 216, Ferrua p. 381). Thomas' nephew, Count Thomas of San Severino, claimed to have heard the story from Thomas himself (FVST pp. 348–9, Ferrua p. 290) and a monk of Fossanova, who knew Thomas quite well, was egged on by Reginald to ask Thomas about it (FVST p. 331, Ferrua pp. 272–3).

154. We learn this from Peter Capucci, who studied in Paris after spending four years in Montpellier round about 1295 (cf. above, note 79) (FVST pp. 398–9, Ferrua pp. 340–1).

155. *Chart.* I p. 321.

156. Ibid. p. 366.

157. Included in the Quodlibets as a.17 of *Quodl.* 7. Weisheipl argues that this disputation formed part of the formalities of Thomas' inception (*Thomas* pp. 104–6).

158. Tolomeo (Ferrua pp. 356–7) dates the work to before Thomas started lecturing as a Master. Cf. Leonine XLI pp. A 12–3.

159. FVST pp. 91–2, Ferrua pp. 60–1.

160. Tocco dates *Contra Impug.* to the pontificate of Clement IV (1264–68) and refers it to a chapter at Anagni. It is supposed to be a response to a work produced by the circle of "William of St. Amour and Siger of Brabant," which had been sent to the pope under the pretext of zeal for the church. The pope asked John of Vercelli, Master of the Dominican Order, to reply to it. Thomas, at the chapter, volunteered to write a reply and did so, with the pope's encouragement, in the form of a plea to the pope for justice. As a result the original book by the friars' enemies was condemned and burned and the Dominicans were

awarded a second chair of theology in Paris, thanks to the support of King Louis. This is nonsense from start to finish. The Dominicans had had their second chair of theology since 1230 (and maybe King Louis helped them then). *Contra Impug.* is not a plea to the pope for justice. There was no General Chapter at Anagni during the pontificate of Clement IV. There was however a Roman Provincial Chapter at Anagni in 1265, at which Thomas was told to create a new studium in Rome (MOPH XX p. 32)—that is the new "chair" resulting from a Chapter at Anagni. The work sent to Clement IV by William of St. Amour was not the *De Periculis*, to which Thomas replied (and which was condemned), but the *Collectiones*, sent to Clement in 1266 (by a bearer, curiously, called "Master Thomas"); Clement did not see any reason to treat this work as posing a threat or needing urgent attention, so he replied politely to William, saying that he had not had time to read his book, but would get someone competent to look at it (*Chart.* I p. 459). The General Chapter of 1268 was held in Viterbo, followed by the Provincial Chapter, and Thomas was presumably present at both, and it was after the Chapters in 1268 that he was reassigned to Paris. In Paris two quite separate crises were brewing, one a recrudescence of the anti-mendicant campaign (to which Thomas responded with *De Perfectione* and *Contra Retrahentes*), whose ringleader was now Gerard of Abbeville rather than William of St. Amour, who had long been in exile from Paris; the other crisis was a philosophical one, posed by a form of Averroistic Aristotelianism that was endangering faith, and Siger emerged as one of its most prominent spokesmen; this controversy elicited from Thomas the *De Unitate Intellectus*. Tocco has gloriously scrambled together the crisis of the 1250s with those of the late 1260s, various academic chairs, various Chapters and various assignments given to Thomas. Not bad for a historian!

161. Dufeil, *Guillame de Saint-Amour* pp. 260–1, is quite right to say that neither Thomas nor Bonaventure was involved in the Anagni condemnation, and it is perfectly clear that there was no need for them to be involved. But Dufeil is wrong to adduce as evidence the dream ascribed to Thomas by Gerald de Frachet, which refers to the events of 1254 (cf. above, note 151).

162. After bringing us up to Thomas' inception, Tocco proceeds to give us a list of Thomas' writings and thereafter treats of his virtues and achievements thematically, concluding with various miracles, leading easily to the account of his last days and death. Much the same scheme is followed by Gui and Calo.

163. FVST pp. 256–8.

164. Tolomeo (Ferrua pp. 357–9) provides a relative date for

Thomas' departure from Paris and knows that he went to Italy where, at some stage, he ran a studium in Rome. After that there is no coherent sequence in his narrative.

165. Cf. QE I p. 272.

166. RSPT 9 (1920) p. 144. The alleged residence in Anagni (1259–61) was already discarded in Walz-Novarina p. 117, in spite of a general adherence to the principle that Thomas was *lector curiae* (p. 119). Thomas' assignment to Orvieto in 1261 has achieved canonical status, thanks to the insertion of Mandonnet's dating into the edition of the text in FVST p. 582, but for all that the date is not directly supported by any evidence. The alleged residence in Viterbo (1267–68) finds apparent support in Weisheipl's curious misreading of Conrad of Sessa (*Thomas* p. 144, corrected in the revised edition, p. 470), but unfortunately Conrad says Orvieto, not Viterbo, so once again we are left without a shred of evidence that Thomas ever lived in Viterbo, and Mandonnet's whole saga was devastatingly exposed for the fantasy it is by R. A. Gauthier, *Angelicum* 51 (1974) pp. 438–42.

167. Ferrua pp. 357–8.

168. *Chart*. I pp. 390–2, FVST pp. 564–5.

169. The oldest catalogues of Thomas' works mention 11 Quodlibets (Grabmann, *Werke* p. 92, FVST p. 388, Ferrua p. 330). *Quodl*. XII was added to the collection later. I-VI form an unvarying sequence and were clearly published as a block, and at least essentially, they represent the Quodlibets from Thomas' second regency. Quodlibets were held twice a year, in Advent and Lent (*Les Genres Littéraires*, pp. 73–4), so I–VI represents three years' worth. It looks as if XII belongs to the same period. This means that VII–XI almost certainly belong to the first regency, and at a rate of two per annum this brings us at least as far as Advent 1258. VII and VIII are certainly contemporary with the beginning of the edited text of *De Veritate* (A. Dondaine, *Secrétaires* pp. 81–2) and IX comes immediately after (J. Isaac, AHDLMA 16 [1948] pp. 145–85; Dondaine, *Secrétaires* p. 82). Cf. I. T. Eschmann, "Catalogue of St. Thomas's Works" in E. Gilson, *The Christian Philosophy of St. Thomas Aquinas* (New York, 1956), p. 392.

170. At least one manuscript of the chronicle of Gerald de Frachet (AGOP XIV 23 f.120ᵛ) contains the information that in 1260 the two Dominican Regent Masters were Peter of Tarentaise and William of Alton.

171. A. Dondaine, *Secrétaires* pp. 63, 83–6.

172. *Chart*. I pp. 385–6, FVST pp. 560–2.

173. The commission was present at the Chapter, as the text makes clear, but its members were not all entitled to be there. Thomas, for instance, was not socius to the provincial (as was suggested in QE I p. 272 and Walz-Novarina p. 112); the socius elected by the Provincial Chapter

was Laurence of Todi (MOPH XX p. 23). They must therefore have been summoned in advance, and this can only have been done by the Master of the Order.

174. At least the germ of a policy can surely be detected in a sequence of moves made by John or under his auspices: sending a German lector (Albert) to graduate in Paris, setting up four extra studia generalia in the Order, sending the lector of Montpellier (Elie Brunet) to graduate in Paris, asking Albert to recommend someone to go to Paris and in the outcome sending Thomas. John seems to have wanted to ensure that Parisian Masters were not a monopoly of the Paris province and that studies at university level were available elsewhere in the Order.

175. Cf. Weisheipl, *Thomas* p. 142.

176. E.g., Walz-Novarina pp. 115–6.

177. P. T. Masetti, *Monumenta et Antiquitates* II (Rome, 1864), p. 268; FVST p. 582.

178. MOPH XX p. 32.

179. V. M. Fontana, *De Romana Provincia* (Rome, 1670), p. 100; FVST p. 582 (where it should be noted that the date is supplied by Laurent without any warrant in the document itself; the year, 1261, is no doubt taken from Mandonnet, and the more precise date given for the Chapter of that year is known from the acts of the previous Chapter, MOPH XX p. 25).

180. FVST p. 326, Ferrua p. 268.

181. Schneyer, *Repertorium* V p. 581, nos. 18–19.

182. FVST p. 98. Ferrua pp. 67–8.

183. Constitutions II 7 (ASOP 3 [1897–8] pp. 112–3).

184. ASOP 3 (1897–98) p. 115.

185. If there is any substance to the tradition that Thomas preached to the people in Viterbo in the time of Clement IV (cf. A. Walz, *Memorie Domenicane* NS 31 [1955] p. 196), we may presume that he did so in 1268 while he was there for the two chapters.

186. Sebastian de Olmeda, *Chronica*, ed. M. Canal Gomez (Rome, 1936), p. 46. There is no mention of Thomas' presence in London in Borselli or Taegio, so Galvano can probably be ruled out as Sebastian's source. Where he found this story we do not know.

187. MOPH II p. 100 (Galvano della Fiamma).

188. Galvano is notoriously unreliable and Sebastian's source is unknown. But in any case both authors claim that Thomas was diffinitor at the respective chapters, which we know to be untrue, since we have the acts of the provincial Chapters and know who was elected diffinitor in each case and who was elected socius to the diffinitor, and Thomas is not the man (MOPH XX pp. 27, 33). Thomas' presence in Bologna in 1267 is al-

legedly confirmed by a letter from Clement IV (FVST p. 570) commissioning Thomas to select two friars, one cleric and one laybrother, to serve, with the permission of their superiors, as companions to a Dominican bishop in Syria, on the assumption that Thomas was being deputed by the pope to raise the matter at the Chapter (cf. Walz-Novarina p. 146); but Clement's letter is dated 14 July 1267 and the Chapter began at Pentecost (5 June), and anyway the pope is clearly asking Thomas personally to select the bishop's companions, not telling him to ask any Chapter to select them. The pope's commission attests the esteem in which Thomas was held, maybe, but it proves nothing about his whereabouts.

189. Potthast II p. 1495.

190. The oldest manuscript of the first part of the *Catena Aurea* (Parma, Palat. 1) dates from 1263; cf. Weisheipl, *Thomas* p. 371.

191. Thomas explains the circumstances of *Contra Errores Graecorum* in his prologue. The text of Nicholas, together with Thomas' work, is edited, with an important introduction, in Leonine XL.

192. Even then it cannot be assumed that Thomas' assignation had anything to do with the papal court. The Provincial Chapter was held in early July (MOPH XX p. 26), some months before the pope moved to Orvieto. But it is impossible to date Thomas' assignation later than 1262 if we take Conrad of Sessa's testimony that Thomas wrote the *Catena Aurea* in Orvieto (FVST pp. 326–7, Ferrua p. 268) to mean what it appears to mean, that he wrote the whole of the work in Orvieto, including the first part.

193. Tocco (FVST p. 114, Ferrua p. 87).

194. R. A. Gauthier, *Summa contra Gentiles* I (Paris, 1961), pp. 47–8.

195. Peter of Montesangiovanni testified that he had known Thomas at Montesangiovanni, Naples and Fossanova, and that he knew him over a period of ten years (FVST p. 330, Ferrua p. 271). Ten years before Thomas' death (i.e., in 1264) it is only at Montesangiovanni that he could have met him.

196. FVST pp. 389–91, Ferrua pp. 331–3. Bartholomew heard the story from Nicholas of Sezze and many other brethren in Anagni; it does not appear to be part of the Naples tradition. This surely indicates that it was not at Christmas 1272, after his return to Naples, that Thomas paid this visit to the cardinal.

197. Masetti, II pp. 267–9.

198. His notes cover the Chapters from 1244–99; he mentions several foundations not noted in the text of the Chapters printed in MOPH XX, but there are very few foundations in the MOPH XX text that he has overlooked (one in 1271, MOPH XX p. 38, and one in 1287, ibid. p. 78). He first goes up to 1298, noting only Chapters at which a foundation was made (and 1275, at which vicariates were established); then he goes back to 1287

and 1297 to note some details about individuals, and concludes with more notes on individuals from 1299. Thus, apart from the last three items, all the Chapters he is interested in provide material about foundations. His heading, "Origo Nonnullorum Conventuum Romanae Provinciae," seems fully justified.

199. He does not mention Thomas' assignation to Rome in 1265, but no foundation was made in that year. No doubt this is also why he does not mention Thomas' assignation to Orvieto. He does mention Thomas' appointment as preacher general in 1260 and the fact that he was a diffinitor at the 1273 chapter, because foundations were made in those years.

200. Masetti prints "1258," but this is clearly a mistake for 1268, as a comparison with MOPH XX p. 34 shows.

201. The academic year ended toward the end of June (cf. A. Dondaine, *Secrétaires* p. 211 note 5).

202. For the date of the Chapter, see Masetti II p. 268.

203. Walz-Novarina p. 117; J. P. Torrell reminds us of this possibility in RSPT 69 (1985) pp. 14–5.

204. Gauthier, *Summa contra Gentiles* I p. 33.

205. Dondaine, *Secrétaires* p. 186.

206. Weisheipl, *Thomas* pp. 142–44, though the testimony of Conrad of Sessa cannot be used, as Weisheipl wants, to support this contention. Conrad is clearly not listing the places where he lived with Thomas in chronological order, and it is probably at the end of Thomas' life that he lived with him in Naples. Conrad claims that he first met Thomas "62 years ago" (i.e., in 1257), which has been used (e.g., by P. R. Diaccini, *Vita di San Tommaso d'Aquino* [Rome, 1934], p. 99) to prove that Thomas was in Italy in 1256–57 in connection with the condemnation of William of St. Amour, but this is absurd: Conrad does not mention Anagni, and he claims he was living with Thomas, not that he saw him on a visit. In 1319 he was seventy-seven years old, so he may be forgiven for having his dates slightly wrong; no doubt he first met Thomas in Orvieto.

207. S. Szabó, ed., *Xenia Thomistica* III, Rome 1925, pp. 30–1 (incidentally "1258" is repeatedly printed instead of 1268); he is followed by Walz-Novarina p. 151 and Gauthier, *Revue Thomiste* 82 (1982) pp. 220–1 notes 31–2 (in spite of his own earlier refutation of Mandonnet!).

208. Gauthier, *Angelicum* 51 (1974) p. 442; Gauthier, Leonine XLV i pp. 286*–7*.

209. FVST pp. 575–80.

210. A. A. King, *Liturgies of the Primatial Sees* (London, 1957), p. 331.

211. Cf. *Missale Ambrosianum* (Milan, 1954), pp. 10–11 for the readings.

212. H. Denifle, in his pioneering study in ALKGMA 2 (1886) pp.

170–5, argues that the original list only went up to 1258 (the date given in Toulouse 487), but there is much more evidence for a list going up to 1259: such a list is found in Madrid, Bibl. Univ. Complut. 147, AGOP XIV 23, Vatican Libr. Reg. lat. 598, and it was known to Gui (ALKGMA 2 p. 176) and Peter of Prussia, ed. cit. pp. 98–9.

213. The 1259 list includes Hugh of Metz, Bartholomew of Tours and Peter, after Florent and Thomas. The fuss over Thomas' inception in 1256 makes it most unlikely that any other Dominican Master incepted in the same year. Florent incepted in 1255 (cf. above, note 144); Peter was regent in 1260, so Hugh and Bartholomew have to be fitted in before him. Therefore Hugh must have incepted in 1257 and Bartholomew in 1258. This means that Peter cannot have incepted before 1259.

214. AGOP XIV 23 f.120ᵛ.

215. "Licenciati a cancellario Parisiensi et actu ordinarie legentes" (MOPH I p. 334).

216. RTAM 3 (1931) pp. 412–22.

217. AFP 4 (1934) p. 104.

218. MOPH XX p. 24.

219. Masetti II p. 268.

220. FVST p. 98, Ferrua pp. 67–8.

221. The 1259 chapter was a provincials' Chapter and the socius elected by the Provence province is named in Douais p. 74. Gerald de Frachet was provincial from 1251–9 (Douais pp. 42, 76; MOPH XXIV pp. 25, 248; MOPH III p. 101).

222. Constitutions II 1 (ASOP 3 [1897–88] p. 98).

223. Humbert, ed. Berthier II pp. 254–5; cf. MOPH XX p. 29.

224. MOPH XX p. 29.

225. MOPH XX p. 32.

226. Cf. L. E. Boyle, *The Setting of the Summa Theologiae of St. Thomas* (Toronto, 1982), pp. 8–11.

227. Santa Sabina was at this time the only fully constituted priory in Rome; the Minerva became a priory some years later (Masetti, I p. 181). Although we are not told so directly, Thomas' studium must have been at Santa Sabina.

228. Ferrua p. 360. There is some uncertainty about the succession in Naples. Archbishop Bernard died in October 1262 (Ughelli, VI col.113) and Ayglerius was not appointed until 29 October 1266 (E. Jordan, *Registres de Clément IV* I p. 103). In between we hear of someone called Dalfinas, who is only described as *electus* (Ughelli VI 113–4), whose dates are not known and whose separate existence is doubted by Eubel (I p. 359). In any case, Thomas can only have been offered the archbishopric between the election of Clement IV and the appointment of Ayglerius.

229. It was probably in December 1262 that he became a cardinal: cf. A. L. Redigonda, *Dizionario Biografico degli Italiani* III (Rome, 1961), p. 343, though it may have been earlier in the year.

230. Some manuscripts of Gerald's chronicle continue the list of Masters up to Baudouin and Annibaldo (MOPH I p. 335). Annibaldo must have graduated in 1262 at the latest, and Baudouin must either already have been a Master or else he was Annibaldo's successor, since the expanded list goes no further. Glorieux identified a Quodlibet as being by Peter of Tarentaise and dated it to 1264 (RTAM 9 [1937] pp. 237–80); the ascription to Peter is convincing, but the alleged reference to events of 1263–64 is much less convincing (pp. 240–41). John Quidort of Paris was present at this disputation (RSPT 19 [1930] pp. 469–74), but we do not know when he was first a Dominican student in Paris. There seems nothing against dating the Quodlibet to 1267–9, as is done by H. D. Simonin in *B. Innocentius Papa V: Studia et Documenta* (Rome, 1943), pp. 236–9, and L. B. Gillon in M. H. Laurent, *Le Bienheureux Innocent V* (Vatican City, 1947), pp. 370–7, in which case it teaches us nothing about when Peter's first regency came to an end. He was twice provincial in Paris and in between he was regent for a second time (1267–69) (MOPH XVIII p. 80), but we do not know when he first became provincial, except that it was not before 1261, when one of his predecessors was absolved (MOPH III p. 110; the provincial absolved in 1261 cannot already be Peter, unless Gui's list, MOPH XVIII p. 80, is completely wrong). The argument that Peter must already have been provincial before Humbert's resignation (advanced, for instance, by Meersseman in MOPH XVIII p. 84) was refuted by Laurent (pp. 67–9), but Laurent's own suggestion (pp. 54–6) that he lost his chair because of complaints about his doctrine is unsupported by any evidence, as H. F. Dondaine points out (Leonine XLII p. 266 note 4). Nor do we know that he became provincial as soon as he vacated his chair. The anonymous Dominican author of the *Annales Colmarienses* and *Basilienses* (who entered the Order in 1238, he tells us, MGH SS XVII p. 214, and was in Paris in 1261, ibid. p. 191) was under the impression that Peter remained a professor for twelve years and only then became provincial (ibid. p. 200), which certainly proves that he was still regent in 1261. I conjecture, tentatively, that Baudouin incepted as his successor in 1261 or 1262.

231. Gilbert was certainly a Master by 1269 (Leonine XLII p. 487). If we assume that Salagnac's list of Masters is roughly chronological at this point, which is far from certain, as Annibaldo is certainly misplaced and the earlier Masters are completely higgledy-piggledy, then we can put Gilbert fairly early, since he is listed straight after Baudouin (MOPH XXII p. 127); this is perhaps confirmed by the collection of sermons in Paris, BN lat. 14952 that includes sermons ascribed to Thomas, Bartholomew of

Tours, Baudouin, Gilbert, Peter (?), William of Luxi and William of Alton, which appears to indicate a period covering Thomas' first regency and the years immediately after it. On this manuscript cf. B. Hauréau, *Notices et Extraits* IV (Paris, 1892), pp. 17–104.

232. MOPH III p. 121.

233. MOPH V pp. 63–5.

234. The text is edited, with an introduction indicating the historical context, in Leonine XLII pp. 259–94.

235. In a document of 7 July 1267 he is listed as teaching in the faculty of theology (*Chart.* I pp. 467–9).

236. MOPH XVIII p. 80.

237. In Salagnac's list he comes immediately after Gilbert (MOPH XXII p. 127), and he is one of the Dominicans whose sermons are found in Paris, BN lat. 14952 (cf. above, note 231).

238. Cf. above, p. 24.

239. MOPH III pp. 125–6. The cherished doctrine that one Dominican chair was reserved for members of the French province, the other for members of other provinces is, at least for this period, decisively refuted by the 1264 Chapter, which specifies that people are to be provided to these chairs "regardless of nation." Cf. above, pp. 102–03, note 77.

240. MOPH III p. 142.

241. For the date see Potthast II p. 1648.

242. In December 1268 Gerard of Abbeville launched the attack in his Christmas Quodlibet and pursued it in a sermon delivered on 31 December in the Franciscan church (cf. Leonine XLI p.B 6). The first response from the mendicants seems to have been made by the Franciscan, Eustace of Arras, probably in his Christmas Quodlibet for 1268 (I. Brady, AFH 62 [1969] pp. 683–4).

243. For the date see MOPH XX p. 35.

244. MOPH XX p. 36.

245. *De Secreto* Prol. (Leonine XLII p. 487). A report on the event, coming from the Dominican archives in Viterbo, makes it clear that the dispute on which the Masters were consulted actually broke out during the Chapter (ibid. p. 475), so there can be no question of Thomas being sent for in advance to serve on this commission.

246. There was one diffinitor among the Masters (*De Secreto* Prol.); four of them (Bonhomme, Peter, Bartholomew and Baudouin) were members of the French province, so were at the Chapter as members of the Provincial Chapter which was to follow. Thomas was not representing his province (MOPH XX p. 35), so Gilbert must have been there as diffinitor for the German province. Thomas' presence is therefore unexplained except on the assumption that he was already in Paris for some other reason.

247. The evidence comes from the Dominican chronicle of Perugia; the relevant text is printed in full by E. Panella, *Memorie Domenicane* NS 14 (1983) pp. 32–3. Nothing is actually stated about when Nicholas studied with Albert, but we learn that he joined the Order in 1255, so can hardly have studied with Albert before he became a bishop. In 1268 Albert was not yet back in Cologne, so Nicholas cannot have gone straight on there after his journey with Thomas. The chronicle also says that Nicholas studied with Thomas. He may already have been his student in Rome, but it seems that he must in any case have studied with him in Paris before going on to Cologne. He later had a distinguished career as teacher and superior and in due course he succeeded another of Thomas' students, Peter d'Andria, as the second provincial of Naples (AFP 32 [1962] pp. 319–20).

248. Thus J. Kirshner, *Dizionario Biografico degli Italiani* XIV (Rome, 1972), p. 523.

249. Mandonnet's reconstruction of Thomas' journey in the winter of 1268–69 was exploded by Gauthier (Leonine XLV i pp. 286*–7*). No fresh evidence has been adduced to show that Thomas did not leave until the winter. Thomas and his companion probably travelled much of the way by boat; it is surely to this journey that we should ascribe the story told by Tocco (FVST p. 112, Ferrua p. 84) that once, when he was going to Paris, he was unperturbed by a storm that terrified the sailors (cf. Gauthier, loc. cit.).

250. Thomas' second regency is noted in the early catalogues (Grabmann, *Werke* pp. 92, 97). According to Tolomeo, his successor in Paris was Romano, who died the year after he incepted and the year before Thomas died (Ferrua p. 369); Tolomeo knew Thomas personally in this period, so his evidence can be trusted. Thomas therefore finished his second regency in 1272. The main evidence for the duration of his regency is provided by the Quodlibets, and much controversy surrounds its interpretation. There is no doubt that I–VI in our editions were early gathered together as a group, and three of them are dated in one or more manuscripts: III to Easter 1270, II to Christmas 1270 and V to Christmas 1271 (F. Pelster, *Gregorianum* 29 [1948] p. 63). Masters who held Quodlibets were expected to publish them as quickly as they could (*Les Genres Littéraires* p. 77), so stray matter from the same period could easily be published with a Quodlibet: in Thomas' own manuscript, for instance, the material from his inception is attached to his first Quodlibet (Dondaine, *Secrétaires* p. 78); since IV very quickly acquired an "appendix" of two questions disputed in Lent 1271 (Leonine XLI p.C 7) it is likely that this Quodlibet belongs to Easter 1271. I probably belongs to Christmas 1269: articles 15 and 16 are closely related to Thomas' contribution to the commission of Masters at the General Chapter of that year and take up a point on which he dissented from

the other six Masters (Leonine XLII p. 488); as we have seen (cf. above, note 245) there is no evidence that the issues were being debated before the Chapter, so the Quodlibet must be later than Pentecost 1269. If I–V thus take up the available slots from Christmas 1269 to Christmas 1271, it is natural to assume that VI belongs to Easter 1272 and most scholars have assumed this to be correct. In this case we can prove that Thomas was regent Master for 1269–72, but not for 1268–69.

251. Conceivably the Order's plans were thrown out by the elevation of Peter of Conflans to the archbishopric of Corinth in February 1268 (Eubel I p. 210); Gui at least implies that he was otherwise set to graduate as a Master in Paris (MOPH XXII p. 127 app. crit.).

252. E.g., Weisheipl, *Thomas* pp. 237–8.

253. Mandonnet, *Siger de Brabant* I (Louvain, 1911), pp. 88–9.

254. Bonaventure, *De Decem Praeceptis* 2:24–5 (Quaracchi ed. V p. 514), *De Donis Spiritus Sancti* 8:15–20 (V pp. 496–8). Cf. F. van Steenberghen, *Maître Siger de Brabant* (Louvain, 1977), pp. 33–46.

255. Cf. above, note 160.

256. It is mentioned en passant in Walz-Novarina p. 149.

257. I. Brady, "Questions at Paris c.1260–1270," AFH 61 (1968) pp. 434–461; Brady, "Background to the Condemnation of 1270: Master William of Baglione OFM," *Franciscan Studies* 30 (1970) pp. 5–48; Brady, "The Questions of Master William of Baglione OFM *De Aeternitate Mundi* (Paris 1266–1267)," *Antonianum* 47 (1972) pp. 362–71, 576–616.

258. Cf. *Franciscan Studies* 30 (1970) pp. 33–4, *Antonianum* 47 (1972) pp. 591, 600–4, 613–4. As van Steenberghen comments (p. 34), the object of William's attack is not, directly, anyone in the Arts faculty; it is Thomas.

259. *Antonianum* 47 (1972) p. 603.

260. *Genres Littéraires* p. 35.

261. In the mid-1260s a thoroughly scandalous row between the two Orders in the south of France (cf. Y. Dossat, *Eglise et Hérésie en France au XIIIᵉ siécle* [London, 1982], XXV pp. 577–9) called forth a papal Bull in 1266 telling them to stop quarrelling in public (BOP I pp. 475–6).

262. Galvano says that Thomas disputed "certain questions about making accusations" in Paris in 1268 (MOPH II p. 100), which would give us evidence that Thomas was already regent in 1268–69, but he is obviously referring to *Quodl*. I, which has to be dated to Christmas 1269 (see above, note 250), and Galvano's whole "life of Thomas" is sheer fantasy anyway. If we assume that Thomas did not occupy his chair until 1269–70, we could account for the fact that *Quodl*. XII was evidently not prepared for publication by supposing that it represents an informal Quodlibet held internally at St. Jacques in 1268–69. But Gauthier has drawn attention to the fact that in *Quodl*. VI Thomas is apparently still citing Aristotle,

Metaph. Λ as "book 11," whereas from the beginning of 1271 he is aware of the real book 11 and cites Λ as "book 12" (RTAM 18 (1951) pp. 87–8, note 52), which suggests that maybe *Quodl.* VI has to be dated earlier than 1272, in which case it cannot be later than Easter 1269, in which case Thomas was already regent in 1268–69. And in that case we can, with great plausibility, regard XII as belonging to Easter 1272 and ascribe the fact that it was not prepared for publication to the strike which was in force in the university.

263. Cf. Tugwell, *Ways of Imperfection* pp. 153–7.

264. *Summa Theol.* I q.66 a.1; *Quodl.* III a.1. For anxieties about the implications for the doctrine of the Eucharist, cf. Henry of Ghent, *Quodl.* I q.10, ed. R. Macken (Louvain/Leiden, 1979), pp. 62:9–14, 67:4–8; William de la Mare in Glorieux, ed., *Correctorium "Quare"* (Paris, 1927), p. 114.

265. *Summa Theol.* I q.46 a.1 and 2; *Quodl.* III a.31, XII a.2 and 7. In his little monograph on the subject, *De Aeternitate Mundi*, Thomas argues that if the idea of an eternal creation is not incoherent, it detracts from omnipotence to deny the possibility of an eternal creation (Leonine XLIII p. 86).

266. *Summa Theol.* I q.76 a.4; *Quodl.* I a.6, XII a.9; Thomas takes up the question of how this affects the identity of Christ's dead body in *Quodl.* II a.1 and IV a.8. For the Masters' view that Thomas' doctrine does lead to dangerous consequences on just this point, see Henry of Ghent, *Quodl.* X q.5, ed. R. Macken (1981), pp. 127–8; William de la Mare p. 129.

267. It was the Arts faculty that petitioned the General Chapter of 1272 not to remove Thomas from Paris and that sent an emotional letter after his death in 1274, asking for copies of various works he had promised them (FVST pp. 583–6).

268. On Siger, see van Steenberghen, op. cit. Many of the suspect doctrines of heterodox Aristotelianism can be found in Siger's writings, but the dating of these is controversial, so it is not certain what role, if any, he played in prompting Bonaventure's outburst in 1267. Van Steenberghen dates the earliest of the controversial works to about 1270 (pp. 50–7), but Gauthier argues for c.1265 (RSPT 67 [1983] pp. 209–12).

From the outset Siger was a serious reader of Thomas' works (cf. Gauthier, art. cit. pp. 212–32). For his later reactions to Thomas and his sensitivity to Thomas' criticisms, see, for example, A. Zimmermann, *Philosophisches Jahrbuch* 75 (1967–68) pp. 206–17; A. Morlasca, *Les Quaestiones super Librum de Causis de Siger de Brabant* (Louvain/Paris, 1972), p. 30; van Steenberghen pp. 56–57, 400; the editions by W. Dunphy and A. Maurer of different reportationes of Siger's *Quaestiones in Metaphysicam* (Louvain, 1981) pp. 30–1 and (Louvain, 1983) pp. 17–8.

269. Siger of Brabant, *De Anima Intellectiva* 3, ed. B. Bazán (Louvain/ Paris, 1972), p. 81.

270. *De Unitate Intellectus*, edited in Leonine XLIII pp. 291–314; on the date and circumstances, see ibid. pp. 248–51.

271. *Chart.* I pp. 486–7.

272. Gregory X was not elected until 1 Sept. 1271 (Potthast II p. 1651).

273. In the period before Lyons II (1274) there was renewed agitation to get the privileges of the friars (which were essential for their work) drastically curtailed, and in self-defense the Dominicans and Franciscans were obliged to make some limited concessions. Cf. R. W. Emery, "The Second Council of Lyons and the Mendicant Orders," *Catholic Historical Review* 39 (1953) pp. 259–60. Cf. MOPH V pp. 96–100.

274. The work is edited in M. Bierbaum, *Bettelorden und Weltgeistlichkeit an der Universität Paris* (Münster, 1920), pp. 37–168; the thesis is announced in chap. 2 (pp. 43–8). On the ascription to Thomas of York, see Dufeil, *Guillame de Saint-Amour* p. 277 note 160.

275. The Quodlibet is edited by A. Teetaert in *Archivio Italiano per la Storia della Pietà* 1 (1951) pp. 168–78; the sermon is edited in Bierbaum, pp. 208–19. For the date of both, see Teetaert, pp. 114–21, and H. F. Dondaine, Leonine XLI p. B 6.

276. Edited by S. Clasen in AFH 31 (1938) pp. 276–329 and 32 (1939) pp. 89–200.

277. Edited by Teetaert, art. cit. pp. 128–68.

278. Edited by H. F. Dondaine, Leonine XLI pp. B 56–62.

279. Bonaventure, *Apologia Pauperum* (Quaracchi ed. vol. VIII pp. 233–330). Pecham's *Tractatus Pauperis* is edited piecemeal in C. L. Kingsford, A. G. Little and F. Tocco, *Fr. Johannis Pecham Tractatus Tres de Paupertate* (Aberdeen, 1910), pp. 21–90; A. van den Wyngaert, ed., *Tractatus Pauperis* (Paris, 1925); F. M. Delorme, ed., *QD de Privilegio Martini Papae IV* (Quaracchi, 1925), pp. 79–88; F. M. Delorme, *Studi Francescani* 29 (1932) pp. 3–47; F. M. Delorme, *Collectanea Franciscana* 14 (1944) pp. 90–120.

280. Cf. especially Pecham's *quaestio* edited by L. Oliger, *Franziskanische Studien* 4 (1917) pp. 139–76.

281. *Quodl.* III a.17; *De Perfectione* (Leonine XLI pp. B 69–111). In what follows I give a brief résumé of the argument of this latter work.

282. Cf. L. Bongianino, *Collectanea Franciscana* 32 (1962) pp. 16–7.

283. Cf. *Summa Theol.* II.II q.188 a.7 for the first point, and q.188 a.6 for the second.

284. Cf. Matthew Paris, *Chron. Mai.* IV (Rolls Series 57) p. 279; it is

obviously against this threat that Kilwardby's letter to Dominican novices is partly directed (Tugwell, *Early Dominicans* pp. 149–152).

285. Kingsford, Little and Tocco, pp. 121–2.

286. Delorme, *Collectanea Franciscana* 14 (1944) pp. 90–120.

287. FVST p. 99, Ferrua pp. 68–9.

288. Cf. I. Brady in *St. Thomas Aquinas 1274–1974, Commemorative Studies* (Toronto, 1974), II pp. 152–4; the text of Pecham is edited ibid. pp. 155–78.

289. Leonine XLIII p. 56 note 10.

290. Ibid. pp. 57–8.

291. *Chart.* I p. 634, FVST p. 643.

292. Bartholomew (FVST p. 374, Ferrua p. 316). The two stories are referred to the same occasion, for example, by Weisheipl, *Thomas* pp. 255–6, and R. Wielockx p. 214 note 152.

293. Leonine XLII p. 488.

294. Cf. Wielockx, pp. 171–2.

295. Cf. above, notes 264–6. Thomas' independent line at the 1269 chapter is taken up in *Quodl.* I a.15 and 16 and IV a.12. Several other articles later feature in anti-Thomist literature: I 4, II 13, III 5, IV 4, XII 11, XII 12 all relate to matters taken up in William de la Mare's *Declarationes* (ed. F. Pelster [Münster, 1956], nos. 58, 21, 17, 30, 1, 28); I 5 is taken up in William's *Correctorium* (in Glorieux, *Correctorium "Quare"* art.16). V 9 is related to the 38th condemned proposition in Giles of Rome (Wielockx p. 56).

296. Grabmann, *Werke* pp. 265–6.

297. Apart from the Matthew commentary, Peter also took down Thomas' conferences on the Ten Commandments and edited them in Latin (Grabmann, *Werke* pp. 93, 98; Bartholomew, FVST p. 389, Ferrua p. 331).

298. Grabmann, *Werke* p. 264.

299. It is now certain that Remigio was a student of Thomas': E. Panella, *Memorie Domenicane* NS 10 (1979) pp. 191–2. Thomas' influence on Remigio shows through repeatedly in his works; for some of his comments on Thomas, including the poem he wrote on his death, see Panella, AFP 54 (1984) pp. 264–8.

300. This is attested by Bartholomew (FVST p. 370, Ferrua p. 313).

301. For the date of Giles' time as bachelor see Wielockx, pp. 236–40.

302. Wielockx pp. 182–3, 190–1, 196, 198–9, 207–8.

303. FVST pp. 383–4, Ferrua pp. 325–6.

304. His constant cheerfulness is commented on by Bartholomew (FVST p. 372, Ferrua p. 315).

305. *Chart.* I pp. 502–3.

306. Cf. above, notes 250 and 262. Either *Quodl.* VI or XII must be allocated to Easter 1272.

307. This is shown by the petition of the Arts faculty to the General Chapter of 1272, asking for Thomas to be sent back (FVST p. 585).

308. William died, a Master in Theology, in June 1274 (MOPH XXII p. 127, Douais p. 202); since 1272 he had been lector in Montpellier (Douais p. 162). From 1266–68 he was lector at Montpellier (Douais pp. 115, 130). The assignations for 1268–71 survive and William is not mentioned. It therefore seems likely that he was bachelor and Master in Paris from 1268–72. This suits his place in Salagnac's list (MOPH XXII p. 127).

309. I. Brady, *St. Thomas 1274–1974* II p. 147 note 16.

310. Tolomeo (Ferrua p. 369).

311. Ferrer is mentioned immediately after Romano in Salagnac's list (MOPH XXII p. 127). We possess a Quodlibet of his dated to Easter 1275 (ALKGMA 3 [1887] p. 320 note). He is not to be confused with the inquisitor Ferrer, on whom see W. L. Wakefield, "Friar Ferrier, Inquisitor," *Heresis* 7 (Dec. 1986) pp. 33–41.

312. MOPH III pp. 164, 167, 171.

313. MOPH XX p. 39. Weisheipl, *Thomas* p. 296, argues that Thomas' brief was not to set up a studium generale, but only a provincial theological studium, but this is not quite fair to the evidence. It is true that the Provincial Chapter of 1269 uses the phrase "studia generalia" to mean provincial studia (MOPH XX p. 36), but that is all the more reason why in 1272 a decision to leave it to Thomas to decide what to do about "the studium generale" cannot refer to another provincial studium. Also Thomas was told to decide about where the studium generale should be and he opted for Naples, where there was already a provincial studium. He had surely not been given the right to take over an existing studium; he could only appropriate Naples in the name of a higher-level studium than the one that was already there.

314. FVST pp. 579–80; Ferrua p. 361 (Tolomeo).

315. His presence in Naples is attested from September (FVST pp. 575–80).

316. Bartholomew lists some of the members of the community, referring apparently to a time when Thomas was still alive (FVST pp. 370–1, Ferrua p. 313). For the presence of Peter d'Andria, cf. below, note 554.

317. FVST pp. 579–80.

318. Cf. Weisheipl, *Thomas* pp. 299–300.

319. FVST p. 583.

320. Tolomeo (Ferrua pp. 363–4).

321. Bartholomew, on the authority of a Dominican tradition going back to Reginald (FVST pp. 376–8, Ferrua pp. 318–20).

322. That Thomas was on his way to the council on the pope's orders was well-known: cf. Tolomeo (Ferrua p. 361), Bartholomew (FVST p. 375, Ferrua p. 317), Nicholas of Fossanova (FVST p. 276, Ferrua p. 213), Peter of Montesangiovanni (FVST p. 330, Ferrua p. 272). Tocco's claim that he was taking with him the *Contra Errores Graecorum* (FVST p. 129, Ferrua p. 104) may be an inference from Tolomeo's remark that Thomas had been summoned to the council as an expert on the doctrinal disputes with the Greeks (Ferrua p. 372), and Gui is no doubt only interpreting Tocco when he takes the further step of saying that Gregory X had told Thomas to bring the book with him (FVST p. 202, Ferrua p. 171). Whether Thomas really did take the book to the council we do not know, but it is highly unlikely that it was as an expert on Greek disputes that he was summoned to the council, as no doctrinal discussions with the Greeks were planned at the council, which was meant simply to solemnize an agreement already worked out in Constantinople (cf. A. Franchi, *Il Concilio II di Lione (1274)* [Rome, 1965], pp. 124–31, 135–8, 169–72).

323. The presence of a servant is indicated by Peter of Montesangiovanni (FVST p. 334, Ferrua p. 275). By the time of Thomas' accident, the party included the dean of Teano and his nephew, abbot Roffredo, who was Bartholomew's informant (FVST pp. 375–6, Ferrua pp. 317–8).

324. Tolomeo (Ferrua p. 361).

325. The story of Thomas' last journey is known from several good witnesses, Nicholas of Fossanova, Peter of Montesangiovanni and Bartholomew in particular (FVST pp. 276–7, 330–2, 375–9; Ferrua pp. 212–4, 271–2, 317–21).

326. The date of Thomas' death is given by Tocco and Gui as the seventh (or Nones) of March (FVST pp. 138, 205; Ferrua pp. 115, 175); in the testimony of Nicholas of Fresolino the "ninth" of March must be an error for "Nones" (FVST p. 280, Ferrua p. 217). According to abbot Nicholas, Thomas stayed in the monastery for about a month (FVST p. 277, Ferrua p. 213). His devout reception of the last rites is described by Peter of Montesangiovanni, who was in attendance, and who also informs us of the people present at his death (FVST pp. 332, 335–6; Ferrua pp. 273, 276–7).

327. FVST p. 291, Ferrua p. 228.

328. Abbot Nicholas (FVST p. 277, Ferrua p. 213).

329. FVST p. 290, Ferrua p. 228.

330. FVST p. 287, Ferrua p. 224.

331. FVST p. 278, Ferrua p. 214.

332. Ibid.; also FVST pp. 336–7, Ferrua p. 278.

333. This is not reported by the monks of Fossanova, but there is no reason to disbelieve the testimony of Bartholomew (FVST p. 379, Ferrua p. 321), except that he is wrong to imply that Thomas' hand had already been removed.

334. FVST pp. 337–8, Ferrua pp. 278–9.

335. FVST pp. 291–2, Ferrua pp. 229–30.

336. FVST p. 394, Ferrua p. 336. The witness, John of Boiano, says that this happened fifteen years after Thomas' death during a Provincial Chapter at Anagni, but in 1289 the Chapter was at Viterbo (MOPH XX p. 90). The Chapter was at Anagni in 1285 (ibid. p. 70) and 1293 (ibid. p. 110). John also says that Hugh was Cardinal of Ostia, but he did not become that until 1294 (Eubel I p. 35). He was first made a cardinal in May 1288 (Eubel I p. 11). Since John is more likely to have the date wrong than the place, we should probably settle for 1293.

337. We have the victim's own testimony (FVST pp. 324–6, Ferrua pp. 265–7).

338. FVST p. 402, Ferrua p. 345.

339. Peter of Montesangiovanni claims to have been an eyewitness of a miracle worked at Thomas' bed immediately after his death (FVST pp. 335–6, Ferrua pp. 276–7), but this cannot be correct. If a miracle had been worked in front of all the monks, surely someone else would have reported it too. And the same miracle is reported by another monk, on the authority of Peter himself, as having taken place later at Thomas' tomb (FVST pp. 289–90, Ferrua p. 227), so Peter's memory has probably overdramatized the scene of Thomas' death.

340. Reported by one monk after another (FVST pp. 279, 281–2, 283–5, 287–9, 292–3, 311–3, 338–40; Ferrua pp. 216, 217–9, 220–2, 225–6, 230–1, 251–3, 280–1).

341. FVST p. 329, Ferrua p. 270. The episode being reported apparently antedates Landulph's consecration as bishop of Vico Equense in about 1301 (Eubel I p. 74).

342. The two canonization processes are full of reports of miracles worked at the tomb for visiting pilgrims, especially in the period leading up to the canonization, but all the pilgrims seem to be local. A party from Naples went to Fossanova in 1318 and received some miracles, but they were on their way to Rome (FVST pp. 274–6, 317–8, 320–2, 360–1; Ferrua pp. 211–2, 258–9, 261–3, 302–3).

343. Cf. FVST pp. 273, 317, 319, 320, 360, 393, 396; Ferrua pp. 210, 258, 260–1, 261, 302, 335, 338.

344. Cf. FVST pp. 322–3, 370, 373, 374; Ferrua pp. 264–5, 312, 313, 315, 316.

345. Bartholomew (FVST p. 381, Ferrua p. 323).

346. This is clear from FVST pp. 373–4, Ferrua pp. 315–6. Bartholomew never claims to have known Thomas personally. On Bartholomew, see A.Nitschke, 'Die Reden des Logotheten Bartholomäus von Capua', *Quellen und Forschungen aus Italienischen Archiven und Bibliotheken* 35 (1955) pp. 226–274; I. Walter and M. Piccialuti, 'Bartolomeo da Capua', in *Dizionario degli Italiani* VI, Rome 1964, 697–704.

347. FVST pp. 370–1, Ferrua p. 313.

348. FVST pp. 386–9, Ferrua pp. 327–31.

349. FVST p. 385, Ferrua p. 327.

350. FVST p. 384, Ferrua p. 326; James made a similar comment in the hearing of Peter Grasso (FVST p. 274, Ferrua pp. 210–1).

351. Cf. James' report of what Giles said (FVST pp. 383–4, Ferrua pp. 325–6).

352. In the Naples canonization process we pick up echoes of Dominicans talking about Thomas in a variety of convents (cf. FVST pp. 328, 349, 369–70, 376, 378, 380–1, 382–3, 389–91, 397–9; Ferrua pp. 269, 290–1, 312, 318, 320, 322–3, 324–5, 331–3, 340–1).

353. FVST pp. 356–8, Ferrua pp. 297–300. Albert of Brescia's *De Officio Sacerdotis* is profoundly dependent on Thomas (cf. M. Grabmann, "Albert von Brescia OP (†1314) und sein Werk 'De officio sacerdotis,' " *Divus Thomas* [Freiburg, 1940] pp. 5–38).

354. FVST pp. 358, 382; Ferrua pp. 299, 324. Evidently he considered it high praise to call someone "a second Thomas Aquinas" (cf. above, p. 225).

355. FVST pp. 583–6.

356. Cf. D. O. Lottin, "Saint Thomas d'Aquin à la faculté des arts de Paris aux approches de 1277," RTAM 16 (1949) pp. 292–313.

357. Cf. van Steenberghen pp. 157–8.

358. On Henry of Ghent's role in the opposition to Thomism, cf. Wielockx, especially pp. 121–178.

359. Giles' letter is known only from Albert's reply (Col. XVII i pp. 31–44). For the date, see van Steenberghen pp. 121–9. The earlier dating proposed by B. Geyer in Col. XVII i p. XXI is unjustified; Giles makes it clear that the opinions he wants Albert to comment on have already been condemned (Col. XVII i p. 31), and there is no reason to imagine that he was in Paris as early as 1270.

360. I. Brady, AFH 62 (1969) pp. 688–9.

361. F. Pelster, RTAM 3 (1931) pp. 397–411.

362. He propounds Thomistic theses in his *Theoremata de Corpore Christi* (c.1274) and defends unicity of form in his *De Anima* (c.1276); see Wielockx pp. 236–40.

363. The letter of 18 January is published in *Chart.* I p. 541, that of 28 April in AFH 18 (1925) pp. 459–60.

364. Cf. Wielockx pp. 100–2.

365. The number of Masters is known from the second Quodlibet of Jean de Pouilly (Wielockx p. 98 note 6).

366. Henry's membership of the commission is known from his second Quodlibet, q.9; cf. Wielockx p. 86 note 41.

367. It was the same commission that was involved in the 7 March condemnation and in the process against Giles (Wielockx p. 79 note 15, citing Jean de Pouilly), and it is clear that Thomas is already seriously implicated in the process against Giles (ibid. pp. 179–215). Evidently Tempier was following a single policy throughout the whole series of operations.

368. II *Sent.* d.32 q.2 a.3 (quoted in Wielockx p. 102 note 22).

369. *Chart.* I pp. 543–555. Cf. R. Hissette, *Enquête sur les 219 articles condamnés à Paris le 7 Mars 1277* (Louvain/Paris, 1977).

370. The fifty-one propositions are known from Giles' apologia, ed. Wielockx pp. 49–59. It can be inferred from *Chart.* I p. 633 that the result of Giles' refusal to recant was that he was debarred from becoming a Master in Theology; cf. also Wielockx p. 178.

371. Henry of Ghent, *Quodl.* X q.5, ed. cit. p. 128.

372. Ibid. p. 127. For the identification of the two dissentients as the two Dominican Masters, cf. L. Hödl, "Neue Nachrichten über die Pariser Verurteilungen der thomasischen Formlehre," *Scholastik* 39 (1964) p. 187; Wielockx p. 87. On the move to censure Thomas, see now R. Wielockx, 'Autour du Procès de Thomas d'Aquin', in A. Zimmermann, ed., *Thomas von Aquin*, Berlin 1988, pp. 413–438.

373. Cf. Hödl pp. 178–96; that there was a list of Thomistic propositions involved in the censure seems clear (cf. Wielockx *Aegidii. . . . Romani Apologia* p. 95 note 75).

374. It is clear from Henry of Ghent, *Quodl.* X q.5, ed. cit. p. 127, that no public condemnation occurred.

375. Between 1276 and 1278 John was engaged in papal diplomatic work in Paris (BOP I pp. 549–67).

376. Cf. A. Callebaut, AFH 18 (1925) p. 461; Wielockx pp. 218–9.

377. Cf. above, pp. 26–27.

378. Potthast II p. 1718.

379. We learn of this from Pecham, who was at the curia at the time: *Chart.* I p. 625.

380. The short text is edited by F. Pelster, *Declarationes Magistri Guilelmi de la Mare OFM de variis sententiis S. Thomae Aquinatis* (Münster, 1956); the long text, the *Correctorium*, is contained, with one of the Dominican

retorts, in P. Glorieux, *Le Correctorium Corruptorii "Quare"* (Paris, 1927). The major work was completed by 1279 at the latest (cf. R. Creytens, AFP 12 [1942] pp. 325–6). On nearly every page of the *Declarationes* William tries to link Thomas' doctrine with the syllabus of 7 March 1277.

381. AFH 26 (1933) p. 139.

382. *Chart.* I pp. 558–9. Van Steenberghen, pp. 147–8, brings out the essentially anti-Thomist thrust of Kilwardby's condemnation.

383. MOPH III p. 199.

384. Giles of Lessine's *De Unitate Formae* is edited by M. de Wulf (Louvain, 1901), as volume I of *Les Philosophes Belges.*

385. Peter's letter has not survived, but its tone can be inferred from Kilwardby's reply, edited in F. Ehrle, *Gesammelte Aufsätze zur englischen Scholastik* (Rome, 1970), pp. 18–54.

386. Cf. above, note 251. If he was a bachelor, all set to become a Master, in 1267–68, he must surely have been in Paris in 1266–67.

387. MOPH III p. 204.

388. Eubel I p. 163.

389. It comes out clearly in his response to Kilwardby's letter to Dominican novices, ed. in Kingsford, Little and Tocco, *Tractatus Tres* pp. 121–147.

390. He claims that the two Orders disagree almost totally about all points on which disagreement is possible (*Chart.* I p. 627).

391. It seems certain that the *Correctorium "Sciendum"* (ed. P. Glorieux [Paris, 1956]) is by Robert Orford (see A. P. Vella, *Robert d'Orford, Reprobationes dictorum a fratre Aegidio* [Paris, 1968], pp. 18–22). There does not seem to be any doubt that the *Correctorium "Circa"* (ed. J. P. Müller, *Le Correctorium Corruptorii de Jean Quidort de Paris* [Rome, 1941]) is by John Quidort (cf. Creytens, art. cit. p. 314). The *Correctorium "Quare"*, probably the first of the series (ed. Glorieux [Paris, 1927]) is generally accepted as being by Richard Knapwell (Kaeppeli, *Scriptores* III p. 306). The *Correctorium "Quaestione"* (ed. J. P. Müller [Rome, 1954]) is probably by William Macclesfield (Kaeppeli, *Scriptores* II p. 118).

392. Cf. Vella p. 22.

393. None of them refers to Pecham's 1284 condemnation or to the second edition of William de la Mare, so they must all have been finished by 1284 (Creytens, art. cit. pp. 327–330).

394. We learn this from Pecham himself (*Chart.* I p. 624). For a good account of the events of these years in England, see W. A. Hinnebusch, *The Early English Friars Preachers* (Rome, 1951), pp. 342–56.

395. In his letter of 7 Dec. 1284 he tries to defend himself against the charge of partisanship, but he cannot resist retorting to the alleged Dominican claim that Dominicans possess more of the truth than the Fran-

ciscans that, in his view, the opposite is the case (i.e., Franciscans have more of the truth than Dominicans) (*Chart.* I pp. 624–6)—hardly an unpartisan remark!

396. Hinnebusch, *Friars Preachers* p. 350.

397. Cf. *Chart.* I p. 625.

398. Cf. Hinnebusch, *Friars Preachers* pp. 351–2.

399. Potthast II p. 1794.

400. Potthast II pp. 1795–6.

401. Cf. Wielockx p. 99.

402. *Chart.* I p. 633. Wielockx, p. 110, rightly draws attention to the way in which the pope circumscribes the bishop's independence in the matter.

403. Cf. Wielockx pp. 111–3, 219–20.

404. Wielockx pp. 221–3 (though he is wrong to say that the pope also confirmed the acts of the Dominican General Chapter of 1286; Dominican Chapters do not and never have received papal confirmation).

405. Henry of Ghent, *Quodl.* X p. 127, app. crit.

406. Ibid.; also Godfrey of Fontaines, *Quodl.* III q.5, ed. M. de Wulf and A. Pelzer (Louvain, 1904), pp. 207–8.

407. Henry of Ghent, *Quodl.* X q.5, p. 126.

408. Potthast II pp. 1823–4.

409. Potthast II p. 1826.

410. Cf. Hinnebusch, *Friars Preachers* pp. 353–5.

411. Text in ASOP 17 (1926) pp. 694–5. For the date, see Tugwell, *Mediaeval Studies* 47 (1985) pp. 16–8.

412. MOPH III p. 235.

413. Although Pecham did not move against Thomism until 1284, Hothum's warning to him suggests that the Dominicans' anticipation of such a move went back some time. Pecham's elevation, coming almost immediately after the visitation ordered by the General Chapter, can easily be believed to have united the Oxford Dominicans in a determination to resist anything that might be attempted against Thomism.

414. Cf. Wielockx p. 184 note 26, p. 190 note 56 and pp. 195–6 note 75. The text is edited in Vella, op. cit.

415. Cf. Wielockx p. 190 note 56. The text is edited by G. Bruni, *Analecta Augustiniana* 17 (1939–40) pp. 429–442, 500–9, 562–76; 18 (1940–1) pp. 95–124, 238–268. On the ascription to Knapwell, see J. Schneider, *Thomas von Sutton, Quaestiones Ordinariae* (Munich, 1977), pp. 66*–7*.

416. Edited by R. A. Gauthier, RTAM 19 (1952) pp. 271–326.

417. It was only after 1313 that lectors were required to use the *Summa* in the course of their lectures on the Sentences (MOPH IV p. 65),

but individual lectors may have decided to introduce such a practice on their own initiative long before it was made compulsory.

418. For instance, Olivi maintained an energetic polemic against Thomism; cf. M. T. d'Alverny, "Un adversaire de St Thomas: Petrus Iohannis Olivi," in *St. Thomas 1274–1974* II pp. 179–218.

419. Cf. Creytens, AFP 12 (1942) pp. 316–27.

420. *Quodl.* X q. 5, p. 126.

421. W. A. Hinnebusch, *History of the Dominican Order* II, pp. 170–1. Some lectors of the Roman province had evidently started using the *Summa* instead of the Sentences in the early fourteenth century, but they were told to stop it in 1308 (MOPH XX p. 169).

422. Boyle, *Setting of the* Summa pp. 15–17.

423. Apart from Albert of Brescia's manual (cf. above, note 353), an important example is the *Summa Confessorum* of John of Freiburg, on which see L. E. Boyle in *St. Thomas 1274–1974* II pp. 245–68.

424. Cf. Thomas' remarks in *Super Boethii de Trinitate* q.2 a.2 ad 7, ed. B. Decker (Leiden, 1959), pp. 84–5.

425. MOPH IV p. 38.

426. MOPH IV pp. 64–5, 72–3, 81.

427. MOPH XXII p. 128.

428. MOPH IV pp. 83–4.

429. FVST p. 378, Ferrua p. 320.

430. FVST p. 147; cf. FVST p. 350, Ferrua p. 291.

431. Tocco was prior of Benevento in 1319 (FVST p. 268, Ferrua p. 204); we do not know when he was elected. Since he was apparently no longer a student when he knew Thomas in Naples, he must have been quite old in 1317.

432. FVST p. 345, Ferrua p. 287. Tocco does not say whether he was in Naples for the whole period of Thomas' last residence there.

433. W. Holtzmann, *Quellen und Forschungen aus italienischen Archiven und Bibliotheken* 18 (1926) pp. 179–80, 189–90.

434. FVST pp. 347–8, Ferrua pp. 289–90.

435. FVST pp. 350–1, Ferrua pp. 291–2.

436. FVST p. 270, Ferrua p. 206.

437. FVST pp. 347–8, Ferrua pp. 289–90.

438. On 12 April 1317 a substantial sum of money was paid to Guillaume Durand, lector of the Dominican house in Bordeaux (cf. MOPH XXIV p. 88), for a lot of the works of St Thomas, and another sum was paid on 18 April for the complete *Summa Theologiae* and *Summa contra Gentiles* (K. H. Schäfer, *Die Ausgaben der apostolischen Kammer unter Johann XXII*, Paderborn 1911, pp. 262–3).

439. A. Dondaine, "La collection dite de Jean XXII et Jacquet Maci," *Scriptorium* 29 (1975) pp. 127–152.

440. The Bull and the depositions are edited in FVST pp. 267–407, Ferrua pp. 203–350.

440a. MOPH IV p. 123.

441. For the texts, see FVST pp. 411–510.

442. Cf. A. Vauchez, *La Sainteté en Occident* (Rome, 1981), pp. 466–8. It seems to have been part of the policy of the Avignon papacy to canonize theologians: cf. Vauchez, in *Scuole degli Ordini Mendicanti* pp. 151–72.

443. Vauchez, *Sainteté en Occident* pp. 49–67.

444. FVST p. 513.

445. FVST pp. 519–30.

446. Mandonnet in *Mélanges Thomistes* (Kain, 1923), p. 45, suggested that the pope's aim was to *popularize the Summa*. If so, he failed. Apart from his own copy (now in the Vatican library, Burgh. lat. 116–119), only one other manuscript is known, and that contains only the potted II.II (Paris, BN lat. 3100), and since it is a very splendid manuscript, it was probably a presentation copy. It seems likely that John XXII wanted the potted *Summa* for his own use. Petrarch, some years later, commented on the pope's appreciation of such 'condensed books' (*Rerum memorandarum libri* 2.91, ed. G. Billanovich, Florence 1945, p. 102). The Borghese manuscripts give us the details about the commissioning and completion of the work: II.II was completed first, on 10 March 1324, then I and I.II on 4 May 1324 (which was perhaps one reason why, on 15 May 1324, the pope presented the Dominican library in Avignon with a copy of I.II, now Musée Calvet MS 255; see L. H. Labande, *Catalogue Général des Manuscrits des Bibliothèques Publiques de France: Départements* XXVII, Paris 1894, pp. 172–3). An even more abbreviated version of II.II was completed on 23 March 1325 (the colophon of this part, in Burgh. lat. 118, proves that the year is regarded as beginning on 25 March). On 17 Sept. 1327 John Dominic received some money from the pope 'in return for long service' (Schäfer, op. cit. p. 502). On 17 October 1331 he finally produced an alphabetic potted Tertia Pars. See A. Maier, *Codices Burghesiani Bibliothecae Vaticanae* (Vatican City, 1952), pp. 152–6.

447. FVST pp. 666–9. Cf. A. Maier, 'Der Widerruf der "Articuli Parisienses" (1277) im Jahr 1325,' AFP 38 (1968) pp. 13–19.

448. There is a commented catalogue of Thomas' works by I. T. Eschmann in Gilson, op. cit. 381–439, and by J. A. Weisheipl in his *Friar Thomas d'Aquino* pp. 355–405.

449. Cf. the sensible remarks of V. J. Bourke in *St. Thomas 1274–1974* I pp. 247–55.

450. As is made clear, for instance, in Gerald's chronicle (MOPH I p. 334), the Master is essentially one who gives ordinary lectures on the "sacred page." Cf. also A. Dondaine, Leonine XXVI p. 1*.

451. Cf. above, note 190.

452. The genuine homilies had been translated into Latin by Burgundio of Pisa in the twelfth century; on the pseudo-Chrysostom (whose inauthenticity was unsuspected in the thirteenth century) see now F. W. Schlatter, *Vigiliae Christianae* 39 (1985) pp. 384–92; the work was probably written in Latin.

453. This is stated in Thomas' dedication of the second part of the work (beginning with Mark) to Annibaldo. On the Greek source, see R. M. Tonneau, *Bulletin Thomiste* 9 (1954–6) pp. 179–80; H. F. Dondaine, RSPT 47 (1963) p. 405.

454. Cf. for example the remarks of C. Dozois, *Revue de l'Université d'Ottawa* 34 (1964) p. 233*, and L. J. Bataillon, *St. Thomas 1274–1974* I pp. 67–75; also H. F. Dondaine, art. cit. pp. 403–6.

455. Leonine XXVI pp. 17*–18*.

456. FVST p. 88, Ferrua p. 56. As A. Dondaine points out (Leonine XXVI p. 25*), Roland of Cremona had earlier attempted a literal commentary on Job (cf. Kaeppeli, *Scriptores* III p. 330), but it was not a success.

457. We have Reginald's own testimony of this in some manuscripts (cf. Grabmann, *Werke* pp. 265–6; Marietti ed. p. VII). Thomas clearly used the *Catena Aurea* (e.g., paras. 1490 and 2627 in the Marietti ed., where Thomas cites Theophylact, cf. *Catena Aurea*, Marietti ed. pp. 483, 590; Thomas knew Theophylact only through his Greek catena: cf. Bataillon, art. cit. p. 74). This proves that the John commentary, at least as it stands now, belongs to the second regency, and there seems little reason to suppose that the whole *reportatio* does not belong to this period. The provost of St. Omer at this time was Adenulf of Anagni, on whom see Grabmann, *Traditio* 5 (1947) pp. 269–83.

458. Tolomeo (Ferrua p. 368).

459. E.g., Grabmann, *Werke* p. 264; Weisheipl, *Thomas* p. 121.

460. H. V. Shooner, *Bulletin Thomiste* 10 (1957–59) pp. 153–7.

461. That Peter d'Andria made a *reportatio* of the Matthew lectures is known from the ancient catalogues (Grabmann, *Werke* pp. 93, 98). An anonymous *reportatio* exists in a manuscript in Basel (B.V.12) and this is almost certainly to be identified as the work of Peter (cf. J. P. Renard, "La *Lectura super Matthaeum* V 20–48 de Thomas d'Aquin," RTAM 50 [1983] pp. 145–8).

462. AFP 32 (1962) p. 319.

463. Léger's name is given in some manuscripts (Grabmann, *Werke* p. 264; Marietti ed., p. VI).

464. Cf. H. F. Dondaine's arguments reported (from a private correspondence) in J. P. Torrell, RSPT 69 (1985) pp. 16–17. More recently M. Arges has argued that the Matthew lectures should be dated to 1263 (*Mediaeval Studies* 49 (1987) pp. 517–523), but I do not find his arguments convincing. The ascription of the *De Ecclesiasticis Dogmatibus* to Augustine in the Léger *reportatio* may well be due to Léger, and the lack of any ascription in the other *reportatio* (which follows Thomas' normal later practice, as Arges shows, art. cit. p. 521 note 20) can quite properly be regarded as fairer to what Thomas actually said. And the argument that Thomas' views on the dove which appeared at Jesus' baptism, as found in the Matthew lectures, are closer to those found in the commentary on the Sentences than to his later views, as found in the lectures on John and in the *Summa Theologiae*, is not decisive; what Thomas says in the Matthew lectures is very close to *Summa Theol.* III q.39 a.6 ad 2, and the discussion of whether the dove was a real animal or not (taken up in III q.39 a.7) is simply not alluded to in the Matthew lectures, which is hardly evidence of a change in Thomas' views.

465. Grabmann, *Werke* pp. 92–3, 97–8.

466. Simonin, *B. Innocentius V* p. 228.

467. FVST p. 218, Ferrua p. 191.

468. According to Weisheipl, *Thomas* p. 373, there are seven manuscripts containing the Hebrews commentary in isolation.

469. FVST p. 88, Ferrua p. 56.

470. Cf. above, note 131.

471. Ferrua pp. 362–3.

472. Para. 41 in the Marietti ed. seems to derive from Proclus (cf. *Super Librum de Causis*, ed. H. D. Saffrey [Fribourg/Louvain, 1954], pp. 79–80). This is pointed out by P. Marc in the Marietti ed. of the *Contra Gentes*, I (Turin, 1967), p. 534. I am indebted to Fr. L. J. Bataillon for drawing my attention to this point.

473. The translation of the *Elements of Theology* is dated to May 1268 in some manuscripts: cf. H. Boese's edition of the Latin text (Louvain 1987) p. 103, and Marc, p. 118.

474. The early catalogues imply that the published commentary written by Thomas went up to 1 Corinthians 10, which perhaps means that the interpolation of the foreign matter between 1 Corinthians 7 and 1 Corinthians 10 antedates the publication of the commentary. The reason for the interpolation is presumably that a part of the *reportatio* was lost, unless we have really lost a part of what Thomas wrote.

475. Cf. Eschmann p. 394. L. J. Bataillon OP has suggested to me

that the Psalms commentary reads much more like the early Isaiah commentary, so it too should perhaps be dated rather to the beginning of Thomas' career in Paris.

476. A commentary on the Canticle is mentioned by Bartholomew and Gui (FVST pp. 388, 219; Ferrua pp. 330, 191), but not by Tolomeo or Tocco, nor does it feature in the oldest catalogues (Grabmann, *Werke* pp. 92–3, 97–8).

477. FVST p. 131, Ferrua p. 107.

478. On the *quaestio disputata* see B. C. Bazán in *Les Genres Littéraires* pp. 31–49.

479. *Quodl.* IV a.18.

480. On Quodlibets see J. F. Wippel in *Les Genres Littéraires* pp. 67–84.

481. Cf. above, note 250.

482. Cf. above, note 169; Eschmann p. 392.

483. The oldest catalogues (Grabmann, *Werke* pp. 92, 97) and Tolomeo (Ferrua p. 357) explicitly assign *De Veritate* to the first Parisian regency. Cf. Leonine XXII i pp. 5*–7*.

484. It is generally agreed that the Boethian commentaries fall within the first regency; on a variety of grounds, P. M. Gils suggests 1257–58 or early 1259 ("Introduction: L'Oeuvre," in the preface to the forthcoming Leonine edition of *Super Boethii de Trinitate*, which I have been able to use in typescript thanks to the kindness of Fr. A. M. Kenzeler of the Leonine Commission). The prologue to *De Trin.* implies that Thomas was intending to comment on all the *Opuscula Sacra* (ed. B. Decker, p. 47 para. 4), and there are several indications in the text that Thomas was envisaging at least a commentary on the whole of *De Trinitate* (cf. Gils, loc. cit.).

485. Various possibilities have been suggested: Thomas may have lectured on Boethius privately within the Dominican studium, or he may have lectured in the university, or he may have chosen the commentary just as a literary form. Cf. Gils, loc. cit.

486. Prol. to the commentary on *De Trin.* (Decker pp. 45–8).

487. Q.1 deals with whether and in what way reason unaided by revelation can know God (Decker pp. 56–79), q.3 a.1 explains why faith is necessary as well (for the point cited here see especially Decker pp. 112–3).

488. Q.2 a.2 (Decker pp. 86–7).

489. Q.2 a.2 (Decker p. 87), and cf. q.2 a.2 ad 7 (Decker pp. 89–90) and q.2 a.1 ad 7 (Decker pp. 84–5).

490. Q.2 a.2 (Decker pp. 85–90).

491. Prol. (Decker pp. 47–8).

492. Q.2 a.1 (Decker p. 83).

493. Q.2 a.3 (Decker pp. 94–5).

494. Expos. proemii (Decker p. 52).

495. The last page of the autograph ends with the cue for the next page, which is in fact the beginning of chapter 3, so clearly when Thomas finished writing the commentary on chapter 2 he fully intended to carry on (cf. Decker p. 43; Gils, loc. cit.).

496. This is Mandonnet's suggestion (RSPT 9 [1920] p. 150), taken up by Gils (loc. cit.), though it is not quite correct to say that the *Contra Gentiles* takes up "exactly" the project announced in the prologue to *De Trin.*: the latter is explicitly a matter of using reason to explore a faith that is presupposed, whereas books I–III of *Contra Gentiles* explicitly consider what can be said without presupposing faith.

497. Meticulous study of Thomas' own manuscript has shown that Thomas composed book I up to chapter 52 before he left Paris: cf. Gauthier, *Summa contra Gentiles* I p. 33. The title *Summa contra Gentiles* is attested in Paris quite early (*Chart.* I p. 646). On the genuine title, cf. Gauthier, *Summa contra Gentiles* pp. 74–5.

498. Cf. Gauthier, *Summa contra Gentiles* pp. 51–9. It can at any rate be presumed that Thomas had finished *Contra Gentiles* before he started on the *Summa Theologiae*.

499. Cf. Gils, loc. cit.

500. MOPH VI i p. 12. For the "traditional" view see, for example, A. Walz, *San Tommaso d'Aquino* (Rome, 1945), p. 96.

501. Gauthier, *Summa contra Gentiles* pp. 60–99.

502. A. Patfoort, *Thomas d'Aquin, les Clés d'une Théologie* (Paris, 1983), pp. 104–130, with references to other discussions sparked off by Gauthier.

503. MOPH V pp. 18–20.

504. MOPH V pp. 39–40 (after the Paris General Chapter of 1256).

505. Cf. MOPH I pp. 151–2. Gerald de Frachet describes people pleading with Humbert to be sent, and it looks as if he is referring to people presenting themselves in person, not just in writing. The 1256 Chapter was a provincials' Chapter (as we learn, for instance, from the 1255 Roman Chapter, which elected a socius to accompany the provincial to the 1256 General Chapter: MOPH XX p. 19). Gerald was at this time provincial of Provence (Gui, in Martène-Durand VI 423), so he must have been present in Paris in 1256; is he not describing what he himself witnessed in his account of these eager volunteers for the missions? Thomas had no occasion to be at the Chapter, but he was presumably in the convent at the time.

506. Ed. Berthier II p. 187.

507. MOPH V p. 19. Humbert's special concern for Arabic studies is noted by Gerald de Frachet (MOPH I p. 151). The General Chapter of

1259 called for the establishment of a special studium for Arabic (MOPH III p. 98).

508. J. Richard, *La Papauté et les Missions d'Orient au Moyen Age (XIII–XIV siècles)* (Rome, 1977), p. 117, toys with the idea of connecting *Contra Gentiles* with Humbert's concerns, but dismisses it on the grounds that the work "seems rather to be intended as an attack on Christian Averroism," The anti-Averroist interpretation of *Contra Gentiles* was proposed by M. M. Gorce in *Mélanges Mandonnet* I (Paris, 1930), pp. 223–43, but in 1961 Gauthier, *Summa contra Gentiles* p. 71, noted that it "has been almost universally rejected," and he refutes it at some length (ibid. pp. 70–87).

509. Already in his initial analysis of d.1 of book I of the Sentences, Thomas recognizes that in speculative ("argumentative") theology the investigation of truth and the destruction of error go hand in hand (I *Sent.* d.1 div. textus); cf. Patfoort pp. 16–24.

510. Cf. below, p. 357.

511. *Contra Gentiles* I 1–2.

512. Ibid. I 9, II 1, III 1, IV 1.

513. Ibid. I 9, IV 1.

514. Cf. Boyle, *Setting of the* Summa, pp. 15–17.

515. *Summa Theol.* II.II q.181 a.3. In III *Sent.* d.35 q.1 a.3 q.1 Thomas is more prepared to allow that teaching (unlike preaching) may be a part of the contemplative life.

516. *Summa Theol.* II.II q.181 a.3. This is the significance of Thomas' famous phrase about "passing on to others what you have contemplated" (II.II q.188 a.6), which occurs precisely in the context of how works like teaching and preaching flow from "contemplation."

517. One of the few points Thomas sticks to in his comments on the "contemplative life" is that the phrase identifies the temperamental bias of the person who loves the pursuit of truth for its own sake, as distinct from the "active life" of the person who is primarily interested in practical results (III *Sent.* d.35 q.1 a.1; *Summa Theol.* II.II q.179 a.1).

518. The 1220 General Chapter added to the Dominican constitutions the declaration that Dominican *studium* should be directed chiefly toward being useful to the souls of others (Thomas, *Constituties* p. 311). Even though it is probable that *studium* was originally intended to mean "zeal," Humbert takes it as meaning "study" (ed. Berthier II p. 41) and it is quite likely that this is how Thomas understood it. Albert in principle undertook all his writing in order to be useful, but it is hard to believe that, for instance, his extensive writings on animals and plants were not primarily motivated by his own personal interest. In the case of Thomas, once the educational purpose of the *Contra Gentiles* is recognized, it is hard to think of anything he wrote simply for the gratification of his own intellec-

tual interests. Thomas' study, however much he may have enjoyed it, does really seem to have been thoroughly directed toward being useful.

519. The Valenciennes Chapter of 1259 re-emphasized the obligation of everyone, including priors, to attend the sessions held by the house lector (MOPH III p. 99).

520. These are among the books Humbert thinks every house ought to have (ed. Berthier II p. 265). Cf. Boyle, *The Setting of the Summa* p. 15.

521. This is attested by Tolomeo, who saw a copy of the new work on I *Sent.* in Lucca, though when he looked for it again it had disappeared (Ferrua p. 368).

522. Boyle, *The Setting of the Summa* pp. 11–2.

523. Prologue to *Summa Theol.* Cf. Boyle, *The Setting of the Summa* pp. 17–20.

524. This is attested in the oldest catalogues (Grabmann, *Werke* pp. 92, 97).

525. Gauthier, *Summa contra Gentiles* I pp. 51–6.

526. Gauthier, *Angelicum* 51 (1974) pp. 452–3; id., Leonine XLV i p. 269*.

527. There are various clues to the dating of the *Summa Theologiae*. Thomas' knowledge of book XI of Aristotle's *Metaphysics* is evident from II.II onward, but he did not yet know it in 1270, when he wrote *De Unitate Intellectus*. So I and I.II were finished by the end of 1270. The Secunda Pars as a whole was published in Paris, so must have been finished before Thomas left there in 1272. The new translation of Themistius makes its appearance in I qq.75–89, which must belong to about 1268. Thomas was still working on III in Naples, when he abandoned all writing, but he may have started it in Paris. Thus the dates given by Tolomeo (Ferrua p. 360) are to some extent confirmed, though he claims that the whole *Summa* was composed between 1265 and 1272 (his reference to the "three parts" cannot be taken to mean I, I.II and II.II, in spite of Eschmann p. 386).

528. Gauthier, Leonine XLV i pp. 283*–8*.

529. Gauthier, Leonine XLVIII App. p. XXIV; but cf. above, note 449, for Bourke's questioning of Gauthier's conclusions.

530. Weisheipl, *Thomas* p. 365.

531. Cf. Marc pp. 412–3.

532. Cf. above, note 527.

533. Cf. *Summa Theol.* I.II q.3 a.8, II.II q.180 a.4 ad 4; I q.1 a.2 and a.4.

534. This may be partly due to the circumstances in which the *Summa* was conceived: the training that young friars were meant to receive was essentially practical, so the whole *Summa* can be seen as an exercise in moral theology.

535. Cf. Patfoort pp. 49–70.

536. III Prol.

537. Cf. J. Owens, "Aquinas as Aristotelian Commentator," *St. Thomas Aquinas 1274–1974* I pp. 213–238.

538. The precise dates have generally not been established, but cf. Eschmann pp. 400–404. Gauthier (Leonine XLV i p. 235*) situates the commentary on the *Physics* against the background of the Averroist problematic of the second regency. The commentary on the *Metaphysics* is particularly problematic, but it looks as if the discovery of book XI occurred while Thomas was working on it, which suggests that the whole work should be dated to the second regency, although it is quite probable that Thomas was able to incorporate or adapt material he had already composed in Rome.

539. Ferrua pp. 358–9.

540. Gauthier, Leonine XLV i pp. 293*–4*, with the comments of B. C. Bazán, RSPT 69 (1985) pp. 533–6, and L. Elders in A. Lobato, ed., *L'Anima nell'Antropologia di S. Tommaso d'Aquino* (Milan, 1987) pp. 49–51.

541. *De Perfectione* 30 (Leonine XLI p. B 111): "If anyone wants to write back against what I have said, I shall be delighted, because there is no better way of disclosing truth and confuting error than by arguing with people who disagree with you."

542. One of the main tactics used in the earliest preaching campaign against the heretics in southern France, in which Dominic was involved from 1206–15, was the public disputation, in which the moderators were supposed to be equally acceptable to both parties, so that the Catholic claims had to win on the basis of arguments, not authority. Cf. M. H. Vicaire, *Histoire de St. Dominique*, rev. ed. (Paris, 1982), I pp. 219–222.

543. Cf. A. Dondaine, Leonine XXVI pp. 17*–18*.

544. Judging from slightly later writings, Pecham was amongst the most strident critics of the "errors" brought into theology by the use of philosophy (e.g., *Chart.* I pp. 625, 627).

545. Leonine I p. 5.

546. FVST p. 345, Ferrua p. 287.

547. For the date of the *De Causis* commentary see the edition by H. D. Saffrey (Fribourg/Louvain 1954), pp. XXXIII–XXXVI. For the recognition of Proclus as the source, ibid. p. 3.

548. FVST p. 585.

549. Cf. below, note 11 on his inaugural lecture.

550. In the Naples canonization process many of the witnesses comment on Thomas' regular occupations of prayer, study, teaching and writing (FVST pp. 274, 278, 317, 319, 322, 326, 328, 330, 346, 363, 369, 372–

3, 384, 393; Ferrua pp. 210, 214, 258, 260, 264, 268, 269, 271, 287, 305, 311, 315, 326, 336), but relatively few mention preaching as being among his normal activities (FVST pp. 274, 326, 346, 369, 393; Ferrua pp. 210, 268, 287, 311, 336). For a good modern study, see J. P. Torrell, "La pratique pastorale d'un théologien du XIII siècle: Thomas d'Aquin prédicateur," *Revue Thomiste* 82 (1982) pp. 213–245. It should be noted that the collection of sermons included in the Piana edition of Thomas and often reprinted is entirely spurious (though it is probably a very early collection of Dominican sermons from before the time of Thomas; cf. L. J. Bataillon, 'Les Sermons attribués à Saint Thomas: Questions d'Authenticité,' in Zimmermann, *Thomas von Aquin*, pp. 325–341, where there is also a list of the known genuine sermons).

551. Grabmann, *Werke* pp. 93, 98.

552. FVST p. 122, Ferrua p. 96.

553. Leonard of Gaeta, on the authority of Reginald, locates the sermons at St. Mary Major's (FVST p. 369, Ferrua p. 312) and this is probably more accurate than Tocco's version, derived from an unnamed informant, according to which Thomas was preaching at St. Peter's (FVST pp. 126–7, Ferrua p. 102).

554. FVST p. 391, Ferrua p. 333; the same series of sermons is also mentioned by another witness (FVST p. 399, Ferrua p. 341). Tocco also remarks on the numbers attending Thomas' sermons, without referring to any specific occasion (FVST p. 345, Ferrua p. 287). According to the catalogues, the conferences on the Lord's Prayer were taken down and edited by Reginald (cf. above, note 551), but the surviving text has been reworked and contains some material which is not by Thomas (B. G. Guyot, AFP 53 [1983] pp. 175–201). The catalogues also list a reportatio by Reginald of a series of conferences on the Creed and a reportatio by Peter d'Andria of some conferences on the commandments. All these conferences were presumably in the vernacular: those on the Lord's Prayer were preached to the populace at large, and there is some manuscript evidence that those on the commandments were delivered in the vernacular (Torrell, RSPT 69 [1985] p. 13); the same can be presumed in the case of the conferences on the Creed (on which see Guyot, *Genres Littéraires* pp. 239–244). D'Andria is not known to have been associated with Thomas before the second Parisian regency, so if the talks on the Creed were in the vernacular, they must also have been given in Naples. It looks as if Peter and Reginald collaborated in Naples to edit a Latin text of all three sets of conferences, working into them some material taken from Thomas' lectures on Matthew (*Bulletin Thomiste* 10 [1957–59] pp. 153–7, 11 [1960–62] pp. 11–4). All of this makes it probable that all three sets of conferences were given during Thomas' final years in Naples between autumn 1272 and the end of 1273. The confer-

ences on the commandments have been edited by J. P. Torrell in RSPT 69 (1985) pp. 5–40, 227–263; he seems unduly hesitant about dating them to 1272–73 (ibid. pp. 9–17).

555. The Naples canonization process naturally draws attention primarily to Thomas' last years in Naples. But Peter Grasso (FVST p. 274, Ferrua pp. 210–1) claims to have picked up information about Thomas in various places, and one of his sources was Reginald, and Conrad of Sessa (FVST pp. 326–7, Ferrua p. 268) lived with Thomas in Orvieto and Rome as well as in Naples, and both of them mention preaching as one of Thomas' regular occupations. At least he probably took his turn at preaching in the priory church when he was in Italy.

556. FVST p. 362, Ferrua p. 304.

557. This is implied by John Coppa's account (FVST p. 391, Ferrua p. 333).

558. Cf. Torrell, *Revue Thomiste* 82 (1982) pp. 223–6.

559. He evidently did so in Rome (cf. above, note 553). He seems to have been conscious of a preacher's responsibility to move his hearers as well as instruct them (Torrell, art. cit. p. 224 note 43).

560. Torrell, art. cit. pp. 224–5, draws our attention to Thomas' fascinating reply to the lector of Besançon, who was wondering about the propriety of using in one's sermons such pious fancies as that our Lady recalled Symeon's prophecy seven times a day every day of her life (Leonine XLII p. 355).

561. This is apparently first reported by Gerson, *Contra Impugnantes Ordinem Carthusiensium*, ed. P. Glorieux, *Oeuvres Complètes* X (Paris, 1973), p. 41.

562. Cf. Vauchez, *Sainteté en Occident* pp. 223–234; for an interesting example of the popular model of sanctity see C. Carozzi, "Une beguine Joachimite: Douceline, soeur d'Hugues de Digne," *Cahiers de Fanjeaux* 10 (1975) pp. 169–201.

563. Remigio refers to him as "very fat" (*pinguissimus*) (AFP 54 [1984] p. 268); elsewhere he is called *grossus* (FVST pp. 291, 323; Ferrua pp. 229, 264).

564. Tocco (FVST pp. 111–2, Ferrua p. 84); cf. Peter of San Felice (FVST p. 323, Ferrua p. 264).

565. FVST pp. 287, 323; Ferrua pp. 225, 264. For the color of his hair, see Tocco (FVST p. 111, Ferrua p. 84) and Nicholas of Piperno (FVST p. 291, Ferrua p. 229).

566. According to Bartholomew's informant, Nicholas of Malasorte, this story was widely known in Paris (FVST p. 376, Ferrua p. 318). Anthony of Brescia heard it too and interprets it as evidence of Thomas' lack of interest in worldly goods (FVST p. 356, Ferrua p. 297).

AQUINAS: INTRODUCTION

567. Anthony of Brescia heard this story from Nicholas of Marcillac (FVST pp. 355, 358–9; Ferrua pp. 297, 300). There is no reason to believe that Nicholas was in Paris in 1259 (cf. above, note 80); he was passing on gossip picked up ten or more years later.

568. Cf. P. M. Gils, "Appendice: S. Thomas Ecrivain," in the forthcoming Leonine edition of the commentary on Boethius' De Trinitate.

569. Ibid., referring to Vat. lat. 9851 f.45ᵛ: "Primum / in nomine / fratris Iohannis." It is not clear if it was the librarian's job to supply parchment or that of the supervisor of scribes (Humbert, ed. Berthier II pp. 266–7).

570. Cf. below, p. 622 note 23. I doubt if Thomas ever thought of poverty in connection with books.

571. Conrad of Sessa (FVST p. 326, Ferrua p. 268).

572. A lay witness, who perhaps had an exaggerated idea of Thomas' failure to turn up for meals (FVST p. 362, Ferrua pp. 303–4). The point is clearly, as John of Naples says, that Thomas was not prepared to give more time than the bare minimum to things he did not find interesting, like eating and sleeping (FVST p. 328, Ferrua p. 269).

573. Peter of Montesangiovanni, who was an eyewitness, was quizzed extensively on this miracle, and even tells us the name of the fishmonger and proves that he knew how to recognize herring. Evidently they bought the whole box and the entire household as well as Thomas enjoyed the fish (FVST pp. 332–4, Ferrua pp. 274–5). Tocco also heard the story from several people at Maenza, and he told the story to abbot Nicholas (FVST p. 279, Ferrua pp. 215–6).

574. Tocco (FVST pp. 104, 122; Ferrua pp. 74–5, 96).

575. Remigio cites a "jocular" remark from him, which does not strike me as funny (AFP 54 [1984] p. 266).

576. This is attested at least for Naples: Bartholomew (FVST p. 374, Ferrua p. 316). Thomas' famous remark on wanting Chrysostom more than Paris (cf. above, note 566) was made when he was returning with some other friars from St. Denis, but we do not know whether it was business or relaxation that took them there.

577. Tocco (FVST p. 98, Ferrua pp. 67–8).

578. This is reported by Bartholomew (FVST p. 373, Ferrua p. 315).

579. Bartholomew (FVST p. 381, Ferrua p. 323).

580. This is commented on by several people, including Bartholomew (FVST pp. 274, 319, 374, 393–4; Ferrua pp. 210, 260, 316, 336).

581. Bartholomew heard this from the brethren in Anagni (FVST pp. 389–90, Ferrua pp. 331–2).

582. Cf. above, p. 219 and note 195. In 1272 Thomas had to devote some time to family business owing to complications arising from the will

of his brother-in-law, Roger d'Aquila, whose executor Thomas was (FVST pp. 575–9); it was in connection with this affair that Thomas had to go to Capua on one occasion, where he was seen by Bartholomew (FVST p. 374, Ferrua p. 316).

583. Tocco (FVST pp. 116–7, Ferrua p. 90). The historical credibility of the story, as it stands, has been cogently impugned by Gauthier, *Contra Gentiles* I pp. 23–5.

584. FVST pp. 571–4, 581; Leccisotti, op. cit., plate IV.

585. Cf. above, p. 211 and notes 131–2. The dedication of the *Compendium Theologiae* to Reginald is no doubt a gesture of appreciation, but the phrase found in some editions, "To his dearest socius, Reginald," is not genuine (it seems to have appeared first in an edition of 1488; cf. Leonine XLII pp. 18, 40).

586. Tolomeo (Ferrua p. 358).

587. Books 8 and 9 of the *Nicomachean Ethics* provide Thomas with the occasion to explore the notion of friendship at length, and his commentary on these books is a full and sympathetic one.

588. *Summa Theol.* II.II q.23 a.1, right at the beginning of the treatise on charity.

589. *Revue Thomiste* 82 (1982) p. 226.

590. It is difficult to imagine Thomas writing anything like the letters of Jordan to the nuns in Bologna, for instance (MOPH XXIII passim).

591. FVST pp. 319, 381; Ferrua pp. 260, 323.

592. *Summa Theol.* II.II q.180 a.7; cf. W. H. Principe, *Thomas Aquinas' Spirituality* (Toronto, 1984), p. 14.

593. FVST pp. 319, 323, 330, 373, 397; Ferrua pp. 260, 264, 271, 315, 340.

594. FVST pp. 323, 373, 397; Ferrua pp. 264, 315, 340.

595. Tocco (FVST pp. 116–7, Ferrua pp. 89–91).

596. Tocco (FVST p. 121, Ferrua p. 95).

597. FVST pp. 319, 322, 326, 328, 330, 392, 397, 400; Ferrua pp. 260, 264, 268, 269, 271, 335, 340, 343.

598. This is brought out, for instance, in Tocco's chapter on Thomas' abstraction (FVST pp. 116–7, Ferrua pp. 89–91). In his treatise on the contemplative life, of which a translation is given below, Thomas (with doubtful success, but apparent unself-consciousness) unites the intellectual and religious senses of "contemplation," which he has inherited from Aristotle and from the Latin Christian tradition, as if they were inseparable. No doubt they were inseparable in his own case.

599. Cf. above, note 249.

600. FVST p. 99, Ferrua pp. 68–9.

601. FVST pp. 322, 373; Ferrua pp. 264, 315.

602. FVST pp. 273–4, 319, 326, 369, 373, 393, 397; Ferrua pp. 210, 260, 268, 311, 315–6, 336, 340.

603. Of the many testimonies, we may note those of Conrad of Sessa, Peter of Montesangiovanni and Bartholomew (FVST pp. 326, 330, 373–4; Ferrua pp. 268, 271, 316).

604. Tocco (FVST p. 103, Ferrua p. 74). Humbert says that lectors should only miss compline for very grave reasons (ed. Berthier II p. 255).

605. Peter of San Felice mentions seeing Thomas in choir in Naples (FVST p. 323, Ferrua p. 264), and Bartholomew implies that Thomas was regular in celebrating the Office (FVST p. 384, Ferrua p. 326), but in neither case is it clear how much conventual Office is really meant. If Thomas normally said Mass and attended another Mass every day, the information that he said Mass in St. Nicholas' chapel in Naples and then attended a second Mass immediately, without even unvesting completely (FVST p. 373, Ferrua pp. 315–6), must mean that he did not attend the conventual Mass. After his two Masses he started work and spent the rest of the day at his various labors (FVST pp. 319, 326, 369; Ferrua pp. 260, 268, 311—"praying" in these accounts would not naturally be used to refer to the liturgy, in the usage of the time), so it appears that he did not attend any Office during the day. John of Caiazzo reports that Thomas was always the first to get up and go into church to say his prayers, but when the other friars started arriving he went back to his room (FVST p. 373, Ferrua p. 315) and the inference that he did not attend matins is borne out by a story Tocco reports from the sacristan of Naples (FVST p. 108, Ferrua p. 79).

606. *De Substantiis Separatis* Prol. (Leonine XL p. D 41:1–4).

607. Cf. H. F. Dondaine, Leonine XL pp. D 6–7.

608. Cf. Humbert, ed. Berthier II pp. 29–30, where lectors are even allowed to miss Office for the sake of relaxation, as long as this is going to help them do their work better.

609. Thomas apparently attended matins in Salerno (FVST p. 107, Ferrua p. 79).

610. It used to be asserted on the authority of a later Dominican bibliography (MOPH XVIII p. 62 no. 33) that William's translations were commissioned by Thomas, but this is certainly not true as it stands, as some of William's translations were made before it is at all reasonable to suppose that he could have been influenced by Thomas. Gauthier argues that there was no direct relationship between the two men at all (Leonine XLV i p. 288*), but L. J. Bataillon informs me that there is some manuscript evidence suggesting that William may have prepared some texts or extracts from texts for Thomas' use.

611. Tocco tells us that Reginald told him that he had been told, in confidence, by Thomas himself, that his knowledge came from God, be-

AQUINAS: INTRODUCTION

cause he always prayed before writing and always had recourse to prayer when he ran into any kind of difficulty (FVST p. 346, Ferrua pp. 287–8). After Thomas' death Reginald proclaimed Thomas' secret publicly, but it looks as if the secret was only that Thomas always prayed when he ran into difficulties, not that all his knowledge was inspired (FVST p. 381, Ferrua p. 323), so Tocco has probably touched up the story to suit the supposed needs of a canonization process (cf. *Scuole degli Ordini Mendicanti* p. 163).

612. *Summa Theol.* II.II q.188 a.6.

613. There was evidently both a family tradition and an Order tradition of this miracle: FVST pp. 347–8, 380–1; Ferrua pp. 289–90, 322–3.

614. FVST p. 373, Ferrua p. 315.

615. Cf. A. Dondaine, *Secrétaires* pp. 15–25.

616. Bartholomew simply says that Thomas dictated to several secretaries (FVST p. 373, Ferrua p. 316); it is Tocco who specifies that he dictated different things to different secretaries at the same time (FVST p. 89, Ferrua p. 58). Dondaine (*Secretaires* p. 18) claims that Caesar and Napoleon had the same ability, without citing any sources. I do not know about Napoleon, but Caesar is said to have used secretaries in the plural in Suetonius I 55:3, but the point is simply that several secretaries were needed to follow what he was dictating, not that he was dictating several things at once. Walz-Novarina, p. 167, cite Origen as another parallel case, but in Eusebius, *Hist. Eccl.* 6:23, we are told explicitly that his seven or so stenographers took turns taking down what he was saying in his lectures.

617. Tocco alleges this on the authority of one of the secretaries (FVST p. 89, Ferrua p. 58).

618. Tocco (FVST pp. 108–9, 113–4; Ferrua pp. 80–1, 85–6).

619. FVST pp. 320, 322, 326, 330, 345, 369, 394, 397; Ferrua pp. 261, 264, 268, 271, 287, 311, 336, 340.

620. *De Veritate* q.11 a.1, q.17 a.5.

621. Thomas would not have agreed with St. Anthony the Great that when you are asked a question about what some passage in the bible means, the proper answer is to say, "I don't know" (*Apophthegmata Patrum* Anthony 17, PG 65:80D).

622. Tocco (FVST p. 103, Ferrua pp. 73–4).

623. That Thomas composed the Office for Corpus Christi, at the request of Urban IV, is affirmed by Tolomeo (Ferrua p. 359) and Tocco (FVST p. 88, Ferrua p. 57) and recent research has tended to validate this claim: cf. W. Breuer, *Die lateinische Eucharistiedichtung des Mittelalters von ihren Anfängen bis zum Ausgang des 13 Jahrhunderts* (Wuppertal, 1970), pp. 244–303; L. J. Bataillon, RSPT 58 (1974) p. 454; P. M. Gy, RSPT 64

343

(1980) pp. 491–507 and RSPT 66 (1982) pp. 81–6. On the other hand Thomas' authorship of *Adoro Devote* now seems very unlikely: cf. Breuer pp. 317–334; Gy, RSPT 66 (1982) pp. 81–6.

624. Principe, p. 13, points suggestively to hints in Thomas' writings of his personal devotion to Christ, which confirms the rather hagiographical accounts of the biographers.

625. This is the tradition of Fossanova (FVST pp. 332, 379; Ferrua pp. 273, 321).

626. Tocco (FVST p. 132, Ferrua p. 108); cf. Bartholomew (FVST p. 379, Ferrua p. 321).

627. Tocco (FVST p. 108, Ferrua pp. 79–80).

628. Tocco (FVST pp. 125–6, Ferrua pp. 100–1).

629. The evidence of Thomas' own manuscript, now Vat. lat. 781, proves the early date of this Quodlibet: cf. Dondaine, *Secrétaires* p. 82.

630. Bartholomew heard the story from a friar who heard it from Reginald (FVST pp. 376–8, Ferrua pp. 318–20).

631. FVST pp. 391–2, Ferrua pp. 333–4.

632. One of the monks of Fossanova thought Thomas looked "50 or 60 years old" at the time of his death (FVST p. 291, Ferrua p. 229), which perhaps implies that he looked older than his age.

633. This is suggested by E. Colledge, *St. Thomas 1274–1974* I p. 26.

634. Tocco (FVST p. 132, Ferrua p. 108).

635. Revelation means that we are enlightened by God's own knowledge (*Summa Theol.* I q. 1 a. 2), but it proposes its message to us in the form of propositions, though the object of faith is not propositions as such, but God (II.II q. 1 a. 1 and a. 2).

636. Cf. Hugh of St. Cher's postil on Matt. 3:12, for instance.

637. Tocco (FVST p. 120, Ferrua p. 94).

638. *Summa Theol.* II.II q. 180 a. 5, q. 175 a. 2.

Part II

I. Thomas' Inaugural Lecture (1256)

1. *Chart.* II pp. 693–4.

2. In Oxford in 1253 there were already the two sessions, one in the evening, one the following morning, as we learn from Adam Marsh's Letter 192 (ed. J. S. Brewer, *Monumenta Franciscana* I [London, 1858], pp. 348–9). Since Oxford almost certainly followed the same practice as Paris, we can infer that the two sessions were also customary in Paris by this time.

3. There is a reference to *principia* in the anti-Dominican statute of February 1252 (*Chart.* I p. 227), but there the word probably refers to the whole ceremony of inception. However, the tradition concerning Thomas' inaugural lecture is early (cf. MOPH I p. 216, where *principium* surely refers to the lecture Thomas has to give). For the different senses of *principium* in the thirteenth century, and for the ceremonies of inception, cf. O. Weijers, *Terminologie des Universités au XIIIe siècle*, Rome 1987, pp. 407–422.

4. Cf. above, p. 215.

5. MOPH I p. 216.

6. E. Panella, *Memorie Domenicane* NS 10 (1979) pp. 207–8.

7. On this manuscript, see G. Pomero, *Memorie Domenicane* NS 11 (1980) pp. 425–6; H. F. Dondaine and H. V. Shooner, *Codices Manuscripti Operum Thomae de Aquino* I (Rome, 1967), pp. 351–2.

8. E.g., Eschmann, p. 428; Weisheipl, *Thomas* pp. 373–4.

9. This seems to be how William of Auxerre interpreted Augustine: *Summa Aurea* IV, ed. cit. pp. 88, 97, 116.

10. Albert, *MT* 1 (Col. XXXVII p. 456:25–38).

11. *De Veritate* q.11 a.1.

12. *Contra Gentiles* III 69.

13. *De Veritate* q.11 a.1.

14. Origen, on 1 Cor. 2:12–5, ed. in *Journal of Theological Studies* 9 (1908) p. 240.

15. *Quodl.* III a.10.

16. *Quodl.* XII a.26.

17. Albert, loc. cit.

18. Cf. Humbert, *De Eruditione Praedicatorum* II xii 139 (Tugwell, *Early Dominicans* p. 224).

19. *Contra Impugnantes* 2.3 (Leonine XLI pp. A 56–7).

20. Humbert of Romans, letter of 1256, MOPH V pp. 32–3.

21. *De Apibus*, Douais 1605, pp. 180–1.

22. *Contra Impugnantes* 2.3 (Leonine XLI pp. A 57–8). Cf. the sermon quoted by L. J. Bataillon, RSPT 67 (1983) p. 432, comparing entry into the university to entry into religious life. The sermon is probably by Adenulf of Anagni, who was an admirer of Thomas (and paid to have his lectures on St. John copied) and a friend of the Dominicans (he preached a sermon on "glorious St. Dominic"—Schneyer, *Repertorium* I p. 50, no. 6).

23. Humbert complains that the secular Masters have made the friars "contemptible" (MOPH V p. 36); for the physical and moral injuries suffered by the Dominicans at this time, see Hinnebusch, *History of the Dominican Order* II pp. 73–4.

24. *Contra Impugnantes* 14.

II. THOMAS' THEOLOGY OF PRAYER

1. I have discussed Thomas' doctrine of prayer, against the background of other theologians and spiritual writers, in "Prayer, Humpty Dumpty and Thomas Aquinas," in B. Davies, ed., *Language, Meaning and God* (London, 1987), pp. 24–50.

2. See H. V. Shooner, *Bulletin Thomiste* 10 (1957–9) pp. 153–7. Shooner argues that the edition of the Matthew lectures must, to some extent, be dependent on the edition of the later conferences, but it seems to me that this is far from certain. It is surely more likely that Thomas assembled his documentation in the first place for his university lectures, not for his popular conferences; the precise citations, to which Shooner points, which are indeed not typical of the *reportatio* of the Matthew lectures, can be interpreted in a way that allows them to be a genuine part of the lectures. The conferences, which were delivered in the vernacular, needed much more editing than the Matthew lectures; it is quite likely that in the process Peter and Reginald looked up some of Thomas' citations to find the exact text. The exact text could then be inserted into the Matthew lectures, where before there was only a rough note. But this does not mean that Thomas had not cited the same texts in the Matthew lectures.

3. PL 176:981–2.

4. *Lettres des premiers Chartreux* II, Sources Chrétiennes 274 (Paris, 1980), pp. 150–170.

5. *Ep.* 130.9.18; *Enarr. in Ps.* 37.14.

6. Marginal Gloss to 1 Thess. 5:17; also Lombard's Gloss (PL 192:309A).

7. IV *Sent.* d.15 p. 2 a.1 q.4.

8. *De Oratione* 5.1.

9. *Stromateis* VII 39.6; the phrase is derived from the popularizing Platonist, Maximus of Tyre 5.8, ed. H. Hobein (Leipzig, 1910) p. 63, who uses it as a way of avoiding the "embarrassment" of supposing that Socrates, when he prayed, was really asking the gods for anything.

10. The definition of *oratio* ("speech") as *oris ratio* ("oral reason") is attested in the Latin grammarians from the third century onward (cf. *Thesaurus Linguae Latinae* s.v.). Jerome distinguishes the biblical sense of the word ("prayer") from this grammatical sense (*Ep.* 140.4), but Cassiodorus already applies the grammarians' definition to *oratio* in the sense of "prayer" (*Expos. in Ps.* 38:13), and thereafter it is cited quite frequently in discussions of prayer.

11. *Opera Omnia* I (Paris, 1674), pp. 336–406.

12. *De Oratione* 14.2.

13. E.g., Ambrose, *De Sacramentis* VI 22–25.

14. E.g., Cassian, *Conf.* 9:11–17.

15. Cf. Tugwell, art. cit. pp. 27–30.

16. This is particularly clear in William of St. Thierry; cf. Tugwell, art. cit. pp. 29–30.

17. This process is already visible in Gregory the Great (e.g., PL 75:1107–8), and it is very clear in Guigo I (e.g., *Meditationes* 243); it is built into the structure of Guigo II's *Scala Claustralium*.

18. So, for instance, Philip the Chancellor can say that prayer, in one sense, refers to "when the soul is caught up into God by contemplation" (*Summa de Bono*, ed. N. Wicki [Berne, 1985], p. 939:145).

19. This definition apparently derives from the pseudo-Augustinian *De Spiritu et Anima* 50 (PL 40:816), but the rather more compact formula into which it evolved rapidly took on a life of its own; cf. Tugwell, art. cit. p. 49 note 10. The degree to which the affective notion of prayer prevailed can be seen, for instance, in Philip the Chancellor's adaptation of the much older description of prayer as "the ascent of the mind to God" (which comes from Evagrius, *De Oratione* 36, and was made known to the Latins through the Latin translation of John Damascene's *De Fide Orthodoxa* 68.1, ed. Buytaert p. 267): Philip reformulates it to read "prayer is ascending to God with pious affection" (p. 332:153–4).

20. Albert, *DN* 3.6, Col. XXXVII p. 104:62–3.

21. *Summa Aurea* IV 11.2, ed. J. Ribaillier (Grottaferrata, 1985), p. 274.

22. Cf. Tugwell, art. cit. p. 25; also Philip the Chancellor, p. 939:140.

23. *Summa Magistri Rolandi Cremonensis* III, ed. A. Cortesi (Bergamo, 1962), pp. 766–7.

24. Ibid. pp. 765–810.

25. *De Rhetorica Divina* 1.

26. IV *Sent.* d.15 q.1 a.4.

27. *Summa Theol.* I q.23 a.8 ad 2.

28. Ibid. I.II q.68 a.2 ad 3.

29. As is suggested, for instance, by William of St. Thierry and Bonaventure: cf. Tugwell, art. cit. pp. 34–5.

30. Cf. Tugwell, art. cit. pp. 47–8; id., *Dominican Ashram* 1 (1982) pp. 128–44.

31. Bede Jarrett, "The Method of Prayer," "Contemplation," *Meditations for Layfolk* (London, 1955), pp. 288–9, 297.

32. Vincent McNabb, *The Craft of Prayer* (London, 1935), p. 10.

III. The Contemplative Life

1. IV *Sent.* d.15 q.4 a.1 q.2 ad 1.

2. Cf., for example, John Blund, *De Anima* 336–7, ed. D. A. Callus and R. W. Hunt (London, 1970) pp. 91–2.

3. Tocco in fact uses the phrase *studii contemplatio* (FVST p. 91, Ferrua p. 60).

4. Third sermon on Evangelists, printed in *Opera Omnia S. Antonii Paduani* (Paris, 1641) p. 432; Tugwell, *Early Dominicans* p. 146.

5. MOPH I p. 112. Cf. Langland's complaint that friars "go to scole / And lerne logyk and lawe and ek contemplacion, / And preche men of Plato, and preue it by Seneca . . . " (*Piers Plowman* B 20.273–5).

6. Prologue, cited in A. J. Minnis, *Medieval Theory of Authorship* (London, 1984) p. 129.

7. *Stimulus Amoris* 11.

8. The tradition essentially goes back to Aristotle, *Eth. Nic.* X 7, and was taken up later by the Platonists, e.g., Albinus, *Didask.* 2. For an interesting survey of its earlier antecedents, see L. B. Carter, *The Quiet Athenian* (Oxford, 1986).

9. E.g., Macrobius, *Comm. in Somn. Scip.* 1.8.8.

10. PL 76:953.

11. Vatican Library, MS Ottob. Lat. 1610 f.15^r–16^v.

12. *Sermones ad Diversos Status* (Hagenau, 1508) fol. a3.

13. Cf. William of Auxerre, *Summa Aurea* III 34.3, ed. cit. p. 653.

14. PL 76:953.

15. Gregory, PL 77:20; Humbert of Romans, ed. Berthier I p. 59; Thomas, III *Sent.* d.35 q.1 a.4 q.2 obi. 2.

16. At least since Justinian, *Novell.* 5.3, the solitary life had been identified as "contemplative," and the problem of justifying it against the charge of selfishness was a real one; cf., for instance, C. Phipps, "Romuald–Model Hermit," in W. J. Sheils, ed., *Monks, Hermits and the Ascetic Tradition* (Oxford, 1985) pp. 65–77. A similar concern seems to underly Guigo I's Carthusian customary 28:3–4 (SC 313 [Paris, 1984] p. 224). Guigo II seems much less sensitive on this point: cf. *Scala Claustralium* 15 (SC 163 [Paris, 1970] pp. 116–8).

17. Cf., for instance, the Marginal Gloss on Luke 10:42.

18. Cf. Gregory, PL 77:26D–27A, cited by Thomas in II.II q.182 a.1 ad 1.

19. The "mixed life" derives from the Stoic refusal to give priority to a purely "contemplative life"; they preferred a "rational life," in which activity and contemplation would both find their proper place (cf. Diogenes Laertius 7.130).

20. III *Sent*. d.35 q.1 a.1.

21. III *Sent*. d.35 q.1 a.4 q.2.

22. II.II q.182 a.2.

23. Cf. *De Perfectione* 7 (Leonine XLI p. B 72).

24. II.II q.182 a.2.

25. Commentary on John, Marietti ed. paras. 2487 and 2640. In *Summa* I q.20 a.4 ad 3 (in the context of a quite different discussion) Thomas refuses to choose between various views on the relative merits of John and Peter, symbolizing (according to Augustine) the contemplative and active lives.

26. II.II q.182 a.1.

27. III *Sent*. d.35 q.1 a.4 q.1 sed contra 2; *Summa* I q.20 a.4 ad 3, taken up in the commentary on John, ed. cit. para. 2640.

28. II.II q.47 a.2.

29. II.II q.181 a.2.

30. II.II q.181 a.3 obi.3 and ad 3.

31. II.II q.83 a.1.

32. II.II q.180 a.3 ad 4.

33. II.II q.83 a.13 ad 2 refer to "contemplation" in connection with praying as the ascent of the mind to God; but this ascent is interpreted strictly with reference to the "contact" needed if a petition is to be presented, ibid. a.1 ad 2.

34. III *Sent*. d.35 q.1 a.3 q.1 obi. 3 and ad 3.

35. II.II q.181 a.3; cf. already *De Veritate* q.11 a.4.

36. II.II q.179 a.1; the same text had already been used in III *Sent*. d.35 q.1 a.1.

37. II.II q.180 a.2 ad 1.

38. II.II q.188 a.8.

39. II.II q.188 a.6.

40. II.II q.182 a.4 ad 1 makes it clear that without the active life there is no fraternal charity at all, and II.II q.25 a.1 shows that fraternal charity is an integral part of charity, inseparable from love of God.

41. II.II q.182 a.4.

42. II.II q.171 prol.

43. For the first point, see II.II q.181 a.1 ad 3; for the second, *De Perfectione* 10 (Leonine XLI p. B 76:82–103).

44. Cf. A. Hayen, RTAM 9 (1937) pp. 219–36; A. Dondaine, *Bulletin Thomiste* 6 (1940–1942) pp. 100–2.

45. III *Sent*. d.35. Cf. Lombard, III *Sent*. d.35.1.5; William of Auxerre III 34, ed. cit. pp. 648–665.

46. III *Sent*. d.35 q.1 a.2 q.1 obi.3, not repudiated by Thomas in his response.

47. Ibid. q.1 a.2 q.1 (ed. Moos p. 1177).
48. II.II q.180 a.2 ad 3.
49. III *Sent.* d.35 q.1 a.2 q.2.
50. There is a very useful appendix on the evolution of Thomas' thought on the gifts in volume XXIV of the Blackfriars *Summa*, pp. 110–130.
51. I.II q.68 a.2.
52. II.II q.45 a.3, q.8 a.3.
53. III *Sent.* d.30 a.4 ad 2.
54. *Civ. Dei.* XIX ch. 1–11.

IV. RELIGIOUS LIFE

1. MOPH V p. 60.
2. *Summa Theol.* II.II q.186 a.8.
3. One wonders what Thomas would have made of the story of the young Franciscan who was asked whether he wanted to go to England; he replied that he did not know, and explained that the reason why he did not know was that "his will was not his own, but his minister's, and so he wanted whatever the minister wanted him to want" (Eccleston, *De Adventu Fratrum*, ed. A. G. Little (Paris, 1909), p. 6). He was so highly regarded by the Franciscans that he became guardian of Oxford while still a novice (ibid. p. 13). He also castrated himself to get rid of carnal temptations (ibid. p. 6).
4. *Summa Theol.* II.II q.104 a.1 ad 1.
5. Ibid. q.104 a.5.
6. Ibid. I.II q.13 a.1.
7. It is clear from what Humbert says, both in the encyclical cited above and in his commentary on the Constitutions (ed. Berthier II p. 53) that the vow of obedience was rarely invoked in the day-to-day business of the Order. The promise of obedience to the Master of the Order, which is the heart of the Dominican profession formula (*Primitive Constitutions* I 16), meant essentially that the Master (or the General Chapter) had the right to deploy all the manpower of the Order as he saw fit, and it was surely in assigning friars to particular places and allocating particular jobs to them that all Dominican superiors most obviously call upon them to fulfill their profession.
8. *Summa Theol.* II.II q.186 a.9. Cf. G. G. Meersseman, in *Ordo Fraternitatis* (Rome, 1977) pp. 1290–1314, on the Dominican "leges mere poenales."
9. It is clear from the 1220 Constitutions that, from the outset, novices are to be encouraged to be "always reading or thinking about some-

thing" (*Prim. Const.* I 13), and that some people have the specific role of being teachers (II 23) and that some people are formally deputed to be students (II 20, II 28–29). Jacques de Vitry, in about 1222, noted how the Dominicans in Bologna met every day for a class on the bible given by one of their number, and he implies that this was a function intended for the whole community (*Historia Occidentalis* 27, ed. J. F. Hinnebusch [Fribourg, 1972], p. 143). On Dominican study, see A. Duval, "L'Etude dans la Législation religieuse de St. Dominique," in *Mélanges M. D. Chenu* (Paris, 1967), pp. 221–247; Dieter Berg, *Armut und Wissenschaft* (Düsseldorf, 1977); P. Amargier, *Etudes sur l'Ordre Dominicain* (Marseilles, 1986), pp. 19–51. For a simple introduction, see J. A. Weisheipl, *The Place of Study in the Ideal of St. Dominic* (River Forest, 1960).

    10. *Prim. Const.* Prol.

    11. Cf. Tugwell, *Early Dominicans* p. 7 with note 42.

    12. *Prim. Const.* Prologue.

    13. The question of shoes is already a major bone of contention, apparently, in the 1240s (cf. the treatise edited in AFP 6 [1936] pp. 153–5; for the date, cf. Tugwell, *Early Dominicans* p. 44 note 88), and at the end of the century the debate is still going on merrily (cf. the treatise of Thomas Sutton edited in AFP 3 [1933] pp. 74–80).

    14. M. T. d'Alverny, in *St. Thomas Aquinas 1274–1974* II p. 179. The Spirituals' dislike of John XXII was caused by his line on poverty; the last straw, in their view, was when he formally declared in 1323 that Christ and the apostles did own possessions (cf. J. Moorman, *History of the Franciscan Order* [Oxford, 1968], pp. 313–317).

    15. How many Dominicans there were in Thomas' time who were attracted by poverty as such it is difficult to say. Jordan's friend Henry seems to have been primarily motivated to join the Order by a desire for poverty (Jordan, *Libellus* 72), and it was presumably their claim to a greater poverty that made the Franciscans an attractive proposition to Dominican novices, a threat that called forth Kilwardby's letter to the novices of the English province (Tugwell, *Early Dominicans* pp. 149–52), dating from about 1270.

    16. It is certainly shared by Kilwardby (see his letter cited in the previous note).

Thomas Aquinas

Inaugural Lecture (1256)

Watering the earth from his things above,
the earth will be filled from the fruit of
your works (Psalm 103:13).

The king of the heavens, the Lord, established this law from all eternity, that the gifts of his providence should reach what is lowest by way of things that are in between. Thus Dionysius, in the fifth chapter of the *Ecclesiastical Hierarchy*, says, "It is a most sacred law of the Godhead that the middle beings should be brought to the most divine light of himself by way of the first beings."[1]

This law is found to apply, not only to spiritual creatures, but also to bodily creatures. As Augustine says in the third book of the *De Trinitate*, "Just as coarser, weaker bodies are arranged so as to be governed by finer, more powerful bodies, similarly all bodies are governed by the breath of life."[2] This is why the Lord uses a metaphor taken from bodily things to express the law, stated in the psalm, which is observed in the communicating of spiritual wisdom: "Watering the mountains . . . " We see with our bodily senses that rain pours down from the things that are above in the clouds, and watered by the rain the mountains produce rivers, and by having its fill of these the earth becomes fertile. Similarly the minds of teachers, symbolized by the mountains, are watered by the things that are above in the wisdom of God, and by their ministry the light of divine wisdom flows down into the minds of students.

So there are four things we may look at in our text: the exalted nature of spiritual teaching, the high standing of those who teach it, the position of those who hear it and the manner of its communication.

The exalted nature of this teaching is indicated by the words, "From things above," on which the Gloss comments, "From the

---

1. PG 3:504C.
2. *De Trinitate* 3.4.9.

more exalted mysteries."³ And there are three ways in which sacred teaching is elevated:

(1) In its source, because this is the wisdom which is described as being "from above" (James 3:17). "The fount of wisdom is the word of God on high" (Ecclus. 1:5).

(2) In the subtlety of its content. "I dwelt in the highest place" (Ecclus. 24:7).⁴ There are some heights of divine wisdom which are reached by everyone, albeit incompletely, because the knowledge of the existence of God is naturally implanted in everyone, as Damascene says;⁵ it is with reference to this that it says in Job 36:25, "Everyone sees him." There are some things which are more exalted, and these are reached only by the minds of the wise, following the guidance of reason alone; of these it says, "What is known of God is manifest in them" (Romans 1:19). Then there are the highest things, which transcend all human reason, and with reference to them it says in Job 28:20–1, "Wisdom is hidden." And in Psalm 17:12, "He made darkness his hiding place." But holy teachers, instructed by the Holy Spirit who "examines even the deep things of God" (1 Cor. 2:10) passed these things on to us in the text of sacred scripture, and these are the highest things, in which this wisdom is said to dwell.

(3) In the sublimity of its goal, because the goal of this teaching is very exalted, namely eternal life. "These things have been written so that you may believe and have life in his name" (John 20:31). "Seek the things that are above" (Col. 3:1).

Because of the exalted nature of this teaching, high standing is also required in those who teach it, and this is why they are symbolized by mountains: "Watering the mountains. . . . " And there are three reasons for this:

(1) Mountains are high. They are raised above the earth and close to the sky. In the same way holy teachers ought to make light of the things of earth and yearn only for the things of heaven. "Our way of life is in heaven" (Phil. 3:20). Accordingly it says of the

---

3. Lombard's Gloss (PL 191:934B).

4. Thomas' text has the reading *altissimis*, which is a recognized variant for the Vulgate *altis*.

5. *De Fide Orthodoxa* 1.2, ed. Buytaert p. 12.

teachers' teacher, Christ, "He will be raised above the hills and the nations shall flow toward him" (Is. 2:2).

(2) They are radiant. The mountains are the first to catch the sun's rays, and holy teachers are likewise the first to receive radiance in their minds. Like mountains, teachers are the first to be enlightened by the rays of divine wisdom. "You shine wonderfully from the everlasting mountains" (Ps. 75:5), that is, from the teachers who share in eternity.[6] "Among them you shine" (Phil. 2:15).

(3) They are a defense, because mountains protect the land from its enemies. In the same way the church's teachers ought to protect the faith against error. "The children of Israel do not trust in lances and arrows, but the mountains defend them."[7] That is why some prophets are rebuked in Ezekiel 13:5, "You did not go up against them."

So all the teachers of sacred scripture ought to be "high" because of the high quality of their lives, so that they will be capable of preaching effectively. As Gregory says in the *Pastoral Rule*, "If your life is despised then unavoidably your preaching will also be despised."[8] "The words of the wise are like goads and like nails deeply fixed" (Eccles. 12:11). Hearts cannot be goaded on or fixed in the fear of God unless they are fixed in an elevated way of life.[9]

They need to be enlightened, so that they can suitably teach by lecturing. "To me, the least of all the saints, the grace has been given to enlighten everyone" (Eph. 3:8–9).

And they need to be well-armed[10] so that they can refute errors by arguing against them. "I will give you a wisdom they will not be able to resist" (Luke 21:15).

---

6. Thomas is following the Lombard's Gloss (PL 191:706CD), interpreting the "everlasting mountains" as referring to apostles, prophets and so on, who are called "eternal" because eternal life is promised through them.

7. Judith 7:8.

8. Actually *Hom. Ev.* 1.12.1 (PL 76:1119A).

9. I think this means that preachers cannot affect other people's hearts unless their own life is exalted.

10. *Muniti* (which I have translated "well-armed") picks up *montium munitionem* above, which I translated "they (mountains) are a defense." I could not think of any convincing way of retaining the verbal link in English.

These three functions, preaching, teaching and disputing,[11] are mentioned in Titus 1:9, "So that he will be capable of exhorting people" (this refers to preaching) "in sound teaching" (this refers to lecturing) "and of defeating those who contradict" (this refers to disputing).

Thirdly, the position of the hearers is symbolized in the metaphor of the earth, so it says, "The earth will be filled. . . . " The earth is lowest: "heaven above and earth below" (Prov. 25:3). Also it is stable and solid: "The earth stands firm forever" (Eccles. 1:4). And it is fertile: "Let the earth bring forth" (Gen. 1:11).

So the hearers of this teaching ought to be as low as the earth, in humility: "Where there is humility, there is wisdom" (Prov. 11:2). They must also be solid in right judgment: "Do not be like children in your minds" (1 Cor. 14:20). And they must be fertile, so that the words of wisdom which they receive will be fruitful in them: "The seed that fell on good ground . . . " (Luke 8:15).

So humility is needed in them with reference to their being students, listening to teaching: "If you bend your ear, you will receive teaching" (Ecclus. 6:34). Right judgment is needed, so that they can assess what they hear: "Does not the ear assess words?" (Job 12:11). And they need fertility, in the sense of that capacity to discover things, which enables a good student to explain a lot on the basis of a few things which he has heard. "Give a wise man the opportunity, and he will obtain more wisdom" (Prov. 9:9).[12]

Three aspects of the manner in which this teaching is acquired are alluded to in our text:
(1) The manner in which it is communicated, with reference both to the magnitude and to the quality of the gift received. The teachers' minds do not have the capacity to hold all that is contained in God's wisdom, and so it does not say, "Pouring things above onto the mountains" but "Watering them from things above."[13] "This is a partial statement" (Job 26:14). In the same

---

11. These are the three tasks of a Parisian Master: cf. Petrus Cantor, *Verbum Abbreviatum* 1 (PL 205:25A); Sorbonne statutes (*Chart.* I p. 507).

12. Thomas' follows the recognized variant in the Vulgate, *Da sapienti occasionem*.

13. *De Superioribus:* already the Latin *de* is moving toward the partitive use of *di, de* etc. in the modern Latin languages.

way the teachers do not pour out before their hearers all that they understand. "He heard secret words which it is not lawful to speak to anyone" (2 Cor. 12:4). So it does not say, "Passing on the fruit of the mountains to the earth," but "giving the earth its fill from the fruit." Gregory mentions this in book XVII of the *Moralia*, in his comment on Job 26:8: "The teacher ought not to preach all that he knows to simple people, because he himself cannot know all that there is in the mysteries of God."[14]

(2) The text alludes secondly to the manner in which this teaching is possessed. God possesses wisdom by nature, and this is why the "things above" are said to be "his," because they are natural to him. "With him is wisdom" (Job 12:13).[15] But teachers share abundantly in knowledge, and so they are said to be "watered from things above." "I will water the garden of plants" (Ecclus. 24:42). But students have an adequate share in knowledge, and this is symbolized by the earth being "filled." "I shall have my fill when your glory appears" (Ps. 16:15).

(3) Thirdly, with reference to the power to communicate, God communicates wisdom by his own power, and so he is said to water the mountains by himself. But teachers can only communicate wisdom in a ministerial role, and so the fruit of the mountains is not ascribed to them, but to the works of God: "From the fruit of your works," it says. "So what is Paul? . . . The ministers of him whom you have believed" (1 Cor. 3:4–5).

But "who is capable of this?" (2 Cor. 2:16). What God requires is ministers who are innocent ("The one who walks a spotless path is the one who has been my minister," Psalm 100:6), intelligent ("An intelligent minister is pleasing to his king," Prov. 14:35), fervent ("You make spirits your messengers and your ministers a burning fire," Psalm 103:4) and obedient ("His ministers who do his will," Psalm 102:21).

However, although no one is adequate for this ministry by himself and from his own resources, he can hope that God will

---

14. *Moralia* 17.26.38 (PL 76:28D).

15. The printed text has "knowledge" (*scientia*); but Thomas elsewhere comments on the text with the standard "wisdom" (*sapientia*) and I have taken the liberty of making the slight emendation necessary here to bring the quotation in line with the Vulgate.

make him adequate. "Not that we are capable of a single thought on our own resources, as if it came from us, but our adequacy is from God" (2 Cor. 3:5). So the teacher should ask God for it. "If people lack wisdom, they should beg for it from God and it will be given them" (James 1:5). May Christ grant this to us. Amen.[16]

---

16. The printed text has: *Oremus. Nobis concedat Christus. Amen.* As Osmund Lewry, O.P., suggested to me, this is a thoroughly unconvincing beginning for a prayer, and we do not expect a formal collect here anyway; so I have emended *oremus* to *quod.*

THOMAS AQUINAS

TEXTS ON PRAYER

Commentary on the Sentences
Book 4, distinction 15, question 4

There are seven questions to be asked about prayer:
(1) What is prayer?
(2) How should we pray?
(3) The kinds of prayer.
(4) What should be asked for in prayer?
(5) To whom can we pray?
(6) To whom is praying properly attributed?
(7) The effectiveness of prayer.

I. What is prayer?

(A) Prayer appears to be an act of the affective part of us:

(1) Augustine defines prayer as "a devout affection of the mind, turned toward God."[1]

(2) Hugh of St. Victor says that prayer is "a kind of devotion arising from compunction."[2] But devotion is a matter of affection, therefore prayer must be too.

(3) The only difference between giving an order and praying is that one involves our relationship to someone superior to us, whereas the other involves our relationship to someone inferior: we give orders to our inferiors, but we entreat our superiors. But the will gives orders to our other powers.

---

1. This "definition" of prayer is derived from the pseudo-Augustinian compilation *De Spiritu et Anima* 50 (PL 40:816), whose source here is Hugh of St. Victor, *De Virtute Orandi* 1 (PL 176:979AB), but Thomas is unlikely to be quoting it directly from *De Spiritu et Anima*. The exact form in which he cites it is already found in Peraldus, *Summa de Virtutibus* III 5.7.2, and in Albert, *De Bono* 3.2.6 (Col. XXVIII p. 147:35–6), III *Sent.* d.9 a.8 (B 28 p. 178). Albert had already realized that *De Spir. et Anim.* was not by Augustine, and it is unlikely that he was aware that this was the source of "Augustine's" definition of prayer (cf. Hiedl, art. cit. p. 116), which had evidently become part of the tradition independently of its source (cf. Petrus Cantor, *Verbum Abbreviatum* 124, PL 205:318B; Alan of Lille, *Expos. super Orationem Dominicam* 4; Alexander of Hales, IV *Sent.* d.31, ed. cit. pp. 494–5; William of Auvergne, *Rhetorica Divina* 1).

2. Paraphrased from *De Virtute Orandi* 1 (PL 176:979AB).

Therefore it is also to the will that it belongs to pray and to ask for things.[3]

(4) Outward prayer is an indication of the inner desire of someone praying. But what is revealed by outward prayer is inner prayer. So inner prayer is nothing other than inner desire, and as such it is a matter of our affections.

On the other hand:

(a) On Psalm 38:13, "God, hear my prayer," the Gloss comments that "prayer is when we display our wishes to God."[4] And displaying or demonstrating is an act of reason. Therefore prayer must be so too.

(b) According to Damascene "prayer is a petition made to God for things that are fitting."[5] And fittingness implies that one thing is adapted to another, and adapting is an act of reason, so prayer will also have to be an act of reason.

(B) Prayer appears to be the act of one of the gifts, not one of the virtues:

(1) According to Hugh of St. Victor prayer is part of contemplation.[6] But contemplation has to do with wisdom, since it is by wisdom that we attain the fulfilment of our higher reason which, as Augustine says, cleaves to the contemplation

---

3. The argument is clearly invalid and Thomas effectively explodes it in the course of his exposition. The fact that the will "gives orders" to our other powers (which Thomas accepts: cf. II *Sent.* d.25 q.1 a.2 ad 4, where he indicates that the will governs the other powers of the soul in the sense that it is the will's orientation toward our goal that governs the activity of our other powers, including the intellect) is adduced as proof that giving orders is an activity proper to the will, but of course it does not show that it is always and only the will that is responsible for giving orders, and it is this stronger claim that is needed if the argument is to demonstrate that it is the will's business both to pray and to command. Thomas, in the course of his discussion, seems to think it unnecessary to point out the fallacy in so many words, but his proof that giving orders is essentially an activity of reason makes it apparent.

4. Lombard's Gloss, PL 191:395D.

5. *De Fide Orthodoxa* 68.1, ed. Buytaert p. 267.

6. Humbert (ed. cit. I p. 155) similarly claims that Bernard says that "prayer is part of contemplation," but so far as I know neither Hugh nor Bernard says this. Thomas' response to this point shows that he has in mind some doctrine of reading, meditation and prayer as parts of contemplation, and just such a doctrine is found in William of Auxerre, *Summa Aurea* III 34.3, ed. cit. p. 653, ascribed to "the masters." It may derive from Hugh of St. Victor's rather different lining up of reading, meditation, prayer and contemplation in *Didasc.* 5.9 (PL 176:797A) and *Alleg. in Novum Test.* 3.3 (PL 175:805A), though Hugh maintains a clear distinction between prayer and contemplation.

of the things of eternity.[7] Therefore prayer is an act of the gift of wisdom.

(2) As Damascene says, "Prayer is an ascent of the intellect to God."[8] But ascending to God is proper to the gift of understanding; this is why the sixth beatitude, "Blessed are the pure in heart for they will see God," is allocated to the gift of understanding, as the Gloss makes clear.[9] So prayer is an act of the gift of understanding.

(3) Gregory says that "to pray is to utter noisy groans in a state of compunction."[10] But groaning is an act of the gift of knowledge because, according to the Gloss[11] and to Augustine,[12] the third beatitude, "Blessed are those who mourn," is attributed to the gift of knowledge. So prayer is the act of a gift.

On the other hand, prayer appears to be the act of one of the virtues:

(a) "Let him ask in faith, not doubting at all" (James 1:6). But faith is one of the virtues, so prayer (which is a form of asking) is an act of one of the virtues.

(b) Augustine says, "Faith believes, and hope and charity pray,"[13] and by praying they obtain what they pray for. But hope and charity are virtues, so prayer is the act of a virtue.

(C) Prayer appears not to be the kind of act which can be commanded:

(1) Nothing which comes from the will is produced by necessity.[14] And prayer is particularly a matter of the will, in that

---

7. Loosely derived from Augustine, *De Trinitate* XII 3.3 and 14.22 (cf. Thomas, *Summa Theol.* II.II q.45 a.3).

8. *De Fide Orthodoxa* 68.1, ed. cit. p. 267.

9. Marginal Gloss on the beatitudes as a whole, attached to Matt. 5:3.

10. *Moralia* XXXIII 23.43 (PL 76:701B).

11. Marginal Gloss on Matt. 5:3.

12. *De Doctrina Christiana* II 7.10 (PL 34:39); cf. *De Sermone Domini* I 4.11 (PL 34:1234), which is the classic text in which Augustine shows how the beatitudes can be distributed among the gifts of the Spirit.

13. *Enchiridion* 2.7 (PL 40:234).

14. The Latin *necessitas* is more comprehensive than the English "necessity," covering a variety of ways in which we may "have" to do something (physical constraint, constraint of circumstances or the call of duty); the argument rests on a naive opposition between wanting to do something and having to do it.

when we pray we ask for whatever we will. Therefore it is not a matter of necessity. So it is not something about which there can be a precept.

(2) Asking seems to be nothing other than revealing some desire of ours to somebody else. But it is superfluous to explain to someone something that he already knows. And the Christian religion contains no superfluous commandments, otherwise it would be a form of superstition.[15] So since all our desires are known to God, it does not seem that prayer can be the object of any commandment.

(3) God is most generous in giving his gifts. And it is more generous to give without being asked because, as Seneca says, "The highest price you can pay for something is the price of your prayers."[16] So God ought not to command prayers for anything he wants to give us. Nor ought he to command prayers for anything he does not want to give us, because we ought not to want anything that God does not want, else our wills will not be conformed to his will. And we ought not to ask for anything that we ought not to want. So there is no way in which prayer can be the object of a commandment.

On the other hand:

(a) On Luke 18:1, "One should pray always," Chrysostom comments, "In saying 'one should,' he is indicating that it is necessary."[17] But in this context "necessity" can only mean the kind of necessity which arises from there being a commandment. Therefore prayer is a matter of precept.

(b) Prayer is listed with fasting and almsgiving, and both of these are subject to commandments.[18] Therefore prayer is too.

---

15. To be superstitious is to sin by excess against the virtue of religion: cf. III *Sent.* d.9 q.1 a.1 q.3 ad 3, where Thomas quotes from Lombard's Gloss on Col. 2:23, defining superstition as "exaggerated religion" (PL 192:278C).

16. *De Beneficiis* II 1.4.

17. I do not know where this comes from.

18. Thomas' comments on IV *Sent.* d.15 are devoted to satisfaction (works of penance undertaken to compensate for one's sins) and the three practices generally regarded as the main works of penance: almsgiving, fasting and prayer. By the time he reaches prayer he has already shown that both almsgiving and fasting are liable to be imposed by precept.

REPLY

(A) In response to the first question we must say that, as Cassiodorus remarks, prayer (*oratio*) is so called as being "the mouth's reason (*oris ratio*)."[19] So by its very name it signifies the expression, by way of the mouth, of some act of the reason.

Even if we take "reason" only in the sense of "speculative reason,"[20] it has two kinds of activity: first, that of making connections and separations, and this activity is expressed orally by the sort of speech (*oratio*) described by the philosopher in the *Peri Hermeneias*. The second activity of reason is moving from one point to another in order to find something out, and in this connection a syllogism can be called a kind of speech (*oratio*).[21]

Because public addresses contain arguments which are meant to persuade people, they too are called "speeches" and those who make them are called "speakers" (*oratores*). And because these speeches, particularly those involved in the kind of case we call a lawsuit, have it as their objective to ask a judge for something—which is why lawyers call advocates' speeches "pleas"—the word *oratio* was taken over to refer also to petitions made to God, as to the judge who is concerned with our activities. It is in this sense that Damascene defines prayer as "a petition made to God for things that are fitting," and it is of *oratio* in this sense that we are speaking here.[22] Therefore the act of

---

19. *Expos. in Psalt.* 39.14, 85 tit. (PL 70:285C, 610C).

20. As distinct from "practical reason" ("speculative reason" being concerned to explore things with a view to understanding them, "practical reason" being concerned with working out how to get things done). In the *Summa Theol.* II.II q.83 a.1 Thomas cuts out this whole, fanciful attempt to derive *oratio* (prayer) from *oratio* (speech) via the activities of speculative reason by locating prayer immediately within the domain of practical reason.

21. Intellectual activity begins with a simple grasp of simple notions (the meaning of individual words); from this it proceeds to sort out ways in which these simple notions may or may not be connected, and on this basis it proceeds to its third activity, which is constructing arguments. The second of these operations was considered to be the subject of Aristotle's *Peri Hermeneias*: cf. Kilwardby, *De Ortu Scientiarum* 517, ed. cit. p. 177, and Thomas' own, much later, commentary on *Peri Hermeneias*, Prologue.

22. It is clear from this discussion that Thomas is not distinguishing between different senses of "prayer," but between different senses of *oratio* ("speech," "prayer"): *oratio* in the sense of prayer means petition. This point is at least obscured by K. D. O'Rourke's translation of the corresponding passage in *Summa Theol.* II.II q.83 a.1 (Blackfriars *Summa* vol. XXXIX p. 49). Thomas shows no interest in the tendency already apparent in some twelfth-century

prayer must be attributed to the same faculty as the act of petition.

Now the way in which human beings are moved differs in two respects from the way in which other animals are moved. First, the object of will or desire is fixed by nature in the case of other animals, but not in the case of human beings. Secondly, with respect to the pursuit of what is wanted or desired, other animals have certain fixed ways and means of fulfilling their desires, and so as soon as there is any movement of desire in them they immediately set their limbs in motion, unless there is something forcibly preventing them; human beings, by contrast, have no fixed ways and means. So in their case reason has a double role to play: it seeks out an appropriate and definite good which it is right to desire, and it fixes the means which are needed in pursuit of this good which is desired. So in our case there is an act of reason both preceding and following the act of the will: a preceding act, taking counsel to discover what it is right for the will to choose, and a subsequent act in the form of a command, instructing each of the means adopted as to what it is supposed to do. This last act of the reason is expressed in words by the imperative mood.

The means which are put to work by the command of reason for the pursuit or attainment of the desired object include not only the powers of the soul and the parts of the body, but also other people; as the philosopher says, "What is done by means of our friends is, in a way, done by ourselves."[23] But our friends, being outside ourselves, are not under our control in the same way as the parts of our own bodies are or the powers of our own souls. So when we use external means like this to achieve our desires, it is sometimes called "giving orders" or "commanding," when the people concerned are subject to our control, and it is sometimes called "asking," when the people concerned are not under our control as our subjects. Sometimes it is even called "entreaty," if the people concerned are superior to us. And "asking" and "entreaty" are as much acts of the rea-

---

writers, such as William of St. Thierry, to separate prayer from petition and make it mean something else (cf. Tugwell, *Ways of Imperfection* pp. 116–7).

23. Aristotle, *Eth. Nic.* III 3.13 (1112b27–8).

son as "giving orders" is. And this is clear from the philosopher's saying that "reason entreats us toward what is best."[24]

It follows, then, that prayer is an act of the reason, bringing the will's desire into relationship with him who is our superior, not subject to our control, namely God. So Damascene's definition, "Prayer is a petition made to God for things that are fitting," displays the essential nature of prayer with the utmost accuracy.

In reply to the points raised above:

(1) There are two different senses in which our affections can be turned toward God. They may be turned toward him in the sense that he is their object, and in this sense turning our affections toward God means loving him. That is not what Augustine is talking about here.

In another sense our affections may be directed toward God as to the one by whom our inner desire is to be fulfilled. And this turning of our affections toward God is brought about by our reason involving God in the pursuit of what our affections desire, in the way we have been explaining. And this kind of turning of our affections toward God is prayer. So the definition proposed here is a material definition:[25] the actual turning toward God is indicated by specifying what it is that is turned to him, just as sometimes we use the word "faith" to mean the things that are believed. There is a similar use of language in the Gloss on 1 Thessalonians 5:17, where it says that "desire for good is

---

24. Ibid. I 13.15 (1102b16). *Deprecatur* is a misleading translation of παρακαλεῖ ("urges").

25. A material definition is one that, by comparison with some other possible definition, fails to encapsulate the full nature of something because it omits all reference to the kind of cause which determines most effectively what something is—e.g., a purely biological account of anger (by contrast with one that specifies what kind of emotion it is) or an account of a house in terms of material, shape, architect and so on, which omits to point out what such a structure is for (cf. IV *Sent.* d.3 a.1 q.1). So the "Augustinian" definition of prayer fails to specify what actually makes the turning of our affections toward God into *prayer* (i.e., the intention to obtain from God the fulfilment of some desire). William of Auvergne, *Rhetorica Divina* 1, similarly comments that the "Augustinian" formula is a "commendation" of prayer rather than a definition.

prayer."[26] in as much as the desire is the thing for whose fulfilment we are praying.

(2) In the case of external petitions, something can be a petition in two ways. It may be a real petition, as when we say, "Give me that." Or it may be something which has an equivalent meaning, as when someone stretches out his hand or explains his needs. Similarly interior prayer made to God is really an act of reason importuning God in a kind of way, as we have said. But reflecting on one's needs and raising one's hope to God, or mentioning something that one desires or even a humbling of one's spirit before God are equivalent in some ways to praying, and it is in this sense that devotion too can be called "prayer," as it is by Hugh of St. Victor.

(3) In asking, commanding or entreating, we call upon something to help us attain our objective or to further some purpose of ours. But it is not the will that does this, since the will, as such, goes straight to its object, which is its goal; it is rather the work of reason, whose business it is to set things in order so that one thing leads to another. So, strictly speaking, issuing commands is not the business of the will.

But there are two senses in which the will is said to issue commands. First, by doing something which can be taken as equivalent to a command. Giving a command initiates some movement, and so any act of the soul which results immediately in any movement can be called "commanding"; and so, since any full-fledged act of appetition results immediately in some movement of our bodily organs, our appetitive powers can be said to be "commanding" such a movement.

Secondly, the will is said to "command" in that commands originate in the will. Calling on someone to help us pursue our goal (which is where commanding comes in) presupposes that we have an appetite for our goal and it is a way of pursuing that goal. For this reason the operational powers or skills and the habits we have which are immediately related to our goal are said to "command" those which are related to the means by which we pursue our goal. And in this

---

26. Lombard's Gloss (PL 192:309A) (from Augustine, *In Ps.* 37:14, PL 36:404).

sense the will, whose object is our goal itself, is said to "command," inasmuch as commanding, which is an act of reason, originates in the will, where our desire for our goal is located.

(4) There are two ways in which a word spoken outwardly can be a sign of something. First, it is an immediate sign of whatever it was primarily established to mean. For example the word "fire" signifies one of the elements. But in another sense a word can signify something indirectly, when the reality to which it primarily refers is itself taken as signifying something else. For example, "fire" signifies charity, because the thing called "fire" is suitable as a symbol of charity, owing to certain points of resemblance.

So exterior, vocal prayer signifies immediately the act of reason of the person praying, if the external prayer too is expressed in the form of a prayer, as in Wisdom 9:4, "Give me wisdom, which sits by your throne." But indirectly it signifies and expresses the desire itself, which underlies it, as we can see from what has been said. And it is in this sense that the definition of prayer given above has to be understood, "Prayer is when we display our wishes to God."

(B) In response to the second question, we must say that prayer is an act of some kind. Now an act is said to be the act of one of the virtues if its definition includes something which belongs to the order of virtue, even if it does not contain everything that is needed for a virtue. So such an act has to be regarded as an act of the virtue to which the factor belongs which entitles it to be classed as a virtue.

Prayer belongs to the general category of acts of petition, and this does not give it any claim to the title of "virtue." Taken by itself like this, unadorned with any feature making it good or bad, it indicates only the act of one of our powers. But Damascene, in the text cited above, adds two specifications which are relevant to the idea of virtue: prayer is a petition made *to God* for things *that are fitting;* that is, it means asking the right person for the right things.

The second of these features does not sufficiently define prayer, because we might be asking some human being for "things that are fitting," and this is not called "prayer." Nor is this feature essential to prayer, because even someone who asks God for things that are not fitting is praying, albeit carnally. So this feature concerns rather the well-being of prayer than the definition of its specific nature.

The only alternative, then, is that it is the specification that it is a petition "made to God" that identifies prayer and draws it into the domain of virtue. And since a petition or entreaty made to a superior carries with it a certain reverence, by means of which it strives to obtain its objective, it follows that the efficacy of prayer in obtaining what is being prayed for derives from its display of reverence toward God.[27] And showing reverence to God is an act of worship, so therefore prayer must be an act produced directly by worship.[28] It is no obstacle to this conclusion that worship is located in the will,[29] not the reason, while prayer is an act of the reason; worship is part of justice and justice uses the acts of all our powers as its material, to pay what is owing to everyone by means of them. Thus justice restrains our capacity for concupiscence to prevent adultery, and it restrains our capacity for anger to prevent murder, and it similarly uses the act of reason in order thereby to show reverence to God.

Since worship is a virtue, not a gift, as we have seen,[30] it follows that prayer must be an act of virtue, not the act of a gift.

In reply to the points raised above:
(1) "Contemplation" is sometimes taken in a strict sense to mean the act of the intellect thinking about the things of God, and in this sense contemplation is an act of wisdom. But in another sense it is taken more generally to mean any act in

---

27. William of Auvergne, *Rhetorica Divina* 1, similarly identifies petition plus reverence as the best way of defining prayer.

28. Prayer is *elicitive* an act of worship. An act is "elicited" from the virtue that is its immediate source and that specifies its immediate objective; it is "commanded" in some cases by another virtue, which subordinates the immediate objective of the act in question to a further objective (cf. IV *Sent.* d.15 q.1 a.1 q.2 ad 1). On this view the immediate purpose of prayer is to offer worship to God, a doctrine that raises questions not tackled by Thomas here, though he offers an incisive answer in *Summa Theol.* II.II q.83 a.3.

29. Cf. Philip the Chancellor's definition of *latria* as "the will to give to God the cult which is due to him" in *Summa de Bono*, ed. cit. p. 963:85–6.

30. The reference is probably to III *Sent.* d.9 q.1 a.1.

which people separate themselves from worldly affairs to attend to God alone, and this occurs in two ways: either inasmuch as people listen to God speaking in the scripture, and this happens in their reading, or inasmuch as they speak to God, and this happens in their prayers.[31] Meditation is related to both reading and prayer as a kind of intermediary between them: as a result of God speaking to us in the scriptures we become present to him in our minds and in our affections through meditation, and once we are made present to him like this, or once we have him present to us, we can speak to him in prayer. Hugh of St. Victor accordingly postulates three parts of contemplation: first reading, then meditation and thirdly prayer.[32] But this does not have to mean that prayer is an act produced immediately by wisdom, even though wisdom prepares the way for prayer by means of meditation.[33]

(2) There are two senses in which the intellect can be said to ascend to God. It can ascend to him in the sense that it ascends to the knowledge of him, and this belongs to the gift of understanding. But this is not what Damascene is talking about here. Or we can ascend to God in the sense that he is the one to whom we are looking for help. As it says in Psalm 122:1, "I have lifted up my eyes to you who dwell in the heavens." And prayer is this kind of ascent. So it does not follow that prayer is an act of the gift of understanding, though it may presuppose such an act, as the second kind of ascent presupposes the first.

(3) Groaning and weeping are not prayer as such, but they are a kind of foundation for prayer. Asking for something is ob-

---

31. This echoes the classic formula, "When you read God is speaking to you, when you pray you are speaking to God"; cf. Tugwell, *Ways of Imperfection* p. 103.

32. Cf. above note 6.

33. Prayer is not an act "elicited" from wisdom; that is, whatever role wisdom may play in the broader context within which we pray, wisdom does not determine the immediate objective of prayer (which is to offer worship to God). It is interesting that Thomas does not make his point in the obvious way, which would have been to say that wisdom might "command" prayer, even though prayer is not "elicited" from wisdom; the implication of this would be to subordinate prayer ultimately to wisdom's objective of contemplation (a subordination achieved, with lasting results, by Guigo II; cf. Tugwell, *Ways of Imperfection* p. 115). Presumably Thomas is happy with the idea that meditation leads to prayer, but does not want to suggest that prayer itself is rigorously directed toward the single goal of contemplation.

viously superfluous where there is nothing you need. So the recognition of one's own wretchedness, in which one sees one's need and one's inability to help oneself, which makes one groan in one's feelings, is reckoned by God as a sort of prayer. For this reason Augustine says that "the business of prayer is conducted more in groans than in words, more in weeping than in speaking."[34]

(a,b) In response to the points raised on the other side we must say that faith, hope and charity are prerequisites for worship, as has already been pointed out;[35] so in this way the act of prayer too is attributed to them. And in addition to this, they have a certain relevance specifically to prayer in its own right and they are necessary preconditions for it, because it is futile to address a petition to someone if you do not believe that he can give you what you want and hope that he is willing to give it to you. And it is presumptuous to ask someone for something unless he is in some way united to you, and such union is brought about by charity.

(C) In response to the third question, we must say that prayer is a matter of precept both in a particular way and in general.

In a particular way those who are officially appointed to be mediators between God and the people, such as the ministers of the church, are obliged by precept to say certain prayers. So it is incumbent on them ex officio to offer prayers to God in the name of the whole church, and for this reason they are bound by the church's law to recite the canonical hours.

In a general way everyone is obliged to pray by virtue of the fact that we are all obliged to procure spiritual benefits for ourselves, and they are given to us by God alone. Therefore there is no other way in which they can be procured except by asking for them from him. Also the fact that we are bound by the commandment of charity to love our neighbor as ourselves means that we are bound to help other people in their need, not only by giving material alms, but also by giving spiritual alms, and one such alms is prayer, as was said above.[36]

---

34. *Ep.* 130.10.20 (PL 33:502).
35. III *Sent.* d.9 q.1 a.1 q.3 ad 1.
36. IV *Sent.* d.15 q.2 a.1 q.2 ad 4.

Furthermore the church appears to have fixed a definite time of prayer for everyone, not just for people who exercise an official ministry in the church, since everyone is obliged by canon law to attend the liturgy on feast days, to align his own intention with the ministers who pray for the people.[37]

In reply to the points raised above:

(1) The fact that something comes from the will is incompatible with absolute necessity and also with the kind of necessity caused by coercion; but it does not exclude the kind of constraint that results from having some particular objective.[38] Love is supremely an instance of something coming from the will, yet it is necessary for anyone who wishes to reach the goal of salvation. And it is in this way that prayer is necessary and a matter of commandment, with respect to those things which we are bound (in the way stated above) to want.

(2) We are commanded to reveal our desires to God not in order to teach him what it is that we desire, but to make us direct our feelings and our intellect toward him.

(3) God accepts our prayers both with regard to what he does want to give us and, sometimes, with regard to what he does not want to give us. In the first case it is so that we will be in a fit state to receive his gift, which we should not be if we were not hoping to obtain from him what we desire. And we should not consider it offensive to subject ourselves to God in prayer, as it is to subject ourselves to another human being, because our whole good consists in our being subject to God, but it does not consist in our being subject to any human being.

With respect to things that God does not want to give us, he accepts our prayers because he wants us to want, devoutly, what he legitimately does not want, as was pointed out at the end of the first book.[39]

---

37. Cf. Gratian, *Decretum* Cons. d.3 c.1–2 (Friedberg I 1353).

38. There are three different kinds of *necessitas:* "absolute necessity" (e.g., the constraints imposed on an animal by its biological constitution), "coercion" (e.g., brainwashing) and "conditional necessity" (if you want to fly to New York, you have to board an airplane that is going in the right direction; but you do not have to want to fly to New York).

39. I *Sent.* d.48 q.1 a.4, where Thomas points out the various levels of will in a human

II. How should we pray?

(A) It would seem that prayer ought to be just mental, and not vocal:

(1) Prayer is meant to be secret and made to God alone, because it is "a petition made to God for things that are fitting." This is why it says in Matthew 6:6, "When you pray, go into your chamber." But vocal prayer is not secret and gives the impression of not being directed to God alone, since he attends to the heart, not to spoken words. So prayer ought not to be spoken aloud.

(2) Prayer is part of contemplation, and contemplation does not reside in any external act, but only in an inward activity. So prayer ought not to be performed with any external sound.

(3) By prayer the intellect is meant to ascend to God, as Damascene says, and the affections are meant to be directed toward him, as Augustine says. But if the soul is occupied in bodily acts, this hinders the ascent of the   ind and of the affections to the things of God, because the soul cannot be engaged with any intensity in several different things at the same time.[1]

On the other hand:

(a) In Psalm 141:2 it says, "With my voice I cried to the Lord."

(b) Prayer is an act of worship, as we have already said, and acts of worship do not consist solely of interior acts, but also of external acts. So prayer ought not to be made only in the heart, but also in the voice.

(B) It appears that prayer ought not to go on for a long time:

---

being. There is first of all bodily appetite, which quite properly desires health, food and so on. Then there is our natural will for such human goods as knowledge and companionship. Finally there is our deliberate will, which sometimes cuts across the desires of the other levels of will: we may find ourselves wanting to undergo a painful operation for the sake of our health, and we may find ourselves sacrificing real human goods for the sake of the service of God. Being conformed to God's will means that our deliberate will has to accept whatever is known to be God's will (and if we are sick, for instance, it is clearly, in one sense, God's will that we should be sick), but this does not negate the propriety of our at the same time willing our own appropriate natural good (e.g., health). Thus even if in fact God does not will to give us something, it may be eminently right and proper to desire it and pray for it, even while we assent to whatever God may want to give or to withhold.

1. Cf. above, note 65 on Albert, *MT* 1.

(1) "When you pray, do not talk a lot" (Matt. 6:7). But if you pray for a long time vocally, you will talk a lot. So at least vocal prayer ought not to be prolonged.

(2) We ought not to go beyond the limits of God's commandment, and the Lord commands us to pray like this, "Our Father, etc." So it looks as if we ought not to add any other prayers.

(3) Prayer is meant to be made to God with confidence. "Let him ask in faith, not doubting at all" (James 1:6). But when we address petitions to other people, it is a sign that we lack confidence if we spin them out at great length; so the reason for prolonging our words is to win over the mind of the person to whom our petition is addressed. So when we are praying to God, we ought not to prolong our prayer.

On the other hand:

(a) "A widow who is truly on her own should devote herself to prayers by day and by night" (1 Tim. 5:5). So prayer ought to be prolonged.

(b) "All the actions of Christ are meant to instruct us."[2] And Christ, as we read in Luke 22:43, "prayed all the longer."

(C) It seems that people ought never to stop praying:

(1) "He told them a parable, that they ought to pray always and not give up" (Luke 18:1).

(2) "Pray without ceasing" (1 Thess. 5:17).

(3) Prayer is a kind of declaration of one's desire to him through whom one looks for its fulfilment. But we are supposed always to desire the things for which we are meant to pray, that is, spiritual benefits. So prayer ought to be going on the whole time.

On the other hand:

(a) When people are praying they cannot give their time to works of mercy, and sometimes we are obliged to give our time to such works. So people ought not to pray the whole time.

(b) According to Hugh of St. Victor prayer is part of contemplation, and people ought not to devote their whole time to

---

2. Cf. Lombard's Gloss on Heb. 5:7 (PL 192:437C).

contemplation, but sometimes they have to come out of themselves and do something. So they ought not to pray the whole time.

(D) Actual attentiveness would seem to be essential in prayer:
    (1) As Gregory says, God does not hear a prayer to which the person praying it is not paying any attention.[3] But the point of praying is that our prayer should be heard by God, so prayer is a waste of time if we are inattentive.
    (2) Hugh of St. Victor says, "If we are turning over something else in our mind while we pray, even if it is something good, we are not without fault."[4]
    (3) "Prayer," according to Damascene, "is an ascent of the intellect to God." But if attentiveness is lacking, our intellect does not ascend to God and in that case there is no real prayer.
    (4) Every virtuous work has to emanate from a deliberate choice. And prayer is a virtuous work. Therefore it has to be attentive, because otherwise there would be no deliberate choice.[5]

    On the other hand:
    (a) Nobody is obliged to do the impossible, and it is impossible to hold one's mind attentive to anything for long, without its being suddenly distracted by something else. Therefore it is not essential to prayer that it should be accompanied the whole time by attentiveness.
    (b) In other meritorious works it is not necessary that we should actually be paying attention to what we are doing the whole time; for instance, a pilgrim does not have to think about his pilgrimage the whole time. So it seems that it is not necessary in the case of prayer either.

(E) It looks as if attentiveness is damaging to prayer:
    (1) As Hugh of St. Victor says, "Pure prayer is when the mind

---

    3. This text occurs in Hugh of St. Victor, *Expos. Reg. Aug.* 3 (PL 176:892B), but has not been found in Gregory.
    4. The source of this quotation is unknown.
    5. Virtuous acts must be deliberate acts (cf. Aristotle, *Eth. Nic.* II 5.4, 1106a3–4), and that implies that we must be paying attention to what we are doing.

is so enflamed with overwhelming devotion that when it turns to God to ask for something it actually forgets its own petition."[6] But if you forget your own petition you are clearly not paying attention to your own prayer. So since it is particularly desirable that prayer should be pure, it looks as if prayer is hindered by attentiveness.

(2) If it is our intention which determines the direction of our prayer, the same is true of all our other outward activities. And in our other outward activities it is extremely unhelpful if we are continually conscious of our intention. As Avicenna says, that way an excellent musician would perform abominably.[7] So attentiveness is harmful to our prayer if it is present the whole time.

(3) The human mind cannot attend to several things at once. And sometimes we ought to pay attention to our objective while we pray or to thinking about the God to whom we are praying; it would spoil our prayer if we did not do this. So it is harmful to us in our prayer if we always pay attention to the prayers we are saying.

On the other hand:

(a) Augustine says, "When you pray to God with psalms and hymns, your heart should be occupied with what your mouth is uttering."[8]

(b) "God is spirit, and those who worship him should worship in spirit and in truth" (John 4:24). So prayer is not damaged by the kind of attentiveness which makes us pray in spirit.[9]

REPLY

(A) In response to the first question we must say that there are two kinds of prayer: private prayer, which individuals make on their

---

6. *De Virtute Orandi* 2 (PL 176:980A).

7. *Sufficientia* 1.14 J (Venice, 1508, repr. Frankfurt, 1961), f.22rb.

8. *Rule of St. Augustine* 2.3 (ed. in L. Verheijen, *La Règle de St. Augustin* [Paris, 1967], I p. 421, and in G. Lawless, *Augustine of Hippo and his Monastic Rule* [Oxford, 1987] p. 84).

9. The move in Latin from *adorare* (worship) to *orare* (pray) is easy; exactly the same use of this text is found in Peraldus (cf. Tugwell, *Early Dominicans* p. 167). The Marginal Gloss on John 4:24 identifies "spirit" as "the innermost temple of the heart," and says that it is in this temple that "prayer is to be made to God."

own behalf, and public prayer, which it is the duty of the ministers of the church to offer, as has been said above. And since public prayer is not offered by the minister simply for himself, but for others, it ought not to be purely mental, it ought to be vocal too, so that other people also will be stirred to devotion by the prayers which are uttered aloud and the minister's purpose will be extended to the rest as they join him in praying. This was also the reason why singing was introduced in the church. Augustine tells us how he wept profusely at the hymns and songs of the church in her sweet singing, and that the sound of them flowed into his ears and truth dripped gently into his heart.[10]

But private prayer is offered by individuals for themselves, and this can be done either aloud or silently depending on what is most helpful to the mind of the person praying.

There are, however, four reasons for adding spoken utterance to one's prayer.[11] First, it is a way in which we can stir ourselves with our words to pray with devotion. Secondly, praying aloud can keep our attention[12] from wandering, because we can concentrate better if we support our feelings[13] with words when we pray. Thirdly, the intensity of our devotion when we pray may result in our starting to pray aloud,[14] because when our higher powers are strongly moved, the effect spills over into our lower powers; so when our mind is kindled by devotion as we pray, we break out spontaneously into weeping and sighing and cries of jubilation and other such noises. Fourthly, we pray aloud to pay a debt of justice, because we

---

10. *Confessions* IX 6.14.

11. Literally "adding the voice to prayer": St. Thomas takes it for granted that all prayer is "mental prayer," in that if there is no act of the mind involved there will be no prayer; so vocal prayer is a matter of "adding the voice."

12. In this passage Thomas makes frequent and rather confusing use of the word *intentio*, which I have had to translate into several different words in English. Here it is more or less equivalent to "attention."

13. *Affectus*, meaning any kind of emotional engagement in our prayer, including (as we have already seen) our desire for what we are praying for and our hope that God will give it to us; it covers more possibilities than are usually envisaged in modern discussions of "feelings in prayer."

14. This classic notion that strong emotion makes prayer noisy (cf. Cassian, *Conf.* 9.27) was vividly exemplified in St. Dominic, who was famous for his noisy praying (cf. Jordan of Saxony, *Libellus* 13).

have to serve the God to whom we offer reverence in prayer not only with our minds, but also with our bodies.

In reply to the points raised above:

(1) As Gregory says, "A good work ought to be performed in public," to edify others, that is, "in such a way that your inner purpose[15] remains secret."[16] So when you are praying in public, if you are seeking only God's glory, not external glory from other people, then your inner purpose remains secret and you are praying to God alone in your inner purpose, even if your neighbor can hear your prayer and be edified by it.

(2) All activities whose immediate object is God himself belong to the contemplative life and are parts of contemplation, taking "contemplation" in its broad sense, and this is true of external activities too, though they are not parts of contemplation if we take "contemplation" in the strict sense of meditating on wisdom. In the same way reading which is directly geared to meditation on the things of God is also taken to be a part of contemplation, and reading is sometimes done aloud.

(3) When two faculties are engaged in the same pursuit they do not hinder each other's functioning, they help each other; for instance, the senses help the imagination[17] when they are directed toward the same object. So when we express our meaning aloud, it does not interfere with the ascent of the intellect to God, unless we take too much trouble over the actual formulation of what we want to say, as some people do who strive to use elaborately structured language in their prayer.[18]

(B) In response to the second question we must say that what is most important in prayer is the devotion of the person praying. So prayer should be extended for as long as the devotion of the

---

15. *Intentio* again.

16. *Hom. Ev.* 11.1 (PL 76:1115B).

17. "Imagination" in the scholastic sense, on which cf. above, note 21 on Albert, *MT* 5.

18. "Elaborately structured language": *verba composita*, the phrase used by Gregory in the passage from which another part was cited above in a.1 B obi. 3.

person praying can be maintained. Therefore if devotion can be maintained for a long time, prayer ought to be prolonged and lengthy, but if prolonging it engenders boredom or distaste then prayer should not be continued any longer. This is why Augustine says, "The brethren in Egypt are said to use frequent prayers, but these are very brief, shot out as it were in a moment.[19] This is to make sure that their intentness,[20] which is so necessary in prayer and which they have vigilantly aroused, does not fade away and become dulled through prolonging their prayers. This same principle of theirs, which shows that intentness should not be allowed to become dulled when it cannot be maintained, also shows that when it does persist it should not be broken off."[21]

In reply to the points raised above:
(1) According to Augustine, "Talking a lot should be banished from prayer, but not praying a lot, provided that a fervent intention continues. 'Talking a lot' in prayer means using an unnecessary number of words to do what has to be done, but praying a lot means importuning him to whom we are praying with a prolonged, devout activity of the heart."[22]
(2) As Augustine says, "We are free to use all kinds of other words" (other than those in the Lord's Prayer, that is) "to express the same things in our prayer; but we should not feel free to change the content of the prayer substantially."[23] So the Lord's precept does not oblige us to use precisely those words, but only to ask for precisely those things from God. As Augustine also says, "Whatever other words we say, whether they are shaped by feelings already present, with a view to their expression, or studied by feelings which come afterward in order to intensify them, if we are praying rightly and properly we shall be saying nothing other than what is contained in the Lord's prayer."[24]

---

19. *Raptim quodammodo iaculatas:* hence the phrase "ejaculatory prayer."
20. *Intentio* again.
21. *Ep.* 130.10.20 (PL 33:501–2).
22. Ibid. (PL 33:502).
23. Ibid. 12.22 (PL 33:503).
24. Ibid. 12.22 (PL 33:502). This rather obscure sentence, which different translators of Augustine interpret in widely divergent ways, seems to be referring to two distinct situ-

(3) We make petitions to other people in order to inform them of what we want and to win their favor with our words. But we make our prayers to God in order to exercise our own desire. And so it is useful to pray for a long time if prolonging the exercise increases our desire.

(C) In response to the third question, we must say that there are two ways in which an act can be said to endure: in itself, or in its momentum or effects. If you throw a stone, your movement lasts, in itself, only as long as you are actually moving the stone with your hand, but the momentum of your act lasts as long as the stone continues moving as a result of the impetus you gave it at the outset. In the same way prayer can be considered as lasting in two ways. It can be said to last in the sense that you actually go on praying, and in this sense people cannot pray continuously or the whole time, because they sometimes have to be engaged in other activities as well. But prayer can be said to last virtually in another sense. The starting point of prayer is desire for eternal life, and this persists in all the other works we do in due order, because all of them should be ordered toward obtaining eternal life, and so the desire for eternal life persists virtually in all the good deeds we do. This is why it says in the Gloss on 1 Thessalonians 5:17, "Anyone who never stops acting well never stops praying."[25]

But the momentum imparted by an initial movement gets continually weaker, so that the stone sometimes comes to rest or starts to move in the opposite direction to that in which it was thrown, unless its movement is given a boost. In the same way, as Augustine says, "Our desire grows tepid because of the cares of life, and so we call our minds back to the business of praying at certain times to make sure that desire does not freeze up entirely, once it has begun to grow cool."[26]

In reply to the points raised above:

(1) When the Lord said that we should pray always, he did not

---

ations: we may start with a feeling and try to find words in which to express it so that the feeling itself will become more apparent, or we may start with some words and, by paying careful attention to them, an appropriate feeling may be fostered.

25. Lombard's Gloss (PL 192:309A).
26. *Ep.* 130.9.18 (PL 33:501).

mean that the act of prayer should never be broken off, but that it should not be broken off as if never to be resumed, which is what people do who give up praying if their prayers are not heard at once. It is by going on praying for a long time that we obtain what we are asking for, as the Lord shows by his parable.[27]

(2) As Augustine says, "Praying without ceasing is nothing but ceaselessly desiring the life of blessedness."[28]

Alternatively we can say that the apostle here means praying without ceasing in the sense of not abandoning the practice of praying at the appointed times, or in the sense that we make the prayers of the poor our own by the help we give them, even when we ourselves stop praying; this is how one of the saints expounds the matter in the *Lives of the Fathers*.[29]

(3) The answer to the third point is clear from what has already been said.

(D) In response to the fourth question, we must say that there is one sense in which actual attentiveness is required for prayer, in order to avoid sin in the case of prescribed prayers and to acquire merit in the case of voluntary prayers, but it is not required in every sense. As we have said, sometimes an act lasts in the sense that the act itself continues as well as its effect, but sometimes the act itself comes to an end but its effect continues; we saw an example of this in the case of a stone being thrown. So continuing in effect is something between a habit and an act: to have a habit is not the same thing as actually doing something, either in the sense that you are doing something now or in the sense that the effect of something you did is still continuing.[30]

Along these lines, then, I say that attentiveness must per-

---

27. Exegetically Thomas is surely correct: praying and not giving up means praying (intermittently) over a long time, not literally praying without ever taking a break; but he is reinterpreting *diuturnitas* and thereby actually changing the terms of the discussion.

28. *Ep.* 130.9.18 (PL 33:501).

29. *Vitae Patrum* III 212, V 12.9 (PL 73:807C, 942C).

30. If I possess the appropriate habit, that means that I *can* play the trumpet when I want to; but this is different from actually playing the trumpet and it is also different from the echoes that linger on when I have finished playing or the recording that preserves my performance for posterity.

sist the whole time that we are praying, in the sense that its effect must continue, but not in the sense that actual attentiveness is required the whole time. And its effect persists if you come to prayer with the intention of obtaining something from God or of rendering him due service, even if in the course of your prayer your mind is distracted by other things, unless the distraction is such that the momentum of your original intention disappears entirely. So it is necessary that we should frequently call our hearts back to us.

In reply to the points raised above:

(1) Gregory must be understood to be referring to prayer without any kind of attentiveness at all.

(2) Hugh is to be understood as referring to people deliberately turning their minds to other things while praying, because then they are not without fault, particularly if they wantonly engage themselves in something which will distract the mind, such as some kind of external work.[31] And if the mind wanders off into something opposed to prayer, that will actually be mortal sin. But if our minds wander off to other things without our noticing, then there is either no fault or only a very slight fault, unless we have to say that there was some fault involved in the things we were thinking about before praying, which prompted the distraction.

(3) The intellect ascends to God when it directs its prayer toward him, and the effect of this ascent lasts throughout the whole prayer.

(4) When we are performing virtuous works, we do not have to be actually choosing to do them the whole time. When you give alms, for instance, you do not have to be thinking about almsgiving the whole time; it suffices that you thought about it once, when you decided to give alms, unless a subsequent thought breaks off your previous intention.

(E) In response to the fifth question, we must say that there can be three kinds of attentiveness in prayer: attentiveness to the words we are using in making our petition, attentiveness to the petition

---

31. If I start doing the washing-up while saying my prayers, for instance, I am courting distraction.

itself, and attentiveness to the context of our petition, such as the need which prompts it, the God to whom we are addressing it, and so on. If any of these kinds of attentiveness is present, our prayer should not be considered inattentive. This means that even people who do not understand the words of their petition can be attentive to their prayer. But it is the last kind of attentiveness which is most commendable, and the second kind is more commendable than the first. And since our soul cannot be strongly attentive to several things at once, the first kind of attentiveness can be damaging and lessen the fruitfulness of our prayer, if it eliminates the second kind, and the second kind of attentiveness can be damaging if it entirely destroys the third. But the converse is not true. Nevertheless attentiveness, taking it quite generally, far from being damaging, is a great help to our prayer, as the quotation from Augustine shows.

In reply to the points raised above:

(1) When the mind is so caught up in love of God that it forgets its own petition, its prayer is not inattentive, but it is the third kind of attentiveness, not the second or first, which is present.

(2) This argument works with reference to the first kind of attentiveness which, if carried too far, will result in ridiculous interruptions in the prayer, if you want to stop at each word and think about how it should be spoken; sometimes it will even result in your making mistakes, because if you are too self-conscious in this way the words will come less readily to your mind. In the case of this sort of attentiveness it is enough that we should be sufficiently alert to speak all the words fully.[32]

(3) Things which are related to each other can, as such, all be understood together at the same time, because the mind, in-

---

32. In the case of the sacraments, it is essential that the words of the sacramental formulae should be adequately spoken, because the words are part of the essence of the rite. Thomas is not particularly bothered about incidental mistakes that do not affect the meaning of the words, but in principle the integrity of the words to be spoken has to be respected (cf. IV *Sent.* d.3 a.2 q.4). The meaning of the prayers we pray is vested objectively in the words, as well as subjectively in the intention of the speaker, so if the words go too far wrong, it will affect the very nature of what we are trying to do. The child who prayed "Lead us not into Penge station" in the Lord's Prayer may have been entirely innocent of malice, but such a mistake really does change the prayer.

asmuch as it takes them precisely as related to each other, makes a single object out of them in grasping their interconnectedness. In the same way the intellect can be attentive simultaneously to prayer and to the goal of prayer. All the same, whichever of them it is attending to, there will be no lack of due attentiveness.

III. The kinds of prayer[1]

(A) The different kinds of prayer appear not to be appropriately distinguished:
(1) In 1 Timothy 2:1 it says, "I entreat you first of all that entreaties should be made and prayers, pleas and thanksgiving." Entreaties are adjurations made for difficult things, as

---

1. This article is a typical medieval exercise in classification, and it involves some fairly arbitrary definitions of terms, as can be seen from the widely divergent senses attributed by different writers to the various words for "prayer." Here I have translated *obsecratio* "entreaty," *oratio* "prayer," *postulatio* "plea" or "pleading" and *supplicatio* "supplication." The crucial text in this exercise is 1 Tim. 2:1 and analyses of prayer based on this text are found as early as Ambrose and Cassian, but there seem to be two significant different traditions of interpretation. Cassian (*Conf.* 9.9–17) takes the four terms listed by St. Paul as designating four kinds (*species*) of prayer and argues that they belong essentially to different people who are at different stages of Christian progress; Ambrose (*Sacr.* 6.22–5) sees them rather as indicating a sequence of elements that should be found in any prayer (i.e., they designate the parts of prayer, as Ambrose says, and can accordingly be employed to analyze the rhetorical structure of a prayer). Nearer to Thomas' own time, the Cistercians developed Cassian's interpretation and used 1 Tim. 2:1 in the context of a theory about spiritual progress, in which people move on from one kind of prayer to another (Bernard, *Serm. de Diversis* 25; William of St. Thierry, *Golden Ep.* 176–80 and cf. *Expos. Cant.* 14–24). The Glossa Ordinaria, on the other hand, followed by Peter Lombard in his Gloss, takes the four terms as indicating the sequence of elements found in the Mass or the sequence of things the church should pray for. Among the Dominicans, Peraldus (op. cit. III 5.7.10) cites William of St. Thierry's account of the "kinds of prayer," but effectively eliminates the suggestion that they represent a sort of progress in prayer; Hugh of St. Cher, in his postil on 1 Tim., follows the Gloss, though he generalizes the point and makes it apply to all prayer (at least all public prayer), not just the Mass, and he also refers to other interpretations, including that of Bernard. Thomas, in his commentary on the Sentences, seems not yet to have clarified exactly what his own position is. He shows no interest whatsoever in any idea of progress from one kind of prayer to another, but he is not yet in a position to make an entirely clear distinction between the question of "kinds of prayer" and the question of "parts of prayer." He is evidently attracted by the prospect of treating "parts of prayer" as a tool for making a rhetorical analysis of prayer, but he is still rather in the grip of the idea of a sequence of things to be prayed for, which slightly confuses the issue.

the Gloss says.[2] But adjuring implies a certain kind of coercion, and so it reduces the element of reverence which there has to be in prayer. So entreaty is not a kind of prayer.[3]

(2) The whole cannot be the same as one of its parts, and all the parts listed here are meant to be parts of prayer; so prayer should not also be listed as one of the parts.

(3) Pleading is the same as petition, but petition is the genus to which prayer belongs, as we have already said. Therefore pleading ought not to be listed as one of the parts of prayer.

(4) All prayer is "petition made to God for things that are fitting," according to Damascene. But thanksgiving is not petition, because it refers to gifts already received. Therefore it is not a form of prayer.

(B) Ambrose's analysis of the parts of prayer also seems to be maladroit:

(1) He says that prayer is divided into praise of God, supplication, pleading and thanksgiving.[4] But, as it says in the *Ethics*, things are praised only with reference to something other than themselves. But God is not subordinated to anything else, in fact everything else has to be referred to him. So he should not be praised, he should rather be honored.[5] Praise of God is therefore not part of prayer.

---

2. Either the marginal Glossa Ordinaria on 1 Tim. 2:1 or Lombard's Gloss (PL 192:336C). *Obsecratio* translates the Greek δέησις, meaning simply "petition," but by stressing the Latin etymology (*ob* + *sacrum*) it is possible to take it as meaning specifically a prayer of the form, "I entreat you by your holy Passion" (cf. Bernard, *Serm. de Div.* 25.1).

3. *Adiuro* was commonly used in contexts that involved spiritual coercion, such as exorcisms or the ritual of the ordeal. Such coercion is clearly incompatible with the reverence which Thomas, following William of Auvergne, has identified above as the distinguishing feature of the kind of petition that is "prayer."

4. *Sacr.* 6.22. Thomas probably knew this text at second hand and seems to be unaware that it is in fact an interpretation of 1 Tim. 2:1, but with "prayer" coming before, rather than after, "entreaty"; Thomas is therefore wrong in supposing that Ambrose took *obsecratio* to mean "praise," because it is actually *oratio* that means "praise" in Ambrose's scheme.

5. *Eth. Nic.* I 12.12 (1101b13–4). Aristotle distinguishes between things we "praise" (ἐπαινετά) and things we "honor" (τίμια). We "praise" (or "congratulate" or "approve of") something with reference to something other than itself, whereas we "honor" (or "value") something for its own sake. If we value sportsmen, we may approve of Jones because he is a good sportsman. In this sense it is, as Aristotle suggests, rather silly and even insulting to "praise the gods."

(2) Praise, properly speaking, involves making some statement about something, but prayer needs the imperative mood rather than the indicative, which is used in statements. So praise is not part of prayer.

(3) All supplication is a kind of plea, so they ought not both to be listed together.

(C) The parts of prayer listed by Hugh of St. Victor also appear to be inappropriate:

(1) He says that there are three parts of prayer: supplication, pleading and insinuation.[6] As Cicero explains, "insinuation" is one form of exordium.[7] But when we approach God we do not need any exordium, because we do not have to win his favor with words. So insinuation is not part of prayer.

(2) The exordium is the first part of a speech (*oratio*). So if the parts of prayer, which is our speaking to God, are analogous to the parts of a speech, it looks as if insinuation ought to be the first part of prayer, not the last.

(3) "Supplication" seems to add to the idea of "plea" an extra nuance of humility in pleading.[8] But a notion that is a refinement of another notion is secondary with regard to that notion, so supplication ought to come after pleading.

(4) In Matthew 7:7 the Lord seems to be laying down three parts of prayer when he says, "Ask and you will receive, seek and you will find, knock and the door will be opened to you." Since these parts are omitted in all the previous analyses, all the lists we have been considering appear to be incomplete.

Reply

(A) In response to the first question, we must say that "parts of

---

6. *De Virtute Orandi* 2 (PL 176:979C); Hugh actually says that these are "kinds" (*species*), not "parts," of prayer.

7. Thomas could be referring either to *De Inventione* I 15.20 or to the pseudo-Ciceronian *Ad Herennium* I 4.6. The purpose of an exordium is to win the favor of the audience, as both texts make clear.

8. Hugh of St. Victor (loc. cit.) says that supplication is "a humble, devout form of praying." Hugh of St. Cher, on Heb. 5:7, connects "supplication" with bodily gestures of humility (thus retaining the very ancient idea of certain postures being characteristic of suppliants), and in monastic texts *supplicatio* often simply means "inclination" or "bow."

prayer" can mean two different things: integral parts of prayer and "parts of prayer" in the sense of things that actually fall within the scope of prayer.[9] The integral parts are identified by reference to the different things which are needed to make up a complete prayer. The things that fall within the scope of prayer are identified by reference to the different things that we ask for in prayer or to different ways of asking for them.

The apostle's list of parts involves both kinds of analysis. Because it is not by our own merits that we presume to obtain the things we ask for from God and because a lack of gratitude for gifts already received blocks the way to obtaining anything more by prayer, a complete prayer requires first of all the commemoration of the holy things in virtue of which we obtain difficult requests, and this is what "entreaty" is all about. This is why the Gloss says that entreaty concerns "difficult things, like the conversion of a sinner."

Secondly there is the actual petition, and that either means asking for things we want in view of our primary petition, and this is "prayer," which is what we call petition for the good things needed in this life, or it means asking for the things which we are primarily concerned to obtain, such as the good things of heaven, and this kind of petition is called "pleading."[10]

Finally there is thanksgiving, which concludes a prayer in such a way as to leave the door open for a later prayer.

As the Gloss points out, the parts of the Mass can be ana-

---

9. "Integral parts" of something are the parts necessary for it to be complete (e.g., the integral parts of a house are its walls, floors, roof, etc.); the other kind of parts referred to here (*partes subiectivae*) are the different things that fall under the heading of something (in this sense cows and lions are "parts" of the genus "animal"). Integral parts of X are not themselves X (a roof is not a house), but *partes subiectivae* of X are X (a lion is an animal).

10. Thomas here follows one of the interpretations suggested by the Glosses on 1 Tim. 2:1. "Entreaty" is for something difficult, like the conversion of a sinner; "prayer" is praying for virtues and other such things which are needed in this life by people who are already converted; "pleading" means praying for the eternal reward that crowns the life of the just. William of St. Thierry, ignoring the order of the words in 1 Tim., takes "pleading" to refer to ordinary petitionary prayer for things in the world, while "prayer" is taken to mean "the affection of someone cleaving to God and a kind of intimate, fond conversation and the stability of an enlightened mind set to enjoy God for as long as it may" (*Golden Ep.* 177, 179). The deployment of the terminology is essentially arbitrary, and Thomas soon abandons his identification of "prayer" as prayer for things in this world.

lyzed in the same way. The words that precede the consecration
are "entreaty," in that they commemorate Christ and his teaching and that of his saints. The words spoken at the consecration
are "prayer," because the sacrament which they effect is a help
for us on our way in this life, which is why it is called "viaticum."[11] What comes after the consecration is "pleading," because there we plead for eternal goods on behalf of the living and
the dead. And the words that follow communion are "thanksgiving."

In reply to the points raised above:

(1) In an oath[12] we call on God's truth, as being more sure, to
attest the truth of what we are saying; similarly in an adjuration we call on a power greater than our own in order to
obtain something that our own weakness cannot obtain. So
an adjuration is always a confession of one's own insufficiency. But sometimes the power called upon in an adjuration is meant to force someone violently to our will, as when
the saints adjure demons to leave the bodies of the possessed,
but at other times it is called upon to woo someone's good
will, and this is what we are doing when we adjure God by
his Son or by his saints, who were more acceptable to him
than we are. And in this way entreaty does not mean any
lessening of reverence.

(2) It is normal for a generic noun to be applied to the species
which has no particular rank (or less than other species) over
and above what is meant by the generic noun. For example
the word "angel," which applies to all ranks of angels, is allocated to the lowest rank of angels. In the same way the
word "prayer" is appropriated to the kind of prayer which
ranks lowest, namely, that in which we ask for good things
belonging to this life.[13]

---

11. "Viaticum" means "provisions for the journey" and was applied to the Eucharist
as such, not just to reception of Holy Communion on one's deathbed. Cf. Lombard, IV *Sent.*
d.8 ch.2.2.

12. "Adjuration" is etymologically derived from *iurare* (take an oath).

13. This position, taken from the Gloss, does not really satisfy, once it is taken up
systematically, because there is no obvious reason why "prayer" should be the generic term,
if in itself it means "praying for things needed in this life," and Thomas' comparison with
"angel" does not help very much, since even the highest angels are "angels," whereas, on the

(3) Pleading implies a certain intensity of desire for what we are asking for, and what is desired primarily and for its own sake is our final goal, so "pleading" adds a particular nuance to the idea of "petition," in that it refers to a specific object of petition, namely, our final goal.

(4) Thanksgiving is mentioned as a part of prayer, but not as if it were a kind of prayer, so there is no reason why the definition of prayer should apply to it.[14]

(B) In response to the second question, we must say that *oratio* in the sense of a prayer made to God has an exordium just as much as *oratio* in the sense of a speech does; that is why the Mass begins with the singing of an introit. But there is this difference between them: the exordium in a speech is aimed at the audience, to make them sympathetic, docile or attentive.[15] But in the case of a prayer an exordium is sometimes needed to stimulate our own desire as we pray, so that we shall present our petitions with devotion.

In an exordium designed to win the good will of the audience there are four ways of proceeding, according to Cicero: we may try to win sympathy by alluding to the person of the judge and praising him, or by alluding to the business in hand and displaying its seriousness, or by alluding to ourselves as petitioners and showing how deserving we are of the audience's support, or by alluding to the person of our opponents and inciting the minds of our hearers against them.[16] But in a prayer made to God we are only pleading for ourselves, not trying to get anyone else into trouble; and the business in hand is God himself, to whom all our desires have to be subordinated. So there are two ways in which our feelings can be stirred to devotion as we pray by a kind of exordium: by adverting to God and praising

---

view being expounded here, other kinds of "prayer" (in the generic sense) are not "prayer" (in the specific sense).

14. In the thirteenth century there was as yet no general tendency to treat thanksgiving as a "form of prayer," though it is already so treated in Bernard, *De Diversis* 25.6. Peraldus, op. cit. III 5.8, treats thanksgiving as being distinct from prayer, though it is often "mingled with prayers." In Thomas' terms, it may be an "integral part" of a prayer, but as such it does not itself have to be prayer.

15. Cf. Cicero, *De Inventione* I 15.20; *Ad Her.* I 4.6.

16. *De Inventione* I 16.22; *Ad Her.* I 4.8.

him, and by adverting to ourselves and reflecting on our own weakness. This is why Ambrose proposes praise of God as a part of prayer: this is the first kind of "exordium." And with reference to the second, he mentions "supplication," which is a "humble, devout form of praying";[17] and this can include the "business in hand," inasmuch as our spirit is humbled by the need which drives us to pray. "Pleading" belongs to the unfolding of our prayer and "thanksgiving" to its conclusion, as we have said.

In reply to the points raised above:

(1) "Praise" is here taken in a broad sense, covering both praise and honor. Alternatively we may say that, though God is not to be referred to anything beyond himself, nevertheless he arranges everything directly so that it is referred to him, and in this sense the notion of praise does apply to him.[18]

(2) Praise is listed as an integral part of prayer, in that it belongs in some way to the completeness of a prayer, but it is not listed as the kind of part that falls within the scope of prayer.[19]

(3) "Supplication" is not listed here precisely as containing the idea of pleading or petition, but with specific reference to the manner of pleading which it denotes.

It can also be said that the parts of prayer listed by Ambrose can be reconciled with those listed by the apostle: entreaty will

---

17. Hugh of St. Victor, *De Virtute Orandi* 2 (PL 176:979C).

18. This is essentially a Greek problem: αἰνεῖν has too much of the connotation "approve of" to be entirely appropriate in connection with God (though it can be used: e.g., Callimachus, *Hymns* 4.6); but its use for a variety of Hebrew words in the Septuagint made it a settled part of Christian vocabulary, so that "praising God" was not really problematic in Christian Greek and it was never problematic in Latin. But in *Summa Theol.* II.II q.91 a.1 ad 1 Thomas uses the "problem" to make quite a nice point: God in himself is "greater than all praise" (Ecclus. 43:33), but he is praised (even "commended") for his works, which benefit us (and therefore, in however special a way, fit into the Aristotelian category of "praiseworthy things"). Here in the commentary on the Sentences Thomas' attempt to evade the problem is less convincing; his point seems to be that praising something is always a matter of relating one thing to another, and that the way in which God makes everything relate to himself does, more or less, satisfy this rubric. Thomas appears not to have been convinced by Albert's solution offered in his lectures in Cologne, at which Thomas was present (FVST p.79, Ferrua p.46): praise is due to the deeds for which we are ourselves responsible, so God can be praised for his deeds, for which he is responsible (*Super Eth.* I 14.84, Col. XIV i p.74:39–41).

19. I.e., praise is not itself prayer.

be identified with praise, inasmuch as we adjure God by things which are pertinent to praising him, and supplication will be identified with prayer, because they both connote a certain reverence. The other two items are identical even in name.

(C) In response to the third question, we must say that Hugh lists the parts of prayer in the sense of things that actually fall within the scope of prayer, and he distinguishes between them on the basis of their different ways of asking for something. A petition is specified by some kind of statement, and such a statement is a form of exposition. So in some cases both petition and statement are involved in a prayer, and this is called "pleading"; as Hugh himself says, "A plea is a statement included within a specific petition." Or only one of them may be involved, so there may be a non-specific petition without any statement, and this is "supplication"; so Hugh says, "Supplication is a humble, devout praying without specifying any particular petition." Or there may be a statement without any petition, and this is "insinuation," which in his view is "signifying what you want without asking for anything, simply by stating your wish."[20]

In reply to the points raised above:

(1) What we said above in (B) deals with this point.

(2) Cicero distinguishes insinuation from exordium in that an exordium is explicit in trying to arouse the audience's good will, docility or attentiveness, whereas insinuation does the same thing in a hidden and roundabout way.[21] So insinuation is properly a matter of saying one thing and intending something else. This is why Hugh uses the name "insinuation" for the kind of prayer in which a statement is made while a petition is intended. He does not mean that it is a sort of exordium, only that it is a way of asking for something that resembles one kind of exordium.

(3) From what we have said it is clear that "pleading" falls between insinuation and supplication;[22] that is why it is placed in the middle of the list.

---

20. *De Virtute Orandi* 2 (PL 176:979C).

21. Cf. Cicero, *De Inventione* I 15.20; *Ad Her.* I 7.11.

22. "Insinuation" (statement without petition) and "supplication" (petition without statement) represent two "extremes"; "pleading" (petition with statement) represents the mean term, as it were.

(4) According to Augustine, the three things mentioned in this text refer to different things which we need to make our way in this life. First, we need health to give us the energy to walk, and "Ask and you will receive" refers to this. Then we need knowledge to guide us, as otherwise we shall not know our way, and "Seek and you will find" refers to this. Thirdly, we need it to be possible for us to arrive, and "Knock and the door will be opened to you" refers to this.[23] So it is clear that different parts of prayer, in the sense of different things that fall within the scope of prayer, are being distinguished here with reference to different objects of petition. So "prayer" in the apostle's list includes asking and seeking, and "pleading" covers "knocking." "Thanksgiving" and "entreaty" are not parts of prayer in this sense and do not refer to distinct objects of petition.

IV. What should be asked for in prayer?

(A) It would seem that we ought not to ask for anything specific when we pray:

(1) It is dangerous to ask for something that we ought not to ask for. But "we do not know what to pray for as we should" (Rom. 8:26). So we ought not to ask for anything specific.

(2) In prayer we ought to cast our hope on God, as it says in Psalm 54:23, "Cast your care upon the Lord." But if you specify some particular thing in your prayer, it does not look as if you are casting your care entirely upon the Lord. So prayer like that is unacceptable.

(3) The only reason for specifying one's petition is to inform someone of what one wants. But the God to whom we pray knows our desires better than we do. So we ought not to ask for anything in particular when we pray.

On the other hand:

(a) The Lord has given us the proper form for our prayer, and the Lord's Prayer contains specific petitions. Therefore it is right to ask for particular things.

(b) Pleading is a part of prayer, and according to Hugh of St.

---

23. *De Sermone Domini* II 21.71–2 (PL 34:1302).

Victor pleading involves a specific petition. So we should ask for particular things.

(B) It seems that we should not ask for temporal things when we pray:

(1) On Matthew 6:33, "Seek first the kingdom of God and all these other things will be added," the Gloss says, "Not that these other things should be sought after the kingdom."[1] So there is no room left for it to be legitimate to ask for temporal things when we pray.

(2) People who pray for things are concerned about them, but we are not meant to be concerned about temporal things, as Matthew 6:25 makes clear, "Do not be concerned about what you are going to eat." So temporal things should not be asked for in prayer.

(3) In prayer we ought to ask only for something which is a real good for us, and temporal things are not our real good, as the quotation from Augustine in the Gloss on Matthew 6:33 makes clear.[2] So we ought not to ask for temporal things when we pray.

On the other hand:

(a) The Lord's Prayer contains the petition, "Give us this day our daily bread," and as the Gloss on Luke 11:3 shows, this is a prayer for bodily bread, not just for spiritual bread.[3] So it is legitimate to pray for temporal things.

(b) Bernard says, "Temporal things are to be asked for inasmuch as our need requires."[4]

(C) It seems as if we ought not to pray for anyone else's good:

(1) In Jeremiah 7:16 it says, "Do not pray for this people."

(2) It is presumptuous to interfere with what is above us. But the overflowing of grace from one person to another is characteristic of the special fullness which there was in Christ as

---

1. Interlinear Glossa Ordinaria.
2. Marginal Glossa Ordinaria, based on Augustine, *De Sermone Domini* II 16.53 (PL 34:1292).
3. Marginal Glossa Ordinaria.
4. *Serm. de Diversis* 25.5.

our Head.[5] So nobody ought to usurp the function of praying for anybody else.

On the other hand:
(a) In Matthew 5:44 it says, "Pray for those who persecute you and revile you."

REPLY

(A) In response to the first question, we must say that three things are achieved by being specific in what we pray for: First, it helps to focus our attention while we pray, and this is very necessary in prayer. Secondly, it makes us aware of our own desire and of how we are progressing in it. Thirdly, it makes us pray more fervently, because the more precisely we concentrate our attention on particular good things, the more earnestly we desire them, as the philosopher remarks in connection with bodily delights in the *Ethics*.[6]

Accordingly Augustine says, "The reason why we also pray to God at certain intervals in specific words is in order to give ourselves a reminder by means of these signals"—this takes up the first point—"and to become aware of how we are progressing in our desire"—this is the second point—"and to stir ourselves to a more eager desire"—this is the third point.[7]

In reply to the points raised above:
(1) Augustine provides the answer to the first point: The apostle's comment is prompted by those temporal afflictions which are often sent to benefit us, but yet we ask to be delivered from them, because they are bad in themselves, even if they are good from a particular point of view. But there are some things we know quite well we should pray for, just as we know we should desire them.
(2) In doubtful cases we have to cast our cares upon God in the sense that if what we are asking for is not in line with what

---

5. Christ, as Head of the church, is the source from which grace flows into the other members of the church: cf. III *Sent.* d.13 q.2 a.1.

6. In Moos' text the reference is given as *Eth. Nic.* III, but there is nothing there to which Thomas could be alluding. He is perhaps thinking of VII 3.5 (1147a25–35).

7. *Ep.* 130.9.18 (PL 33:501).

is good for us, the matter is to be left in God's hands. The Lord gave us a model for this way of praying when he said, "Not as I will, but as you will" (Matt. 26:39).

(3) The answer to the third point is clear from what has been said already.

(B) In response to the second question, we must say that prayer is a way of carrying out a desire, and so it is lawful to ask in prayer for whatever it is lawful to desire, in the same way that it is lawful to desire it. But there are two distinctions we need to notice with regard to our desires. First, some things are desired for their own sake, while others are desired for the sake of something else. Secondly, some things, such as the virtues, cannot be desired too much, while other things, like bodily pleasures and wealth, can be desired to excess.

Temporal goods are to be desired for the sake of something else and in a restrained way, that is, in proportion to our need of them in order to pursue our life in this world. And so they can be prayed for in the same way.

In reply to the points raised above:

(1) Temporal goods should not be sought first or second as if they were a primary objective, but they can be sought as things we desire for the sake of something else; this kind of desiring is a matter of choosing rather than wanting in the strict sense, because what we want is our final goal.[8]

(2) What is forbidden by the Lord's words here is excessive concern, not necessary concern.

(3) Temporal things are not, as such, our real good, but they are good for us inasmuch as they contribute to our pursuit of something else. In this way they fall under the heading of "useful goods."[9] And in this sense they can be prayed for.

---

8. Cf. Aristotle, *Eth. Nic.* III 2.4 (1111b26–7): we "will" or "want" our ultimate objective, we "choose" the things that will lead us to that objective (e.g., we "want" to get rid of a headache, so we "choose" to take a pill). Thomas is suggesting that temporal goods are "chosen" in this sense, rather than "willed."

9. The division of "good" into "noble, pleasant and useful" (*honestum, delectabile, utile*) probably derives from Aristotle, *Eth. Nic.* VIII 2.2 (1155b19), but it had become commonplace in the schools (cf. William of Auxerre, *Summa Aurea* II 8.2.9.3, ed. cit. p. 221; Thomas, *Summa Theol.* I q.5 a.6). In the *Summa Theol.* Thomas ascribes it to Ambrose (cf. *De Officiis* 1.27, PL 16:31–2), but William of Auxerre, loc. cit., ascribes it to Aristotle.

As the philosopher says, "People ought not to pray for them" (temporal things, that is) "they ought to pray that they will use them well."[10]

(C) In response to the third question, we must say that, since we are bound by the commandment of love to love our neighbors as ourselves, we must want for them the same things that we want for ourselves, and so we can pray for the same things for them as we can for ourselves.

In reply to the points raised above:

(1) The Lord forbids the prophet to pray, because there were reasons in the people why his prayer could not be heard, namely, their uncorrected faults and final impenitence, as the Gloss on this passage says.[11]

(2) When you pray, you are not trying to obtain anything on the strength of yourself, but on the strength of the one to whom you are praying. And so when you pray for someone else, you are not laying claim to any grace of fullness in yourself, you are ascribing it to the one you are praying to, whom you are asking to give grace to your neighbor.

V. To whom can we pray?

(A) It appears that prayer should be addressed only to God:

(1) This follows from the definition of prayer; as Damascene says, "Prayer is the ascent of the intellect to God."

(2) We have already said that prayer is an act of worship, and worship is due to God alone. So the same must be true of prayer too.

(3) The power of prayer is due more to feeling than to spoken words because, as Augustine says, "This business is conducted more in groans than in spoken words."[1] But only

---

10. This is apparently a reference to Aristotle, *Eth. Nic.* V 1 (1129b4–6), where Aristotle says that people pray for things that are good in themselves, but not necessarily good for certain individuals; instead they ought to pray that such things will be good *for them*. Albert comments on this that "the good use of these things is better than the things themselves" (*Super Ethica* V 2.374, Col. XIV i p. 317:40), which may have influenced Thomas here.

11. Marginal Gloss on Jer. 7:16.

1. *Ep.* 130.10.20 (PL33:502).

God can perceive the thoughts and feelings of people's hearts, so it is only to him that prayer is made.

On the other hand:

(a) It says in Job 5:1, "Call and see if there is anyone who will answer you, turn to one of the saints." So prayer can be made to God's saints as well as to himself.

(b) "Supplication" is one kind of prayer, and we can supplicate other human beings. Therefore we can pray to them.

(B) It looks as if prayer can be addressed even to saints who are not in heaven:

(1) We only address our prayer to saints inasmuch as they are closer to God than we are, because it is through things which are closer to him that God sends out the rays of his goodness to things which are further away, as Dionysius says.[2] But even the saints who are in this world are in a higher state than we are. So we ought to pray to them.

(2) The people in purgatory are already sure of their salvation. So they are in a better position than we are. So we can pray to them.

(3) In the *Dialogues* we read that Paschasius was revealed to St. Germanus, the bishop of Capua, as being in purgatory, yet he worked a miracle after his death.[3] Along the same lines it seems that there is no reason why prayer should not be addressed to people who are not in heaven.[4]

On the other hand:

(a) We should not pray to the same people that we pray for, and we pray for all the saints who are either in this world or in purgatory. Therefore we ought not to pray to them.

(b) We only pray to the saints inasmuch as they enjoy a full participation in the Godhead. But they participate fully in the Godhead only inasmuch as they participate in beatitude, as

---

2. This is not an exact citation from Dionysius; the wording resembles *DN* 4.1 (PG 3:693B), but the meaning is closer to such texts as *CH* 13.3 (ed. cit. pp. 151–5) and *EH* 5.4 (PG 3:504D).

3. Gregory, *Dial.* 4.40 (PL 77:396–7).

4. In the medieval mind there was a close link between praying to the saints and expecting (or desiring) a miracle, so the argument here is that if someone in purgatory can work miracles, then it is clearly appropriate to address prayers to that person.

Boethius says.[5] So we should pray only to the saints who are in bliss.

(C) We seem to pray to God with reference to one of the divine Persons rather than the divine essence:

(1) We ought to pray in the way that Christ taught us, and he taught us to address our prayer to the Person of the Father: "If you ask anything of the Father" (John 16:23). So it is with reference to a divine Person that we pray to God.

(2) Anything which is attributed to God with reference to the divine nature applies equally to the Trinity as a whole and to each of the Persons. But the church does not address any prayers to the Holy Spirit.[6] So it is not with reference to the divine nature that we pray to God, but with reference to a divine Person.

On the other hand:

(a) We pray to someone inasmuch as he can give us a share in the good that is his. But it is because he is good that it belongs to God to give us a share in himself. So, since goodness is an attribute of God's essence, it seems that it is with reference to the divine nature that we address our prayers to God.

REPLY

(A) In response to the first question, we must say that what we ask for in prayer is the life of blessedness, as Augustine points out, because everything else that we ask for is desired simply in view of blessedness.[7] And it is only God who directly gives us blessedness.[8] But the saints help us to obtain it. And so prayer

---

5. Cf. the argument in Boethius, *Consol. Phil.* III pr. 10.

6. Originally all formal prayers were meant to be addressed to the Father, but by this time some collects were being interpreted as addressed to the Son. The position implied here is identical with the assertion made by Hugh of St. Cher: "All prayers are addressed to the Father or the Son, but none is addressed to the Holy Spirit" (*Tractatus super Missam*, ed. G. Sölch [Münster, 1940], p. 15). Cf. J. A. Jungmann, *The Mass of the Roman Rite* [New York, 1951], I p. 380 note 25.

7. Cf. *Ep.* 130.4.9 (PL 33:497), where Augustine tells Proba to pray for "a life of blessedness" and points out that this is what everyone is looking for, saints and sinners alike, though sinners are looking for it in the wrong place. In the same letter 7.14 (PL 33:499) he adds that all other desires are to be referred to the desire for the life of blessedness.

8. Cf. ibid. 9.18 (PL 33:501).

is addressed directly and properly to God, because it is from him that we hope to obtain what we are asking for when we pray. But we turn to the saints when we pray, because it is by their help that we obtain what we are hoping for. This is why Cassiodorus says that "prayer," properly speaking, is addressed to God, while we "beseech" the saints.[9]

In reply to the points raised above:

(1) A definition has to contain the elements which belong to something without qualification. And although in one sense we can pray to the saints, as to people who intercede for us, all the same it is to God that prayer, in its proper and unqualified sense, is addressed.

(2) Prayer is an act of worship. But when we pray to the saints we are not offering worship to them, but to him from whom we hope for the fulfilment of our petition.

(3) The saints know, in the Word, everything that pertains to their own glory.[10] And it is greatly to their glory that they are able to help others, as a kind of fellow-workers with God. Therefore they immediately see in the Word the desires of those who call upon them.

(a) This text teaches us to turn to one of the saints not in the sense that our prayers are directed primarily to them, but inasmuch as they can act as intermediaries for our prayers.

(b) *Oratio*, as we have already seen, is used of prayer by analogy with a forensic speech. The speech is actually addressed only to the judge, though supplications or other kinds of petition may be made to other people who are in a better position than we are. Similarly in the case of prayer, it is God alone who is actually addressed by our prayer, but we can supplicate others even in the sense of addressing our supplications to them.

(B) In response to the second question, we must say that we only ask for something from someone who has it. So, since the life of blessedness is what we ask for when we pray, prayer (in some

---

9. *In Ps.* 60.1 (PL 70:424D). Cassiodorus' distinction between *oratio* and *deprecatio* ("beseeching") is entirely arbitrary.

10. Cf. below, note 6 on *Summa Theol.* II.II q.83 a.4.

sense) is addressed only to those saints who possess the life of blessedness and not to those who are in this world or in purgatory, although we can address supplications or other kinds of petition to those who are in this world.[11]

In reply to the points raised above:

(1) The saints who are in this world are in a higher state than we are and they can pray for us, but they have not yet reached such a level of superiority as to possess that beatitude which we do not possess.

(2) Although people in purgatory are in a state of greater certainty than we are, they are in greater distress; also they are not in a position to merit anything.[12] So rather than praying for us, they need us to pray for them.

(3) In the case of miracles what is primarily looked for is the faith and devotion of the person praying. This is why the Lord himself said to the woman he healed, "Your faith has saved you" (Matt. 9:22). Because of Paschasius' outstanding merits, he was believed to be in heaven, and for that reason people prayed to him and their prayer was heard at the time because of the faith of the people praying and to express approval of his life; it does not mean that he was praying for others while he was in purgatory.

(C) In response to the third question, we must say that prayer is addressed primarily to God, inasmuch as he is blessed and the bestower of blessedness on others. And since it is with reference to his essence that this is said of him, it must be with reference to his essential attributes that we pray to him.

In reply to the points raised above:

(1) All the attributes of the divine essence are in the other Per-

---

11. This argument, which implies that the saints in heaven actually give us beatitude as their own gift to us, as if they were the (or at least a) source of our beatitude, is painfully inadequate; in *Summa Theol.* II.II q.83 a.4 ad 3 Thomas deals with this question much more satisfactorily. In this period there was great devotion to praying for the souls in purgatory, but the later devotion of invoking the prayers of the Holy Souls was unknown.

12. This does not imply that the saints in heaven can still merit (cf. II *Sent.* d.11 q.2 a.1); the contrast is between us on earth, who can merit, and the souls in purgatory, which cannot. It was this helplessness of the souls in purgatory that supposedly persuaded St. Dominic's friend, Bertrand of Garrigues, that he ought to say the Mass for the dead more often (MOPH I pp. 287–8).

sons from the Father. So we can, in a way, trace things back from the other Persons to the Father, as Hilary makes clear.[13] Because of this the Father is also called "principle of the whole Godhead."[14] Christ was leading us back to the Father in a similar way, as to the source which has no source,[15] when he taught us to direct our prayers to the Father through the Son.

(2) It belongs to the Holy Spirit as a personal attribute that he is called "Gift." So it is more appropriate that we should ask for him than that we should ask for anything from him, although the church obviously does address some prayers to him as well, and also some hymns which take the place of prayers, like *Nunc Sancte Nobis Spiritus* and *Veni Creator Spiritus*.[16]

VI. To whom is praying properly attributed?

(A) It seems that praying is attributable to a divine Person:

---

13. It is not clear what passage of Hilary Thomas has in mind, but cf. *De Trinitate* 8.20 (PL 10:251A), *De Synodis* 20.54 (PL 10:519B), which show how it is possible to move from saying that the Holy Spirit "receives from the Son" to saying that he "proceeds from the Father," or from saying that he is "sent by the Son" to saying that he is "sent by the Father," on the principle that the Son's works are the Father's works and what he has he has from the Father.

14. Augustine, *De Trinitate* IV 20.29, as rephrased by Lombard, I *Sent.* d.29 c.1.2.

15. The Father is *principium non de principio*, the Son is *principium de principio* (cf. Lombard, I *Sent.* d.29 c.3.3); the Father is the source that has no source, the Son is the source (of the Holy Spirit and of creatures) that has a source (the Father).

16. The hymn *Nunc Sancte Nobis Spiritus* ("Come, Holy Ghost, Who Ever One" in Newman's version) was already traditional in the ninth century, when it is cited (and ascribed to Ambrose) by Hincmar, *De una et non trina deitate* 17 (PL 125:589C); it was used as the hymn for terce. *Veni Creator Spiritus* ("Come, Holy Ghost, Our Souls Inspire" in the famous version by John Cosin) probably dates from the late ninth century and was used in the Divine Office at Pentecost and on many other occasions; in the Dominican rite it was sung during the clothing of novices, for instance (cf. Tugwell, AFP 53 [1983] pp. 27–9), and St. Dominic was remembered to have sung it during his travels (*Bologna Canonization Process* 21, MOPH XVI p. 140). When Thomas says that these hymns are recited *loco orationum* he cannot mean that they replace formal collects, but that they are used in situations in which a corresponding prayer could equally well have been said. The "prayers" which Thomas mentions are similarly not formal collects but, presumably, such texts as the antiphon *Veni Sancte Spiritus* ("Come, Holy Spirit, fill the hearts of your faithful") used, for instance, in the Dominican prayers for a General Chapter (*Ordinarium*, ed. F. M. Guerrini [Rome, 1921], p. 125) and in the Divine Office for Pentecost (AFP 52 [1982] p. 55).

(1) Anyone who can receive something can pray.[1] But it is quite in order to say that one divine Person receives from another, as the Son and the Holy Spirit do. So a divine Person can pray.

(2) "I will ask the Father and he will give you another comforter" (John 14:16). It is the Son who says this. Therefore there is nothing wrong in saying that the Son prays.

(3) It says in Romans 8:26, "The Spirit pleads with unutterable groans." And the Holy Spirit is the third Person of the Trinity. Therefore it is in order to say that a divine Person prays.

On the other hand:

(a) Praying implies a lack of power in the person praying, and this cannot be ascribed to a divine Person. So prayer is not properly attributable to a divine Person.

(b) Prayer is an act of worship, and "worship" means "service of God."[2] And service of God is not something that a divine Person can suitably be said to perform. So the same must be true of praying as well.

(B) It appears that we should not attribute praying to the saints in heaven either:

(1) The saints in heaven are conformed to Christ in his humanity. And it is not right to ascribe prayer to Christ in his humanity, as otherwise we should say, "Christ, pray for us."[3] Therefore it is not right to ascribe prayer to the other saints either.[4]

(2) The saints in heaven are equal to the angels of God (Matt. 22:30). And praying is not attributable to angels because, as we have seen, prayer is an act of reason and there are no acts of reason in the angels, since reason arises "in the shadow of

---

1. Since we ask for things in order to receive them, this argument suggests, a capacity to receive something from someone implies a capacity to ask someone for something and therefore to pray. Praying and receiving seem to rest on the same basis of dependence on someone.

2. This interpretation of "latreia" (worship) is taken from the Marginal Gloss on Matt. 4:10.

3. The point seems to be that if the humanity of Christ prayed for us in heaven, we should say, "Christ, pray for us"; no point is implied about whether Christ as a man on earth really prayed.

4. The Latin *sanctus* can be used of Christ (the "saint of saints," *sanctus sanctorum*) and of angels; hence the reference to "the other saints" here and in the next point.

intelligence," as Isaac says.[5] Therefore prayer is not attributable to the other saints in heaven either.

(3) Anyone who prays for someone else merits something for someone else. But the saints in heaven are not in a position to merit anything. Therefore they are not in a position to pray.

On the other hand:

(a) We say, "St. Peter, pray for us."

(b) The saints in heaven are more fervent in charity than they were on earth, and charity makes the saints on earth pray for people; all the more, therefore, do the saints in heaven pray for us.

(C) It appears that even brute animals pray:

(1) In Psalm 146:9 it says that God "gives the beasts their food and the young crows that call upon him." And calling upon God is praying to him. Therefore even irrational animals pray.

(2) Prayer is an appetite declaring itself. And the brute animals, in their own way, desire the good which is God. Therefore they pray.

On the other hand:

(a) Prayer is made only to God and God cannot be known except by the intellect, which brute animals lack. Therefore they cannot be said to pray.

REPLY

(A) In response to the first question, we must say that prayer requires there to be a distinction between the person praying and the person prayed to, because nobody asks for something from himself. And prayer is made to God on the basis of his essential attributes, in which no distinction is made between the divine

---

5. Isaac Israeli, *Liber de Definitionibus*, ed. J. T. Muckle, *Archives d'Histoire Doctrinale et Littéraire du Moyen Age* 11 (1937–8) p. 313:25–7. "Intelligence" here is used to mean a higher intellectual power than "reason"; where reason has to toil discursively, "intelligence" simply sees what is what. The same distinction is made later on in terms of "intellect" and "reason." The angels do not reason discursively, so they are "intellectual" rather than "rational" beings.

Persons. Therefore one Person cannot be said to pray to another.

In reply to the points raised above:

(1) The imparting and receiving which occurs between the divine Persons is a matter of natural fecundity, not a free gift,[6] and it is to obtain free gifts that we pray.

(2) The Son says this of himself, not because of the Person he is, but in virtue of our nature which he assumed.

(3) The Holy Spirit is said to "plead" inasmuch as he makes us plead.[7]

(B) In response to the second question, we must say that some heretics have maintained that the saints cannot help us by praying for us, because we all receive what our deeds have deserved.[8] But this is contrary to the article of faith about the "communion of saints" which results from charity.[9] So since the saints in heaven also have the most perfect charity, it falls to them to pray for us, though not for themselves, since everything they desire is theirs.

In reply to the points raised above:

(1) Christ, in his humanity, does pray for us. The reason why we do not say, "Christ, pray for us," is that "Christ" implies

---

6. According to the classic Trinitarian theology, the Father did not "choose" to beget the Son, he begot him by nature (*Fides Damasi*, in H. Denzinger and A. Schönmetzer, *Enchiridion Symbolorum, Definitionum, Declarationum* no. 71).

7. Cf. Marginal Gloss on Romans 8:26, or Lombard's Gloss (PL 191:1447A).

8. Vigilantius denied that the saints pray for us (cf. Jerome's response, *Contra Vigilantium* 6, PL 23 [1845]:344), but Thomas is probably thinking of more contemporary heretics: the Waldensians were by this time denying that we can be helped by the prayers of the saints (cf. the document from about 1215 printed in AFP 29 [1959] p. 275; Moneta of Cremona, *Adv. Catharos et Valdenses* IV 9.4), and this is probably because of their insistence on each individual's responsibility (cf. K. V. Selge, *Die ersten Waldenser* [Berlin, 1967], I pp. 154–5).

9. Against the moralizing individualism of the Waldensians it is indeed necessary to stress that the saints share what they have with one another (the "communion of saints" in its traditional sense)—a point made dramatically in the dream of Peter of Aubenas reported in the *Vitae Fratrum* (MOPH I pp. 183–4); but the communion of saints can only be relevant to the question of their prayers for us on the assumption that they are actually giving us a share in what is theirs by praying for us, which makes little sense. Cf. above, note 11 to article V. Thomas uses a different argument in *Summa Theol.* II.II q.83 a.11.

the eternal subject[10] whose part is not to pray for us but to help us. That is why we say, "Christ, hear us," or "Have mercy on us." And in this way we avoid the heresies of Arius and Nestorius too.[11]

(2) Intellect possesses in a much more noble way anything that reason possesses, because anything that a lower power can do, a higher power can also do. And so the angels, who are intellectual beings, can pray.

(3) Some people say that the saints are not in a position to merit anything with regard to their essential reward, but they can merit something with regard to their incidental reward,[12] and can therefore also merit things for other people. But meriting is confined to people who are still on the way, in this world. So we must say that there is a difference between obtaining things by prayer and meriting things; this will be discussed shortly. So even if the saints cannot merit anything, they can obtain things for us by their prayers.

(C) In response to the third question, we must say that praying is in no way attributable to brute animals, and that for three reasons. First, they have no share in the life of blessedness, which is the primary object of all petition. Secondly, they have no apprehension of the God to whom prayer is offered. And thirdly,

---

10. *Suppositum*, which Thomas uses as equivalent to *hypostasis*. The doctrine of the hypostatic union means that, though we can distinguish between the divinity of Christ and his humanity, there is only one person there, of whom it is always correct to say that he is the Son of God. His humanity is not the humanity of anyone else except the Son of God. Cf. III *Sent.* d.6 q.1 a.1 q.2.

11. Asking Christ to pray for us could easily be taken to imply Arianism (the belief that the Son of God is a creature) or Nestorianism (the belief that there is in Christ a human person distinct from the divine Person).

12. There was evidently an opinion in the schools that the angels are in a position to merit, and so it could be argued that the saints are similarly in a position to merit the increase of their reward, which will come at the Judgment (i.e., the glory of the resurrected body); cf. Roland of Cremona, *Summa* III, ed. A. Cortesi (Bergamo, 1962), p. 805. The essential reward is the vision of God, and this the saints already have; the "incidental" extras are such things as the resurrected body. If one of the incidental glories of a preacher is that he is escorted by all those whom he converted (Humbert of Romans, *De Erud. Pred.* I 5.54, in Tugwell, *Early Dominicans* p. 200), it could presumably be argued that the saints could increase their incidental glory by increasing the number of their "clients," but I do not know any evidence that anyone actually did argue this.

asking is an act of reason, as we have seen, since it involves a certain kind of planning.

In reply to the points raised above:

(1) As Augustine says, brute animals are said to obey God's commands, not as if they understood his instructions, but inasmuch as they are moved by God by their natural instincts;[13] in the same way they are said to "call upon God" in an extended sense, inasmuch as they have a natural desire for something which they obtain from God.

(2) "Appetite," as we said above,[14] implies only a straightforward movement toward the desired object, but "prayer" or "petition" implies a certain planning, and this involves reason. So brute animals can be said to have "appetites," but they cannot be said to ask for things or to pray for things.

VII. The effectiveness of prayer

(A) Prayer appears not to be a work of satisfaction:[1]

(1) All prayer is either vocal or mental. Mental prayer is not a work of satisfaction because it is enjoyable rather than painful.[2] Nor is vocal prayer a work of satisfaction because, as Isidore says, "It is not the sound of our voices that reconciles us to God, but the pure, straightforward purpose which is in our minds."[3] Therefore prayer is not part of satisfaction.

---

13. *Super Gen. ad Litt.* IX 14.24-5.

14. The reference is probably to III *Sent.* d.27 q.1 a.2.

1. By this time it was commonplace to say that penance (meaning both the sacrament and the virtue) consists of contrition, confession and satisfaction (what we now call "the penance"): cf. Lombard, IV *Sent.* d.16 ch.1.1; William of Auxerre, *Summa Aurea* IV 8.2, ed. cit. IV pp. 198–201; Raymund of Peñafort, *Summa de Poenitentia* (Rome, 1603) p. 442. It was also commonplace to identify the three works of satisfaction as prayer, fasting and almsgiving (William of Auxerre pp. 272–9; Raymund pp. 467–8).

2. Latin *poena* (from which "penance" derives) enfolds both "punishment" and "pain," making it appear self-evident that if something is not painful it cannot count as a punishment (or penance). The point raised here about prayer being delightful and therefore not penitential is discussed in William of Auxerre, pp. 273–5; the argument that prayer is "sweet" (which William does not entirely accept) is based on two proof texts (Eccles. 10:1, traditionally interpreted as referring to prayer, and Apoc. 5:8, interpreted in the light of Exod. 30:1), rather than directly on psychological experience.

3. Cf. *De Summo Bono* III 7.29 (PL 83:678A).

(2) Worship, as we saw in the previous distinction,[4] is a distinct virtue from penance. And satisfaction is an act of the virtue of penance, while prayer is an act of worship. So prayer is not a work of satisfaction.

(3) Works of satisfaction are performed in order to reconcile someone whom we have offended, but prayer comes after reconciliation; it seems rather presumptuous to ask for something from someone we have offended. So prayer is not a work of satisfaction.

On the other hand:

(a) Jerome says that the plagues of our mind are healed by prayer, just as those of the body are healed by fasting.[5] And fasting is a work of satisfaction, therefore prayer must be too.

(b) In prayer we ask to be released from what we owe, and we do not do this in vain, since the practice was instituted by the Lord. And it is by penance that we are released from what we owe. So prayer does belong to some part of penance, and that part can only be satisfaction. Therefore prayer is a work of satisfaction.

(B) Prayer appears not to be meritorious:

(1) A meritorious work involves focussing one's purpose on God alone, because any mercenary intention empties our deeds of their capacity to merit. But when we pray we do not only have our eye on God, we have it on our own needs, for which we are asking for help. So prayer is not a meritorious work.

(2) If prayer is meritorious, what it will merit most of all is the granting of its plea. But it does not merit the granting of its plea, because sometimes even the prayer of someone who is in a state of charity is not heard. Therefore prayer is not meritorious.

---

4. In IV *Sent.* d.14 q.1 a.1 q.5 Thomas has shown that penance and religion are both, in some sense, parts of the virtue of justice.

5. Cf. pseudo-Jerome (PL 30:616C), quoted in the marginal Gloss on Mark 9:28; this text is cited, for instance, in William of Auxerre, p. 273, and Raymund of Peñafort, *Summa de Poenitentia* p. 469. Thomas has rephrased the text slightly.

(3) Nature does not use two means to achieve something that can be achieved by one, because there is nothing in the works of nature which proves to be pointless, and the same principle applies even more to the works of grace. But deeds are a sufficient way of acquiring merit. So it looks as if prayer is not meritorious.

On the other hand:

(a) Any virtuous work can be meritorious, and prayer is a virtuous work, as we have seen. Therefore it is meritorious.

(b) It says in Psalm 34:13, "My prayer will return to my bosom."[6] So something accrues from prayer to the person praying, and so prayer does appear to merit that something.

(C) There appears to be something wrong with the list of conditions which make prayer efficacious:

(1) The Gloss on Luke 11:5, on the parable, "Which of you has a friend . . . ," says that four conditions have to be met if prayer is to be efficacious: one must be praying piously, for oneself, perseveringly and with relevance to one's salvation.[7] Anyone in a state of sin lacks the virtue of piety, but in fact the prayer of sinners is sometimes heard, because miracles can be worked even by sinners. So prayer does not have to be made piously in order to be efficacious.

(2) A prayer which comes from charity is always efficacious: "If you abide in me and my words abide in you, you will ask for whatever you want, and it will be done for you" (John 15:7)—and abiding in God is the result of charity as 1 John

---

6. Although Thomas' text of the Psalm has *in sinu meo convertetur* (and this is the text found in the Dominican liturgy), his comment shows that the ablative has in fact to be treated as if it were accusative, and in his commentary on this Psalm Thomas in fact glosses *in sinu, id est ad meipsum*. His interpretation follows the marginal Gloss on *oratio mea*, which takes the clause to mean that a prayer that has no effect elsewhere returns to the person praying, along the lines of "Your peace will return to yourselves" (Matt. 10:13), an interpretation based on that of Cassiodorus (PL 70:246CD).

7. The four "conditions of impetration" were by this time conventional, but William of Auxerre, op. cit. III 27.3.1, ed. cit. pp. 517–8, is aware that there is some doubt about where they came from. "Piously" and "perseveringly" are found in the interlinear Gloss on Matt. 7:8, but there is nothing in the Glossa Ordinaria on Luke 11; however Hugh of St. Cher does mention the four conditions together on Luke 11:10, which suggests that Thomas is perhaps thinking of his distinguished Dominican confrère rather than the Glossa Ordinaria.

4:16 makes clear. And any prayer which is made piously comes from charity and is therefore efficacious. So there is no need to add any other conditions.

(3) The greater the charity, the more efficacious it is in meriting. And the more people it embraces, the greater the charity is. So it seems that a prayer which is made for other people because of charity is more efficacious than a prayer which is made for oneself. So praying for oneself is not a necessary condition.

(4) The reason why a prayer can result in merit is the same as the reason why a deed results in merit: in both cases merit is due to charity. But a deed resulting from charity is meritorious, even if one does not go on doing it. So persevering in prayer is not a necessary condition for efficaciousness.

(5) A desire or a petition for things which are relevant to salvation does not move God to anger. But sometimes God grants the prayers of people whose petition makes him angry, as he did when the children of Israel asked for a king and in his indignation he gave them one.[8] So asking for things relevant to our salvation is not a necessary condition for our prayer to be efficacious.

In addition, it looks as if many more conditions are required:

(a) We must ask with faith and confidence: "They should plead in faith, not doubting at all" (James 1:6). And prayer has to be humble: "He looked on the prayer of the humble and did not spurn their entreaty" (Psalm 101:18). Also the poverty of the petitioner contributes to the efficaciousness of prayer: "The Lord heard the desire of the poor" (Psalm 9:38). So does fervor in one's devotion: this is why Augustine says, "The more fervent the feeling that goes before, the more noble will be the effect that comes after."[9] So the four conditions that are listed are not sufficient.[10]

---

8. Cf. Augustine, *Ep.* 130.14.26 (PL 33:504), which cites this example (from 1 Sam. 8) among others to show that God sometimes grants people's petitions in anger.

9. *Ep.* 130.9.18 (PL 33:501).

10. Raymund of Peñafort, *Summa de Poenitentia* p. 469, lists thirteen things that are required in prayer, though he does not explicitly contend that they are conditions of impetration.

Reply

(A) In response to the first question, we must say that satisfaction relates both to past guilt, offering compensation for the offense it caused, and to future guilt, against which it is a prophylactic.[11] And in both ways it falls within the scope of prayer. "The beginning and root of sin is pride" (Ecclus. 10:15). Therefore by subjecting our spirit humbly to God in prayer we both offer compensation for the pride involved in our previous offenses and remove the opportunity for future guilt by cutting it off at the root. So prayer is fully in line with the definition of satisfaction.

In reply to the points raised above:

(1) Both mental and vocal prayer count as works of satisfaction, provided they are made in charity. Vocal prayer is a work of satisfaction because it involves an outward labor and so does have an element of painfulness about it.[12] And inasmuch as the force of the original intention with which someone begins praying persists, it also counts as a meritorious good work. And these are the two things required for a work of satisfaction.[13] So we can see how we can respond to the text cited from Isidore: it is not the sound of our voice as such that reconciles us to God, but only insofar as the effect of a pure purpose persists in our prayer.

Similarly mental prayer is also a work of satisfaction. Although it is enjoyable, there is a certain painfulness attached to it too. As Gregory says, "To pray is to utter bitter groans in a state of compunction," either because of one's sins or because of one's delay in reaching heaven.[14] Furthermore the raising of the mind is itself an affliction to the

---

11. According to a current definition ascribed to Augustine, "satisfaction means cutting out the causes of sin" (in fact, Gennadius, *De Eccl. Dogm.* 54, PL 58:994C): cf. Gratian, *Decretum* C.33 q.3 d.3 c.3 (Friedberg I 1211); William of Auxerre IV 11.1 p. 269.

12. Raymund lists prayer as one form of mortification of the flesh (p. 468).

13. Thomas has demonstrated in IV *Sent.* d.15 q.1 a.1 q.1 that satisfaction is necessarily a matter of performing a virtuous, therefore meritorious, work.

14. Gregory, *Moralia* XXXIII 23.43 (PL 76:701B); the two suggested reasons for groaning are the same as those given in a similar context in William of Auxerre, op. cit. IV 11.2 pp. 274–5.

flesh, as we have already noted;[15] and any affliction of the flesh affects the mind too, inasmuch as they are united with one another, and it also affects the proud spirit, whose wound is healed by prayer. Prayer cannot be humble without a certain element of pain.

(2) There is nothing odd in the act of one virtue being commanded by a quite different virtue. For instance an act of temperance is sometimes commanded by the virtue of fortitude. So an act of worship can similarly be commanded by the virtue of penance, in which case it will be a work of satisfaction, just as there used to be sacrifices for sins in the old law and there still are.[16]

(3) If we have upset another human being, the very fact that we humbly ask for pardon soothes the person we have offended; this is much more powerfully the case when we are dealing with God in all his mercy.

(B) In response to the second question, we must say that it is charity which accounts for all our works being meritorious. So since it is possible sometimes for prayer to be inspired by charity, it can clearly be meritorious in exactly the same way that any other deeds inspired by charity are meritorious.

In response to the points raised above:

(1) Having your eye on something other than God in the sense of making something other than God your primary objective does destroy the basis for meriting. But attending to something else as a means by which we can come to God does not interfere with merit. And it is in this way that prayer attends to the relieving of our own needs.

(2) Acts of all other virtues derive their merit from the force of charity. And charity's *object* is what other virtues have as

---

15. IV *Sent*. d.15 q.1 a.4 q.3.

16. The "sacrifices" offered under the New Testament are all sorts of interior and external acts that can be considered as offering something to God: cf. Peraldus, op. cit. III 5.5, where the "sacrifices" listed range from the sacrifice of a contrite heart to the sacrifice involved in being generous to people in need, and obviously some of these "sacrifices" will also count as works of satisfaction.

their *goal*.[17] So in the acts of the other virtues merit is not just a matter of meriting the acts themselves, but of meriting their goal.[18] In the case of prayer, what we are actually asking for is only the object of our prayer, not our own goal. So it does not matter if there is no meriting to be looked for with reference to what we are praying for.

(3) Our deeds are not sufficient by themselves to obtain all we need, and so it is necessary that God's mercy should make up the deficiency. And this mercy is what prayer entreats. And so the merit of prayer is needed to make up the deficiency of all our other merits.[19] This is why Gregory says, "These two things have a great need to go together, so that

---

17. The growing tendency to distinguish between "object" (*obiectum*) and "goal" (*finis*) in thirteenth-century writers remains to be studied in detail. In a rough-and-ready way, in a context like the present, it is a distinction between immediate and ultimate objectives. The distinction, as applied to virtues, is related to the distinction between the "object" and the "goal" of a human act (which can also be made in terms of a distinction between the goal of the act and the goal of the agent), and also the distinction between the object of a human faculty and the orientation of that faculty to some further goal. The goal of all that we do in our lives is God or beatitude, and God is also the object of charity (it is he whom we love by charity); other virtues have their own objects (particular objectives), but these must be subordinated to the fundamental objective of charity. Cf. O. Lottin, *Psychologie et Morale aux XII*ᵉ *et XIII*ᵉ *Siècles*, IV, Louvain/Gembloux, 1954, pp. 489–495; L. Dewan, " 'Obiectum,' notes on the invention of a word," AHDLMA 48 (1982) pp. 37–96.

18. *Meritum in actibus aliarum virtutum non est solum illius actus, sed finis*: the genitives are nicely ambiguous! Does the merit belong to the goal, not just the act itself? Or does it merit the goal, not just the act? The former makes more sense (how does merit merit the act which is meritorious?), but the argument seems to require the latter: to answer the point at issue, Thomas has to explain why prayer (if it is meritorious at all) does not necessarily merit the thing being prayed for, and his argument seems to be that the thing prayed for is only the object, not the goal, of the prayer, and merit is more to do with goals than with objects, because what merits is charity, and charity is directly related to the goal, not to any lesser object; therefore there is no reason why meriting, in the case of prayer, should be located with reference to the object of prayer, provided there is room for meriting with reference to the goal. But the argument is not particularly limpid.

19. The point Thomas is answering and Thomas' answer both seem rather absurd. The argument that our deeds acquire merit enough, so prayer is not needed, overlooks the obvious fact that prayer is itself a kind of deed and is therefore meritorious (if it is meritorious), not over against our deeds, but merely as one kind of deed over against others (so the argument could equally well be proposed that we can merit enough by going to Mass, so do not need to do anything else). The answer seems to require a distinction between what we obtain by our own deeds and what we obtain from God, which is quite unsatisfactory, or a belief that our charitable deeds fall short of meriting heaven, so that they need to be topped up by another kind of merit, which implies a rather peculiar idea of charity and of merit.

prayer supports what we do and what we do supports our prayer."[20]

(C) In response to the third question, we must say that prayer has two aims: its own object and our goal.[21] Therefore it has two kinds of efficacity: it is effective in meriting with regard to our goal, which is eternal life, which is the final point of reference for all merit; and it is effective in impetrating what is being prayed for, and this is the object of prayer.

The difference between these two is that merit implies a relationship of justice between merit and reward, because it is a matter of justice to pay a reward to someone as having earned it, whereas impetration implies a relationship of mercy or generosity on the part of the giver. So merit contains within itself the reason why it attains to its reward, whereas the prayer of someone wanting to impetrate does not contain within itself any reason why it should succeed, such a reason being located rather in the purpose or generosity of the giver. This shows clearly that prayer which is inspired by charity always has the effect of meriting, but it does not always have the effect of impetrating, because there may be something militating against impetration in the providence of the God to whom the prayer is made.

It is to eliminate these obstacles to impetration that the four conditions listed above are specified: if they are met, prayer will always be efficacious in impetrating. There may be an obstacle on the part of the person praying: you may be praying in an unruly way, and it is to prevent this that it says that prayer must be made piously, implying the element of worship (which is another name for piety) which must govern our way of praying. Or there may be an obstacle on the part of the thing being prayed for: sometimes people pray for things which would not be good for them, and so it says that prayer must be for things which are relevant to salvation. Or there may be an obstacle on the part of the person being prayed for, and this obstacle may be present at the time when the prayer is being made; but if you

---

20. *Moralia* XVIII 5.10 (PL 76:42D).

21. There is the object (or goal) of the act (in the case of prayer, this means obtaining what we are praying for) and the goal of the agent (in this case, as in the case of all other virtuous deeds, God or beatitude).

are praying for yourself, there cannot be any such obstacle provided you are praying piously, but there may be such an obstacle if you are praying for someone else, so the further condition is laid down that prayer should be for oneself. Or this obstacle may arise in the interval between the prayer and its fulfilment, and this is eliminated by the condition that prayer must be persevering.

In reply to the points raised above:

(1) These conditions are not necessary for impetration in the sense that nothing is impetrated if one of them is missing, because sometimes people's prayers are heard when they are praying for someone else. What is meant is that if all these conditions are met, then prayer will always be effective in impetrating. After all, the power to impetrate depends more on the intentions of the person being prayed to than on the merits of the person praying, which is why sometimes even the prayers of sinners are heard, when their prayer is in line with God's purpose.

We must also realize that even someone who lacks the virtue of piety can sometimes pray piously, just as someone who lacks the habit of justice can sometimes perform just deeds.[22] In this way even sinners can sometimes pray piously.

(2) The will is more concerned with our goal than with anything which is asked for in view of our goal. So when God sees that what we are asking for is incompatible with the goal in view of which we are piously praying, he hears our desire better by not doing what we are asking for than he would if he did do it. So we have to take what the Lord says in a strict sense: "Whatever you *want*. . . . " The goal underlying our petition is our own salvation and God's glory. And it would be contrary to God's glory to save an impenitent sinner, and it would be contrary to our salvation if God were to give us something inimical to salvation at our request. Therefore our desire is heard, even though we do not impetrate what

---

22. Thomas, following Aristotle, regards the possession of a virtue as a stable condition, a "habit," a way of being; it justifies us in saying that someone "*is* virtuous" in some way. An isolated virtuous deed (an act of generosity, say, by a habitual miser) does not prove the existence of a real virtue.

we are praying for if we pray without persevering or for someone else or for things which are inimical to our salvation.[23]

(3) A prayer which is made for someone else out of charity is always effective in terms of the merit of the person praying, but what we are talking about now is effectiveness in impetrating.

(4) Impetration means the achievement of what we are asking for, but merit does not mean the achievement of anything, only the establishment of a just claim on something. So if some obstacle arises, because of human instability, it interferes with impetration because it prevents the achievement of what we were praying for, but it does not interfere with the justice of our claim, and so it does not remove our merit. So we can merit even without persevering, but we do not impetrate without persevering.[24]

(5) All of us have beatitude as the final goal of our desires, as the thing we desire most of all. So God really hears the people whose petitions he does not grant, if they are asking for something that would get in the way of beatitude, more than he hears the people whose petitions he does grant. So when God answers prayers in this way, in indignation, this should not really be called impetration.

(a) All these extra conditions required on the part of the person praying, as such, are contained in the requirement of piety, which includes all the facets of virtue governing human acts on the part of the human agent.

---

23. Thomas is probably influenced by Augustine's comment on John 15:7 (*In Io. Ev.* tr.81.4), which explains that whatever we want will be granted only inasmuch as we are asking for things that we want in Christ, that is, for things that are genuinely going to be good for our salvation. On this basis it can be argued that prayer made in charity is always efficacious in obtaining what we really *want*, even if it does not succeed in obtaining what we are actually asking for.

24. Even if we are in a state of sin for the time being, our previously acquired merits "keep," as it were, and will continue to entitle us to our reward in readiness for the time when we become fit to receive it. Cf. IV *Sent.* d.14 q.2 a.3 q.3.

Quaestiones Disputatae De Veritate, Question 6, Article 6

Can predestination be helped by the prayers of the saints?[1]

Surely predestination cannot be helped by the prayers of the saints:

(1) Whatever can be helped can also be hindered,[2] and predestination cannot be hindered, therefore it cannot be helped by anything.

(2) If anything produces the same results whether or not you add something else to it, it is not helped by that something else. But predestination must produce its effect, since it cannot be falsified, whether or not any prayer is offered. Therefore predestination is not helped by prayers.

(3) Nothing eternal can be preceded by anything in time. But prayer happens in time, while predestination is eternal. Therefore prayer cannot precede predestination, and so it cannot help it.

(4) The members of the mystical body resemble the members of the natural body, as 1 Corinthians 12:12 makes clear. And in the natural body one member does not acquire its perfection by means of any other member; therefore the same thing must be true of the mystical body. But the members of the mystical body

---

1. The question whether predestination is "helped by prayers" is raised in Gregory, *Dial.* 1.8 (PL 77:188B), the main instance alleged to show that it is being Isaac's prayer in Gen. 25:21; Gregory affirms that "what the saints effect by praying is predestined to be obtained by prayers." His text is quoted in the Marginal Gloss on Gen. 25:21, which ensured that the issue was on the agenda for medieval theologians. Cf. Alexander of Hales, I *Sent.* d.41.11, ed. cit. I pp.418–9; William of Auxerre, *Summa Aurea* I 9.3.4.III, ed. cit. I pp.192–3; Bonaventure, I *Sent.* d.41 a.1 q.1, Quaracchi ed. I pp. 728–9; and Thomas himself, I *Sent.* d.41 q.1 a.4.

2. If something can be helped, that implies that it is to some extent dependent on some outside factor for its achievement; and if this factor were to let it down, it would be prevented from realizing its achievement. The help that I receive from my typewriter, when it is working, is inseparable from the hindrance I receive from it when it is not working.

are made perfect particularly through the effects of predestination. Therefore human beings are not helped toward the attainment of the effects of predestination by the prayers of anyone else.

On the other hand:

(a) It says in Genesis 25:21 that Isaac "entreated God on behalf of Rebecca his wife, because she was barren, and God heard him and granted it to Rebecca that she should conceive," and Jacob was born as a result of this conception, and he had been predestined from all eternity. And this predestination would never have been fulfilled if Jacob had not been born, and it was Isaac's prayer that won the birth of Jacob. Therefore predestination is helped by prayers.

(b) In a sermon on the conversion of St. Paul[3] we find the Lord being presented as saying, "It was in my mind to destroy you, had not my servant Stephen prayed for you." Therefore Stephen's prayer rescued Paul from reprobation. Therefore it was by means of Stephen's prayer that Paul was predestined. So predestination is helped by prayers.

(c) It is possible for someone to merit the first grace for someone else,[4] so on the same basis it is possible to merit the final grace for someone else. But anyone who receives the final grace is predestined. So one person can be helped by the prayers of another to be predestined.

(d) Gregory prayed for Trajan and freed him from Hell, as Damascene tells us in a sermon on the dead,[5] and so it looks as if he was freed from the company of the reprobate by Gregory's prayers. Therefore predestination is helped by prayers.

(e) The members of the mystical body are like the members of the natural body, and in the natural body one member is helped by another. Therefore the same must be true in the mystical body. So the same conclusion follows yet again.

---

3. The precise sermon that Thomas has in mind has not been identified, but cf. Peraldus' sermon on St. Stephen, printed in the 1674 ed. of William of Auvergne, II pp.379–80.

4. For this argument, cf. Alex. of Hales, loc. cit. It was generally conceded that, in a loose way (*ex congruo*), one can merit the first grace for someone else: one can be such a person that it is appropriate (congruous) that one's prayers for someone's conversion should be heard. Cf. Thomas, II *Sent.* d.27 q.1 a.6.

5. *De His Qui in Fide Dormierunt* 16 (PG 95:261–4).

REPLY

There are two different ways of understanding the proposition that predestination is helped by the prayers of the saints. It can mean that the prayers of the saints help someone to be predestined, and this cannot be true either of prayers as they exist in themselves, because they are temporal whereas predestination is eternal, or of prayers as they exist in God's foreknowledge, because, as we have already seen, God's foreknowledge of people's merits, whether their own or those of others, is not the cause of predestination.[6] Or we can take the proposition to mean that predestination is helped by the prayers of the saints in the sense that prayer helps people to obtain the effects of predestination, just as people are helped by various tools to accomplish their work. And it is in this sense that this question has been debated by all those who believe that there is a divine providence over human affairs. But different people have come to different conclusions.

Some people, impressed by the inflexibility of God's plan, have argued that things like prayer and sacrifice cannot do any good at all. This is supposed to be the position of the Epicureans, who said that all things happen inflexibly as a result of the arrangement of the higher bodies, which they called gods.

Others have claimed that sacrifices and prayers do have an effect, precisely because they bring about a change in the plans of those whose business it is to decide about human acts. This is said to be the view of the Stoics, who maintained that all things are governed by certain spirits, which they called gods. And when they had decided on something, prayers and sacrifices could win a change in their decision, so they claimed, by placating the gods' minds.[7] And Avicenna seems almost to have fallen into this belief at the end of his *Metaphysics*, where he maintains that everything that goes on in the realm of human acts, derived from the human will, can be traced back to the will of the heavenly souls—he maintains that the heavenly bodies have souls. As heavenly bodies affect human bodies, so on his view do heavenly souls have an effect on human souls, and it

---

6. *De Veritate* q.6 a.2.
7. This very garbled account of the doctrines of the Epicureans and Stoics seems to be derived, as the Leonine editor suggests, from Albert, *Phys.* 2.2.19 (Col. IV i pp. 126–7).

is in accordance with their fancy that whatever happens here below unfolds. So, on his view, sacrifices and prayers influence these heavenly souls to conceive of the things we want to happen to us.[8]

These positions are foreign to the faith because the first of them eliminates free will, while the second one takes away the certainty of predestination. So we have to say instead that God's predestination never changes, but nevertheless prayers and other good works do influence people's attainment of the effects of predestination. In any chain of causes we have to notice not only the link between the first cause and the final effect, but also the link between the secondary cause and the effect and the link between the first cause and the secondary cause, because the secondary cause is connected with the effect only by virtue of the way in which it is directed by the first cause. It is the first cause which gives the secondary cause the capacity to contribute to the effect, as the *Liber de Causis* shows.[9]

So my position is that the effect of predestination is human salvation, which results from predestination as from its first cause, but there can be many other proximate causes which serve as instruments appointed by God's predestination in view of human salvation, just as a craftsman uses his tools to bring about the products of his craft. So if it is as the effect of God's predestination that such and such a person is saved, it is also the effect of predestination that this particular individual is saved by means of the prayers of such and such a person and by means of such and such merits. And this is what Gregory says in book I of the *Dialogues:* "What holy people bring about by praying was predestined to be obtained by prayers."[10] And this is why, as Boethius says, "When prayers are right, they cannot be ineffective."[11]

In reply to the points raised above:

(1) Nothing can interfere with the working out of predestination, so predestination cannot be thwarted. But many things are involved in the working out of predestination as intermediary

---

8. Cf. Avicenna, *De Philosophia Prima* 10.1, ed. cit. pp.527–9.

9. *Liber de Causis* 1.

10. *Dial.* 1.8 (PL 77:188B).

11. *Consol. Phil.* V pr. 6 (in the context of Boethius' demonstration that God's foreknowledge does not eliminate free will).

causes, and they are said to help predestination in the way indicated above.

(2) Inasmuch as it is predestined that such and such an individual should be saved by the prayers of such and such a person, these prayers cannot be taken away without taking away predestination, any more than you could eliminate the human salvation which is the result of predestination.[12]

(3) This argument works in the sense that prayer does not help predestination in the sense of being a cause of predestination; this has to be conceded.

(4) The effects of predestination, namely grace and glory, are not a form of first perfection, but rather a form of second perfection.[13] And the members of the natural body may not help each other to attain their first perfection, but they do help each other's second perfection. And there is in fact one member in the body which is the first to be formed and does then help toward the formation of the other members, namely the heart.[14] So the argument starts from a false premiss.

(a) This we concede.

---

12. The argument in (2) was that if X is predestined then X is bound to be saved; therefore the presence or absence of other factors cannot make any difference. Thomas' answer is that if X is predestined, the whole process by which X comes to be saved is included within the predestination of X, so that removing any of the factors involved is tantamount to removing that whole chunk, so to speak, of predestination. It would be like saying that if God wants the kettle to boil, then it will boil and it cannot make any difference whether or not we put the kettle on the fire.

13. Cf. *De Veritate* q.1 a.10 ad 3 contra: "First perfection is the form of a thing, by which it has its being, so nothing loses this perfection as long as it remains in being; second perfection is a thing's functioning (*operatio*)." The distinction is based on Aristotle's distinction between two senses of "actualization" (cf. *Metaph.* θ 6, 1048b6–9); cf. especially *De Anima* 2.1 (412a10–11), to which Thomas refers in II *Sent.* d.15 q.3 a.1. As an untutored innocent, I am merely *capable* of learning about how a computer works; in due course this capacity may be actualized, so that I *know* how a computer works: this knowledge is a first perfection. On that basis I can sometimes actually be using my knowledge of how a computer works, which actualizes my knowledge in a different sense: this is a second perfection. The point Thomas is making here is that grace and glory are more like a second than a first perfection; they do not produce a new kind of entity, but a new kind of functioning.

14. For the sake of argument it may be conceded that one part of the body does not contribute to the first perfection of other parts of the body, but it may still contribute to their second perfection: my toes may not play any role in the physical formation of my hands, but they may well help my hands to function (by helping me to keep my balance, for instance). But actually, according to Aristotelian zoology, the heart plays a role even in the first perfection of the other parts of the animal body (*De Gen. Anim.* 2.1, 735a14–26).

(b) Paul was never reprobate in the plan of God's decision, which is unchangeable, but only in the plan of God's verdict, which refers to lower causes and is sometimes changed.[15] So it does not follow that prayer was the cause of his being predestined, but only that it helped toward the fulfilment of predestination.

(c) Although predestination and final grace go together,[16] it is not necessarily the case that whatever is in any way a cause of final grace is also a cause of predestination, as is clear from what has already been said.

(d) Although Trajan was in the place of the reprobate, he was not simply reprobate; it was predestined that he should be saved by the prayers of Gregory.

(e) This we concede.

---

15. The distinction between God's *sententia* ("verdict") and his *consilium* ("decision") goes back to Gregory, *Moralia* 16.10.14 (PL 75:1127B–D); it is developed at some length in the Marginal Gloss on Isaiah 38:1. God's verdict is mutable because it refers to the operation of lower causes, whether natural or moral (cf. Hugh of St. Cher's postil on Isaiah 38:5; William of Auxerre, *Summa Aurea* II 7.2.3, ed. cit. II p.155; Thomas, *Expos. super Isaiam* 38:1, Leonine vol. XXVIII p.162). "God's 'decision' means his eternal plan which never alters . . . his 'verdict' means something to which certain causes point—'verdicts' are delivered in court on the merits of some case. Sometimes the thing pointed to by such causes is eternally planned by God, and in this case 'decision' and 'verdict' are the same. But sometimes the thing pointed to by such causes is not eternally planned by God, and then God's 'decision' and his 'verdict' do not refer to the same thing" (*De Veritate* q.12 a.11 ad 3). In the case of Paul, the ordinary outcome of the way he was heading was damnation; but in fact, something intervened to change his course. God's verdict means the verdict that would be delivered on the way the future apostle was heading before his conversion, regardless of the fact that God actually intended to make him a saint.

16. *Convertuntur:* they are inseparable, in the sense that it is impossible to have one without the other; but it does not follow that the cause of one is the cause of the other in every possible way. Alex. of Hales, loc. cit., makes exactly the same point.

Summa Contra Gentiles III
chapters 95–96

The immutability of divine providence
does not mean that prayer is unprofitable.

We must also consider that the immutability of providence does not mean that prayer is unprofitable, any more than it means that there is no room for contingency within the domain of providence. Prayer is not made to God in order to get the eternal plan of providence changed, because this is impossible; its purpose is that people should obtain what they desire from God. It is appropriate that God should assent to the pious desires of rational creatures; not as if our desires moved the immovable God, but it is a consequence of his own goodness that he brings about what they desire in a suitable way. All things naturally desire the good, as has been shown above;[1] and it belongs to the excellence of God's goodness to distribute being and well-being to everything in an ordered way. It follows that, in line with his own goodness, he fulfils the pious desires which are unfolded in prayer.[2]

Again. It belongs to a mover to bring that which is moved to its destination, so it is by one and the same nature that a thing is moved toward its destination and that it arrives there and that it then rests there. Now every desire is a kind of movement toward the good, and there could be nothing like this in things unless it came from God, who is good by virtue of his own essence, and who is the very source of goodness; every mover moves things toward something like itself.[3] So it belongs to God, in his goodness, to bring to a fitting outcome the fitting desires which are expressed in prayers.

---

1. *Contra Gentiles* III 3.
2. It is an aspect of God's goodness that he does not just produce random phenomena; he produces an ordered cosmos, in which things are linked to each other by causal connections. The connection between prayer and the obtaining of what is prayed for is an instance of this more general pattern.
3. Any influence from A to B is in principle designed to make B, in some way or another, more like A. Obviously the effect of heat is to make things hot, but the same principle

Besides. The closer things are to their mover, the more effectively they follow the influence of the mover. The things that are closest to the fire are the ones that are most heated by it. And intellectual beings are closer to God than inanimate natural beings. So the influence of the divine movement is more effective in intellectual beings than in any other natural beings. But natural bodies share in the divine movement to the extent that they derive from it a natural appetite for the good and also the fulfilment of that appetite when they attain their own particular goals. Much more, then, do intellectual beings attain the fulfilment of their desires, which they offer to God in prayer.

Furthermore. It is part of friendship that people who love should wish the desire of those they love to be fulfilled, inasmuch as they want the good and the perfection of the ones they love. This is why it is said to be proper to friends that they want the same thing.[4] Now it has been shown above that God loves his creatures, and he loves each one the more, the more it shares in his own goodness, which is the first and primary object of his love.[5] Therefore he wants the desires of his rational creatures to be fulfilled, because they share most perfectly of all creatures in the goodness of God. And his will is an accomplisher of things, because he is the cause of things by his will, as has been shown above.[6] So it belongs to the divine goodness to fulfil the desires of rational creatures which are put to him in prayer.

Moreover. Goodness in creatures is derived from God's goodness in accordance with a certain similarity. And it is plainly something particularly commendable in human beings that they should not refuse people who come to them with legitimate requests; it is this that wins people the name of being generous, kind, merciful and concerned. So it belongs especially to God's goodness to hear pious prayers.

Because of this it says in the Psalms "He will do the will of those

---

applies even when, for instance, I move a piece of chalk: it does not make the chalk look like me, but it does mean that the location of the chalk now corresponds better to some idea I had in my mind about where it should be.

4. Sallust, *Catiline* 20.4, quoted in William of Auxerre's treatise on prayer in *Summa Aurea* III 27.3.1, ed. cit. p.518:26.

5. *Contra Gentiles* I 74–5.

6. Ibid. II 23.

who fear him and he will hear their prayers and save them" (Ps. 144:19). And in Matthew 7:8 the Lord says, "Everyone who asks, receives and everyone who seeks, finds and to one who knocks the door will be opened."

Nor is it awkward if sometimes the petitions of people who pray are not accepted by God. We have shown that God fulfils the desires of his rational creatures on the principle that he desires their good. But it sometimes happens that what is asked for is not a true good, but only something that appears to be good, while it is strictly speaking bad. So a prayer of this kind cannot be heard by God. This is why it says, "You ask and do not receive, because you ask badly" (James 4:3).

Similarly we showed that it is appropriate for God to fulfil desires on the basis of the fact that he moves people to desire. But a moving object is not brought to the goal of its movement by its mover unless the movement continues. So if the movement of desire is not sustained by insistent prayer, it is not unfitting if the prayer does not gain the effect it should. This is why the Lord says in Luke 18:1, "It is necessary to pray always and not give up." And in 1 Thessalonians 5:17 the apostle says, "Pray without ceasing."

Again. We showed that God properly fulfils the desire of his rational creatures inasmuch as such creatures are close to him. And we come close to him by contemplation and devout affection and a humble, firm purpose. So any prayer which does not come close to God in this way is not going to be heard by God. So it says in the Psalms, "He looked on the prayer of the humble" (Ps. 101:18). "Let him ask in faith, not doubting at all" (James 1:6).

Further. We showed that God hears the wishes of the pious on the basis of friendship. So it would not be fitting that the prayers of people who turn away from God's friendship should be heard. Thus is says in Proverbs 28:9, "If you turn your ear away from hearing the law, your prayer will be detestable." And in Isaiah 1:15, "When you multiply prayers I will not listen to you, for your hands are full of blood."

This is the source of the fact that sometimes God's friends are not heard when they pray for people who are not God's friends. "Do not pray for this people or undertake praise and prayer on their behalf, do not get in my way, because I will not listen to you" (Jer. 7:16).

It also sometimes happens that people refuse their friends' petitions because of friendship, because they know that what they are asking for would be harmful or that the opposite of what they are asking for would be more beneficial. A doctor, for instance, sometimes refuses his patients what they ask for because he reckons that it would not help them to gain bodily health. So, since we have shown that it is out of the love that he has for his rational creatures that God fulfils the desires which they put to him in prayer, it is not surprising if sometimes he does not even fulfil the petitions of people whom he particularly loves, in order to fulfil something which will be more helpful for their salvation. This is why he did not take away Paul's sting in the flesh, even though he asked three times for it to be removed, because he foresaw that it was useful for him as a way of preserving his humility (2 Cor. 12:8–9). For the same reason the Lord says to some people in Matthew 20:22, "You do not know what you are asking." And it says in Romans 8:26, "We do not know what to pray for as we ought." This is why Augustine says in his letter to Paulinus and Therasia, "The Lord is good in often not granting what we want, in order to give us something that we would prefer."[7]

It is clear, then, from what we have said, that the cause of some of the things that are done by God is prayers and pious desires. And we have already shown[8] that divine providence does not exclude other causes; on the contrary, it arranges them, so that the pattern which he has fixed in his own mind will be imposed on things. And so there is no contradiction between secondary causes and providence, secondary causes in fact bring about the accomplishment of providence. In the same way prayers are effective with God, without undoing the immutable ordering of divine providence, because it falls within the ordering of providence precisely that such and such a petition should be granted to such and such a person. So to claim that we should not pray in order to obtain anything from God, on the grounds that the ordering of his providence is immutable, is like saying that we should not walk in order to arrive at some place and that we should not eat in order to be fed, all of which is patently absurd.

So what we have been saying eliminates two errors concerning

---

7. Augustine, *Ep.* 31.1 (PL 33:121).
8. *Contra Gentiles* III 77.

prayer. Some people maintained that there is no benefit to be had from prayer. This was asserted both by people, like the Epicureans, who denied divine providence entirely, and by people, like some of the Peripatetics, who withdrew human affairs from the competence of divine providence; and the same doctrine was also maintained by people, like the Stoics, who believed that everything which is subject to providence comes about by necessity.[9] All these positions lead to the conclusion that prayer is without profit, and as a consequence any worship of the Godhead is in vain. This error is alluded to in Malachi 3:14, "You said, 'Anyone who serves God is a fool. What have we gained from keeping his commandments and walking sadly before the Lord of hosts?' "

Some people, on the other hand, alleged that the divine plan could be altered by prayers, as the Egyptians claimed that fate could be influenced by prayers and certain images and by fumigations and

---

9. Thomas' account here reflects the traditional Platonist critique of other philosophical schools much more accurately than the rather garbled picture he gave in *De Veritate* 6.6. His main source appears to be Nemesius, *De Natura Hominis* 35–43, which he knew in Burgundio's Latin version (in which the work was ascribed to Gregory of Nyssa). There is a critical edition of the Greek text of Nemesius by M. Morani (Leipzig 1987), and of Burgundio's Latin text by G. Verbeke and J. R. Moncho (Leiden 1975). In *Contra Gentiles* III 73 Thomas explicitly refers to Nemesius for the Stoic view of providence, and in *Summa Theol.* I q.116 a.3 he cites him as his source for the Egyptian belief that fate can be manipulated by religious practices. For the Epicureans, see Nemesius 43 (Morani p.127:1–8, Verbeke pp.160–161). For the Peripatetics, cf. ibid. (Morani p.127:12–21, Verbeke p.161); on the Platonist contention that the Peripatetics denied that providence reaches to the particulars of the sublunar world, cf. R.W. Sharples, *Alexander of Aphrodisias on Fate*, London 1983, p.25, and fragment 3 of Atticus (ed. E.des Places, Paris 1977, p.48, from Eusebius, *Praep. Ev.* XV 5.7–8). In *Contra Gentiles* III 75 Thomas notes the ascription of this doctrine to Aristotle, but points out that it cannot be derived from anything Aristotle says. On the Stoics, cf. Nemesius 43 (Morani p.126:22–25, Verbeke p.160:94–96) and also 35 (Morani pp.105–106, Verbeke pp.134–135). That these doctrines make nonsense of prayer is suggested by Nemesius several times: cf. 35 (Morani p.104:17, Verbeke p.133:63–64), 42 (Morani p.122:8, Verbeke p.155:68–69); on the alleged incompatibility of determinism with belief in prayer, cf. Sharples, op. cit. pp.150–151. There is in fact a confusion which Thomas never seems entirely to have resolved: it is perfectly legitimate for a determinist to contend that prayer is effective, provided that he regards our prayers as themselves determined, and this is actually fairly close to Thomas' own position, as he expounds it later on in this chapter. What would make prayer meaningless would be the belief that nothing we can do can make any real difference to what happens. The problem of reconciling human freedom with all-pervasive divine causality is a real one, but it is not strictly relevant to the discussion of whether prayer makes sense. Thomas was not particularly allergic to determinism, so long as the source of 'fate' was seen to be God and not just some ineluctable causal nexus: cf. *Contra Gentiles* III 93; *Quodl.* XII q.4 a.1 (probably disputed at Easter 1272). On the Egyptians, cf. Nemesius 36 (Morani p.106:15–20, Verbeke p.135:14–19).

incantations. And some passages in scripture, at first sight, appear to conform to this opinion. In Isaiah 38:1–5, for instance, it says that Isaiah, on the Lord's instructions, told King Hezekiah, "Thus says the Lord: make arrangements for your house, because you are going to die, not live." Then after Hezekiah's prayer the word of the Lord came to Isaiah saying, "Go and say to Hezekiah: I have heard your prayer. See, I will add fifteen years to your days." And in Jeremiah 18:7–8 it says, in the person of the Lord, "I will suddenly speak against the people and against the kingdom, to root out and destroy and scatter it. If this people repents of its evil, which I have spoken against it, I too will repent of the evil which I thought to do to it." And in Joel 2:13–4, "Turn to the Lord your God, because he is kind and merciful; who knows if God will turn and pardon us?"

If these passages are taken at their face value they lead to awkward conclusions. It follows, first, that God's will is changeable, and also that things happen to God in time; further, that some of the things which happen in time in creatures are the cause of something in God. And these are plainly impossible, as is clear from what has been said above.[10] They also contradict texts in scripture, which contain the statement of infallible truth. It says in Numbers 23:19, "God is not like a human being, that he should lie, or like a son of

---

10. Thomas' classic account of why we must not say things like this about God is developed at length in book I of *Contra Gentiles*, from chapter 13 onward. For an excellent modern discussion, see B. Davies, *Thinking about God* pp.148–72. The doctrine that God is changeless and that he is not acted upon by creatures has met with some disfavor in recent times, often, it appears, for rather sentimental reasons; but it is worth reflecting that the implications of any other doctrine are not particularly attractive, even sentimentally. If we allow that God is acted on by creatures, so that he and we are engaged jointly in creating the future, then the only way in which his omnipotence can be secured (so that he will still be the Lord "who does whatever he wills in heaven and on earth," Ps. 134:6) is by making him an exceedingly unequal partner in the game, so that he can always outmaneuver his creatures to achieve the triumph of his own will. Is such a picture of a God who is, as it were, competing with us so unfairly really more attractive than the classic account, according to which God is not competing with us at all, but simply giving us to ourselves? If God is both acted on by his creatures and not necessarily guaranteed always to prevail, then omnipotence has to be sacrificed; and then what hope have we left? If God is in the soup with us, then we have no hope that does not deceive, because the risk remains that God may eventually be defeated. The classic account maintains our hope, because it does not allow that anything can interfere with the working out of God's purpose; and it frees us from any sense of having to compete with God. We belong, as free agents, within the sphere of secondary causes, competing with other secondary causes, the whole thing being created and deployed by God. Our acts are, indeed, caused by God; but then, if we find an insult in the very fact of being created, of being caused, we might as well pack our bags and set off to sample the joys of reigning in hell.

man, that he should change. He has spoken and will he not do it? He has given his word, will he not fulfil it?' And in 1 Samuel 15:29, "He who triumphs in Israel will not spare or be swayed by any change of heart; he is not a human being, that he should repent." And in Malachi 3:6, "I am the Lord, I do not change."

If you examine these matters carefully, you will find that the whole mistake involved here arises from a failure to pay sufficient attention to the difference between the universal pattern and particular patterns. When a whole lot of effects are related to one another because they have a common cause, the pattern will inevitably be the more all-encompassing the more universal the cause is. So a pattern derived from the universal cause, which is God, must necessarily enfold everything. So there is nothing to stop some particular pattern being changed by prayer or in any other way, because there is something outside that pattern which can change it. So it is not surprising that the Egyptians, who referred the pattern of human affairs to the heavenly bodies, maintained that the fate which comes from the stars can be changed by certain prayers and rites, because God is outside and above the heavenly bodies and he can prevent the effect which would have followed from the influence of the stars on lower beings. But nothing can be postulated outside the pattern which enfolds everything, by which the arrangement deriving from the universal cause could be deflected. For this reason the Stoics, who took seriously the dependence of the whole pattern of everything on the universal cause, maintained that the pattern appointed by God cannot be altered in any respect. But then again they departed from their awareness of the universal pattern by declaring prayers to be quite useless, because this implies that they thought that human wishes and desires, from which prayers proceed, are not contained within the universal pattern. When they claim that exactly the same thing will result from the universal pattern, whether or not prayers are made, they are clearly detaching the wishes of the people praying from that universal pattern, because if these wishes are contained within that pattern, then certain results will follow, by God's ordinance, by means of these wishes as by means of any other cause. So denying that prayer has any results is exactly the same as denying the results of all other causes. And if the immutability of God's pattern does not deprive other causes of their results, neither does it take away the efficacy of prayer. So prayers are effective, not as if they changed the pattern of God's plan, but as themselves falling within the scope of that pattern.

But there is nothing to stop any particular pattern produced by some lower cause being changed as a result of prayers, because such a change is wrought by God, who is superior to all causes and, as such, is not constrained by any pattern derived from any cause; on the contrary, whatever constraint may follow from a lower cause is subject to him, as having been appointed by him. So God is said to "turn" or "repent" inasmuch as some part of the pattern of lower causes, appointed by God, is changed as a result of the prayers of pious people. It does not mean that his eternal plan is changed, but that some effect which he produces is changed. This is why Gregory says that God does not change his plan, even if he sometimes changes his verdict.[11] He does not change the verdict which expresses his eternal plan, but only the verdict which expresses the pattern of lower causes, under which Hezekiah was going to die or some people was to be overthrown because of its sins. This kind of change of verdict is metaphorically called God's repentance, inasmuch as God behaves like someone who is repenting, who is changing what he had done. In the same way God is said to be "angry" metaphorically, inasmuch as when he punishes people he produces the same effect as someone who is angry.[12]

---

11. Gregory, *Mor.* 16.10.14 (PL75:1127B–D). Cf. above, note 15 on *De Veritate* 6.6.
12. Cf. *Contra Gentiles* I 91.

From the First Lectures on St. Paul

1 Corinthians 14:13–15

13. So anyone who speaks in a tongue should pray to interpret.
14. For if I pray with a tongue, my spirit prays, but my mind is without benefit.
15. What then? I will pray with my spirit, I will also pray with my mind. I will sing psalms with my spirit, I will also sing psalms with my mind.

Above (1 Cor. 14:1–4) the apostle has shown the superiority of the gift of prophecy over the gift of tongues on the basis of their use in exhortation; here he makes the same point on the basis of their role in prayer. These are the two things for which we use a tongue: prayer and exhortation.

In connection with this, he does two things: first, he indicates the need to pray (verse 13), then he shows how the gift of prophecy is worth more in prayer than the gift of tongues (verse 14).

So he says, first of all: I have explained that the gift of tongues without the gift of prophecy achieves nothing; therefore, since interpreting is an act of prophecy, which is superior to the gift of tongues, "anyone who speaks in tongues," speaking things which are unknown, that is, or strange, or some hidden mysteries, "should pray" to God "to interpret," that is, to be given the gift of interpretation,[1] "praying that God will open for us the door of speech" (Col. 4:3).

The Gloss takes *oret* in a different sense. *Orare* has two meanings: to pray to God, or to urge. So the meaning would be, "Anyone who speaks in a tongue should speak, that is, urge, in such a way as to interpret." And the Gloss takes *orare* in this sense throughout the

---

1. From the Interlinear Gloss or Lombard's Gloss (PL 191:1666D).

chapter.[2] But this is not what the apostle means; he is using the word in the sense of "pray to God."

"For if I pray. . . . " It must be realized that there are two kinds of prayer: one is private, when people pray in themselves and for themselves; the other is public, when someone prays in the presence of the people and for other people. And in each of them the use of the gift of prophecy and of the gift of tongues arises. So he wants to show that in each of them the gift of prophecy is more valuable than the gift of tongues.

With reference to private prayer, he says that if there is some simple person saying his prayers, reciting a psalm or the Our Father, and he does not understand what he is saying, then he is praying "with a tongue" and it makes no difference whether he is praying in words granted to him by the Holy Spirit or in the words of others. And if there is someone else praying and he understands what he is saying, he is praying and prophesying. It is beyond doubt that the one who prays and understands gains more than the one who is only praying with a tongue, who does not understand what he is saying. The one who understands gains refreshment both in his intellect and in his feelings, whereas the mind of the person who does not understand does not benefit from any refreshment. So since it is better to be refreshed in one's feelings and in one's intellect than in one's feelings alone, it is clear that the gift of prophecy is more valuable in prayer than the gift of tongues on its own.

This is why he says, "He should pray to interpret," "because if I pray with a tongue," that is, if I use the gift of tongues in my prayer, so that I utter various things which I do not understand, then "my spirit," that is, the Holy Spirit who is given to me, "prays," inclining me and moving me to pray. Nevertheless I acquire merit in my prayer, because the very fact that I am moved by the Holy Spirit is a merit. "We do not know what to pray for as we ought, but the Holy Spirit himself makes us plead" (Rom. 8:26).[3]

Alternatively, "my spirit," that is, my reason, "prays," that is, bids me utter things which make for good, whether in my own words or in those of other people (the saints).

---

2. The Glossa Ordinaria and Lombard's Gloss both offer this as one way of reading the text, and it is strongly endorsed by Hugh of St. Cher; but as a matter of fact, Thomas is quite right to reject it, as the Greek unambiguously means "pray."

3. The citation from Romans incorporates the Gloss, "makes us pray."

Or "my spirit," that is, my imaginative faculty, "prays," inasmuch as there are sounds or bodily images in my imagination alone, without them being understood by the intellect.[4] That is why he goes on, "But my mind," that is, my intellect, "is without benefit."

So prophecy or interpretation is better in prayer than the gift of tongues.

But is it true that, when people pray without understanding what they are saying, they are always without the benefit of their prayer?

We must say that there are two kinds of benefit resulting from prayer. One is the merit which accrues to us; the other is the spiritual consolation and devotion which is conceived because of prayer. And as far as the benefit of spiritual devotion goes, anyone who is not paying attention to his prayer or who does not understand his prayer does lose this benefit. But as far as merit is concerned, such a person should not be said to lose that benefit, because in that case a great many prayers would be without merit, since it is hardly possible to say a single Our Father without our minds wandering off to other things.

So we must say that when someone is distracted from what he is saying during his prayer, or when someone engaged in some meritorious work does not constantly reflect with every move he makes that he is doing this for God, they do not lose the basis for meriting. The reason for this is that in all meritorious activities whose orientation is toward the right goal, it is not required that the intention of the person doing them should be concentrated on that goal in every single action; the initial impetus which inspired the person's purpose remains in effect throughout the entire operation, even if he is sometimes distracted while performing specific parts of it. And this initial impetus makes the whole work meritorious, unless it is intercepted by some contrary feeling which turns the work aside from its original orientation and redirects it in an opposite direction.

And we must realize that there are three different kinds of attention. We can pay attention to the words we are saying, and this is sometimes harmful, in as much as it hinders devotion. Or we can pay attention to the meaning of the words, and this can be harmful,

---

4. For these three senses of *spiritus*, cf. Lombard's Gloss (PL 191:1667A). For *spiritus* taken in the sense of "imagination," cf. Kilwardby, *De Spiritu Fantastico* 1, ed. P. O. Lewry (Oxford, 1987), p.55. Kilwardby refers back to Augustine, *De Trin.* 14.16.22.

though not very much. Or thirdly, we can pay attention to our objective, and this is better and more or less necessary.

What the apostle says about being "without benefit" refers to the benefit of spiritual refreshment.

"What then?" people might say, "Since praying with a tongue brings no benefit to the mind, and the spirit alone prays, should we therefore not pray with our spirit?"

The apostle disposes of this by saying that we should pray in both ways, with our spirit and with our mind, because we are meant to serve God with all that we have from God, and we have both our spirit and our mind from him and so we ought to pray with both. "With all his heart he praised the Lord" (Ecclus. 47:10). So he says, "I will pray with my spirit, I will also pray with my mind; I will sing psalms with my spirit. . . . "

He says, "I will pray and I will sing psalms" like this because prayer is directed either to entreating God ("I will pray") or to praising him ("I will sing psalms").[5] These two are mentioned in James 5:13, "Is any of you sad? He should pray calmly and sing psalms." "Sing psalms to the Lord" (Ps. 9:12).

So, "I will pray with my spirit," that is, with my imagination, "and with my mind," that is, my will.[6]

1 Timothy 2:1

So I entreat you first of all that entreaties should be made
and prayers, pleas and thanksgiving, for everybody.

Because it is the case that Christ came to save sinners, therefore "I entreat you first of all. . . . " He plainly shows here that of all the things which are needed for the Christian life the most important is prayer, which is effective against the hazards of temptation and in making progress in good. "The persistent prayer of the righteous is very effective" (James 5:16).

---

5. This suggestion that praise is a form of prayer is most unusual in Thomas.

6. This has surely gotten garbled. The Interlinear Gloss proposes "with the will" as an interpretation of "with my spirit," and this may be what Thomas meant; surely "with my mind" must have been interpreted as "with my intellect," as above (and as in the Interlinear Gloss).

So he analyzes prayer into four parts: entreaties, prayers, pleas and thanksgiving; three of these concern benefits to be obtained by prayer, and one concerns benefits already received.

In the case of prayer for benefits to be obtained, three things are required. First, we must show some reason why our prayer should be granted. Secondly, we must show that our case is a reasonable one. Thirdly, we formulate our petition. And we should do in prayer what secular speakers do. We must first think up some reason why our petition should be granted, and this reason is not our own merits but God's mercy. "It is not on the strength of our righteousness that we pour out our supplications before your face, but because of your abundant mercies" (Daniel 9:18). And this is what "entreaty" is, an appeal to certain holy things, as when we say, "By your passion and cross deliver us, O Lord."[7]

Once we have thought out the grounds for our petition to be granted, we need to meditate on the fact that this holy thing to which we appeal is the cause of our salvation. So "prayer" is required, which is an "ascent of the mind to God."[8] "As for me, I directed my prayer to you, Lord" (Ps. 68:14).[9] And it is called "prayer" (*oratio*) from *oris ratio* (the mouth's reason). The urgings of public speakers are called "speeches" (*orationes*), because they are aiming at persuasion, but the two cases are not the same. In the case of our speeches to God, we are not aiming to change God's mind, because he is always ready for anything good; our purpose is that our own hearts should be raised to God in prayer.

Thirdly, "pleas." "Let him plead in faith, not doubting at all" (James 1:6).

· Then thanksgiving for the gifts we have received. "Give thanks at all times" (1 Thess. 5:18). "In all prayer and entreaty, together with thanksgiving, let your petitions be made known to God" (Phil. 4:6).

Accordingly this is the style of prayer used in the church of

---

7. From the Litany of the Saints.

8. Damascene, *De Fide Orthodoxa* 68.1, ed. Buytaert p.267. Thomas here abandons his earlier relegation of "prayer" to the lowly role of meaning prayer for this-worldly blessings, but as the comments that follow reveal, he now drifts toward aligning "prayer" with meditation, and has not yet found how to integrate "prayer" (in the narrower sense, now taken to be "ascent of the intellect to God") into his account of prayer in general (meaning petition).

9. The Vulgate text of the Psalm lacks a verb: *dirigebam* is supplied in the Lombard's Gloss (PL 191:632D).

God: "Almighty, eternal God" (notice the ascent of the mind, which is "prayer") "who gave such and such a blessing to your church" (thanksgiving) "grant, we beseech you" (plea) "through our Lord Jesus Christ" (entreaty).

Similarly in the Mass everything up to the consecration of the Body and Blood is "entreaty," because so far it all concerns the remembrance of holy things which provide the basis for our confidence that we shall obtain our petition. At the mystery of the consecration there is "prayer," because we meditate on what Christ did. The rest, up to communion, is "plea" for the living and dead and for ourselves. At the end comes thanksgiving.[10]

Or these four terms can be referred to four things which we want to obtain in prayer: "entreaty" being referred to obtaining difficult things, such as the conversion of sinners, "prayer" being when we implore grace for people who are already converted, so that they will make progress. We "plead" that rewards will be given for people's merits, and "thanksgiving" is for benefits already received.[11]

Then, when he says, "For everybody," he shows for whom we should pray. And he says that we should pray for everybody. The reason for this is that prayer is the interpreter of our desire; in praying we ask for what we desire. And charity requires that we should desire good for all the people to whom our charity extends. "Pray for one another, that you may be saved" (James 5:16).

---

10. This application of the text to the Mass comes from the Marginal Gloss.
11. This interpretation too is suggested in the Marginal Gloss.

From the Lectures on St. John

John 16:23

On that day you will not ask anything of me. Truly I say
to you, if you ask the Father for something in my name,
he will give it to you.

"On that day you will not ask anything of me." According to
Augustine, the Greek for "ask" here is a word which can mean either
"ask for something" or "ask a question about something,"[1] so "on
that day you will not ask anything of me" can be understood in two
ways: you will not ask me for anything, or you will not put any
questions to me.

So he says, "On that day." What that day is is shown by what
has gone before (16:22): "I shall see you again," which can be taken
either as referring to his resurrection or to our vision of him in glory.

Chrysostom takes it in the first way: "On that day," that is,
when I rise from the dead, "you will not ask anything of me," that
is, you will not say things like, "Show us the Father."[2] But Augustine raises a difficulty about this interpretation: after the resurrection the apostles say, "Will you at this time restore the kingdom to
Israel?" (Acts 1:6),[3] and Peter says, "And what about him?" (John
21:21).

But in support of Chrysostom's interpretation we must say that
by "that day" the Lord means not only the day of his resurrection,
but also the day on which they were to be instructed by the Holy
Spirit. "When he comes, the Spirit of truth, he will teach you all
truth" (John 16:13). Speaking like this about "that day," without
making distinctions, he includes the coming of the Holy Spirit in it.

---

1. Augustine, *Tr. in Ev. Io.* 101.4. As it happens, Augustine is correct.
2. Chrysostom, *Hom. Io.* 79.1–2 (PG 59:428). Thomas had produced a précis of this
passage in the *Catena Aurea* on John 16:23, and he is probably using his own précis here.
Before him, all that Thomas takes from Chrysostom had already been used by Hugh of St.
Cher in his postil.
3. Augustine, loc. cit.

So "on that day," when the Holy Spirit is given, "you will not ask anything of me," because you will know everything by the Holy Spirit.[4] "His anointing teaches you about everything" (1 John 2:27).

Again, still following Chrysostom, "on that day" of the coming of the Holy Spirit "you will not ask anything of me" because you will have no need to ask me.[5]

But surely the apostles did make some prayers to Christ after the resurrection? "Because of this three times I asked the Lord" (meaning Christ) (2 Cor. 12:8).[6] In response, we must say that there were two natures in Christ: his human nature, by means of which he is the mediator between God and human beings (1 Tim. 2:5), and his divine nature, in which he is one with the Father. As man, Christ was not the kind of mediator who would never unite us with God, like some mediators who never bring together the parties on either side. He does unite us with the Father. And our union with Christ in his divine nature is the same as our union with the Father. That is why he says: you will not need to use my mediation, as man. So "on that day you will not ask me," as a mediator,[7] because you will have access to God for yourselves; but you will ask me as God. And even though Christ does intercede for us, as the apostle says (Rom. 8:34), the church does not address him as an intercessor, so we do not say, "Christ, pray for us"; she asks him as God, cleaving to him as God by love and faith.

Augustine takes the text as referring to the day of our vision in glory:[8] "on that day," when I see you in glory, "you will not ask me," that is, you will not ask me for anything, because there will be nothing left to desire, since all good things will be more than abundant for us in our heavenly home. "You will fill me with happiness with your face" (Ps. 15:10). "I shall have my fill when your glory appears" (Ps. 16:15). Again, "you will not ask any questions," because you will be full of the knowledge of God. "In your light we shall see light" (Ps. 35:10).

---

4. Cf. Chrysostom, as used by Hugh of St. Cher and in the *Catena Aurea*.

5. This is clearly moving on to the other interpretation of "ask," meaning petition (this is clearer in Hugh of St. Cher and in the *Catena Aurea*). The reference is to the same passage of Chrysostom.

6. Augustine, loc. cit., followed by Hugh of St. Cher, uses the much clearer example of Stephen's prayer to Christ in Acts 7:58.

7. Cf. Chrysostom, as used in Hugh of St. Cher and the *Catena Aurea*.

8. Augustine, op. cit. 101.5.

But there is a difficulty about both interpretations, since the saints in heaven pray, according to Job 5:1, "Call and see if anyone will respond, and turn to one of the saints." And in 2 Maccabees 15:14 it says, "This is he who prays much for the people." Nor can it be said that they pray for other people but not for themselves, because it says in Apocalypse 6:10, "How long will you not avenge our blood?"

Also, the saints ask questions. They will be the equals of the angels, as it says in Matthew 22:30, and the angels ask questions: "Who is the king of glory?" (Ps. 23:8) and "Who is this who comes from Edom?" (Is. 63:1), where, according to Dionysius, it is angels who are speaking.[9] Therefore the saints also ask questions.

There is a twofold reply to both these difficulties.[10] First, the time of glory can be taken in two ways, referring to the beginning of glory or to its full consummation. The time of the beginning of glory lasts up to the day of judgment. The saints have received glory, as far as the soul is concerned, but there is still something they are waiting to receive: for themselves, they are waiting for the glory of the body, and in connection with others, they are waiting for the number of the elect to be filled up. So up to the day of judgment they can both make petitions and ask questions, though not about the essentials of beatitude. But the time of complete glory comes after the day of judgment, and then there is nothing left to ask for, nothing left to be known. And it is of that day that he says, "On that day," the day of perfect glory, you will ask for nothing and you will ask no questions.

As for what is said about the angels asking questions, it is true with reference to the mysteries of the humanity and the Incarnation of Christ, but not with reference to the mysteries of the Godhead.

"Truly I say to you. . . . " Here he promises the chance to obtain things by prayer. There are two ways in which it can be seen to follow on from what has gone before. According to Chrysostom[11] it refers to the time of Christ's resurrection and the coming of the Holy Spirit, so that it means: it is true that on that day, the day of

---

9. Cf. Dionysius, *CH* 7.3, ed. cit. pp.113–4.
10. The text appears to be promising two responses, but in fact there is only one.
11. The same passage as before.

the resurrection and the Holy Spirit, you will not ask anything of me, but you will have my help, because "in my name you will ask the Father," to whom you will have access through me.

Alternatively, according to Augustine,[12] "on that day" of my glory "you will not ask anything," but in the meantime, while you are living in the wretchedness of this exile, "if you ask the Father for anything, he will give it to you." And on this interpretation "If you ask the Father . . . " does not refer to "that day," but to the time which precedes it.

The Lord lays down seven conditions for a good prayer.[13] The first is that we should ask for spiritual things, when he says, "If you ask for something." Anything which is merely earthly, even if it is something in itself, is nothing by comparison with spiritual things.[14] "I considered wealth to be nothing in comparison with her" (Wisdom 7:8). "I looked at the earth, and it was empty and nothing" (Jer. 4:23). But on the other hand, in Matthew 6:11, the Lord teaches us to ask for temporal things: "Give us this day our daily bread." But then we must say that a temporal thing that is sought with reference to something spiritual is already something.

The second condition is that we should persevere in our prayer. This is why he says, literally, "If you shall have asked . . . ," implying perseverance.[15] "It is necessary to pray always and not give up" (Luke 18:1). "Pray without ceasing" (1 Thess. 5:17).

---

12. Cf. Augustine, op. cit. 101.5.

13. There seems to have been something of a tradition in Paris of trying to derive the four "conditions of impetration" from Augustine's comments on John 16:23–4 (cf. William of Auxerre, *Summa Aurea* III 27.3.1, ed. cit. pp. 517–8), and Hugh of St. Cher lists the standard conditions in his comment on John 16:23 (prayer must be pious, persevering, for something conducive to salvation, for oneself). Thomas' list of seven qualities of a good prayer is a development of the standard list and also a first sign that he wants to shift the discussion away from conditions of impetration, to concentrate rather on what makes a "good prayer"; his attempt is interesting, if not entirely felicitous. He succeeds much better in *Summa Theol.* II.II q.83 a.15.

14. Cf. Augustine, op. cit. 102.2. Hugh of St. Cher includes the requirement that one should be praying for eternal, not temporal, things under the requirement that one must be praying for things conducive to salvation, and finds the textual basis for this in the words "something" and "in my name," which Thomas treats separately as indicating two different aspects of a good prayer.

15. Augustine mentions perseverance in op. cit. 102.2. It is attached to the form of the verb (*petieritis*) by Hugh of St. Cher (on the utterly mysterious grounds that the verb is subjunctive) and by William of Auxerre (loc. cit. p.518) on the slightly more plausible grounds that the verb is future perfect ("if you shall have asked . . . ").

The third condition is that we should pray in harmony: he says, "If you (plural) ask." "If two of you agree on earth about anything at all which you are asking for, it will be done for you by my Father who is in heaven" (Matt. 18:19). Accordingly the Gloss on Romans 15:30 says that it is impossible for the prayers of many not to be heard.[16]

The fourth condition is that prayer should come from filial affection.[17] "If you ask the *Father* . . . " If your prayer comes from fear, then it is not your Father you are asking, but your master or your enemy. "If you know how to give good things to your children, how much more will your Father who is in heaven give good gifts to those who ask him?" (Matt. 7:11).

The fifth condition is that prayer should be made piously, that is, with humility: "He looked on the prayer of the humble and did not spurn their entreaties" (Ps. 101:18). Also with faith that we shall obtain what we are asking for: "Let him ask in faith, not doubting at all" (James 1:6). Also with an eye on the due order of things: "You ask and do not receive, because you ask badly" (James 4:3). With reference to this he says, "In my name," the name of "Savior," that is; we pray in that name when we ask for things that are relevant to salvation and in such a way that we can thereby attain to salvation.[18] "There is no other name under heaven which is given to us in which we must be saved" (Acts 4:12).

The sixth condition is that prayer should be made at the right time. That is why he says, "He will give." We should not give up immediately if we do not receive; it will be given us even if it is de-

---

16. Lombard's Gloss (PL 191:1526D). This condition is original to Thomas, and it is not entirely satisfactory, as praying in harmony with other people (especially if it is taken to mean, as the authorities cited imply, conspiring with other people to pray for a common intention) cannot be regarded as a sine qua non either for impetration or for a good prayer. This condition does not feature in *Summa Theol.*, loc. cit.

17. Thomas redistributes the traditional items, so that "piously" is united with "praying for things conducive to salvation" and attached to the words "in my name," whereas Hugh of St. Cher (with more etymological cogency) attaches "piously" to the principle of praying as a child to one's Father (*pietas* in Latin having a strong connotation of loyalty to one's parents, as is exemplified famously in *pius Aeneas*).

18. The interpretation of praying in Christ's name as meaning praying in the name of the Savior, therefore praying for things conducive to salvation, comes from Augustine, op. cit. 73.3. Thomas, not entirely convincingly, connects it with the moral requirements for a good prayer, which he in turn subsumes under the traditional rubric of praying piously. A moral interpretation of "piously" is already found in William of Auxerre, loc. cit., though William refers to the theological virtues, not to humility and faith.

layed in order that we may receive it at the proper time, so that our desire may grow all the greater. "You give them their food at the proper time" (Ps. 144:15).[19]

The seventh condition is that we should pray for ourselves. So he says "to you," because sometimes we are not heard when we pray for others, because the ill deserts of the people being prayed for prevent it. "Do not pray for this people" (Jer. 7:16). "If Moses and Samuel were to stand before me, my soul is not well disposed toward this people" (Jer. 15:1).[20]

---

19. The principle that God will give his gifts at the appropriate time is noted by Augustine, op. cit. 102.1, but obviously nothing follows from this about *praying* at the right time, nor does Augustine suggest that it does. The only sense that can be made of moving from the timing of the gift to the timing of the prayer is that we must be prepared to go on praying, which has already been listed under the traditional heading of perseverance. Nor is there any obvious reason why perseverance in praying for something should be required just because God may delay the gift of that something: once we have prayed for it, we can surely quite properly leave the matter in God's hands and not feel any need to refer to it again. Augustine's doctrine of perseverance in prayer seems to mean only that we must go on praying for the total and final good of beatitude, and this makes sense; in a matter of such magnitude, stopping praying for it might easily be a sign of loss of interest in it, if only because desire for beatitude should be intense enough to make us clamor continuously for it.

20. The condition of "praying for oneself" comes from Augustine, op. cit. 102.1. As a condition for impetration, this may be a sound principle—so long as it is understood that it is not a necessary condition for impetration as such, but only one of the necessary conditions for guaranteed impetration. As a condition for a good prayer, it is clearly preposterous, and it does not reappear in *Summa Theol.*, loc. cit.

From the Lectures on St. Matthew

Matthew 6:5–8.[1]

5. When you pray, you shall not be like the hypocrites, who love to pray standing in the synagogues and at street corners, in order to be seen by other people. Truly I tell you, they have received their reward.
6. But when you pray, enter into your bedroom and shut the door and pray to your Father in secret, and your Father who sees in secret will reward you.
7. When you pray do not talk a lot, as the Gentiles do, for they think that they will be heard because they talk a lot;
8. so do not imitate them, for your Father knows what you need before you ask him.

"When you pray." The Lord has been explaining above, about almsgiving, that it should not be done for the sake of human glory. Here he shows that the same is true of prayer. And he does two things: first, he teaches the right way to pray, and secondly (starting at verse 9) he teaches what we ought to ask for in prayer.

In connection with the first point he does two things: first, he teaches us to avoid the vanity of hypocrites in our prayer, and secondly, he teaches us to avoid the vanity of the Gentiles (at verse 7).

Under the first heading he does two things: first, he excludes the wrong way to pray, and secondly, he specifies the proper way to pray (at verse 6). He excludes the wrong way of praying by citing the example of hypocrites. So first he excludes this model, then he elaborates on it ("who love . . . "), and thirdly, he indicates his reason ("Truly I tell you . . . ").

It is appropriate enough that he deals with prayer here, after almsgiving. It says in Ecclus. 18:23, "Before prayer prepare your

---

1. Only the *reportatio* of Peter d'Andria (hereafter P) survives of the lectures on Matt. 6:5–8.

soul,"[2] and it is by good works, among which almsgiving is pre-eminent, that the soul is prepared for prayer. "Let us lift up our hearts, with our hands, to the Lord" (Lam. 3:41), and this happens when our good works are in harmony with our prayer.[3]

It should be noted that the Lord is not trying to encourage us to pray, he is teaching us the proper way to pray: "*When* you pray. . . ."[4]

By "hypocrites" is meant people who are only putting on a show, who do[5] everything for the sake of human praise; and although this is a vice which should be avoided in all we do, it is particularly to be avoided in prayer, as Chrysostom says,[6] because prayer is a kind of sacrifice which we offer to God from the depth of our heart. "May my prayer be directed like incense in your sight" (Ps. 140:2). It is not lawful for a sacrifice to be offered to anyone except God. But if prayer is made for the sake of human glory, the sacrifice is offered to other human beings; so people like this are idolaters.

Hypocrites are described with reference to their desires, to place, to pride and to their intention.[7]

With reference to the first point he says, "Who love. . . . " It sometimes happens that holy people feel a certain titillation of vainglory, but this does not mean that they are to be counted as hypocrites, unless they do this on purpose. "In the desire of his soul he drew in the wind of self-love" (Jer. 2:24).

There are two kinds of hypocrite, be it noticed, who patently seek human glory: first, people who pray in public places, which is

---

2. The manuscript has *oratio ante orationem*, but it is clear that a reference to Ecclus. 18:23 is intended.

3. "Hands" is taken to mean "works" (cf. the Interlinear Gloss), so this text can be used to support the call for a conjunction of good works and prayer,

4. The manuscript has *cum angelis*, underlined as if it were a lemma, so I presume Thomas was not identifying the proper way of praying in terms of its being "with the angels," but that he was identifying which part of the Matthean text he was discussing, and this must be "when you pray. . . . " For the point that Christ is teaching us how to pray, not giving us an exhortation to pray, cf. Rabanus Maurus ad loc. (PL 107:816D). In Peraldus, *Summa de Virtutibus* III 5.7 the commendation of prayer (ch.3) is a distinct topic from "how to pray" (ch.8).

5. Reading *faciunt* for the manuscript *fatuum*.

6. *Hom. Matt.* 19.3.

7. For the last two items the manuscript text is corrupt, but the restoration seems reasonably certain.

why it says "in the synagogues," where the populace used to assemble. "The synagogue of the peoples" (Ps. 7:8).[8] The other kind is people who pray in private places and seek glory from their very avoidance of glory.[9] They do not want entirely to aim at secrecy, even though they love private places. This is the point of "in the synagogues and at street corners." If they were genuinely looking for a way to be secret, they would not make for a street corner, they would make for their own chamber. Or we can say in general that any open place is public, but there are two kinds of public place, one designated[10] for prayer, namely the synagogue, and one not designated for prayer, namely street corners. A corner is properly a place where two lines intersect, so that there is a crossroads there,[11] and this is a very public place and it is not designated for prayer. "The stones of the sanctuary have been scattered at the head of every street" (Lam. 4:1).

It should also be noted that one of the things which make for prayer is humility. "The entreaty of the humble and meek has always been pleasing to you" (Jdt 9:16). "He has looked on the prayer of the humble" (Ps. 101:18). But these people look proud because they "stand."[12]

But surely there is no place where it is forbidden to pray. "I want the men to pray in every place" (1 Tim. 2:8). "Bless the Lord God in churches" (Ps. 67:27).[13] What has to be said is that there is no sin unless there is the intention, "in order to be seen by other people." And, as Chrysostom says, if wanting to be seen by other people is damaging in other things we do, it is specially damaging

---

8. Cf. Lombard's Gloss on this Psalm (PL 191:114CD), interpreting "synagogue" as meaning "assembly."

9. This interpretation is traditional: cf. Pseudo-Chrysostom, *Op. Imp. in Matt.* 13 (PG 56:709); Marginal Gloss; Hugh of St. Cher.

10. Here and a few words on I read *deputatum* for the manuscript *deputant*.

11. Cf. Rabanus ad loc. (PL 107:816A).

12. This accords with the interpretation of the Interlinear Gloss. Hugh of St. Cher broke with this exegetical tradition and points out that standing was the normal posture for prayer among the Jews.

13. *Ecclesiis* in the psalter obviously does not mean "churches," but Christian interpreters applied it to their own situation and so "churches" seems to be the best translation, though the emphasis is on the assembled Christians rather than on the buildings (cf. Lombard's Gloss, PL 191:615B). The problem of reconciling praying in church with the Matthean text is raised in Chrysostom, *Hom. Matt.* 19.3, and in Pseudo-Chrysostom, loc. cit. (PG 56:709), the latter citing Ps. 67:27.

in prayer,[14] because it spoils prayer both from the point of view of its objective and from the point of view of its substance, because even if our purpose in praying is good it is almost impossible to stop our minds wandering all over the place, so it is much harder when we are praying because of human glory. This is the point of "in order to be seen. . . . "

So should we never pray in a public place? We must realize that the Lord[15] means to ban a certain way of praying, so as to remove vainglory,[16] and vainglory is only sought in connection with something peculiar to some individual, because when many people are all following the same practice nobody looks for any glory from anyone else. This is why the Lord eliminates any individual way of praying, that is to say, that nobody should pray in a place which is not designated for prayer, unless it is someone of sufficient standing to be able to get other people to pray too. So according to Chrysostom "at street corners" is to be taken as applying to any way in which you would appear to be different from the other people with whom you are associated.[17]

"Truly I say to you." Here he indicates[18] his reason, and he says two things: "reward" and "their." A "reward"[19] is the way in which people are supported by their labor; so when we do something for the sake of human glory, human glory is our reward. But we ought to wait for the true glory, which comes from God. And that is something common, whereas they have helped themselves.[20] "Whatever people sow, that they will reap" (Gal. 6:8).

---

14. Chrysostom, loc. cit.

15. Reading *dominus* for the manuscript *deus*.

16. The Latin literally says, "The Lord intends to ban a way of praying by which vainglory is taken away," but the sense is clear.

17. Cf. Pseudo-Chrysostom, loc. cit.

18. The manuscript has the word garbled, but *assignat* is clearly intended.

19. After "reward" there is an unintelligible word; the sense seems complete without it.

20. The text of this paragraph is obscure, but there are explicitly two points to be made, one about *mercedem* and one about *suam*. The first point is clearly that we get what we are working for, so if we are working for human glory, that is what we shall get. The second point appears to be that divine glory is nobody's private property, and the hypocrites have usurped a private glory to which they have no right, so that part of their offense is to seek a glory which will be "theirs." But I am not too sure that this is really what Thomas said. If *commune* is not the right reading (and it is underlined as if it were a lemma, so perhaps we should read "And that is the point of 'they have received' " or something of the kind), then

"But when you pray. . . . " Here he lays down what the proper way to pray is, and first he lays it down, then he gives the reason for it ("and your Father . . . "). So he says, "When you pray," that is, when you are disposing yourself to pray, "enter into your bedroom." This is interpreted in three ways. First, it is taken literally as referring to the privacy of one's room. But are not people who go to church doing the opposite?[21] We must say that the Lord is speaking of private prayer, and that should be made only in a private place, for three reasons. First, it accords with the faith, because in that way you are confessing that God is present everywhere. "Lord, my every desire is before you and my groaning is not hidden from you" (Ps. 37:10). "I fill heaven and earth, says the Lord" (Jer. 23:24). Secondly, praying with a lot of people is liable to be disturbed, but prayer made in secret is peaceful. "I will lead her into solitude" (Hos. 2:14). Thirdly, it avoids vainglory. "David went in" to pray "in the presence of the Lord," alone, that is.[22]

"And shut the door," literally, to shut out even the possibility of anyone approaching.

Secondly, "bedroom" can be taken more inwardly to mean the secrecy of the heart. "What you say in your hearts and are contrite on your beds" (Ps. 4:5). The "door" is your mouth: "Set a door to your mouth" (Ecclus. 28:28), that is, pray silently. And there are three reasons for this. First, it attests your faith, because in this way you confess that God knows the thoughts of people's hearts. "Human beings see only what appears, but God sees the heart" (1 Sam. 16:7). Secondly, it is not right[23] that other people should know your petitions. "My secret is for me" (Is. 24:16). Thirdly, if you speak out loud, you would disturb others. "The hammer and the axe were not heard in the house" (3 Kings 6:7).

But what shall we say about public prayer? We must say that the Lord is speaking about private prayer, in which the benefit of a

---

quia usurpaverunt (which I have translated, not too happily, "whereas they have helped themselves") would have to be a comment on *suam*, presumably meaning the same point as that found in the Interlinear Gloss: they have received their own reward, not God's.

21. Cf. above, note 13; clearly the citation of Ps. 67:27 would be more in place here.

22. The manuscript refers to "2 Kings 14" and cites "Going in with David to pray before the Lord." This is not an exact quotation, nor does there seem to be anything in 2 Kings (2 Sam.) 14 to which Thomas could be referring. I presume that the intended text is either 2 Sam. 7:18 or 12:16 or 12:20.

23. Reading *decet* for the manuscript *debet*.

single individual is sought. But benefit is sought in public prayer too, the benefit of the whole crowd, and because some people are stirred to devotion by this sort of loud praying, for this reason the practice of singing was established. So Augustine says in his *Confessions* that St. Athanasius wanted everything to be said in a low voice, so that he would not derive an undue enjoyment from the singing, but St. Augustine himself, before his conversion, was greatly helped by this kind of singing, so he did not dare to oppose it; he approves of it.[24]

But the question now is whether people praying in a private place ought to utter words or not. Here we must make a distinction: sometimes words are used deliberately, but sometimes they come from the impulse of the heart, because, as it says in Job 4:2, "Who can hold in a speech once it has been conceived?" So some people are carried away by the very impetus of their spirit to utter some words.[25]

Now words can be considered from two points of view: they can be thought of as a debt and in that case they have to be rendered by the mouth. "With my voice I cried to the Lord" (Ps. 3:5). Or words can be thought of as helping us to pray, and in this case we must distinguish between beginning and end, because "the end of a prayer is better than its beginning" (Eccles. 7:9).[26] If at the beginning of your prayer your feelings are stirred to pray devoutly by means of words, then it is helpful to utter words, but when your feelings are already[27] stirred you should not utter words, you should put the lid on, because feelings are emptied by words, just as hot water dwindles because of evaporation; this is clear from a grief that is expressed to other people. "My heart was hot within me" (Ps. 38:4). "I said, I will not speak in the Lord's name, and a kind of fire developed in my heart" (Jer. 20:9). This is how Chrysostom expounds "shut the door."[28]

---

24. *Conf.* X 33.50.

25. In the manuscript this is followed by *hoc est orans* and a word of which I can make no sense. It looks as if this ought to be another of the retrospective lemmata favored in this *reportatio*.

26. *Oratio* here was originally meant to be "speech," but the Marginal Gloss discusses it in terms of "prayer," and Roland of Cremona devotes a small section of his treatise on prayer to it (*Summa* III, ed. cit. pp.768–9).

27. The sense seems to require *iam* rather than the manuscript *non*.

28. Cf. Chrysostom, *Hom.* 9.3; Pseudo-Chrysostom (PG 56:710).

A third interpretation is offered by Augustine, taking "bed-room" as signifying the heart and the "door" as the outer senses and also imagination, because such a person ought to enter his own heart and shut his senses and his imagination so that nothing can enter within except what belongs to prayer.[29] And Cyprian specifies two reasons: first, it is shocking if you do not pay attention to what you are saying when you are talking to any king, and secondly, how can you expect God to take any notice of you if you are taking no notice of yourself?[30] This is the door alluded to in Apocalypse 3:20, "I stand at the door and knock."

"And your Father. . . . " Here the Lord specifies the reason. Nobody prays except to someone who sees, and in the case of God "everything is bare and open to his sight" (Heb. 4:13).

"In secret," either the secrecy of the heart or a secret place.

"Will reward you. . . . "

"When you pray. . . . " Here he teaches us to avoid the second fault, namely the Gentiles' practice of talking a lot. And on this subject he does three things. First, he teaches us to avoid the example of the Gentiles, secondly ("for they think . . . ") he explains their intention, and thirdly ("for your Father knows . . . ")[31] he specifies the reason. So he says, "When you pray," and notice that he does not say, "Do not pray a lot," because that would be contrary to Romans 12:12, "Being insistent on prayer," and Luke 22:43, "Being in agony he prayed all the longer," and Luke 6:12, "He spent the night in prayer." What he says is, "Do not talk a lot."[32] In his book on prayer Augustine says, "There should not be much talking, but there should be much praying, provided that a fervent intention does not fail."[33] But "much" and "little," "great" and "small" are relative terms. "Much" can be taken in two ways: it can be taken with reference to the praying, which is an ascent to God;[34] or people can be "talking a lot" when their words go beyond the limits of prayer, in one of two senses: the words may be about unlawful things, and then they are damaging; or they may be uttered when there is no

---

29. *De Sermone Domini* II 3.11.
30. *De Oratione Dominica* 31.
31. The manuscript *nobiscum* (evidently meant to be a lemma) cannot be right.
32. The manuscript *noli ri* is meaningless.
33. *Ep.* 130.10.20 (PL 33:502).
34. Reading *ascensus* for the manuscript *assensus*.

devotion present, and then people get bored and praying becomes hateful. So Augustine says that the monks in Egypt used frequent, but brief, prayers, because they saw that devotion was necessary to anyone praying, and that will be dissipated by a great number of words.[35] That is why the practice was established in the church of saying different things at different Hours. "Do not say anything idly, nor should your heart be quick to utter any speech before God" (Eccles. 5:1). And Augustine says that this business, the business of prayer, is conducted more with groans than with words.[36]

"As the Gentiles do." The Gentiles worshipped demons as being gods. "All the gods of the nations are demons" (Ps. 95:5). On demons there are two points to be considered.[37] They do not know the inner secrets of our hearts except insofar as they are displayed to them, and so it was necessary for the Gentiles to explain everything in words. "They shouted with a loud voice" (3 Kings 18:28).[38] And demons' feelings can be changed, so they can be changed by words. Accordingly Augustine says that Plato said that they are swayed by words.[39] But God knows everything and is not affected by words. "I am God and I do not change" (Mal. 3:6). "God is not like a human being, liable to change" (Num. 23:19). "He will not spare them because of words well-formed for entreaty" (Job 41:3).[40] This is the point of "for they think. . . . "

"So do not imitate them." Why? "For your Father knows. . . . " "Lord, my every desire is before you" (Ps. 37:10). So if he knows, we do not have to multiply words.

But it may be said: if God knows what we need, why do we pray? Jerome answers that we do not make petitions in words in order to indicate what we want, but in order to ask for it.[41] And again

---

35. *Ep.* 130.10.20 (PL 33:501), though Augustine says "intention," not "devotion."

36. Ibid. (PL 33:502).

37. The manuscript text is garbled, but this is almost certainly what was meant.

38. The manuscript text refers to "3 Kings 14: they shout more loudly"; I presume that 3 Kings 18:28 is the passage intended.

39. The reference is perhaps to *Civ. Dei* VIII 17–18, where Augustine cites Apuleius, *De Deo Socratis* 6 and 13, according to which demons are the go-between mediating between us and the gods (cf. Plato, *Symp.* 202e); they take our prayers to the gods and are themselves influenced by gifts. In fact Apuleius also says (13) that they are influenced by prayers, but Augustine does not quote this.

40. The text is garbled in the manuscript and the reference is given as Job 14. Job 41:3 seems to be the most promising candidate.

41. Cf. Jerome, *in Matt.* I 6.8, cited by Hugh of St. Cher.

it could be asked why we utter words, and Augustine answers that there is a difference between the prayers we make to other people and the prayers we make to God:[42] in the case of other human beings, words can be very effective in swaying them, but in the case of God our words are useful in helping us to raise our hearts to him.[43] And so Augustine says that, though our hearts ought always to be turned toward God, we should sometimes pray in words so that our desire does not fail.[44] And, as Chrysostom says, as a result of frequent prayer we become intimate with God and he with us.[45] Moses spoke with God face to face (Exod. 33:11). Again, another result is humility, from the thought of God's excellence and our own weakness. "I will speak to my Lord, though I am but dust and ashes" (Gen. 18:27). And another result is that there is an orientation[46] in our actions and we seek help from God. "I lifted up my eyes to the mountains, from where my help will come" (Ps. 120:1). "Whatever you do, do it all in the name of the Lord Jesus, giving thanks to God" (Col. 3:17).

Matthew 6:9–15.[47]

9. So you shall pray like this: "Our Father, who art in the heavens, hallowed be thy name,

10. Thy kingdom come, thy will be done, on earth as it is in heaven.

11. Give us this day our supersubstantial bread.

---

42. Before *Deo* the manuscript has a meaningless word, which I have simply omitted.

43. I think the reference is probably to *Ep.* 130.9.18 (cf. next note), but it may be to *De Sermone Domini* II 3.12.

44. *Ep.* 130.9.18 (possibly meant to be a continuation of the citation from Augustine which immediately precedes it; cf. previous note).

45. *Hom. Matt.* 19.4, as interpreted in the Latin version used by Thomas in the *Catena Aurea*.

46. The manuscript text, *homo ex hoc in actibus suis dirigit*, is not satisfactory; it is tempting to emend to *dirigitur* ("another result is that we are guided in our actions"), but the quotation from Col. 3:17 implies that the point is not that we are guided, but that we "direct" our actions toward God. So I have tried to translate the text as it stands.

47. I have taken the text of the lectures on Matt. 6:9–15 primarily from P, but I have also used the other *reportatio*, by Léger de Besançon (hereafter L), for which I have used the Marietti edition and one manuscript (Vatican Libr., Urb. lat. 25). Obvious emendations to P, especially those supported by L, I have made without comment. All passages taken from L are indicated in the notes.

12. And forgive us our debts, as we too forgive our debtors.
13. And lead us not into temptation, but deliver us from evil. Amen."
14. For if you forgive other people their sins, your heavenly Father will also forgive you your trespasses,
15. but if you do not forgive other people, nor will your Father forgive you your sins.

"So you shall pray like this." Above the Lord has taught us the proper manner in which we should pray, that is, that we must avoid both the vanity of hypocrites and the much-speaking of the Gentiles. Here he teaches us what we ought to ask for in prayer. And in this connection he does two things: first, he gives the title of the prayer,[48] then he proposes the prayer itself.

The connection with what has gone before is this: "I have told you not to talk a lot when you pray, so, in order to talk in few words, you shall pray like this."[49]

Notice that the Lord does not say, "You shall pray this," but "You shall pray like this." He does not rule out the possibility of our praying in other words, but he is teaching us the correct way of praying. As Augustine says in his book on prayer to Proba, people are not praying as they ought to if they are not asking for something contained in the Lord's Prayer.[50] All the same, it is appropriate to use these very words because, as Cyprian says in his book on the Lord's Prayer, it is a friendly and intimate prayer to entreat the Lord on the basis of something that is his own. And he provides an illustration: it is a common practice of advocates to put into people's mouths some words which they should say in court; so this prayer is the safest of all, having been shaped by our advocate, who is the wisest possible advocate, since in him "all the treasures of wisdom and knowledge are hidden" (Col. 2:3). So, as Cyprian says, since we

---

48. *Titulus orationis:* this cannot refer to the opening words of the prayer ("Our Father"), since these are treated as part of the prayer; so presumably *titulus* must mean "title" in the sense of "status" or something like that, referring to the few words used to introduce the prayer.

49. Reading *ut paucis loquamini sic orabitis* for the manuscript *ut paucis loquebaris sic eruditis.*

50. Augustine, *Ep.* 130.12.22 (PL 33:502).

have Christ as our advocate with the Father for our sins, when we pray over our sins we should pronounce the words of our advocate.[51] "We have an advocate with the Father" (1 John 2:1). This is why it says, "Let us approach with confidence to the throne of grace" (Heb. 4:16). "Let him ask in faith" (James 1:6).

This prayer has three qualities: brevity, completeness and effectiveness.[52] There are two reasons for its brevity: it means that everyone can easily learn it,[53] both great and small, learned and unlearned,[54] because he is "the same Lord of all, who is rich toward all who call on him" (Rom. 10:12). Secondly, it is to give us confidence that we shall easily obtain what we are asking for.[55] "The Lord will make a shortened word upon the earth" (Is. 10:23).[56]

It is also complete. As Augustine says, anything that can be contained in other prayers is contained in this one. So he says that if we are praying appropriately and correctly, then whatever words we may be using we are not saying anything other than what is laid down in the Lord's Prayer.[57] God himself gave us this prayer[58] and "God's works are complete" (Deut. 32:4).

It is effective because, according to Damascene, prayer is a petition made to God for things that are fitting.[59] "You ask and you do not receive because you ask badly" (James 4:3). But knowing what we ought to ask for is extremely difficult, as is knowing what we ought to desire. "We do not know what we ought to pray for, but the Spirit himself entreats for us" (Rom. 8:26). Because the Lord himself taught us this prayer, it is particularly effective.[60] This is

---

51. Cyprian, *De Oratione Dominica* 3.

52. Thomas' "three qualities" correspond fairly closely to the five qualities listed in Peraldus' sermon on prayer (Tugwell, *Early Dominicans* p.169). It is likely that Thomas knew this sermon, to which Peraldus refers in his treatise on prayer in the *Summa de Virtutibus* III 5.7.10.

53. Cf. Cyprian, op. cit. 28 (including the quotation of Is. 10:23).

54. "Learned and unlearned" is taken from L.

55. Cf. the Marginal Gloss.

56. The citation from Isaiah comes here in L; P, less plausibly, has it after "It is also complete" in the next paragraph. It is cited in the form found in Rom. 9:28.

57. Augustine, *Ep.* 130.12.22 (PL 33:502).

58. This clause is taken from L. For the point, cf. Peraldus' sermon in Tugwell, *Early Dominicans* p.169 (the first quality of the prayer).

59. Damascene, *De Fide Orthodoxa* 68.1, ed. Buytaert p.267.

60. This corresponds to Peraldus' "fifth quality" (*virtus*), which Peraldus also connects with the Lord's authorship of the prayer: "It is most unlikely that Christ would have for-

---

why it says in Luke 11:1–2, "Lord, teach us to pray . . . and he said to them, 'When you pray, say "Our Father." ' "

In this prayer the Lord does two things: first, he gives us the prayer, then he indicates a reason for it ("if you forgive . . . ").

You must realize that in all speeches (*oratio*), including those of orators, the good will of the addressee is won first before any petition is made.[61] So this should be done in a speech addressed to God, just as it is in a speech addressed to human beings. But the purpose is not the same in each case. In the case of human beings we win their good will inasmuch as we influence their minds, but in the case of God it is a matter of our raising our minds to him.[62]

Accordingly the Lord specifies two things which we need when we pray in order to win good will: we must believe that the one we are praying to is willing to give and that he is able to give. So he says, "Father," because if he is a Father he wills what is best for his children,[63] and "who art in the heavens" because if he is in heaven he can do whatever he wills.[64]

Five things are achieved by saying "Father." First, it instructs us in our faith,[65] and faith is necessary for people who pray. There have been three errors which preclude prayer; two entirely destroy prayer and the third concedes more than it should,[66] and they are all eliminated by the Lord's saying "Our Father." Some people have

---

mulated the petitions it contains unless he meant to grant them" (loc. cit.). The connection with Rom. 8:26 and the suggestion that the Lord's Prayer is a remedy for our ignorance of what we ought to pray for is also found in Hugh of St. Cher (f.23[ra]).

61. "Our Father" is interpreted as a form of *captatio benevolentiae* in Augustine, *De Sermone Domini* II 4.15, in the Interlinear Gloss and in Hugh of St. Cher (f.23[ra]).

62. Peraldus treats "Our Father," not as *captatio benevolentiae*, but as "preparation for prayer", Tugwell (pp.170–1; *De Virtutibus* III 5.7.4), rather along the lines suggested here; it seems more logical to abandon the attempt to find a *captatio* in the Lord's Prayer.

63. The comment "because if . . . " is taken from L. On the point being made, cf. below, note 75.

64. The comment "because if . . . " is taken from L. Peraldus regards the twofold confidence that God is both willing and able to give us things as a necessary part of the "preparation for prayer" summed up in "Our Father" (cf. above, note 62). Hugh of St. Cher also interprets "who art in the heavens" as indicating God's ability to give us things (f.23[rb]). Thomas appears to be thinking of Ps. 113:11, "Our God is in heaven, he does whatever he wills."

65. This dogmatic insert seems to have no parallel in earlier commentaries on Matthew; it anticipates the discussion in *Summa Theol.* II.II q.83 a.2.

66. L presents the material slightly differently, listing at this point only two errors which destroy prayer, and this is perhaps more logical, as the third error does not preclude prayer, only misinterprets it.

said that God is not concerned about human affairs. "They have said, 'The Lord has abandoned the earth' " (Ezek. 9:9). On this view it is a waste of time asking God for anything. Other people have said that there is a divine providence and that it does make provision for everything, but it subjects everything to the constraint of necessity, so there is no need to pray because, if God is making provision, then it will happen just so.[67] The third error concedes too much, saying that God arranges everything by his providence, but his divine plan is changed by prayer.

All these errors are eliminated by the Lord saying, "Our Father who art in the heavens." If he is a Father, then he does exercise providence over his children:[68] "Your providence, Father, guides it" (Wis. 14:3).[69] And the second error is also eliminated: "father" is relative to "children," as "master" is to "servant,"[70] so in calling God "Father" we are calling ourselves his children (*liberi*).[71] Almost nowhere in scripture do we find God called the Father of inanimate creatures, though there is an exception in Job 38:28, "Who is the rain's father?" So "Father" is relative to "son" and "son" implies freedom.[72] So we are not subjected to the constraint of necessity. And by saying, "Who art in the heavens," he excludes any mutability from God's plan, showing that everything is unchanging because he is unchanging.[73] So the prayer makes us believe that God arranges everything in accordance with the nature of things, so that effects

---

67. "And that it does make provision for everything" and "so there is no need . . . just so" come from L.

68. "Over his children" comes from L. Cf. Peraldus, *De Virt.* III 5.7.4.

69. The manuscript has *Sap. 12, Tu autem pater*, but it must be Wis. 14:3 that is meant.

70. "Master" and "servant" is the classic example of the kind of relative term described by Aristotle in *Cat.* 7 (6b28–33), that is, terms which are mutually dependent (if there is no servant there can be no master and vice versa).

71. Cf. Jerome, *in Matt.* I 6.9, though Jerome has *se filios confitentur* and both *reportationes* of Thomas use the word *liberos*. *Liberi* ("children") is connected, probably rightly, with *liberi* ("free") (cf. Isidore, *Etym.* IX 5.17), allowing Thomas to pass easily from the point that we must be God's children, if he is our Father, to the inference that we must therefore be free.

72. The Pauline doctrine that the children are free (cf. Gal. 4:1–7) joins forces here with the etymological implications of *liberi* to make the claim that *filius habet rationem libertatis*.

73. "Showing . . . he is unchanging" comes from L (for the text, see H. V. Shooner, "La 'Lectura in Matthaeum' de S. Thomas," *Angelicum* 33 [1956] p.132). "Heaven" represents divine immutability because it is the "first unchanged changer," which is at the source of all change in the visible world (cf. Albert, *DN* 4.59, Col. XXXVII p.166:43–4; *De Caelo* 2.1, Col. V i p.105—also probably composed while Thomas was still in Cologne in 1250–51).

follow from causes. It is by providence that human beings achieve their goals by their own activity. So prayer does not alter providence nor will it be outside providence, it falls within providence: God's providence arranges for such and such a boon to be granted to us by means of such and such a prayer.[74] So we are, first of all, instructed in our faith by the words "Our Father."

Secondly, these words raise our hopes. If God is our Father, he is willing to give us things.[75] As it says below (Matt. 7:11), "If you who are evil know how to give good things to your children, how much more will your Father who is in heaven give good things to those who ask him?"

Thirdly, they serve to stimulate charity.[76] It is natural for children to love their father and vice versa. "Children, obey your parents in the Lord" (Eph. 6:1).[77]

Fourthly,[78] we are invited to imitate God.[79] "Be imitators of God, like dearest children" (Eph. 5:1). "So that you may be children of your Father" (Matt. 5:45).[80] Children ought to imitate their father as far as they can. "You will call me 'Father' and you will not cease to come after me" (Jer. 3:19).

Fifthly,[81] we are called to humility.[82] "If I am your Father, where is my honor?" (Mal. 1:6).

In saying "Our Father"[83] our feelings for our neighbors are set in order. "Is there not one Father of us all?" (Mal. 2:10). If we all have one Father, none of us ought to despise any of our neighbors on the grounds of birth.[84]

---

74. These three sentences are conflated from L and P.

75. Cf. Augustine, *De Sermone Domini* II 4.16.

76. Ibid.

77. The citation from Ephesians is taken from L. Lombard's Gloss on Eph. 6:1 (PL 192:217C) treats it as equivalent to "Honor your father and mother," which is in turn identified as part of the second precept of charity.

78. P does not have "fourthly" here, and L does not number the successive points.

79. This clause comes here in L; in P it comes after the citation of Eph. 5:1 (and in P it is introduced with "thirdly"!).

80. The citation from Matt. is taken from L (as found in the Marietti ed.; it is not in the manuscript I have consulted).

81. P says "fourthly."

82. Cf. Augustine, *De Sermone Domini* II 4.16.

83. These words are taken from L; P says "fifthly" and presents this point as the final item in the discussion of "Father."

84. Cf. Augustine, *De Sermone Domini* II 4.16. This sentence is taken from L, as found in Marietti; the manuscript of L I have used has a deformed text.

But why do we not say, "My Father"? There are two reasons. First, Christ wanted to reserve that to himself as his own, because he is God's Son by nature, whereas we are his children by adoption and that is common to all of us. "I am ascending to my Father and to your Father" (John 20:17), because he is "mine" in a different sense from that in which he is "yours."[85] Secondly, as Chrysostom says, the Lord is teaching us not to make private prayers, but to pray generally for the whole people; this kind of prayer is more acceptable to God. In Chrysostom's words, "In God's eyes a prayer is more pleasing if it comes from fraternal love rather than from need."[86] "Pray for one another" (James 5:16).

The second thing belonging to the winning of good will is "Who art in the heavens," and this is interpreted in two ways. First, literally, with reference to the bodily heavens. Not that he is confined there. " 'Do I not fill heaven and earth?' says the Lord" (Jer. 23:24). The reason for saying, "Who art in the heavens," is that the heavens are the highest part of creation. "Heaven is my seat" (Is. 66:1). This makes provision for the weak[87] who are unable to rise above bodily things. Augustine says that this is the reason why we pray toward the East, because the movement of the sky is from the East, and God is above our spirit just as the sky is above our body. So we are given to understand that our spirit ought to turn to God, just as we turn our bodies to the sky when we pray.[88] So he says "Who art in the heavens" to raise our attention away from the things of earth[89] "to an incorruptible inheritance . . . preserved in heaven" (1 Pet. 1:4).

Alternatively, the heavens can be taken to mean the saints,[90] as in Isaiah 1:2, "Hear, you heavens." "You dwell in your holy one" (Ps. 21:4). And he says this to give us a greater confidence in obtaining what we pray for, because he is not far from us.[91] "You are in us, Lord" (Jer. 14:9).

---

85. The last phrase is taken from L. Cf. Marginal Gloss here and Interlinear Gloss to John 20:17.

86. Pseudo-Chrysostom, *Op. Imp. in Matt.* 14 (PG 56:711), quoted in Hugh of St. Cher (f.23rb).

87. This phrase is taken from L.

88. Augustine, *De Sermone Domini* II 5.18.

89. Cf. Chrysostom, *Hom. Matt.* 19.4.

90. Cf. Augustine, *De Sermone Domini* II 5.17.

91. Reading *longe* (supported by L); the manuscript of P has *in lege*.

"Hallowed be thy name." After the winning of good will, he now moves on to the petitions.[92] First, let us take them in general, then in detail. And there are three things we have to consider with reference to these petitions. Petition serves desire, because what we ask for is what we want to have. Now in this prayer all that we can desire is contained. Secondly, it is contained in the order in which we ought to desire things. Thirdly, these petitions correspond to the gifts and beatitudes.[93]

We must realize that people naturally desire two things: to obtain good and to avoid ill.[94] In the prayer four good things to be desired are laid down. And the primary objective of desire is the goal it is aiming at, the things which lead to that goal being secondary. And the ultimate goal of everything is God. So the first thing to be desired has to be God's honor. "Do everything to the glory of God" (1 Cor. 10:31). And this is what we ask for first: "Hallowed be thy name."

Among the things which belong to us, our final goal is eternal life,[95] and this is what we ask for in "Thy kingdom come." The third thing we have to ask for is the things that lead to our goal, that is, that we may have virtue and good merits, and this is what we do in "Thy will be done." And there is nothing other than this that we ask for in connection with the virtues.[96] So the point of our beatitude is God, and the point of the virtues is beatitude. But we need support, both temporal and spiritual, such as the church's sacraments, and this is what we ask for when we say "our bread," meaning external bread or sacramental bread. And in these four things all our good is contained.

As for what is ill, we avoid that inasmuch as it hinders good. The first good, God's honor, cannot be hindered, because God is honored if there is righteousness, and if there is evil he is similarly honored inasmuch as he punishes it, even though he is not honored

92. This sentence is taken from L.

93. The connection between the gifts of the Holy Spirit, the beatitudes and the petitions of the Lord's Prayer was first suggested by Augustine, *De Sermone Domini* II 11.38, and was thereafter classic.

94. Cf. the Interlinear Gloss and Hugh of St. Cher (f.23ra).

95. Instead of "eternal life" L has "God's glory."

96. I.e., we pray for virtues solely because of a desire for beatitude (not, for instance, because we want the satisfying feeling that we are virtuous); at least, I presume this is what Thomas means.

as far as the sinner has anything to do with it. But sin hinders beatitude, and so this is the first ill to be taken away, when we say, "Forgive us." Temptation is opposed to the good consisting of the virtues, and so we ask, "Lead us not into temptation." And any lack whatsoever is opposed to the necessities of life, and so, "Deliver us from evil."

It is clear, then, that whatever is desired is all contained in the Lord's Prayer.

The gifts of the Holy Spirit can be fitted to these petitions in different ways, either ascending or descending.[97] Ascending, we can attach the first petition to fear, inasmuch as fear produces poverty of spirit and makes us seek God's honor, so that we say, "Hallowed be thy name." Descending, we can say that the final gift, that of wisdom, which makes people into God's children, goes with this petition.

We need to look at this petition, "Hallowed be thy name." It appears to be inappropriate, because God's name is always holy, so how do we ask for it to be hallowed?[98] The saints offer several interpretations. First of all Augustine, and I think his is the most literal interpretation: "Hallowed be thy name," that is, may your name, which is always holy, appear holy among human beings, and this is what it means to honor God, because it does not mean any increase of glory for God, but it does mean that we grow in the knowledge of his glory.[99] "As you were made holy in us in their sight, so you will be magnified in our sight in them, so that they may know you as we know you" (Ecclus. 36:4–5). And "Hallowed be thy name" comes appropriately enough after "Our Father who art in the heavens" because nothing is such plain evidence that we are children of God, since a good son reveals the honor of his father.

According to Chrysostom it means "Hallowed be thy name by our deeds," as if he said, "Make us live in such a way that your name will be seen to be holy because of our deeds."[100] "Hallow the Lord

---

97. Cf. the Marginal Gloss. Hugh of St. Cher (f.23ʳᵃ) refuses to enter into the niceties of how the gifts and petitions are to be correlated: "We leave that for people to argue about."
98. The last clause is taken from L.
99. Augustine, *Ep*. 130.11.21 (PL 33:502).
100. Chrysostom, *Hom. Matt*. 19.4.

Christ in your hearts . . . so that your detractors may be put to shame, who abuse your good conduct in Christ" (1 Pet. 3:15–6).[101]

Or, according to Cyprian, "Hallowed be thy name" means "sanctify us in your name."[102] "Sanctify them in your name" (John 14).[103] "And he will be your sanctification" (Is. 8:14).[104] And we must realize that "hallowed" is taken first to mean that those who are not holy should become holy, because this prayer is made for the whole human race; secondly, it means that people should persevere in holiness, and thirdly, that if there is any alloy mixed in with holiness it should be removed. Every day we need sanctifying in the face of our daily sins.

"Thy kingdom come." This petition can correspond either to the gift of understanding, which purifies the heart, or to the gift of piety.[105]

"Thy kingdom come." According to Chrysostom and Augustine the kingdom of God is eternal life,[106] and I think that this is the literal interpretation. So we ask, "Thy kingdom come," that is, make us come to and share in eternal beatitude. "Come, you blessed of my Father, possess the kingdom which has been prepared for you" (Matt. 25:34). "I am preparing a kingdom for you" (Luke 22:29).

Alternatively, according to Augustine, God began to reign from the time when he redeemed the world.[107] "All power is given to me" (Matt. 28:18).[108] So "thy kingdom come," that is, the con-

---

101. The manuscript gives no precise indication of what text from "Peter 3" is intended, but 1 Pet. 3:15 seems the most likely.

102. Cyprian, *De Oratione Dominica* 12.

103. This is a completely dud reference; there is no such text in John, nor is there anything similar in John 14. What the manuscript offers looks like a conflation of John 17:11 and 17:17.

104. The manuscript of P has a dud reference, but this is probably what Thomas meant.

105. "Understanding" is suggested in the Interlinear Gloss, "piety" in the Marginal Gloss.

106. Pseudo-Chrysostom, *Op. Imp. in Matt.* 14 (PG 56:711); it is not clear what text of Augustine is meant, but it could be *De Sermone Domini* II 6.20 or *Enchiridion* 30.115 (cf. Dozois, Revue de l'université d'Ottawa. 33, 1963 p.45*).

107. Dozois, art. cit. p.42*, refers to this citation as unidentifiable, but perhaps Augustine should not be cited for this particular point, but for the interpretation developed in the rest of the paragraph (cf. below, note 110). L has "God," P has "Christ."

108. This must be the text envisaged, though the manuscript says "John."

summation of your kingdom, and this will be when he puts his enemies under his feet.[109] So "thy kingdom come," that is, "Lord, come to judgment, so that the glory of your kingdom may be manifested." "When these things begin to happen . . . know that the kingdom of God is near" (Luke 21:28–31). And the saints desire the coming of Christ because then they will possess perfect glory.[110] "And not only for me, but for those too who love his coming" (2 Tim. 4:8).

But against this it says, "Woe to those who desire the day of the Lord,"[111] because, according to Jerome, it takes a confident conscience not to fear the judge.[112]

Alternatively, "Thy kingdom come," that is, may the reign of sin be destroyed and you, Lord, reign over us. When we are slaves to righteousness then God reigns, but when we are slaves to sin the devil reigns. "So do not let sin reign in your mortal body" (Rom. 6:12).[113] "They have not rejected you, they have rejected me from reigning over them" (1 Sam. 8:7).

And notice that people who had proved themselves to be children by saying "Our Father" could properly enough ask, "Thy kingdom come." Children are entitled to an inheritance.[114] But this kingdom is in heaven, so you cannot go there unless you are made heavenly, so it is appropriate that the next petition is "Thy will be done," that is, make us imitators of those who are in heaven. "As we have borne the image of the earthly man, so let us bear the image of the heavenly" (1 Cor. 15:49)

And notice that he does not say, "Thy will be done," as if God were doing our will,[115] but because his will is fulfilled through us, which wills everyone to be saved (1 Tim. 2:4). "This is God's will, your sanctification" (1 Thess. 4:3).[116] "Teach me to do your will" (Ps. 142:10). So we ask that God's will may be fulfilled by means of

---

109. 1 Cor. 15:25.
110. Augustine, *De Sermone Domini* II 6.20.
111. Amos 5:18.
112. Jerome, *in Matt.* I 6.10.
113. Cf. Jerome, op. cit. I 6.10.
114. Cf. Marginal Gloss.
115. The point being made is probably that of Augustine, *De Sermone Domini* II 6.21, "So those who do God's will are those in whom God's will is done, not because they are causing God to will, but because they are doing what he wills."
116. The manuscript simply has "Thess." without further specification, but 1 Thess. 4:3 is probably what was meant.

us, and it would be pointless to ask for this unless it came from God, so "Thy will be done," because it is God who works in us.[117] Thus the error of Pelagius is destroyed, who said that we do not need God's help.

"As it is in heaven." This is interpreted in several ways by Augustine.[118] First, like this: "As it is in heaven," that is, as the angels in heaven do your will, so may we fulfil your will on earth. "You servants of his who do his will" (Ps. 102:21) (this refers to the angels). And this destroys the error of Origen, who maintained that angels can sin.[119] Alternatively, "Thy will be done on earth as it is in heaven," that is, in the church as it is in Christ. The earth is made fertile by the sky, which is why the Gentiles called the sky gods masculine and the earth gods feminine. "I have come down from heaven . . . to do the will of him who sent me" (John 6:38). Or by "heavens" we can understand the saints, whose "conduct is in heaven,"[120] and by "earth" we can understand sinners.[121] As heaven is to earth, so saints are to sinners. So it is equivalent to "Lord, convert sinners to do your will as the righteous do."[122] "Lord, as you enlighten my lamp, so enlighten my darkness" (Ps. 17:29).[123] Or "Thy will be done . . . ": the relationship between flesh and spirit in a human being is like that between earth and heaven in the universe. As far as lies in it, spirit does the will of God, but flesh rebels. "I see another law in my members" (Rom. 7:23). So "Thy will be done," that is, as spirit is in harmony with your will, so may flesh be.[124] "Create a pure heart in me" (Ps. 50:12).

All these petitions are in part begun in this life, but they will be brought to fulfilment in the life to come.[125]

---

117. This sentence is taken from L. Cf. Cyprian, *De Oratione Dominica* 14.
118. Augustine, *De Sermone Domini* II 6.21–4, offers all the interpretations mentioned here.
119. Cf. Jerome, *in Matt.* I 6.10.
120. Phil. 3:20.
121. This last clause is taken from L.
122. This last phrase is taken from L.
123. This sentence is taken from L Lombard's Gloss on Ps. 17:29 (PL 191:198B) effectively identifies the "lamp" with the saints and the apostles and the "darkness" with sinners.
124. This sentence is taken from L.
125. Cf. Augustine, *De Sermone Domini* II 10.36 and the Marginal Gloss.

Chrysostom relates "as it is in heaven" to all that has gone before: so "Hallowed be thy name on earth as it is in heaven"[126] and "Thy kingdom come on earth as in heaven" and so on.[127]

Also notice, according to Chrysostom, that he did not say, "Let us hallow," or "Hallow," but neutrally, "Hallowed be. . . . " Nor did he say, "Let us go to your kingdom," or "Come," but he kept to an impersonal formula throughout, and this is because two things are required for our salvation: the grace of God and our free will. If he had said, "Hallow," he would have left no room for free will, and if he had said, "Let us do your will," he would have ascribed everything to free will. But he spoke neutrally: "Thy will be done" and so on.[128]

"Our bread." After teaching us to ask for God's glory, eternal life and the action of the virtues by which we merit eternal life, he teaches us here to ask for all the things that are necessary for this present life.[129] But "our bread" is interpreted in four ways. It can be interpreted of four kinds of bread. First, of that bread which is Christ,[130] who says of himself,[131] "I am the bread of life" (John 6:48). And he is "bread" particularly inasmuch as he is contained in the sacrament of the altar. "The bread which I shall give is my flesh" (John 6:52). "My flesh is real food" (John 6:56). And it says "our bread" because this is not bread for absolutely anyone, it is the bread of the faithful.[132] "A child is born for us" (Is. 9:6). It is as a result of becoming members of Christ in baptism that people can share in this bread. And so it should in no way be given to the unbaptized or to unbelievers.

"Supersubstantial." Jerome says that in Greek this is *hyperousion*, which Symmachus translated as "chief" or "outstanding."[133]

---

126. I have added this clause from Pseudo-Chrysostom.

127. Pseudo-Chrysostom, *Op. Imp. in Matt.* 14 (PG 56:712), cited by Hugh of St. Cher (f.24rb).

128. Pseudo-Chrysostom, ibid., cited by Hugh of St Cher, ibid.

129. Cf. Augustine, *De Sermone Domini* II 7.25.

130. This interpretation is specially argued for by Augustine, *De Sermone Domini* II 7.25–7, but is also mentioned by most of the other commentators.

131. "Who says of himself" is taken from L.

132. Cf. Cyprian, op. cit. 18.

133. Jerome, op. cit. I 6.11.

The old translation has "daily."[134] That this bread is supersubstantial, that is, above all substances,[135] is shown by Ephesians 1:20–1, "Setting him above every principality and power. . . . "

He says "daily" because it ought to be received every day, but not by every individual. This is why it says in the book on *The Dogmas of the Church*, "I neither commend nor criticize daily reception."[136] But it ought to be received every day in the church, or at least the faithful should receive it spiritually in faith, even if not sacramentally.[137] In the Eastern church, though, it is not received daily in the church, because they do not have a daily celebration of Mass, but only once a week; but Augustine says that this practice is accepted,[138] so it is enough that Christians receive this bread spiritually every day without receiving it sacramentally.

"Give us." If it is "our bread," why does it say, "Give us"? Cyprian: "Give us," that is, make us live in such a way that we can receive this bread to our profit and not be made unfit to receive it by sin, because it is not "given" to people who receive it unworthily, but they take it to their detriment. "People who eat and drink unworthily are eating and drinking a judgment on themselves" (1 Cor. 11:29). So if we make this petition we are asking for nothing else but that we may persevere in good, that is, that our holiness may not be contaminated with anything else which is opposed to it.[139]

At this point Augustine[140] raises a difficulty: This prayer is said at all hours of the day, even at compline. So are we asking God to give us this bread at that time of day? We must say in response that "today" is taken in two different senses. Sometimes it refers to one particular day, but sometimes it refers to the whole of this present life. This is alluded to in Hebrews 3:15, "While it is called 'today' ". So the meaning of the petition is: grant that we may be able to receive this bread throughout this present life. And it is with reason that he says, "Give us today," because this sacramental bread is nec-

---

134. "Daily" is the text commented on by Augustine, for instance, *De Sermone Domini* II 7.25.

135. Cf. Hugh of St. Cher, f.23ᵛᵇ.

136. Gennadius, *De Eccl. Dogm.* 53 (PL 58:994); L identifies the author as "Augustine," and in fact Gennadius' work was often ascribed to Augustine.

137. "Even if not sacramentally" is taken from L.

138. This clause is taken from L. Augustine, *De Sermone Domini* II 7.26.

139. In this paragraph I have merged the two *reportationes*. Cyprian, op. cit. 18.

140. Augustine, *De Sermone Domini* II 7.26–7.

essary only in this life; when we see him as he is, we shall not need sacraments and signs, once we have obtained the reality.[141] So this unique and special bread is only necessary during this present time, and if now we receive it each day in particular, then we shall receive it continuously.[142]

The second way of understanding "bread" is to take it as referring to God, that is, the Godhead.[143] "Blessed is anyone who eats bread in the kingdom of God" (Luke 14:15).[144] "Human beings have eaten the bread of angels" (Ps. 77:25).[145] So "Give us this day," that is, so that we may be able to enjoy it in the kind of way that is possible in this life.[146]

Thirdly, "bread" can be taken as referring to God's commandments,[147] which are the bread of wisdom. "Come, eat my bread," as wisdom says (Prov. 9:5). Anyone who seeks into the teachings of salvation,[148] who keeps the precepts of wisdom, eats this bread. "My bread is to do the will of him who sent me" (John 4:34). At present[149] these precepts are bread, because it is with some difficulty that they are chewed in our reflections on them and in our practice, but afterward they will be drink, because they will nourish us without difficulty.[149a]

Fourthly, "bread" can be taken literally as meaning bodily bread.[150] Earlier the Lord said, "Hallowed be thy name"[151] and "Thy will be done," wanting us to be heavenly in fulfilling God's

---

141. This clause is taken from L.

142. Cf. Augustine, *De Sermone Domini* II 7.27 and the Marginal Gloss.

143. For this interpretation, cf. Jerome, op. cit. I 6.11, the Marginal Gloss and Hugh of St. Cher, f.23vb.

144. For the interpretation of the bread as meaning God, cf. the Marginal Gloss and Hugh of St. Cher on Luke 14:15.

145. The bread of angels is Christ: cf. Lombard's Gloss on Ps. 77:25 (PL 191:732A).

146. Cf. Jerome, op. cit. I 6.11, interpreting the apocryphal version, "Give us today tomorrow's bread."

147. For this interpretation, cf. the Marginal Gloss; Peraldus (Tugwell, *Early Dominicans* p.174) offers "teaching" as one meaning of "bread."

148. This clause is taken from L.

149. Reading *nunc* for the manuscript *non*.

149a. Cf. Marginal Gloss on Matt. 6:9, derived from Augustine, *De Sermone Domini* II 10.37.

150. This interpretation is favored by Chrysostom, *Hom. Matt.* 19.5, and by Pseudo-Chrysostom, *Op. Imp. in Matt.* 14 (PG 56:713), but it is also mentioned by Cyprian, op. cit. 19, and Jerome, op. cit. I 6.11, both citing the same text from 1 Tim. 6:8 that Thomas cites.

151. "Hallowed be thy name" is taken from L.

will; but mindful of our weakness he now teaches us to ask also for the temporal things which are necessary to support life.[152] So he does not teach us to ask for anything splendid or superfluous, but to ask for what is needed. "Having nourishment and clothes to cover us, we are content with that" (1 Tim. 6:8). This is how Jacob prayed: "If he gives me bread to eat and clothes to wear . . . " (Gen. 28:20).

He says "*our* bread" for two reasons, according to Chrysostom, to prevent people from appropriating temporal things to themselves: first, because nobody ought to eat bread obtained by stealing; they should eat bread that comes from their own labor. And secondly, the temporal boons which are given to us because of our need should be accepted in such a way that we share them with others.[153] "I have not eaten my morsel of bread alone" (Job 31:17).

Why is it that he says "supersubstantial"?[154] Augustine[155] says, in his book on prayer to Proba, that it is because whatever is pre-eminent and primary in anything that belongs[156] to our resources stands for all of it, and bread is what we most need. "The beginning of our life is water and bread" (Ecclus. 29:28). And this is what "supersubstantial" means: bread is the prime instance of what we need and stands for all the essentials of life.[157]

But if we read "daily," there are two reasons for saying it, according to Cyprian.[158] First, it is so that you will not seek temporal things on a long-term basis, because if you did you would be contradicting yourself. You said, "Thy kingdom come," but as long as we are in the body we are in exile from the Lord (2 Cor. 5:6), so if you say, "Thy kingdom come," and ask for long life, you are contradicting yourself. The second reason is to prevent superfluity, because what is needed is enough for the day. So "daily" is directed against extravagant people who spend more on one dinner than would be necessary over many days.[159]

---

152. Cf. Chrysostom, op. cit. 19.5.

153. Pseudo-Chrysostom, op. cit. 14 (PG 56:713–4), cited by Hugh of St. Cher, f.24rb.

154. This sentence is taken from L.

155. Augustine, *Ep.* 130.11.21 (PL 33:502).

156. Reading *pertinentibus* for the manuscript *particularibus*.

157. The last clause is taken from L.

158. Cf. Cyprian, op. cit. 19–20, but the second reason is almost certainly taken, not from Cyprian, but from Pseudo-Chrysostom, op. cit. 14 (PG 56:713) (cited by Hugh of St. Cher, f.24rb). In L neither reason is attributed to any authority.

159. The second reason is taken essentially from L.

But if it is "our bread," why does it say, "Give us"? There are two reasons according to Chrysostom. First, temporal goods are held by good and bad people alike,[160] but not in the same way: good people have them to their profit, but bad people to their detriment, because they make bad use of them, so they are not "given" to bad people, because they abuse them, and this comes from the devil, not from God. And secondly,[161] he says that it is like someone offering a loaf of bread to a priest for it to be blessed and then asking for it back. In such circumstances one could say, "Give me the bread which is mine; it is mine because I own it, give it to me by blessing it."[162]

He says "this day" because he did not want us to make it a long-term petition.

But Augustine[163] raises a question here. In what follows the Lord teaches us not to be anxious about temporal things. "Do not be anxious . . . " (Matt. 6:31). So it looks as if we ought not to pray for temporal things. But here he is teaching us to ask for them.[164] Augustine's answer is that we can pray for everything that is lawfully desired,[165] because it is from God that we hope to receive what we desire and whatever we hope to receive from God can be asked for. And we can lawfully desire what we need for this life, not only enough to stay alive, but enough to meet the requirements of our position in life—a king needs more than a count; so it is lawful to ask for these things.[166] But desiring is not the same thing as being anxious about something, as if it were our final goal, and that is what the Lord forbids, as will be explained later on.[167]

A further question arises about "Give us this day": it looks as if we ought to desire things for one day at a time. So all those who desire differently are sinning, and in that case human life will collapse, because no one will gather in the harvest in summer to provide

---

160. This last clause is taken from L.

161. "Secondly" is taken from L.

162. Reading *sanctificatione* for the manuscript *sanctificationi*. Pseudo-Chrysostom, op. cit. 14 (PG 56:713), cited by Hugh of St. Cher, f.24rb.

163. The manuscript has *apostolus*.

164. This sentence is taken from L. Augustine, *De Sermone Domini* II 7.25.

165. This principle is repeated in II.II q.83 a.6, where it is also ascribed to Augustine; see note 7 there.

166. This sentence is taken from L.

167. Augustine, *Ep.* 130.6.12 (PL 33:498–9).

food for the winter.[168] So we must say that the Lord did not intend to forbid people to take thought for the future; what he forbids is that we should anticipate things by presuming to worry before it is time. If some concern is laid upon you now, that is what you should be worrying about, not something that may become your responsibility in the future.[169]

"And forgive us." Here he begins to formulate the petitions which concern the taking away of evil, and he puts first the petition by which the single most important ill is taken away, namely guilt. So "And forgive us." It is shocking[170] if someone who lives by the things of God lives against God.[171] Sins are called "debts" because our sins put us under an obligation to God, like a debt. If you have taken something from someone, then you are bound in justice to return it, and when you sin you are usurping something that belongs to God, because it is his right that every will should be aligned in accordance with his will; so you are stealing something from God and are bound to restitution. You pay your debt when you endure something in accordance with God's will contrary to your own will. "I forgave all your debt . . . " (Matt. 18:32).[172] So "forgive us our debts," that is, our sins. "Forgive me so that I may be refreshed" (Ps. 38:14).

This passage refutes two heresies, those of Pelagius and Novatian.[173] Pelagius said that some perfect people were able to live without sin during this life and to fulfil Ephesians 5:27, "To display for himself a glorious church without spot or wrinkle." But if this were the case, then there would be some people who could not say this prayer, whereas the Lord gave the prayer to all of us, and so we

---

168. This point is perhaps inspired by Augustine, *De Sermone Domini* II 17.57, and Pseudo-Chrysostom, op. cit. 14 (PG 56:713) (cited by Hugh of St. Cher, f.24rb).

169. Cf. Chrysostom, *Hom. Matt.* 22.4, cited more explicitly in Thomas' lectures on John (para. 1820 in the Marietti edition).

170. Reading *indignum* (supported by L) for the manuscript *impugnare*.

171. In the Marietti ed. of L this sentence is ascribed to Jerome, but it has not been found in his works (cf. Dozois, art. cit. p.43*). The manuscript of L which I have used has *ideo*, and there is no trace of any ascription to Jerome in P, so it was probably a false clue all along.

172. This citation is meant only to show that "debts" means "sins"; it is used for this purpose in Cyprian, op. cit. 22.

173. Novatian is not named in L, and in the manuscript of P he is regularly called "Novatus."

all have some sin.[174] "The righteous will fall seven times a day" (Prov. 24:16). "If we say that we have no sin, we deceive ourselves" (1 John 1:8). Novatian said that anyone who sins mortally after baptism cannot do penance, but in that case it would be useless for us to say, "Forgive us." And the Lord would not have taught us to ask unless he were willing to forgive.[175] "He gave them power to become children of God" (John 1:12), by adoption, that is, through grace, and this would not be true if sins were not forgiven.[176]

"As we too forgive our debtors." People can be debtors in two senses: either because they have sinned against us, or because they owe us money or something of the kind.[177] We are not being urged to forgive the second sort of debt, but to forgive any sin whatsoever, even with the loss of our temporal goods.[178] It would be outrageous for me to ask God for mercy and not grant mercy to my fellow servant. "One human being cherishes wrath against another and then asks for help from God" (Ecclus. 28:3). "Forgive your neighbor who harms you."[179]

But what are we to say of those who refuse to forgive, but still say the Our Father? It looks as if they ought never to say it, because they are lying. So it is reported that some people used to miss out the clause, "As we forgive our debtors." But this is faulted by Chrysostom on two grounds: first, because it does not respect the church's pattern in praying, and secondly, because no prayer is ac-

---

174. This sentence is taken from L.

175. This sentence is taken from L. Cf. Chrysostom, op. cit. 19.5.

176. This clause is taken from L. John 1:12 was taken to refer to the whole process leading from the initial grace of conversion to our final assumption into glory (cf. Hugh of St. Cher, ad loc.), but if it is to support Thomas' point here it has to be taken in a very strict sense: "To as many as have received him," i.e., who are already believers, "he has given power to become children of God," i.e., they are not at the moment children of God (though they have already received him), therefore they must have fallen from grace, therefore they can only become children of God (again) by having postbaptismal sins forgiven. If Thomas was using this verse for this purpose, he was pushing his luck!

177. "Or something of the kind" is taken from L. Cf. Hugh of St. Cher, f.23va.

178. L has: "Even if someone's offense against me is a matter of not paying money, I am bound to forgive the offense, but not the debt." Hugh of St. Cher says that if you are perfect, you will let your debtor off payment as well as forgiving the sin, but if you are not perfect, you can claim the money back (provided the debtor can in fact pay it). And even Hugh's position is considerably more "worldly" than that of Augustine, *De Sermone Domini* II 8.28.

179. The manuscript just has *dimitte proximo*, but it looks as if another text from Ecclesiasticus is meant, and Ecclus. 28:2 (*relinque proximo*) is the most likely.

ceptable to God if it does not retain what Christ composed.[180] So we must maintain that people do not sin if they say the Our Father, whatever state of ill will and grave sin they may be in, because people in that situation should do whatever good they can, like almsgiving and prayers, which do not merit eternal life,[181] but do prepare the way for the recovery of grace. Nor is someone in this position lying, because the prayer is pronounced, not in the name of the individual, but in the name of the whole church, and there is no doubt that the church forgives the debts of all those who are in the church. But a person in such a position loses the benefit of it, because only people who forgive gain the benefit.[182]

Augustine raises the question whether it is only those who forgive offenses who are forgiven by the Lord.[183] It looks as if this benefit is gained[184] only by people who forgive offenses. But Augustine answers the question, as far as this particular discussion is concerned—love of enemies has been discussed above[185]—by saying that God wants us to forgive offenses in the same way that he forgives our guilt, and he does not forgive us unless we ask.[186] So anyone who is so disposed as to be ready to forgive anyone who asks pardon does not lose the benefit, so long as in general he does not hate anyone, as has been said above.[187]

"And lead us not into temptation." Another text has a different petition, "Do not bring us into temptation," and there is another

---

180. Pseudo-Chrysostom, op. cit. 14 (PG 56:714), cited by Hugh of St. Cher, f.24va.

181. This clause is from L. No works performed out of a state of grace can merit eternal life, according to the traditional Augustinian doctrine, because merit is always the product of grace.

182. The manuscript has *soli consecuntur qui fructum dimittunt;* I have transposed *qui* and *fructum.*

183. This sentence is taken from L.

184. The manuscript has "not gained."

185. On Matt. 5:44. Thomas takes a much less hard line than Augustine, which is no doubt why he specifies that he is using Augustine here only for a very limited purpose, to establish the principle that our practice of forgiveness should be modelled on that of God. Augustine uses the commandment that we should love our enemies to prove that we have to forgive even people who do not ask for forgiveness, a conclusion which Thomas is reluctant to endorse.

186. I have corrected the text of P in the light of L.

187. Augustine, *De Sermone Domini* II 8.29; but the locus classicus is *Enchiridion* 19.73–4, cited in Lombard, III *Sent.* d.30.2 and Philip the Chancellor, *Summa de Bono,* ed. cit. pp.728–9.

reading, "Do not let us be led into temptation."[188] The interpretation is as follows. God does not tempt anyone, although he allows us to be tempted.[189] And it does not say, "Do not permit us to be tempted," because temptation is useful. People are tempted so that they may become known to themselves and to other people; they are already known to God. "What does anyone know, who has not been tempted?" (Ecclus. 34:9). But being "led into temptation" means succumbing to temptation.[190] So it says, "Lead us not," that is, do not permit us to succumb. It is like someone saying, "I want to be warmed by the fire, but not burned."[191] "God is faithful, who does not permit you to be tempted more than you can endure" (1 Cor. 10:13).

This petition makes nonsense of Pelagius' error on two points. He said that people could stand firm (which is not different from not succumbing to temptation) by their own free will, without God's help. He also claimed that it is not for God to change people's will. But if this were so, it would not say, "Lead us not into temptation," which is the same as saying, "Make us not consent to temptation." So it is in his power to change our will or not to change it. "It is God who works in us both to will and to do according to his good pleasure" (Phil. 2:13).

"But deliver us from evil." This is the last petition. "Deliver us" from past, present and future evil,[192] from the evil of guilt, of punishment and of all ill. As Augustine says, every Christian in any kind of trouble pours out tears at these words and utters groans.[193] "Rescue me from my enemies, my God" (Ps. 58:2). "I myself will comfort you, who are you that you should be afraid?" (Is. 51:12).

"Amen," that is, "So be it" in Hebrew.[194] Nobody has been

---

188. Reading *inferas* for the manuscript *inpera*. The alleged version with *ne sinas* is unknown, but Cyprian, op. cit. 25, offers a version with *ne patiaris*, and L implies that Thomas did refer to Cyprian for something here. All three versions are in fact mentioned by Augustine, *De Sermone Domini* II 9.30.

189. Cf. Augustine, *De Sermone Domini* II 9.30.

190. This sentence is taken from L. Cf. Augustine, *De Sermone Domini* II 9.30.

191. Augustine, *De Sermone Domini* II 9.32.

192. Cf. the prayer after the Lord's Prayer in the (old) text of the Mass.

193. Augustine, *Ep.* 130.11.21 (PL 33:502).

194. "In Hebrew" is taken from L.

willing to translate it, out of reverence, because the Lord frequently used the word. By it we are given confidence that we shall obtain what we pray for, provided we observe all that has been said and are the kind of people who forgive and so on.[195]

In the Greek[196] three more phrases are added, on which Chrysostom comments:[197] first, "For thine is the kingdom," then "and the power and the glory, Amen." And these correspond to three earlier phrases: "Thine is the kingdom" to "Thy kingdom come," "the power" to "Thy will be done" and "the glory" to "Our Father" and to everything else which relates to God's honor. Alternatively, it is tantamount to: "You can do these elevated things because you are a king, and so no one can hinder you;[198] yours is the power, so you can give a kingdom, and yours is the glory, so 'Not to us, Lord, not to us, but to your name give the glory' " (Ps. 113:9).[199]

"For if you forgive. . . ." The Lord attached a condition in his prayer, "Forgive us as we too forgive," and this condition might seem burdensome to people, so the Lord explains the reason for it. And in this connection he does two things: first, he shows that this condition is profitable, then secondly, he shows that it is necessary. It is profitable because by it we obtain the forgiveness of our sins: "If you forgive other people their sins," by which they have sinned against you, "then your heavenly Father will also forgive you your trespasses," which you have committed against him. "Forgive your neighbor who harms you and then when you pray your sins will be forgiven" (Ecclus. 28:2).

But notice that he says, "If you forgive. . . ." As long as human beings live innocently they are gods,[200] but when they sin they fall into the human condition: "I said to you, 'You are gods' . . . but you will die like human beings" (Ps. 81:6–7).[201] So you, who are gods and spiritual people, are to forgive sinful human beings. Again, notice that he says, "Our Father who art in the heavens." The cause

---

195. This clause is taken from L. Cf. Marginal Gloss on Matt. 6:9.

196. L says "Greek," but P has "Hebrew."

197. Pseudo-Chrysostom, op. cit. 14 (PG 56:714), in Hugh of St. Cher, f.24ᵛᵃ.

198. The manuscript simply has *et ideo nullus potest;* I have guessed what the completion of the clause was meant to be.

199. L's *reportatio* breaks off at this point.

200. The Latin text of Matt. 6:14–5 has *hominibus* ("human beings"), which is picked up in the comment, but I have translated it "other people" to make it less unwieldy.

201. Cf. Jerome, op. cit. I 6.14.

of the offenses which occur among people is always to do with something earthly, so heavenly people who have a Father in heaven ought to be free of all quarrels over earthly things. "Be merciful as your Father is merciful . . . " (Luke 6:36).

This condition is also necessary, because without it there is no forgiveness of sins, because "if you do not forgive. . . . " And this is not surprising, because no sin can ever be forgiven without charity. "Charity covers all faults" (Prov. 10:12). If you have hatred for your brethren, you are not in charity and so your sin is not forgiven. "One human being cherishes wrath against another and then asks for help from God" (Ecclus. 28:3). "There is judgment without mercy for anyone who does not practice mercy" (James 2:13).

But one might think, if this is so and offenses are to be forgiven, that the church sins when she does not forgive. We must say that she would sin if she did not forgive a sinner who asked for pardon. If the sinner does not ask[202] for pardon and she does not forgive because of hatred, then she sins, but if it is for the good of the sinner or of other people, to avoid encouraging them to evil ways, that is, then she does not sin.

---

202. Reading *petat* for the manuscript *peccat*.

Prayer
Summa Theologiae II.II
Question 83

Next we must consider prayer, and this raises seventeen questions:
  (1) Is prayer an act of our appetitive power or of our cognitive power?
  (2) Is it appropriate to pray to God?
  (3) Is prayer an act of religion?
  (4) Should we only pray to God?
  (5) Should we ask for particular things when we pray?
  (6) Should we ask for temporal things in prayer?
  (7) Should we pray for other people?
  (8) Should we pray for our enemies?
  (9) The seven petitions in the Lord's Prayer.
(10) Is prayer peculiar to rational creatures?
(11) Do the saints in heaven pray for us?
(12) Ought prayer to be vocal?
(13) Is attentiveness necessary for prayer?
(14) Ought prayer to go on for a long time?
(15) Is prayer meritorious?
(16) Do sinners obtain anything from God by praying?
(17) The kinds of prayer.

I. Is prayer an act of our appetitive power?[1]

Prayer appears to be an act of our appetitive power:
(1) It is prayer's business to be heard, but what is heard by God is

---

1. I.e., is prayer simply a matter of desire, or is it essentially an activity of reason? Notice that the question has changed slightly since the commentary on the Sentences, where Thomas asks whether prayer is an activity of our affective part; by now Thomas apparently does not consider the affective view of prayer to be even worth discussing.

desire: "The Lord heard the desire of the poor."[2] Therefore prayer is desire. And desiring is an act of our appetitive power, so prayer must be so too.

(2) Dionysius says, "Before all we do it is useful to begin with prayer, handing ourselves over to God and uniting ourselves with him."[3] But union with God is the result of love, which belongs to our appetitive power. So prayer belongs to our appetitive power.

(3) The philosopher lays down that the intellectual part of us has two different kinds of activity. The first is the understanding of simple units of meaning, that is to say, grasping what each thing is. The second is making or breaking connections, that is to say, grasping that something is or is not the case. Then there is also a third activity, reasoning, that is, moving from what we know to what we do not know.[4] Prayer does not fall within any of these activities, so it is not an act of our intellectual power, but of our appetitive power.

On the other hand:

(a) Isidore says, "Praying (*orare*) is the same as talking."[5] And talking is a matter of the intellect. So prayer is not an act of our appetitive power, but of our intellectual power.

Reply

As Cassiodorus says on Psalm 38, prayer (*oratio*) is so called as being the mouth's reason (*oris ratio*).[6] Now the difference between speculative and practical reason is that speculative reason simply grasps things, whereas practical reason causes things as well as grasping them. And there are two ways in which one thing causes another. It may be a full-fledged cause of something, in that it makes

---

2. Psalm 9:38.

3. A paraphrase of Dionysius, *DN* 3.1 (PG 3:680D).

4. This account of the three intellectual activities follows the beginning of the proemium to Thomas' commentary on Aristotle's *Peri Hermeneias* almost verbatim (and the commentary is more or less exactly contemporary with the *Secunda Secundae*); in the commentary Thomas cites Aristotle, *De Anima* 3.6 (430a26–8) for the "two" intellectual activities.

5. Isidore, *Etymologiae* 10.195. Isidore is commenting on *orator* in its classical sense and his comment is not meant to have anything to do with *oratio* in the sense of "prayer."

6. Cassiodorus, *Expos. in Psalt.* 39.14, 85 tit. (PL 70:285C, 610C).

it inevitable that that particular thing will result, but for this to happen the effect must be entirely within the power of that cause. Or one thing may cause another in a less complete way in the sense that it just prepares the way for something, when the effect is not totally within the power of the clause.[7] So reason also can be the cause of things in two ways. In some cases it makes it necessary for something to result: it is in this way that it belongs to reason not only to give orders to our own lower powers and to our bodily limbs, but also to other people who are subject to us; this is done by giving orders. In other cases reason can only try to induce something to happen, preparing the way, as it were, for something to happen: in this way reason asks for something to be done by people who are not subject to us, whether they are our equals or our superiors. But both giving orders and asking or entreating imply a certain arranging of things, a planning to bring about something by using certain means, and so they are the concern of reason, since arranging things is a rational activity. This is why the philosopher says that "reason entreats us toward what is best."[8] And it is in this sense that we are here discussing *oratio*, as meaning a kind of entreaty or petition, in line with Augustine's comment that "prayer is a kind of petition."[9] And Damascene also says that "prayer is a petition made to God for things that are fitting."[10] Thus it is clear that prayer (*oratio* in the sense presently under discussion) is an act of our reason.

In reply to the points raised above:

(1) The Lord is said to hear the desire of the poor either inasmuch as it is desire that prompts their petition, since petition is a kind of presentation of desire, or in order to show how quickly he hears, inasmuch as God hears the poor before they formulate their prayer, while it is still only a desire in their hearts. "Before they call, I will hear them" (Is. 65:24).

(2) As we have already said,[11] the will activates the reason to move

---

7. The weaker kind of cause causes *disponendo;* Thomas discusses *causa disponens* in his commentary on *Metaph.* V (para. 767 in the Marietti edition): it is a kind of cause which "prepares the material." The fire can oblige the water to boil, but it can only "dispose" it for being made into tea.

8. *Eth. Nic.* III 13 (1102b16).

9. No reference in Augustine has been identified, but cf. Isidore, *Etym.* 6.19.59 for a very similar text.

10. *De Fide Orthodoxa* 68.1, ed. Buytaert p.267.

11. Cf. *Summa Theol.* I q.82 a.4, I.II q.9 a.1.

toward its own goal, so there is nothing to stop an act of reason, instigated by the will, aiming at the goal of charity, namely union with God. And there are two senses in which prayer, moved by charity in the will, aims at God: with reference to the object of petition, inasmuch as the chief thing we should ask for in prayer is that we may be united with God, as it says in Psalm 26:4, "One thing I have asked for from the Lord and this is what I will seek, to dwell in the Lord's house all the days of my life."[12] Secondly, with reference to the person praying, a petitioner has to approach the person to whom the petition is to be made; if we are asking another human being for something, this means approaching physically, but to ask God for something we have to approach him in our minds. So Dionysius, in the same passage, says that "when we call upon God in our prayers, we are present to him with our minds unveiled."[13] And in this sense Damascene says that prayer is "an ascent of the mind to God."[14]

(3) The three activities listed all belong to speculative reason; but practical reason has the further role of causing something either by giving orders or by petition, as we have already said.

II. Is it appropriate to pray?

On the face of it, it is not appropriate to pray:

(1) Prayer seems to be needed to give information about what we want to the person we are asking for something. But, as it says, "Your Father knows that you need all these things."[1] So it is not appropriate to pray to God.

(2) Prayer is a way in which we change the mind of the person to whom we are praying, so that he will do what is being asked of him. But God's mind cannot be changed or deflected. "Furthermore he who triumphs in Israel will not spare, nor will he be deflected by any repentance."[2] So it looks as if it is not appropriate to pray to God.

---

12. In Lombard's Gloss (PL 191:270A) this petition is interpreted as meaning "one thing I have asked for, namely God himself."

13. *DN* 3.1 (PG 3:680B).

14. Damascene, loc. cit.

1. Matt. 6:32.

2. 1 Sam. 15:29; the context makes it clear that the meaning is that God is not going to repent and change his mind.

(3) It is more generous to give something without waiting to be asked than it is to give something to someone who asks for it. As Seneca says, "The highest price you can pay for something is the price of your prayers."[3] But God is extremely generous. So it is apparently not appropriate that we should pray to God.

On the other hand:

(a) "One should pray always and not give up."[4]

REPLY

Among the ancients there were three different kinds of mistake made about prayer.

Some people maintained that human affairs are not governed by divine providence, and it follows from this view that it is futile to pray and indeed to worship God at all. Of them it says, "You have said, 'Anyone who serves God is a fool.' "[5]

Secondly, there is the opinion of those who maintained that everything comes about by necessity, including human affairs, either because of the unchangingness of God's providence or because of the absolute control of the stars or because of the way in which causes are linked together.[6] This view leaves no room for prayer to be useful.

Thirdly, there is the opinion that human affairs are governed by divine providence and that they do not come about by necessity; but then people went on to say that the arrangements of God's providence could be altered and that God's providence is changed by prayers and other features of divine worship.

All these views have been rejected.[7] So what we have to do now is find some way of indicating the usefulness of prayer which neither

---

3. *De Beneficiis* II 1.4.
4. Luke 18:1.
5. Malachi 3:14.
6. I.e., the three obvious kinds of determinism: theological determinism (what is willed by God must of necessity transpire), astrological determinism and physical determinism.
7. In I q.22 a.2 ad 4 Thomas has shown that human affairs are governed by providence, and in I q.22 a.4 he has argued that providence does not exclude contingency and free will. In I q.115 a.6 astrological determinism is refuted and in the process physical determinism is also excluded.

makes out that human affairs, in being governed by divine providence, are all subject to necessity nor supposes that God's plans can be changed.

We can shed light on the problem by bearing in mind that divine providence does not merely arrange what effects are to occur; it also arranges the causes of these effects and the relationships between them. And among other causes, some things are caused by human acts. So human beings have to do certain things, not so as to change God's plan by their acts, but in order to bring about certain effects by their acts, according to the pattern planned by God. The same thing applies also to natural causes.[8] Similarly in the case of prayer we do not pray in order to change God's plan, but in order to obtain by our prayers those things which God planned to bring about by means of prayers, in order, as Gregory says, that our prayers should entitle us to receive what almighty God planned from all eternity to give us.[9]

In reply to the points raised above:

(1) We do not have to present our prayers to God in order to disclose to him our needs and desires, but in order to make ourselves realize that we need to have recourse to his help in these matters.

(2) As we have already said, our prayer is not designed to change God's plan; the purpose of prayer is to obtain by our entreaties what God has already planned.

(3) God gives us many things out of sheer generosity, without being asked. The reason why he wants to give us some things in response to our petition is that it is profitable for us to acquire a certain confidence in running to him and to recognize that he is the source of all that is good for us. So Chrysostom says, "Consider what a joy is granted you, what glory is bestowed upon you, that you can speak with God in your prayers, that you can engage in conversation with Christ and plead for whatever you want, whatever you desire."[10]

---

8. In I q.22 a.3 and a.4 Thomas has shown how divine providence arranges both causes and effects, so that secondary causes really do contribute to the production of their effects.

9. Cf. *Dial.* 1.8 (PL 77:188B).

10. This text is quoted from a longer passage cited by Thomas in the *Catena Aurea* on Luke 18:1; its source has not been identified.

III. Is prayer an act of religion?

Prayer appears not to be an act of religion:

(1) Religion is part of the virtue of justice and, as such, it is located in the will. But prayer, as we have seen, concerns the intellectual part of us. So prayer appears to be an activity of the gift of understanding, by which the mind rises toward God, rather than an act of religion.

(2) Acts of worship fall under the constraint of a precept. But it does not look as if prayer falls under any such constraint; it surely originates simply in our free will, since all it is is a petition for things that we want. So prayer appears not to be an act of religion.

(3) It is the business of the virtue of religion to make us offer worship and sacred rites to the divine nature. But prayer does not seem to offer anything to God; instead it seeks to obtain something from him. So prayer is not an act of religion.

On the other hand:

(a) It says, "Let my prayer be directed like incense in your sight," on which the Gloss says that "as an image of this, under the Old Law, incense was said to be offered as a sweet smell to the Lord."[1] But this kind of thing belongs to the virtue of religion, so prayer too is an act of religion.

REPLY

As we said above,[2] the proper business of religion is offering reverence and honor to God, and so any way in which reverence is offered to God is part of religion. And by praying we offer God reverence, inasmuch as we subject ourselves to him and profess, by praying, that we need him as the author of all that is good for us. So prayer is obviously and properly an act of religion.

In reply to the points raised above:

(1) As has already been said,[3] the will moves the other powers of

---

1. Psalm 140:2, with Lombard's Gloss (PL 191:1235C), referring rather vaguely to Exod. 29.
2. II.II q.81 a.1, citing Cicero, *De Inventione* II 53.161.
3. I q.82 a.4.

the soul in view of its own goal, and this is how religion, located in the will, directs the acts of our other powers in view of giving reverence to God. And of all the other powers of the soul the most elevated and the one which is nearest to the will is the intellect. Therefore after devotion, which concerns the will itself, prayer, which belongs to our intellectual part, is the most important act of religion, as by it religion moves our intellect toward God.

(2) Not only is asking for what we desire a matter of precept, so is desiring rightly. Desiring falls within the scope of the commandment of charity, but asking comes under the commandment found in Matthew, "Ask and you will receive,"[4] and this is a commandment concerning religion.

(3) By praying we hand over our own minds to God, subjecting them to him in reverence and in a way presenting them to him; this is shown by the text from Dionysius.[5] So since the human mind is superior to all the external things which are put to God's service, whether our own bodily members or anything else, prayer excels all other acts of religion.

IV. Should we only pray to God?

It looks as if we should only pray to God:

(1) Prayer, as we have seen, is an act of religion, and it is only God who should be worshipped by religion. So it is only to God that we should pray.

(2) It is a waste of time addressing a prayer to someone who has no knowledge of our prayer. And it is only God who knows our prayers, for two reasons. First, prayer is often more a matter of an interior activity than a matter of speaking anything aloud, in line with what the apostle says: "I will pray with the spirit, I will also pray with the mind."[1] And interior acts like this are known only to God. Secondly, as Augustine says, the dead, even the saints, do not know what the living are doing, not even their own children.[2] So we should address prayer only to God.

---

4. Actually John 16:24.
5. The reference is to the text cited in a.1 ad 2.
1. 1 Cor. 14:15.
2. Interlinear Gloss on Isaiah 63:16, based on Augustine, *De Cura pro Mortuis Gerenda* 16.19 (PL 40:606) with an eye on ibid. 13.16 (PL 40:604).

(3) If we do address prayer to some of the saints, that is only inasmuch as they are united with God. But some people living in this world and also the souls in purgatory are closely united with God by grace, but we do not pray to them. So we ought not to pray to the saints in paradise either.

On the other hand:

(a) It says in Job 5:1, "Call and see if there is anyone who will answer you, turn to one of the saints."

REPLY

There are two senses in which we address a prayer to someone: we may want them to fulfill our prayer, or we may want them to obtain for us the fulfilment of our prayer. In the first sense prayer is addressed to God alone, because all our prayers ought to aim ultimately at the acquisition of grace and glory, and they are given by God alone: "The Lord will give grace and glory."[3] But in the second sense we address prayer to the angels and the saints, not because we want them to let God know what we want, but because we want our petitions to be successful through their intercession and merits. That is why it says, "The smoke of the incense rose up before God from the prayers of the saints, from the hand of the angel."[4] The church's practice in prayer also teaches us the same lesson: we ask the Holy Trinity to have mercy on us, but we ask all the other holy ones to pray for us.[5]

In reply to the points raised above:

(1) When we pray we are offering worship, in accordance with the virtue of religion, only to him from whom we seek to obtain what we are asking for, because in praying we profess him to be the author of all that is good for us. We are not offering worship to the people we invoke as our intercessors before God.

(2) The dead, if we take into account only their own natural state, do not know what is going on in this world, and in particular they do not know the inner movement of our hearts. But, as

---

3. Psalm 83:12.
4. Apoc. 8:4.
5. Cf. the Litany of the Saints, containing both "Holy Trinity, one God, have mercy on us" and innumerable invocations of the form, "St. Peter, pray for us."

Gregory says,[6] the blessed are shown in the Word whatever it is proper for them to know of our affairs, even the inner movements of our hearts; and it is especially proper to their exalted condition that they should know the petitions that are addressed to them, whether expressed aloud or made only in someone's heart. So the petitions which we address to them are known to them because God reveals them to them.

(3) People in this world or in purgatory do not yet enjoy the vision of the Word which would enable them to know what we are thinking or saying, and so we do not beg for their intercession by praying, but, in the case of the living, we ask for their intercession by talking to them.

V. Should we ask God for particular things when we pray?

It looks as if we ought not to ask God for anything in particular when we pray:

(1) As Damascene says, "Prayer is a petition made to God for things which are fitting," so any prayer asking for something which is not helpful will have no effect. "You ask and do not receive, because you ask badly."[1] But, as it says, "We do not know what to pray for as we ought."[2] Therefore we ought not to ask for anything in particular in prayer.

(2) If you ask someone for something specific, you are trying to influence that person's will to do what you want. But our aim should not be to make God want what we want, but rather to make ourselves want what he wants, as the Gloss says on Psalm 32:1.[3] So we should not ask God for anything in particular when we pray.

(3) We should not ask God for anything evil and, when it comes to good, God is inviting us. And it is futile to ask people for some-

---

6. Cf. Gregory, *Mor.* 12.21.26 (PL 75:999B), quoted in I q.89 a.8, but the point is made in language that owes more to later discussions such as Lombard, IV *Sent.* d.45 ch.6, and William of Auxerre, *Summa Aurea* III 27.6, ed. cit. p.543, than it does to Gregory.

1. James 4:3.

2. Romans 8:26.

3. Lombard's Gloss (PL 191:325D) interprets *recti* as meaning "those who direct their hearts according to the will of God, which is the norm, preferring the will of him who is better than they are to their own will."

thing they are inviting you to accept. So there is nothing specific that we should ask God for in prayer.

On the other hand:

(a) The Lord taught his disciples to ask specifically for the things contained in the petitions in the Lord's Prayer.

REPLY

As Maximus Valerius tells us, "Socrates thought we should ask nothing more from the immortal gods except that they would grant us good things, because they know what is good for each individual, whereas we often ask for things it would be better for us not to obtain."[4] In some ways this view is correct, at least so far as those things are concerned which can turn out badly and which we can use badly or well, such as wealth which, as he goes on to say, "has been a disaster for many people, and honors which have ruined people, and kingdoms which we often see coming to a wretched end, and splendid marriages which sometimes completely destroy families."[5] But there are some things which we cannot use badly, things which cannot turn out badly: the things by which we are made blessed or by which we earn beatitude. The saints ask for these things unconditionally when they pray: "Show us your face and we shall be saved,"[6] or "Lead me in the way of your commandments."[7]

In reply to the points raised above:

(1) Although of ourselves we do not know what we ought to pray for, the Spirit, as the same text says, helps our weakness by inspiring us with holy desires and so making us plead rightly.[8] This is why the Lord says that true worshippers must worship "in spirit and in truth."[9]

(2) When we ask for things in prayer which are relevant to our salvation, then we are conforming our wills to the will of God, of which it says that "he wills everyone to be saved."[10]

---

4. Valerius Maximus, *Facta et Dicta Memorabilia* VII 2.6 Ext. 1.

5. Ibid.

6. Psalm 79:4.

7. Psalm 118:35.

8. Romans 8:26, on which the Marginal Gloss and Lombard's Gloss (PL 191:1447A) say that the Holy Spirit pleads in the sense that he makes us plead.

9. John 4:23.

10. 1 Tim. 2:4.

(3) God invites us to good, but we move to accept it, not by taking bodily steps, but by pious desires and devout prayers.[11]

VI. Should we ask God for temporal things in prayer?

It seems that we should not ask God for temporal things in prayer:

(1) What we ask for in prayer we are seeking, and we are not meant to seek temporal things: it says, "Seek first the kingdom of God and its righteousness and all these things (temporal things, that is) will be added for you."[1] They are not to be sought, it says,[2] they are to be added to what is sought. So temporal things should not be asked for when we pray to God.

(2) People only ask for things when they are concerned about them. But we are not meant to have any concern about temporal things. As it says, "Do not be concerned about your life, about what you are going to eat."[3] So we ought not to ask for temporal things in prayer.

(3) Our minds should be raised to God by our prayer, but if we ask for temporal things they descend to matters that are beneath them, contrary to what the apostle says, "Not looking at what is seen, but at what is not seen; for what is seen is temporal, but what is not seen is eternal."[4] So we ought not to ask God for temporal things when we pray.

(4) We should only ask God for things that are good and for things that are useful.[5] But sometimes temporal things are harmful

---

11. The objection was that there does not seem to be anything in particular to ask for: we should not ask for anything bad and God has got in first with respect to everything good by inviting us to accept it. Thomas' answer rests on the principle that prayer is one of the ways in which we make ourselves able to receive God's gifts: cf. Augustine, *Enarr. in Ps.* 102.10 (PL 37:1324), "God wants to give, but he only gives to one who asks, to make sure he does not give to someone who cannot receive."

1. Matt. 6:33.

2. The Interlinear Gloss on Matt. 6:33 interprets it as indicating that temporal things are not to be sought at all.

3. Matt. 6:25.

4. 2 Cor. 4:18.

5. *Bona* and *utilia*: i.e., following Augustine's distinction, things which can be treated as ends (meaning, strictly, things to do with heaven) and things which are useful as leading to our goal, but which must not be treated as ends in their own right.

when we have them, not only spiritually but even temporally. So they should not be prayed for.

On the other hand:
(a) It says, "Give me just the necessities of life."[6]

REPLY

As Augustine says, it is lawful to pray for what it is lawful to desire.[7] And it is lawful to desire temporal things, not as an end in themselves or as our primary object, but as supports which help us on our way toward beatitude, inasmuch as they serve to sustain our bodily life and play an instrumental role in our virtuous deeds, as the philosopher also says.[8] Therefore it is legitimate to pray for temporal things. And this is what Augustine says. "If you want enough to live off and no more, there is nothing wrong in that; and you do not want it for its own sake, but for your bodily health and to secure circumstances that suit your position, so that you will not be out of place among the people you have to live with. If you have these things, you should pray to keep them, and if you do not have them, you should pray to get them."[9]

In reply to the points raised above:
(1) Temporal things are to be sought, not as our primary object, but in second place. So Augustine says, "In saying that the former (the kingdom of God) should be sought first, he indicated that the latter (temporal goods) should be sought afterward—meaning that they come afterward in rank, not in time. The former is sought as a good, the latter only as something we need."[10]
(2) What is forbidden is not absolutely any concern about temporal things, but an exaggerated concern for them, outside the proper context, as explained above.[11]

---

6. Proverbs 30:8.
7. This is not a genuine quotation from Augustine and is, in fact, almost a quotation from Thomas himself (IV *Sent.* d.15 q.4 a.4 B); although Augustine usually speaks rather less positively about prayer for temporal things, Thomas' general principle can be inferred from Augustine, *Ep.* 130, which deals with what it is right to desire and what it is right to pray for in tandem.
8. *Eth. Nic.* I 8.9.15 (1099a31–b2).
9. *Ep.* 130.6.12–7.13 (PL 33:498–9).
10. *De Sermone Domini* II 16.53.
11. Presumably Thomas is referring to the discussion in this very article. I have trans-

(3) When our mind turns to temporal things in order to rest in them, then it does remain weighed down in them. But when it turns to them with a view to attaining beatitude, far from being weighed down by them it rather raises them up.[12]

(4) By the sheer fact that we are not asking for temporal things as if they were what we primarily wanted, but only in view of something else, what we are asking for is that God will grant them to us only in so far as they help our salvation.

VII. Should we pray for other people?

It appears that we ought not to pray for other people:

(1) When we pray we ought to follow the pattern which the Lord gave us, and in the Lord's Prayer we make petitions for ourselves, not for others: "Give us this day our daily bread," and so on. So we ought not to pray for other people.

(2) The point of praying is to be heard. But one of the conditions required for prayer to be heard is that people should be praying for themselves. So on the text, "If you ask the Father for anything in my name, he will give it to you," Augustine says, "People are all heard on their own behalf, but not on behalf of everyone; that is why it does not simply say, 'He will give it,' it says, 'He will give it to you.' "[1] So it seems that we should not pray for other people, but only for ourselves.

(3) We are forbidden to pray for other people if they are wicked: "Do not pray for this people and do not get in my way, because I will not listen to you."[2] And there is no need to pray for good people, because they can pray for themselves and have their prayers heard. So it looks as if we ought not to pray for other people.

On the other hand:

(a) It says, "Pray for one another that you may be saved."[3]

lated *inordinata* "out of context": it refers to a desire for temporal things that is not properly "ordered" to desire for the kingdom of God.

12. The variant "it is rather raised up" (adopted in the Latin text of the Blackfriars *Summa*, though not in the translation) seems less convincing.

1. John 16:23; Augustine, *Tract. in Io. Ev.* 102.1.
2. Jeremiah 7:16.
3. James 5:16.

Reply

As we have already said, we should pray for whatever we should desire. And we ought to desire good things not only for ourselves, but also for others. This is an essential part of the love we are meant to bestow on our neighbors, as we have seen above.[4] Therefore charity requires us to pray for other people. So Chrysostom says, "We are forced by need to pray for ourselves, but we are urged to pray for others by fraternal charity. And in God's eyes a prayer that is commended by fraternal charity is more pleasing than one which comes from need."[5]

In reply to the points raised above:

(1) As Cyprian says, "The reason for our saying 'Our Father' and not 'My Father' and 'Give us,' not 'Give me,' is that the teacher of unity did not want prayer to be made in a state of isolation, with everyone praying only for themselves; he wanted one person to pray for all, just as he bore all of us in himself alone."[6]

(2) Praying for oneself is laid down as a condition which is needed if there is to be any certainty of the prayer being granted, but it is not a necessary condition for prayer being meritorious. It sometimes happens that we do not obtain what we are praying for for someone else, in spite of the fact that we are praying piously, perseveringly and for things relevant to salvation, because there is an obstacle in the person we are praying for. "Even if Moses and Samuel were to stand before me, my heart is not toward this people."[7] Nevertheless this kind of prayer will be meritorious for the person praying, who is praying out of charity: "My prayer will return to my bosom," on which the Gloss says, "That is, even if my prayer does not benefit them, nevertheless I am not cheated of my reward."[8]

(3) We should pray even for sinners, that they may be converted, and for the righteous, that they may persevere and make progress. But our prayers are only heard for some sinners, not for all; they are heard for those who are predestined, but not for those

---

4. Cf. II.II q.23 a.1.
5. Pseudo-Chrysostom, *Op. Imp. in Matt.* 14.9 (PG 56:711).
6. Cyprian, *De Oratione Dominica* 8.
7. Jeremiah 15:1.
8. Psalm 34:13, with the Interlinear Gloss.

whose death is foreknown by God.[9] It is the same as with fraternal correction, which has an effect on the predestined, but not on the reprobate. "No one can correct someone whom God despises."[10] This is why it says, "If you know your brother is committing a sin which is not fatal, you should ask and life will be given to the one who is sinning, but not fatally."[11] But since we cannot distinguish between the predestined and the reprobate, as Augustine says, and so should not deny anyone the benefit of fraternal correction, on the same basis we should not deny anyone the help of our prayers.[12]

There are three reasons why we should pray for the righteous. First, because when many people pray, their prayers are heard all the more readily, as the Gloss on Romans 15:30 says: "The apostle does well to ask for the prayers of people who are inferior to him, because when many who are of little account come together in unanimity they become great, and it is impossible that the prayers of many should fail to obtain what they are praying for,"[13] provided, of course, that they are praying for something that can be granted. Secondly, it is so that many people will give thanks to God for the blessings bestowed on the righteous, which also do good to many others, as the apostle makes clear.[14] Thirdly, it is to prevent the great becoming proud at the thought that they do not need the intercessions of lesser folk.

VIII. Should we pray for our enemies?

It appears that we ought not to pray for our enemies:

(1) It says in Romans 15:4 that "whatever is written is written for our instruction." And in sacred scripture there are a lot of curses

---

9. In the classic terminology, those who are to be saved are "predestined" by God, while those who are going to be damned are said to be "foreknown," not "predestined."

10. Ecclesiastes 7:14.

11. 1 John 5:16.

12. Augustine, *De Correptione et Gratia* 16.49.

13. Lombard's Gloss (PL 191:1526D).

14. Cf. Thomas' own commentary on Romans 15:30, in which the third reason for the apostle's request for prayers is "so that while many pray, many will also give thanks when their prayer is heard, in line with 2 Cor. 1:11;" this suggests that what "the apostle makes clear" in our present passage is not the benefit derived by others from the blessings given to the righteous, but the principle of many people giving thanks for these blessings.

pronounced against people's enemies, such as "Let all my enemies be put to shame and confused, let them turn back quickly
and be thoroughly put to shame."[1] So we too ought to pray
against our enemies rather than for them.

(2) If you take vengeance on your enemies, it results in their harm.
But the saints ask for vengeance on their enemies, as in Apocalypse 6:10, "How long will you not avenge our blood on those
who dwell in the land?" That is why they also rejoice when vengeance is taken on the wicked: "The righteous will rejoice to see
vengeance."[2] So we ought not to pray for our enemies, we ought
rather to pray against them.

(3) What we do and what we pray ought not to contradict each
other. But sometimes we lawfully fight against our enemies, otherwise all wars would be unlawful, which we have seen not to
be the case.[3] So we should not pray for our enemies.

On the other hand:

(a) "Pray for those who persecute and abuse you."[4]

REPLY

Praying for someone else is a work of charity, as we have seen.
So we are bound to pray for our enemies in the same way that we
are bound to love them. How we are bound to love them we have
already seen, in the treatise on charity[5]: we must love their human
nature, not their guilt, and what we are commanded to do is love
them in general, not to show love to any particular enemy, except
in the sense that we must be inwardly ready in our minds to show
love specifically to some enemy and offer help in case of real need,
or if we are asked for pardon. But, simply speaking, to love our enemies individually and to help them in particular ways is a work of
perfection. In the same way it is a matter of obligation not to exclude
our enemies from the general prayers we make for other people, but
it is a work of perfection, not of obligation, to pray for them in particular, except in special circumstances.

---

1. Psalm 6:11.
2. Psalm 57:11.
3. II.II q.40 a.1.
4. Matt. 5:44.
5. II.II q.25 articles 8 and 9.

In reply to the points raised above:

(1) The curses in the bible can be understood in four ways. First, as Augustine says, the prophets often predict the future in the form of a curse.[6] Secondly, God sometimes sends temporal harm to sinners to convert them. Thirdly, the curses may be understood not as a prayer against the people themselves, but as a prayer against the reign of sin, that is, as a prayer that sins will be destroyed through the conversion of sinners. Fourthly, the saints conform their will to God's justice with regard to the damnation of those who persevere in sin.

(2) In the same book Augustine says that the martyrs' revenge is the overthrowing of the reign of sin, under which they suffered so greatly.[7] Or, as has been said, they plead for vengeance not by saying anything but by the logic of what they are, as the blood of Abel cried out from the ground.[8] And they rejoice in vengeance, not for its own sake, but because of God's justice.

(3) It is lawful to fight against one's enemies to restrain their sins, which is good for them and for others, and in this sense it is also lawful in prayer to ask for certain temporal misfortunes to befall them to bring them to their senses. So what we pray and what we do will not contradict each other.

IX. Are the seven petitions in the Lord's Prayer appropriately specified?

The seven petitions in the Lord's Prayer appear to be specified inappropriately:

(1) It is idle to ask for something to be hallowed which is always holy. And God's name is always holy: "Holy is his name."[1] And his kingdom is everlasting: "Your kingdom, Lord, is a kingdom forever."[2] And God's will is always fulfilled: "All that I will shall be done."[3] So it is idle to ask for God's name to be hallowed and for his kingdom to come and for his will to be done.

---

6. *De Sermone Domini* I 21.72.

7. Ibid. 22.77.

8. Pseudo-Augustine, *Quaest. Vet. et Nov. Test.* 68 (PL 35:2262).

1. Luke 1:49.

2. Psalm 144:13.

3. Isaiah 46:10.

(2) Departing from evil comes before attaining to good, so it is clearly inappropriate for the petitions relating to the attainment of good to be placed before the petitions relating to the taking away of evil.

(3) The point of asking for something is to obtain it as a gift. But the chief gift of God is the Holy Spirit and the things which are given to us through him. So it looks as if the petitions are inappropriately laid out, since they do not correspond to the gifts of the Holy Spirit.

(4) According to Luke there are only five petitions in the Lord's Prayer, so it was superfluous for Matthew to list seven.

(5) It seems silly to try and win the good will of someone who anticipates us with good will. And God does get in first with his good will toward us, since "he loved us first," as it says in 1 John 4:10. So it is unnecessary to say "Our Father who art in heaven" before the petitions, since this seems to be designed to win good will.[4]

On the other hand:

(a) The authority of Christ who appointed the prayer is sufficient.

REPLY

The Lord's Prayer is the most perfect prayer of all because, as Augustine says, if we pray rightly and properly we cannot say anything except what is contained in this prayer the Lord gave us.[5] Because prayer is a kind of presentation of our desire before God, we can only rightly pray for what we can rightly desire, we also pray for things in the order in which they should be desired. So this prayer not only instructs our pleading, it also gives shape to our whole affective life.[6]

Now obviously the first thing our desire lights on is our goal, and then the things that lead to the goal. And our goal is God.[7] And

---

4. For the interpretation of the opening words of the Lord's Prayer as a kind of *captatio benevolentiae* see Thomas' commentary on Matthew, above.

5. *Ep.* 130.12.22 (PL 33:502).

6. *Informativa totius nostri affectus*, literally "such that it informs our whole feeling."

7. This sums up the demonstration given (following Aristotle) in I.II q.1. What moves the will in the first place is some kind of goal, and only in the light of this do the means toward the realization of that goal become attractive: there is nothing particularly attractive about

our affection is directed toward him in two ways: first, in the sense
that we will his glory,[8] and secondly, in the sense that we want to
enjoy his glory. The first of these pertains to that love by which we
love God in himself, and the second pertains to that love by which
we love ourselves in God.[9] So the first petition is "Hallowed be thy
name," which is a petition for God's glory, and the second is "Thy
kingdom come," which is a petition that we may come to the glory
of his kingdom.[10]

There are two ways in which something can set us on our way
toward our goal: directly or incidentally.[11] We are directly set on

boarding the London train unless you actually want to go to London—or unless you just happen to like trains, in which case travelling by train is a goal in its own right. But beyond our
particular goals there is an overarching goal, which we cannot help but want: beatitude (cf. I
q.82 a.1). And in fact, even though we may not always appreciate this, the ultimate goal of
all of us is God because true, complete human happiness consists in union with God by
knowledge and love. Therefore, however obscurely, all our appetites fall into place with reference to our movement toward God and are otherwise doomed to incoherence and frustration. For an excellent account of Aristotle's and Thomas's ideas about goals and ultimate
goals, cf. R. McInerny, *Ethica Thomistica* (Washington, D.C. 1982), pp. 11–33.

8. Cf. Chrysostom, *Hom. Matt.* 19.4, quoted in the *Catena Aurea* on Matt. 6:9.

9. Cf. II.II q.26 a.3, where Thomas tackles the argument that if we love God we must
to the same extent love enjoying God, which is a form of self-love; therefore we cannot help
but love ourselves as much as we love God. His answer is that "God's goodness is greater in
itself than we are able to share by enjoying him, therefore simply speaking we love God more
than ourselves." Love of God, in Thomas' view, means friendship with God, and friendship
means willing the good of the other, but it also involves a certain reciprocity based on some
kind of sharing; in the case of friendship with God, the basis for such friendship is God's
sharing of his own beatitude with us (II.II q.23 a.1). Thus love of God for himself and enjoying him (sharing his beatitude) cannot be separated into two distinct goals. If we did not
love God, we should not enjoy sharing in his life, so in that sense loving God comes before
loving ourselves in him; but there is no room for any divorce between the two aspects of love
("altruistic" and "selfish," as it might be): charity (with both its commandments) is a single
virtue (II.II q.23 a.5) because love of God and love of self are inseparable, and love of neighbor
means willing for other people what we will for ourselves and doing so for God's sake (because
we love him). Thomas' doctrine of friendship with God makes nonsense of the Romantic idea
of being willing to sacrifice one's own bliss so long as God was content (the doctrine found
later among the Quietists in the guise of "pure love"); it also undercuts the late thirteenth-
century dispute about whether our goal is to be identified as God himself or as our awareness
of our own union with him (John of Paris taught the latter: cf. J. P. Muller, "La thèse de Jean
Quidort sur la béatitude formelle," in *Mélanges Auguste Pelzer* [Louvain, 1947], pp. 493–511;
a similar view was propounded by Durandus of St. Pourçain: I *Sent.* d.1 q.2. Eckhart energetically resisted such a doctrine: cf. E. zum Brunn and A. de Libera, *Maître Eckhart, Méta-
physique du Verbe et Théologie Négative* [Paris, 1984], p. 81 note 13; S. Tugwell, *Reflections on the
Beatitudes* [London, 1980], p. 4).

10. This interpretation of "Thy kingdom come" effectively follows the Marginal
Gloss, which takes it to be a petition for the kingdom in which the saints will reign with God.

11. *Per se* or *per accidens*: we are set on our way toward London by the London train

our way by any good which helps us[12] toward our goal, and things can be helpful toward the goal of beatitude in two ways. There is a kind of good which is immediately relevant in its own right to the attainment of the goal, and this has to do with the ways in which we merit beatitude by obeying God; and it is with reference to this that we pray, "Thy will be done on earth as it is in heaven." In another sense things can assist instrumentally by giving us some kind of help in meriting, and this is what the next petition is about, "Give us this day our daily bread," whether it is taken to mean the sacramental bread whose daily use is profitable to us (and this can be taken to mean all the other sacraments too) or whether it is understood in the sense of bodily bread, meaning all the necessities of life, as Augustine says,[13] because the Eucharist is the chief sacrament and bread is our chief food. This is why in Matthew's gospel it says "supersubstantial bread," meaning "chief" according to Jerome's commentary.[14]

We are set on our way incidentally by the removal of obstacles, and there are three obstacles blocking our path toward beatitude: first of all sin, which directly shuts us out from the kingdom—"Neither fornicators nor idolaters shall possess the kingdom of God."[15] This is dealt with in the petition, "Forgive us our trespasses." Then there is temptation, which hinders our observance of God's will, and this is dealt with in "Lead us not into temptation"; this is not a petition that we may not be tempted at all, but that we may not be overcome by temptation, which is what is meant by being "led into temptation."[16] Thirdly, there is the painfulness of our present condition, which prevents us from living to the full; and with reference to this it says, "Deliver us from evil."[17]

---

per se (the train is actually going to take us there); we are set on our way *per accidens* by the cancellation of all our engagements so that we are free to go to London (but the cancellation of our engagements does not of itself get us anywhere).

12. *Utile:* a good which is a means, not an end.

13. A loose paraphrase of part of Augustine, *Ep.* 130.11.21 (PL 33:502).

14. Jerome, *in Matt.* I 6.11 (quoted in the *Catena Aurea* on Matt. 6:11).

15. 1 Cor. 6:9.

16. This is the interpretation of "Lead us not into temptation" found in the Interlinear Gloss; cf. Augustine, *De Sermone Domini* II 9.30–34.

17. In III *Sent.* d.34 q.1 a.6 Thomas claims to be following Augustine in identifying the last three petitions of the Lord's Prayer as pleas for help against (1) guilt, (2) temptation and (3) pain (punishment); the reference is probably to *De Sermone Domini* II 10.37.

In reply to the points raised above:

(1) As Augustine says, "Hallowed be thy name" does not imply that God's name is not holy; it is a petition that his name may be treated as holy by human beings, which concerns the propagation of God's glory among us. And we do not say, "Thy kingdom come," as if God were not already reigning but, as Augustine says, we are stirring up our own desire toward that kingdom so that it may come to us and we may reign in it. And "Thy will be done" is rightly understood as meaning "May thy precepts be obeyed"; "On earth as it is in heaven" means "May they be obeyed by human beings as they are by the angels." So these three petitions will be fully realized in the life to come, whereas the other four petitions concern the needs of this present life, as Augustine says.[18]

(2) Since prayer is a presentation of desire, the order of the petitions does not correspond to the order in which things are carried out but to the order in which we want or intend things; and here it is the goal which comes first and then the things that lead to the goal, and the attainment of good comes before the removal of evil.

(3) Augustine fits the seven petitions to the gifts and the beatitudes: "If it is the fear of God which makes the poor in spirit blessed, let us ask that God's name may be hallowed among us by a chaste fear. If it is piety which makes the meek blessed, let us ask for his kingdom to come, so that we may become meek and not resist it. If it is knowledge that makes mourners blessed, let us pray that his will will be done, and then we shall stop mourning. If it is fortitude which makes the hungry blessed, let us pray that our daily bread may be given us. If it is counsel which makes the merciful blessed, let us forgive other people's sins so that our own trespasses may be forgiven. If it is understanding which makes the pure of heart blessed, let us pray that we may not have a divided heart, seeking temporal things which cause us to be tempted. If it is wisdom which makes the peacemakers blessed, because they will be called children of God, let us pray to be

---

18. This whole paragraph comes essentially from Augustine, *De Sermone Domini* II 5.19–6.21, except that the comment on "stirring up our own desire" comes from *Ep.* 130.11.21 (PL 33:502), and the concluding sentence is a paraphrase of *De Sermone Domini* II 10.36–7.

delivered from evil, because this very deliverance will make us God's free children."[19]

(4) As Augustine says, Luke included five petitions, not seven, in the Lord's Prayer; he shows us that the third petition is a kind of repetition of the two which precede it and by omitting it he makes it easier to understand this, because the principle object of God's will is that we should know his holiness and reign with him. As for the petition which Matthew adds at the end, "Deliver us from evil," Luke does not add it, to make us all realize that we are delivered from evil precisely in not being led into temptation.[20]

(5) We do not proffer our prayers to God in order to make him change his mind, but in order to stimulate our own confidence in pleading; and this confidence is particularly aroused by the consideration of his love for us, which wills our good (and this is why we say, "Our Father"), and by the consideration of his supremacy, which means that he has the power to do good to us (and this is why we say, "Who art in heaven").[21]

X. Is prayer peculiar to rational creatures?

Prayer does not appear to be peculiar to rational creatures:

(1) Anyone who can receive something can ask for something. But uncreated Persons too, namely the Son and the Holy Spirit, can be said to receive. Therefore they can also be regarded as praying. And indeed the Son says, "I will ask the Father,"[1] and the apostle says of the Holy Spirit, "The Spirit pleads on our behalf."[2]

(2) Angels are higher than rational creatures, since they are intellectual beings. But they have their share in praying. This is why it says, "Worship him, all his angels."[3] So praying is not peculiar to rational creatures.

---

19. *De Sermone Domini* II 11.38, quoted in the slightly abbreviated form found in the *Catena Aurea* on Matt. 6:13 (cf. C. Dozois, art. cit. p. 240*).

20. *Enchiridion* 30.116.

21. Cf. above, Thomas' exposition of "who art in heaven" in his commentary on Matthew.

1. John 14:16.

2. Romans 8:26.

3. Psalms 96:7.

(3) Any being that calls upon God (which is done chiefly by praying) can pray. And animals can be said to call upon God: "He
gives the beasts their food and the young crows that call upon
him."[4] So praying is not peculiar to rational creatures.

On the other hand:

(a) Prayer is an act of reason, as we saw above, and it is because of
reason that a creature is called "rational." So praying is peculiar
to rational creatures.

REPLY

As we have already seen, prayer is an act of reason in which
one entreats someone superior to oneself, just as giving orders is an
act of reason by which someone inferior to oneself is directed to do
something. So praying properly belongs to beings that have reason
and have someone superior to them who can be entreated. There is
nothing superior to the divine Persons, and brute animals lack reason. Therefore neither divine Persons nor brute animals can properly be said to pray. Praying is peculiar to rational creatures.

In reply to the points raised above:

(1) Divine Persons are such as to receive things by nature, whereas
praying belongs to those who receive things by grace. The Son
is said to "ask" or "pray" with reference to the nature he assumed, human nature, that is, not with reference to his Godhead. And the Holy Spirit is said to "plead" inasmuch as he
makes us plead.

(2) Intellect and reason, as we have said above, are not two distinct
powers in us; the difference between them is that between perfect and imperfect.[5] So sometimes intellectual creatures, which
is what the angels are, are distinguished from rational creatures,
but sometimes they are included under the same heading. And

---

4. Psalm 146:9.

5. I q.79 a.8. "Reason" in this context refers to the capacity to "reason," to move from
one point to another in pursuit of understanding; "intellect" is the understanding which results from this process, so is the "perfection" toward which reason aspires. The angels are not
"rational," in that they can simply understand without going through the process of reasoning.

it is in this sense that praying is said to be peculiar to rational creatures.[6]

(3) Young crows are said to call upon God because of the natural desire which makes all things in their own way desire the goodness of God.[7] It is similar to the way in which even brute animals are said to obey God because of their natural instinct by which they are moved by God.

XI. Do the saints in heaven pray for us?

It looks as if the saints in heaven do not pray for us:

(1) Anything that people do is more meritorious for themselves than for anyone else. But the saints in heaven do not merit anything for themselves nor do they pray for themselves, since they have already arrived at their destination. So they do not pray for us either.[1]

(2) The saints conform their wills perfectly to God, so that they will nothing except what God wills. But what God wills is always fulfilled. So it would be pointless for the saints to pray for us.[2]

(3) If the saints in heaven are in a higher position than we are, so are the souls in purgatory, because they are no longer able to sin.

---

6. I.e., when prayer is said to be peculiar to rational creatures, "rational" is being used to exclude sub-rational beings, not supra-rational beings like the angels.

7. Cf. I.II q.109 a.3 and the splendid chapters on God as the goal of the whole creation in *Contra Gentiles* III 16–24.

1. Both this objection and the answer to it seem to be a bit confused. The traditional problem concerned meriting, because it was generally assumed that obtaining something by prayer meant (more or less) deserving to obtain it; i.e., it was a form of merit (cf. especially the confusion between meriting and impetrating which is apparent in Roland of Cremona's *Summa* III, ed. cit. pp. 773–82); the problem of whether the saints pray for us tended therefore to become a discussion of the saints' merits (cf. William of Auxerre, *Summa Aurea* III 27.6, ed. cit. pp. 541–7; Thomas, IV *Sent.* d.45 q.3 a.3 obi. 4), and it seems reasonable to say that if they cannot merit anything for themselves they cannot merit anything for us either—merit is essentially related to one's own reward and meriting things for others is only a spin-off from that. But by now Thomas has become even more insistent on distinguishing between merit and impetration: cf. I.II q.114 a.6 ad 2, "Impetration in prayer rests on mercy, whereas merit in the strict sense rests on justice, and so we obtain many things from God's mercy by praying, which we do not deserve in justice." That is presumably why here he feels obliged to mention the idea that the saints do not pray for themselves as something distinct from the idea that they do not merit anything for themselves; but there seems no reason why it should even be suggested that their not praying for themselves should entail their not praying for us.

2. A standard difficulty: cf. William of Auxerre p. 541.

But people in purgatory do not pray for us, we pray for them. So neither do the saints in heaven pray for us.

(4) If the saints in heaven did pray for us, the prayer of the higher saints would be the most efficacious. So we ought not to beg for the intercession of lower saints, but only of the higher ones.[3]

(5) Peter's soul is not Peter. So if the souls of the saints prayed for us, while they are separated from the body, we ought not to call "St. Peter" to pray for us, but rather his soul. And this is the opposite of what the church actually does. So at least until the resurrection the saints do not pray for us.[4]

On the other hand:

(a) It says in 2 Maccabees 15:14, "This is he who prays a lot for the people and for the whole of the holy city, Jeremiah the prophet of God."

REPLY

As Jerome says, it was Vigilantius' mistake to believe that "while we live we can pray for each other, but once we are dead nobody's prayer for anyone else will be heard, particularly since the martyrs, for all their prayers, are unable to obtain vengeance for their blood."[5] Such a view is entirely wrong. Prayer for other people, as we have seen, derives from charity and so the saints in heaven, whose charity is more perfect than ours, pray all the more for people in this world who can be helped by their prayers; and since they are more closely united to God, their prayers are proportionately more effective. It is characteristic of the way God has arranged his creation that there should be a flowing out of excellence from higher beings to those that are lower down, just as the air receives its radiance from the sun.[6] This is why it says of Christ him-

---

3. Cf. William of Auxerre p. 546.

4. Cf. William of Auxerre pp. 546–7.

5. According to Jerome, *Contra Vigilantium* 6 (PL 23 [1845]:344B) this is an actual quotation from Vigilantius.

6. This Dionysian principle provides the essential theological justification for prayer to the saints: we do not pray to the saints because we doubt the sufficiency or the readiness of God's own mercy, but because it is God's own will that his creatures should in various ways be the bearers of his gifts to one another and that we should be dependent not only directly on him but also indirectly, by being dependent on those who are (in any sense) higher than we are. This is a basic principle of both the natural and the supernatural order.

self, "Entering into the presence of God by way of himself to intercede for us. . . . "[7] For this reason Jerome retorts to Vigilantius, "If the apostles and martyrs pray for other people while they are still in the body, when they still need to worry about themselves, how much more will they do so after they have won their crowns, their victories and their triumphs?"[8]

In reply to the points raised above:

(1) The saints in heaven are blessed and so they lack no part of beatitude except the glorification of their bodies, for which they do pray. But they pray for us, who do lack the final realization of beatitude, and their prayers are effective in obtaining things from God because of their previous merits and because God accepts their prayers.[9]

(2) The saints obtain by their prayers whatever God wants to happen as a result of their prayers; what they ask for is what they reckon is to be accomplished by their prayers in accordance with God's will.[10]

(3) Even if the people in purgatory are in a higher state than we are in the sense that they cannot sin, they are in a lower state because of the pains they suffer,[11] and from this point of view they are more in a position to be prayed for than to pray.

(4) God wants lower beings to be helped by all higher beings, and so it is proper not just to seek help from the higher saints, but also from the lower ones; otherwise we should have to confine ourselves to begging mercy from God alone. And sometimes it

---

7. Heb. 7:25, reading *accedens* rather than the more common variant, *accedentes*.

8. Jerome, loc. cit.

9. In IV *Sent.* d.45 q.3 a.3 ad 4 Thomas, as here, says that the saints merited on earth the right to be heard thereafter, but he also points out that meriting and impetrating are two different things, so the fact that the saints are not now in a position to merit does not affect the question whether they are in a position to impetrate. Here Thomas seems to feel obliged to add the further remark that the saints do still pray for themselves, a doctrine evidently based on Apoc. 6:10.

10. This is the standard answer. Cf. Roland of Cremona, pp. 802, 806–7, pointing out that if it were accepted that the saints' prayers are superfluous because God is going to do what he wants anyway, the same argument would prove that it was useless for us to do anything at all. This discussion played an important part in the development of Thomas' theology of prayer (cf. *De Veritate* q.6 a.6; *Summa Theol.* II.II q.83 a.2).

11. It was universally assumed that the pains of purgatory far exceed any pains we can experience in this life: cf. Augustine, *Enarr; in Ps.* 37.3; Pseudo-Augustine, *De vera et falsa Poenitentia* 18.34 (PL 40:1128); Lombard, IV *Sent.* d.21 ch.2.

happens that it is more effective to beg for the help of one of the lower saints, either because we pray with greater devotion or because God wants to display the sanctity of that particular saint.[12]

(5) We invoke the saints by the names by which they were known in this world because it was here that in their lifetime they merited the right to pray for us, and also these are the names by which they are best known to us. Also by so doing we hint at our faith in the resurrection, as when it says, "I am the God of Abraham, etc."[13]

XII. Ought prayer to be vocal?

It appears that prayer ought not to be vocal:

(1) As we have seen, prayer is addressed primarily to God, and God knows what our heart is saying. So vocal prayer is pointless.

(2) By praying our minds are meant to ascend to God, as we have said. But speaking aloud draws us back from the ascent of contemplation toward God, just as other affairs of the senses do. So we should not use any kind of noise in our prayers.[1]

(3) Prayer should be offered to God in secret: "When you pray, enter into your chamber and shut the door and pray to your Father in secret."[2] But if you pray aloud, you make your prayer public. So prayer ought not to be vocal.

On the other hand:

(a) "With my voice I cried to the Lord, with my voice I entreated the Lord."[3]

---

12. Cf. William of Auxerre p. 546, for the first point. This justifies the evident fact that people have their favorite saints. For the second point, cf. Humbert of Romans' sermon outline "For a New Saint" in *De Eruditione Predicatorum* (as yet unpublished): "On the occasion of new saints the Lord usually grants more favors through them . . . these are the fruits of a canonization."

13. Cf. Matt. 22:31–2.

1. *Vox* includes animal noises as well as articulate words (cf. William of Sherwood, *Introd. in Logicam* 1.1.1, ed. C. H. Lohr, *Traditio* 39 [1983] p.223, defining *vox* as a noise "coming from a living being's mouth" as distinct from the noise made by trees). What Thomas says here applies as much to shrieks and hallooing as it does to the utterance of sober prose.

2. Matt. 6:6.

3. Psalm 141:2.

REPLY

There are two kinds of prayer, the prayer of the community and the prayer of an individual. The prayer of the community is the prayer offered to God through the church's ministers on behalf of the whole people of believers, and so this kind of prayer has to be such that the whole people, on whose behalf it is made, can be aware of it, and this is impossible if it is not made vocally. So it is quite reasonable that the church's ministers are instructed to pronounce prayers of this kind not just aloud but loudly,[4] so that everyone can know what is being said.

The prayer of individuals, however, is offered by different people on their own account, whether they are praying for themselves or for others. And it is not essential to this kind of prayer that it should be made aloud. But there are three reasons for using your voice as well[5] in this kind of prayer.

First, it can help to arouse that inner devotion by which our minds are raised to God when we pray. External signs, either in the form of spoken words or in the form of certain gestures, stimulate our minds to grasp things better and this in turn stimulates our affections. This is why Augustine says that by using words and other signs we arouse ourselves all the more eagerly to the enhancement of holy desire.[6] For this reason we should use spoken words and other such signs in our private prayer inasmuch as they help to stir our minds inwardly. And if they become a distraction or an obstacle in any way they should be abandoned, and this applies particularly to people whose minds are sufficiently prepared for devotion without this kind of thing. This is why the psalmist said, "My heart spoke to you, my face sought you."[7] And Hannah is said to have been "speaking in her heart."[8]

The second reason for adding vocal prayer to our prayer is to

---

4. Since Thomas says *institutum est*, I presume he has in mind some official regulation, but I do not know of there being any such at this time.

5. *Adiungitur vox tali orationi:* prayer, as such, involves an inner act, so vocal prayer is "added" to the inner prayer.

6. Cf. Augustine, *Ep.* 130.9.18 (PL 33:501), though Augustine is there making a rather different point, explaining why we sometimes pray explicitly, on top of the constant implicit prayer of faith, hope and charity.

7. Psalm 26:8.

8. 1 Sam. 1:13.

pay a kind of debt, to serve God, that is, with all that we have received from him, with the body as well as the mind. And this applies particularly to prayer as a form of penance. This is why it says in Hosea, "Take away all our sin and accept what is good and we will repay the sacrifice of our lips."[9]

The third reason for adding vocal prayer is that when the soul is powerfully moved the effect of this spills over into the body. "My heart rejoiced and my tongue exulted."[10]

In reply to the points raised above:

(1) The purpose of vocal prayer is not to reveal anything to God which he did not know, but to stir the minds of the people praying and of others toward God.

(2) Irrelevant words do distract the mind and get in the way of our devotion as we pray, but words which mean something relevant to devotion arouse our minds, particularly if we are rather lacking in devotion.

(3) As Chrysostom says, the Lord forbids us to pray in community with the intention of being seen by the community. That is why we should not do anything strange, to attract people's attention, when we pray; you should not cry out to make other people listen to you or publicly beat your breast or stretch out your hands to make the populace look at you.[11] But on the other hand, as Augustine says, it is not being seen by other people which is wrong, it is doing all this in order to be seen by other people.[12]

XIII. Is attentiveness necessary for prayer?[1]

Surely attentiveness is necessary for prayer:

(1) It says, "God is spirit and those who worship him must worship in spirit and in truth."[2] But prayer is not "in spirit" if it is not

---

9. Hosea 14:3.

10. Psalm 15:9.

11. Pseudo-Chrysostom, *Op. Imp. in Matt.* 13.5 (PG 56:709), more or less as abridged in the *Catena Aurea* on Matt. 6:5.

12. *De Sermone Domini* II 3.10, quoted in the *Catena Aurea* immediately after the passage just cited from pseudo-Chrysostom.

1. The question has to be taken in a strong sense: Is attentiveness in prayer a necessary condition for there being prayer at all? Is inattentive "prayer" going to count as prayer?

2. John 4:24.

attentive. So it is a necessary condition of prayer that it should be attentive.

(2) Prayer is an ascent of the intellect to God. But if we are not attentive to our prayer, our intellect does not ascend to God. So it is necessary for prayer to be attentive.

(3) It is essential to prayer that it should be completely without sin. But if your mind happens to wander while you are praying, you are not without sin, because it looks as if you are mocking God, as you would be if you were talking to another human being without paying attention to your own words. This is why Basil says that we must not be slack when we beg God's help nor must our minds be wandering hither and thither, because otherwise we shall not only fail to obtain what we are praying for, we shall anger God instead.[3] So it is necessary for prayer to be attentive.

On the other hand:

(a) Even holy people sometimes find that their minds wander while they are praying. As it says, "My heart abandoned me."[4]

REPLY

This question arises chiefly in connection with vocal prayer. And we must realize that something can be said to be necessary in two ways: it can be necessary in the sense that it enables us to reach our goal better, and in this sense attentiveness is absolutely necessary in prayer. Or something can be necessary in the sense that without it the matter in hand will be unable to achieve its purpose at all. Now prayer produces three different kinds of result. First of all, there is the result which is common to all acts which are shaped by charity, and that is merit. And to achieve this result it is not essential that we should be attentive to our prayer the whole way through; the force of our initial intention when we come to our prayer makes the whole prayer meritorious, as happens in the case of other meritorious deeds too.

The second result of prayer is its own proper result, namely, that we obtain what we were praying for. And for this result too our

---

3. Pseudo-Basil, *Constitutiones Monasticae* 1.4 (PG 31:1333A); this is one of the texts Thomas had had translated for the *Catena Aurea*, and this passage is cited on Luke 11:9.

4. Psalm 39:13.

initial intention is sufficient, because this is what God primarily takes note of. If the initial intention is lacking, then prayer is neither meritorious nor capable of obtaining anything that it asks for.[5] As Gregory says, God does not hear a prayer of which the person praying it takes no notice.[6]

The third result of prayer is one which occurs straightaway, a certain kind of spiritual refreshment. And for this attentiveness in prayer is required. This is why it says, "If I pray with my tongue, my mind receives no benefit."[7]

But we must realize that we can pay attention to vocal prayer in three different ways. We can pay attention to the actual words, to make sure that we do not make any mistakes in reciting them. And we can pay attention to the meaning of the words. And we can pay attention to the goal of our prayer, God himself, and to the thing for which we are praying. And it is this last which is most necessary, and even the most uneducated people are capable of this kind of attention. And sometimes, as Hugh of St. Victor says, our minds are so intensely carried away toward God by this third kind of attentiveness that they actually forget all the rest.[8]

In reply to the points raised above:

(1) Anyone who comes to prayer by the prompting of the Spirit is praying "in spirit and in truth," even if later on some weakness makes the mind begin to wander.

(2) The human mind, because of the weakness of our nature, cannot long remain on high, because the soul is dragged down by the burden of human frailty. And this is why we find that when the mind of someone praying is ascending to God by contemplation,[9] it suddenly begins to wander because of some weakness.

---

5. Strictly speaking, if there is no initial intention to pray there can be no praying, since it is intention that specifies the nature of what we do (cf. I.II q.1 a.3); but we may be saying prayers, even if we have no intention of praying, so at least materially our activity can be called "praying."

6. This text occurs in Hugh of St. Victor, *Expos. Reg. Aug.* 3 (PL 176:892B), but has not been found in Gregory.

7. 1 Cor. 14:14.

8. Cf. *De Virtute Orandi* 2 (PL 176:980A).

9. In his comment on 1 Tim. Thomas connected prayer (as 'the rising of the mind to God') with meditation; in the *Summa* (II.II q.83 a.1 and a.17) he identifies the 'rising of the mind' as being the establishment of the contact necessary for a petition to be presented. Here it is likely that he is using 'contemplation' in a very weak sense, to mean essentially 'looking towards God', without any necessary connotation of serious intellectual involvement.

(3) If you deliberately make your mind wander while you are praying, this is a sin and it does interfere with the fruitfulness of your prayer. Augustine warns us against this when he says, "When you are praying to God with psalms and hymns, your heart should be occupied with what your mouth is saying."[10] But when the mind wanders unintentionally, that does not take away the fruitfulness of your prayer. So Basil says, "But if you are weakened by sin and cannot concentrate on your prayer, control yourself as much as you can and God will pardon you, because it is not out of carelessness but only out of frailty that you are not able to stand before him as you should."[11]

XIV. Ought prayer to go on for a long time?

It looks as if prayer ought not to go on for a long time:

(1) It says, "When you pray, do not talk a lot."[1] But if you pray for a long time you must talk a lot, particularly if you are praying vocally. So prayer ought not to be prolonged.

(2) Prayer unfolds desire. And the more your desire is restricted to one thing the holier it is: "One thing I have asked the Lord for and this I will seek."[2] So prayer too is all the more acceptable to God the shorter it is.

(3) It is surely unlawful for us to go beyond the limits set by God, particularly in matters concerning the worship of God: "Give the people a solemn warning not to want to go beyond the limits appointed for them to see God, otherwise a great crowd of them will perish."[3] And God has fixed the limits of our prayer by establishing the Lord's Prayer, as we can see from Matthew 6:9–13. So it is not lawful for us to extend our prayer any further.

On the other hand it looks as if we ought to pray constantly:

(a) The Lord says, "One must pray always and not give up."[4] And in 1 Thessalonians 5:17 it says, "Pray without ceasing."

---

10. *Rule of St Augustine* 2.3 (ed. L. Verheijen I p.421; Lawless p. 84).
11. Pseudo-Basil 1.4 (PG 31:1333BC), quoted in *Catena Aurea*, loc. cit.
1. Matt. 6:7.
2. Psalm 26:4.
3. Exod. 19:21.
4. Luke 18:1.

REPLY

We can talk about prayer in two different ways. We can talk about it with reference to what it is in itself, or we can talk about it with reference to what causes it. And the cause of prayer is charitable desire, which ought to be the source of prayer; and charitable desire ought to be in us continually, at least virtually, if not as something we are conscious of directly.[5] And the effect of such desire persists in everything that we do because of charity. We ought to do everything for the glory of God, as it says in 1 Corinthians 10:31, and in this sense prayer ought to be continuous. This is why Augustine says, "In our very faith, hope and charity we are always praying because of the constancy of our desire."[6]

But prayer itself, as a specific activity, cannot be persistent because we have to devote ourselves to other works. But, as Augustine says, "For this reason we also entreat God in words at certain intervals of times and seasons[7] so that by these signs of things we may encourage ourselves and discover in ourselves what progress we are making in our desire and rouse ourselves the more eagerly to do this[8]."[9]

Now whatever we are dealing with, its quantity ought to be proportionate to its purpose. Medicine, for instance, has to be taken in the right quantity to restore the patient to health. So it is proper for prayer to last as long as it is helpful in stimulating the fervor of our inner desire. When it goes beyond this limit, so that it cannot be prolonged further without boredom, it ought not to be continued any longer. So, as Augustine tells us, "The brethren in Egypt are said to use frequent prayers, but these are very brief, shot out as it were in a moment. This is to make sure that their intentness, which is so necessary in prayer and which they have vigilantly aroused, does not fade away and become dulled through prolonging their

---

5. *Vel actu vel virtute:* either in the sense that we are actually engaged in desiring something (we are making an act of desire) or in the sense that we are doing something prompted by desire, even if we are not particularly conscious of the desire at the moment.

6. *Ep.* 130.9.18 (PL 33:501).

7. *Per certa intervalla horarum et temporum:* presumably this refers to different times of day and different seasons of the year or month or week.

8. "Do this" apparently refers to the continual "prayer" of faith, hope and charity, consisting in continual desire.

9. *Ep.* 130.9.18 (PL 33:501).

prayers. This same principle of theirs, which shows that intentness should not be allowed to become dulled when it cannot be maintained, also shows clearly enough that when it does persist it should not be broken off."[10] Notice has to be taken of this principle with regard to the intentness of the individual in private prayer, and similarly in public prayer it has to be applied to the devotion of the people.

In reply to the points raised above:

(1) As Augustine says, "Praying for a long time is not the same thing as talking a lot. Of the Lord himself we read that he spent the whole night praying and that he prayed all the longer, to give us an example."[11] Later on he says, "Talking a lot should be banished from prayer, but not praying a lot, provided that a fervent intention continues. 'Talking a lot' in prayer means using an unnecessary number of words to do what has to be done, but praying a lot means importuning him to whom we are praying with a prolonged, devout stirring of the heart. And very often this business is conducted more with groans than with words, with weeping rather than with talking."[12]

(2) Prolixity in prayer does not consist in asking for many different things, but in having a constant feeling of desire for one thing.

(3) The Lord did not appoint this prayer to oblige us to use only these words when we pray, but because these are the things that our intention should always be set on obtaining when we pray, however we express or think of them.

(a)[13] We pray continuously either inasmuch as our desire is continuous, as we have already said, or in the sense that we do not give up praying at the appointed times,[14] or with reference to the effect our prayer has on us, leaving us more devout even after we have finished praying, or with reference to the effect we have on other people, as for instance when our kindness prompts someone to pray for us even when we ourselves have stopped praying.

---

10. *Ep.* 130.10.20 (PL 33:501–2).

11. *Ep.* 130.10.19 (PL 33:501).

12. *Ep.* 130.10.20 (PL 33:502).

13. This is one of the few cases where Thomas treats the *sed contra* as an "objection" calling for an answer. In his view no absolute answer to the question is correct.

14. This interpretation is suggested by the Interlinear Gloss and by Hugh of St. Cher; it probably refers to the set times for the Divine Office, as in the Gloss of Haimo of Auxerre (PL 117:775C), which is the source of the Interlinear Gloss here.

XV. *Is prayer meritorious?*

Prayer does not appear to be meritorious:

(1) Merit comes from grace, but prayer comes before grace, seeing that grace itself is one of the things won by prayer: "Your Father in heaven will give a good spirit to those who ask him."[1] So prayer is not a meritorious act.

(2) If prayer merits anything, it surely must particularly merit the thing that is being prayed for. But it does not always merit this, since often even the prayers of the saints are not heard. Paul, for instance, was not heard when he asked for the sting in his flesh to be removed.[2] So prayer is not a meritorious act.

(3) Prayer relies particularly on faith: "They should ask in faith, not doubting at all."[3] But faith is not sufficient for merit, as the case of people with unformed faith[4] makes clear. So prayer is not a meritorious act.

On the other hand:

(a) On Psalm 34:13, "My prayer will return to my bosom," the Gloss says, "Even if it does them no good, at least I shall not be deprived of my reward."[5] And a reward is owed to nothing except merit. Therefore prayer does count as meritorious.

REPLY

Apart from the immediate result of spiritual consolation, prayer is capable of yielding two results in the future, as we have seen: it is capable of meriting, and it is capable of obtaining what is being prayed for. Prayer, like any other virtuous act, has the result of meriting inasmuch as it derives from the root of charity, whose proper object is the eternal good, the enjoyment of which is the reward which our merits earn. Prayer comes from charity by way of

---

1. Luke 11:13.

2. 2 Cor. 12:7–9; the problem posed by Paul's unanswered prayer is discussed at length in William of Auxerre, *Summa Aurea* III 27.4, ed. cit. pp.526–34, and the essential problem is how his prayer could be meritorious without being answered, or conversely how it could avoid being demeritorious if it was not a prayer that could be answered.

3. James 1:6.

4. I.e., people who have the faith, but are not in a state of charity.

5. Cf. Interlinear Gloss.

the virtue of religion, since prayer is an act of religion, as we have
seen, and it is accompanied by various other virtues which are necessary for the goodness of prayer, namely humility and faith. It belongs to the virtue of religion to offer the prayer to God, but it is to
charity that the desire belongs for the thing whose fulfillment we
are praying for. Faith is necessary with reference to the God to
whom we are praying, because we must believe that we can obtain
from him the things we are asking for. And humility is necessary
with reference to ourselves, who acknowledge our need by making
our petition. Devotion is also needed, but this too belongs to the
virtue of religion, and it is the first act of religion and is necessary
for all the rest that follow.[6]

As for the other result of prayer, its obtaining what we are
praying for, this depends on the grace of the God to whom we are
praying, who is also the one who incites us to pray. This is why
Augustine says, "He would not encourage us to ask unless he
wanted to give,"[7] and Chrysostom says, "He never denies his blessings to people who pray, since it is he who kindly urges them on not
to give up praying."[8]

In reply to the points raised above:
(1) Prayer without sanctifying grace is not meritorious, any more
    than any other virtuous act is. Yet the prayer which wins sanc-
    tifying grace does originate in some kind of grace, a kind of free
    gift, since praying itself is a sort of gift from God, as Augustine
    says.[9]
(2) Sometimes the merit of prayer points primarily at something
    other than what is being prayed for. Merit, after all, is princi-
    pally directed toward our beatitude, whereas our petitions di-
    rectly reach out sometimes to other things, as we have seen. So
    if you are praying for something else for yourself and it is not
    going to help you toward beatitude, then you will not merit it,

---

6. In Thomas' understanding "devotion" means the readiness to give oneself unhesitatingly to the service of God and, so, to God himself (II.II q.82 a.1 and a.2). A lack of this
disposition would clearly prevent the carrying out of any acts of religion, including prayer,
except perhaps in a halting and inadequate way.

7. *Serm.* 105.1.1 (PL 38:619), quoted in Peraldus, *Summa de Virt.* III 5.7.3.

8. From a text in the Greek florilegium translated for Thomas, which he used in the
Catena Aurea on Luke 18:1; its source in Chrysostom has not been found.

9. Cf. *De Dono Perseverantiae* 23.64.

and indeed sometimes you will lose merit by asking for it and wanting it, for instance, if you were to ask God for the accomplishment of some sin, which is not a pious prayer.

Sometimes what we pray for is neither necessary for salvation nor patently contrary to salvation, and then we can merit eternal life by our prayer, but without meriting the thing we are asking for. This is why Augustine says that someone praying faithfully for the necessities of this life is both mercifully heard and mercifully not heard, because the doctor knows better than the patient what is going to be useful to someone who is sick.[10] This is the reason why even Paul was not heard when he asked for the sting in his flesh to be removed; it was not expedient.

But if what is asked for is helpful toward beatitude, as being relevant for our salvation, then we merit it not only by praying but also by doing other good works. And so we shall undoubtedly receive what we are asking for, though only at the proper time. "Some things are not denied, but put off so that they can be given at the appropriate time," as Augustine says.[11] But of course this can be thwarted if we do not persevere in asking, so for this reason Basil says, "Sometimes you ask and do not receive because you pleaded wrongly, either without faith or without seriousness or for something that would do you no good or else you gave up pleading."[12]

Because we cannot strictly merit eternal life for anyone else, as we have said above,[13] it follows that we sometimes cannot strictly merit for someone else the things which lead to eternal life. For this reason we are not always heard when we pray for other people, as we have already noticed. This is why four conditions are laid down which, if they are all present at once, will ensure that one always obtains what one is asking for: one must be praying for oneself, for things that are necessary for salvation, piously and with perseverance.

(3) Prayer relies principally on faith with respect to its capacity to obtain things from God, but not with respect to its capacity to

---

10. Prosper, *Sent. Aug.* 213 (PL 51:457A).

11. *Tract. in Io. Ev.* 102.1.

12. Pseudo-Basil 1.5 (PG 31:1335C); cf. *Catena Aurea* on Luke 11:9.

13. I.II q.114 a.6, though there the question is whether one can merit the first grace for someone else.

merit, because this relies chiefly on charity. It is by faith that we have some knowledge of God's omnipotence and mercy, and it is from these that prayer obtains what it asks for.

XVI. Do sinners obtain anything from God by praying?

It looks as if sinners do not obtain anything from God by praying:

(1) It says, "We know that God does not hear sinners,"[1] and this tallies with "If you turn your ears aside to avoid hearing the law, your prayer will be an abomination."[2] But prayer that is an abomination does not obtain anything from God. So sinners do not obtain anything from God.

(2) The righteous obtain from God what they merit, as has been said above.[3] But sinners cannot merit anything, because they are without grace, and they also lack charity, which is what gives force to piety as the Gloss on 2 Timothy 3:5 says ("Having the appearance of piety but denying its force"), and so they cannot pray piously, which is one of the conditions required for obtaining anything by prayer, as has been said above.[4] So sinners do not obtain anything by praying.

(3) Chrysostom says, "The Father does not gladly listen to a prayer which the Son has not dictated."[5] But in the prayer which Christ dictated it says, "Forgive us our trespasses as we forgive those who trespass against us," and sinners do not do this. Therefore they are either lying, if they say these words, and so do not deserve to be heard, or else, if they do not say these words, they

---

1. John 9:31.
2. Proverbs 28:9.
3. This picks up some of what has been said in art. 15, but it ignores the crucial distinction Thomas has made between meriting and impetrating.
4. This is a double-pronged attack. Sinners cannot merit, since they lack grace (and so, on the assumption that impetration depends on merit, it follows that they cannot impetrate). In any case they cannot meet the conventional conditions for impetration, which include piety which, with the help of the Interlinear Gloss on 2 Tim. 3:5, it is possible to reduce to charity which, by definition, sinners lack ("sinners," of course, meaning people not in a state of grace). So (assuming that the "conditions of impetration" are all necessary conditions for impetration, which Thomas does not in fact believe) on neither count can sinners impetrate.
5. Pseudo-Chrysostom, *Op. Imp. in Matt.* 14.14 (PG 53:714).

are not heard because they have abandoned the pattern of prayer laid down by Christ.

On the other hand:

(a) Augustine says, "If God did not hear sinners, the publican would have been praying in vain when he said, 'Lord, be merciful to me a sinner.' "[6] And Chrysostom says, "Everyone who asks receives: everyone, that is, whether they are righteous or sinners."[7]

REPLY

There are two ways of looking at sinners: we may think of their human nature, which God loves, or we may think of their guilt, which God hates. So if a sinner prays for something precisely as a sinner, that is to say, in pursuance of some sinful desire, then God mercifully does not hear such a prayer, though sometimes he may hear it with a view to vengeance, letting a sinner fall even more deeply into sin. As Augustine says, "There are some things which he denies in mercy and grants in wrath."[8] But if sinners pray because of some good desire coming from their human nature, then God does hear them, not as a matter of justice, because sinners do not deserve this, but out of sheer mercy, provided the four conditions listed above are met, that is to say, provided it is a prayer made for oneself, for things necessary for salvation, made piously and perseveringly.

In reply to the points raised above:

(1) As Augustine points out, this was said by the blind man before he was anointed, that is, before he was completely enlightened.[9] So it is not a valid observation. Though it can be taken as true if it is understood as referring to sinners precisely as such, and it is in this sense too that their prayer is said to be an abomination.

(2) Sinners cannot pray piously in one sense: their prayer is not conditioned by a solidly established virtue of piety.[10] Nevertheless

---

6. *Tract. in Io. Ev.* 44.13.
7. Pseudo-Chrysostom 18.18 (PG 53:732).
8. *Serm.* 354.7.7 (PL 39:1567).
9. *Tract. in Io. Ev.* 44.13.
10. Literally "their prayer is not informed by the habit of the virtue."

their prayer can be pious in the sense that they can ask for something which belongs to piety, just as a person who is not really just can sometimes will something just, as we have seen above.[11] The prayer of such people is not meritorious, but it can have power to obtain what is being prayed for, since merit is based on justice, whereas winning an answer to prayer rests on grace.[12]

(3) As we have seen, the Lord's Prayer is recited in the name of the church as a whole, so if people who are individually not willing to forgive their neighbors' sins say the Lord's Prayer, they are not lying, even though they are saying something which is not true of them as individuals, because it is true of the church, though such people are deservedly outside the church and so do not benefit from this prayer. But sometimes even sinners are prepared to forgive people who are in their debt, and in this way their own prayers are heard. As it says, "Do not hold on to the sins of your neighbor who does you harm and then your sins will be forgiven when you pray."[13]

XVII. Are the parts of prayer properly listed as being entreaties, prayers, pleas and thanksgivings?

On the face of it, entreaties, prayers, pleas and thanksgivings are inappropriately listed as the parts of prayer:

(1) Entreaty appears to be a form of adjuration and, as Origen says, people who want to live according to the gospel ought not to adjure anyone, because if it is wrong to swear, it must be wrong

---

11. Cf. II.II q.59 a.2, where Thomas actually discusses the converse question, whether it is possible to commit an unjust act without thereby becoming an unjust person; his answer is that it is possible to produce the occasional act which conflicts with one's habitual state of mind, without thereby changing one's essential position.

12. Not, of course, sanctifying grace in this context; but if God answers the prayers of any of us this is essentially due simply to his gracious good will. The answer to this point and the article as a whole spell out some of the implications of the distinction between meriting and impetrating: sinners cannot merit, but they can fulfil the conditions for impetration and so pray a prayer that is certain to be fulfilled (so from that point of view their position is not different from that of the person who is in a condition to merit, since it is only when these conditions are met that merit and impetration coincide). And this does not, of course, mean that sinners can oblige God to save them; they can only pray at all, let alone pray piously and perseveringly and for things relevant to salvation, because God's grace is leading them toward conversion and final perseverance.

13. Ecclesiasticus 28:2.

to adjure.[1] Therefore it is inappropriate that entreaty should be listed as a part of prayer.

(2) According to Damascene prayer is "a petition made to God for things that are fitting," so it is inappropriate to distinguish between prayers and pleas.

(3) Thanksgiving looks back to the past, whereas the other things in the list look to the future, and the past comes before the future, so it is inappropriate for thanksgivings to be listed after the rest.

On the other hand:

(a) There is the text cited from the apostle.[2]

REPLY

Three things are needed for there to be a prayer. First, the person praying must approach the God to whom the prayer is addressed, and this is indicated by the word "prayer," because prayer is "an ascent of the intellect to God."[3] Then there has to be a petition, and this is indicated by the word "plea"; and the petition may be formulated quite precisely, and some people reserve the word "plea" to this sort of petition, or it may be formulated vaguely, as when we ask God to help us, and some people call this "supplication." Or sometimes we simply state what is the case, for example, "Look, he whom you love is ill,"[4] and this they call "insinuation."[5] Thirdly, there has to be a basis for the granting of our prayer, whether on God's side or on ours. On God's side the basis for granting our prayer is his own holiness, for the sake of which we ask to be heard: "For your own sake, my God, turn your ear;"[6] and this is

---

1. *Super Matt. Comm. Ser.* 110 (PG 13:1757C). "Adjuring" is a form of swearing (*iurare*), so the inference is not implausible in Latin or in Greek.

2. 1 Tim. 2:1, from which the list is taken.

3. In the commentary on the Sentences Thomas took "prayer" to mean specifically "petition for the things needed for this life," but here he follows Bonaventure (IV *Sent.* d.15 p. 2 a.1 q.4, Quaracchi ed. IV p. 368) in accepting Damascene's phrase as identifying the precise meaning of the word. But where Bonaventure says that "prayer" properly means "an ascent to God to enjoy something or to obtain something or to pay a debt," Thomas confines its application strictly to the context of petition.

4. John 11:3.

5. Thomas is here following Hugh of St. Victor's interpretation of the terminology (*De Virtute Orandi* 2, PL 176:979C).

6. Daniel 9:17-8.

what entreaty is about, because entreaty is a calling on holy things to support our plea,[7] as when we say, "By your birth, deliver us, O Lord."[8] The basis for the granting of our prayer on our side is thanksgiving, because by giving thanks for the blessings we have already received we deserve to receive yet greater blessings, as it says in one of the collects.[9]

This is why it says in the Gloss that what comes before the consecration in the Mass is "entreaties," because there certain holy things are commemorated, and what happens at the actual consecration is "prayers," because that is the time when the mind ought specially to be raised toward God, and then the petitions which follow the consecration are "pleas" and the thanksgivings are what comes at the end.[10]

In many of the church's collects the same pattern can be observed, as for example in the collect for Trinity Sunday: "Almighty eternal God" has to do with the ascent to God which is "prayer." "Who gave your servants, etc." has to do with thanksgiving. "Grant, we beseech you" has to do with "pleading." And "Through our Lord, etc." at the end has to do with "entreaty."[11]

There is a different interpretation in the *Conferences of the Fathers:* entreaty is crying out because of one's sins, prayer is when we vow something to God, pleading is when we ask for something for other people, and thanksgiving is what the mind repays to God by way of unutterable ecstasies.[12] But the first interpretation is better.

In reply to the points raised above:
(1) Entreaty is not an adjuration used with a view to compelling anyone, which is what is forbidden, it is an adjuration used with a view to begging for mercy.
(2) "Prayer," taken in its general sense, includes all the items on the

---

7. *Per sacra contestatio* is probably meant as an "etymology" of *obsecratio.*

8. Found in some versions of the Litany of the Saints.

9. Postcommunion for Friday of the September Ember Days (Prototype of the Dominican liturgy, AGOP XIV L 1 f.407ᵛ).

10. Cf. Marginal Gloss to 1 Tim. 2:1.

11. AGOP XIV L 1 f.47ʳ: "Almighty eternal God, who gave your servants the grace to acknowledge the glory of the everlasting Trinity in the confession of the true faith and to adore the Unity in the power of your majesty, we beseech you that we may always be kept safe from all that is hostile to us by our firmness in this same faith, through our Lord. . . . "

12. Cassian, *Conf.* 9.11-14.

list, but inasmuch as it is distinguished from the others it properly means an ascent to God.

(3) When we are talking about several different things, the ones that are past come before the ones that are future; but where we are talking about one and the same thing, it is future before it is past.[13] So we thank God for his other blessings before we embark on our pleading, but in the case of any individual blessing we first plead for it and only at the end, once we have received it, do we give thanks for it. But prayer comes before pleading, since that is how we approach the God to whom we are going to address our petition. And entreaty comes before prayer, because it is the thought of God's goodness which gives us the courage to approach him.[14]

---

13. At 11:00 a.m. my breakfast is past and my lunch (at noon, say) is still in the future, and there is no doubt that breakfast comes before lunch on this reckoning. But at 11:00 a.m. my lunch is future and it may be a long time before it is past—I may still be toying with a final liqueur at 3:00 p.m.; so from this point of view my lunch is decidedly future before it is past.

14. Thomas appears to be totally unconcerned to safeguard the order in which the items are listed in the Pauline text. He explains in what sense thanksgiving for past benefits can be pushed to the head of the list, and he offers an explanation of the order given in the text with thanksgiving at the end. But his unconcern to find a sequence in the text is apparent, as in the body of the article he proposes a logical sequence that does not correspond to the ordering of the items in the text, and the collect form to which he appeals as an illustration has the items in yet another different order.

From the Commentary on Romans

Romans 8:26–27

26. Similarly the Spirit helps our weakness. For we do not know what to pray for as we ought, but the Spirit himself pleads for us with unutterable groans,
27. and he who searches hearts knows what the Spirit desires, because he is pleading for the saints in accordance with God.

We have been told that our mortal bodies will be made alive through the Holy Spirit, when our weakness is taken away; similarly even in the situation of this life, in which we are still subject to weakness, "the Spirit helps our weakness," even if he does not completely remove it. "The Spirit lifted me up and raised me up and I went off, bitter in the indignation of my spirit," finding that weakness had not entirely gone, "for the hand of the Lord was with me, strengthening me"—it was in this that the Spirit raised me up (Ezek. 3:14). "The spirit is ready, but the flesh is weak" (Matt. 26:41).

Then he explains this by saying, "We do not know what to pray for." And first, he shows our need of the Spirit's help, which concerns the weakness of this present life; then he shows the manner of his help ("the Spirit himself . . . "). Thirdly, he shows the effectiveness of his help ("He who searches . . . ").

So, first, he says: I am right in saying that "the Spirit helps our weakness," because we suffer weakness in this regard, that "we do not know what to pray for as we ought." "A man whose way is hidden, and God has surrounded him with darkness" (Job 3:23). And notice that the apostle says that there are two things we do not know: what to ask for when we pray and the manner in which we ought to ask for it. And both of these contentions appear to be false.

We do, first of all, know what to pray for, because the Lord taught it to us: "Hallowed be thy name, etc." (Matt. 6:9). But we must say that we can indeed know in a general way what it is ap-

520

propriate for us to pray for, but we cannot know how to apply this in specific ways. (1) If we desire to do some virtuous deed (and that is what it means to fulfil the will of God on earth, as it is fulfilled in heaven), it can come about that that particular virtuous deed is not suitable for this or that individual. For instance, the quiet of contemplation is not right for someone who can obtain useful results in some form of activity, and vice versa, as Gregory says in the *Moralia* on Job 5:26.[1] So it says in Proverbs 14:12, "There is a way which seems right to someone, but its end leads to death."

(2) Someone may be desiring some temporal good to support life (and this is what it means to ask for daily bread), but the particular good becomes a risk of death. Many people have perished because of wealth. "Wealth that is preserved for the ill of its master" (Eccles. 5:12).

(3) Someone may desire to be freed from the harassment of some temptation, when in fact that temptation is serving to preserve humility. For instance, Paul asked to have the sting in his flesh taken away, but it had been given to him to prevent the greatness of his revelations making him conceited, as it says in 2 Corinthians 12:7.

Similarly it looks as if we know how we ought to pray: "Let him plead in faith, without doubting at all" (James 1:6). To this we must say that we can know in general, but we cannot entirely distinguish each particular motion of our heart, whether for instance we are asking for such and such a thing out of anger or out of zeal for righteousness. So in Matthew 20:20–3 the petition of the sons of Zebedee is rebuked because, even though they appeared to be pleading for a share in God's glory, yet their petition came from a certain vainglory or conceit.

Then he says, "But the Spirit himself . . . ," establishing the manner in which the Holy Spirit helps us. "The Spirit pleads for us with unutterable groanings." This appears to lend support to the error of Arius and Macedonius, who maintained that the Holy Spirit was a creature and beneath the Father and the Son, because pleading is something that inferiors do. But if we infer from what the apostle says (that he "pleads") that he is a passible creature inferior to the Father, it follows as well from the same text (that he "pleads with groans") that he is a passible creature lacking beatitude,

---

1. Gregory, *Moralia* 6.37.57 (PL 75:761–2).

something that no heretic has ever claimed, because groaning comes from grief, which has to do with wretchedness.[2]

So we must interpret "pleads" as meaning that he makes us plead, just as in Genesis 22:12, "Now I know that you fear the Lord" means "I have made you know."[3]

The Holy Spirit makes us plead inasmuch as he causes right desires in us. Pleading is a certain unfolding of our desires, and right desires come from charitable love, and this is produced in us by the Holy Spirit. "The charity of God is poured out in our hearts by the Holy Spirit, who is given to us" (Rom. 5:5). With the Holy Spirit directing and prompting our hearts, even our desires cannot help but be useful to us. "I am the Lord your God, who teach you useful things" (Is. 48:17). Therefore the apostle adds "for us."

If something we greatly desire and pray for with desire is delayed, we endure such a delay with distress and groaning, so he goes on, "with groans," groans caused in our hearts by the Holy Spirit, inasmuch as he makes us desire the things of heaven, which are not given to the soul immediately. This is the groaning of the dove[4] produced by the Holy Spirit in us: "Her handmaids were driven out, groaning like doves" (Nahum 2:7).

And he says, "unutterable," either because they are about something unutterable,[5] namely the glory of heaven ("He heard secret words which it is not lawful for anyone to speak," 2 Cor. 12:4), or because the very movements of the heart cannot adequately be expressed, in that they come from the Holy Spirit. "Who will express the tally of the heavens?" (Job 38:37).

Then, saying, "He who searches hearts . . . ," the apostle demonstrates the effectiveness of the help with which the Holy Spirit assists us. "He who searches hearts" is God and it is peculiar to him. "God who searches hearts and reins" (Ps. 7:10). And he is said to search hearts, not in the sense that he discovers the secrets of our hearts by investigating them, but because he knows clearly all that is lurking in our hearts. "I will search Jerusalem with lights" (Zeph. 1:12).

---

2. *Miseria* is the opposite of beatitude (cf. II.II q.30 a.1).

3. Cf. Lombard's Gloss (PL 191:1447BC), also quoting Gen. 22:12. From here onward Thomas follows the general drift of the Lombard's Gloss fairly closely.

4. Cf. PL 191:1447C.

5. Cf. PL 191:1447A.

God, who searches hearts, "knows" (meaning "approves,"[6] as in 2 Tim. 2:19, "The Lord knows those who are his own") "what the Spirit desires," makes us desire, that is. "Lord, my every desire is before you" (Ps. 37:10).

The desires which the Holy Spirit produces in the saints are acceptable to God for the reason that he "pleads for the saints," makes them plead, that is, "in accordance with God," in accordance, that is, with God's good pleasure. "The desire of the righteous is entirely good" (Prov. 11:23). As an example of this, the Lord said to the Father, "Not as I want, but as you want" (Matt. 26:39).

---

6. Cf. PL 191:1448A.

Thomas Aquinas

Texts on the Contemplative Life

Prologue to the Commentary on Boethius' *De Hebdomadibus*

> Run ahead into your house and gather yourself there and play there and pursue your thoughts. (Ecclus. 32:15–16)

The advantage which the study of wisdom has is that it is to a greater degree self-sufficient in pursuing its business. When we are engaged in outward activities we need many things to help us, but in the contemplation of wisdom we work all the more effectively, the more we dwell alone with ourselves. So, in the words cited above, the wise man calls us back to ourselves: "Run ahead into your house," that is, be anxious to return from external things to your own mind, before anything else gets hold of it and any other anxiety distracts it. That is why it says in Wisdom 8:16, "I will enter my house and rest with her," with wisdom, that is.

The first requirement, then, for the contemplation of wisdom is that we should take complete possession of our minds before anything else does, so that we can fill the whole house with the contemplation of wisdom. But it is also necessary that we ourselves should be fully present there, concentrating in such a way that our aim is not diverted to other matters. Accordingly the text goes on, "And gather yourself there," that is, draw together your whole intention. And when our interior house is entirely emptied like this and we are fully present there in our intention, the text tells us what we should do: "And play there."

There are two features of play which make it appropriate to compare the contemplation of wisdom to playing. First, we enjoy playing, and there is the greatest enjoyment of all to be had in the contemplation of wisdom. As Wisdom says in Ecclesiasticus 24:27, "My spirit is sweeter than honey."

Secondly, playing has no purpose beyond itself; what we do in play is done for its own sake. And the same applies to the pleasure of wisdom. If we are enjoying thinking about the things we long for or the things we are proposing to do, this kind of enjoyment looks

527

beyond itself to something else which we are eager to attain, and if we fail to attain it or if there is a delay in attaining it, our pleasure is mingled with a proportionate distress. As it says in Proverbs 14:13, "Laughter will be mixed with grief." But the contemplation of wisdom contains within itself the cause of its own enjoyment, and so it is not exposed to the kind of anxiety that goes with waiting for something which we lack. This is why it says in Wisdom 8:16, "Her company is without bitterness" (the company of wisdom, that is) "and there is no boredom in living with her." It is for this reason that divine Wisdom compares her enjoyment to playing in Proverbs 8:30, "I enjoyed myself every single day, playing before him," each "single day" meaning the consideration of some different truth. So our text goes on, "Pursue your thoughts," the thoughts, that is, by means of which we obtain knowledge of the truth.

From the Prologue to the Commentary on St. John

I saw the Lord sitting on a high, elevated throne and the house was full of his majesty,[1] and the things which were beneath him filled the temple (Isaiah 6:1).

The words quoted here are the words of someone contemplating, and if we take them as coming from the mouth of John the evangelist they are quite apt as a comment on his gospel. As Augustine says, the other evangelists instruct us about the active life in their gospels, but John instructs us also about the contemplative life in his gospel.[2]

In the words quoted above, the contemplation of John is depicted under three headings, in line with the three ways in which he contemplated the Godhead of the Lord Jesus. It is depicted as being high, expansive and complete. It is high, because he "saw the Lord sitting on a high, elevated throne." It is expansive, because "the house was full of his majesty." It is complete, because "the things which were beneath him filled the temple."

On the first point, we should realize that the height, the sublimity of contemplation consists chiefly in the contemplation and knowledge of God. "Lift up your eyes on high and consider who made these" (Is. 40:26). So we lift up the eyes of our contemplation on high when we see and contemplate the very Creator of all things. Since John, then, rose above every creature, above the very mountains, the very skies, the angels themselves, and reached the Creator of all, as Augustine says,[3] clearly his contemplation was very high. And so he says, "I saw the Lord sitting on a high throne." And because, as John himself says, "Isaiah said this when he saw his glory," Christ's, that is, "and it was about him that he spoke" (John 12:41),

---

1. This phrase, which is not found in current editions of the Vulgate, occurs in some Parisian manuscripts from the time of Thomas.
2. Augustine, *De Consensu Evang.* 1.5 (PL 34:1046).
3. Augustine, *Tr. in Io. Ev.* 1.5.

this means that the Lord sitting on the high, elevated throne is Christ.

In this contemplation of John's about the Word incarnate, four kinds of height are identified: authority (which is why he says "the Lord"), eternity ("sitting"), natural rank or nobility ("on a high throne") and truth which baffles our understanding ("elevated"). These were, in fact, the four ways in which the ancient philosophers came to the contemplation of God.

Some of them came to the knowledge of God by way of his authority, and this is the most effective way. We see that in the domain of nature things act purposively and attain useful and definite objectives and, since they lack understanding, they cannot direct themselves toward any goal unless they are moved and directed by the mind of someone guiding them. So the movement of natural objects toward a definite goal is itself evidence of there being something higher by which they are directed and guided toward their goal. And so, since the whole course of nature proceeds and is directed in an orderly way toward its goal, we must of necessity posit something higher which directs all these things and governs them as their Lord. And this is God. It is this authority to govern which is indicated as belonging to the Word of God when it says "Lord." Accordingly in the Psalms it says, "You lord it over the power of the sea, you control the movement of its waves" (Ps. 88:10). "Yours is the kingdom, yours is the power,"[4] as if to say, "You are the Lord of nature, the governor of all things." John reveals that he has this knowledge about the Word when he says, "He came to what was his own," into the world, that is, because the whole world is his own (John 1:11).

Others came to the knowledge of God by way of his eternity. They saw that whatever exists in things is changeable, and the nobler anything is in the scale of things the less changeable it is. For instance, lower bodies are changeable both in their substance and in their location, but the heavenly bodies, which are nobler, are unchangeable in their substance and undergo only change of place.[5]

---

4. It is not clear whether this is intended as part of the quotation from Psalm 88 (there is nothing in the Psalm at all like it) or whether it is meant to be an allusion to the supplementary phrase used at the end of the Lord's Prayer ("thine is the kingdom, the power . . . ").

5. According to Aristotelian cosmology, the heavenly bodies are not liable to the sort

Along these lines it can obviously be inferred that the first principle of all things, the highest and most noble of all, is immutable and eternal. And this eternity of the Word is implied by the prophet when he says "sitting," that is, presiding in eternity with absolutely no change at all. "Your seat, O God, is forever" (Ps. 44:7). "Jesus Christ, yesterday and today, the same forever" (Heb. 13:8). It is to display this eternity that John says, "In the beginning was the Word" (John 1:1).

Some people came to the knowledge of God by way of his rank; these were the Platonists. They saw that all the things that possess some quality by participation presuppose something primary and supreme which possesses that quality by virtue of its own essence, just as everything that is on fire by participation presupposes fire which is such by virtue of its own essence.[6] So since everything which exists participates in existence and exists by participating in existence, there must be something at the summit of everything which exists by virtue of its own essence. And that is God, who is the utterly sufficient, worthy and complete cause of all existence, from whom everything that exists derives its share in existence. This rank is revealed in the words "on a high throne," which Dionysius says refers to the divine nature.[7] "The Lord is high above all nations" (Ps. 112:4). John points to this rank when he says, "The Word was God" ("the Word" being the subject of the sentence and "God" the predicate).[8]

Some came to the knowledge of God by way of the incomprehensibility of his truth. Every truth which our intellect can contain is limited because, as Augustine says, anything that is known is within the limits of the knower's grasp,[9] and if it is limited it is also defined and particular, and so there must be a first, supreme truth,

---

of change and decay which all bodies on earth undergo; the only change which affects them is local motion. Cf. Aristotle, *De Caelo* 1.3.

6. According to Platonist metaphysics, the qualities that we see in the complex creatures around us are all derivative; at a higher level there must be uncomplex and pure versions of the diluted and confused qualities found here below, and these must be the source of whatever share in these qualities is exhibited by the world around us. Cf. Thomas, *In Lib. de Causis* 16, ed. cit. p. 94.

7. Dionysius, *CH* 13.4 (ed. cit. pp. 156–7).

8. John 1:1. In Latin *Deus erat Verbum* is syntactically ambiguous and could be read as meaning, "God was the Word."

9. Augustine, *Civ. Dei* 12.19.

which surpasses all understanding and is incomprehensible and unlimited. And that is God. So it says in Psalm 8:2, "Your splendor, O God, is raised high above the heavens," that is, above all created intellects, those of angels as well as our own.[10] And that is because, as the apostle says, he "dwells in unapproachable light" (1 Tim. 6:16). The incomprehensibility of his truth is indicated in our text when it says "elevated," too high, that is, for the knowledge of any created intellect. And John implies this incomprehensibility when he says, "No one has ever seen God" (John 1:18).

So John's contemplation, which he passes on to us in his gospel, was high with reference to the authority, eternity, rank and incomprehensibility of the Word.

It was also expansive. Contemplation is expansive when someone is able to see in some cause all the effects produced by that cause, knowing, that is, not only the nature of the cause but also the power with which it pours itself out into many things. This outpouring is spoken of in Ecclesiasticus 24:35, "Who fills with wisdom like the Phison," and in Psalm 64:10, "The river of God is filled with water," because divine wisdom is expansive[11] with regard to the knowledge of everything. "He gave me true knowledge of all that is" (Wis. 7:17). So John the evangelist's contemplation was expansive because after being raised up to contemplate the nature and essence of the divine Word he says, "In the beginning was the Word and the Word was with God," and then he immediately goes on to indicate the power of the Word with which he pours himself out into all things, "By him all things were made" (John 1:1,3). So in our text, after the prophet has said, "I saw the Lord sitting . . . ," he goes on with a reference to his power, "And the house was full of his majesty," that is, the whole fullness of things and of the universe comes from the majesty and power of the Word of God, by whom all things were made and by whose light everyone coming into this world is enlightened (John 1:3,9). "The Lord's is the earth and its fullness" (Ps. 23:1).

John's contemplation was also complete. Contemplation is complete when the person contemplating is brought and raised to

---

10. This is one of the interpretations found in Lombard's Gloss on Ps. 8:2 (PL 191:123D).

11. The text transmitted by the manuscripts seems to have *altitudinem*, but surely Thomas meant *amplitudinem*; anyway, that is what I have translated.

the high level of the things contemplated; if you remain down below in the depths, however high your contemplation may be, it would not be complete. So if it is to be complete it must rise up and reach the very goal of the thing contemplated, cleaving and assenting in heart and mind to the truth contemplated. "Do you know the ways of the clouds," that is, the contemplations of preachers,[12] "Do you know that they are completely perfect?" (Job 37:16)[13] inasmuch as they cleave firmly in heart and mind to the high truth they contemplate. So because John not only taught us how Jesus Christ, the Word of God, is God, high above all things, and how all things were made through him, but he also taught us that we are sanctified through him and that we cleave to him by the grace which he pours into us ("From his fullness we have all received," John 1:16), it is evident that his contemplation was complete. And this completeness is revealed when our text goes on, "And the things that were beneath him filled the temple," because, as it says in 1 Corinthians 11:3, "Christ's head is God," so what is under him is the sacraments of his humanity, by which the faithful are filled with the fullness of grace. So "the things which were under him," that is, the sacraments of his humanity, "filled the temple," that is, the faithful who are the "holy temple of God," as it says in 1 Corinthians 3:17, inasmuch as all the faithful receive something from Christ's fullness of grace by means of the sacraments of his humanity.

So John's contemplation was high, expansive and complete.

And it should be noticed that these three kinds of contemplation are distributed between different sciences. The completeness of contemplation belongs to moral science, which is concerned with our final goal. Its expansiveness and fullness belong to natural science, which looks at the things that proceed from God. The height of contemplation, as far as the philosophical sciences are concerned, belongs to metaphysics. But what these sciences possess separately the gospel of John contains all together, and therefore it is utterly complete.

---

12. Cf. Gregory's interpretation of Job 37:16 in *Moralia* XXVII 37.61–2 (PL 76:435–6), much of which was taken up into the Marginal Gloss.

13. This is a very inexact citation; the Vulgate text suggests that by "they" Thomas probably meant "kinds of knowledge" (*scientiae*) rather than "clouds."

Active and
Contemplative Life
Summa Theologiae II.II
Questions 179–182

Next we must look at the active and contemplative lives, and there are four topics to be examined:
(1) The division of life into active and contemplative;
(2) The contemplative life;
(3) The active life;
(4) The comparison between the active and contemplative lives.

QUESTION 179: The division of life into active and contemplative

The first topic contains two questions:
(1) Whether the division of life into active and contemplative is appropriate;
(2) Whether it is adequate.

Article 1: Is the division of life into active and contemplative appropriate?

The division of life into active and contemplative appears to be inappropriate:
(1) It is by its essence that the soul is the principle of life. As the philosopher says, "For living creatures life is their being."[1] But it is by its powers that the soul is the principle of activity and contemplation. So it is apparently not appropriate to divide life into active and contemplative.[2]

---

1. Aristotle, *De Anima* 2.4 (415b13).
2. This objection challenges the propriety of the phrases "active life" and "contemplative life" on the grounds that action/contemplation belong to a different level of inquiry from

534

(2) Life comes before intellect, because life is already present in living creatures by virtue of the vegetative soul, as the philosopher makes clear.[3] But "active" and "contemplative" (or "speculative" and "practical") are specific kinds of intellectual operation, as we can see from the *De Anima*.[4] And it is not proper to use the specific characteristics of something that comes later in an analysis of something that comes first.[5]

(3) The word "life" implies movement, as Dionysius shows.[6] But contemplation consists more in repose, as is suggested by Wisdom 8:16, "I will enter my house and rest with her." So it looks as if the division of life into active and contemplative is inappropriate.[7]

On the other hand:

Gregory says, "There are two lives about which almighty God instructs us by means of his holy word: the active and the contemplative."[8]

REPLY

Beings are properly called "living" if they have it in themselves to move and to do things. But any being is particularly characterized

life. By virtue of the "essence" of my soul I *am* the particular kind of living creature that I am, and my being alive cannot be divorced from my being alive as this particular kind of living creature. Different ways of being alive must therefore refer to being alive as different kinds of living being: I may be alive as a chimpanzee or a cauliflower or a human being. Being "active" or "contemplative" is therefore not a matter of being alive in a particular kind of way, but simply of using the powers that I have as a living being in a particular kind of way.

3. The vegetative soul, in Aristotelian terminology, is what makes something alive to the extent that it can grow, reproduce and so on; it is common to plants, animals and human beings, and as such it is the first kind of life. Cf. Aristotle, *De Anima* 2.4 (415a23–5).

4. Aristotle, *De Anima* 3.10 (433a14–5).

5. This raises much the same difficulty as the first objection, but more from the point of view of methodology. To talk of "active" and "contemplative" lives suggests a misleading kind of classification, like talking of different kinds of tiger as if they were different kinds of animal: differences of species should not be regarded as constituting a difference of genus. Within the genus "life" we can identify "intellectual life" as a species; it is within the species "intellectual life" that the difference between "active" and "contemplative" arises.

6. Dionysius, *DN* 6.1 (PG 3:856AB), on which Thomas comments (para. 678 in the Marietti edition): "Among bodies, those are properly described as living which have the capacity for movement in themselves . . . and since any kind of activity is in some way movement, anything that has the source of its activity in itself . . . is called living."

7. The objection this time is that "contemplation" is not really "life" at all, but rather, as it were, a matter of taking a break from life.

8. *Hom. Ezek.* 2.2.7 (PL 76:952D).

in itself by whatever is proper to it and whatever it is most inclined to. So each living being is shown to be alive by the function which is most proper to it and to which it is most inclined; for instance, the life of a plant is said to consist in its absorbing nourishment and in its propagating itself, while the life of an animal is identified as consisting in sense-perception and movement. But the life of human beings is identified as consisting in their understanding things and their acting rationally.

On the same basis, within the domain of human life, the life of any one individual seems to be identifiable as the thing he most enjoys and in which he is most interested, which will also be the thing he most wants to share with a friend, as it says in the *Ethics*.[9]

So, since some people particularly devote themselves to the contemplation of truth, while others apply themselves particularly to outward works, this is why it is appropriate to divide human life into "active" and "contemplative."[10]

In response to the points raised above:

(1) The proper form of each being, which makes it actually exist, is the principle of its proper activity. So living is said to be the being of living creatures because living creatures act in such and such a way by virtue of the fact that they have their being through their form.[11]

(2) Life in its most general sense is not divided into active and contemplative; the distinction concerns human life, which is specified by the possession of intellect. So the distinction between different kinds of human life is the same as the distinction between different kinds of intellect.

(3) Contemplation does involve resting from external movements, but all the same, contemplating itself is a kind of movement of the intellect, inasmuch as any activity can be called a movement, in the same sense in which the philosopher says that perceiving

---

9. Aristotle, *Eth. Nic.* 9.12 (1172a1–3).

10. I.e., the distinction between "active" and "contemplative" life is a matter of intellectual bias: some people apply their minds primarily to the attempt to understand the truth for its own sake, whereas other people apply their minds chiefly to the attempt to get something done.

11. Thomas refuses to distinguish between what makes, say, a tiger *alive* and what makes it *alive as a tiger*. So if you are the kind of person whose bias is toward understanding truth for its own sake, what makes you alive is what makes you alive *as that kind of person*, so that it is appropriate to say that your life is a contemplative life.

and understanding are kinds of movement, meaning by "movement" the operation of some complete being.[12] In the same sense Dionysius lists three movements of the soul in contemplation: straight, circular and spiral.[13]

Article 2: Is the division of life into active and contemplative adequate?

The division of life into active and contemplative appears to be inadequate:[1]

(1) The philosopher says that there are three main kinds of life: self-indulgent, civic (which seems to be the same as the active life) and contemplative.[2] So the division into active and contemplative is inadequate.

(2) Augustine lists three kinds of life: leisurely (which belongs to contemplation), busy (which belongs to the active life), and then he adds a third kind of life which is a compound of the other two.[3] So it looks as if the division into active and contemplative is insufficient.

(3) Human life takes on different forms in accordance with the different activities in which people are interested. But there are more than two kinds of activity in which people are interested. So surely life ought to be divided up under more headings than just "active" and "contemplative."

On the other hand:

These two lives are symbolized by Jacob's two wives, the active life by Leah and the contemplative by Rachel; also by the two women who gave the Lord hospitality, the contemplative life being symbolized by Mary, the active by Martha, as Gregory says.[4] And this symbolism would not work if there were

---

12. Aristotle distinguishes between the movement (or change) that brings some being to its maturity (e.g., growth) and the movement a being can perform once it has reached its maturity (*De Anima* 3.7, 431a6–7); perceiving and thinking are movements in the latter sense (ibid. 431a8).

13. Dionysius, *DN* 4.9 (PG 3:705AB).

1. A scholastic *divisio* is meant to be a complete analysis of something, so that if it fails to account for some part of its subject it is an inadequate division.

2. Aristotle, *Eth. Nic.* 1.5 (1095b17–19).

3. Augustine, *Civ. Dei* 19.1–2.

4. *Moralia* 6.37.61 (PL 75:764B–D).

more than two types of life. So life is adequately divided into active and contemplative.

Reply

The division into active and contemplative life is meant to apply to human life, and so it concerns different kinds of human understanding. And understanding is divided into active and contemplative, because the purpose of intellectual knowledge is either the sheer knowledge of truth (which is a matter of contemplative understanding) or some outward act (which is a matter of practical or active understanding). So it is sufficient to divide life into active and contemplative.

In response to the points raised above:

(1) The life of self-indulgence takes bodily enjoyment as its goal, and this is something we share with the animals. So, as the philosopher says in the passage referred to, this is a "bestial life."[5] That is why it is not included in this present analysis, whereby human life is divided into active and contemplative.

(2) Intermediaries are made up of extremes,[6] and so are implicitly contained within them: tepid is contained in hot and cold, pale is contained in white and black. In the same way something compounded of active and contemplative is contained within these two terms. But in any mixture there is one ingredient which predominates, and so it is in the intermediary kind of life: sometimes the contemplative element predominates, sometimes the active.[7]

---

5. *Eth. Nic.* 1095b20. The refusal to treat the life of self-indulgence as a genuinely "human" life rests on Aristotle's argument in *Eth. Nic.* 1.7 that human good must be identified with something which is specifically human, i.e., something we do not have in common with plants and animals. The point is not that the specifically human capacity for rational thought puts us under an obligation to use it, but that if we try to live as if we did not possess it we cannot actually succeed in being happy; in a more modern idiom, we shall not be "being ourselves."

6. Cf. Aristotle, *Physics* 1.5 (188b23–24), with Thomas' comments (para. 78 in the Marietti edition), showing that only the opposites constitute the real ultimate principles.

7. Thomas disallows the notion of the "mixed life" as being an unnecessary complication. The active and contemplative lives are identified with reference to an intellectual bias one way or the other; there is no reason to suppose that this bias will normally be so intense as to exclude entirely the less favored facet of life. Even the most dedicated intellectual must

(3) All the human activities in which people are interested are part of the active life, if they are geared to the needs of the present life in accordance with right reason, because it is the business of the active life to provide for the needs of this present life by means of properly ordered activities. But if what people are interested in serves any kind of lust, then it belongs to the life of self-indulgence, which does not fall within the active life.[8] And human interests aimed at the study of truth belong to the contemplative life.

QUESTION 180: *The contemplative life*

Next we must look at the contemplative life, and this raises eight questions:
(1) Whether the contemplative life belongs entirely to the intellect, or whether feelings come into it as well;
(2) Whether the moral virtues belong to the contemplative life;
(3) Whether the contemplative life consists in just one act, or in several;
(4) Whether the consideration of all sorts of truth belongs to the contemplative life;
(5) Whether the contemplative life in this world can rise to the vision of God;
(6) The contemplative movements listed by Dionysius;
(7) The delightfulness of contemplation;
(8) The lastingness of contemplation.

Article 1: *Is the contemplative life quite independent of feelings and confined to the intellect?*

It looks as if the contemplative life has nothing to do with feelings, and belongs entirely in the intellect:

---

sometimes turn his mind to practical matters, and even the most energetically active person is liable sometimes to read the newspaper just out of interest. But in everyone there will be some bias one way or the other. So treating the "mixed life" as a third kind of life would be like treating "gin and tonic" as a third kind of substance, distinct from both gin and tonic. However mixed up in practice the two ingredients may be, there are still only two ingredients.

8. Thomas covertly brings in here the traditional Christian notion of the active life as consisting in the pursuit of the moral virtues. In that sense it cannot contain anything which is not in accordance with moral virtue.

(1) The philosopher says that the goal of contemplation is truth.[1] And truth is entirely a matter for the intellect. So apparently the contemplative life is wholly intellectual.

(2) Gregory says that Rachel, whose name means "sight of the first principle," signifies the contemplative life.[2] But seeing a principle is properly the business of the intellect. So the contemplative life belongs properly to the intellect.

(3) Gregory says that it is part of the contemplative life to rest from external activity.[3] But our emotional or appetitive power makes us turn to outward activities.[4] So it seems that the contemplative life has no connection with our appetitive power.

On the other hand:

Gregory also says that the contemplative life means holding on to the love of God and of neighbor with all our mind, and to cleave solely to desire for our Creator.[5] But desire and love concern our emotional or appetitive power, as we have seen.[6] So the contemplative life too has something to do with our emotional or appetitive power.

REPLY

We must say that "the contemplative life" refers to the life of people whose primary aim is the contemplation of truth. And aiming at something, as we have seen,[7] is an activity of the will, because what we aim at is our objective, and this is the object of the will. So the contemplative life belongs to the intellect, if what we are thinking of is the actual nature of its activity. But with reference to the motive which inspires its functioning, that is the business of the will, which moves all our other powers, including the intellect, to perform their own acts, as we have seen.[8]

---

1. Aristotle, *Metaph.* α 1 (993b20–1).

2. *Moralia* 6.37.61 (PL 75:764B).

3. *Hom. Ezek.* 2.2.8 (PL 76:953AB).

4. The suggestion is that wanting something or getting excited about something naturally prompts us to set about doing something about it.

5. *Hom. Ezek.* 2.2.8 (PL 76:953AB).

6. I.II q.26 a.1.

7. I.II q.12 a.1.

8. I q.82 a.4.

Our appetitive power prompts us to look into something, whether with the senses or with the intellect, in two ways: sometimes it is because we love the object of our vision; as it says in Matthew 6:21, "Where your treasure is, there is your heart too." Sometimes it is because we love the knowledge itself which we gain by looking into something.[9] This is why Gregory locates the contemplative life in the love of God, inasmuch as it is love of God which fires people to look at his beauty. And because we all enjoy obtaining what we love, the contemplative life culminates in enjoyment, which is a matter of our feelings; and this in turn makes love more intense.

In response to the points raised above:
(1) Truth, precisely as the goal of contemplation, functions as a good which is desirable, lovable and enjoyable. From this point of view it does concern our appetitive power.
(2) We are drawn to the vision of the first principle, God, by love of him. So Gregory says that the contemplative life disdains all other concerns and is on fire with yearning to see the face of its Creator.[10]
(3) The appetitive power not only moves the limbs of our bodies to perform outward works, it also moves the intellect to perform the activity of contemplation, as we have explained.

Article 2: Do the moral virtues belong to the contemplative life?

Surely the moral virtues do belong to the contemplative life:
(1) Gregory says that the contemplative life means holding on to the love of God and of neighbor with all our mind.[1] But all the moral virtues whose acts are covered by the precepts of the Law can be seen as facets of the love of God and of our neighbor, because

---

9. In III *Sent.* d.35 q.1 a.2 q.1 Thomas uses much the same distinction in order to distinguish between the "contemplation of the philosophers" and that of the saints, but here he does not even seem to be terribly interested in separating the two kinds of interest from each other, let alone in allocating them to different people. He takes up the point again in q.180 a.7, and it is clear that he in no way disapproves of the delight there can be simply in knowing. Like everything else, though, it becomes fully good only in the context of charity.

10. *Hom. Ezek.* 2.2.8 (PL 76:953B).

1. *Hom. Ezek.* 2.2.8 (PL 76:953A).

"charity is the fulfilment of the Law" (Rom. 13:10). So it looks as if the moral virtues do belong to the contemplative life.

(2) The contemplative life is directed primarily toward the contemplation of God. Gregory says that it disdains all other concerns and is on fire with yearning to see the face of its Creator.[2] But the only way to achieve this is purity, which is caused by moral virtue, because it says in Matthew 5:8, "Blessed are the pure in heart, because they will see God." And in Hebrews 12:14 it says, "Pursue peace with everyone and also holiness, without which no one will see God." So apparently the moral virtues do belong to the contemplative life.

(3) Gregory says that the contemplative life is beautiful in the soul; that is why it is symbolized by Rachel, who had a beautiful face (Gen. 29:17).[3] But it is to the moral virtues that we look for beauty in the soul, and in particular to temperance, as Ambrose says.[4] So it seems that the moral virtues do belong to the contemplative life.

On the other hand:

The moral virtues are geared to external activities, and Gregory says that it is part of the contemplative life to rest from external activities.[5] Therefore the moral virtues do not belong to the contemplative life.

REPLY

There are two ways in which something can belong to the contemplative life: as an essential part of the contemplative life, or as something that prepares us for the contemplative life. Now the moral virtues do not belong to the essence of the contemplative life, because the goal of the contemplative life is the consideration of truth. But in the case of the moral virtues, as the philosopher says, knowing (which is an aspect of the consideration of truth) carries

---

2. Ibid. (PL 76:953B).

3. *Hom. Ezek.* 2.2.10 (PL 76:954C).

4. *De Officiis* 1.43.209 (PL 16:86B).

5. *Moralia* VI is indicated in the text, but this is in fact part of the passage Thomas has already cited several times from *Hom. Ezek.* 2.2.8 (PL 76:953AB).

little weight.[6] This is why he declares the moral virtues to be involved in active happiness, not contemplative.[7]

But the moral virtues do belong to the contemplative life in a preparatory role. The act of contemplation, in which the contemplative life essentially consists, is hindered both by tempestuous passions, which distract the soul's attention away from the objects of the mind to the objects of the senses, and by external disturbances. The moral virtues, however, check the violence of our passions and calm the disturbances involved in external activities.[8] In this way the moral virtues are part of the contemplative life inasmuch as they fit us for it.

In response to the points raised above:
(1) As we have seen, the contemplative life is motivated by our feelings, and in this sense love of God and of neighbor is necessary for the contemplative life.[9] But motives do not enter into the essence of anything, though they prepare and complete things.[10] So it does not follow that the moral virtues belong essentially to the contemplative life.
(2) Holiness or purity is due to the virtues which deal with the passions that obstruct the limpidity of our reason. And peace is caused by justice, the virtue concerned with our deeds—"The work of justice is peace" (Is. 32:17)—inasmuch as someone who refrains from wronging other people removes the occasion for litigation and disturbances. And in this way the moral virtues prepare the way for the contemplative life inasmuch as they cause peace and purity.

---

6. Aristotle, *Eth. Nic.* 2.4 (1105b2–3).

7. Ibid. 10.8 (1178a9-22), with Thomas' comment (Marietti ed. para. 2111).

8. The moral virtues make for the smooth functioning of life, which involves (a) the proper ordering of our emotions, so that we are not at the mercy of riotous and irrelevant feelings, and (b) an ability to do whatever we do without undue turbulence.

9. So far as I know, Thomas nowhere explains how love of neighbor is a necessary disposition for the contemplative life, but cf. above, pp. 283–84.

10. Motives do not enter into the essence of an act, because the same act can be performed for a variety of different motives without ceasing to be the same act. If I go to the opera to show off, or because my youngest daughter is singing in it, or because I am being paid to review it, whatever my motives may be, I am still going to the opera. However, whatever motivates an act will both take the first steps toward getting it done and see it through to its completion. Preparing something in view of some goal and seeing it through to that goal belong to the same agent (I.II q.98 a.2).

(3) Beauty, as we saw above,[11] consists in a certain radiance and in proper proportions. And both of these are found in the reason, where they are rooted: it is to reason that the light belongs which makes things clear, and it is reason's business to arrange the proportions of things. Therefore beauty is found in its own right and essentially in the contemplative life, which consists in the activity of reason. This is why it says in Wisdom 8:2, with reference to the contemplation of wisdom, "I became a lover of her beauty." In the moral virtues, on the other hand, beauty is found only secondarily, inasmuch as they participate in reason's order, and it is found in this way particularly in temperance, which restrains the lusts which most darken the light of reason. This is why the virtue of chastity most fits people for contemplation, inasmuch as sexual delights are the most calculated to hold the mind down under the sway of the senses, as Augustine says.[12]

Article 3: Are there several acts belonging to the contemplative life?

It looks as if several different acts belong to the contemplative life:

(1) Richard of St. Victor distinguishes between contemplation, meditation and cogitation,[1] but they all seem to belong to the contemplative life. So the contemplative life contains several different acts.

(2) The apostle says, "We, with unveiled face reflecting[2] the glory of the Lord, are transformed into the same radiance" (2 Cor. 3:18). But this belongs to the contemplative life. So in addition to the three items already mentioned, reflection also belongs to the contemplative life.

(3) Bernard says that the first and greatest contemplation is "wondering at his majesty."[3] But according to Damascene wonder is

---

11. II.II q.145 a.2.

12. *Solil.* 1.10.17 (PL 32:878).

1. *Benjamin Major* 1.3 (PL 196:66C).

2. The Latin is *speculantes*, which suggests a link with "speculation," sometimes more or less identified with "contemplation"; I have tried to preserve something of the Latin word-play by using the word "reflect."

3. *De Consideratione* 5.14.32.

listed as a kind of fear.[4] So it appears that several different acts are involved in the contemplative life.

(4) Prayer, reading and meditation are said to belong to the contemplative life.[5] Listening is also part of it, because it says of Mary, who symbolizes the contemplative life, that she "sat at the feet of the Lord and listened to his words" (Luke 10:39). So it looks as if several acts are needed for the contemplative life.

On the other hand:
"Life" in this context means the activity in which someone is most interested. So if the contemplative life has more than one activity, then there will be several contemplative lives, not just one.

REPLY

We must point out that what we are discussing here is the contemplative life as it concerns human beings. And the difference between us and the angels, as Dionysius makes clear, is that angels look at the truth with a direct grasp of it,[6] whereas we have to start with many different things and proceed step by step from there before we reach the point where we can see truth in its simplicity. So there is one act in which the contemplative life comes to its final fulfilment, namely the contemplation of truth, and this is what gives it its unity, but several activities are involved on the way to this final act; some of them concern the acceptance of the principles on the basis of which we proceed to the contemplation of truth, while others are a matter of making deductions from these principles to bring us to the truth of what we want to know. The final act, which completes the process, is the actual contemplation of the truth.

In response to the points raised above:
(1) According to Richard of St. Victor, cogitation appears to involve looking at many things from which we hope to gather some single truth;[7] so under this heading we may include the sense-

---

4. *De Fide Orthodoxa* 29, ed. cit. pp. 121–2.

5. Cf. above, p. 364 note 6.

6. Dionysius, *DN* 7.2 (PG 3:868B); cf. Thomas, *Summa Theol.* I q.58 a.3–4.

7. *Benjamin Major* 1.3 (PL 196:66–7). This text from Richard is the basis of the whole of the answer to the first objection.

perceptions which give us the knowledge of certain effects, the use of imagination, the application of discursive reasoning to various signs, or anything else that can lead us to the knowledge of the truth we are aiming at. Though Augustine suggests that every actual operation of the intellect can be called "cogitation."[8]

"Meditation" seems to refer to the rational process leading from the various relevant principles to the contemplation of some truth. And "consideration" refers to the same thing, according to Bernard,[9] although the philosopher suggests that every operation of the intellect is called "consideration."[10]

"Contemplation" refers to the actual, simple, looking at the truth. So Richard says that contemplation is a penetrating and unhindered gazing of the mind at the things that are there to be seen, while meditation is the way a mind looks at things when it is engaged in seeking truth; cogitation is the glance of a mind which is prone to wandering.[11]

(2) As Augustine's gloss on the passage points out, *speculantes* comes from *speculum* (mirror), not from *specula* (observatory).[12] And seeing something in a mirror means seeing a cause by means of an effect, in which its likeness is apparent. So speculation can surely be regarded as a form of meditation.

(3) Wonder is a kind of fear which results from an awareness of something which is too great for our capacity. Therefore it is an act which follows from the contemplation of some high truth. And we have already said that contemplation culminates in our feelings.

(4) There are two ways in which people come to the knowledge of truth. One way is by means of what we receive from others. So with regard to what we receive from God prayer is necessary: "I called and the spirit of Wisdom came to me" (Wis. 7:7). With regard to what we receive from other people, listening is necessary, inasmuch as we receive things from people speaking to us, and reading is necessary, inasmuch as we receive things that are transmitted in writing. The other way of coming to the

---

8. *De Trinitate* 14.6.8–14.7.10.
9. *De Consideratione* 2.2.5.
10. Aristotle, *De Anima* 2.1 (412a11).
11. *Benjamin Major* 1.4 (PL 196:67D).
12. Marginal Gloss on 2 Cor. 3:18.

knowledge of truth is by people undertaking their own study, and so meditation is needed.[13]

Article 4: Does the contemplative life consist solely in the contemplation of God or also in the consideration of all sorts of truths?

The contemplative life appears to consist not only in the contemplation of God, but also in the consideration of all sorts of truths:

(1) It says in Psalms 138:14, "Your works are wonderful and my soul will know them greatly." But the knowledge of God's works comes about by way of some kind of contemplation of truth. So it looks as if it is the business of the contemplative life not only to contemplate the truth of God, but also to contemplate any other truth.

(2) Bernard says that the first contemplation is wondering at his majesty, the second concerns God's judgments, the third his kindnesses and the fourth is contemplation of his promises.[1] But of these four only the first is about the truth of God, while the others are about the effects which he produces. So the contemplative life does not consist solely in looking at the truth of God; it consists also in looking at the truth about the effects of God.

(3) Richard of St. Victor distinguishes six kinds of contemplations, of which the first involves only the imagination, our attention being directed to bodily things, while the second involves the imagination governed by reason, inasmuch as we look at the ordering and arrangement of the things our senses perceive. The third kind involves reason dependent on imagination, when we are raised by our examination of visible things to the realm of invisible things. The fourth involves reason working on its own terms, when the mind attends to invisible things which are unknown to imagination. The fifth is above reason, when by God's revelation we know things which human reason cannot compre-

---

13. Thomas evidently sees no need to distinguish between "meditation" and "study," and in medieval Latin *meditatio* has a well-established academic sense: cf., for instance, E. Jeauneau, "Jean de Salisbury et la Lecture des Philosophes," in M. Wilks, ed., *The World of John of Salisbury* (Oxford, 1984), pp. 78–81; Vincent of Beauvais, *De Eruditione Filiorum Nobilium*, ed. A. Steiner (Cambridge, Mass.: 1938), 5.32 (p. 22) and 17 (pp. 62–4).

1. *De Consid.* 5.14.32.

hend, and the sixth is above reason and in spite of it, when by God's enlightening we know things which appear to contradict human reason, such as what we learn about the mystery of the Trinity.[2] But of these it is surely only the last which concerns the truth of God. So contemplation is not only a matter of the truth of God; it involves also the truth which is studied in creatures.

(4) What we look for in the contemplative life is the contemplation of truth in as much as this is what fulfils us as human beings. But all kinds of truth fulfil the human intellect.[3] So the contemplative life consists in all sorts of contemplation of truth.

On the other hand:
Gregory says that what is sought in contemplation is the first principle, namely God.[4]

Reply

As we have seen, there are two ways in which things belong to the contemplative life: primarily or secondarily and preparatorily. What belongs to the contemplative life primarily is the contemplation of the truth of God, because it is this kind of contemplation which is the goal of human life as a whole. So Augustine says that the contemplation of God is promised to us as the goal of all that we do and as the eternal perfection of our joys.[5] In the life to come such contemplation will be perfect, when we see God "face to face," and it will accordingly make us perfectly happy, but for the moment we are capable only of an imperfect contemplation of the truth of God, "in a mirror and obscurely,"[6] from which we obtain a kind of beginning of bliss, which starts here on earth, but is to be completed in the life to come. This is why the philosopher locates our ultimate happiness as human beings in the contemplation of the most excellent intelligible object.[7]

---

2. *Benjamin Major* 1.6 (PL 196:70B).

3. The knowledge of any truth, to some extent, fulfils our minds, because truth is what our minds are designed for (cf. I q.16 a.6 ad 1); so truth of any kind is a "perfecting of the intellect" in the sense that, in however small a way, it actualizes our intellectual potential.

4. *Moralia* 6.37.61 (PL 75:764B).

5. *De Trin.* 1.8.17.

6. 1 Cor. 13:12.

7. Aristotle, *Eth. Nic.* 10.7, with Thomas' comments (Marietti ed. para. 2087).

However, since we are led to the contemplation of God by way of his effects, in line with Romans 1:20, "The invisible things of God are seen in that they are understood by means of what he has made," the contemplation of God's effects is also a part of the contemplative life, but in a secondary role, namely that of leading us to the knowledge of God. So Augustine says that when we consider creatures we should not engage in an idle curiosity, which must sometime come to an end, we should make them a step toward the immortal realities which last forever.[8]

From all that we have said it is clear that there is a sort of sequence of four things which belong to the contemplative life: first the moral virtues, then the various acts other than contemplation, then thirdly the contemplation of God's effects and fourthly and finally the actual contemplation of the truth of God.[9]

In response to the points raised above:

(1) David was seeking knowledge of God's works in order to be led to God, which is why elsewhere he says, "I will meditate on all your works and on what your hands have made, I have stretched out my hands toward you" (Ps. 142:5–6).

(2) By considering God's judgments we are led to the contemplation of his justice, and by considering his kindnesses and promises we are led to the knowledge of his mercy and goodness, as by their effects either shown or due to be shown.

(3) This list specifies the stages by which we rise through creatures to the contemplation of God. In the first stage there is our perception of the objects of our senses. In the second stage there is a movement from the objects of the senses to those of the intellect. In the third stage there is an assessment of the objects of the senses in the light of the objects of the intellect. In the fourth stage there is a consideration of the things of the intellect to which the things of the senses lead us, but without further reference to the senses. In the fifth stage there is a contemplation of realities accessible only to the intellect, which the world of the senses could never disclose, but which can be grasped by reason. In the sixth stage there is a consideration of realities accessible

---

8. *De Vera Religione* 29.52 (PL 34:145).

9. Thomas comes very close to the classic Greek scheme as found, for instance, in Evagrius, according to which the Christian life is made up of practical science (ethics), natural science and theology (cf. Evagrius, *Praktikos* 1).

to the intellect, which reason can neither discover nor grasp, realities, that is, which involve a high contemplation of the truth of God,[10] and it is in this truth that contemplation finally reaches its perfection.

(4) The ultimate perfection of the human intellect is the truth of God. Other truths fulfil the intellect in view of the truth of God.[11]

Article 5: Can the contemplative life, in the conditions of this life, reach the vision of God's essence?

It seems that the contemplative life can reach the vision of God's essence in the conditions of this life:

(1) In Genesis 32:30 Jacob says, "I have seen God face to face and my soul is saved." But seeing God's face means seeing God's essence. So it looks as if it is possible for someone in this present life to reach out in contemplation to see God in his essence.

(2) Gregory says that contemplatives return inward into themselves in their exploration of spiritual things and do not in any way take with them any shadow of bodily things, or if they have brought any such shadow with them they shoo it away by making the necessary distinctions. What they desire to see is the unlimited light; therefore they suppress all the images that belong to their own limitedness, and in striving to reach that which is above them they overcome what they themselves are.[1] But all that

---

10. Richard relates his sixth stage to things which "appear to be contrary to reason," which Thomas rather misleadingly quoted as if Richard had simply spoken of things contrary to reason; but in his own reinterpretation of this doctrine, Thomas suppresses even the appearance of irrationality. Reason may not be able to grasp some things, but that does not mean that there is any warrant for supposing that they are contrary to reason.

11. Any truth is a "perfection of the intellect" in one sense, but not in the sense that it crowns our whole intellectual endeavor. But there is a real continuity, nevertheless, between the limited "perfections" produced by stray bits of knowledge and the overall perfection which goes with beatitude: Thomas does not envisage a movement in which the mind leaves behind some objects in order to concentrate on higher things, but rather a movement toward an ever more all-encompassing understanding. So the limited "perfection" associated with bits and pieces of truth can be seen as relevant to the hope of final perfection, because there is an "order" (*ordo*) in which bits of truth are objectively related to the First Truth, God. The vision of God would give us omniscience, if we could totally comprehend it; failing that, it does at any rate draw into a single focus all that we do know about things (I q.12 a.8).

1. *Moralia* 6.37.59 (PL 75:763C).

stops people from seeing God's essence, which is the unlimited light, is the need we have to attend to bodily images. So apparently contemplation in this life can reach as far as the vision of the unlimited light in its essence.

(3) Gregory says that the whole of creation seems cramped to a soul which sees the Creator, and so the man of God (St. Benedict), who saw on his tower a globe of fire and the angels returning to heaven, could undoubtedly not see these things except in the light of God.[2] But St. Benedict was still alive in this world, so contemplation in this life can reach as far as the vision of God's essence.

On the other hand:

Gregory says that as long as we are alive in this mortal flesh no one is so proficient in the power of contemplation as to be able to fix the eyes of the mind on the actual radiance of unlimited light.[3]

REPLY

As Augustine says, no one who sees God is living in this mortal life which we live in these bodily senses. Unless in some way you die out of this life, either by leaving the body entirely or by being rapt out of the senses of the flesh, you cannot be raised to that vision.[4] We dealt with this more fully earlier on, when we were discussing rapture and the vision of God.[5]

So we must say that there are two possible ways of being in this life: we may be actually in this life, inasmuch as we are actually using our bodily senses, and in that case it is quite impossible for contemplation in this life to attain to the vision of God's essence. Or we may be in this life potentially, but not actually, in the sense that the soul is joined to the mortal body as its form, but without using the bodily senses or even imagination; this is what happens in rapture. And in that case contemplation in this life can attain to the vision of God's essence. So the highest level of contemplation in this life is

---

2. *Dial.* 2.35 (PL 66:200AB).
3. *Hom. Ezek.* 2.2.14 (PL 76:956AB).
4. *Super Gen. ad Litt.* 12.27.55.
5. II.II q.175 a.3–5.

the kind attained by Paul in a rapture,[6] in which he was in a condition midway between that of this present life and that of the life to come.

In response to the points raised above:

(1) As Dionysius says, if anyone who sees God understands what he has seen, he has not seen God himself but one of the things which are his.[7] And Gregory says that almighty God is definitely not seen now in his splendor, but the soul looks at something which is under his splendor, by which it can make straightforward progress and afterward reach the glory of seeing God.[8] So when Jacob said, "I have seen God face to face," this must not be taken to mean that he saw God's essence, but that he saw some form, an imaginary form, that is,[9] in which God spoke to him; alternatively, since it is by their faces that we recognize people, he called his knowledge of God God's "face," as Gregory's gloss on the passage suggests.[10]

(2) Human contemplation in the conditions of this life cannot dispense with images, because it is natural to human beings to see intelligible forms in images, as the philosopher says.[11] But intellectual knowledge does not actually stop at these images; in them it contemplates intelligible truth in its purity, and this applies not only to natural knowledge but also to what we know by revelation. As Dionysius says, the divine radiance manifests the hierarchies of angels in certain figurative symbols, and by its power we are brought back to the simple ray,[12] that is, to the simple knowledge of intelligible truth. And this is how we must take what Gregory says: people do not take with them any shadow of bodily things when they contemplate because their

---

6. 2 Cor. 12:2–4.

7. *Ep.* 1 (PG 3:1065A).

8. *Hom. Ezek.* 2.2.14 (PL 76:956B).

9. The scholastics distinguish between different kinds of divine revelation. Sometimes something is revealed to the bodily senses, sometimes to the imagination (so that the mind is conscious of images, but without any actual sense-perception) and sometimes to the intellect without any sensory or quasi-sensory phenomena (cf. II.II q.173 a.2). Thomas here identifies Jacob's vision as belonging to the second kind. There is, of course, no implication that Jacob was "only imagining things."

10. *Moralia* 23.6.12 (PL 76:293A), taken up into the Glossa Ordinaria.

11. Aristotle, *De Anima* 3.7 (431a16–17).

12. *CH* 1.2 (ed. cit. p.71).

contemplation does not stop at any such shadow but comes to rest rather in looking at intelligible truth.

(3) These words of Gregory's do not give us to understand that St. Benedict in this vision saw God in his essence; he wants to point out that all creation seems cramped to anyone who sees the Creator and that therefore everything can easily be seen by means of the illumination of God's light. So he goes on to say that however little people see of the light of the Creator, all that is created becomes small for them.[13]

Article 6: Is it appropriate to distinguish three kinds of movement in the contemplative act: circular, straight and spiral?

The distinction between three kinds of movement (circular, straight and spiral) in the contemplative act[1] seems inappropriate:

(1) Contemplation belongs only to repose; "I will enter into my house and rest with her" (Wis. 8:16). And movement is the opposite of repose. So the acts of the contemplative life should not be called "movements."

(2) The activity of the contemplative life belongs to the intellect, and as far as the intellect goes human beings are at one with the angels. But Dionysius specifies these movements in different ways in us and in the angels. He says that the angels' circular movement centers on their enlightenment about the beautiful and the good, while he gives several different specifications of the circular movement of the soul: first, it is the soul's entering into itself from external things; secondly, it is a certain orbiting of its powers, by which the soul is freed from going astray and from external concerns, and thirdly, it is its union with things which are above it.[2]

He similarly gives different descriptions of their straight move-

---

13. *Dial.* 2.35 (PL 66:200A). Thomas' interpretation seems to be a wanton misinterpretation of Gregory's text. Where Gregory's moral is that creation is not worth seeing, by comparison with the divine light, Thomas wants him to mean that creation is easy to see in the divine light.

1. Dionysius, *DN* 4.8–9 (PG 3:704D-705B) is explicitly the source of this analysis.

2. The angels' circular movement is expounded in *DN* 4.8, that of the soul in 4.9; cf. Thomas' commentary, Marietti ed. paras. 375–6.

ments. The angels' straight movement is, he says, their going forth to exercise providential care over the things which are beneath them. But he identifies the soul's straight movement in two ways: first, by its going out to the things which are round about it, and secondly, by its rising from external things to more unified contemplations.[3]

He also specifies their spiral movements differently. He identifies the spiral movement of the angels in terms of their making provision for those that have less, while remaining unchanged in their relationship to God. But the soul's spiral movement he identifies with its being enlightened rationally and in a diffuse way by different kinds of divine knowledge.[4]

So it does not appear that the workings of contemplation are properly identified in these ways.[5]

(3) Richard of St. Victor proposes quite a few other ways of specifying the movements of contemplation, by comparing them to the birds of the air: some of them now rise up to heights above themselves, and now sink down to what is beneath them and can be seen doing this over and over again. Others keep on turning aside to the right or to the left. Some often move backward or forward. Some go round in a kind of circle, making larger or smaller circuits. Some stay in one place, hanging more or less immobile.[6] So it looks as if there are more than just the three movements of contemplation.

On the other hand there is the authoritative text of Dionysius.

REPLY

As we have noted above, the working of the intellect, in which contemplation essentially consists, is called a "movement" in the sense of being the movement of a complete being, as the philosopher says.[7] Since we reach the knowledge of intelligible realities by way

---

3. Ibid. (Thomas' commentary is in para. 378).

4. Ibid. (Thomas' commentary is in para. 377).

5. The point of the objection is that, since we and the angels are both intellectual beings, any analysis of the workings of the intellect ought to apply equally both to us and to them; if Dionysius' analysis does not in fact apply isomorphically to both parties, then there must be something wrong with it.

6. *Benjamin Major* 1.5 (PL 196:68D–69A).

7. See note 12 on q.179 a.1.

of the things of the senses, and the workings of the senses always involve some kind of movement, this means that the workings of the intellect too are described as kinds of movement, and they are specified by analogy with different sorts of movement.

In the case of bodily movement, the most complete and primary sort is movement from one place to another, as is shown in the *Physics*.[8] That is why the analogy of local motion is used most readily in giving an account of the workings of the intellect. And local motion is particularized in three ways: there is circular movement, in which something moves uniformly around a single center. And there is straight movement, in which something moves from one point to another. And thirdly there is spiral movement, which is a mixture of the other two.

So in the workings of the intellect whatever is straightforwardly uniform is ascribed to circular movement. And the intellectual function of moving from one point to another is ascribed to straight movement. And a function which combines a certain uniformity with a certain movement from one point to another is ascribed to spiral movement.

In response to the points raised above:

(1) Outward, bodily movements are contrary to the repose of contemplation, which is understood to mean a repose from outward occupations. But the movement involved in the workings of the intellect is a facet of the repose of contemplation.

(2) The human intellect does share a common genus with that of the angels, but the intellectual power of the angels is far more exalted than ours is. That is why these movements have to be identified in different ways in the angels and in human souls, in line with the different relationships they have to uniformity. The angels' intellects have a uniform knowledge in two senses: they do not pick up intelligible truth from a range of compound realities,[9] nor do they understand it discursively, since they can just

---

8. *Phys.* Θ 7 (260a26-9). In Greek κίνησις ("movement") is used also of other kinds of change.

9. "Intelligible truth" is simple, whereas the things we perceive by our senses are complex. Any given dog I can see (smell, hear, touch, etc.) is confusing, because his dogginess is mixed up with all the idiosyncrasies that make him *this* dog. The human mind only arrives at the simple, intellectual notion of "dog" by a process of abstraction from the various dogs it has met. The angels can know what "dog" means far more straightforwardly. It is difficult for us to see the tree for the trees, but the angels do not have this problem.

see it. But the soul's intellect does derive intelligible truth from the things of the senses, and it understands it by means of a certain discursive act of the reason.

Dionysius accordingly identifies the angels' circular movement in terms of their seeing God uniformly and ceaselessly, without beginning or end, like a circular movement which has no beginning or end and travels uniformly round a single center. But in the soul there are two kinds of diversification which have to be removed first, before it can come to this sort of uniformity: first, the diversification caused by the variety there is in external things, and this is removed by the abandonment of external things, and this is the first feature which Dionysius identifies in the soul's circular movement, its leaving external things to enter into itself. The second diversification which has to be removed is the one caused by discursive reasoning, and this is done inasmuch as all the soul's workings are reduced to a simple contemplation of intelligible truth. And this is the second thing he declares to be needed, a uniform orbiting of its intellectual powers, that is, the abandonment of discursive reasoning and a fixing of the soul's gaze in the contemplation of one unified truth. And in this working of the soul there is no going astray; this is clear, because there is no possibility of making mistakes about the understanding of first principles, which we know by simply seeing them.[10] On the basis of these two preliminaries, there follows a third uniformity which is like that of the angels, in which the soul ignores all else and settles down to the sheer contemplation of God. So, in Dionysius' words, "having become uniform, in a way that is united with" (that is, conformed to) "the unified powers, it is led to the beautiful and the good."[11]

In the case of the angels "straight movement" cannot be taken to mean that their thought moves from one point to another; it

---

10. It is impossible to make mistakes about first principles, or to argue about them. Once we understand what is meant by saying that the part cannot be greater than the whole, we cannot help but understand the truth of the principle; we just *see* it. If someone cannot see it, we can only infer that he has not understood what we are talking about. For instance, we cannot make any sense of the idea that maybe after all we were mistaken in believing that the part cannot be greater than the whole and that that is why our interlocutor remains puzzled.

11. *DN* 4.9. How Thomas understood the syntax of this rather opaque sentence is made clear in his commentary (para. 376). The "unified powers" he takes to be the angels.

can only refer to the order of their providential concern, in which a higher angel enlightens lower angels through those that are in between. So Dionysius says that the angels move straight ahead when they come forth to look after those that are beneath them, "passing through everything in a straight line," that is, in line with the right ordering in which things are arranged. But in the soul Dionysius relates straight movement to its moving from the external things of the senses to the knowledge of intelligible things.

He ascribes a spiral movement to the angels, that is, a movement made up of straight and circular, inasmuch as they make provision for their inferiors in accordance with their contemplation of God. But there is a spiral movement in the soul, a movement likewise compounded of straight and circular, inasmuch as it uses divine enlightenment in its reasoning.

(3) All these different movements which are identified in terms of up and down, right and left, backward and forward and various kinds of circle, all fall within the scope of straight or spiral movement, because they all signify discursive reasoning. If our thought moves from genus to species or from whole to part, as Richard explains, there will be a movement up and down. If we move from one opposite to another, there will be a movement right and left. If we move from causes to effects, there will be a movement backward and forward. If we are thinking about the accidents attached to something, there will be a big or small circuit depending on whether the accidents are more or less closely connected to their subject.[12]

When our discursive reasoning moves from the things of the senses to the things of the intellect along the path of natural reason, that is an instance of straight movement. When it does so in the light of divine illuminations, that will be an instance of spiral movement, as we have seen. Of the things he lists it is only immobility which belongs to circular movement.

So it is clear that Dionysius' description of the movements of contemplation is far more satisfactory and penetrating.[13]

---

12. Richard of St. Victor, *Benjamin Major* 1.5 (PL 196:69B–D).
13. Richard's categories correspond only to incidental differences, whereas Dionysius' list constitutes a real analysis of the different kinds of intellectual operation. Conceivably

Article 7: Is contemplation enjoyable?

It does not look as if contemplation is enjoyable:

(1) Enjoyment concerns our appetitive power, but contemplation belongs essentially in the intellect. So enjoyment would seem to have nothing to do with contemplation

(2) Any kind of combat or struggle hinders enjoyment, and there is a combat and a struggle in contemplation. As Gregory says, when the soul tries to contemplate God it seems to be caught up in a kind of struggle in which sometimes it wins a sort of victory, inasmuch as it tastes something of the unlimited light in its understanding and feeling, but at other times it suffers a setback, in that even while it tastes it falls away again.[1] So there is no delight in the contemplative life.

(3) Enjoyment depends on the degree of perfection attained in any activity, as it says in the *Ethics*.[2] But in this life contemplation is imperfect: "Now we see in a mirror, obscurely" (1 Cor. 13:12). So the contemplative life appears not to be enjoyable.

(4) Enjoyment is prevented by any bodily wound, and contemplation causes a bodily wound. This is why we read in Genesis 32:30–2 that Jacob was lame in one foot after saying, "I have seen the Lord face to face," because "he had touched the sinew of his thigh and it was paralyzed." So there appears to be no enjoyment in the contemplative life.

On the other hand:
It is of the contemplation of wisdom that it says in Wisdom 8:16, "Her company is without bitterness and there is no boredom in living with her, but only happiness and joy." And Gregory says that the charm of the contemplative life is most appealing.[3]

Thomas' declaration of loyalty to Dionysius is also in part prompted by his preference for the honest intellectualism of the Greek father, rather than the highly charged emotional piety of the Victorine.

1. *Hom. Ezek.* 2.2.12 (PL 76:955BC).

2. Aristotle, *Eth. Nic.* 10.4.5 (1174b14–23), with Thomas' commentary on it (Marietti ed. para. 2022).

3. *Hom. Ezek.* 2.2.13 (PL 76:956A); I have slightly adapted the Leonine text in the light of Gregory's actual words.

REPLY

Contemplation can be enjoyable in two ways. It can be enjoyable by virtue of the activity itself, because every creature enjoys activities which suit its own nature or disposition, and contemplation of truth does suit human nature, in that we are rational animals, so that everyone naturally has a desire for knowledge.[4] As a result everyone enjoys knowing truth. And this becomes even more enjoyable if you have the habit of wisdom and knowledge,[5] so that you can contemplate without difficulty.

The other way in which contemplation can be enjoyable depends on the object contemplated: it is enjoyable to contemplate something that we love. This happens in the case of bodily vision too, which is enjoyable not only because seeing itself is pleasant, but also inasmuch as what we see is somebody that we love. So since the contemplative life consists supremely in the contemplation of God, to which we are moved by charity, as we have already noted, it follows that the contemplative life not only contains the pleasure which attends contemplation as such, it is also enjoyable because of our love of God.

And on both counts it is more enjoyable than any other human pleasure. Spiritual enjoyment surpasses bodily enjoyment, as we noted in the discussion of the passions[6]; and the love with which we love God in charity surpasses every love. So that is why it says in Psalm 33:9, "Taste and see that the Lord is sweet."

In response to the points raised above:

(1) Although the contemplative life does reside essentially in the intellect, it has its beginning in our feelings, inasmuch as it is charity that inspires people to contemplate God. And since ends correspond to beginnings, it follows that the end and goal of the contemplative life is also located in the feelings, in our enjoy-

---

4. This is Aristotle's famous principle: *Metaph.* A 1 (980a21).

5. "Habit" here translates the same word as "disposition" in the previous sentence: *habitus*, which is used to refer to any more or less stable condition of something, such as the regular practice of any particular virtue or skill is likely to induce. "Habitual knowledge," for instance, means the state of knowing something, so that the knowledge in question is, so to speak, "on tap" in your mind.

6. I.II q.31 a.5.

ment of the vision of the beloved object; and our enjoyment of the beloved object further encourages love. So Gregory says that when people see the one they love, they blaze up in even greater love of him.[7] And this is the final perfection of the contemplative life, that the truth of God should be not only seen, but loved.

(2) When some external thing causes us conflict or struggle, that does prevent us from enjoying it, because we do not enjoy anything that we are fighting against. But when we are fighting for something, we enjoy it all the more when we obtain it, other things being equal; as Augustine says, the greater the danger in the battle, the greater is the joy in victory.[8] Now in the case of contemplation conflict and struggle are not caused by any opposition on the part of the truth we are contemplating; they come from the inadequacy of our own intellect and from our corruptible bodies, which drag us down, as it says in Wisdom 9:15, "The body, which gets corrupted, weighs down the soul and our earthly dwelling-place oppresses the mind which is thinking of many things." This is why, when we do reach the contemplation of truth, we love it all the more keenly, and at the same time we are all the more inclined to detest our own inadequacy and the burden of the corruptible body, so that we will say with the apostle, "Wretch that I am, who will free me from the body of this death?"[9] As Gregory says, once God is known by desire and understanding, he dries up all the pleasures of the flesh.[10]

(3) The contemplation of God in this life is imperfect by comparison with heavenly contemplation, and the enjoyment of contemplation in this live is similarly imperfect by comparison with the enjoyment of contemplation in heaven, of which it says in Psalm 35:9, "You will give them to drink of the torrent of pleasure." But the contemplation of the things of God which we have in this life, even if it is imperfect, is still more enjoyable than any other contemplation, however perfect, because of the superiority of what it contemplates. This is why the philosopher says, "Our speculation about those noble and divine beings may be more limited, but if we can only touch them a little, they have

---

7. *Hom. Ezek.* 2.2.9 (PL 76:954A).
8. *Confessions* 8.3.7.
9. Romans 7:24.
10. *Hom. Ezek.* 2.2.13 (PL 76:955C).

something about them which is more enjoyable than all that is down here, because of the nobility of the knowledge of them."[11] This is also why Gregory says that the charm of the contemplative life is very appealing: it snatches the soul above itself, opens the things of heaven to it and reveals spiritual things to the eyes of the mind.[12]

(4) After his contemplation Jacob was lame in one foot because, as Gregory says, it is inevitably with a weakening of love for this world that people grow strong in the love of God. So once we know the sweetness of God, one of our feet remains healthy and the other is lame. Everyone who is lame in one foot leans solely on his healthy foot.[13]

Article 8: Is the contemplative life long-lasting?

The contemplative life does not appear to be long-lasting:

(1) The contemplative life consists essentially in the business of the intellect, and all the intellectual accomplishments of this life are brought to nothing, according to 1 Corinthians 13:8 ("if prophecies, they shall come to nothing; if tongues, they will cease; if knowledge, it will be destroyed"). So the contemplative life comes to nothing.

(2) Some people get a taste of the sweetness of contemplation, but in a moment and fleetingly. Thus Augustine says, "You lead me into a great and unwonted feeling inwardly, to I know not what sweetness, but I return here with my tiresome burdens."[1] Gregory also says, in his comment on Job 4:15 ("When a spirit passed by in my presence"), "The mind is not fixed for long in the pleasure of inner contemplation, because it is beaten back by the sheer immensity of light and called back to itself."[2] So the contemplative life is not long-lasting.

(3) Something that is not natural to human beings cannot last long.

---

11. Aristotle, *Part. Anim.* 1.5 (644b25–34); we may wonder whether Thomas was as enthusiastic about the rest of what Aristotle says here, about the worthwhileness of studying even the most dingy of creatures.

12. *Hom. Ezek.* 2.2.13 (PL 76:956A).

13. Ibid. (PL 76:955CD).

1. *Confessions* 10.40.75.

2. *Moralia* 5.33.58 (PL 75:711C).

And the contemplative life is, as the philosopher says, better than a human life.[3] So it looks as if the contemplative life is not long-lasting.

On the other hand:

The Lord says, "Mary has chosen the best part, which will not be taken away from her" (Luke 10:42). This is because, as Gregory says, the contemplative life begins here, in such a way that it will be brought to perfection in heaven.[4]

REPLY

There are two senses in which something can be called "long-lasting": with reference to what it is in itself, or with reference to us. In itself it is obvious that the contemplative life is long-lasting in two ways: (1) in that its concern is with things which are incorruptible and unchanging, and (2) because there is nothing opposing it, since, as it says in the *Topics*, there is nothing opposed to the delight there is in speculation.[5]

Even as far as we are concerned the contemplative life is long-lasting, for two reasons: it falls within the capacity of the incorruptible part of the soul, the intellect, that is, and so it can last beyond the end of this life; and there is no bodily labor involved in the works of the contemplative life, so it is more possible for us to go on performing such works continuously, as the philosopher says.[6]

In response to the points raised above:

(1) Our way of contemplating here is not the same as it will be in heaven, but the contemplative life is said to persist because of the charity in which it begins and ends. And this is what Gregory is saying. "The contemplative life begins here, in such a way that it will be brought to perfection in heaven, because the fire of love, which begins to burn here, will blaze up even more in love of him, when it sees him whom it loves."[7]

---

3. Aristotle, *Eth. Nic.* 10.7.8 (1177b26–7).

4. *Hom. Ezek.* 2.2.9 (PL 76:954A).

5. Aristotle, *Topics* 1.15 (106a36–b1). Actually Aristotle says that "there is nothing opposed to the pleasure of seeing that the diagonal is incommensurate with the side"! The more general claim that there is nothing opposed to the pleasure of speculation is found in Nemesius, *Nat. Hom.* 18 (Morani p. 76:18–19; Verbeke p. 96:85–86).

6. Aristotle, *Eth. Nic.* 10.7.2 (1177a21–2).

7. *Hom. Ezek.* 2.2.9 (PL 76:954A).

(2) No activity can last for long at its highest pitch. And the height of contemplation is that it should reach the uniformity of contemplation of God, as Dionysius says in the text cited above.[8] So at this level contemplation cannot last for long, but all the same it can go on for a long time as far as the other acts of contemplation are concerned.

(3) The philosopher says that the contemplative life is suprahuman because our capacity for it rests on there being "something divine in us," namely the intellect,[9] which is in itself incorruptible and impassible, so that its activity can last longer.[10]

QUESTION 181: The active life

Next we must look at the active life, and this raises four questions:

(1) Whether all the works of the moral virtues belong to the active life;
(2) Whether prudence belongs to the active life;
(3) Whether teaching belongs to the active life;
(4) How long-lasting the active life is.

Article 1: Do all the works of the moral virtues belong to the active life?

It looks as if not all the acts of the moral virtues belong to the active life:

(1) The active life appears to consist solely in things which relate to other people. Gregory says that the active life means giving bread to the hungry and then he lists many activities which concern other people, ending up with "distributing to each individ-

---

8. *DN* 4.9 (PG 3:705A); cf. above, q.180 a.6.

9. Aristotle, *Eth. Nic.* 10.7.7 (1177b27–8); for the identification of the "something divine" as the intellect, cf. ibid. 10.7.1 (1177a13–7).

10. For the incorruptibility and impassibility of the intellect, cf. Aristotle, *De Anima* 1.4 (408b18–25) and 3.5 (430a22–5) (the latter probably being the passage envisaged in I q.79 a.2 obi.2). The intellect is not corruptible, in Thomas' view, because it is not attached as such to any bodily organ.

ual what each one needs."[1] But not all the acts of the moral virtues involve our dealings with other people, but only those which relate to justice and its subsidiaries, as we have already seen.[2] Therefore the active life does not include the acts of all the moral virtues.

(2) Gregory says that the active life is symbolized by Leah, who was half-blind but fruitful: "being occupied in doing things, she sees less, but by inspiring her neighbors to imitate her, sometimes by word, sometimes by example, she brings many children to birth in good works."[3] But this surely is less a matter of the moral virtues than it is of that charity by which we love our neighbor. So it looks as if the works of the moral virtues do not belong to the active life.

(3) As we have seen, the moral virtues fit us for the contemplative life. But whatever is responsible for preparing for something is also responsible for bringing it to completion, so evidently the moral virtues do not belong to the active life.[4]

On the other hand:
Isidore says that all vices must first be drained off in the active life by the practice of good works, so that one can then pass on to contemplating God in the contemplative life with the eye of one's mind now pure.[5] But this draining off of all vices can only be brought about by the acts of the moral virtues. Therefore these do belong to the active life.

---

1. *Hom. Ezek.* 2.2.8 (PL 76:953A). Thomas has inherited a muddle, of which he was apparently only dimly aware: in the older Christian usage, the term "active life" was used to mean precisely the cultivation of the moral virtues, but Gregory established the other possibility of taking "active life" to mean a life of service to others. This muddle affects both Thomas' discussion of the active life in itself and his discussion of the relationships between the active and contemplative lives, and indeed it causes confusion in quite a few medieval writers.

2. II.II q.58 a.8.

3. *Hom. Ezek.* 2.2.10 (PL 76:954C).

4. The force of this objection is to suggest that the moral virtues actually belong to the contemplative life, on the grounds that planning for something has to be ascribed to the same agent as seeing something through to completion. In the ordinary course of events, if we see workmen clearing a site by a big notice announcing the imminent opening of a new cricket pitch, and then some weeks later we see other workmen laying down turf and marking out wickets and boundaries and so on, we shall be right in assuming that it was one and the same person or organization who planned the whole operation.

5. *Sent.* 3.15.3 (PL 83:690A).

Reply

As we have already noted, the distinction between the active and contemplative lives is based on the different interests of different people who concentrate on different aims in their lives. One kind of interest is looking at the truth, and this is the aim of the contemplative life; the other is external activity, and this is the aim of the active life. Now it is obvious that it is not primarily the contemplation of truth that is sought in the moral virtues; they are geared to doing things. This is why the philosopher says that in the matter of virtue knowledge carries little or no weight.[6] So clearly the moral virtues belong essentially to the active life. The philosopher accordingly makes active happiness the goal of the moral virtues.[7]

In response to the points raised above:
(1) Of all the moral virtues justice is the most notable, as the philosopher shows, this being the virtue which governs our relationships with other people.[8] This is why the active life is described in terms of things which concern other people, not because that is all that it involves, but because it consists primarily in that sort of thing.
(2) It is possible to turn one's neighbors to good by one's example through practicing all the moral virtues, and this is something that Gregory attributes to the active life.[9]
(3) When one virtue is subordinated to the goal of another virtue, in some way it acquires the identity of that virtue, and similarly, in the case of someone using the things that belong to the active life solely inasmuch as they are a preparation for the contemplative life, they are included within the contemplative life.[10] But in the case of people who apply themselves to the works of the moral virtues as being good in themselves and not as a preparation for the contemplative life, the moral virtues belong to the

---

6. Aristotle, *Eth. Nic.* 2.4 (1105b2–3).

7. Ibid. 10.8 (1178a9–22), with Thomas' comments (Marietti ed. para. 2111).

8. Ibid. 5.1.15 (1129b27–33).

9. The answers to the first two objections are attempts, in effect, to reconcile the two different senses of "active life"; they are perhaps not very successful.

10. There is, I think, no suggestion that Thomas would actually approve of such a radical subordination of the moral virtues to the contemplative life. Notice the firm text he quotes from Gregory in q.182 a.4 ad 1.

active life. Although it can be said that the active life as such is a preparation for the contemplative life.[11]

Article 2: Does prudence belong to the active life?

Surely prudence does not belong to the active life:

(1) The active life concerns our appetitive power, just as the contemplative life concerns our cognitive power. And prudence has more to do with our cognitive power than with our appetitive power.[1] Therefore prudence does not belong to the active life.

(2) Gregory says that the active life, being occupied in doing things, sees less, which is why it is symbolized by Leah who was bleary-eyed.[2] But prudence requires clear eyes, if people are to make right judgments about what has to be done. So it looks as if prudence does not belong to the active life.

(3) Prudence falls half way between the moral virtues and the intellectual virtues. We have already seen that the moral virtues belong to the active life, and the intellectual virtues similarly belong to the contemplative life. So it looks as if prudence belongs neither to the active life nor to the contemplative life, but to the intermediate kind of life postulated by Augustine.[3]

On the other hand:

The philosopher says that prudence is related to active happiness, which is the business of the moral virtues.[4]

REPLY

As we have already noted, if A is subordinated to B, so that B is the purpose of A, especially in moral matters, then A comes to

---

11. This point is developed slightly more fully in q.182 a.4 ad 3. The importance of recognizing that even a life which is straightforwardly active is all the same a preparation for the contemplative life is that it safeguards the possibility of treating a purely active life in this world as a legitimate way of preparing for the contemplative life of heaven.

1. The active life is motivated by the various desires that set us our practical objectives; but prudence is not a matter of desire, but of making rational judgments which will sometimes even go against our desires. So it looks as if we are dealing with two very different kinds of thing.

2. *Hom. Ezek.* 2.2.10 (PL 76:954C).

3. *Civ. Dei* 19.1–2 (cf. above, q.179 a.2).

4. Aristotle, *Eth. Nic.* 10.8.3 (1178a16–7).

share in the identity of B. As the philosopher says, if you commit adultery in order to steal something, you are called a thief rather than an adulterer.[5]

Now it is clear that the knowledge involved in prudence is subordinated to the practice of the moral virtues, because that is its goal; as it says in the *Ethics*, it is a correct rational attitude to human actions.[6] This is why the principles of prudence are constituted by the goals of the moral virtues, as the philosopher also says in the same book.[7] We have already remarked that the moral virtues belong to the contemplative life in the case of someone who subordinates them to the repose of contemplation, and the same can be said of the knowledge involved in prudence, but in itself it is geared to the practice of the moral virtues, and as such it belongs intrinsically to the active life, always provided that we are taking "prudence" in its strict sense, as indicated by the philosopher.

If we take "prudence" in a broader sense, to include all sorts of human knowledge,[8] then prudence would belong partly to the contemplative life, along the lines of what Cicero says: "We are right in generally regarding as the most prudent and wise person the one who can most sharply and quickly see the truth and explain the reason for it."[9]

In response to the points raised above:

(1) As we concluded above, the specific identity of moral acts depends on their objective.[10] So any knowledge whose purpose is simply knowledge of truth belongs to the contemplative life, but prudential knowledge, whose goal is located rather in some act of our appetitive power, belongs to the ac-

---

5. Ibid. 5.2.4 (1130a24–8).

6. Ibid. 6.5.6 (1140b20–1), though in fact this definition is a scholastic paraphrase derived from Aristotle.

7. Ibid. 6.5.6 (1140b16–7).

8. *Prudentia* was the conventional equivalent of φρόνησις, which had a wider application than just "prudence." For the range of meanings available in the early thirteenth century, cf. Peraldus, *Summa de Virtutibus* III 2.1.

9. *De Officiis* 1.5.16.

10. I.II q.1 a.3. If the conjuror, in all innocence, actually does saw the lady in half by mistake, the proper description of what he is doing is still "performing a trick," not "committing murder." If I tap my fingers randomly along the top of my desk, knowing full well that sooner or later I shall probably push a button which sets off an explosion, the proper description of my act is (something like) "playing with fire," not "tapping my fingers on my desk."

tive life.[11]

(2) Being engaged in external business makes people see less in the sphere of the objects of the mind which are detached from the world of the senses in which the active life operates. But being engaged in the external affairs of the active life gives people a clearer vision in their judgment about human activities, which is the concern of prudence, both because of their experience and because that is what their minds are concentrated on. As Sallust says, your mind is most effective where you apply it.[12]

(3) Prudence is said to be midway between the intellectual virtues and the moral virtues inasmuch as it is located in our reason, like the intellectual virtues, but its field of operation coincides entirely with that of the moral virtues. But Augustine's "third kind of life" is midway between the active and contemplative lives only with reference to its various concerns: sometimes it is engaged in the contemplation of truth and sometimes it is engaged with external things.[13]

Article 3: Is teaching a work of the active life or of the contemplative?

Teaching is surely a work of the contemplative life rather than the active:[1]

---

11. It is important to bear in mind that for Thomas the active life, as such, is a kind of intellectual life (otherwise it would not be a human life); mindless performance of certain acts is not "the active life." And inasmuch as our acts presuppose a certain vision of life, it is part of the active life to have a vision of life, so long as our main interest is practical rather than speculative. So, in Thomas' language, it is superfluous and misleading to talk about bringing in a "contemplative" dimension into the active life (Thomas had talked rather like that in III *Sent.* d.35 q.1 a.3 q.2, ed. Moos p. 1184, but he does not do so now). If there is no thought, no purpose conceived by the mind, no view of life commanding what we do, the result is not an "active life" needing a "contemplative dimension" to complete it; it is simply not a properly human life at all, and as such it cannot be called an "active life" in Thomas' sense of the phrase.

12. *Catiline* 51.3.

13. Prudence is a genuinely "hybrid" virtue, inasmuch as it is both intellectual and practical, but the "mixed life" is a pseudo-category. The active and contemplative lives are defined only on the basis of people's temperamental bias, not on the basis of their style of life. So whatever your style of life (and you may not always be able to indulge your temperamental preferences), your own personal bias will remain whatever it is. Cf. the comments of M.E. Mason, *Active Life and Contemplative Life, A Study of the Concepts from Plato to the Present*, Milwaukee 1961, pp. 96–8.

1. In q.181 and q.182, especially from q.181 a.3 onwards, it is clear that Thomas is

ACTIVE AND CONTEMPLATIVE LIFE

(1) Gregory says that people who are perfect tell their brethren about the good things of heaven which they have been able to contemplate, and set their hearts on fire with love of inner radiance.[2] And this is the business of teaching. So teaching is a work of the contemplative life.

(2) Acts and habits must surely be classified as belonging to the same kind of life. But teaching is an activity of wisdom; as the philosopher says at the beginning of the *Metaphysics*, the ability to teach is evidence that you know something.[3] So since wisdom and knowledge belong to the contemplative life, it looks as if teaching must also be part of the contemplative life.[4]

(3) Prayer is as much a part of the contemplative life as contemplation is. And when you pray for someone else, it is still part of the contemplative life. So it looks as if it is part of the contemplative life to bring to someone else's notice, by teaching, some truth that you have thought about.[5]

On the other hand:

---

unable to stick rigorously to his identification of the active and contemplative lives in terms of temperamental bias. Even if a bias one way or the other implies a bias towards one sort of occupation rather than another, the crucial question ought to be that of how any sort of occupation can be motivated by the twofold precept of charity, whichever way the individual's bias inclines. But Thomas is driven by the conventions of the game to try to allocate specific occupations to one 'life' or the other, and to try to relate the two 'lives' to each other as if they were ingredients in a single life rather than distinct lives pertaining to distinct people. In principle Thomas' fundamental insight about temperamental bias could have been pursued more ruthlessly at the expense of such conventional doctrines as that the active life is a necessary preparation for the contemplative life, and that prelates ought to excel in both lives, and it could have made for a much more profound exploration of the 'active' and 'contemplative' dimensions to such tasks as teaching.

2. *Hom. Ezek.* 1.5.13 (PL 76:827A).

3. Aristotle, *Metaph.* A 1 (981b7–8).

4. The argument is that wisdom and knowledge are clearly intellectual virtues. Virtues are, in Aristotelian ethics, identified as 'habits', that is, stable conditions in a person facilitating a particular kind of behaviour. Virtuous acts spring from virtuous habits, and clearly there would be something odd about ascribing the habit to one kind of life and the acts it produces to another kind of life. So if teaching is an 'act of wisdom', it must come from the habit of wisdom, which is an intellectual (contemplative) virtue. Therefore teaching must belong within the domain of the contemplative life.

5. 'Thought about' translates *meditatum*. The argument in this objection presupposes the commonplace of the schools that prayer and meditation are part of the contemplative life. If benefiting someone else by your prayer is part of the contemplative life, why should benefiting someone else by your meditation not also be a part of the contemplative life?

Gregory says that the active life means giving bread to the hungry and instructing the ignorant with a word of wisdom.[6]

REPLY

The act of teaching has two objects.[7] Teaching takes place by way of talking, and talking is an audible sign of an inner thought. So one object of teaching is the content or object of your thought. And from this point of view teaching sometimes concerns the active life and sometimes the contemplative life. It concerns the active life when you conceive some truth inwardly in your mind with a view to being guided by it in what you do outwardly. It concerns the contemplative life when you conceive some speculative truth which you enjoy looking at and derive pleasure from your love of it. So Augustine says, "They should choose the better part" (the contemplative life, that is) "and devote their time to the word and be avid for the joys of doctrine[8] and occupy themselves with the knowledge that brings salvation."[9] Doctrine or "teaching" is here clearly presented as part of the contemplative life.

The other object of teaching concerns the hearing of what is said, and from this point of view the object of teaching is the hearer. And as far as this object is concerned all teaching belongs to the active life, as do all external activities.

In response to the points raised above:

(1) The text cited is expressly talking about teaching from the point of view of its content, revolving as it does round the consideration and love of truth.

(2) Habits and acts are at one in their object.[10] So it is clear that this argument is effective with reference to the content of people's inner thoughts. The ability to teach belongs to people who are wise and who know something inasmuch as they can express

---

6. *Hom. Ezek.* 2.2.8 (PL 76:953A).

7. In Latin the verb 'to teach' (*docere*) takes two objects, just as in English (we can say 'I am teaching Latin' or 'I am teaching the sixth-formers').

8. *Doctrina* can mean either the activity of teaching, as in the bulk of this article, or the content of teaching (someone's 'teaching' or 'doctrine'), as here.

9. *Serm.* 104.1.2 (PL 38:616).

10. Having the habitual capacity to do X and actually doing X have precisely X in common.

their inner thought in words, so that they can lead somebody else to an understanding of the truth.[11]

(3) Praying for someone else is not a matter of doing anything to the person for whom you are praying; the act of prayer is addressed only to God, who is truth for the intellect.[12] But if you teach someone else you are doing something which relates to that person directly and it involves an external activity. So the case is not the same.[13]

Article 4: Does the active life endure after this life?

It looks as if the active life does endure after this life:

(1) As we have seen, the acts of the moral virtues belong to the active life, and the moral virtues remain after this life, as Augustine says.[1] So it appears that the active life remains after this life.

(2) Teaching other people is part of the active life, as we have noted. But in the life to come, in which we shall be "like the angels,"[2] there will still be the possibility of teaching, just as there is clearly teaching among the angels, one of whom enlightens, pu-

---

11. The point of the answer is that teaching is an act of wisdom in as much as teaching and wisdom have the content of teaching in common, and this is one of the 'objects' of teaching. It can therefore serve as the point which the habit of wisdom and this particular act of wisdom have in common. It does not therefore imply that wisdom and teaching have everything else or anything else at all in common.

12. This seems a rather desperate way of dealing with prayer as part of the contemplative life. The objection to which Thomas is replying presupposes a much vaguer use of the phrase 'contemplative life' (cf. Thomas' comment in IV *Sent.* d.15 q.4 a.1 (B) ad 1), such that any religious exercise can count as 'contemplative'. Although (in a rather loose sense) there is an element of 'contemplation' involved in prayer (II.II q.83 a.13), the primary aim of prayer is to get something done (ibid.), so it will depend on what is being prayed for whether any particular prayer is 'active' or 'contemplative'. It is not at all clear in what sense asking God to cure aunty's rheumatism could be described as a 'contemplative' operation. The fact that God is 'truth for the intellect' is, on the face of it, utterly irrelevant to it.

13. The objection suggests that the extension of a contemplative act to make it benefit someone else does not mean that the act thereby ceases to be contemplative; prayer for other people is cited as an example. Instead of saying that prayer is not always and necessarily a contemplative act (which would surely be the right answer to give, in view of II.II q.83 a.1), Thomas argues that even praying for other people is an activity directed towards God (and therefore contemplative, in a sense much looser than that theoretically espoused by Thomas), whereas teaching is an activity formally directed towards other people (which, on Gregory's principles, must therefore be classified as belonging to the 'active life').

1. *De Trin.* 14.9.12.
2. Cf. Matt. 22:30.

rifies and perfects another, which refers to their acquisition of knowledge, as Dionysius makes clear.[3] So apparently the active life does remain after this life.

(3) Something that is intrinsically more capable of lasting seems to stand a better chance of remaining after this life, and the active life does appear to be more lasting in itself. As Gregory says, we can remain fixed in the active life, whereas we are quite unable to remain with our minds attentive in the contemplative life.[4] So the active life is much more capable of enduring after this life than the contemplative life is.

On the other hand:

Gregory says, "The active life is terminated together with this world, but the contemplative life begins here in such a way that it will be brought to perfection in heaven."[5]

REPLY

The goal of the active life resides in external deeds, which become part of the contemplative life if they are subordinated to the repose of contemplation. But in the life of blessedness to come all business about external works will lapse, and if there are any external deeds they will have reference to the goal of contemplation.[6] As Augustine says at the end of *De Civitate Dei*, "There we shall be at leisure and see, we shall see and love, we shall love and give praise." And in the same book he has already said that God will be seen without end there, loved without tedium and praised without weariness, and that this gift and this feeling and this activity will be there in everyone.[7]

In response to the points raised above:

(1) As we said above, the moral virtues will remain, but only with reference to the acts which directly concern our goal, not with reference to the acts which concern our movement toward our

---

3. *CH* 8.1 (ed. cit. p.122), interpreted in the light of 7.3 (ed. cit. p.113); cf. *Summa Theol.* I q.106 a.1.

4. *Hom. Ezek.* 1.5.12 (PL 76:825D–826A).

5. Ibid. 2.2.9 (PL 76:954A).

6. I.e., after the resurrection there may be some kind of "external" (bodily) activity, but there will be no more "business" interfering with our freedom to contemplate God.

7. *Civ. Dei* 22.30.

goal.[8] And that means the kinds of act by which they constitute the repose of contemplation, which Augustine is referring to in the passage cited above, when he says that we shall be "at leisure," which must be taken not only to indicate freedom from external harassment, but also freedom from all inner disturbance caused by passion.

(2) The contemplative life, as we have seen, consists supremely in the contemplation of God. And with reference to that no angel teaches another because, as it says in Matthew 18:10 about the "little ones' angels," which belong to one of the lower ranks, they "always see the face of the Father." Similarly in our own case, in the life to come no one will teach anyone else about God, but we shall all "see him as he is" (1 John 3:2). And this is what Jeremiah is referring to when he says, "No longer shall a man teach his neighbor, saying, 'Know the Lord,' because they will all know me, from the least of them to the greatest" (Jer. 31:34).

What the angels do teach each other about, by purifying, enlightening and perfecting, is things which concern the "dispensation of the mysteries of God."[9] From this point of view they do have some part in the active life for as long as the world lasts, and this is because they are involved in the administration of the lower creation. This is what is meant by Jacob seeing angels ascending on the ladder (which has to do with contemplation) and descending (which has to do with activity).[10] But, as Gregory says, they do not go forth from the vision of God in such a way as to lose the joys of inner contemplation.[11] So in their case there is no distinction between the active and contemplative lives,[12] as there is in our case, because we are held back from contemplation by the works of the active life. Nor does the promise made to us mean that we shall be like the angels in their administration of the lower creation, which is not our business, as it is theirs, because our nature does not have that rank in the scheme of things; we are promised that we shall be like them in seeing God.

---

8. I.II q.67 a.1.

9. Cf. 1 Cor. 4:1.

10. Gen. 28:12.

11. *Moralia* 2.3.3 (PL 75:556C).

12. Similarly there is no distinction in God between speculative and practical knowledge (I q.14 a.16). It is rather a pity, perhaps, that Thomas did not pursue the matter further with regard to a possible overcoming in human beings of the dichotomy between the two lives.

(3) In the conditions of this world the active life can outlast the contemplative life, not because of any quality inhering in either of the two lives in itself, but only because of our inadequacy; we are dragged down from the heights of contemplation by the burden of our bodies. So Gregory continues, in the passage cited, "The mind is banished from the immensity of that great height by its own weakness and falls back upon itself."[13]

QUESTION 182: *The comparison between the active and Contemplative Lives*

Next we must look at the comparison between the active and contemplative lives, and this raises four questions:
(1) Which is preferable or more worthwhile;
(2) Which is more meritorious;
(3) Whether the contemplative life is hindered by the active;
(4) The order in which the two lives come.

Article 1: *Is the active life preferable to the contemplative?*

It looks as if the active life is preferable to the contemplative:
(1) "What belongs to the better is surely better," as the philosopher says.[1] And the active life belongs to superiors, to people in charge, that is, who hold a position of honor and power. That is why Augustine says that what we do in this life should not be motivated by love of honor and power.[2] So the active life appears to be preferable to the contemplative.
(2) In all our habits and acts it belongs to the one that is superior[3] to give orders; for example, it is military competence which issues instructions, as being superior, to the skill of the people who make bridles.[4] But it belongs to the active life to give directions and instructions about the contemplative life, as is clear

---

13. *Hom. Ezek.* 1.5.12 (PL 76:826A).
1. Aristotle, *Topics* 3.1 (116b12–13).
2. *Civ. Dei* 19.19.
3. *Potior* can mean "preferable," "more powerful," "superior"; I have kept to "preferable" where possible in translating this article, but in the second objection the point is clearly that the active life appears to be in the commanding position.
4. Cf. Aristotle, *Eth. Nic.* 1.1.4 (1094a9–13).

from Exodus 19:20, where Moses is told, "Go down and adjure the people not to try and exceed the limits set for the vision of God." Therefore the active life is superior to the contemplative.

(3) No one ought to be taken away from something more important to be put to work on things of less importance; as the apostle says in 1 Corinthians 12:31, "Aspire to the better gifts." But people are taken away from their contemplative situation to become engaged in the active life, as is plainly the case with those who are transferred to a position of authority in the church. So it looks as if the active life is preferable to the contemplative.

On the other hand:
In Luke 10:42 the Lord says, "Mary has chosen the best part and it will not be taken away from her." And Mary symbolizes the contemplative life, so the contemplative life is preferable to the active.

REPLY

There is no reason why something which is in itself superior should not be surpassed by something else in some particular regard. So we must say that the contemplative life, as such, is better than the active life, and this is proved by the philosopher on eight counts:[5]

(i) The contemplative life engages what is best in us, namely

---

5. Aristotle, *Eth. Nic.* 10.7.2–9 (1177a19–78a7). Aristotle's eight reasons for claiming that the contemplative life is best are on the whole frankly self-centered, and this does not seem to bother Thomas. The contemplative life enables us to function at our best, and it is less liable to a lot of inconveniences than the active life is, it is something we pursue for its own sake, it is more intensely enjoyable, it already has the quality of "holiday" about it which is one of the things we seek in most of the other occupations we engage in. . . . Thomas would not be too impressed by "altruistic" arguments against this picture; love of others at the expense of love of self is usually dishonest and can be pernicious. True self-sacrifice is never innocent of "selfishness," because true self-sacrifice means that you actually want to sacrifice yourself, because of love, and nothing less would satisfy you. The trouble comes when we try to deny that we are seeking our own happiness. Creation exists to give glory to God, and it gives glory to God by thriving, not by making itself miserable. Mortification as an end in itself is sick, not sanctifying. Its true function can only be seen in the context of a whole discipline of learning how to be truly happy, in accordance with our God-given nature and our God-given calling to share in his own divine life (which is the only fully satisfying human happiness there is). Thomas, as we shall see below, was totally unprepared to accept the common view that a hard life was automatically a better life.

our intellect, and it engages it with regard to its own proper object, namely intelligible reality, whereas the active life is busy with externals. So Rachel, who symbolizes the contemplative life, has a name which means "vision of the principle," while the active life is symbolized by Leah who was bleary-eyed, as Gregory says.[6]

(ii) The contemplative life is less liable to interruption, even if we cannot stay for long at the highest level of contemplation, as was explained above. That is why Mary, who symbolizes the contemplative life, is described as "sitting at the Lord's feet" persistently.[7]

(iii) The contemplative life is more enjoyable than the active. Thus Augustine says that Martha was troubled, while Mary feasted.[8]

(iv) People are more self-sufficient in the contemplative life, because they need fewer things. Accordingly it says in Luke 10:41, "Martha, Martha, you are worried and troubled about a great many things."

(v) The contemplative life is loved more for its own sake, while the active life has something other than itself in view. So it says in Psalm 26:4, "One thing I have sought from the Lord, and this is what I will look for: to live in the house of the Lord all the days of my life, so that I may see the Lord's will."

(vi) The contemplative life consists in a certain leisure and repose. "Be quiet and see that I am God" (Ps. 45:11).

(vii) The contemplative life is centered on the things of God, whereas the active life is about human affairs. So Augustine says, "In the beginning was the Word; that is what Mary was listening to. The Word was made flesh; that is what Martha was serving."[9]

(viii) The contemplative life concerns that in us which is most properly ours, namely our intellect; but our lower powers too share in the workings of the active life, and they are common to us and to brute animals. That is why in Psalm 35:7–10, after "You will save both human beings and beasts, Lord," it adds something specifically human: "In your light we shall see light."

The Lord adds a ninth argument in Luke 10:42 when he says, "Mary has chosen the best part and it will not be taken away from

---

6. *Moralia* 6.37.61 (PL 75:764B).
7. Luke 10:39.
8. *Serm.* 103.2.3 (PL 38:614).
9. Ibid. 104.2.3 (PL 38:617).

her." Augustine interprets this to mean, "You have not chosen a bad part, but she has chosen a better; and I will tell you why it is better: because it will not be taken away from her. One day the burden of need will be taken away from you, but the delights of truth are eternal."[10]

Nevertheless in some circumstances and in some particular respect the active life has to be given preference because of the needs of this present life. The philosopher too acknowledges this, when he says that doing philosophy is better than making money, but making money is better for someone who is suffering want.[11]

In response to the points raised above:

(1) Ecclesiastical superiors are not meant to be confined to the active life; they should also be outstanding in the contemplative life. As Gregory says, "A ruler in the church should be pre-eminent in action and also, more than all the rest, be held high in contemplation."[12]

(2) The contemplative life involves a certain liberty of mind. Gregory says that the contemplative life passes over into a certain inner freedom, thinking not of temporal affairs, but of the things of eternity.[13] And Boethius says, "Human souls will necessarily be more free when they concentrate on gazing at the mind of God, and less free when they sink down to the level of bodies."[14] This makes it clear that the active life does not give orders to the contemplative life as such; it calls for certain works of the active life as a preparation for the contemplative life, and in so doing it is more the servant than the mistress of the contemplative life. And this is what Gregory says: the active life is called servitude, while the contemplative life is called freedom.[15]

(3) People are sometimes called away from contemplation to undertake some of the works of the active life because of something that is needed in this present life, but not in such a way as to be obliged to abandon contemplation entirely. As Augustine says, the love of truth seeks a holy leisure, but the needs of love un-

---

10. Ibid. 103.4.5 (PL 38:615).
11. Aristotle, *Topics* 3.2 (118a10–11).
12. *Reg. Past.* 2.1 (PL 77:26D–27A).
13. *Hom. Ezek.* 1.3.13 (PL 76:812A).
14. *Cons. Phil.* V pr. 2.
15. *Hom. Ezek.* 1.3.9 (PL 76:809D).

dertake whatever business is fair (business of the active life, that is); if no one imposes this burden on you, you should use the time to see and examine the truth, but if such a burden is laid upon you, you should accept it because of the demands of charity. But even so you should not completely abandon your joy in the truth, in case you lose its delights and are crushed by your obligations.[16] It is clear, then, that when people are called to the active life from the contemplative life, this is not a matter of taking something away from them, but of adding something more.

Article 2: Is the active life more meritorious than the contemplative?

On the face of it, the active life is more meritorious than the contemplative:

(1) When we talk about "merit" we imply that some payment is due.[1] And payment is owed in return for work: "People will all receive their reward according to their work" (1 Cor. 3:8). But work is associated with the active life, while the contemplative life goes with repose. As Gregory says, people who turn to God must first toil at their work, that is, they must first receive Leah, if they are afterward to rest in the embrace of Rachel to "see the principle."[2] So the active life is more meritorious than the contemplative.

(2) The contemplative life is a kind of beginning of the happiness of the life to come. On John 21:22 ("I want him to remain until I come") Augustine says, "This can be stated more plainly: perfect activity, shaped by the model of my passion, is to follow me, but the beginning of contemplation is to remain until I come and it will be made perfect when I come."[3] And Gregory says that the contemplative life begins here in such a way as to be brought to perfection in heaven.[4] But in the life to come we shall not be in a position to merit; we shall be in the position of receiving the reward of our merits. So the contemplative life appears to fit the

---

16. *Civ. Dei* 19.19.
1. To "merit" (*mereri*) is the same as to "earn."
2. *Hom. Ezek.* 2.2.10 (PL 76:954B).
3. *In Io. Ev.* 124.5.
4. *Hom. Ezek.* 2.2.9 (PL 76:954A).

notion of "merit" less than the active life does; it accords more with the notion of "reward."

(3) Gregory says that no sacrifice is more acceptable to God than zeal for souls.[5] But zeal for souls makes people turn to the concerns of the active life. So it seems that the contemplative life is not more meritorious than the active life.

On the other hand:
Gregory says, "The merits of the active life are great, but those of the contemplative life are greater."[6]

REPLY

Merit is rooted in charity, as we have seen.[7] And charity consists in loving God and our neighbor, as we noted above,[8] but loving God for his own sake is more meritorious than loving our neighbor, as our earlier discussion makes clear.[9] So things that relate directly to the love of God are more meritorious in general than anything that relates directly to the love of our neighbor for the sake of God.

Now the contemplative life relates directly and immediately to the love of God. Augustine says that holy leisure, the leisure of the contemplative life, that is, is what the love of truth looks for[10]—the truth of God, that is, which is the major interest of the contemplative life, as we have seen. The active life, on the other hand, is aimed more directly at the love of our neighbor, because it "bustles about in busy service," as it says in Luke 10:40. So in general the contemplative life, as such, is more meritorious than the active life. And that is what Gregory says. "The contemplative life is more meritorious than the active, because the active life toils at the works of this present life," in which our neighbors need to be helped, "but the contemplative life already savors inwardly a taste of the repose of the world to come,"[11] in its contemplation of God, that is.

---

5. Ibid. 1.12.30 (PL 76:932C). This text is, not surprisingly, quoted by Humbert of Romans in his demonstration that preaching is particularly pleasing to God (*De Erud. Praed.* 1.4.25; Tugwell, *Early Dominicans* p. 191).

6. *Moralia* 6.37.61 (PL 75:764D).

7. I.II q.114 a.4.

8. II.II q.25 a.1.

9. II.II q.27 a.8.

10. *Civ. Dei* 19.19.

11. *Hom. Ezek.* 1.3.9 (PL 76:809B).

Nevertheless it may happen in practice that some people merit more in the works of the active life than other people do in the works of the contemplative life. For instance, out of an abundance of love of God, someone may for a time endure being parted from the delights of contemplation of God in order to fulfill the will of God for the sake of his glory. Thus the apostle said, "I wanted to be anathema from Christ myself for the sake of my brethren" (Rom. 9:3), on which Chrysostom comments: "His whole mind was so flooded with the love of Christ that he could make light even of what was dearest of all to him, namely being with Christ, if in this way he could please Christ."[12]

In response to the points raised above:

(1) Outward labor works for the increase of our incidental reward, but the increase of merit with regard to our essential reward consists primarily in charity.[13] Enduring outward labor for Christ's sake is a sign of charity, but it is a much clearer sign of charity to abandon all that belongs to this life and enjoy giving one's attention solely to the contemplation of God.

(2) In the state of happiness which is to come we reach perfection, so there is no room left for any further progress to be made by way of meriting. But if there were room for such progress, merit would be more effective there because of the greater charity there is there. But in this present life contemplation goes with a certain imperfection and so it does have room for improvement, and therefore it does not eliminate the basis for meriting. On the contrary, it makes for an increase of merit because of its greater practice of the love of God.

(3) A spiritual sacrifice is made to God when anything is offered to him. And of all the goods we possess, the one which is most acceptable to God is our own soul, if this is offered to him in sacrifice. Our own soul is the first thing we should offer to him, according to Ecclesiasticus 30:24, "Have mercy on your soul and give pleasure to God." The second thing we should offer is the souls of other people, according to Apocalypse 22:17, "Anyone

---

12. *De Compunctione* 1.7 (PG 47:405).

13. The essential reward given to people in heaven is the vision of God; the incidental reward consists of "extras," like haloes. Conventionally these extras constitute the reward given to particular good works, such as preaching or martyrdom, whereas the essential reward is given to charity.

who hears should say, 'Come.' " And the more closely we join our own soul or the souls of others to God, the more acceptable the sacrifice becomes to him. So it is more pleasing to God that we apply our own soul and the souls of others to contemplation than it is if we apply them to activity.

So saying that zeal for souls is the most acceptable sacrifice we can offer to God does not mean putting the merit of the active life before that of the contemplative life; what it shows is that it is more meritorious to offer your own soul and the souls of others to God than it is to offer any other gift of external things.

Article 3: Is the contemplative life hindered by the active life?

It looks as if the contemplative life is hindered by the active life:

(1) The contemplative life needs a certain inner leisureliness. "Be quiet and see that I am God" (Ps. 45:11). But the active life is restless: "Martha, Martha, you are worried and disturbed about many things" (Luke 10:41). Therefore the active life does interfere with the contemplative life.

(2) The contemplative life calls for clear vision. But the active life interferes with the clarity of vision. As Gregory says, it is bleary-eyed and fertile, and because it is caught up in doing things, it sees less.[1] Therefore it does interfere with the contemplative life.

(3) Opposites hinder each other, and the active and contemplative lives appear to be the opposite of each other, because the active life is concerned with a great many things, whereas the contemplative life applies itself to the contemplation of a single object. So they are strictly opposites. So it looks as if the contemplative life is hindered by the active life.

On the other hand:
Gregory says that people who desire to hold the citadel of contemplation must first prove themselves in the field by practicing good works.[2]

---

1. *Hom. Ezek.* 2.2.10 (PL 954C).
2. *Moralia* 6.37.59 (PL 75:763C).

Reply

The active life can be looked at from two points of view. If we consider it from the point of view of its concern for and practice of outward works, then it is obvious that it does hinder the contemplative life, in that it is impossible to be engaged in external works and to be free for the contemplation of God at the same time.

But if we consider the active life with reference to its ordering and harmonizing of the inner passions of the soul, then it must be seen as helping the contemplative life, which is hindered by the disorder of our inner passions. So Gregory says, "When people desire to hold the citadel of contemplation, they must first prove themselves in the field by practicing works, to discover earnestly whether they no longer do any harm to their neighbors, whether they bear with equanimity any harm they suffer from their neighbors, whether their minds do not take pleasure in being offered temporal goods and so lose their grip, and whether they are not unduly hurt and upset if they lose temporal goods. Then they must calculate whether, when they return inwardly to themselves, they do not bring with them any shadow of temporal things when they explore the things of the spirit, or at least whether they shoo it away, if they have perhaps brought such a shadow with them, by making the necessary distinctions."[3] So the practice of the active life is beneficial for the contemplative life in that it calms our inner passions, which are the source of the images which interfere with contemplation.

This shows how we should answer the points raised above, because they all make valid observations about being engaged in external works, but not about the result of the active life, namely the tempering of the passions.

Article 4: Does the active life precede the contemplative life?

It looks as if the active life does not precede the contemplative life:

(1) The contemplative life relates directly to the love of God, whereas the active life relates to the love of our neighbor. And the love of God comes before love of neighbor, inasmuch as it is

---

3. Ibid.

for God's sake that our neighbor is loved. So apparently the contemplative life comes before the active life.

(2) Gregory says, "You must realize that the right order in life is to move from the active life toward the contemplative life, while at the same time it is often useful to turn one's mind back from the contemplative life to the active life."[1] So it is not enough to say that the active life precedes the contemplative.

(3) There is surely no need for things that pertain to different people to be in any sequence. And the active and contemplative lives do pertain to different people. As Gregory says, often people who could have contemplated God in peace have fallen because of the pressure of their commitments; and often people who would have lived well if they had been engaged in human affairs, are slain by the sword of their own repose.[2] So the active life does not precede the contemplative.

On the other hand:
Gregory says, "The active life comes before the contemplative in time, because we move toward contemplation on the basis of good works."[3]

REPLY

There are two senses in which one thing can be said to precede another. If we are asking which comes first intrinsically, then we must say that the contemplative life comes before the active life, inasmuch as the objects to which it applies itself are prior and better; that is why it inspires and guides the active life. Our higher reason, which is responsible for contemplation, is related to our lower reason, which is responsible for our activities, as a husband is related to his wife, who is meant to be guided by her husband, as Augustine says.[4]

In another sense, though, we say that something comes first with reference to us, and that means that it is the first to be brought to birth. And in this sense the active life precedes the contemplative,

---

1. *Hom. Ezek.* 2.2.11 (PL 76:954D–955A).
2. *Moralia* 6.37.57 (PL 75:761D).
3. *Hom. Ezek.* 1.3.9 (PL 76:809B).
4. *De Trin.* 12.3.3.

because it prepares us for the contemplative life, as is clear from what we have already said. And preparing the material, when we are talking about how things come into being, precedes the appearance of form, even though intrinsically and naturally the form comes first.[5]

In response to the points raised above:

(1) The aim of the contemplative life is not just the love of God, but the perfect love of God, whereas the active life is necessary for any level of love of our neighbor. So Gregory says, "People can enter heaven without the contemplative life, so long as they take the trouble to do the good they can, but they cannot enter heaven without the active life, if they do not take the trouble to do the good they can."[6] And this also makes it clear that the active life comes before the contemplative life, on the principle that what is common to all comes into being before anything that is confined to the perfect.[7]

(2) In terms of how they come into existence, the movement is from the active life to the contemplative; but there is a return from the contemplative life to the active in terms of guidance, the active life being guided by the contemplative. In the same way we acquire moral habits by performing moral acts, but once we have acquired a habit we perform its acts all the more perfectly, as it says in the *Ethics*.[8]

(3) People who are vulnerable to their passions because of their drive to do things are, as such, better suited to the active life because of the restlessness of their spirit. That is why Gregory says that some people are so restless that they find it much harder work if they have to stop working, because the disturb-

---

5. In Aristotelian terms, before (say) a bundle of damp twigs can acquire the form of fire, it must be prepared (dried out and so on); on the other hand, if the form of fire did not already exist it would be impossible even to dry out the twigs. Aristotle habitually presumes that what is prior by nature (the fire in this case) comes later in the "order of production" (cf. *Phys.* Θ 7, 261a14; *Metaph.* A 8, 989a15–16).

6. *Hom. Ezek.* 1.3.10 (PL 76:809D–810A).

7. Obviously there have to be hats before there can be perfect hats, and where perfection is the product of some process of maturing there must be immature specimens before you can hope for mature specimens. But this principle sits ill with Thomas' starting point, that the active and contemplative lives belong to different people, and it sits even less happily with his own doctrine that the different lives are defined in terms of differences of temperament.

8. Aristotle, *Eth. Nic.* 2.4 (1105a17–b18).

584

ance of their hearts is so much the worse, the more time they have for thought.[9] But some people naturally have a purity and quietness of soul which makes them suited to the contemplative life, and if they are put to work the whole time in doing things it does them harm. So Gregory says that some people's minds are so leisurely that if they are caught up by the labor of some business, they collapse at the very outset of their work.[10] But, as he goes on to say, love often stimulates even lazy minds to work, and fear holds restless souls in check and makes them contemplate.[11]

So people who are more adapted to the active life can be prepared for the contemplative life by their practice of the active life, and those who are more adapted to the contemplative life can all the same undertake the practices of the active life in order thereby to become more fit for contemplation.

---

9. *Moralia* 6.37.57 (PL 75:761C).
10. Ibid.
11. Ibid. 6.37.58 (PL 75:762D).

Thomas Aquinas

Texts on Religious Life

Obedience and the Vows
De Perfectione, Chapter 13

The error of those who take it upon themselves to lessen the merit of obedience and the vows.

The devil resents human perfection. He has therefore raised up various pretentious and rebellious teachers to attack the ways of perfection. The first way of perfection (poverty) was attacked by Vigilantius, and Jerome replied to him in these words: "He claims that it is better to make use of one's possessions and distribute the income from one's property little by little. There is no need for me to answer such a claim, the answer is given by the Lord himself: 'If you want to be perfect, go and sell all that you have and give it to the poor and come, follow me.' He is addressing someone who wants to be perfect, who is ready, with the apostles, to abandon father, ship and nets. The way of life you recommend ranks second or third. We accept it too, provided it is recognized that the best comes before the second best, and the second best before the third."[1]

It is to preclude this error that is says in the *Ecclesiastical Dogmas*, "It is a good thing to provide resources for the poor on a regular basis, but it is better to give away everything at once with the intention of following Christ and, free from worldly cares, to be poor with Christ."[2]

The second way of perfection (chastity) was attacked by Jovinian, who made marriage equal to virginity. His error is manifestly refuted by Jerome in the book which he wrote against him. Augustine also refers to his error in his *Retractationes*: "Jovinian's heresy tried to make the merit of holy virgins the same as that of married chastity, and it was so influential in Rome that even some nuns, who

---

1. Jerome, *Contra Vigilantium* 14 (PL 23:350D–351A), quoting Matt. 19:21. In Thomas' time there were some people who wanted to revive Vigilantius' contention that wealth was an aid to virtue: cf. A. Murray in G. J. Cuming and D. Baker, eds., *Popular Belief and Practice* (Cambridge, 1972), p. 91.

2. Gennadius, *De Eccles. Dogm.* 38 (PL 42:1219).

had never before incurred any suspicion of unchastity, are said to have fallen and got married. Our holy mother, the church, has resisted this monstrosity with the utmost fidelity and vigor."[3] This is why it says in the *Ecclesiastical Dogmas* that it is the part of a Jovinian, not a Christian, to place marriage on the same level as virginity consecrated to God or to believe that people who abstain from wine or meat out of a desire to chastise their bodies do not acquire any extra merit thereby.[4]

These old intrigues were not enough for the devil, so in our own time, we are told, he has incited certain people who are attacking the vow of obedience and all other vows in general, saying that it is more praiseworthy to perform virtuous deeds without being under a vow or under obedience than to be constrained to practice them by a vow or by obedience.[5] Some of them, it is said, have reached such a degree of madness that they claim that a vow which has been made to enter religion can be ignored without any harm to one's salvation,[6] and this error is apparently being supported by various empty and silly arguments. They say, for instance, that an act is more praiseworthy and meritorious the more voluntary it is, but the more one is constrained to do something the less voluntary it is; they infer that it is more praiseworthy and meritorious to perform virtuous deeds by one's own free choice without the constraint of a vow or of obedience than it is to be compelled to perform them by a vow or by obedience. As evidence of this they apparently cite what Prosper says in book II of his *De Vita Contemplativa:* "We ought to practice abstinence and fasting in such a way as not to subject ourselves to any obligation of fasting, in case we start doing something voluntary unwillingly instead of doing it with devotion."[7] They

---

3. Augustine, *Retract.* 2.22.1 (PL 32:639).

4. Gennadius 35 (PL 42:1219).

5. Thomas is rather insistent that he knows about these doctrines only by hearsay; their exponents should perhaps be sought among the "pseudo-apostles," who maintained that "it is more perfect to live without a vow than with one," according to Bernard Gui (*Manuel de l'Inquisiteur*, ed. G. Mollat [Paris, 1964], I p. 92). The Dominicans themselves were very sensitive to the risk that obedience could diminish the value of people's acts: cf. Tugwell, *Early Dominicans* pp. 19–24, 434, 439, 441.

6. This was evidently a matter of interest to some students, as it was raised in a Quodlibetal disputation (*Quodl.* III a.12).

7. Pseudo-Prosper (actually Julianus Pomerius), *De Vit. Cont.* 24.1 (PL 59:470B).

could also allege to the same effect the words of the apostle: "Each of them as they have purposed in their hearts, not sadly or under constraint, because God loves a cheerful giver" (2 Cor. 9:7). It is necessary, then, to show clearly that these contentions are false and to demolish their stupid arguments.

We may begin our demonstration of the falsity of this error with what it says in Psalm 75:12, "Make vows and fulfil them to the Lord your God." The Gloss comments on this, "It should be noticed that there are some vows to God which are common to all of us, without which there is no salvation, such as the vow of faith made in baptism, and even if we do not make these promises we are still bound to keep them. With regard to vows of this sort everyone is commanded, 'Make vows and keep them.' Other vows are personal to particular individuals, such as chastity, virginity and such like. We are invited, but not commanded, to make vows of this kind; what is commanded is that we should keep them. The actual vowing is recommended to our choice, but once we have made such a vow, its fulfilment is demanded of us."[8]

So some vows are a matter of precept, while others are a matter of counsel, but in both cases we have to conclude that it is better to do good with a vow than without it. It is obvious that everyone is bound, by God's commandment, to those things which are required for salvation, and it would be quite wrong to imagine that any of God's commandments is pointless. But the purpose of every commandment is charity, as the apostle says (1 Tim. 1:5), so any commandment to do something would be pointless if doing it were not more characteristic of charity than not doing it. Now we are commanded not only to believe and to refrain from stealing, but also to vow these things. Therefore believing under a vow and not stealing under a vow and other such things must be more appropriate to charity than doing them without such a vow. And anything that is more proper to charity is more praiseworthy and more meritorious; therefore it is more praiseworthy and more meritorious to do things with a vow than without.

Further, there is a counsel not only to practice virginity or chastity, but also to make vows about them, as the quotation from

---

8. Lombard's Gloss (PL 191:708D–709A).

the Gloss shows. And we have already said that such counsels are not offered except in connection with some greater good.[9] Therefore it is better to practice virginity with a vow than without, and the same applies to other things too.

Of all good works, the practice of virginity usually receives special commendation, and we are invited to practice it by the Lord, when he says, "Anyone who can take this, should take it" (Matt. 19:12). But virginity itself is made commendable by being vowed. As Augustine says, "Virginity is not honored because it is virginity, but because it is dedicated to God, vowed and kept by pious self-control. . . . What we acclaim in virgins is not that they are virgins, but that they are consecrated to God by their pious self-control."[10] A fortiori, then, other works are rendered more praiseworthy by being dedicated to God by a vow.

Again, any particular good becomes better if another good is added to it. And there can be no doubt that promising something good is itself a good thing. If you make someone a promise, you are regarded as already giving them something good, which is why people say "thank you" when they are promised something. And a vow is a promise made to God: "If you have vowed anything to God, do not delay fulfilling it, because a faithless and foolish promise is displeasing to him" (Eccles. 5:3). So it is better to do something and to vow it than simply to do it without making a vow.

Again, the more you give people the more you deserve from them in return. If you do something for someone without a vow, you are giving them no more than what you actually do for love of them, but if in addition you make a vow, you are not just giving what you do, you are also giving over your capacity and freedom to do it. You are making it impossible for yourself not to do something which previously you could quite properly not have done. Therefore doing something under a vow is more deserving in God's sight than doing it without a vow.

It also contributes to the excellence of a good work if the will is firmly committed to good, just as it makes us more guilty if our will is obstinately fixed on something bad. Now clearly if you vow

---

9. *De Perfectione* 7.

10. Augustine, *De Sancta Virginitate* 8 and 11 (PL 40:400–1).

something you are committing your will to the matter of your vow, so when you perform the good deed which you have vowed, it comes from a committed will. So, just as it affects the seriousness of your guilt if you do evil of set purpose, because that is what it means to sin out of malice, similarly it makes for an increase of merit if you perform a good work under a vow.

Moreover, anything that we do is more or less praiseworthy depending on whether it comes from a more or less important virtue, because it is the virtue which determines the quality of the deed. And it can happen that a lower virtue is called into play by a higher virtue, as for instance when an act of justice is called forth by charity; and it much better to perform an act of a lower virtue at the behest of a higher virtue—an act of justice is better if it proceeds from charity. Now obviously specific good deeds which we do belong to specific lower virtues: fasting belongs to the virtue of abstinence, sexual restraint to chastity, and so on. But making a vow is strictly speaking an act of the virtue of worship, which is undoubtedly to be reckoned as more important than abstinence or chastity or any other such virtue. Worshipping God takes precedence over being rightly disposed toward our neighbor or toward ourselves. So any feat of abstinence or chastity or any other such virtue which is inferior to the virtue of worship is enhanced by being performed under a vow.

Our argument is further supported by the pious zeal of the church, which encourages people to make vows and lavishes indulgences and privileges upon people who vow to go and help in the Holy Land or elsewhere in defense of the church. She would not encourage people to make vows if it were better to do good deeds without a vow, because it would be contrary to the apostle's exhortation, "Aspire to the better gifts" (1 Cor. 12:31). If it were better to do good deeds without a vow, the church, far from encouraging vows, would discourage them either by banning them or by urging people not to make them. And, since it is the church's purpose to lead her faithful toward a better state, she would release them all from any vows they had made, so that their good deeds would be more praiseworthy.

It is clear, then, that this kind of position is at odds with the general tenets and the opinion of the church, and should therefore be condemned as heretical.

It is easy enough to provide an abundant answer to the objections which have been raised.

First, it is claimed that a good deed performed under a vow is less spontaneous, but this is certainly not true always and in every case, because many people fulfil their vows with such eagerness that even if they had not made a vow they would readily not only perform the deed itself but also make a vow to do it.

Secondly, even if we grant that a particular good deed which is done because of a vow or under obedience is in itself not spontaneous, being performed solely because of the constraint of the vow or because of a reluctance to go against obedience, even in this case it is more praiseworthy and meritorious than the same deed performed with a ready will but without a vow. Even if there is no spontaneous eagerness to perform the specific deed in question—fasting, for instance—there is still a ready desire to keep the vow and to be obedient, and this is worth far more than fasting and it is far more meritorious. So the person who keeps a vow in this way is more deserving than someone who fasts spontaneously. And the will to keep one's vow or to be obedient is reckoned all the more prompt, the more unattractive in itself the will finds the deed undertaken because of a vow or out of obedience. So Jerome says to the monk Rusticus, "The point I am leading up to in all this is that I want you to learn not to leave yourself subject to your own will. . . . Do not do what you want to do, eat what you are told to eat, have nothing except what you receive, wear the clothes that you are given, do your allotted work, be subject to someone you have not chosen, go tired to bed and nod off even while you are walking and be forced to get up before you have had your fill of sleep."[11] This shows that it is relevant to the merit of a good deed that we should do or endure for God's sake things which we would not wish to do or endure for their own sake, because the degree of our will's readiness to love God can be inferred from the degree to which we do or endure for his sake things which are repugnant to our own will. This is why we particularly praise the martyrs, because they endured so much more for God's love that the human will would never choose. So Eleazar, in the midst of his torments, said to God,

---

11. Jerome, *Ep.* 125.15 (PL 22:1080–1).

"I endure terrible bodily pains, but in my soul I am glad to suffer them because of the fear of you" (2 Macc. 6:30). [12]

Thirdly, in the case of people who do not retain even the will to keep their vow or to be obedient, it is clear that in the sight of God, who judges hearts, they are reckoned to be breaking their vow and transgressing against obedience. And if they do keep their vow or do what they are commanded to do simply out of human fear or embarrassment, this would not be meritorious in God's eyes, because it would not be done out of any desire to please God, but simply because of human constraint. But even so the vow, if it was made out of charity, was not useless, because the act of vowing was more meritorious than the act of someone else simply fasting, and this merit is not lost, provided the inner disobedience is repented of.

This indicates how we should answer the texts cited above: they are referring to human constraint and to situations in which people do what they have sworn or vowed to do simply because they are embarrassed or afraid of other people; they are not referring to the kind of constraint which results from aiming to love God, [13] which may make people do or endure things which they would otherwise not want in order to fulfil the will of God. This is clear from the words of the apostle, "Not sadly or under constraint"; sadness is caused by human constraint, but it is taken away or at least diminished when we are constrained by the love of God. It is also clear from what Prosper says, "In case we do something voluntary unwillingly instead of doing it with devotion"; the constraint which results from love of God does not lessen devotion, it increases it.

Something that Augustine says shows that this kind of constraint is good and desirable. In a letter to Armentarius and Paulina

---

12. The point is not that doing or suffering what goes against the grain is intrinsically better; that Thomas always denies. It is better in some circumstances inasmuch as it attests a greater love of God. Also what Thomas says here underlines the doctrine that we can be commanded to do (or suffer) something, but we cannot be commanded to like it (cf. II.II q. 104 a. 5); Thomas' doctrine is much more restrained than that of Humbert of Romans (ed. Berthier I pp. 5–6) and it formally excludes the later doctrine of St. Ignatius Loyola, according to which merely doing what one is told hardly even counts as religious obedience, by comparison with the real obedience of the will and the mind (see his letter to the Jesuits in Portugal, 26 March 1553, *Monumenta Ignatiana, Epist.* IV 669–681).

13. Thomas distinguishes between the kind of constraint that simply pushes me to do something I do not want to do, and the kind of constraint that arises precisely from wanting to do something: if I want to go for a ride on a train, then I am constrained to buy a ticket.

he says, "Because you have now made a vow and bound yourself, it is not lawful for you to act otherwise. Before you made yourself liable under a vow, you were free to remain at a lower level, though we should not applaud a freedom which means that we are not obliged to do something which it is profitable to do. But now your promise is lodged with God and so I am not inviting you to a great righteousness" (that is, to the chastity which he had already vowed, as appears from what has been said above), "instead I am trying to deter you from great wickedness, because if you do not fulfil your vow you will not be in the same position that you would have been in if you had never made such a vow. If you had not made the vow, you would have been lower, but not worse; but now if, God forbid, you break the pledge you have given to God, you will be as much more wretched as you will be more blessed if you keep it. And this should not make you wish you had not made your vow; on the contrary, you should be glad that you are no longer free to do what you would once have been free to do to your disadvantage. So proceed fearlessly, fulfil in deed what you have promised in words, and he himself who is looking for this fulfilment will help you. It is a happy constraint, which drives us on to what is better."[14]

These words also make it clear that it is mistaken to claim that people are not bound to fulfil a vow to enter religion.

---

14. Augustine, *Ep.* 127.8 (PL 33:487).

Obedience
Summa Theologiae II.II
Question 104 a.5

It would appear that subjects are bound to obey their superiors in everything:

(1) The apostle says, "Children, obey your parents in everything . . . slaves, obey your earthly masters in everything" (Col. 3:20,22); so on the same principle other types of subjects ought to obey their superiors in everything.

(2) Superiors are intermediaries between God and their subjects; as it says in Deuteronomy 5:5, "I was the trustee and intermediary between God and you at that time, to declare his words to you." Now it is impossible to go from one end of something to the other without going through the middle. So the precepts of a superior should be regarded as the precepts of God.[1] This is why the apostle says, "You received me as the angel of God, as Christ Jesus himself" (Gal. 4:14) and "When you received from us the word in which God was heard, you did not receive it as a human word, but as God's word, which indeed it is" (1 Thess. 2:13). So people ought to obey their superiors in everything, just as they have to obey God in everything.

(3) Religious make a vow of obedience at their profession in just the same way as they make a vow of chastity and poverty. And a religious is bound to observe chastity and poverty in everything, so the same must apply to obedience too.

On the other hand:

It says in Acts 5:29, "It is necessary to obey God rather than human beings." And sometimes the commands of superiors are contrary to God. Therefore superiors are not to be obeyed in everything.

---

1. The argument rests on the spatial analogy implicit in the idea of "intermediary": if C is midway between A and B, you cannot go from A to B without passing C. So, if superiors are intermediaries between us and God, the only way in which God's commands will reach us is through our superiors, and the only way we can offer obedience to God is by obeying our superiors.

REPLY

As we have seen, people respond to the authority of those who command them by a kind of contraint of justice, just as things in nature are affected by the power of whatever acts on them by the constraint of nature.[2] Now there may be two reasons why a natural object is not in fact affected by something that would naturally affect it: it may be prevented by the presence of another more powerful influence—fire, for instance, cannot burn wood if it is counteracted by the more powerful effect of water. Or it may be because the object to be affected is not subordinated in that regard to the thing that is trying to affect it, so that it is partly receptive of its influence, but not totally—for example, a liquid is sometimes subject to heat sufficiently for it to become hot, but not sufficiently for it to be dried up or consumed entirely.[3]

In the same way there are two reasons why subjects may not be obliged to obey their superiors in everything. One is because of a precept from a higher authority. On Romans 13:2 ("Those who disobey win condemnation for themselves") the Gloss comments, "If a superintendant tells you to do something contrary to the orders of the proconsul, are you meant to do it? Or if the proconsul tells you to do one thing, when the emperor has told you to do something else, is there any doubt that you should ignore the one and serve the other? So if the emperor tells you to do one thing and God another, you ought to ignore the emperor and obey God."[4]

Secondly, subjects are not obliged to obey their superiors if they give orders in an area in which they do not have authority over them. Seneca says, "It is mistaken to suppose that servitude applies to anyone as a whole; the better part is exempt from it: bodies are liable to it and are subject to masters, but the mind remains autonomous."[5] And so in everything that concerns the

---

2. II.II q.104 a.1.

3. The same heat will evaporate one liquid while only heating another, so it is not simply a question of the two parties to the deal, but of their relationship to one another.

4. Lombard's Gloss on Rom. 13:2 (PL 191:1505BC).

5. Seneca, *De Beneficiis* 3.20.1.

inner activity of the will, we are not obliged to obey any human being, but only God.

It is in our external, bodily activities that we are obliged to obey one another. And even here we must say that we are not obliged to obey other human beings in things which concern our bodily nature, because we are all equal in our nature. In such matters only God is to be obeyed. This applies to such things as bodily nourishment and having children. So servants are not obliged to obey their masters, nor are children obliged to obey their parents in things like getting married or remaining celibate.

But in the ordering of human affairs and activities subjects are obliged to obey their superiors in accordance with the nature of their specific authority. Soldiers must obey the commander of the army in anything that concerns war. Servants must obey their master in anything that concerns the proper work of servants. Children must obey their father in anything that concerns their education or the administration of the household. And so on.

In response to the points raised above:

(1) When the apostle says, "in everything," we must take him to mean everything that is involved in a father's or a master's authority.

(2) We are subject to God in everything without qualification, inwardly and outwardly. And so we are bound to obey God in everything. But subjects are not subject to their superiors in everything, but only with regard to certain things. Within their own sphere of authority superiors are intermediaries between God and their subjects, but in everything else people are subject to God without intermediaries and he himself instructs them by means of the natural law and the written law.

(3) Religious make profession of obedience with reference to the regular life, and here they are subject to their superiors. And so it is only in connection with things that might be pertinent to the regular life that they are bound to obey. And this kind of obedience is sufficient for salvation. However, if they want to obey in other things too, that is a matter of a higher perfection, always provided that it does not mean doing things which are contrary to God or to the rule they have professed, because that kind of obedience would be unlawful.

So we can distinguish three types of obedience: one which

is sufficient for salvation, which obeys in those things to which it is strictly bound; one which is perfect and obeys in everything that is not unlawful, and one which is undiscriminating and foolish, which obeys even in things that are unlawful.

Sin and The Rule
Summa Theologiae II.II
Question 186 a.9

Is it always a mortal sin if religious contravene what it says in their Rule?

It looks as if it is always a mortal sin for religious to contravene what it says in their Rule:[1]

(1) Doing anything contrary to your vow is the kind of sin that brings damnation, as we can see from what the apostle says about widows who want to marry: "They incur damnation because they have made their first promise void."[2] But religious are bound to their Rule by the vow involved in their profession. Therefore they commit mortal sin by contravening the contents of their Rule.

(2) A Rule is like a law to which religious are subject. And breaking any of the commandments of the law is a mortal sin. So it looks as if a monk who contravenes what it says in his Rule commits mortal sin.

(3) Contempt for the law makes for mortal sin. But if someone keeps

---

1. This was a "topical" question; it had been raised in a Quodlibetal disputation at Christmas 1269 (I a.20) in the form, "Is it a mortal sin for a monk to eat meat?" In his response Thomas generalizes the discussion and tackles the question whether it is a sin for a religious to contravene any of the contents of his Rule (which is the question aired in q.186 a.9); though Thomas confines himself to male religious, his comments would no doubt be the same about women religious. The background to the question is probably to be sought in the many-sided controversies that surrounded the early Dominicans, which seem to have tempted some of the brethren to score points off their critics by accusing them of being in mortal sin. The General Chapter of 1234 admonishes the friars "not to preach that it is a mortal sin for monks to eat meat" (MOPH III p. 4:23–4). In similar vein an Oxford Dominican precipitated a major row with the Franciscans in 1269 by "proving" that they were all in a state of mortal sin because of the possessions they owned contrary to their Rule (cf. A. G. Little, *The Grey Friars in Oxford* [Oxford, 1892], pp. 320–35).

2. 1 Tim. 5:12. Lombard's Gloss (PL 192:353CD) points out that Paul must be talking about widows who have made a vow of chastity, and the same comment is made by Thomas in his lectures on 1 Timothy (Marietti ed., para.204).

on doing something he should not do it appears that his sin is rooted in a refusal to take the law seriously. So if a religious goes against what it says in his Rule frequently he is surely committing mortal sin.

On the other hand:
Religious life is safer than life in the world. That is why Gregory compares life in the world to a tossing sea and religious life to a calm harbor.[3] But if every infringement of any of the contents of the Rule constituted mortal sin for a religious, religious life would be extremely dangerous[4] because of all its observances. So not every single infringement of the contents of the Rule is mortal sin.

REPLY

As we have seen, the contents of a Rule are of two kinds.[5] There are some things in the Rule which indicate the purpose of the whole Rule, for instance, things which concern the practice of the virtues; offending against these things does constitute mortal sin, at least in the case of things which are commanded universally.[6] In the case of things which go beyond the obligations of the universal commandments there is not necessarily any mortal sin, unless the infringement comes from contempt for the Rule.[7] As we have already said, a religious is not obliged to be perfect, but only to be moving in the direction of perfection,[8] and refusing to take perfection seriously is incompatible with that.

The other kind of thing contained in a Rule concerns external

---

3. Gregory, *Ep. ad Leandrum* 1 (PL 75:511AB), at the beginning of the *Moralia*.

4. In his Quodlibetal Thomas says that on this view religious life would be a "death-trap."

5. II.II q.186 a.7 ad 2.

6. In his Quodlibetal Thomas says bluntly that in general nothing will be a mortal sin for a religious that would not be a mortal sin for anyone else.

7. In the Quodlibetal Thomas also suggests that giving scandal (in the strict sense of doing or saying something that is likely to make somebody else fall into sin) might make something not intrinsically sinful into a serious sin. But II.II q.43 a.4 makes it seem unlikely that a religious could actually commit scandal on such a scale as to make it a mortal sin without doing something which would in any case amount to mortal sin.

8. II.II q.186 a.2.

practices, and this includes all external observances.[9] Of these some are binding on religious because of the vow involved in their profession. But what their profession chiefly concerns is the three things we have noted above: poverty, chastity and obedience;[10] all the rest is subordinate to these. So any infringement of these three does constitute mortal sin. But there is not necessarily any mortal sin involved in breaking the other contents of the Rule, except in two cases: contempt for the Rule is directly contrary to one's profession, in which one vowed to live the regular life, so that does involve mortal sin; so does disregarding a formal precept,[11] whether delivered by word of mouth by the superior or written into the Rule, because that would be contrary to the vow of obedience.

In response to the points raised above:

(1) Someone who makes profession of a Rule is not vowing to keep everything that is in the Rule; what he is vowing is to lead the regular life,[12] which consists essentially in the three things listed above. That is why in some religious orders people make profession in rather more cautious terms and do not make profession of the Rule, but promise to live in accordance with the Rule,[13]

---

9. "Observances" in Thomas' language includes poverty, chastity and obedience as well as the details of monastic routine.

10. Thomas argues that the essence of religious profession is the promise of poverty, chastity and obedience (II.II q.186 a.7), and therefore a vow of religion can be interpreted in terms of these three practices; but in Thomas' time it was not normal for the actual formula of profession to contain the "three vows" explicitly and Thomas' argument does not require that it should.

11. A formal precept has a special force which other regulations do not have; it means something that has been quite specifically presented to the subject as a "test case" of obedience, so that failure to obey will automatically mean a serious breach of the profession of obedience, i.e., grave sin.

12. "Regular life," by definition, means life according to the Rule (*regula*), but Thomas sees this as consisting (a) in the practice of poverty, chastity and obedience, and (b) in the acceptance of a certain ideal expressed in the Rule; he does not seem sympathetic to the idea that the religious life is vested in all the details of the Rule, even though such an idea is at least implicit in the Prologue to the Dominican Constitutions (Tugwell, *Early Dominicans* pp. 456–7). Thomas does not specify which religious he had in mind, but probably the ones who were rash enough to promise "to keep the Rule" are the Franciscans; no early Franciscan profession formula has survived, but it is implied in the *Regula Bullata* 2.11 that they did make such a promise at their profession, and certainly by 1260 the formula includes the words, "I vow . . . to keep the Rule of the Friars Minor" (AFH 34 [1941] p. 40). Hugh of Digne, in his commentary on the Franciscan Rule (ed. D. Flood [Grottaferrata, 1979], p. 102), specifically notes that Franciscans promise to "keep the Rule," not to "live according to the Rule."

13. As Thomas' Quodlibetal makes clear, this is his interpretation of the Benedictine

which means aiming to shape their behavior in line with the Rule, taking the Rule as a kind of model. And this is destroyed by contempt for the Rule.

In other religious orders there is an even more cautious profession of "obedience in accordance with the Rule,"[14] so that only an offense against some precept contained in the Rule will be directly contrary to one's profession and infringement or neglect of any of the rest will merely be venial sin. But, as we have seen, this kind of thing is meant to facilitate the keeping of the main vows,[15] whereas committing venial sin, as we have also seen, facilitates mortal sin,[16] inasmuch as it interferes with the things that dispose us to keep the primary precepts of Christ's law, which are the precepts of charity.

---

profession of "conversion of manners according to the Rule." In the Rule of St. Benedict (58:17) it does not say "according to the Rule," and the later monastic formula involved a promise of "conversion of manners and obedience according to the Rule" (cf. AFP 39 [1969] p. 9; *Revue Bénédictine* 44 [1932] p. 37), which looks more like the next kind of profession mentioned by Thomas. But Thomas is in fact right to distinguish between the monastic profession formula and the one he alludes to next, because the monastic formula is a promise of obedience to a way of life, whereas the promise of "obedience according to the Rule" (without any mention of "conversion of manners") is strictly a promise of obedience to the superior, not to a whole way of life (cf. next note).

14. In his Quodlibetal Thomas presents this formula as being the *cautissima et securissima forma* of the Dominicans, and indeed the Dominicans did (and do) promise "obedience . . . in accordance with the Rule" (for the text in the constitutions in force at this time see ASOP 3 [1897–8] p. 55), but a similar formula is normal also in the profession of canons regular (e.g., J. Siegwart, ed., *Die Consuetudines des Augustiner-Chorherrenstiftes Marbach im Elsass* [Fribourg, 1965], para. 140; Pl. F. Lefèvre, ed., *Les Statuts de Prémontré Réformés sur les Ordres de Grégoire IX et d'Innocent IV* [Louvain, 1946], I 14; A. Carrier, ed., *Coutumier du XI siècle de l'Ordre de Saint-Ruf* [Sherbrooke, 1950], ch. 7). It should be noticed that in all these formulae obedience is promised, not to the Rule, but to the superior, and Thomas' comment suggests that it is the authority of the superior that makes certain parts of a religious Rule binding in conscience, so that infringement of them would amount to mortal sin (cf. his comments in the Quodlibetal). In his commentary on the Constitutions Humbert of Romans identifies eleven parts of the Dominican Constitutions that have the force of a precept (ed. cit. II p. 53); two of them are based on the authority of the Rule of St. Augustine, and in one of these cases the authority of the legislator is specifically invoked, and in the other nine cases the General Chapter that incorporated the relevant texts into the Constitutions explicitly refers to its own authority and makes it unambiguous that a precept (or prohibition) is being issued in such a way as to call upon the vow of obedience. Without such a formal declaration on the part of the legislator, no Rule or Constitution can have the force of a precept. Hugh of Digne, by contrast, regards it as a bad innovation to treat as precepts only those which are explicitly formulated as such (ed. cit. p. 106).

15. II.II q.186 a.7 ad 2.

16. I.II q.88 a.3.

In one religious order, that of the Friars Preachers, infringements and omissions of this kind, as such, do not involve any guilt at all, mortal or venial; they merely make people liable to the appointed punishment, because their obligation to keep these things is of this kind.[17] There could still be mortal sin involved, though, because of carelessness, lust or contempt.

(2) Not all the contents of the law are communicated in the form of precepts, some are put before us as decrees or regulations carrying some definite punishment in the case of infraction. Similarly in civil law people do not always deserve capital punishment for the transgression of some statute in the law. And in the church's law there are rulings and decrees whose infringement does not mean mortal sin. It is the same with decrees contained in a Rule.

(3) Doing something or breaking some regulation out of contempt means that your will refuses to be subject to the guidance of the law or Rule and that that is why you are acting contrary to the law or Rule. But if you are led to do something contrary to the regulations of the law or Rule for some particular reason, such as concupiscence or anger, then that is the cause of your sin, not contempt, and this remains true even if you keep on committing the same sin for the same reason or a reason like it. As Augustine says, not all sins are committed because of proud contempt.[18] But committing some sin frequently does prepare the way for contempt: "The wicked, when they reach the depths, make light of it" (Prov. 18:3).

---

17. In 1236 the Dominicans wrote into their Constitutions a declaration to this effect (ASOP 3 [1897–8] p. 33; Tugwell, *Early Dominicans*, p. 457), and we learn from Humbert (ed. Berthier II p. 46) that it was Dominic himself who insisted on this principle.

18. Augustine, *De Natura et Gratia* 29.33.

Study
Contra Impugnantes Dei Cultum et Religionem Chap. 11

Now we must see how they[1] turn the fact that religious apply themselves to study into a way of insulting them.

(1) In 2 Timothy 3 we are warned about certain people who are going to pose a threat to the church and one of the things said against them is that they will be "always learning and never reaching knowledge of the truth" (2 Tim. 3:7). On this basis our critics want to arouse suspicion against religious because they study.

(2) In his comment on Job 16:10 ("My enemy looked at me with terrible eyes"), Gregory comments: "Truth incarnate chose poor, uneducated, simple men to be his preachers; by contrast the man of damnation, whom the apostate angel adopts at the end of the world to preach his lies, will choose cunning, devious men who possess the knowledge of this world."[2] On this basis our critics make out that these religious are precursors of the Antichrist because they are resplendent with knowledge as they exercise their task of preaching.

(3) On Apocalypse 13:11 ("I saw another beast rising from the earth and it had two horns like a lamb"), the Gloss comments: "Having described the tribulation that is to come about through the Antichrist and his princes, he adds another one which will be brought about by his apostles, whom he will scatter throughout the world." The Gloss interprets "rising" to mean "being successful in preaching," and another Gloss comments on "it had two horns," "They will pretend to possess the innocence and purity of life and the true doctrine and miracles that Christ pos-

---

1. Chiefly William of St. Amour, the ringleader at this time of the Parisian attack on the mendicants, who is responsible at any rate for the first three points raised here, as the Leonine editor indicates.

2. Gregory, *Moralia* 13.10.13 (PL 75:1023C).

sessed and gave to his disciples; or they will appropriate to themselves the two testaments."³ So it looks as if people who are successful in preaching, thanks to their knowledge of the two testaments, with a pretense of holiness, are the apostles of the Antichrist.

(4) It says in 1 Corinthians 8:1, "Knowledge puffs up, but charity builds up." Religious are especially meant to cultivate humility; therefore they ought to refrain from the study of knowledge.

(5) Gregory says that St. Benedict, who was noted for his religious life, "abandoned the study of letters in a knowing ignorance and a wise lack of learning."⁴ So religious ought to follow his example and abandon the pursuit of knowledge.

(6) In 2 Thessalonians 3:11 the apostle rebukes people who give up manual labor⁵ and abandon themselves to curiosity and idleness. But curiosity is what the pursuit of knowledge is all about. Therefore religious ought not to give up manual labor in order to abandon themselves to study.

---

3. The first and third citations come from the Marginal Gloss, the second from the Interlinear Gloss.

4. Gregory, *Dial.* 2 Prol. (PL 66:126A).

5. Controversy over manual labor had been going on on several fronts. Apart from a long-standing opposition between manual labor and intellectual work (cf. J. LeGoff in Wilpert, *Beiträge zum Berufsbewusstsein* . . . pp. 18, 21), the Cistercians had made manual labor a crucial part of their monastic ideology (cf. C. J. Holdsworth, "The Blessings of Work: The Cistercian View," in D. Baker, ed., *Sanctity and Secularity* [Oxford, 1973], pp. 59–76). It was chiefly Cistercians who made it an objection to the Waldensians (and in due course the Poor Catholics) that they did not do any manual labor, but the Catharists also raised the same objection (cf. *Cahiers de Fanjeaux* 2 [1967] p. 155; Durandus of Osca, *Liber Antiheresis*, ed. K. V. Selge [Berlin, 1967], p. 77; on the spiritual kinship between Catharists and Cistercians, cf. *Cahiers de Fanjeaux* 21 [1986] p. 318). The reformed canons on the whole imitated the Cistercians in incorporating manual labor into their way of life, but the Dominicans had never done this and Humbert of Romans makes exemption from labor one of the "perks" of the preaching life (*De Erud. Praed.* 1.5.33; Tugwell, *Early Dominicans* p. 194). St. Francis seems to have become progressively more insistent on manual labor (cf. the strong statement in his *Testamentum* 20), and the "primitive" wing of his Order followed suit (cf. the life of Bl. Giles para. 5, ed. W. W. Seton, [Manchester, 1918], p. 60), but the clerical wing of the Order, which rapidly gained control, maintained that spiritual work, being superior, constituted a reason for not doing manual labor (cf. Hugh of Digne, ed. cit. p. 141); but Hugh of Digne (who was probably writing in 1252, only a few years before Thomas' *Contra Impugnantes*) reveals that it was being debated within the Order whether or not there was a precept obliging the friars to do manual labor (ed. cit. pp.139–44). The secular opponents of the mendicants eagerly latched on to the Cistercian conviction that manual labor was an essential part of religious life and attacked the mendicants on this basis for not practicing it (cf. William of St. Amour, *De Periculis* 12; *Responsiones* 7 (AHDLMA 18 [1951] p. 341).

It is not our critics who originated this way of thinking; it was Julian the Apostate who debarred the servants of Christ from the study of letters, as the *Ecclesiastical History* tells us.[6] Our critics reveal themselves to be followers of the Apostate when they forbid religious to study, which is patently contrary to scripture.

In Isaiah 5:13 it says, "My people is led away captive because they had no knowledge," and the Gloss adds the comment, "Because they refused to have any."[7] A deliberate lack of knowledge would not be punished unless the pursuit of knowledge were praiseworthy.

In Hosea 4:5–6 it says, "At night I made your mother keep silent. My people were dumb because they had no knowledge. Because you rejected knowledge, I will reject you from serving as my priest." This clearly shows that people are punished for lacking knowledge.

In Psalm 118:66 it says, "Teach me goodness and discipline and knowledge," which the Gloss interprets as meaning: "Goodness, that is, inspire me with charity. Discipline, that is, give me patience. Knowledge, that is, enlighten my mind, because that knowledge is useful by which people come to know themselves."[8]

Writing to the monk Rusticus, Jerome says, "Never let your book leave your hands or your eyes. . . . Love knowledge of the scriptures and you will not love the vices of the flesh."[9]

In a letter to the monk, Paulinus, Jerome says, "Holy boorishness benefits only itself, and however much the example of its way of life may edify the church of Christ, it does just as much harm if it does not put up any opposition to the church's wreckers."[10] Evidently the knowledge of the saints is preferable to the holiness of simpletons.

In the same letter he lists the books of the bible and then says, "I ask you, dearest brother, living among these books, meditating on them, knowing nothing but them and looking for nothing else, doesn't that seem like living in the kingdom of heaven already here

---

6. Cf. Rufinus' version of Eusebius 10.32 (PL 21:501C); Cassiodorus, *Hist. Trip.* 6.17 (PL 69:1040D).

7. Interlinear Gloss.

8. Lombard's Gloss (PL 191:1076D).

9. Jerome, *Ep.* 125.11 (PL 22:1078).

10. Ibid. 53.3 (PL 22:542).

on earth?"[11] Obviously it is a heavenly way of life to spend one's days in the study of sacred scripture.

That the study of scripture is particularly appropriate for people who are appointed to the task of preaching is clear from what the apostle says in 1 Timothy 4:13, "Until I come, apply yourself to reading, to exhortation and to teaching," which makes it clear that studious reading is a prerequisite for people who propose to exhort and teach.

Jerome says in his letter to Rusticus, "Spend much time in learning what you are later to teach," and he also says to him, "If you are tickled by a desire to be a cleric, learn something that you can teach."[12]

Gregory says in his *Pastoral Rule*, "It is absolutely necessary that people who are active as preachers should not withdraw from the studious practice of sacred reading."[13]

Furthermore, the life of religious is chiefly directed to contemplation, and "reading is part of contemplation," as Hugh of St. Victor says.[14] Therefore it is proper for religious to devote themselves to study.

Again, the people who are best suited to the acquisition of knowledge are those who are the most detached from the cares of the flesh. "To whom will he teach knowledge and whom will he make to understand the message? Those who are weaned from milk and torn from the breasts" (Is. 28:9). And the Commentator says, on the seventh book of the *Physics*, that chastity and the other virtues by which the lusts of the flesh are restrained are particularly useful in the pursuit of the speculative sciences.[15] So the study of letters is particularly suitable for religious, since they are more dedicated than other people to taming the lusts of the flesh because of their chastity and abstinence.

That they can laudably devote themselves to the study of secular subjects as well as the study of sacred texts is manifestly to be inferred from what Jerome says in a letter to the monk Pammachius:

---

11. Ibid. 53.9 (PL 22:549).
12. Ibid. 125.18 (PL 22:1082), 125.8 (PL 22:1077).
13. Gregory, *Reg. Past.* 2.11 (PL 77:50A).
14. Cf. above p. 364, note 6.
15. Averroes, *In Phys.* 7 comm. 20.

"If you love the captive woman, that is, secular wisdom, and are enthralled by her beauty, shave her head and cut off the lure of her hair and her bejewelled words as well as paring her nails, wash her with the nitre of prophecy and then rest with her and say, 'Her left hand is under my head and her right hand will embrace me,' and the captive woman will give you much offspring and she will become an Israelite instead of a woman of Moab."[16] It is clear from this that it is lawful even for monks to learn secular sciences, provided they prune away anything wrong that is found there, in accordance with the rule of sacred scripture.

Again, Augustine says, "If those who are called philosophers say anything true and adapted to our faith, particularly the Platonists, far from shunning their words, we ought to claim them back for our own use as having being unjustly appropriated by the philosophers."[17]

On Daniel 1:8 ("Daniel proposed in his heart . . . ") the Gloss comments: "He refuses to eat from the king's table in case he would be defiled, so if he had thought the wisdom and teaching of the Egyptians to be sinful he would never have learned it; but he learns it, not to follow it, but to assess it and refute it. If someone who is ignorant of their art writes against the astrologers, or someone who is innocent of philosophy campaigns against philosophers, even the most laughable people will laugh at them."[18]

From all of these texts it is clear that study among religious should be commended and particularly study of the scriptures, especially in the case of people who are appointed to be preachers.

In response to the points raised above:

(1) When it says in 2 Timothy 3:7, "Always learning and never reaching knowledge of the truth," what is being criticized is not the fact that they are always learning, but the fact that they never reach knowledge of the truth, and this is what happens to people whose study makes them go astray from the truth of the faith or from uprightness. That is why the apostle goes on to say, "Reprobates whose mind is corrupt with regard to the faith" (2 Tim. 3:8).

---

16. Jerome, *Ep.* 66.8 (PL 22:644), alluding to Deut. 21:11–2 and Cant. 2:6; the Moabitess becoming an Israelite is probably an allusion to Ruth.

17. Augustine, *De Doctrina Christiana* 2.40.60.

18. Marginal Gloss (from Jerome, *Super Dan.* ad loc., PL 25:497A).

STUDY

(2) When Gregory says that the Antichrist will have preachers who possess this world's knowledge, he is referring to people who use human knowledge to lead people to worldly desires and sins. Gregory goes on immediately to cite Isaiah 18:1–2, "Woe to the land, the winged cymbal, which sends its envoys on the sea, in vessels of papyrus across the waters," on which he comments: "From papyrus paper is made. So what is meant by papyrus, if not secular knowledge? So the vessels of papyrus are the hearts of secular teachers. So sending envoys across the waters in vessels of papyrus means investing your preaching in the beliefs of people who are wise according to the flesh and enticing an unstable people into guilt."[19]

(3) This gloss refers to the preachers whom the Antichrist will scatter throughout the world after his coming, as is plain from much of what it says. But it does not follow that knowledge of the two testaments is to be regarded as a bad thing in religious, just because these preachers will abuse it, unless you are prepared to say that innocence and purity of life are also to be regarded as a bad thing because these preachers will fake them—which would be absurd.

(4) As for the point that "knowledge puffs up," this must be taken as meaning knowledge without charity, which is why the Gloss on this text says, "Knowledge puffs up if it is on its own. . . . So add charity to knowledge and knowledge will be profitable."[20] So knowledge is less dangerous in people who are applying themselves to the works of charity. And if knowledge had to be shunned because sometimes it makes people conceited, good works would have to be shunned on the same principle, because, as Augustine says, "pride lies in wait for good works to ruin them."[21]

(5) In response to the point about St. Benedict we must note that he did not abandon study as if he were recoiling from knowledge or study, but because of his fear of worldly life and society. That is why Gregory says, just before the passage quoted, "He had been sent to study the liberal arts in Rome, but he saw that many people engaged in them were proceeding along the precipitous

---

19. Gregory, *Moralia* 13.10.13 (PL 75:1023C–1024A).
20. Lombard's Gloss (PL 191:1601CD).
21. Augustine, *Rule* 1.7 (ed. L. Verheijen, I p. 420; Lawless p. 82).

611

way of vice and he pulled back his foot just when he was on the verge of going into the world, for fear that, if he touched anything of its knowledge, he too would later go headlong over the appalling cliff."[22] So in our own day too it is commendable that people abandon the secular life of students and pass over to religious life, in which they can give their time to study.

(6) "Curiosity" implies an exaggerated and disproportionate interest, so it is not only in the study of letters but in all the pursuits which occupy people's minds that any exaggerated interest, which produces curiosity, is a fault. But what the apostle is reprimanding in the text cited is the curiosity of people who were taking a degrading interest in other people's affairs in the hope of filling their bellies, as the Gloss explains.[23] And calling people who are giving their time to the study of sacred scripture "abandoned to idleness" is contrary to the Gloss on Psalm 118:82, which says, "People who do nothing but study the word of God are not being idle, nor is the person who works outwardly of more value than the person whose study is devoted to knowing God. Wisdom is the greatest of all works, and Mary, who listened, is put before Martha, who served."[24]

---

22. Gregory, *Dial*. Prol. (PL 66:126A).
23. Lombard's Gloss (PL 192:325C), taken from the Marginal Glossa Ordinaria.
24. Lombard's Gloss (PL 191:1085B).

Study
Quodlibetal Question I a.14

*Is someone who is capable of teaching others
nevertheless bound
to abandon the study of theology in order
to concentrate on the salvation of others?*

It looks as if someone who is capable of taking care of the salvation of souls is committing a sin if he spends his time in study:[1]

(1) It says in Galatians 6:10, "While we have time, let us do good." And waste of time is the worst kind of waste. So people ought not to spend all their time in study, putting off devoting their attention to the salvation of souls.

(2) Those who are perfect are bound to do what is best. Religious are perfect. Therefore religious in particular ought to leave study and apply themselves to the salvation of souls.

(3) Going astray in your morals is worse than going astray with your feet. But a superior is bound to call his subjects back, if he sees them going off course with their feet. So he is much more bound to call them back if he sees them going astray in their morals. And it is going astray to omit what is best. So a superior ought to force his subjects to drop study and turn their attention to the salvation of souls.

On the other side of the dispute, established custom counts as an argument.[2]

---

1. This seems to be a specifically Dominican question, prompted by the growing number of more or less permanent academics in the Order. One of the reasons for the increase in the number of academics was the Order's adoption of the program of studies drawn up by the commission of which Thomas was a member at the General Chapter of 1259. At first sight it appears to be contrary to the essential purpose of the Order (preaching and the salvation of souls, according to the Constitutions, ASOP 3 [1897–98] pp.32–3) that many of its best men should devote their whole lives to study and teaching. In this Quodlibet Thomas gives his emphatic defense of Dominican academics. His claim that teachers of theology, by teaching the preachers, do more than the preachers themselves do (if a preacher influences a thousand people, and a teacher teaches fifty preachers, the teacher indirectly influences fifty thousand people) is of a piece with Humbert's readiness to give far more dispensations to teachers than to preachers, on the grounds that the teachers make the preachers, but preachers can always be replaced (ed. Berthier II p.34).

2. Evidently by this time (1269) it was established practice that a significant number

Reply

A comparison can be made between two things either in general terms or with reference to some particular situation. There is no reason why something that is, in itself, preferable should not in some particular situation be less preferable. Doing philosophy is, in itself, better than making money, but in time of need making money should be given priority.[3] A precious pearl is worth more than a loaf of bread, but if you are starving you would rather have the loaf; as is says in Lamentations 1:11, "They have given all their valuables for food to revive their soul."

It must be borne in mind that in any human construction the person who plans it and is called its designer is, as such, superior to any manual laborer who carries out the work according to someone else's specifications.[4] That is why, in the case of building, the person who designs the building, even though he does no work with his hands, is paid more than the manual laborers who carve the wood and cut the stones. And in the case of spiritual building there are the equivalent of the manual laborers, who apply themselves to looking after people's souls in specific ways by administering the sacraments to them or something else of the kind. But the equivalent of the architect in this work of spiritual building is the bishops, who give the orders and plan how these other workers ought to carry out their task. This is why they are called "bishops," which means "superintendents." In a similar way teachers of theology are a kind of "architects." They investigate and teach how others ought to further the salvation of souls. So teaching theology, as such, is better and more meritorious, provided it is done with a good intention, than caring for the salvation of this or that person in particular. This is why the apostle says of himself, "Christ did not send me to baptize, but to preach the gospel" (1 Cor. 1:17), in spite of the fact that baptizing is a work which is supremely useful for the salvation of souls. Again, in 2 Timothy 2:2 the same apostle says, "Entrust these things to faithful people who will be capable of teaching others too." Rea-

---

of Dominicans remained academics all their lives, so that Thomas can appeal without further ado to "custom" (which has the force of law, according to II.II q.147 a.5 ad 3).

3. Aristotle, *Topica* 3.2 (118a10–11).

4. Cf. Aristotle, *Metaph. A* 1 (981a30–b1).

son itself shows that it is better to give an education in the things that pertain to salvation to people who can derive benefit from it for themselves and for others than it is to give instruction to simple people who can only benefit from it for themselves. However in some situations, if there is an urgent need, bishops and teachers may have to abandon their own task and devote themselves to the salvation of individual souls.

In response to the points raised above:

(1) Someone who is doing the better thing by teaching theology or who is preparing to do so by studying is not wasting any time.

(2) People can be called "perfect" in two different senses. They can be called perfect because they have attained perfection or because they are in a state of perfection.[5] Human perfection consists in charity, which unites us with God. So, with reference to the love of God, it says in Genesis 17:1, "Walk in my sight and be perfect," and with reference to the love of neighbor the Lord tells us to love our enemies and then sums up his teaching by saying, "So you are to be perfect" (Matt. 5:44–8). As for states of perfection, people are said to be in a state of perfection when they are publicly committed to something that has some connection with perfection, and that may mean one of two things. Something may be connected with perfection in the sense that it is a preliminary to perfection, preparing people for perfection, such as poverty, chastity and so on, which draw people away from the cares of worldly affairs so that they can devote themselves in greater freedom to the things of God; things like this are a sort of tool of perfection. As Jerome says in his comment

---

5. Thomas gives here a brief résumé of the doctrine of perfection he was very shortly to expound at length in his *De Perfectione*. He insists on the distinction between actual perfection and states of perfection, and the latter he identifies in a fairly deflationary way. What makes a state of perfection a "state" is that it involves a public ("solemn") commitment, either religious profession of some kind or episcopal consecration. And religious profession puts one into a "state of perfection" in that it commits people to three practices that are, in general, efficient means of acquiring actual perfection, actual perfection meaning always the perfection of charity. So Thomas does not concede that poverty, chastity or obedience are in themselves perfections (contrary to the claim being made by some Franciscans that perfection is actually constituted by material poverty; cf. Thomas of York, *Manus Que contra Omnipotentem* 2–3, ed. M. Bierbaum, *Bettelorden und Weltgeistlichkeit an der Universität Paris* [Münster, 1920], pp.43–8).

on Matthew 19:27, it is not enough for Peter to say, "See, we have left everything," he adds the really perfect thing, "And we have followed you." So people who practice voluntary poverty and chastity have got something which is a preparation for perfection, but they are not yet said to be in a state of perfection, unless they commit themselves to such practices by solemn profession. To be in a "state" of some kind implies something public and permanent, as we can see in the case of civic freedom, marriage and things like that.

Another way in which something is connected with the perfection of charity is by being a consequence of it, and that means taking on a responsibility for the souls of others. It is a mark of perfect charity to give up the delights of the contemplative life for God's sake, though one would prefer not to, and take up the business of the active life to win the salvation of one's neighbors. So people who attend to the salvation of their neighbors are in possession of one of the consequences of perfection, but they are not in a state of perfection, except for bishops, who are publicly consecrated to undertake responsibility for souls. Archdeacons and parish priests are rather in the position of being deputed to do a certain job than in that of being placed in a state of perfection. So only religious and bishops are called "perfect," in the sense of being in a state of perfection, which is why religious sometimes become bishops, but never archdeacons or parish priests. So if it is said that those who are perfect are bound to do what is best, this is true if it is meant to apply to those who are in possession of perfect charity and are perfect in that sense, for people like that are bound by an inner law which puts them under an obligation by prompting their will, and so they are obliged by their degree of perfection to do exactly what they do. But if the same claim is made about people who are called "perfect" because they are in a state of perfection, that is, bishops and religious, it is not true, because bishops are bound only within the limits of the pastoral responsibility they have undertaken and religious are bound only by the things to which their profession commits them. Otherwise there would be an unlimited obligation, and nature, art and law are all characterized by limits. But even if we grant that the perfect are always bound to do what is best, it would not prove the point being made, as is clear from our discussion.

(3) Though a superior is bound to call his subjects back from every kind of evil, he is not bound to lead them into everything that is best. And anyway this argument is irrelevant too in the present context, as are all the rest.[6]

---

6. "All the rest" implies that there may have been other arguments brought forward against the Dominican academics of the same kind as the ones Thomas dismisses as irrelevant.

Poverty
Summa Theologiae II.II
Question 188 a.7

Does it detract from the perfection of religious
life to possess anything in common?

Surely it does detract from the perfection of religious life to possess something in common:[1]

(1) The Lord says, "If you want to be perfect, go and sell all you have and give to the poor,"[2] which makes it clear that it is part of the perfection of the Christian life to do without worldly wealth. But if you possess something in common you are not doing without worldly wealth. Therefore you will evidently not fully attain the perfection of the Christian life.

(2) It is part of the perfection envisaged by the counsels that we should be without worldly cares. That is why the apostle, in his advice about virginity, says, "I want you to be free from care."[3] But keeping something in reserve for the future is an aspect of worrying about this present life. And the Lord forbids his disciples this kind of worry: "Do not be anxious for tomorrow."[4] So, on the face of it, possessing something in common does detract from the perfection of the Christian life.

(3) Common wealth belongs in a sort of way to the individuals in the community. That is why Jerome says about some such people, "They are richer as monks than they were in the world, and under Christ in his poverty they possess resources they never had under the devil in his wealth. The church sighs to find people rich, who were beggars when they belonged to the world."[5]

---

1. The Franciscans were arguing insistently that it did detract from the perfection of religious life to own anything in common: cf. John Pecham, *Tractatus Pauperis 5*, ed. A. van den Wyngaert (Paris, 1925), pp. 48–69 (written in 1270).

2. Matt. 19.21.

3. 1 Cor. 7:32.

4. Matt. 6:34.

5. Jerome, *Ep.* 60.11 (PL 22:596).

It detracts from the perfection of religious life for an individual to possess any personal wealth, so it also detracts from the perfection of religious life to have anything in common.

(4) Gregory tells the story of a certain very holy man called Isaac, whose disciples humbly intimated that he should accept for the use of the monastery any properties that he was offered; but he, anxious to guard his poverty, kept to his firm decision, saying, "A monk who seeks property on earth is no monk."[6] And this refers to common property, offered to the monastery for the use of all the monks. So possessing anything in common clearly eliminates the perfection of religious life.

(5) When the Lord was explaining to his disciples the perfection of religious life he said, "Do not possess gold or silver or money in your purse or a bag when you travel."[7] In these words, as Jerome says, he is attacking the philosophers who are popularly called "stick-and-bag-men"[8] for carrying their stores with them, while despising the world and treating everything as nothing.[9] So it appears that it does detract from the perfection of religious life to keep anything in reserve, whether privately or in common.

On the other hand:

Prosper says, and this is cited in the *Decretum*, "It is sufficiently demonstrated both that private property should be despised for the sake of perfection and that it is possible without any risk to perfection to possess the church's resources, which are of course held in common."[10]

REPLY

As we have said above, perfection does not consist essentially in poverty, but in following Christ.[11] As Jerome says, "Because it is not enough to abandon everything Peter adds what is really perfect,

---

6. Gregory, *Dial.* 3.14 (PL 77:245A).

7. Matt. 10:9–10.

8. This seems to have been a nickname for the Cynics (cf. *Greek Anthology* XI 410.1), who were the "mendicants" among the ancient philosophers.

9. Jerome, *in Matt.* I 10.10.

10. Julianus Pomerius, *De Vita Cont.* 2.9 (PL 59:453BC), quoted (and attributed to Prosper) in Gratian, *Decretum* C.12 q.1 c.13 (ed. Friedberg I col.681).

11. II.II q.184 a.3, especially the ad 1.

namely, 'We have followed you.' "[12] Poverty is a tool or a practice whereby we may come to perfection. This is why abba Moses says, "Fasting, keeping vigil, reciting the scriptures, nakedness, lacking all resources, these things are not perfection, but they are the tools of perfection."[13]

The lack of all resources, or poverty, is a tool of perfection inasmuch as various obstacles to charity are removed by the absence of wealth. There are three important obstacles of this kind. The first is the anxiety which often accompanies wealth. This is why the Lord says, "The seed sown among thorns is the person who hears the word and then the cares of this world and the deceitfulness of riches choke the word."[14] The second obstacle is love of wealth, which increases with the possession of wealth. So Jerome says that, because it is difficult to make light of wealth if you possess it, the Lord did not say that it is "impossible" for anyone who is rich to enter the kingdom of heaven, but that it is "difficult."[15] The third obstacle is vainglory or conceit, which is a product of wealth. As it says in Psalm 48:7, "They trust in their strength, they glory in the quantity of their riches."

The first obstacle cannot be entirely divorced from riches, whether they are great or small, because people cannot help but be anxious in some way or another about obtaining or protecting external goods. But if such things are only sought or possessed in small quantities, enough for the sheer maintenance of life, then the anxiety that goes with them does not get in the way to any great extent. It does not therefore detract from the perfection of the Christian life, because the Lord does not ban all anxiety, but only excessive and harmful anxiety. So on the text, "Do not be anxious about your lives, wondering what you are going to eat," Augustine comments, "He does not say that they should not take steps to obtain what they need of these things, he says that they should not have their eye on these things and do what they are told to do, in the way of preaching the gospel, for the sake of these things."[16] But an abundant possession of wealth makes for a corresponding abundance of anxiety, and

---

12. Jerome, *in Matt.* III 19.27.
13. Cassian, *Conf.* 1.7.
14. Matt. 13:22.
15. Jerome, *in Matt.* III 19.23.
16. Augustine, *De Opere Monachorum* 26.34 (PL 40:573), commenting on Matt. 6:25.

this does greatly distract and hinder people's minds from being totally given to God's service. And the other two obstacles, love of wealth and conceit or glorying in wealth, do not arise except in the case of abundant wealth.

It does make a difference, however, with regard to this whether wealth, be it abundant or modest, is possessed privately or in common. Anxiety over one's private wealth is part of the self-love with which people love themselves in a worldly way, but anxiety over common goods is part of charitable love, which "does not seek its own,"[17] but attends to the common interest. And since religious life is meant to serve the perfection of charity, which is made perfect by a love of God which goes so far as to make light of oneself,[18] the possession of any private property is quite incompatible with the perfection of religious life.[19] But anxiety over the goods of the community can be a part of charity, even though it may interfere with some higher act of charity, such as the contemplation of God or the instruction of one's neighbors.

This makes it clear that owning vast wealth in common,

---

17. 1 Cor. 13:5.

18. Augustine, *Civ. Dei* 14.28.

19. Common ownership is not incompatible with effective private control. By this time the Dominicans effectively recognized that certain things, especially books, "belonged" to individual friars for all practical purposes. As early as 1233 a General Chapter refers to "the books of deceased brethren," and says they should be given to someone else rather than sold outside the Order (MOPH III p. 4:5–7), and in 1234 the Chapter rules that the brethren may not sell each other books at a higher price than they themselves paid for them (ibid. p. 5:12–3). At any rate by 1251 there is evidence of individual friars having (effectively) their "own" money to spend on books (Douais p. 45 III). Is it too fanciful to see in II.II q.66 a.2 a reflection of Thomas' views of community life, as found in a Dominican context: The advantage of a system of private property is that people are more likely to get round to obtaining something for themselves than they are for the community (if it is for the community most people will leave it to someone else to go and get it); it also makes for less confusion if individuals are responsible for getting things for themselves; and finally it is less likely that people will quarrel over things. And there is no harm in private property, as long as people are generous in lending things. That sounds to me like a comment on Dominican life! In the stricter days at the beginning of the Order, when the rule was made that nobody was to be granted any guaranteed right to the use of any book (*Primitive Constitutions* I 15, in A. H. Thomas p. 325; this regulation was probably added in the early 1230s, and it stayed in the constitutions in II 14 after Raymund of Peñafort's revision of them and after Humbert's revision), it was apparently necessary to establish procedures at the General Chapter for resolving quarrels between the brethren about books (*Prim. Const.* II 21, ed. cit. p. 357). Later on Richard de Bury singles out the Dominicans for special praise because of their unrivalled generosity in lending their books (*Philobiblon* 8, ed. A. Altamura [Naples, 1954] p. 103).

whether in the form of possessions or in the form of properties,[20] is an obstacle to perfection, even if it does not absolutely prevent it.[21] But owning external things in common, whether possessions or properties, enough to sustain one's life, does not interfere with the perfection of religious life, if poverty is considered in relationship to the common goal of all forms of religious life, namely the freedom to concentrate on God's service.[22]

If we consider poverty in relationship with the specific purposes of different kinds of religious life, then, in view of their different goals, different degrees of poverty will be appropriate to them. And, from the point of view of poverty, each form of religious life will be more or less perfect depending on how well its poverty is adapted to its purpose.

It is clear that the outward, bodily works of the active life call for a good supply of external goods, while few things are needed for contemplation.[23] So the philosopher says that many things are needed for the accomplishment of deeds, and the greater and better the deed is, the more will be needed; but speculation needs none of these things for its functioning. All it needs are the essentials, and everything more will be a hindrance to it.[24] So a religious order which is devoted to the bodily activities of the active life, like the military orders or the hospitallers, would obviously be imperfect if it lacked common wealth.

---

20. *Mobilia siue immobilia*, literally "movable or immovable" (cf. French "meubles" and "immeubles").

21. In a propaganda document for the Dominicans, trying to prove that they are the best Order, an unknown writer turns St. Bernard's eulogy of the Cistercians against them and claims his tribute rather for the Dominicans; the Dominicans are much closer to the poverty of the apostolic church, whereas the Cistercians, "far from selling fields, acquire one field after another" (AFP 6 [1936] p. 148). T. Kaeppeli, who edited the document, suggests it may come from the period of the Oxford quarrel with the Franciscans (1269–70) (ibid. p. 144), but it seems to me to belong more to the 1240s, the time of the quarrel reported by Matthew Paris (cf. below, note 16 on II.II q.188 a.6).

22. Thomas argues that religious life is essentially about the service of God in II.II q.186 a.1.

23. What about books? Thomas is absolutely silent about this facet of the question. Kilwardby, in his letter to Dominican novices (written in 1269–70, probably) appears to maintain that books are needed for the work of the Order and are therefore not covered even by the Pauline principle of austerity (1 Tim. 6:8), which only applies to bodily requirements (Tugwell, *Early Dominicans* p. 152). On Dominicans' books cf. Amargier, *Études sur l'Ordre Dominicain* pp. 53–78.

24. Aristotle, *Ethics* 10.8.5–6 (1178b1–5).

Religious orders devoted to the contemplative life, on the other hand, are more or less perfect depending on how free their poverty makes them from anxiety about temporal things. Any form of religious life is hindered by concern about temporal things in proportion to the degree of concern about spiritual things which is required for it. And it is obvious that a religious order founded for the purpose of contemplating and passing on to others what it has contemplated by teaching and preaching calls for a greater concern about spiritual things than one founded solely for contemplation. So that kind of religious order needs the kind of poverty which involves the least anxiety. And clearly what makes for the least anxiety is the practice of keeping the things that people need to use after obtaining them at some suitable time.[25]

So three levels of poverty befit the three classes of religious order which we identified above. Orders devoted to the bodily works of the active life need to have plenty of wealth in common. Orders devoted to contemplation are best served by having modest possessions, unless they are also expected to offer hospitality and to help the poor, either personally or through their agents. But Orders devoted to passing on to others what they have contemplated need a way of life that is to the greatest extent possible unencumbered by external concerns, and this is achieved by keeping their few necessities of life after obtaining them at some suitable time.

And this is what the Lord, who instituted poverty, taught by his own example. He had a purse, entrusted to Judas, in which the offerings that he was given were kept (John 12:6).[26] It is no objection

---

25. Thomas is here touching on the slightly different problem of whether it is proper to keep things in store (whether or not you are regarded as owning them). Both Dominic and Francis favored living from one day to the next, without keeping anything in reserve for tomorrow (for Dominic, see MOPH XVI p. 150; for Francis, cf. K. Esser, *Anfänge und ursprüngliche Zielsetzungen des Ordens der Minderbrüder* [Leiden, 1966], pp. 251–2), but this was soon found to be a nuisance. In 1240 the Dominican General Chapter legitimized the practice of keeping enough basic supplies for a year in advance (MOPH III p. 15:23–4), and evidently the Franciscans too made some concessions in the matter: according to Hugh of Digne bread and wine could be kept for a week and some other supplies for a month at a time, and there were some friars who wanted permission to store enough for a year at a time (ed. cit. pp. 134, 160). Thomas of Cantimpré, though, indicates that the Franciscans were still going out to beg every day in about 1260, while the Dominicans contented themselves with an annual quest in the late summer (Tugwell, *Early Dominicans* p. 134). Whereas Hugh of Digne regards it as an unfortunate, if necessary, concession to keep anything in store (ed. cit. p. 135), Thomas plainly regards it as a perfection, if what you are trying to do is thereby facilitated.

26. Franciscan writers were quick to point out that it was Judas who had the purse,

to this that Jerome says, "If you care to raise a difficulty about the fact that Judas was carrying money in the purse, we reply that he considered it wrong to turn to his own use the money that was meant for the poor,"[27] by paying the tax, that is. This does not contradict what we are saying, because the foremost among those "poor" were his own disciples, for whose needs the money in Christ's purse was spent: in John 4:8 it says that the disciples "went into the city to buy food" and in John 13:29 that they "thought, since Judas had the purse, that Jesus had said to him, 'Buy what we need for the festival,' or told him to give something to the needy."

This makes it clear that it is in line with the perfection that Christ taught by his example to keep money or anything else in common either for the support of the religious themselves or for the support of other poor people. Similarly, after the Resurrection the disciples, from whom all religious life derives,[28] kept the money raised from selling people's estates and "gave to each one according to the needs of each."[29]

In response to the points raised above:

(1) As we have already explained,[30] the Lord's words do not mean that poverty in itself is perfection, but that it is a tool of perfection and, as we have shown,[31] the least of the three main tools of perfection, because the vow of chastity is more important than the vow of poverty and the vow of obedience is more important than either of them. And since tools are not wanted for their own sake, but for the sake of the purpose they are used for, it is not true that anything is better just because it uses bigger tools; what makes it better is that its tools are better adapted to its purpose. A doctor does not cure his patients any the better just because

---

and they seem to have used "purse-owner" as a routine term of abuse. Cf. Pecham, *Contra Kilwardby*, in Kingsford, Little and Tocco p. 131; *Regula non Bullata* 8.7; Francis, *Admon.* 4.3.

27. Jerome, *In Matt.* III 17.27 (commenting on why Christ could not pay the temple tax in Matt. 17:23–6, even though Judas was carrying a purse with money in it).

28. The belief that religious life goes back to the apostles and the Jerusalem community, propagated by Cassian (*Conf.* 18.5), was by this time commonplace.

29. Acts 4:34–5.

30. II.II q.184 a.3 ad 1.

31. Cf. II.II q.186 a.8, though Thomas does not strictly prove that poverty is lower than chastity; but it is implied, inasmuch as obedience is rated highest, as offering the highest gift to God (ourselves as a whole), and clearly chastity offers God a higher gift (our bodies) than poverty, which merely concerns external goods.

he gives them more medicine, but only inasmuch as he gives them the medicine that suits their diseases. In the same way the excellence of a religious order is not measured by the degree of its poverty, but by the extent to which its poverty is adapted to the purpose of religious life in general and the specific purpose of the particular Order. And even if it were to be granted that increased poverty would make an Order more perfect precisely in being poorer, it will still not make it more perfect in any unqualified sense. There might be another Order which was superior in matters concerning chastity and obedience, and in that case it would be more perfect in general terms, in that its superiority concerns things which are themselves, in general terms, superior.

(2) When the Lord says, "Do not be anxious for tomorrow," this does not mean that nothing is to be kept in reserve for the future. That would in fact be dangerous, as St. Anthony shows, when he says, "We have seen people pursuing such a lack of all resources that they could not bear to have even one day's livelihood or even one penny left over," and various other similar things, "and we have seen them suddenly beguiled in such a way that they could not bring the work they had started to a fitting conclusion."[32] And, as Augustine says, if the Lord's saying, "Do not be anxious for tomorrow," were taken to mean that nothing should be set aside for the next day, it could not be followed by people who shut themselves away from the sight of other people for days on end, living in a great concentration on their prayers. And he goes on, "Or maybe they are all the holier the less like birds they are?"[33] Later on he says, "If the gospel is quoted at them to persuade them to keep nothing back for the next day, they reply, 'So why did the Lord himself have a purse in which to keep his money all together? Why was grain sent to the holy fathers so long in advance, when there was a famine impending? Why did the apostles collect what was required for the needs of the saints?' "[34]

According to Jerome, what is meant by "Do not be anxious for tomorrow" is this: "It is enough for us to think about the pres-

---

32. Cassian, *Conf.* 2.2.
33. Augustine, *De Opere Monachorum* 23.29 (PL 40:570–1).
34. Ibid. 24.31 (PL 40:571).

ent; the future is uncertain, let us leave it to God."[35] According to Chrysostom what it means is: "The labor you endure to get what is necessary is labor enough; do not add to it by seeking more than you need."[36] According to Augustine it means: "When we are doing something good, we should not be thinking of temporal things, which is what is meant by 'tomorrow,' but of the things of eternity."[37]

(3) Jerome's words apply where there is an excess of wealth which is treated as private property or which is abused in such a way that all the individuals in the community become cocky and begin to run riot. But they do not apply to modest wealth, kept in common solely to provide the sustenance which all the individuals need, because the fact that the individuals use what they need to stay alive is justified by exactly the same principle that justifies the community as a whole in keeping its resources.

(4) Isaac refused to accept possessions because he was afraid that it would lead to unnecessary wealth, whose abuse would then interfere with the perfection of religious life. So Gregory goes on to say, "He was as afraid to lose his carefree poverty as rich misers are keen to keep their doomed wealth."[38] But it does not say that he refused to accept certain necessities which could be kept in common in order to sustain their lives.

(5) The philosopher calls bread and wine and things like that "natural wealth" and he calls money "artificial wealth."[39] On that basis some philosophers refused to use money, but they used other things, and this was meant to be "living according to nature."[40] So Jerome, on the passage quoted, cites the Lord's verdict, forbidding both kinds of wealth in the same terms, to show that it comes to the same thing whether we have money or whether we have other things that life needs.[41] But though the

---

35. Jerome, *in Matt.* I 6.34.

36. Pseudo-Chrysostom, *Op. Imp.* 16 (PG 56:724).

37. Augustine, *De Sermone Domini* II 17.56.

38. Gregory, *Dial.* 2.14 (PL 77:245B).

39. Aristotle, *Pol.* 1.9 (1257b19–20), with Thomas' comment on it (Marietti ed. para.121).

40. Life "according to nature" was a widely accepted ideal among ancient philosophers, and the Cynics were certainly among those who espoused it. What Thomas' source is for the belief that they regarded money as "unnatural," I do not know.

41. This is Thomas' interpretation of Jerome rather than Jerome's interpretation of the gospel.

Lord ruled that such things should not be carried with them on their journeys by the people he sent out to preach, he did not say that they should not be kept in common. But we have already shown above how these words of the Lord are to be understood.[42]

---

42. II.II q.185 a.6 and 2.

The Best Religious Order
Summa Theologiae II.II
Question 188 a.6

Is a religious order devoted to the contemplative life better than one devoted to the works of the active life?

It does not look as if a religious order[1] devoted to the contemplative life is better than one devoted to the works of the active life:

(1) It says in the Decretals, "A greater good is preferable to a lesser good and in the same way the benefit of the community is preferable to the benefit of individuals, and in this case teaching is rightly put before silence and concern before contemplation and toil before rest."[2] But what makes a religious order better is that its goal is a greater good. So religious orders which are geared to the active life are presumably better than those which are geared to the contemplative life.

(2) Every form of religious life is meant to lead to the perfection of charity, as we have already argued.[3] But on Hebrews 12:4 ("You have not yet resisted to the point of shedding your blood") the Gloss says, "There is no love more perfect in this life than that which the martyrs attained, who struggled with sin even to the point of shedding their blood."[4] And struggling to the point of shedding one's blood belongs properly to the military orders, and they are part of the active life. So it looks as if that kind of religious life is best.

(3) Any religious order is surely all the more perfect the more strict and austere it is. But there is no reason why some forms of active religious life should not be more austere in their observances

---

1. It is difficult to translate *religio* consistently, and I have not tried to do so in this article; it covers both what we call a "religious order" and its "religious life."

2. Decretals of Gregory IX, 3.31.18 (ed. E. Friedberg, *Corpus Iuris Canonici* II [Leipzig, 1881], col. 576).

3. II.II q.186 a.1

4. Lombard's Gloss (PL 192:501D).

than religious orders aiming at the contemplative life. And so they are superior.

On the other hand:
The Lord says that the "best part" is Mary's, and she symbolizes the contemplative life.

REPLY

As we have seen, the distinction between different forms of religious life is drawn chiefly on the basis of their objectives, and secondarily on the basis of their practices.[5] And since we cannot say that one thing is better than another except on the basis of some point on which the two things differ, we must look for the superiority of one form of religious life over another chiefly in the light of their objectives and secondarily on the basis of their practices. But this calls for two different kinds of comparison. If we are comparing their objectives, that is an absolute comparison, because objectives are pursued for their own sake. But if we are comparing them on the basis of their practices, that is a relative comparison, because practices are not pursued for their own sake, but for the sake of some objective. So one kind of religious life is better than the other inasmuch as it is focused on an objective which is intrinsically superior, either because it is a greater good or because it serves a greater number of goods. But if the goal of two different religious orders is identical, then one is better than the other in a secondary way, not because its practices are quantitively greater, but because they are better adapted to the objective that order has in view. So in the *Conferences of the Fathers* Anthony's verdict is cited, giving priority to discretion, by which people regulate everything else, rather than to such observances as fasting and keeping vigil.[6]

The active life has two different kinds of work. One kind flows from the fullness of contemplation, such as teaching and preaching. This is why Gregory says that Psalm 144:7, "They will blurt out the memory of your sweetness," applies to the perfect returning from their contemplation.[7] And this is better than mere contempla-

---

5. II.II q.188 a.1.
6. Cassian, *Conferences* 2.2–4.
7. Gregory, *Hom. Ezek.* 1.5.12 (PL 76:826B).

tion. It is a greater thing to give light than simply to have light, and in the same way it is a greater thing to pass on to others what you have contemplated than just to contemplate.[8] The other kind of active work consists entirely in external business, like almsgiving, hospitality,[9] and such like. And these are inferior to the works of contemplation, except in an emergency, as what we said above makes clear.[10]

So the highest rating among religious orders must be awarded to those which are geared to teaching and preaching, and they are the ones that are closest to the perfection of the bishops. Here as in other things "the borders of the first level of reality are joined to the beginnings of the second level," as Dionysius says.[11] The second place is awarded to forms of religious life aiming at contemplation. And the third place is awarded to those which are busy about external activities.

Within each of these categories there is room for degrees of superiority inasmuch as one religious order may be devoted to a higher activity than another in the same class. Among the works of the active life redeeming captives is higher than running hostels,[12] and among the works of the contemplative life prayer is superior to reading.[13]

---

8. This is the source of the famous Dominican adage, *contemplari et contemplata aliis tradere* (taken over by the Second Vatican Council and applied to all priests: *Presbyterorum Ordinis* 13). It has often been misunderstood by being taken out of the context of Thomas' thoroughly intellectual understanding of *contemplatio*. It would not be too misleading to translate him as saying "pass on to others what you have studied."

9. "Hospitality," taking in "guests" (*hospites*), especially in the present context, probably means something more than just being nice to the odd visitor and envisages the fairly systematic provision of accommodation and care for poor pilgrims and other travellers and for the sick, this being a corporal work of mercy practiced on quite a significant scale in this period. Our modern words "hostel," "hospice," "hotel," "hospital," all derive from this same Latin root, indicating something of the breadth of its application.

10. II.II q.182 a.1.

11. Dionysius, *DN* 7.3 (PG 3:872B).

12. The Trinitarian Order was founded in 1198 for the purpose of ransoming captives (there is a useful article on this Order by G. Cippollone in *Cahiers de Fanjeaux* 18 [1983] pp. 135–56); the Mercedarians were founded in about 1220 for the same purpose. There were various groups of religious involved in running hostels for poor pilgrims, hospices for the sick, and so on, the most renowned being the Hospitallers, founded at the end of the eleventh century. In his *De Eruditione Predicatorum* Humbert of Romans provides material for sermons to Trinitarians, Hospitallers, brothers and sisters living in hospitals and brothers and sisters living in leprosaria.

13. Reading and prayer were the two classic components of Christian piety (cf. Tug-

We can also consider other ways in which one religious order can be better than another: it may be designed to do more works or its regulations may be better adapted to the achievement of its purpose.[14]

In response to the points raised above:

(1) This decretal is talking about the orientation of the active life to the salvation of souls.[15]

(2) Military orders are more directly designed to lead to the shedding of their enemies' blood than to the shedding of their own blood, which is the special privilege of martyrs. But there is nothing to stop religious of this kind attaining the merit of martyrdom in some cases and in that respect excelling other religious, just as in some cases active works are sometimes given precedence over contemplation.

(3) It is not the strictness and austerity of its observances that makes a form of religious life particularly commendable, as St. Anthony says.[16] As it says in Isaiah 58:5, "Is this the fast I have

---

well, *Ways of Imperfection* p. 103) and it was conventional also to say that, if it was necessary to choose between them, prayer should be given priority (cf. Isidore, *Sent.* 3.8.1, PL 83:679A). But in the thirteenth century the mood of piety was changing and reading was going out of fashion, especially in "devout" circles, so the shrewd author of the *Ancrene Riwle* evidently considered it necessary to turn the tables: "Often, dear sisters, you should pray less for to read the more" (M 286; modern English translation by M. B. Salu [London, 1955], p. 127—though "fixed prayers" is perhaps rather an overtranslation). Jordan of Saxony refused to give any priority to either of them, suggesting that choosing between prayer and study was like choosing between eating and drinking (MOPH I p. 146; Tugwell, *Early Dominicans* p. 131); Thomas would probably have agreed, though he might have pointed out that prayer does have a certain priority, in that even when we read we need enlightenment from God and should therefore pray before we read (this was certainly Thomas' own practice: cf. Tocco, FVST pp. 104–5, Ferrua pp. 75–6; the tradition of the Order has passed down a prayer which is supposedly the one Thomas used before he studied or lectured: E. Martène and U. Durand, *Veterum Scriptorum et Monumentorum Amplissima Collectio* VI [Paris, 1724], cols. 563–4; and cf. AFP 1 [1931] p. 224).

14. Thus Kilwardby argued against Franciscan attempts to lure Dominican novices away that the Dominicans are best because their régime is the best adapted to their purpose (Tugwell, *Early Dominicans* p. 150), and implicitly Thomas argues the same point in II.II q.188 a.7.

15. This rather cryptic response is unnecessarily opaque! The Decretal makes a distinction between the legitimacy (in some circumstances) of religious transferring to a different Order and the legitimacy of bishops abandoning their pastoral responsibilities. The text quoted in the objection is part of the explanation of why bishops (unlike religious) cannot just opt out of their commitments in quest of a more contemplative life.

16. Cassian 2.2. In his quiet way, Thomas is here challenging a principle that was accepted by almost all his contemporaries and was indeed by now accepted by the law of the

chosen, to afflict your soul for a day?" Austerity is taken up by religious life as being necessary to mortify the flesh but, if it is practiced without discretion it carries with it the risk of faltering, as St. Anthony points out.[17] So no religious life is superior just because it has more austere observances; what makes a form of religious life better is that its observances are more intelligently adapted to its purpose. For instance, self-control is more effectively served by mortifying the flesh by abstaining from food and drink, which is a matter of hunger and thirst, than by taking away people's clothes, which is a matter of cold and nakedness, or by bodily labor.[18]

---

church! By this time it was accepted that a religious could transfer to a stricter (*arctior*) form of religious life, even without his superior's consent, on the assumption that a stricter life was more perfect; and the classic official text for this in law was precisely the letter of Innocent III contained in the Decretal cited in the first objection of this article! Cf. J. Hourlier, *Histoire du Droit et des Institutions de l'Église en Occident*, vol. 10, *L'Age Classique: Les Religieux* [Éditions Cujas, 1974], pp. 244–9; A. H. Thomas, *De oudste Constituties van de Dominicanen* [Louvain, 1965], pp. 64–5; B. M. Bolton in W. J. Sheils, *Monks, Hermits and the Ascetic Tradition* pp. 176–7. *Arctior* means not just stricter, but more austere (cf. what Jordan of Saxony says about the earliest Dominican constitutions in *Libellus* 42), so I have tried to incorporate both notions into my translation. The whole matter was of some concern to the Dominicans, as the Franciscans claimed that theirs was the *arctior vita* and that therefore Dominicans could (and should) become Franciscans (cf. Matthew Paris, *Chronica Maiora*, ed. H. R. Luard [Rolls Series 1872–84] IV p. 279); it was no doubt in a desperate attempt to show that the Dominicans were really more austere than the Franciscans that Kilwardby turned the Franciscan boast of not wearing shoes against them and pointed out that the Dominicans did not indulge in the pleasant practice of not wearing shoes in summer (Tugwell, *Early Dominicans* p. 150). Thomas clearly thinks that the whole argument about who is most austere is silly, and he thinks that degrees of austerity are irrelevant to the discussion of whether or not it is proper for religious to move from one Order to another (II.II q.189 a.8).

17. Cassian, loc. cit.

18. The proper territory of self-control (*continentia*) is disordered appetites for things like food and sex (II.II q.155 a.2), so abstaining from food and drink is directly pertinent to it, whereas forcing people to wear less is not directly or obviously moderating any unduly hectic desire (and might, if carried far enough, actually stimulate an undue appetite for food, in pursuit of warmth, or for sex); similarly bodily labor has no direct connection with the moderation of our appetites.

Abbreviations and
Select Bibliography

AFH = *Archivum Franciscanum Historicum.*

AFP = *Archivum Fratrum Praedicatorum.*

AGOP = Dominican Archives, Santa Sabina, Rome.

AHDLMA = *Archives d'Histoire Doctrinale et Littéraire du Moyen Age.*

Alberto di Castello. *Cronica de Magistris Generalibus.* In *Tabula Privilegiorum.* Venice, 1504.

ALKGMA = *Archiv für Litteratur- und Kirchengeschichte des Mittelalters.*

AMDU = G. Meyer and A. Zimmermann, eds. *Albertus Magnus–Doctor Universalis 1280/1980.* Mainz, 1980.

Anim. = Albert. *De Animalibus.* Ed. H. Stadler. Beiträge XV–XVI. Münster, 1916, 1921.

Archives de Philosophie 43 (1980) 4: VIIe centenaire d'Albert le Grand.

ASOP = *Analecta (Sacri) Ordinis Praedicatorum.*

AT = A. Fries, ed. *Albertus Magnus, Ausgewählte Texte.* Darmstadt, 1981. (Cited by the number of the text, in places where Fries offers a more reliable edition than any other which is available.)

B = A. Borgnet, ed. *B.Alberti Magni Opera Omnia.* Paris, 1890–9. (Cited by volume number and page numbers.)

Beiträge = *Beiträge zur Geschichte der Philosophie (und Theologie) des Mittelalters.*

Bonaventure. *Opera Omnia.* Quaracchi, 1882–1902.

BOP = *Bullarium Ordinis Praedicatorum* I. Ed. A. Bremond. Rome, 1729.

Boyle, L. E. *The Setting of the* Summa Theologiae *of Saint Thomas.* Toronto, 1982.

Callaey, F. "La Vita del B. Alberto Magno." ASOP 20 (1932) pp. 475–530.

CC = Corpus Christianorum, Turnhout.

CH = Dionysius. *Celestial Hierarchy.* Ed. R. Roques, G. Heil and M. de Gandillac (SC 58bis). Paris, 1970.

Chart. = H. Denifle and E. Chatelain, eds. *Chartularium Universitatis Parisiensis.* Paris, 1889–97.

Chenu, M. D. *Introduction à l'Étude de Saint Thomas d'Aquin.* Montreal/Paris, 1950.

Col. = Editio Coloniensis of the works of Albert. (Cited by volume and page numbers, sometimes with line numbers as well).

Const. = Dominican Constitutions. (Cited according to various editions, see p. 101, note 54.)

Craemer-Ruegenberg, I. *Albertus Magnus.* Munich, 1980.

Creytens, R., and Künzle, P., eds. *Xenia Medii Aevi Historiam Illustrantia Oblata Thomae Kaeppeli OP.* Rome, 1978.

Davies, B., ed. *Language, Meaning and God, Essays in Honour of Herbert McCabe OP.* London, 1987.

Dion. Ep. = Dionysius. *Epistles.*

DN = Dionysius. *Divine Names.*

Dondaine, A. *Secrétaires de Saint Thomas.* Rome, 1956.

Douais, C., ed. *Acta Capitulorum Provincialium Ordinis Fratrum Praedicatorum.* Toulouse, 1894.

Dufeil, M. M. *Guillaume de Saint-Amour et la Polémique Universitaire Parisienne 1250–1259.* Paris, 1972.

Eckert, W. P. Biographical introduction to AT, pp. VII–XXX.

EH = Dionysius. *Ecclesiastical Hierarchy.*

Entrich, M., ed. *Albertus Magnus, sein Leben und seine Bedeutung.* Graz/Vienna/Cologne, 1982.

Eubel, C. *Hierarchia Catholica Medii Aevi* I. repr. Padua, 1968.

Ferrua, A., ed. *Thomae Aquinatis Vitae Fontes Praecipuae.* Alba, 1968.

Foster, K. *The Life of St. Thomas Aquinas: Biographical Documents.* London, 1959.

Freed, J. B. *The Friars and German Society.* Cambridge, Mass., 1977.

FVST = *Fontes Vitae Sancti Thomae.* Ed. D. Prümmer and M. H. Laurent in fascicles attached to *Revue Thomiste* (1911–1937).

Grabmann, M. *Die Werke des hl. Thomas von Aquin.* Beiträge XXII/1–2. Münster, 1949.

Herford, Henry of. *Liber de Rebus Memorabilibus.* Ed. A. Potthast. Göttingen, 1859.

Hinnebusch, W. A. *History of the Dominican Order.* New York, 1966, 1973.

Hödl, L. "Albert der Grosse und die Wende der lateinischen Philosophie im 13 Jahrhundert." In *Virtus Politica* (Festgabe für Alfons Hufnagel), Stuttgart/Bad Cannstatt, 1974, pp. 251–275.

————."Über die averroistische Wende der lateinischen Philosophie des Mittelalters im 13 Jahrhundert." RTAM 39 (1972), pp. 171–204.

Hugh of St. Cher. *Postillae in Bibliam.* Venice, 1703.

Humbert of Romans. *Opera de Vita Regulari.* Ed. J. J. Berthier. Rome, 1888; reprinted Turin, 1956.

Kaeppeli, T. *Scriptores Ordinis Praedicatorum Medii Aevi.* Rome, 1970ff.

Kovach, F.J. and R.W.Shahan, eds., *Albert the Great: Commemorative Essays.* Norman, Oklahoma 1980.

Leccisotti, T., *S Tommaso d'Aquino e Montecassino.* Montecassino, 1965.

Leg. Col. = Anon. Life of Albert. Ed. P. von Loë. *Analecta Bollandiana* 19 (1900): 272–84.

Leonine = Editio Leonina of the works of St. Thomas Aquinas.

Loë, P. von. "De Vita et Scriptis B. Alberti Magni." *Analecta Bollandiana* 20 (1901): 273–316.

Lombard, Peter. *Sententiae in IV Libris Distinctae.* Grottaferrata, 1971, 1981.

Luis of Valladolid. *Tabula Alberti Magni.* In ASOP 20 (1932): 752–61.

Mandonnet, P. "Thomas d'Aquin, novice prêcheur." *Revue Thomiste* 7 (1924): 243–67, 370–90, 529–47; 8 (1925): 222–49, 393–416, 489–533.

Martène, E., and U.Durand, eds. *Veterum Scriptorum . . . Amplissima Collectio* VI. Paris, 1724.

MGH (SS) = Monumenta Germaniae Historica (Scriptores).

McInerny, R. *Ethica Thomistica.* Washington, D.C., 1982.

————. *St. Thomas Aquinas.* repr. Notre Dame, 1982.

MOPH = Monumenta Ordinis Praedicatorum Historica.

MT = Dionysius, *Mystical Theology.*

Ostlender, H., ed. *Studia Albertina.* Beiträge Supplementband IV. Münster, 1952.

Patfoort, A. *Thomas d'Aquin, les Clés d'une Théologie.* Paris, 1983.

Peter of Prussia. *Legenda Alberti Magni.* With [Albert], *De Adhaerendo Deo.* Antwerp, 1621.

ABBREVIATIONS AND SELECT BIBLIOGRAPHY

PG = Migne. *Patrologia Graeca.*

Philip the Chancellor. *Summa de Bono.* Ed. N. Wicki. Berne, 1985.

Pieper, J. *The Silence of St. Thomas.* New York, 1957.

PL = Migne. *Patrologia Latina.*

Potthast = A. Potthast. *Regesta Pontificum Romanorum 1198–1304.* Berlin, 1874–75. (Cited either by the number of the document referred to or by page number.)

Prim. Const. = A. H. Thomas. *De oudste Constituties van de Dominicanen.* Louvain, 1965.

Principe, W. H. *Thomas Aquinas' Spirituality.* Toronto, 1984.

QE = J. Quétif and J. Echard. *Scriptores Ordinis Praedicatorum.* Paris, 1719, 1721.

QF = Quellen and Forschungen zur Geschichte des Dominikanerordens in Deutschland.

Revue des Sciences Philosophiques et Théologiques 65 (1981) 1: Pour le VIIe centenaire d'Albert le Grand.

RIS = Muratori. *Rerum Italicarum Scriptores.*

RSPT = *Revue des Sciences Philosophiques et Théologiques.*

RTAM = *Recherches de Théologie Ancienne et Médiévale.*

Rudolph of Nijmegen. *Legenda Alberti Magni.* Ed. H. C. Scheeben. Cologne, 1928.

St. Thomas Aquinas 1274–1974, Commemorative Studies. Toronto, 1974.

SC = Sources Chrétiennes. Paris.

Scheeben, H. C. *Albert der Grosse: zur Chronologie seines Lebens,* QF 27. Vechta, 1931.

Schneyer, J. B. *Repertorium der lateinischen Sermones des Mittelalters.* Beiträge XLIII 1–9. Münster, 1969–1980.

Scuole degli Ordini Mendicanti (Convegni del Centro di Studi sulla Spiritualità Medievale XVII). Todi, 1978.

Thomassen, B. *Metaphysik als Lebensform: Untersuchungen zur Grundlegung der Metaphysik im Metaphysikkommentar Alberts des Grossen.* Beiträge NF 27. Münster, 1985.

Tugwell, S. *Early Dominicans* (Classics of Western Spirituality). New York, 1982.

Vicaire, M. H. *Histoire de St. Dominique,* revised ed. Paris, 1982.

Walz, A. and P. Novarina. *Saint Thomas d'Aquin.* Louvain, 1962.

Weisheipl, *Albert* = J. A. Weisheipl, ed. *Albertus Magnus and the Sciences.* Toronto, 1980.

Weisheipl, *Thomas* = J. A. Weisheipl. *Friar Thomas d'Aquino*. Revised edition. Washington, D.C., 1983.

Wicki, N. *Die Lehre von her himmlischen Seligkeit in der mittelalterlichen Scholastik von Petrus Lombardus bis Thomas von Aquin*. Fribourg, 1954.

Wielockx, R., ed. *Aegidii Romani Opera Omnia III 1: Apologia*. Florence, 1985.

William of Auvergne. *Opera Omnia*. Paris, 1674; reprinted Frankfurt, 1963.

William of Auxerre. *Summa Aurea*. Ed. J. Ribaillier. Grottaferrata, 1980–1986.

Zimmermann, A., ed., *Thomas von Aquin: Werk and Wirkung im Licht neuerer Forschungen*, Berlin, 1988.

Index to Introductions

INDEX TO INTRODUCTIONS

INDEX TO INTRODUCTIONS

Index to Text

Other Volumes in this Series

TYPESET IN JANSON BY
PUBLISHERS PHOTOTYPE INTERNATIONAL, CARLSTADT, NEW JERSEY.
PRINTED AND BOUND BY
R. R. DONNELLEY, HARRISONBURG, VIRGINIA.